Crime and Madness in Modern Austria: Myth, Metaphor and Cultural Realities

Crime and Madness in Modern Austria: Myth, Metaphor and Cultural Realities

Edited by

Rebecca S. Thomas

Cambridge Scholars Publishing

Crime and Madness in Modern Austria:
Myth, Metaphor and Cultural Realities,
Edited by Rebecca S. Thomas

This book first published 2008 by

Cambridge Scholars Publishing

15 Angerton Gardens, Newcastle, NE5 2JA, UK

British Library Cataloguing in Publication Data
A catalogue record for this book is available from the British Library

ISBN (10): 1-84718-546-0, ISBN (13): 9781847185464

TABLE OF CONTENTS

Madness, Literature, Theater and Visual Art

(War) Crimes and Terror

Crime and Madness: Reality and Metaphor in Postwar Literature

Madness and Crime in a Postmodern Mood: Contemporary Film and Detective Novels

ACKNOWLEDGEMENTS

I extend many thanks to my friends and colleagues from the Modern Austrian Literature and Culture Association for their energetic and thoughtful collaboration in both the concept and completion of this volume. Thanks also to the Wake Forest University for providing a course reduction for a semester so that work on the project could proceed, and to my colleagues and friends in the Department of German and Russian who encouraged and supported my efforts at every stage. I am also indebted to my students at Wake Forest from the 2006 senior seminar in Austrian Literature as well as the 2007 Flow House Austrian Literature and Culture course for their enthusiasm, curiosity, and insightful discussion. Thanks specifically to my student and friend, Kevin Duck, for providing hours of technical support in the formatting and layout process. Unending gratitude goes to Chuck Thomas for his patience, support, and historical expertise throughout. Finally, particular thanks go to my friend Mary Fahnestock-Thomas for her invaluable editorial contributions, her unflagging patience, brutal honesty and perennial good cheer.

INTRODUCTION

REBECCA S. THOMAS

There is nothing particularly Austrian about madness and crime. There is, however, a specifically Austrian confrontation with these experiences beyond cultural norms that reveals much about both the criminal and the mad(wo)man, and even more about the culture that defines and encounters them. Medical and legal determinations are not based exclusively on objective science or law, but issue also from cultural assumptions and beliefs about the very nature of the criminal and the mad. This volume explores the experience of the criminal and the insane, as well as the ways in which Austrian history, cultural attitudes, prejudices and politics have defined the categories of illness and madness, and determined medical and legal responses to them. The essays contained here are interdisciplinary and multi-perspectival. Some treat shifts in medical and legal practices and institutions over time, others examine the ways in which times of war or social upheaval effect our understanding of madness and crime. Still other essays treat representations of madness and crime, as either theme or metaphor, in literature and art. The essays at hand continually revise, deconstruct, relativize and redefine the labels of crime and madness, which have frequently been used as fulcra to promote a political or social agenda.

In Michel Foucault's groundbreaking and controversial volume *History and Madness* (1961), the author posits madness as the phenomenon beyond reason and cultural control that engenders a visceral fear within ordered society. He surveys the changing definitions of and responses to madness from the medieval period to the modern age as a means of understanding the shifting roles and relative authority of reason to unreason over centuries of Western Civilization. In his study, he interrogates institutions such as asylums and their practices, as well as the art and literature of the various ages that takes madness as its subject and theme. The present volume seeks to revisit the general spirit of Foucault's project within the limited geo-cultural sphere of modern Austria, and to expand the inquiry to explicitly include both madness and crime, which are frequently conflated or conjoined in medical and legal analyses as well as in popular conceptions and art. The time and space of the query are contracted to focus on modern Austrian culture, that is, Austria from the late 19th century to the present day.

Madness and crime have always provoked the reflex of control. Control may be physical, in the form of the straight jacket or the shackle, incarceration in the asylum or the prison, or removal through ostracism or death. It may come in the form of scientific or philosophical categorization, or the creation and enforcement of laws and statutes. Despite controlling efforts, however, madness and crime elude final mastery, and continue to represent the absolute other beyond cohesive bonds of cultural identification and belonging.

Madness and Modernity

In Hans Gabriel's opening essay, he argues for a re-reading of the comfortable, Biedermeier world view traditionally ascribed to Adalbert Stifter. Instead, he proposes a reading of Stifter's novels *Abdias* and *Mountain Crystals* that reveals a grave unease with the recognition of reason's inability to master what Stifter posits as the irrationality of the natural world. Traditional world views in which the universe and nature are assumed to be ordered and rational objects whose secrets could be disclosed through objective, scientific observation, give way to modern view characterized by skepticism regarding both the rational structure of the universe and reason's capacity to comprehend or represent it. Gabriel's essay forms the bridge out of the 19th century into the modern era under consideration in this volume.

The essays that follow treat iconic works of Viennese Modernism. They reveal a fascination with the limits of reason, defining the causes and symptoms of madness, and the link between crime and the irrational. The correspondences among the representations in science, literature, art and music are striking, and reveal a profound fascination with understanding and representing dissonances beneath the veneer of cultural stability. Katherine Arens' essay on Sigmund Freud explores the "medicalizing of the subject" in Freud's discourse and practice of psychoanalysis, and reveals the mythmaking regarding the definition of mental illness, the authority of psychoanalysis as a discipline, and of Freud as a cultural icon. In his essay on Gustav Klimt and Robert Musil, Stefan Kutzenberger offers an interpretation of how both Klimt and Musil dissect and represent the pathologies of Viennese society in modernity. In each, metaphors of illness, madness and violence abound as markers of a culture out of joint and beyond the control of reason. Robert Musil links psychoanalysis with the crime narrative in his depiction of Moosbrugger, the psychopathic sex murderer in his epic novel *The Man Without Qualities*. Musil's musings on the conjunction and disjunction of reason and irrationality in modern man and society also reveal the polarities and correspondences between science and art. His project is largely one of situating madness, crime, unreason, and the irrational within a rationalized culture in which the logic of science and commerce dominated. In his famous university paintings, Gustav Klimt was also concerned with representing the elements of life beyond the control of medicine, philosophy and law, calling into question both the limits of reason and the achievements of culture. Lyle Barkhymer's essay on Alban Berg' *Wozzeck* explores the individual's impotence in the face of biological and cultural forces which, often irrational themselves, lead to a descent into madness and crime. Barkhymer provides an analysis of the text as well as the musicological representation of madness and crime in the opera.

Gender, Madness and Law

Given the relationship between power and medical and legal classification, it is not surprising that women have often been pathologized as mad or criminal. Sigmund Freud's theories of sexuality propounded at the beginning of the twentieth century were based entirely on the model of the male norm and female aberration. His studies on hysteria and the biological predisposition of the female subject to mental instability could only reinforce prevailing stereotypes of the sort codified by Otto Weininger[1] in *Sex and Character*. Freud's essays on the theory of sexuality and Weininger's magnum opus *Sex and Character* were particularly influential in purveying negative stereotypes about the female body and mind.

The guise of scientific and socio-historical discourse lent legitimacy to both Freud's and Weininger's claims that women are aberrant per se. Each emphasized the role of gender in assessing proclivities towards madness and crime. It is no accident that Freud's theories came under vigorous critique during the early 20th centuries as the women's movement gained momentum, and as women were becoming increasingly visible within the public sphere. Susanne Hochreiter explores the courage and insight of Rosa Mayreder, who fought tirelessly to deconstruct the false assumptions and mythologies about women's "nature" and concomitant inferior and limited social status that issued from the new sciences. The hegemony of scientific discourse at the time, the status of which had been enhanced by quantum advances in scientific understanding and technological progress, reinforced the quality of these pseudo-scientific assertions as unassailable by non-specialists, and imbedded the accompanying assumptions about women and gender more firmly in the popular imagination. Hochreiter explores how Rosa Mayreder resists and rejects the categorizations of stereotypical or real behaviors of women as mad or criminal, and demands a more humane, inclusive rhetoric that does not stigmatize difference but seeks to understand and expand the pallet of human responses to the world.

Gender is also central to several highly visible legal conundra. The debates hovering around the criminalization of abortion, prostitution and sex trafficking, along with the consequences of juridical outcomes for medical practice are subjects for both historical inquiry and artistic representation. The question of whether or not to criminalize these actions has always been highly politicized, with arguments proffered from across the political and ideological spectrum decrying the immorality of various diametrically opposed legal positions. Should a woman receiving an illegal abortion, the physician performing the procedure, or both be tried in court? Should the prostitute or her client or both be held legally accountable in cases of prostitution? How should the legal status of prostitution or sex trafficking effect the availability and confidentiality of medical care? Gender and, less obviously immigrant status and ethnicity, play significant roles in making these legal and medical determinations. Essays in this volume treat the specifically Austrian manifestations of the intersection of gender, madness and crime. Sarah Painitz's essay explores Mela Hartwig's treatment of Austrian abortion laws in *The Crime* and *TheFantastical Paragraph.* Painitz's essays also reveal a strong feminist reaction against Freud's influence. In their tandem essays, Lesley Bart and Lorely French explore Austria's wrangling with the realities and representation of prostitution and sex trafficking. Bart gives a historical overview of the legal, political and feminist-theoretical debates surrounding the issue, while Lorely French interprets the literary representation of the same in Marlene Streeruwitz's recent novel *Jessica.* Each of the essays in this section reinforces repeatedly the repression and rebellion at the intersection of psychiatry, law, and gender.

Madness and the Arts

The relationship of the arts to madness and crime is multi-dimensional. Since the early 19th century in the literature of the German speaking world, madness has been linked to genius and seen as a virtual precondition for artistic production. To be "irrational" is to be gifted with a special vision that, much like the role of the jester, the fool, or the blind in classical literature, endows the seer with the capacity to look behind the curtain of manner and form and to speak truth about underlying or transcendent truths regarding society and its foibles. The mad in literature and art are often gifted with access to a deeper, more authentic perception. In his essay on madness in Austrian literature, Geoff Howse explores the tension between real sufferings of real people with mental illness and fictional representations of madness. Howse investigates key works of Austrian literature and what they reveal about the interface between the mad and society, and how the discourse of the mad is mediated by "patrons.," who allow the reader to follow the mad person to "the vanishing point of the uninterpretable" (Howse, 176).

A survey of institutions involved in the treatment of mental illness gives insight into changing attitudes about psychiatry and assessments of the nature of mental illness *per se,* but also into the politics and culture of institutions and the effects of these non-medical judgments on patient care. Here one also witnesses the complex interplay between madness and art in terms of both production and representation. The essays in this section that treat asylum planning and practices at the turn of the century conjoin the realms of art and science in a way particular to the age, the emblem of which may be Otto Wagner's architectural plan for the church at the Viennese mental asylum *Steinhof.* Neo-romanticism that was prevalent in literary and artistic theory at the time emphasized the cult of genius often linked with eccentricity or madness. The finely attuned nerves of the artist are invoked by the playful adaptation of the term *neu-romantik* (German for neo-romantic) to *neuro-mantic* by contemporaries who emphasized the neurotic hypersensitivity they diagnosed in turn-of-the-century artists. As Luke Heighton explores in his essay on art in the asylum, the self-representation of the mad became an object of both clinical and aesthetic fascination during this time. Heighton explores the intersection of aesthetic and psychiatric theory at the turn of the century through an examination of two expositions (1898 and 1908) featuring works by psychiatric patients and an in-depth look at the work of the manic-depressive painter Joseph Karl Raedler. The essay provides a fascinating reception history of the art of the insane in Austria, as well as clues to its interpretation.

In addition to pondering the relationship between madness and genius and the representation of psychological states in art, the effect of the arts on the mentally ill as consumers rather than producers was also a hotly debated topic among medical professionals and patient advocates. This resulted not only in the construction of architectural masterpieces such as Wagner's church at Steinhof, but also the installation of theaters in a number of asylums such as Mauer-Öhling. These theaters were intended to entertain, but also to contribute to a healing. Julie M. Johnson explores the theory and practice of therapeutic theater at Mauer-Öhling. In her essay, Pamela Saur explores Gerhard Roth's fascination with the asylum *Gugging*, a therapeutic center in which the patients are encouraged to produce and exhibit art. Saur provides an overview of the development of practices at Gugging, as well as an analysis of Roth's essayistic and fictional treatments of the asylum as a representation of Austrian attitudes and a reflection of Austrian culture.

(War) Crimes and Terror

While characterizations of crime in the era between the collapse of empire and the end of the Second World War were largely metaphorical for cultural dislocation and angst accompanying modernism, the paradigm shifted radically in the wake of the horrific events of World War II and the holocaust. Whereas the First World War's primary cultural significance for Austria was the crescendo towards the collapse of a centuries-old political and cultural order that left a void of cultural identity and stability, the Second World War and the Shoah imprinted historical realities upon the Austrian national identity from which it would spend decades trying to hide. If the legal system relies on disclosing the truth about events to establish innocence or guilt, it is apparent that a national obviation of the facts regarding Austrian involvement in the war and the holocaust would jeopardize the state's ability to function as an unbiased arbiter and authority on matters of right and wrong.

The case of Austrian reluctance to come to terms with its past and atone for its culpability in a war in which it had backed the unrighteous cause of Nazism is complicated further when one contemplates the demand of the victors that war crimes be prosecuted in the post-war era. How is responsibility to be assigned within a military structure that relies on obedience to authority and orders? What, within the brutal economy of war, counts as a war crime? Does the reality of war relativize what may properly be held as mad or criminal? Is the distinction merely one of state sanction versus rogue vigilante action? In this section, crime and madness are diffused onto a broader canvass of national political engagement. There are multiple layers of complexity associated with the paradigm, in which war abrogates norms of restraint and violence. Perhaps the most significant of these is whether and how crime and justice can be defined and served within the wartime ethos.

Winfried Garscha considers the "excesses of violence" in the final phases of the war. From his position as an archivist with the Austrian Research Center for Post War Trials, Garscha has a unique vantage on both the nature of war crimes committed and the implications of the post war prosecution and sentencing of those criminals involved.

In his essay on the bombing campaigns in South Tirol in the 1960s, Georg Grote provides an overview of the events surrounding these campaigns, along with a historiography of the writing and re-writing of the events in Tirolean history. He explores the changing views of the activists as freedom fighters and terrorists, and considers the importance of the mythmaking surrounding the bombers, in which they achieve a status of "founding fathers" of Tirolean regional identity.

Theodore Fiedler gives a detailed analysis of Austrian author Peter Handke's controversial "uncritical pro-Serbian views on the bloody unraveling of Yugoslavia in the 1990s" (Fiedler, 306) and the justice pursued against Serbian war criminals by the Hague Tribunal. The former Yugoslavia's historical connection to the Habsburg Empire along with Handke's position as one of the best-known post-war Austrian writers makes his literary and polemical responses to these events of central interest to the study of conflicting Austrian attitudes regarding terror, war crimes and Austria's role in the New Europe.

Günter Haika compares and contrasts two divergent Austrian confrontations with the terror attacks of September 11. This essay provides close analysis of two works by the contemporary Austrian authors Kathrin Röggla and Paulus Hochgatterer, and provides uniquely Austrian perspectives on America's response to terror and its consequences for global culture.

Crime and Madness: Reality and Metaphor

In the post war period, in addition to the concrete, although far from straight-forward, issues of dealing with war crimes, was the founding myth of Austria's victim status during the Anschluss, the period during WWII in which Austria disappeared as an independent nation state after its annexation into greater Germany. The notion that the Second Republic depended on repressed memory of the truth regarding events related to the war, war crimes and the holocaust for its identity as well as economic and political recovery became a fixture of Austrian discourse in the era following the Waldheim election in 1986. It is not accidental that critics such as Gerhard Roth, in his monumental, multivolume work *The Archives of Silence*, fixates on characters who are criminal and insane, and on the legal and medical systems which are authorized to diagnose and treat them. In the preface to *The Story of Darkness*, volume six of the cycle, Roth's stated intentions might be generalized as the project of his generation: "From the beginning I intended to write a novel about Austria, about the openly apparent insanity of Austrian history, and the hidden madness of Austrian everyday life." The essays in this section are bound by the authors' concern for the lingering effects of past crimes on contemporary culture, and on the persistent effects the madness of war exercises over fundamental, defining issues within both the medical and legal communities. These essays focus on literal and metaphorical representations of madness in fiction, and on postwar literature as a mirror of societal dysfunction.

In her essay, Dagmar Lorenz contrasts Elias Canetti's critique of prewar Austrian bourgeois society with Veza Canettis' fictional representations of the Anschluss and war years. In each case, she focuses on representations of crime and madness as keys to representing Austrian society's descent into the moral and intellectual abyss of Nazism.

Thomas Bernhard was among the most outspoken and controversial postwar authors to take on the Oedipal struggle of criticizing the previous generation for its complicity in war crimes and the holocaust. Joseph Moser provides analyses of Bernhard's first novel, *Frost*, and his final novel, *Extinction*, through which he follows Bernhard's aggressive case against what he deemed the pervasive criminality of Austrian culture both during and after the war. Moser explores Bernhard's contention that Austria's embrace of Nazism was related to faschistoid tendencies in the Austrian clerical state prior to the war, thus undermining the contention that Nazism was an external ill forcibly imposed on Austria by the Germans and focusing on the particularly Austrian manifestation of fascism and anti-Semitism.

Rebecca Thomas's essay treating Doron Rabinovici's *Search for M.*, follows the path of historical continuities preceding and flowing from Austria's complicity in the holocaust and war into the second generation of holocaust survivors. As a young Jewish writer with personal ties to both Austria and Israel, Rabinovici addresses the need for personal and national healing. In the novel, psychological dysfunction and crime hover between realistic depiction of history and loss, and metaphorical representation of a culture whose repressed memories of guilt and suffering continue to deform it.

Taken together, these essays suggest that madness and crime constitute an extended metaphor for the preconditions and consequences of Austria's embrace of Nazism.

Madness and Crime in a Postmodern Mood

In Austrian postmodern fiction and cinema, the final inversion of madness and normality triumphs in representations of the world as madhouse narrated through fracture, disjuncture, and multi-perspectival forms. The reading and viewing of these works replicates popular notions of madness and socio-pathological states of mind, in which reason is undermined as a myth and a nexus of events seemingly unrelated by causality or sense washes over the viewer who experiences the rootlessness of the mind unmoored from an ordered universe. The dissolution of all external authority, systems of order and meaning is made palpable through the aesthetic representation of the discourses of madness and crime.

In her essay on Wolf Haas, Helga Schreckenberger explores the author's use of the popular fiction format of the detective novel as a vehicle for representing, commenting on and deconstructing Austrian postwar identities. Postmodernism dismantles boundaries between high and low culture, and this trend probed in Schreckenberger's essay, which probes the potential of popular detective fiction as a vehicle for representing a critical agenda. Schreckenberger illuminates the ways, both structural and linguistic, in which Haas's crime novels dismantel the postwar construction of a pastoral Austrian identity.

Robert von Dassanowsky's essay on Alois Hotschnigg's novel *Leonardo's Hands* examines the ways in which Hotschnigg's prose proceeds from and leads to a postmodern perspective in which individual and national identities are unmasked as not merely false, but indeed totally fictional. Here questions of guilt and crime are both historically bound to the reception of the holocaust and war, and simultaneously transcendent of this historical specificity in their conclusions about the ultimate irrationality of existence itself. Reason and sanity are here revealed as illusory constructs. Dassanowsky pursues Hotschnigg's postmodern claims that the apparently cohesive meta-narrative of national and personal identity obscures what is, in reality, a "collage of individual mythologies" (Dassanowsky, 446). Placing Hotschnigg firmly in the tradition of Schnitzler and Kafka, Dassanowsky provides a uniquely Austrian take on the central questions posed by postmodernist discourses of reason and madness.

Finally, Oliver Speck delivers an analysis of the ways in which Michael Haneke's films stage madness and crime as acts of defiance against an increasingly malignant postmodern global consumer culture. In the course of his essay, Speck initiates the reader into Haneke's varying forms of cinematic madness, all of which lead the viewer to an experience of the journey away from the notion of a normative truth against which madness or sanity might be measured, and instead into a fragmented perspective on the world as composed of multiple competing truths. The discourse of madness is thus transformed into a vehicle of liberation from "the global culture of so-called post modernity" (Speck, 463).

Conclusion

In the final analysis, this volume has its strength in the kaleidoscopic, multi-perspectival approach that seeks to represent and understand the juncture of reality, metaphor and myth with respect to mental illness and crime in Austrian literature and culture. From the real sufferings of human beings afflicted with mental illness, to the social and moral imperatives implied by research into political rather than medical or legal classification of madness and crime, the survey of developing attitudes and trends in policy and practice reveals much about Austria's cultural self-awareness and self-creation. The metamorphoses in clinical and legal institutions tell us about Austrian views and values in particular historical moments. The aesthetic treatments and representations of madness and crime render complex legal, medical, moral and political issues comprehensible on both intellectual and visceral levels. It is largely on the basis of these aesthetic renderings that the horizon of possibilities regarding inclusion or exclusion from the ranks of the socially acceptable is expanded. The relationship of the essays to one another has much in common with the correspondences Sigmund Freud perceived between his systematic, clinical findings and Arthur Schnitzler's intuitive, artistic representations of the psyche. The distance between their disciplines was more one of method than of substance in the end. Both diagnosed the political and societal ills of modern life, while shedding light on the cultural roots and causes. The collection of essays presented here illuminates the shifts in practice and representation of madness and crime in modern Austria. It belongs to the specifically Austrian content of this volume that iconic Austrian figures such as Freud, Weininger, Scnhitzler, Kafka, and Musil, are invoked repeatedly by the authors and critics whose own diagnosis of the Austrian condition remains connected to the cultural narrative of Austrian modernism. The interdisciplinary approach of the volume, drawing on specialists from the fields of Austrian history, psychology, art history, musicology, film studies and literature produces a rich whole in which the boundaries between "reality" and "fiction" are largely deconstructed along with the categories of madness and criminality themselves. From these investigations proceeds the clear insight that cultural responses to crime and madness are often steeped in mythmaking as much as objective policy and practice. Conversely, literary and metaphorical representations of crime and madness reveal attitudes and cultural realities about the Austrian society that produced them and which they reflect. The essays collected here, by way of correspondences and co-illumination, serve to explicate and reveal the changing attitudes and values of modern Austria through how it classifies, treats, thematizes and represents crime and madness as subversions of constructed norms. This volume thus turns out to be as much about the normative narratives shaping modern Austrian identity and cultural politics as of the purported aberrations at the margins.

Works Cited

Berg, Alban. 1955. *Wozzeck, Oper in 3 Akten, Op. 7.* Edited by H. E. Apostel. Vienna: Universal Edition.

Bernhard, Thomas. 1986. *Extinction.* Chicago: University of Chicago Press.

—. *Frost.* 1963. Translated by Michael Hofmann. New York: Knopf, 2006.

Foucault, Michael. 1965. *Madness and Civilization; a history of insanity in the Age of Reason.* Trans. Richard Howard. New York: Pantheon.

Hotschnig, Alois. 1989. *Aus. Eine Erzählung.* Frankfurt a. M.: Luchterhand.

—. *Leonardo's Hands.* 1999. Trans. Peter Filkins. Lincoln: University of Nebraska Press.

Musil, Robert. 1995. *The Man Without Qualities.* Trans. Sophie Wilkins, ed. Burton Pike. New York: Alfred A. Knopf, Inc.

Rabinovici, Doron. 2000. *The Search for M.* trans. Francis Sharp. Riverside Ariadne Press.

Roth, Gerhard. 1999. *The Story of Darkness.* Trans. Helga Schreckenberger. Riverside, CA: Aridadne Press.

Schorske, Carl. *Fin-de-Siecle Vienna: Politics and Culture.* 1979. New York: Knopf.

Stifter, Adalbert.1994. *Abdias.* Trans. Helen Watanabe-O'Kelly. In *Brigitta and Other Tales.* London: Penguin (21-95).

—. *Rock Crystal.* Trans. Harry Steinhauer. In *Deutsche Erzählungen–German Stories: A Bilingual Anthology.* 1984. Ed by Harry Steinhauer. Berkeley: University of California Press (148-250).

Streruwitz, Marlene. *Jessica, 30. Roman.* 2004. Frankfurt a. M.: S. Fischer.

Weininger, Otto..*Sex and Character. An Investigation of Fundamental Principles*. 2005. Edited by Daniel Steuer with Laura Marcus. Bloomington: Indiana University Press.

Notes

[1] It is perhaps worth noting that Weininger's own tendency towards mental instability and schizophrenia culminated in suicide.

CHAPTER ONE

"THE FINAL IRRATIONALITY OF EXISTENCE": THE LANGUAGE OF MADNESS AND THE MADNESS OF LANGUAGE IN STIFTER'S *ABDIAS* AND *BERGKRISTALL*

HANS GABRIEL

The name and the work of Adalbert Stifter still evoke for many Friedrich Hebbel's contemporaneous description of him as the quintessentially Biedermeier "man of endless [narrative] studies."[1] In *Fin de Siècle Vienna,* for example, Carl Schorske uses Stifter's famous (and famously long) novel *Der Nachsommer* to exemplify mid-nineteenth-century Austrian efforts to establish a reassuring aesthetic safe haven or "garden" in the wake of the failed revolutions of 1848. "To illustrate and propagate his concept of *Bildung,*" writes Schorske, "compounded of Benedictine world piety, German humanism, and Biedermeier conventionality, Stifter gave to the world his novel *Der Nachsommer*" (283).[2] Until fairly recently, what literary-critical debate there was regarding Stifter's work revolved primarily around the question of whether one supported or rejected this more or less universally acknowledged "Biedermeier conventionality." As one critic writes citing another, "In general, Stifter scholarship ranges from 'confessional confirmation and apology on the one hand, [to] ideological accusations and rejection on the other.'"[3] Hardly the sort of work, or so it would seem, where one would expect to encounter extreme states such as madness.

In the last two decades or so, however, scholarly readings of Stifter's work have shown an increasingly radical departure from this traditional assessment, as recent book titles such as *The Mania for Moderation, Adalbert Stifters schrecklich schöne Welt (Adalbert Stifter's Terribly Beautiful World)* and *Geborgenheit und Gefährdung* (*Security and Peril)* make evident. Hebbel famously criticizes Stifter in his own day for what he calls an "overrated Talent for minutiae that describes [the most common] things in a broad and wide-ranging manner."[4] And an anonymous English contemporary of Stifter's speaks of an "effect like that of a highly finished doorway leading into mere vacant space" ("Studies by Adalbert Stifter," 853). Recently, however, one critic admiringly claims for Stifter, "beneath the surface of Biedermeier solidity [...] a vision of fracture, emptiness, meaninglessness not only more radical than that of any nineteenth-century author, but more radical than the vision of any twentieth-century author [...]" (Ragg-Kirkby, 11).[5] Another concludes approvingly that reading Stifter's *Abdias* is "a matter of semiotics and [...] a matter of antisemiotics [...] at once" (Metz, 232).[6] In other words, critics no longer want to see Stifter, as Schorske does, as an author seeking to cultivate a "garden" of "Biedermeier conventionality" that turn-of-the-century Viennese art will subsequently "transform" and then "explode."[7] On the contrary, many of these critics' conclusions give the impression that Stifter's work never even seeks to plant the seeds for such a garden.

The presence of such radically opposing emphases in critical readings of Stifter implies a corresponding and somewhat paradoxical coexistence of support for both views *within* his texts themselves. And as hyperbolic as some of their conclusions may be, modern critics have come to acknowledge this paradoxical coexistence.[8] Thomas Mann's famous pronouncement regarding Stifter may therefore no longer be as accurate as when he first wrote it. "More seldom," writes Mann, "[...] has it been observed that behind the quiet, inward exactitude of precisely Stifter's observation of nature, a tendency to the excessive, the catastrophic, the pathological is at work."[9] Nevertheless, the carefully controlled interdependence of the two extremes in Stifter's work still deserves critical attention. As a direct response to Hebbel's one-sided attack, Stifter's *Preface to [the story collection] "Many-colored Stones"* of 1854 outlines the underlying aesthetic/philosophical principles on which this paradoxical coexistence of "quiet exactitude" and "catastrophic (pathological) excess" is based. Nowhere is this coexistence more carefully established, however, than in two of Stifter's best-known short prose works, namely *Abdias* and *Bergkristall* (literally "Mountain Crystal," usually translated as "Rock Crystal"). Neither solely reflective nor merely destructive of comforting bourgeois norms or "Biedermeier conventionality," their representations of madness and of natural extremes reveal both a narrative acknowledgment of the impossibility of rendering these states intelligible and an unwavering determination to continue to do so. The result is a masterful simultaneous illustration in these mid-nineteenth-century Austrian narratives of both the inadequacy and the creative potential of literary representation. The paradoxical structure and content of Stifter's narratives present in "gentle," indirect fashion the frightening threat of madness that accompanies, at least potentially, the failure or limits of human reason. In so doing, they offer a critique of language and representation that anticipates that of Nietzsche's early writings and prefigures the full-blown ironic *Sprachskepsis*, or "language skepticism," of turn-of-the-century Austrian literature.[10]

Stifter's preface to his *Novelle* collection *Bunte Steine* (*Many-colored Stones*) has received a great deal of critical attention, and it is well beyond the focus and scope of this piece to review this discussion.[11] A brief look at the *Vorrede* or *Preface* itself, however, highlights just what is at stake for Stifter in the literary treatment of "the pathological" and "catastrophic" in each of his *Novellen*. In the *Preface*, physical reality is said to point to a decidedly moral underlying natural and social force—which Stifter's narrator calls the "gentle law." This underlying reality is presented as an absolute, self-evident truth:

> We want [*wir wollen*] to try to observe the gentle law that guides the human race. [...] There are forces that work toward the survival of mankind as a whole that may not be checked by individual forces. [...] It is the law of these forces, the law that wants everyone to be respected, honored, and unthreatened beside the other [...]. (1-6, 3-4)[12]

The multivalence of the combination "wir wollen" in Stifter's text here underscores the crucial, insurmountable paradox in his program. "*We want to* try to discern an overarching moral 'gentle law' from physical evidence," is the translation most closely in line with modern German usage. In Stifter's day, however, the combination retains something of the sense of "We *will*" try to do so, as well as the sense of "*Let us*" try to do so. Like the meaning of the modal verb here, Stifter's description of the process by which the intangible moral "law" he posits is gleaned from and supported by physical evidence is neither strictly scientific nor solely a matter of faith and human desire. Rather, like the ambivalence between what one "will" and what one "wants to" find, it hovers uneasily but unavoidably and unabashedly between a quasi-scientific, pseudo-objective production and testing of hypotheses on the one hand and a quasi-religious belief in an underlying but imperceptible "gentle law of nature" on the other. Modern readers will recognize the structure used by proponents of intelligent design, where perceivable physical data are used to try to support a belief in the morality and/or rationality ("intelligence") of an assumed but imperceptible underlying universal order or "design."

Here, however, the *Preface*'s description of how the subsequent literary data is to be read - indeed, the very fact that it prefaces these literary examples with this description - underscores an awareness that the cart will necessarily always come before the horse; that a comprehensible human explanation of unfathomable natural processes will always precede and never fully encompass the observed physical data that ostensibly support it. Certainly this admission then renders any such explanation fundamentally incomplete or unverifiable. Yet Stifter's narrator nonetheless remains determined to use his powers of literary representation to continue to test our hypotheses and/or faith. We will, we want to, let us try, using an understanding of our existence that is paradoxically located between rational scientific hypothesis and irrational religious faith, to collect and (re)present physical evidence that appears to support this understanding.

As Harmut Laufhütte points out with specific reference to *Abdias* in his essay "Von der Modernität eines Unmodernen," it is this consciously paradoxical self-positioning, more than anything else, that yields in Stifter's work "the modernity of an unmodern man." The paradox remains, based on a faith in the absolute existence of a rational and/or moral order on the one hand, and on its necessarily mediated or experimental basis on the other. In the calculated interdependence with which the *Preface* presents the opposing sides, it becomes a point of reference and a structural model for the representation of natural and psychological extremes in the *Novellen* that follow. Unlike *Bergkristall, Abdias* is not among the collection of stories introduced by the preface, and its publication precedes that of *Many-colored Stones*. In its efforts to represent Abdias's madness, however, this earlier narrative mirrors exactly the structure outlined in the *Preface.* Thus, it, too, presents itself as one of the touchstones of Stifter's aesthetic program, ironically and consciously generated by Stifter himself. In these stories, Stifter confronts some of the most extreme manifestations of human and natural existence imaginable, where the sense of reason that frames and guides the process breaks down. He therefore essentially compromises his own efforts in advance. Yet by leaving no stone unturned in his efforts to glimpse the "gentle law" that he himself posits, he nonetheless hopes to encourage his readers to continue to seek it out as well. The ongoing determination to observe this "gentle law," even in the face of inscrutable physical data, then itself becomes final irrefutable evidence of such a law's continued hypothetical existence.

The *Novelle* form Stifter adopts to represent these extreme states proves useful for more than just its brevity. By the time Stifter first published *Abdias* and *Bergkristall* in the 1840s, the *Novelle*, or short narrative tale, had already achieved considerable status as a genre in

German-language literature.[13] Its specific definition had been the subject of literary-critical debate since the German Romantics borrowed the term from Boccaccio and Cervantes around the beginning of the century.[14] While critical debate about the generic definition of the *Novelle* remains to this day, there is general consensus, now as then, regarding the importance of characteristics such as narrative economy, a frame story, and a crucial unusual central figure or event. In his *Gespräche mit Eckermann* from the same period in which Stifter first published versions of *Bergkristall* and *Abdias,* Goethe offered what remains the most famous definition of the *Novelle*: "What is the *Novelle*," he asks rhetorically, "other than an actually occurring unheard-of given event [Begebenheit]?"[15]

The inherent paradox in Goethe's characterization of the *Novelle* as an "unheard-of [but] given event" echoes perfectly the "quiet exactitude" with which "the excessive, the catastrophic, the pathological" are represented in Stifter's texts. In both *Abdias* and *Bergkristall,* Stifter's narrator then expands this general understanding of the genre to mirror the structure of the *Preface* within the *Novellen* themselves. As he does with the preface that frames the collection of "many-colored stones," Stifter's narrator eschews the traditional, specifically located frame story that often introduces individual *Novellen.* Instead, he frames each one with an abstract philosophical introduction that both insists on and denies a metaphysical explanation for the "unheard-of given events" that follow. The inclusion, within the narrative itself, of an abstract metaphysical frame introducing the "unheard-of, actually occurring given event" then takes the paradox in Goethe's definition from a physical to a linguistic or representational level. Whatever degree of "truth" the representation of the event itself loses in its failure to corroborate a rational overarching moral law in any clearly determinable way, it simultaneously stands to gain in that its inexplicability makes it appear all the more persuasively "given" rather than authorially manipulated. The reverse is then of course also true. The more neatly or comprehensibly the representations fit or support the conceptual frame in which they are packaged, the less persuasive they become as actual "Begebenheiten" or "given things." A close look at *Abdias* and *Bergkristall*—"the harmless things that follow," as the *Preface* calls the *Novellen* it frames (6)[16]—reveals the centrality of this representational paradox as Stifter's mid-century texts seek ways to represent convincingly the extreme reality they portray.

The narrator of *Abdias* begins his frame, and the *Novelle* as a whole, by indicating what appears from a human perspective to be an inequality in the workings of the universe. "There are people," Stifter's text begins,

> on whom such a series of misfortunes falls out of the blue that they finally stand and let the hail-storm roll over them, just as there are others whom good fortune visits with such extraordinary willfulness that it seems as though the laws of Nature had been reversed in a given case so that things should turn out solely for their good. (21)[17]

This relativizing gesture, in which this physical state of affairs is shown to yield an overarching but humanly constructed "explanation," is equally immediate: "In this way the ancients arrived at the concept of fate, we at the milder one of destiny" (21).[18] Equally immediate again, however, is the narrative assertion of something extrahuman, something "real" after all: "But there is indeed [really], too, something terrifying in the indifferent innocence with which the laws of Nature operate." This assertion is then immediately relativized in its turn as being merely the way "it seems to us": "so that it seems to us as though an invisible arm were reaching out of the clouds and enacting the incomprehensible before our eyes."

This back-and-forth in the *Novelle*'s opening lines between what supposedly *is* and what only appears to us to be prefigures a similar oscillation in the presentation of the life of the title character. Abdias is a North African Jew visited by one misfortune after another. After a hundred pages or so, during which his desert home has been pillaged, his wife has died, he has moved to a remote Austrian valley, and his beloved daughter, Ditha, has first been cured of her blindness by one lightning strike, then killed several years later by another, "Abdias the Jew," as Stifter's narrator calls him, finally dies. "Abdias still lived thirty years after Ditha's death," we read. "No one knows for how long after that. [...] No one knew how old he had been. Many said that it was much more than a hundred years. [...] So ended the life and career of Abdias the Jew" (95).[19] In the *Novelle*'s final words as in its initial ones, a masterfully controlled narrative oscillation predominates. The last sentence, which relates Abdias's death, appears with its initial "so" to offer a sense of closure, of unequivocal certainty. Yet coming as it does immediately after the revelation that no one knows when he actually died, the "so" also links this final narrative assertion to the irresolvable uncertainty surrounding Abdias's death and indeed most of his life: "so (in this indeterminable way) ended the life and career of the Jew Abdias."

The narrative's description of Abdias's death only underscores this linguistic ambivalence further. In keeping with the uncertainty associated with the actual death, the narrative takes great pains to distance itself from any description of the actual occurrence at all. "Many people saw him sitting on the bench before his house," we read at the end of one paragraph. "One day he no longer sat there," the next paragraph begins; "the sun shone on the empty spot and on his fresh grave mound, from where the tips of the grass already peeped out" (95).[20] This crucial event is hardly mentioned at all, and it is only reported well after the fact, as the tufts of grass already sprouting ironically emphasize. Indeed, Abdias himself doesn't know when his death actually occurs: "He sat for many years […] and he did not know how long he had been sitting […]" (94).[21]

This simultaneous narrative assertiveness and shyness in the description of Abdias's end returns the reader to the frame with which Stifter's narrator begins the tale. As he does at the end, the narrator takes pains at the beginning to anchor or frame his narrative and his protagonist in a reality ostensibly verified by actual eyewitnesses. "It is the Jew Abdias whose story I want to tell," he writes,

> Anyone who perhaps has heard of him or who has even sometime seen the bent ninety-year-old figure sitting in front of the little white house […] should […] as he reads, bring his image once more before his eyes […] since we have simply tried to show what Abdias was like. (23)[22]

In other words, the narrator once again tries to convince the reader of the veracity or objectivity of his linguistically constructed scene by equating it with what has supposedly actually been physically seen. But he immediately takes a step back from this equation and ties it to a blatantly poetic metaphor. "A serene chain of flowers hangs through the infinity of the universe," he writes, "and transmits its shimmer into men's hearts—the chain of cause and effect—and into man's brain was cast the most beautiful of these flowers, reason, the eye of the soul, in order to attach the chain to it" (22).[23]

However beautiful this metaphor may be, the narrator's recourse to it here to frame the supposed equivalence of physical and mental perception completely contradicts the realistic and objective status that he has just worked so hard to establish. The reader recognizes once more the same oscillation that informs the structure of the *Preface* and the uncertain certainty of the *Novelle*'s conclusion. This movement continues, as the narrator feels compelled to try to explain this discrepancy by taking yet another framing step backwards before actually beginning his story. "For the ancients this [flower chain] was fate," he writes, "frightful, final, inflexible cause of events, farther than which one cannot see and beyond which nothing more exists […] for us it is destiny" (21).[24] This final move leads the reader back to the opening lines quoted earlier, where this "Fatum," in its turn, is described as deriving from an inscrutable state of affairs in which some people are visited by great misfortune while others seem inordinately fortunate.

Ironically, the narrator can only really begin and end his explanation of how human reason allows him to relate an objectively descriptive narrative at the point where this supposed connection falls apart, at the point where there is no longer any objectively verifiable corroborating physical data. His replacement of inscrutable "Fate" and "Destiny" with his more comforting notion of a "flower chain of cause and effect" dependent on human reason occurs with the now-familiar mix of narrative self-assurance and uncertainty:

> But in fact perhaps there is neither fate as the final irrationality of existence nor is its individual occurrence visited upon us; rather, a serene chain of flowers hangs through the infinity of the universe [...]. (22)[25]

Thus, the narrator matches almost verbatim the rhetorical stance with which, only a few lines earlier, he admits the terrifyingly inhuman impassivity with which natural laws function. "But there is indeed, too, something terrifying in the indifferent innocence with which the laws of Nature operate [...]" (21).[26] Which "but" is more accurate, "but in fact" (*Aber eigentlich*) or "but indeed/really" (*aber wirklich)*? The answer, of course, is neither and both. Not surprisingly, the only thing that the narrator can "eigentlich" or "wirklich" project with absolute conviction at the end of this introductory frame is the same sense of uneasy uncertainty that pervades the *Novelle*'s conclusion. As a result, Stifter's narrator begins the inconclusive conclusion of this frame, and the transition to the story itself, with the same ambivalent "wir wollen," used in the *Preface*:

> Let us not *[wir wollen [...] nicht]* ponder the nature of these things further but simply tell of a man who exemplifies much of this and of whom it is uncertain which is stranger, his destiny or his heart. In any case one is [tempted] by the course of lives like his [...] into a gloomy brooding about providence, destiny and the ultimate cause of all things. (22)[27]

Here again, in other words, "We don't want to" and "will not" and "let us not" stop trying to comprehend the "ultimate basis of all things" in humanly constructed representations, even as we acknowledge their uncertainty and inadequacy.

The story's conclusion gives us no other choice. In a final aside that seems almost too casual, the narrator divulges why Abdias himself can no longer be sure of how long he has been sitting. The reason (as far as can be reasonably determined) is precisely inscrutable unreason: it is madness. "He sat for many years, [...] and he did not know how long he had sat, *for according to reliable statements, he had gone mad*" (95; my emphasis).[28] Given the overabundance of direct seeing and of allusions to eyes, blindness, and vision in the story, the indirectness with which this insanity is registered contains a level of irony that matches that of the (non)description of Abdias's death. In one impressively minimal narrative stroke, Stifter's narrator has concretized his abstract and unrepresentable "final irrationality of existence" into an ostensibly real figure that one or the other of his readers supposedly "had even seen sitting before his little white house" (22).[29] At the same time, the indirectness and generality with which this concrete "final irrationality" of Abdias's existence is registered renders it almost completely undefined. It may be hard to believe that so fleeting and indefinite a narrative moment could carry within it all the awesome weight and power of the "frightful, final, inflexible cause of events." Yet the narrative structure here is merely taking pains to reflect the "indifferent innocence with which," as it claims, "the laws of Nature operate [...]" (3).[30] After all, no one, not even Abdias himself, even knows how long his madness actually lasts.

This narrative uncertainty befits the incomprehensible state of unreason or insanity, and the narrative's refusal to describe this state in any detail paradoxically places Abdias's madness at the very center of the text. Unequipped to comprehend this madness, the reader must look elsewhere to find more concrete "Begebenheiten," or "given events," that offer insight into it. Stifter's narrator obliges in his characteristically ambivalent way throughout the text, but nowhere more prominently than in the repeated appearance and effects of lightning strikes. Once again, the *Preface to Many-colored Stones* proves helpful for reading *Abdias*. The narrator outlines there why this particular extreme natural phenomenon so suits his aesthetic perspective, and connects it metaphorically to the sense of sight that figures so prominently in *Abdias*:

> If we had a sensory organ for electricity and the magnetism emanating from it, such as we have eyes for the light, what a great world, what an abundance of immense phenomena would be open to us. But if we do not have this physical eye, we have the mental eye of science, and this teaches us that the electrical and magnetic forces act upon a huge scene, that it is spread over the whole earth and through the whole sky, that it flows around everything [...]. Lightning is just a small feature of this force, which itself is something great in nature. (*Preface* 2)[31]

Here, human reason is "the mental eye of science"; in the introductory frame of *Abdias,* it is "the eye of the soul." In both cases, lightning becomes the illustrative physical example of the difference between what is perceived by "the physical eye" and the "eye of science/the mental eye of the soul."

To illustrate what it refers to as the "dispassion of Nature," the introductory section of *Abdias* offers the following scenario:

> There the Bedouin rides between the dark cloud of his sky and the yellow sand of his desert: then a light, glittering spark leaps onto his head, he feels an unfamiliar shiver run through his nerves, still hears drunkenly the thunder in his ears, and then nothing more for all eternity. (21)[32]

The generality of this seemingly hypothetical example is complemented by not one, but two actual lightning strikes in the story itself. The two strikes then complement one another as well. The first one hits the house with Abdias's beloved daughter Ditha inside. Instead of killing her as in the frame example, however, it miraculously restores her vision.

> When the rain was scarcely beginning to trickle softly down the roofs, there was a great crash of thunder accompanied by a flash that lit up the whole house with dazzling brightness. Immediately Abdias realized that the lightning had hit the house. […] The lightning had passed through [Ditha's room], [and] had struck ceiling and floor so that there was thick smoke in the room. […] Ditha was […] unharmed. (79)[33]

Both the fleeting nature of the actual strike and the inevitably secondary human apprehension of it are finely rendered here. In the hypothetical frame example, the Bedouin can only "drunkenly" apprehend after the fact what has already occurred to him as he dies. Within the story, Abdias can also only "realize" physically what, by the time he does so, has also already finished happening, namely, "that the lightning had hit his house." As the narrative switches to the pluperfect tense to describe the physical effects of the lightning on Ditha's room, it becomes clear that any deeper understanding of what has happened will remain frighteningly secondary and incomplete. Indeed, in introducing the lightning strike, the narrator emphasizes both the actuality of the event and the human uncertainty regarding its greater significance. In doing so, he echoes the ironic description of lightning in his own *Preface to Many-colored Stones* as "merely a very small feature" of a great natural force. His description also repeats almost verbatim Goethe's famous definition of the *Novelle*. "A wonderful [given] event happened," writes Stifter's narrator, using the same term (*Begebenheit*) that Goethe uses:

> A given event that will remain a wonder until those great widespread forces of Nature have been fathomed […]. Hitherto they [such events] have

been scarecely more than merely wonderful for us and their nature is not even vaguely known to us. (78)[34]

The ironic secondariness of this last characterization—*uns fast noch nicht einmal in Ahnungen bekannt*—is almost impossible to render fully in English. Translated directly, it describes the "wonderful event" as "almost not yet familiar to us even in premonitions," recalling as it does so the rhetorical gestures with which the narrative counterbalances its reporting of Abdias's madness and death. Here, too, only the obvious physical facts remain, in poignantly inadequate testament to the inscrutable "wonder" of what has already occurred. "The same thunderstorm that had made Ditha see had smashed the roof of his house with its hail-stones and flattened his neighbor's harvest," notes the narrator. "Now, as he [Abdias] stood in the wet grass, it was all over" (80).[35]

The second actual lightning strike then complements both the physical effects and the miraculousness of the first. Since it kills Ditha this time, this final lightning strike returns the reader to the scenario in the opening frame. Its effect within the story, meanwhile, is even more momentous, even more extreme. For just this reason, the text represents it with even less descriptive fanfare. Once again, "it is all over" even as one tries to perceive, register, or understand it. In fact, in this case, nothing has really even begun. The strike that cured Ditha's blindness occurred "when the rain was scarcely beginning to trickle softly down the roofs." The lightning strike that kills her, by contrast, occurs without any accompanying precipitation at all, as the reader once again learns after the fact. "Not a drop of rain fell, only the thin clouds trickled across the sky like quickly-drawn veils" (94).[36] The deadly strike, meanwhile, is so physically insignificant that it doesn't even interrupt the conversation Abdias and Ditha are having. It only registers at all in that it causes Ditha to fall silent. Like the reader taking in the minimalistic description of Abdias's madness and death, Abdias only perceives the lightning strike in passing out of the corner of his eye. And like the "gentle law" described in the *Preface to Many-colored Stones*, it too occurs ever so "gently" or "softly" (*sanft*):

> She fell silent suddenly. He thought he had seen a soft (*sanft)* light shining at the side of the sheaves. [...] When he looked at her, it was all over already. After the brightness a short, hoarse crack had followed and Ditha leaned back against a sheaf and was dead. (93-94)[37]

A final narrative description and distancing links this strike to the previous one and renders it perfectly ambivalent. In an ironic inversion of the birth of Christ, two shepherds are the first to learn of Ditha's wondrous death. "The new marvel and the judgment, as they called it, flew immediately round the country" (94). The narrative appears to be referring to the news of what has happened—to the secondary human understanding of the "wonderful given event." It could just as well be referring to the storm itself, however—to the physical event the meaning or sense of which remains "almost not yet even comprehensible to us in premonitions." In any case, the way in which it describes the storm's effects leads the reader both directly to Abdias's madness and back to the narrative's opening frame.

> The thunderstorm that had kissed the child's life away from her head with its soft flame poured down blessings on everyone and finished, *like the one that had given her eyes light,* with a beautiful rainbow far off to the east. (94; my translation in italics)[38]

On the one hand, as the final "wonderful event" whose incomprehensibility leads to Abdias's inscrutable madness, this storm quite literally "kisses the life away from [Abdias's] head with its soft flame" as well. This wondrous physical event therefore stands in for the otherwise unrepresentable fall into madness that it produces even before Abdias finally dies. Once his madness has set in, Abdias's death becomes little more than an insignificant afterthought. On the other hand, this description also recalls the "soft, gleaming spark" that "leaps onto the head" of the Bedouin, killing him in the hypothetical example of the *Novelle*'s opening frame.

In other words, the reader is directed back to the undeniable but unfathomable condition—the "final irrationality of existence"—that mark the *Novelle*'s beginning and end. As the narrative records the destructive effect of the hail on Abdias's roof, it also notes Abdias's obliviousness to it: "But he had noticed nothing of it" (80).[39] This image recalls once more the *Novelle*'s opening line, which speaks of people renouncing all hope of understanding in the face of a "hail-storm" of misfortune. This opening generalization assumes concrete form as madness overcomes Abdias and his obliviousness becomes complete:

> After this event Abdias sat on the little bench in front of his house, saying nothing but looking at the sun. [...] One sun after another passed away, one summer after another, and he did not know how long he had been sitting, for, according to reliable statements, he had gone mad. (94)[40]

In its own paradoxical way and in its own paradoxical example, Stifter's narrative is therefore able to represent Abdias's inscrutable madness after all; not as the absence of reason, but as the loss of the desire, when faced with the incomprehensibility of existence, to try nonetheless to construct a humanly comprehensible scenario. Again, it is for *this* reason, and not because we can "really" (*wirklich)* or "actually" (*eigentlich)* do so with any final authority, that both the *Preface to Many-colored Stones* and the opening frame of *Abdias* assert that "wir wollen"—we want to, we will, and let us - observe an intelligible design in even the most extreme and unintelligible of physical data. Instead of just standing there and "letting this hailstorm of inscrutable misfortune roll over us" as Abdias finally does, the reader, like the narrative, must continue, if only "almost not yet even in premonitions," to try to represent and understand this "final irrationality of existence":

> And let him who has never heard of the man follow us too, if he likes, to the end, since we have simply tried to show what Abdias was like. Then let him judge the Jew Abdias according to the promptings of his heart. (23)[41]

This inconclusive imperative, along with its attendant representational irony and its oscillating perspective, is equally central to *Bergkristall*. The unexpectedly heavy snowstorm that forces the children Conrad and Sanna to spend the night atop the mountain presents a decisive natural "event" that is just as "wonderful," just as extreme and unexpected, as the lightning strikes in *Abdias*. Of course, in their reactions, neither the children nor the villagers succumb to the madness that overcomes Abdias. Their socio-cultural traditions and their connection and sensitivity to their natural environment appear to make them better adapted to cope mentally and physically with its unfathomable vicissitudes. The survival of the children and the strengthening of social ties between the two villages do not, however, imply that the threat of madness and/or deviance is absent here. On the contrary (as Thomas Mann noted), in its description, the narrative remains committed to acknowledging the dangerous irrationality or "madness" that lurks just beneath the surface of their lives and of its own inability to render comprehensible what it struggles vainly to describe.

Once again, these actual events—"the harmless things that follow"—come after a lengthy conceptual introduction that frames them. In the case of *Bergkristall,* it is the discussion of Christmas Eve, with all its familiar and comforting cultural significance.[42] "Our church observes various holidays," the narrative begins, "that affect the heart deeply. [...] One of the most beautiful holidays is celebrated by the church almost in the middle of winter [...]—the feast of Christmas" (*Rock Crystal*, 149).[43] The frame describes how, like the reader of *Abdias* and like Abdias himself, the children are not able to experience the wonderful moment itself. Rather, like the description in *Abdias*'s opening frame of how the various notions of fate are derived, *Bergkristall*'s opening description emphasizes how fundamentally the children's understanding of Christmas depends on their inability to see or know exactly what really happens:

> The church holiday is tied up with a domestic one. In almost all Christian countries the custom has spread of showing children the arrival of the Christ child—[…] the most wonderful [child] that ever was on earth—as a happy, splendid, solemn thing […].
>
> The children are not permitted to come until the sign is given that the Holy Christ has been there and has left behind the gifts which He has brought. Then the door is opened [and] the little ones are permitted to enter […]. Sometimes they hear in their dreams the tones of the midnight bells which call the grown-ups to worship in church; then they imagine that the little angels are now moving through heaven or the Holy Christ is returning home after visiting all children […]. (150-51)[44]

In other words, the narrative takes pains to describe the "wonderful event" of Christmas as something that is staged by the parents and that the children understand only on a very limited and not at all accurate basis. Even as it does so, however, the narrative also emphasizes the fact that nonetheless, or perhaps for this very reason, their limited understanding carries them through the darkest hours of life, insulating them from the madness that ultimately claims Abdias. It is a celebration, the reader is told,

> which continues to affect us throughout our whole lives; and sometimes, even in our old age, in the midst of troubled, melancholy, or touching memories, it flies on bright, glittering wings through the desolate, sad, and empty night sky like a backward glance into a time now past. (150-51)[45]

In both respects, the initial conceptual frame describing the children's understanding of the "wonderful event" that is Christmas foreshadows their efforts to understand the "wonderful events" that befall them in the particular Christmas story that follows. Moreover, as was the case in *Abdias,* this general frame once again becomes a way for the narrative to remind its considerably more world-weary adult readers that they still need and want to emulate the children. It is "because this holiday has such a lasting effect," the initial frame concludes, that "[…] we like to be present when children celebrate it and rejoice in it" (153).[46]

The narrative framing then moves to a description of the particular mountain—the *Berg* of the story's title—where the two children will spend their Christmas Eve. Significantly, the very first description of the mountain already juxtaposes its reality with its appearance from the human perspective of the village: "Toward the south of the village one sees a snowy mountain whose gleaming horns seem to be almost directly above the house tops but are in fact not so near" (155).[47] Some paragraphs later we read,

> But from the lower regions the recent winter snow [...] recedes and a vague iridescence of blue and green becomes visible; this is the glacial striation that is exposed and sends its greetings to the inhabitants below. At the edge of this iridescence, where from a distance it looks like a border of broken jewels, it is, from close up, a mixture of wild, gigantic blocks, slabs and debris, crowded together and piled in confusion over one another. (159)[48]

Like the lightning strikes and Abdias's madness, this extreme natural setting of "wild, gigantic blocks, slabs and debris" is ironically only describable in its indistinguishability. In the original German, it is not something that is even described as "green" or "blue." Rather, the colors are themselves blurred and then nominalized, replacing the indistinguishable objects from which they emanate with "an indefinite shimmering of greenish and bluish." This is all the villagers, from their distanced human physical perspective, are allowed by nature to perceive: indefinite, shimmering colors benignly, as it seems to them, "sending their greetings" down to them. Still, their reasoned understanding of the mountain and its features appears to make even their limited perception enough. They appreciate the mountain as a powerful force of nature, and their reasoned observation of it over time allows them to adjust their behavior in accordance with even the slightest changes in its appearance. Their doing so provides a concrete example of the activity of the "mental eye of science" described theoretically in the *Preface*, and of "reason, the eye of the soul" as described philosophically in the frame of *Abdias*: "The inhabitants of the valley call the slight variations great ones, note them well, and calculate the progress of the year by them" (159).[49]

Meanwhile, the narrator's description of what this indefinite iridescence actually is has provided the specific extreme setting in which the children later find themselves:

> "We have now got to the ice," said the boy, "we're on the mountain, Sanna, you know, the one we see from our garden looking so white in the sunshine. [...] Do you still remember how we often used to sit in the garden in the afternoon, how really beautiful it was, how the bees buzzed

> around us, the linden trees smelled sweet and the sun shone in the sky?" (209)[50]

In terms of their character, the narrative has already positioned the children at the same poles evident in the *Preface,* in *Abdias*, and in the multivalent construction "wir wollen":

> The boy Conrad already had the serious character of his father, and the girl Susanna, named after her mother, or Sanna, as she was called for short, had much faith in his knowledge, judgment, and power and yielded absolutely to his leadership, just as her mother yielded absolutely to the leadership of the father, to whom she attributed unerring judgment and ability. (179)[51]

The younger girl, in other words, is lead by her "faith" in the "knowledge, judgment and power" that guide her "serious" older brother. Both children underscore this general characterization of them as they react to the "force of nature" atop the mountain. As Conrad reasons his way back home to the village, his plan of action is simultaneously supported by both the strength of his reasoning *and* by Sanna's unwavering faith, registered repeatedly in her affirmative refrain "Yes, Conrad":

> "Do you see now, Sanna, since we're at the ice now, we'll go down over the blue color, then through the forests where the rocks are, then over the meadows, then through the green leaf woods, and then we'll be in the valley of Gschaid and find our village easily."
> "Yes, Conrad," said the girl. (211)[52]

The forests, the meadows, the woods—all are described as such in Conrad's plan with comforting familiarity. The "blue color," however, is different. In the case of the rocks and ice, Conrad cannot rely on the actual terrain, but must depend instead on its appearance from the village. In imitation of his father and the rest of the villagers, he substitutes the sensory data he knows—the color as seen from the village below—for the terrain itself. And like the children in whose minds the sights and sounds of the staged Christmas festivities become the "coming of the Christ child," Sanna and Conrad continue to display a childlike dependence here on blind faith on the one hand and on logical deduction based on ever more limited sensory data on the other. Earlier, Conrad repeatedly uses the phrase "wir wollen" as he encourages them to use their senses to get their bearings. First, he tells Sanna to stop and look around: "We'll stop for a moment and look about ["*Wir wollen* ein wenig stehenbleiben und herumsehen," (my emphasis)], perhaps we'll see something." Several pages later, he tells her to stop and listen "We'll stop for a while and listen [*wir wollen* ein wenig stehen bleiben und horchen, (my emphasis)]; maybe we can hear something from the valley." Both efforts yield the same negative result: "But they saw nothing"; "But they heard nothing" (201, 205).[53] The children are learning the hard way that the map is not the territory.

Nevertheless, as they reach "the blue color," Conrad redoubles his efforts. He seeks to compensate for their growing sense of helplessness and uncertainty by presenting all the more forcefully the "knowledge, judgment and power" that Sanna believes him to possess. His description of the indescribable and daunting *terra incognita* in which the children unexpectedly find themselves as "the blue color" is of absolutely no practical use to them as they try to navigate it. Still, it allows him to enact the survival tactic that the opening frame describes with regard to the power of children's memories of Christmas festivities. By referencing their memory of this region's appearance from the comfortable perspective of their garden on a bright summer day, he allows this perspective, however inaccurate and useless in practical terms, to "fly [to them] through the desolate, sad and empty night sky." In addition, this time, instead of saying "wir wollen," he substitutes the more definite future-tense form "wir werden" as he lays out his plan of action: "*We will* go down over the blue color [...]": "so *werden wir* über die blaue Farbe hinabgehen [...]" (my emphasis).

Conrad is clearly just whistling in the dark. With the apparent "indifferent innocence" of nature itself, the narrative's pithy description immediately and effortlessly unmasks Conrad's reason and Sanna's faith in it alike. Only two simple descriptive sentences are needed to put things into their proper perspective: "The children now went into the ice where it was accessible. They were tiny mobile points in these enormous chunks" (211).[54] It is not the children alone, however, whose reasoned human perspective becomes meaningless in "the blue color"—"as blue," the reader is told, "as nothing else in the world." [55] When the narrative notes that "because there was no shadow, there could be no judgment about the size of things" (207),[56] it also acknowledges its own inability to represent this extreme natural situation any more comfortingly or intelligibly than they can. Thus, atop the mountain, the children and the narrative alike struggle, "with the courage of ignorance, [to] clamber[ ] into the ice" (213),[57] as both search with increasing futility for distinguishing physical characteristics from which they can draw reasoned perspectives or conclusions. The children are reduced to Conrad's increasingly ineffectual rational efforts on the one hand and to Sanna's increasingly irrational blind faith in them on the other. Initially meaningful in its comforting expression of unwavering faith, her repeated refrain "Ja, Konrad" becomes almost maddening to the reader in its increasing meaninglessness and emptiness. The narrative, meanwhile, must resort to paradoxical descriptions that both creatively expand and self-admittedly transgress the limits of linguistic sense or reason. "It seemed," we read, "to be a great expanse of light and yet one could not see three paces ahead; everything was enveloped, *if one may say so,* in a single white darkness [...]" (206; my emphasis).[58]

We are presented, "if one may say so," with a figurative and figural madness; a point where human reason and comprehensible linguistic description fail. Both the children and the narrative actually reach the point—described conceptually in the opening frame of *Abdias*—"farther than which one cannot see and beyond which nothing more exists": "They intended to climb down again on the other side. But there was no other side. As far as the eyes of the children could reach there was nothing but ice" (213).[59] The disparaging comment of Stifter's English contemporary regarding *Abdias* assumes unintended significance here as it sums up the situation perfectly: "The effect is like that of a highly finished doorway leading into mere vacant space." At this point, Conrad tells Sanna that they cannot continue, and she agrees as always. For the first and only time, however, the grammatical structure of his question forces Sanna to agree with a "nein" rather than her customary "ja, Konrad." As empty as her "ja" may have become, reading the "nein" without his name attached to it evokes a new measure of terrifying absence, emptiness, and inscrutability.

Abdias's arrival at this moment marked his descent into an equally inscrutable actual madness. "With the courage of ignorance," however, the narrative and the children adhere to the social, cultural, and linguistic framework that the text has worked so hard to establish. The situation atop the mountain reveals just how tenuous, just how "ignorant" this framework is. And yet, however incomprehensibly, by clinging tenaciously to it, the narrator and the protagonists are literally and literarily able to "talk themselves out" of this moment of figurative and figural madness. Both soldier on, managing to find a way out that appears once again to reincorporate and realign their physical and their conceptual perspective of things. And both even come to happy ends, as mother and children are absorbed into the familiar human world of the villagers, whose socio-cultural traditions are thereby reaffirmed. We are told that the villagers, too, will self-assuredly narrate the terrifying event in their own way "for years to come, when the mountain is seen especially clearly on bright days or when strangers are told about its peculiarities" (247).[60] Their understanding of the children's miraculous survival as their own personal reenactment of the Christmas miracle ironically equates them with the children who enjoy *their* staging of Christ's coming each year. However distanced and inaccurate it may be, it allows them to account for things in a way that improves their ability to interact with nature and each other.

And yet, by representing this miraculous *avoidance* of impending madness by the narrator and protagonists alike, *Bergkristall* underscores even more "gently" than *Abdias* the same frightening incommensurability of our rational human perspective *vis-a-vis* the reality it purports to represent. Almost imperceptibly, but nonetheless fundamentally, the confrontation of their reason and their faith with the mountain ice/crystal has affected the "courage of ignorance" that had allowed them comfortably to perceive and to represent their surroundings in their self-assured way. Thus, as the *Novelle* ends, the narrative underscores the ineradicable aftereffects of this brush with madness with one more narrative oscillation. With a final "but" that echoes those of *Abdias*'s opening frame as well as those contradicting the best efforts of the children and the narrator to see and hear something atop the mountain, the final scene ironically leaves the children in exactly the same setting that Conrad invokes on the mountain in his utterly futile attempt to gain control of the situation:

> But the children will not forget the mountain and will now study it still more seriously when they are in the garden, when, as in the past, the sun shines very beautifully, the linden tree gives off its fragrance, the bees hum, and it looks down on them, as beautiful and as blue as the gentle firmament. (249)[61]

This final scene also recalls Schorske's metaphor of the garden. In its description of the children's hard-won new perspective, however, Stifter's narrative clearly already emphasizes "the transformation of the garden" that Schorske attributes to subsequent decades, even as it continues to describe the cozy comfort the garden affords the children. Actually, the last word doesn't even belong to them, but to the indescribably blue "Bergkristall" of the *Novelle*'s title, now both close and distant, both familiar and inscrutable, that looks "gently" but utterly unfathomably down on them.

Thus, *Bergkristall* ends where *Abdias*'s frame and story also begin and end: with the "gentlest" possible physical manifestation of an ominously impassive and inscrutable "final irrationality of existence." And even when Stifter's reader, his narrator, and his protagonists all still manage to retreat from the edge, as we do in *Bergkristall,* we are left with the inescapable awareness that "that way madness lies." In the Austrian literature of the end of the nineteenth century, this "final irrationality of existence" is given much more radical and direct expression. In Hofmannsthal's lyric drama *Der Tor und der Tod (Death and the Fool*) of 1893, for example, Death himself appears on stage and speaks to Claudio and the audience. As he claims Claudio's life and makes his final exit, Death both marvels at and mocks "the fool" Claudio for being human—for being one of "those wondrous beings, / Who explain what is inexplicable, / […] / Master confusion and set it right / And still find ways in the eternal night" (*Death and the Fool*, 66).[62] Stifter's mid-century narratives confront his characters, his readers, and his narrators with similarly extreme test cases, stripping away their "courage of ignorance" *vis-à-vis* this "final irrationality of existence." And yet, whether his characters somehow "still find ways" back from the brink of madness like the children and the villagers, or actually go mad like Abdias, Stifter's narrators continue to try to convince themselves and their readers that "wir wollen": that we want to and we will, and so let us keep on trying to observe an underlying "gentle law" in even "the final irrationality of existence."

This highly ambivalent and paradoxical conviction does not stop Stifter's narrators from representing the possibility that, in addition to inexplicable success and irreversible madness, the stripping away of the "courage of ignorance" might also spawn radically deviant behavior. As Abdias sits out the end of his days in front of his little white house, the narrative reveals that, "Once he awoke again and wanted to go to Africa to stick a knife into Melek's heart, but he could no longer do it (94).[63] And in the *Novelle*'s opening frame, Stifter's narrator has already voiced this possibility in general terms. "The strong submit to [fate] humbly," he notes; "the weak rebel against it complainingly, and the base are dully amazed when the monstrous occurs, or go mad and commit crimes" (21).[64] Speaking from the middle of the nineteenth century, the narrators of *Abdias* and *Bergkristall* do not yet cultivate this possibility any further. Neither do they ignore or deny it, however. Instead, they consciously and conscientiously plant it in the otherwise picture-perfect Biedermeier tranquility of the final garden settings with which both *Novellen* end. Far from being "exploded" or even "transformed," in other words, the gardens in which "Abdias the Jew" sits in quiet but inscrutable madness and on which the impossibly blue "mountain ice/crystal" gazes impassively down on a summer day already demonstrate a gentle but undeniable prescience, "almost not yet familiar to us even in premonitions," of the more radical representations of madness and criminality in the Austrian art and literature that follow.

Works Cited

Adalbert Stifters schrecklich schöne Welt. Jahrbuch des Adalbert Stifter Institutes 1. Linz: Adalbert Stifter Institut, 1993.

Amann, Klaus. "Adalbert Stifters *Nachsommer.* Studie zur didaktischen Struktur des Romans." *Wiener Arbeiten zur deutschen Literatur* 8. Vienna: Braumüller, 1977.

Doppler, Alfred. "Das sanfte Gesetz und die unsanfte Natur in Stifters Erzählungen." In *Geborgenheit und Gefährdung in der epischen und malerischen Welt Adalbert Stifters.* Deutsche Chronik 55. Edited by Jattie Enklaar and Hans Ester. Würzburg: Könighausen & Neumann, 2006. 13-22.

Downing, Eric. "Common Ground: Conditions of Realism in Stifter's 'Vorrede.'" *Colloquia Germanica* 28.1 (1995): 35-53.

Gabriel, Hans. "Prescribing Reality: The Preface as a Device of Literary Realism in Auerbach, Keller, and Stifter." *Colloquia Germanica* 32.4 (1999): 325-44.

Eckermann, Johann Peter. "Gespräch vom 29. Januar 1827." In *Gespräche mit Goethe in den letzten Jahren seines Lebens.* Edited by Heinz Schlaffer. *Johann Wolfgang Goethe. Sämtliche Werke nach Epochen seines Schaffens. Münchner Ausgabe* 19. Edited by Karl Richter. Munich: Hanser, 1986. 200-05.

Hebbel, Friedrich. "Das Komma im Frack." In *Friedrich Hebbel Werke* 3. Edited by Gerhard Fricke et. al. Munich: Hanser, 1965. 683-85.

Hofmannsthal, Hugo von. *Der Tor und der Tod.* Frankfurt a. M.: Insel, 1984.

—. *Death and the Fool.* Trans. Alfred Schwarz. In *Three Plays*. Detroit: Wayne State University Press, 1966. 43-66.

Laufhütte, Hartmut. "Von der Modernität eines Unmodernen. Anläßlich der Erzählung *Abdias* von Adalbert Stifter." In *Adalbert Stifters schrecklich schöne Welt.* In *Adalbert Stifters schrecklich schöne Welt. Jahrbuch des Adalbert Stifter Institutes* 1. Linz: Adalbert Stifter Institut, 1993, 65-75.

Mann, Thomas. *Die Entstehung des Doktor Faustus: Roman eines Romans*. Amsterdam: Bermann-Fischer, 1949.

Metz, Joseph. "The Jew as Sign in Stifter's *Abdias*. *Germanic Review* 77.3 (2002): 219-32.

Nietzsche, Friedrich. *The Birth of Tragedy*. Translated by Douglas Smith. Oxford: Oxford University Press, 2000.
—. *On the Advantage and Disadvantage of History for Life.* Translated by Peter Preuss. Indianapolis, IN: Hackett Publishing, 1980.
—. *On Truth and Lies in a Nonmoral Sense.* Translated by Keith Ansell Pearson and Duncan Large. In *The Nietzsche Reader.* Edited by Keith Ansell Pearson and Duncan Large. London: Blackwell, 2006. 114-23.
Paulin, Roger. *The Brief Compass: The 19th-century German Novelle.* Oxford: Clarendon Press, 1985.
Ragg-Kirkby, Helena. *Adalbert Stifter's Late Prose: The Mania for Moderation*. New York: Camden House, 2000.
Schorske, Carl. *Fin de Siècle Vienna Politics and Culture.* New York: Vintage Books, 1980.
Stern, J. P. *Reinterpretations: Seven Studies in 19th-Century German Literature.* New York: Basic Books, 1964.
Stifter, Adalbert. *Abdias.* Translated by Helen Watanabe-O'Kelly. In *Brigitta and Other Tales.* London: Penguin, 1994. 21-95.
—. *Gesammelte Werke in sechs Bänden.* Frankfurt a. M.: Insel, 1959.
—. *Preface to Many-colored Stones.* Translated by Jeffrey Sammons. In *German Novellas of Realism I.* Edited by Jeffrey Sammons. The German Library, vol. 37. New York: Continuum, 1989. 1-6.
—. *Rock Crystal.* Translated by Harry Steinhauer. In *Deutsche Erzählungen–German Stories: A Bilingual Anthology.* Edited by Harry Steinhauer. Berkeley: University of California Press, 1984. 148-250.
"Studies by Adalbert Stifter." *The Athenaeum* 1087 (26 Aug. 1848): 851-53.
Swales, Martin. *The German Novelle.* Princeton, NJ: The Princeton University Press, 1977.
Swales, Martin and Erica. *Adalbert Stifter: A Critical Study.* Cambridge: Cambridge University Press, 1984.
Weinhold, Ulrike. "Uneigentliche Eigentlichkeit zum Problem der Authentizität in Stifters *Nachsommer.*" *Neuphilologus* 68 (1984): 247-58.

Notes

[1] "D[er] Mann der ewigen Studien" (Hebbel, 685; my translation).

[2] The metaphor of the garden is Schorske's, and he takes it from Stifter's novel. For Schorske's discussion of *Der Nachsommer,* see his chapter entitled "The Transformation of the Garden." The subsequent chapter, in which he discusses the work of Kokoschka and Schönberg, bears the title "The Explosion in the Garden."

[3] "Überhaupt bewegt sich die Stifter-Forschung zwischen 'bekenntnishafte(m) Nachvollzug und Apologie auf der einen Seite, Ideologievorwurf und Ablehnung auf der anderen" (Weinhold, 248; my translation). She is citing Amann, 134.
[4] "[Ein] überschätzte[s] Diminutiv-Talent, [das] breit und weitläufig [die Dinge] beschreibt" (Hebbel, 685; my translation).
[5] Ragg-Kirkby argues persuasively for the importance of both sides in Stifter's late prose, as her title suggests. For her own excellent summary of Stifter criticism and how and where she fits into it, see her Introduction and Conclusion.
[6] Metz, too, pays admirably close attention to both sides, and he also concludes convincingly that what is ultimately at stake is the potential and the limitation of linguistic representation. I merely want to suggest that his conclusions, like Ragg-Kirkby's, tend to overcompensate for the traditional readings of Stifter, pushing Stifter's texts too far in a postmodern direction. My readings will, I hope, support and clarify the idea that Stifter's "vision of meaninglessness," to repeat Ragg-Kirkby, is itself meant to be an integral and ineradicable component of the meaning of his texts rather than their final word.
[7] Again, these are Schorske's terms and this is his basic conclusion. See his chapters "The Transformation of the Garden" and "The Explosion in the Garden."
[8] J. P. Stern's comments on Stifter remain among the most readable and insightful overviews in English (see chapter 6, 239-300, "Propitiations: Adalbert Stifter"). Otherwise, before the recent work of Ragg-Kirkby and Metz, Erica and Martin Swales offer the most balanced critical reading in this regard of Stifter in general and *Bergkristall* in particular. I am also indebted to recent articles in German by Alfred Doppler, Hartmut Laufhütte, and Ulrike Weinhold for their attention to this unresolved coexistence of perspective in Stifter's texts.
[9] "Seltener [...] ist beobachtet worden, daß hinter der stillen, innigen Genauigkeit gerade seiner Naturbetrachtung eine Neigung zum Exzessiven, Elementar-Katastrophalen, Pathologischen wirksam ist [...]" (124; my translation). Mann goes on to cite *Bergkristall* and *Abdias* as two primary examples of his observation.
[10] I use the term "gentle"—*sanft* in German—in anticipation of its repeated appearance at crucial moments in Stifter's writings. The centrality of the term to the paradoxical structure of his aesthetic program will become clear in the course of my readings. As regards Nietzsche, I am thinking here in particular of his description of the function of asthetics in *The Birth of Tragedy (Die Geburt der Tragödie)*, of the human need to build one's own "horizon" in *On the Advantage and Disadvantage of History for Life (Vom Nutzen und Nachteil der Historie für das Leben),* and of his critique of language as a metaphorical "lie in an extra-moral sense" in his essay *On Truth and Lie in an Extra-moral Sense (Über Wahrheit und Lüge im aussermoralischen Sinne*).
[11] My own discussion of Stifter's Preface in conjunction with those of Auerbach and Keller provides a more in-depth view of how I read its structure and function. Eric Downing also provides a good sense of the status of this discussion as well as a careful reading of the Preface in English.
[12] The original German reads as follows: "Wir wollen das sanfte Gesetz erblicken suchen, wodurch das menschliche Geschlecht geleitet wird [...]. Es gibt [...]

Kräfte, die nach dem Bestehen der gesamten Menschheit hinwirken, die durch die Einzelkräfte nicht beschränkt werden dürfen. Es ist das Gesetz dieser Kräfte, […] das Gesetz, das will, daß jeder geachtet, geehrt, ungefährdet neben dem anderen bestehe […]" (*Gesammelte Werke* 3:7-14,10-11).

[13] For this reason, and because the genre is particularly well-developed in German-language literature of this period, I retain the German term *Novelle* rather than using the less clearly defined, if more recognizable, English term "Novella."

[14] For a good overview in English of the development of the *Novelle* and the debate surrounding its definition, see Martin Swales, *The German Novelle*, or, more recently, Roger Paulin, *The Brief Compass The 19th-century German Novelle*. Paulin's study also contains an appendix of famous pronouncements on the genre by Goethe and others in the original German.

[15] "Was ist die Novelle anderes als eine sich ereignete unerhörte Begebenheit?" (203; my translation).

[16] "D[ie] harmlosen folgenden Dinge[ ]" (*Gesammelte Werke* 3:14).

[17] "Es gibt Menschen, auf welche eine solche Reihe Ungemach aus heiterm Himmel fällt, daß sie endlich dastehen und das hagelnde Gewitter über sich ergehen lassen: so wie es auch andere gibt, die das Glück mit solchen ausgesuchten Eigensinne heimsucht, daß es scheint, als kehrten sich in einem gegebenen Falle die Naturgesetze um, damit es nur zu ihrem Heile ausschlage (*Gesammelte Werke* 2:7).

[18] "Auf diesem Wege sinde die Alten zu dem Begriffe des Fatums gekommen, wir zu dem milderen des Schicksals. Aber es liegt auch wirklich etwas Schauderndes in der gelassenen Unschuld, womit die Naturgesetze wirken, daß uns ist, als lange ein unsichtbarer Arm aus der Wolke, und tue vor unseren Augen das Unbegreifliche" (*Gesammelte Werke* 2:7).

[19] "Dreißig Jahre nach dem Tode Dithas lebte Abdias noch, wie lange nachher, weiß man nicht […]. Wie alt er geworden war, wußte man nicht. Manche sagten, es seien weit über hundert Jahre gewesen […]. So endete das Leben und die Laufbahn des Juden Abdias" (*Gesammelte Werke* 2:114).

[20] "Eines Tages saß er nicht mehr dort, die Sonne schien auf den leeren Platz, und auf seinen frischen Grabhügel, aus dem bereits Spitzen von Gräsern hervorsahen" (*Gesammelte Werke* 2:114).

[21] "Er saß viele Jahre […]—und er wußte nicht, wie lange er gesessen war […]" (*Gesammelte Werke* 2:114).

[22] "Es ist der Jude Abdias, von dem ich erzählen will. Wer vielleicht von ihm gehört hat, oder wer etwa gar noch die neunzigjährige gebückte Gestalt einst vor dem weißen Häuschen hat sitzen gesehen, […] er halte sich in diesen Zeilen noch einmal sein Bild vor die Augen […] da wir sein Wesen einfach aufzustellen versucht haben […]" (*Gesammelte Werke* 2:9).

[23] "Eine heitere Blumenkette hängt durch die Unendlichkeit des Alls, und sendet ihren Schimmer in die Herzen—die Kette der Ursachen und Wirkungen—und in das Haupt des Menschen ward die schönste dieser Blumen geworfen, die Vernunft, das Auge der Seele, die Kette daran anzuknüpfen" (*Gesammelte Werke* 2:8).

[24] "Dieses war den Alten Fatum, furchtbarer letzter starrer Grund des Geschehenden, über den man nicht hinaus sieht, und jenseits dessen auch nichts mehr ist [...]; uns ist es Schicksal" (*Gesammelte Werke* 2:8).

[25] "Aber eigentlich mag es weder ein Fatum geben als letzte Unvernunft des Seins, noch auch wird das einzelne [Schicksal] auf uns gesendet; sondern eine heitere Blumenkette hängt durch die Unendlichkeit des Alls" (*Gesammelte Werke* 2:8).

[26] "Aber es liegt auch wirklich etwas Schauderndes in der gelassenen Unschuld, womit die Naturgesetze wirken [...]" (*Gesammelte Werke* 2:7).

[27] "Wir wollen nicht weiter grübeln, wie es sei in diesen Dingen, sondern weiter schlechthin von einem Manne erzählen, an dem sich manches davon darstellte, und von dem es ungewiß ist, ob sein Schicksal ein seltsameres Ding sei, oder sein Herz . Auf jeden Fall wird man durch Lebenswege wie der seine [...] in ein düsteres Grübeln hineingelockt über Vorsicht, Schicksal und letzten Grund aller Dinge" (*Gesammelte Werke* 2:9).

[28] "Er saß viele Jahre, [...] und er wußte nicht, wie lange er gesessen war, *denn nach glaublichen Aussagen war er wahnsinnig gewesen"* (*Gesammelte Werke* 2:114; my emphasis).

[29] "etwa gar noch einst vor dem weißen Häuschen hat sitzen gesehen" (*Gesammelte Werke* 2:9).

[30] "d[ie] gelassene[ ] Unschuld, womit die Naturgesetze wirken" (*Gesammelte Werke* 2:7).

[31] "Wenn wir, so wie wir für das Licht die Augen haben, auch für die Elektrizität [...] ein Sinneswerkzeug hätten, welche große Welt, welche Fülle von unermeßlichen Erscheinungen würde uns da aufgetan sein. Wenn wir aber dieses leibliche Auge nicht haben, so haben wir dafür das geistige der Wissenschaft, und diese lehrt uns, daß die elektrische [...] Kraft auf einem ungeheuren Schauplatz wirke, daß sie auf der ganzen Erde und durch den ganzen Himmel verbreitet sei, daß sie alles umfließe [...]. Der Blitz ist nur ein ganz kleines Merkmal dieser Kraft, sie selber aber ist ein Großes in der Natur" (*Gesammelte Werke*3:9).

[32] "Dort reitet der Beduine zwischen der dunklen Wolke seines Himmels und dem gelben Sande seiner Wüste: da springt ein leichter glänzender Funke auf sein Haupt, er fühlt durch seine Nerven ein unbekanntes Rieseln, hört noch trunken den Wolkendonner in seinen Ohren, und dann auf ewig nichts mehr" (*Gesammelte Werke* 2:7).

[33] "Da der Regen noch kaum leise auf die Dächer niederträufelte, geschah ein schmetternder Schlag, von Feuer begeleitet, das das ganze Haus in einen blendenden Schein setzte. Abdias erkannte augenblicklich, daß der Blitz in sein Haus gefahren sei. [...] Der Blitz war durch [Dithas Zimmer] gegangen, er hatte die Decke und den Boden durchgeschlagen, daß dicker Staub in der Stube war, [...] Ditha war unbeschädigt" (*Gesammelte Werke* 2:91).

[34] "Es geschah eine wundervolle Begebenheit, eine Begebenheit, die so lange wundervoll bleiben wird, bis man nicht jene großen, verbreiteten Kräfte der Natur wird ergründet haben [...]. Bisher sind sie [diese Begebenheiten] uns kaum noch mehr als bloß wunderlich und ihr Wesen ist uns fast noch nicht einmal in Ahnungen bekannt" (*Gesammelte Werke* 2:90).

[35] "Dasselbe Gewitter, welches Ditha sehend gemacht hatte, hatte ihm mit Hagel das Hausdach und seinen Nachbarn die Ernte zerschlagen [...]. Jetzt, da er im nassen Grase stand, war alles vorüber" (*Gesammelte Werke* 2:94).
[36] "Kein Tropfen Regen fiel, nur die dünnen Wolken rieselten, wie schnell gezogene Schleier, über den Himmel" (*Gesammelte Werke* 2:113).
[37] "Sie schwieg plötzlich. Ihm war es, als hätte er seitwärts an der Garbe einen *sanften* Schein lodern gesehen. [...] Da er hinblickte, war schon alles vorüber. Es war auf den Schein ein kurzes heiseres Krachen gefolgt, und Ditha lehnte gegen eine Garbe zurück, und war tot" (*Gesammelte Werke* 2:113).
[38] "Das Gewitter, welches dem Kinde mit seiner wiechen Flamme das Leben vom Haupte geküßt hatte, schüttelte an dem Tage noch auf alle Wesen reichlichen Segen herab, und hatte, wie jenes, das ihr das Augenlicht gegeben, mit einem schönen Regenbogen im weiten Morgen geschlossen" (*Gesammelte Werke* 2:114).
[39] "er aber hatte nichts davon gemerkt" (*Gesammelte Werke* 2:94).
[40] "Abdias saß nach diesem Ereignisse au dem Bänkchen vor seinem Hause, und sagte nichts, sondern er schaute die Sonne an. [...]—Und er wußte nicht, wie lange er gesessen war, denn nach glaublichen Aussagen war er wahnsinnig geworden" (*Gesammelte Werke* 2:114).
[41] "Und auch derjenige, der nie etwas von diesem Manne gehört hat, folge uns, wenn es ihm gefällt, bis zu Ende, da wir sein Wesen einfach aufzustellen versucht haben, und dann urteile er über den Juden Abdias, wie es ihm sein Herz nur immer eingibt" (*Gesammelte Werke* 2:9).
[42] The story's original title, *Der heilige Abend,* connects the children's miraculous survival even more directly with the Christmas miracle.
[43] "Unsere Kirche feiert verschiedene Feste, welche zum Herzen dringen. [...] Eines der schönsten Feste feiert die Kirche fast mitten im Winter, [...] das Fest der Weihnacht" (*Gesammelte Werke* 3:181).
[44] "Mit dem Kirchenfeste ist auch ein häusliches verbunden. Es hat sich in fast allen christlichen Ländern verbreitet, daß man den Kindern die Ankunft des Christkindleins—auch eines Kindes, des wunderbarsten, das je auf der Welt war—als ein heiteres, glänzendes, feierliches Ding zeigt [...]. Die Kinder dürfen nicht eher kommen, als bis das Zeichen gegeben wird, daß der heilige Christ zugegen gewesen ist und die Geschenke, die er mitgebracht, hinterlassen hat [...]. Wenn sie [die Kinder] dann zuweilen in ihre Träume hinein die Glockentöne der Mitternacht hören, [...] dann mag es ihnen sein, als zögen jetzt die Englein durch den Himmel, oder als kehre der Heilige Christ nach Hause, welche nunmehr bei allen Kindern gewesen ist [...]" (*Gesammelte Werke* 3:182).
[45] "das durch das ganze Leben fortwirkt und manchmal noch spät im Alter bei trüben, schwermütigen oder rührenden Erinnerungen gleichsam als Rückblick in die einstige Zeit mit den bunten, schimmernden Fittichen durch den öden, traurigen und ausgeleerten Nachthimmel fliegt" (*Gesammelte Werke* 3:182).
[46] "So stehen wir so gerne dabei, wenn Kinder dasselbe [dieses Fest] begehen und sich darüber freuen..." (*Gesammelte Werke* 3:183).

[47] "Gegen Mittag sieht man von dem Dorfe einen Schneeberg, der mit seinen glänzenden Hörnern fast oberhalb der Hausdächer zu sein scheint, aber in der Tat doch nicht so nahe ist" (*Gesammelte Werke* 3:185).

[48] "Aber es weicht von ihren unteren Teilen der Winterschnee, und es wird das unbestimmte Schillern von Bläulich und Grünlich sichtbar, das das Geschiebe von Eis ist, das dann bloßliegt und auf die Bewohner unten hinabgrüßt. Am Rande dieses Schillerns, wo es von ferne wie ein Saum von Edelsteinsplittern aussieht, ist es in der Nähe ein Gemenge wilder, riesenhafter Blöcke, Platten und Trümmer" (*Gesammelte Werke* 3:187).

[49] "Die Bewohner des Tales heißen die geringen Veränderungen große, bemerken sie wohl und berechnen an ihnen den Fortschritt des Jahres" (*Gesammelte Werke* 3:188).

[50] "Wir sind jetzt bis zu dem Eis gekommen," sagte der Knabe, "Wir sind auf dem Berge, Sanna, weißt du, den man von unserem Garten aus im Sonnenscheine so weiß sieht […] wie es recht schön war, wie die Bienen um uns summten, die Linden dufteten und die Sonne von dem Himmel schien?" (*Gesammelte Werke* 3:217-18).

[51] "Der Knabe Konrad hatte schon das ernste Wesen seines Vaters, und das Mädchen Susanna, nach ihrer Mutter so genannt, oder, wie man es zur Abkurzung nannte, Sanna, hatte viel Glauben zu seinen Kenntnissen, seiner Einsicht und seiner Macht und gab sich unbedingt unter seiner Leitung, gerade so wie die Mutter sich unbedingt unter die Leitung des Vaters gab, dem sie alle Einsicht und Geschicklichkeit zutraute" (*Gesammelte Werke* 3:199-200).

[52] "'Siehst du nun, Sanna, weil wir jetzt bei dem Eise sind, so werden wir über die blaue Farbe hinabgehen, dann durch die Wälder, […] dann über die Wiesen, und dann durch die grünen Laubwälder, und dann werden wir in dem Tale von Gschaid sein und recht leicht unser Dorf finden.'
'Ja, Konrad,' sagte das Mädchen" (*Gesammelte Werke* 3:218).

[53] "Vielleicht erblicken wir etwas. Sie erblickten aber nichts." "[Wir wollen stehen bleiben und horchen], ob wir nicht etwas hören können […]. Sie blieben nun stehen, aber sie hörten nichts" (*Gesammelte Werke* 3:212, 214).

[54] "Die Kinder gingen nun in das Eis hinein, wo es zugänglich war. Sie waren winzigkleine wandelde Punkte in diesen ungeheuern Stücken" (*Gesammelte Werke* 3:218).

[55] "die blaue Farbe" […] "so blau, wie gar nichts in der Welt ist" (*Gesammelte Werke* 3:218-19).

[56] "[…] Weil kein Schatten war, so war kein Urteil über die Größe der Dinge" (*Gesammelte Werke* 3:215).

[57] "Mit dem Starkmute der Unwissenheit kletterten sie in das Eis hinein" (*Gesammelte Werke* 3:220).

[58] "Es schien eine große Lichtfülle zu sein, und doch konnte man nicht drei Schritte vor sich sehen; alles war, wenn man so sagen darf, in eine einzige weiße Finsternis gehüllt" (*Gesammelte Werke* 3:215).

[59] "Jenseits wollten sie wieder hinabklettern. Aber es gab kein Jenseits. So weit die Augen der Kinder reichen konnten, war lauter Eis" (*Gesammelte Werke* 3:220).

[60] "Man wird noch nach Jahren davon reden, wenn man den Berg an heiteren Tagen besonders deutlich sieht, oder wenn man den Fremden von seinen Merkwürdigkeiten erzählt" (*Gesammelte Werke* 3:240).
[61] "Die Kinder aber werden den Berg nicht vergessen und werden ihn jetzt noch ernster betrachten, wenn sie in dem Garten sind, wenn wie in der Vergangenheit die Sonne sehr schön scheint, der Lindenbaum duftet, die Bienen summen und er [der Berg] so schön und so blau wie das sanfte Firmament auf sie herniederschaut" (*Gesammelte Werke* 3:240).
[62] "Wie wundervoll sind diese Wesen, / Die, was nicht deutbar, dennoch deuten, / Was nie geschrieben wurde, lesen, / Verworrenes beherrschend binden / Und Wege noch im Ewig-Dunkeln finden" (*Der Tor und der Tod*, 31).
[63] "Auf einmal erwachte er wieder und wollte jetzt nach Afrika reisen, um Melek ein Messer in das Herz zu stoßen; aber er konnte nicht mehr; denn seine Diener mußten ihn am Morgen aus dem Hause tragen bringen, und mittags und abends wieder hinein" (*Gesammelte Werke* 2:114).
[64] "Der Starke unterwirft sich [dem Schicksal] auch ergeben, der Schwache stürmt mit Klagen darwider, und der Gemeine staunt dumpf, wenn das Ungeheure geschieht, oder er wird wahnwitzig und begeht Frevel" (*Gesammelte Werke* 2:8).

CHAPTER TWO

DISCIPLINING PSYCHOANALYSIS INTO VIENNESE MODERNISM: FREUD'S NEW SCIENCE AND THE MEDICALIZED SUBJECT

KATHERINE ARENS

From the first, Freud was at pains to define psychoanalysis, most often by claiming it as a new discipline, alongside psychiatry, psychology, and other sciences of culture of his era (such as anthropology). His new discipline, however, was anything but straightforwardly defined. As Freud himself acknowledged, his "science" was very much seeking a role for itself among the professional claims of the practitioners of several different disciplines and their institutional contexts. Most often, he set his work over and against medical psychiatry and the experimental psychology of his day, as he defined his particular therapeutic approach to mind.

Yet Freud's own origin myth is very incomplete, no matter how convincingly it has become the master narrative of psychoanalysis's heroic creation and titanic cultural battles. As the numerous memoirs and biographies from within the Freudian movement attest, psychoanalysis was incubated as an outsider discipline—not to be contained, evaluated, or judged against any of its peers. Early Freudians (including Freud himself) had frequent recourse to this genesis narrative: they often interpreted confrontations or rejection in terms of this "us/them" boundary, claiming that their new work was rejected by embedded orthodoxies or outmoded institutions, or as personal or "ideological" conflicts within a fragile, but threatened movement that promised to change the world.[1]

These narratives capture one dimension of the Freudian movement: he managed to take this outsider role seriously and so to evolve his own institutional base, including publishing venues, meetings, and credentialing organizations. Indirectly, these narratives also explain many of the consequences of Freudianism's forced emigration during the Nazi era, as Freud's original institutional bases were in part lost and new coalitions of practice were sought by émigrés trying to defeat these new historical opponents. Today we remember this diaspora of Freudianism as a further series of triumphs: Anna Freud's Hampstead Clinic in England, and its connection to public health and to children's war trauma; the US's combats between the International Psychoanalytic Association and the American Medical Association; the triumphalist tales of analysts preserved in Hollywood films, from Anatole Litvak's 1948 film *The Snake Pit* (where an analyst saves patients from psychiatry) through the more questionable images of the field offered by Barbra Streisand (as director, *The Mirror Has Two Faces* [1996], and *The Prince of Tides* [1991]).

The present essay will willfully ignore these seductive narratives in order to reclaim an often overlooked dimension of Freud's work: what the philosopher Michèle Le Dœuff calls a *Philosophical Imaginary* (1989; *Imaginaire philosophique*, 1980). There, Le Dœuff takes up the case of philosophy to show how a formalist science of any sort is a discipline which authorizes its users in a particular way, creating an authorized subject of its knowledge—the image of its "approved user" and day-to-day practices: "Philosophical discourse is inscribed and declares its status as philosophy through a break with myth, fable, the poetic, the domain of the image. . . . It is, indeed, a very odd commonplace to associate philosophy with a certain logos thought of as defining itself through opposition to other types of discourse" (1).

In another of her major works, *Hipparchia's Choice* (1991; *L'Étude et le rouet*, 1989), Le Dœuff traces how philosophy substitutes professionals for a profession, the arbiters of knowledge for the knowledge itself, noting that "there is always something of the philosopher in philosophy and that thus the latter remains an indiscipline" (135). In this volume, Le Dœuff outlines how philosophers dominate by producing knowledge that they define as their field. Thus philosophy is a discipline identified through the personae of the teacher, the guru, or the professional controlling its production and distribution of knowledge. These philosophers explain, explicate, or elucidate canonical texts for insiders and use their mastery of technical terminology to decide who may act as authorized readers of these texts. As proof for these assertions, Le Dœuff offers her analysis of the discipline's "philosophical imaginary" (2): each "philosophical imaginary" is the set of culture-bound images that centers the knowledge valued by the philosophy of any particular era.[2]

It is straightforward to take up the equivalent for Freudianism—what might be called the "psychoanalytic imaginary"—in order to see the implications of Freud's work in its Viennese context as it produces social images of wellness and illness that resonate through other texts of the era, defining the individual at the *fin de siècle*. The source for this discussion is an appeal to the text that offers the most comprehensive archive of Freudian theory as it evolved in Vienna, before it went into the diaspora and responded to the needs of other cultures. As we shall see in reading *An Outline of Psychoanalysis* (*Abriß der Psychoanalyse*, originally 1940), Freud's psychoanalytic imaginary points not to one specific therapeutic discipline, but rather to several unreconciled, disjunct, and even unreconcilable definitions of how individuals need to be rescued from culture.

The *Outline*, in this reading, reveals Freudianism as a particular cultural force from *fin de siècle* Vienna. Against the specifically Austrian scientific constellation of socialized medicine in which Freud's work originated, the images of illness, therapy, and cure preserved in Freudianism emerge as a kind of cultural reactionism claiming to cure individuals but actually in many cases blaming the victims, medicalizing what others might see as part of society, and envisioning individuals in isolation rather than as part of a cultural community. From this perspective, the subject of the Freudian "cure" ends up as determined psycho-somatically in ways that deny the effects of her social objectification and historical determinism, and the analyst becomes an agent of social regression.

Freud: Model versus Institution

In many ways a problematic text, the *Outline* was probably begun in 1938, when Freud was in English exile. The form in which we know it might not be that intended by Freud: the last chapter is disarmingly short. Nonetheless, it was published in 1940, after Freud's death, with the editor referring to it as "incomplete" rather than "unfinished," for it is a lucid, condensed overview of the terminology central to psychoanalytic theory in all its variants.

The work is divided into three parts: "The Mind and its Workings," "The Practical Task," and "The Theoretical Yield." The first of these is most important for the present discussion, since its five chapters each present a different model of the mind. Each uses a different central metaphor to build the architecture of its particular theory focus. They are summarized in the following table:

Model	Epistemological Claim	Possible Institutional Configurations
Psychical Apparatus agencies: id/ego/superego	synchronic, a phenomenology of mental processes (internal to mind); stresses internal management and self-preservation in face of affects	behavior modification, based on internal balancing "weak ego"), normative (i.e., fixing a behavior in order to facilitate socialization; the self as victim of society
Theory of Instincts libido/anti-libido Eros/destructive impulse	soma-world interface, stressing conservation of energy level of the individual with respect to desires in outside world; dynamics of mind/world as put into play by the body, in synchronic frame	phasic-behavioral research, favors sociobiology and acculturation; dovetails with work on body-mind chemistry; rarely used in psychotherapy
Development of Sexual Function oral/anal/phallic/latent/genital phase	stresses diachronic socialization, preservation of species in self/other relations	little interest in acculturation; stress on parents as source of sexual-social identity problems; playrooms and workrooms for acting out and re-learning "normal" sex behaviors correlating with normative sexual identity
Psychical Qualities unconscious/preconscious/conscious	depth-of-processing model; stresses storage and retrieval of memory vis-à-vis acculturation, internal phenomena	trauma repair and reequilibration; optimalization therapy, sports psychology, individual therapy; classic talking cure about wishes and assertion of self
Dream Interpretation latent and manifest contents; mind as semiotic system	criteria for general semiotic process; originality versus life experience, censorship, representability, and communication norms -- explored within individuals	stress on cultural communication and communicability; semiotic research in the Western tradition, using libraries; often turns into Jungianism, using *metaphors* as *archetypes*

Table 2-1 Freud's Models: An Overview

A review of this inventory can allow us to project this overly familiar theory into more concrete contexts—to trace what might be the sources and nexes of social power implicated in each. Freud uses the term "phenomenology" to describe how he evolves this inventory of terms, each taking up specific relations between the mind and the world and implying motivations for the mind's acts.

The first of Freud's five models is presented under the title "The Psychical Apparatus." Here, Freud describes what he calls in other contexts "agencies": the id, ego, and superego (2). The terminology recalls, on the one hand, older physiology and faculty psychology that assumed the cerebral location of mental functions and affects. In the *Outline*, however, Freud's definitions refute many of the stereotypes we have of them. The id, for example, emerges as containing more than just the stereotyped "instincts":

> [The id] contains everything that is inherited, that is present at birth, that is laid down in the constitution—above all, therefore, the instincts, which originate from the somatic organization and which find a first psychical expression here in forms unknown to us. (2)

The ego develops out of the id to direct the individual in self preservation:

> by becoming aware of stimuli, by storing up experiences about them (in the memory), by avoiding excessively strong stimuli (through flight), by dealing with moderate stimuli (through adaptation) and finally by learning to bring about expedient changes in the external world. . . . (2)

In dealing with the outside world, the ego manages, guides, defers, and satisfies the demands of the id (or surrenders itself to it in sleep) as "a particular distribution of mental energy" (3). The third agency, the superego, summarizes effects of the individual's parents, "family, racial and national traditions," and the demands of the social milieu (3), all of which are internalized on the individual's long growth into maturity. It is the voice of a culture's habits and customs, passing on survival messages to the group that individuals have learned.

In these distinctions, Freud describes the mind functioning synchronically, balancing its responsibilities to its organic host, its own conscious wants, and its remembered sociohistorical context. This model has often been translated into a very specific strategy for therapy: a call to help the individual ego balancing demands from various sources. A "weak ego" may need help balancing the demands made on it; "overdeveloped" id responses may require behavior modification aimed at establishing the individual's socialization (conformity with established norms); "superego" demands must be contextualized, so that the individual learns to respect the demands of the outside world, while not succumbing to them utterly.

Freud thus uses these terminological distinctions to account for dominance within an individual mind, as part of an individual psychic reality. This model guides an analyst to pay attention to how a person gratifies wishes and whims, or relies on authority, or deals with stress on a sense of self. Cast this way, the analyst is authorized to plot possible social-behavioral modifications to an individual's reaction patterns, to help an individual resocialize him- or herself by balancing the demands of the three agencies. The pressures imposed by the superego on the id must be made conscious, while the ego learns to craft its gratification on socially acceptable patterns. This model, then, allows the individual to be evaluated socially-normatively, to stress the *outside* world as a force pressing inward and overpowering the mind, and the individual mind as potentially too weak to deal with it.

Freud's second model reverses this optic, looking at how internal somatic forces put pressure on the mind and press toward external expression. His "Theory of the Instincts" explores "somatic demands on the mind" as expressed in two forms of instinct: the libido and anti-libido, also known, respectively, as *Eros* and the destructive instinct, later called *Thanatos* (5). Eros is a positive instinct, one that documents how an individual joins with others and reinforces a sense of self; Thanatos is negative, pointing toward dissolution and disintegration of identity. Popular shorthand equates these forces with "love and death," identifying these instincts as part of an individual's narcissistic search to attach itself to or avoid objects in the outside world as the id joins its demands to the ego or super-ego, often overcoming them. The analyst seeks evidence of these two instincts as documenting an individual mind's attempt to maintain balance while confronting the world's demands—to conserve energy as the id's somatic demands are displaced, suppressed, or delayed by the ego or superego.

Freud's first two models thus offer two complementary pictures of the mind interacting with the world based on an individual's *id* trying to make or sustain an *ego*-identity in the face of the *superego*—on the moment when somatic demands meet social prohibitions, and an individual emerges as a set of defining choices. One result of the confrontation is internal: the mind becomes ego when the outside impinges on the individual. Another result is external, as the mind engages in a play of self-assertion and destruction vis-à-vis the outside world, emerging with its distinctive pattern of "instincts" that have the potential to undermine the ego's structural stability of the ego.

These two models both operate as dialectical models, pitting the mind against the world—requiring therapy to overcome anything from social anxiety to more severe forms of the ego-in-crisis, helping the individual contain the instincts that threaten the *stability* of a mental architecture. Yet as Freudian therapy, they draw attention particularly to the individual under stress, rather than to the external threats themselves. What, for example, might threaten the individual ego through the anti-libido; what does the libido express about the ego as a balance point between biological determinism and social construction?

Freud's third model answers this question in part by addressing the id/libido under the rubric of the "Development of the Sexual Function." Here he projects the mind-world dialectic into a diachronic framework, seeking to define one facet of individual identity in an evolution of sexual identity—a "phenomenology of the subject" as it correlates with the dynamics and economics of the libido and the structural balance among the id, ego, and superego (13).[3] This is the most (in)famous of Freud's models in the US context, outlining the famous sequence of phases in sexual development, from oral, through anal, phallic, latent, and genital phases of sexuality.

Freud summarizes this developmental sequence as dealing with "how those energies (in the main, the libido) organize themselves into a physiological function which preserves the species" (14)—how social functions are organized to further essentially biological aims. The oral phase describes an individual still largely functioning as id, taking the world into it; the anal, that individual's negative reaction as an emergent ego, when the powers that be in the world deny that wholeness with the world. Subsequently, external prohibitions determine an individual's development more than do instincts. The phallic stage, the stage of Oedipal conflicts, pits the now-individual ego against its family role-models, particularly against the father's authority. The result of the conflict is latency, a withdrawal into self due to implied threat and castration anxiety, and then the individual again emerges into a connection with the world's others and to genital sexuality—a socially scripted connection defined as maturity.

Freudian sex therapy has, in its historical norms of appearance, reified a certain set of social norms as biological necessities. U.S. Freudian therapy of the 1950s, for example, took this model all too seriously as a literal and normative description about appropriate individual development. As many Woody Allen films assure us, the mother is responsible for early-life traumas, the father for later social trauma related to identity, and homosexuality is the result of a developmental error: an individual learns to identify with the opposite-sex parent rather than a more appropriate same-sex one, leading to social misadaptation and a sell-out of the biological imperatives.

At this point, the *Outline* radically shifts focus from the structure and function of the mind to its contents, taking Freud's phenomenology of the mind in a different direction—focusing on mental presentations rather than on the mind's structure or development (14). Freud calls his fourth model, "Psychical Qualities," a "topographical dissection of the psychical apparatus" (20). Yet he is actually asking about psychic localization, asking *where* in the mind information is stored—how deeply buried or easily accessible to the mind it is, classified as either unconscious, preconscious, or conscious data. Such representations might be repressed (rendered inaccessible), as in the case of somatic desires inappropriate to the certain moment. A great number of impressions lie at the borders of accessibility in the preconscious, waiting to be called on by the conscious mind, as it attempts to reassert or maintain an equilibrium with the world. Other data is taken in, registered, and stored in the mind in light of its *tolerability* to the individual, and Freud evaluates that cultural input in terms of its potential to inflict injury or inhibit development. His topographical description, then, reveals a mental landscape of impressions conditioned by education, personal tastes, or acculturation—its "susceptibility to culture" (58). This model stresses what has been taken into the field of identity and being.

That topography reveals itself in dreams, as Freud's fifth and final models sketches. His most famous model for therapy, his dream interpretation, focuses on how the latent contents of the mind become manifest. This model is the inverse of the prior one, aligned to speak about data-retrieval from the mind rather than its storage in it: dreams retrieve a store of culturally bound materials to communicate with the mind, placing it squarely within the communication and symbolic norms of the culture. Dream semiotics—the way dreams "speak" of experience—combines shared cultural source materials with individual instincts to facilitate a mind coming to clarity about itself, to symbolize its wants and needs. From this point of view, dreams operate at the boundary between the "normal" and "abnormal" minds, where the former is judged by the conventionality of its symbols and the latter by its idiosyncrasies. Later in the text, when speaking of "The Theoretical Yield" of psychoanalysis, Freud casts dream interpretation as the key to therapeutics—as the key to the contentious interface between mind and world.

These five models are all familiar today, at least in part, as belonging to the Freudian legacy. The twentieth century had Freudian films, Freudian couches and jokes, Freudian models for art, Freudian legacy wars, and even Freud action figures. Yet what we tend to forget is how

Freud's work succeeded in popular culture while ultimately creating a fortress around itself as a discipline. That space of popular culture has obscured in many ways what we may now revisit as the psychoanalytic imaginary—the way in which Freudian psychoanalysis originally structured itself as a region of power with practitioners of very specific sorts.

Projecting Freud Back into Vienna

The five models pursued here do not exhaust the interface of the mind and world. As the *Outline* indirectly documents, each model constitutes a *different* frame of reference, and a different image about what kinds of illness may result from the mind's interface with the world. Each could, in consequence, have emerged as a completely *different* discipline, rather than as warring branches of "Freudian" analysis. There is in this presentation no unified "psychoanalytic theory"; there is only a set of (mostly complementary) descriptions of how and why minds interface with the world.

Turning to what those models imply for the self in society, we can uncover a very different image of what psychoanalysis thought of the self and what positions therapists might need to assume. Freud's five models tell us very different things about therapists and therapy (see again the chart above).

The id/ego/superego model stresses the self as a victim of society and prescribes a "cure" in strengthening the ego. The theory of the instincts focuses on biology, and thus is very little used in "the talking cure" familiar from the US popular media. Freud's model for sexual development leads to the classic popular image of individuals as created by their relation to their parents and their own sexual traumas. A focus on the conscious and unconscious contents of mind offers an image of how trauma can be repaired, repressions overcome, and healthier selves created. Freudian dream analysis complicates how the mind reveals itself and how its conscious and unconscious stores of experience can be revealed.

It took later generations to formalize this work into therapeutic practice: Freud had, for example, described the set-up of psychoanalytic practice as a conflict of authority between the patient and the analyst. But the *Outline* reveals that the discipline of psychoanalysis had in many ways not yet transcended its nineteenth-century roots. These five models oscillate between two poles of description: on the one hand, finding the etiology of mental diseases in the interaction of self and society, but then implicitly turning to a more medicalized, somatic model where the individual mind is very much conditioned by neurology or physiology. In very striking terms, the overall space of this model tends to turn an individual's knowledge of cultural phenomena from *memory* into *symptoms*. Community and history might seem to play a part in causing illness, but ultimately family and the individual's constitution are most determining of states of wellness or illness.

The *Outline* reveals a discipline that ascribes little or no positive value to community or to the memories that might be called cultural tradition. No wonder, then, that the Freudian movement managed to exclude several early followers whose work attempted to factor cultural and community experience into their treatment of mental illness. Otto Fenichel's great discussions of the social origins of the neuroses and Karen Horney's explorations of female psychology as socially constructed were both early casualties of mainstream Freudianism—in the intellectual history of the Freudian movement, they are remembered as outsiders, no matter how favorably their work might have been received outside psychoanalysis.[4]

And here emerge specific consequences for the intellectual histories of Austria, Austro-Hungary, and Europe: Freudian images of repression and sexual maladaptation have been taken as characteristic of mainstream Austro-Hungarian culture, particularly in Vienna, but also in Budapest, home of many analysts (see Lukacs). Freud's patients, drawn from a very narrow band of the social spectrum, have all too often been taken as representing the Viennese and Central European bourgeoisie in general. Vienna has, in essence, been taken prisoner in historians' collective memory as *Freud's* Vienna: his psychoanalysis paints a picture of a *fin de siècle* culture that besieges individuals, and of individuals who are at the mercy of their biology. This Vienna does not have history so much as a distinctive symptomology. These images, moreover, occlude other historical truths of the era. The Austro-Hungary of the *fin de siècle* was, for example, also the birthplace of several kinds of socialized medicine and social welfare—*Red Vienna*, as described by John W. Boyer (1981) and Anson Rabinbach (1983); it was regarded as a culture of liberalism by Pieter Judson (1996), and its commitment to socialized medicine is amply documented in Arthur Schnitzler's medical reviews (republished in 1988). That liberalism made the city an environment very conscious of social determinism and of society's responsibility to individuals, not just the site of individual struggle and repression.[5]

Nonetheless, the subject of Freudian psychoanalysis ends up seeming like nothing so much as the victim of society favored in modernism. The consequences for intellectual history are profound: when the intellectual models at the basis of psychoanalysis convey an image of an individual pitted against society, they tacitly characterize Viennese society as a force of negativity, opposition, and repression—in fact, the dominant image of rot underlies the golden veneer of *fin de siècle* Vienna in the popular mind, no matter what historians might prove to the contrary. The psychoanalytic imaginary of the *Outline's* psychoanalysis thus clearly aligns itself with turn-of-the-century modernist critiques of traditional society, a particular moment of cultural reaction: this psychoanalysis claims for itself the social power of *medical* practice and places it at the service of individualism, offering a vision of individuals suffering under a society that must devalue the group's influence. Freudianism "cures" individuals by returning them to their individual integrity and their biological essences, envisioning their health as recaptured in isolation rather than as part of a cultural community. Social signification, social objectification, and historical determinism recede in interest.

The intellectual history consonant with this psychoanalytic imaginary, in turn, aligns very closely with Freud's own most cherished image of his place as an analyst and a figure of power. His overwhelming sense of marginalization in Vienna is incontestable, no matter how much more current scholarship has pointed out his integration into the city's intellectual and social life.[6] His own disciplinary politics required him to be cast as an outsider, a self-definition for analysts exacerbated in the Freudian diaspora of the Second World War. Where Freud, heroic Nietzschean superman of therapy, created his own institution, his disciples were forced into alternate institutions to retain jobs and career identity—and usually into private practice. As Freud's followers attempted to rebuild institutional bases outside of Austro-Hungary and Berlin, they had to assert their abilities to self-credential rather than submit to the authority of agencies like the American Medical Association; among the casualties of this shift, for example, was lay analysis. Thus, in a very real sense the scattering of European psychoanalysis in the 1930s encouraged therapists to assume extreme versions of their own roles, defining themselves outside of Europe's institutions, figuring themselves and their therapeutic practice as bulwarks against society's corrosive effects.

Freud, on a ship bound for New York Harbor, quipped to Jung that "we are bringing them the plague," a remark that takes on a new salience in this context. He was indeed bringing a kind of plague—a new collective of professional therapists who enforced the image of individuals at the mercy of their environment. Freud had created a medicalized discipline of culture and empowered it to declare history and traditions the enemy of individuals. That discipline's power derived from the image of individualism it imposed onto the twentieth century: an individual rendered too weak by the nurture of his or her family to resist the imbrication of culture and society on personal identity. The psychoanalytic imaginary reveals to us not only one version of modern individualism, but also a force whose agency has occluded the social and communal innovations of a Viennese intellectual community not determined completely by Freud and his origin myth.

Works Cited

Boyer, John W. *Political Radicalism in Late Imperial Vienna: The Origins of the Christian Social Movement, 1848-1897*. Chicago: University of Chicago Press, 1981.

Fenichel, Otto. *The Psychoanalytic Theory of Neurosis*. New York: W. W. Norton, 1945.

Freud, Sigmund. *An Outline of Psycho-Analysis*. Trans. and ed. James Strachey. New York: W. W. Norton, 1949.

Gay, Peter. *Freud: A Life for Our Time*. New York: W. W. Norton, 1988.

Horney, Karen. *Feminine Psychology*. Ed. Harold Kelman. New York: W. W. Norton, 1967.

Jacoby, Russell. *The Repression of Psychoanalysis: Otto Fenichel and the Political Freudians*. New York: Basic Books, 1983; Chicago: University of Chicago Press, 1986.

Judson, Pieter M. *Exclusive Revolutionaries: Liberal Politics, Social Experience, and National Identity in the Austrian Empire, 1848-1914*. Ann Arbor: University of Michigan Press, 1996.

Le Dœuff, Michèle. *Hipparchia's Choice: An Essay Concerning Women, Philosophy, etc.* Trans. Trista Selous. Oxford: Blackwell, 1991. [*L'Étude et le rouet*, 1989].

—. *The Philosophical Imaginary*. Trans. Colin Gordon. Stanford, CA: Stanford University Press, 1989. [*L'Imaginaire philosophique*, 1980].

Lesky, Erna. *The Vienna Medical School of the Nineteenth Century*. Trans. L. Williams and I. S. Levij. Baltimore, MD: Johns Hopkins University Press, 1976.

Lukacs, John. *Budapest 1900: A Historical Portrait of a City and Its Culture*. 1988. New York: Grove Press, 1990.

McGrath, William J. *Freud's Discovery of Psychoanalysis: The Politics of Hysteria*. Ithaca, NY: Cornell University Press, 1986.

Quinn, Susan. *A Mind of Her Own: The Life of Karen Horney*. New York: Summit Books, 1987.

Rabinbach, Anson. *The Crisis of Austrian Socialism: From Red Vienna to Civil War, 1927-1934*. Chicago: University of Chicago Press, 1983.

Schnitzler, Arthur. *Medizinische Schriften*. Ed. Horst Thomé. Vienna: P. Zsolnay, 1988.

Notes

[1] Compare the accounts of arguments between camps of Freud's followers enumerated in Peter Gay's *Freud: A Life for Our Time*.
[2] Le Dœuff most likely derives this term in analogy to the work of Jacques Lacan and Julia Kristeva in psychoanalysis. For them, the available images (symbols, terms) that a culture uses to signify or communicate its values are referred to as the symbolic order. Individuals develop their own identity by inserting themselves into this symbolic order—by entering into the community, and into its values. As they do so, they develop their own sense of how these relationships work: their imaginary. Le Dœuff calls the sense of professionalism shared by the community of philosophers in any culture the philosophical imaginary—a description which shares the idea that this is a group of professionals sharing a discourse community and engaged in a shared sense of power and prerogative.
[3] This equation with phenomenology is no accident. See William J. McGrath's assessment of what Freud knew of Brentano.
[4] For Fenichel's story, see Russell Jacoby, *The Repression of Psychoanalysis: Otto Fenichel and the Political Freudians*; for Horney's, Susan Quinn's *A Mind of Her Own: The Life of Karen Horney*.
[5] For the history of medicine in Vienna, see Erna Lesky, *The Vienna Medical School of the Nineteenth Century*.
[6] One of the first of these great reevaluations is again McGrath's *Freud's Discovery of Psychoanalysis* (1986), which identifies Freud's reading in philosophy; see Peter Gay's biography (1988) for the best overview of Freud's work and context.

CHAPTER THREE

"BECAUSE THAT'S PATHOLOGICAL!" MANIFESTATIONS OF MADNESS IN 1900 VIENNA IN THE WORKS OF KLIMT AND MUSIL

STEFAN KUTZENBERGER

TRANSLATED BY MARIA MORRISON

In 1900, when after years of work Gustav Klimt first unveiled his large-format painting "Philosophy," it aroused such a scandal that the artist was almost immediately declared insane. Not only did the entangled naked bodies in the painting cause a furor, the ambiguous imagery of the allegory excited heated debate, particularly among the positivistic professors of philosophy. It seems, however, that more than that it was the totality of the depicted life that elicited such a sense of public discomfort. The painting unites all of the stages of life (from infancy to old age) and all conditions (from lustful devotion to bitter envy), as well as Knowledge (as allegory in the form of a woman's head) and Ignorance (in the form of a sphinx emerging from the cosmic murk). The juxtaposition of these oppositions on a single canvas demonstrates Klimt's unquestionable arrival in modernity, that epoch in which "the flare of insight into the unity in the symbol of polarity, the concurrence of opposites," was suddenly possible.[1] If the preceding historicism depicted only unambiguous slices of society and parts of life (mostly mythologized), it was now possible for the artist to begin the attempt to portray life as a totality, with all of its inconsistencies and paradoxes. Surely the greatest attempt to produce such a total artwork is Musil's immense but unfinished novel *The Man without Qualities*. Not coincidentally, the book's central argument revolves around the question of the boundary between normality and insanity. Musil offers a minute dissection of the very society which Gustav Klimt, as creator of "Philosophy," pathologized.[2]

Points of Contact between Klimt and Musil

Gustav Klimt (1862-1918, Vienna) and Robert Musil (1880-1942, Klagenfurt-Geneva) never met. Klimt never read Musil; in fact, as likely as not, he was unaware of the latter's existence. Musil mentions Klimt three times in his diaries and twice in his letters. We know that on the 22 February 1907 he saw Klimt's three faculty paintings (Philosophy, 1899/1907; Medicine 1900/1907; and Jurisprudence 1903/1907) in the Keller and Reiner Gallery in Berlin. He called them "inconceivable … lyrical … and much more."[3] Even if we know of no other encounter between the author and the painter's work, we can assume that Musil would have been familiar with Klimt, for he had always been interested in art, worked as an art critic from time to time for newspapers such as the *Prager Presse* and the *Deutsche Allgemeine Zeitung* (see *Gesammelte Werke*, 9), and was married to a painter who had attended Lovis Corinth's School of Painting for Women. Whereas Klimt, in his lifetime, was considered the greatest Austrian artist and had multiple well-heeled patrons, Musil was known only among a small group of literati; at the end of his life he was forced to constantly send begging letters in order to secure enough money to live.

The two artists share an exceptionally time-consuming work style; as a consequence both can claim only a fairly small body of work. Gustav Klimt is famous for having repainted his pictures again and again. Indeed, even paintings which had already been exhibited and which were thought finished were amended and repainted. (For example, in "Death and Life" [1910/1915] one can still detect traces of Klimt's repainting on the frame. This is also true of all three faculty paintings, for which Alice Strobl lists seven different versions between 1900 and 1907 [151].) Klimt himself speaks of the years of "fumbling, agonizing work" invested in his art (qtd. in Vergo, 92). Needless to say, this "fumbling and agonizing work" is characteristic of Robert Musil's oeuvre as well; in fact, Musil elevated this kind of work to a principle: "The principle of art is never-ending variation" (*Gesammelte Werke*, 7:868).

Gustav Klimt's career began very successfully and very much in keeping with the Zeitgeist. Already as a sixteen-year-old student at the Kunstgewerbeschule (School of Applied Arts), Klimt had the opportunity to participate in designing the pageant by Hans Makart in honor of the Silver Wedding anniversary of the imperial couple, Emperor Franz Joseph I and Empress Elisabeth.[4] Hans Makart, who only the year before had presented his monumental painting *The Entry of Charles V in Antwerp* in the Wiener Künstlerhaus (Artists House in Vienna), had been commissioned to take over the artistic design of the pageant in 1879 (Bernhard, 254). [5] On Sunday, 27 April 1879, the pageant finally took place. It was a kind of living tableau, which extended from the Rotunda in the Prater to the Ring. All three thousand participants were magnificently clad in specially-made costumes from the age of Dürer. The pageant, with an audience of over 350,000, marked the zenith of Makart's career. The report in *Die Neue Freie Presse* (The New Free Press) on the following day spanned three columns and five entire pages:

> Today, our bright, beautiful Vienna, with its artistic sensibility, truly proved itself an imperial city, a designation which it carries with pride. As festive, cordial, and grand as the homage paid to the imperial couple throughout the week was, the homage of the Viennese people themselves far exceeded it.[6]

At the same time the pageant was one of the final presentations of the strengthened bourgeoisie, which, despite its diversity, still formed a whole. The people still believed in a God-given world order founded on the imperial family, upon which they could build and maintain their future.

This pinnacle of historicism heralded not only the death of that artistic epoch, but also the end of the unified worldview of an entire age. With the beginning of the classic modern age there is no longer a single, God-given truth; truth disintegrates into a multiplicity of truths. Particularly in literature this multiplicity of perspectives will be seen as the only viable means of capturing reality. In the arts in general what qualifies as good is no longer that which is beautiful and conforms to an ideal truth (*Wahrheitsideal*), only that which is novel. The Avant Garde (i.e., classic modernism) explicitly rejects the past. If Art movements once lasted for decades, now the most diverse isms followed each other in rapid succession:

> As a reaction against fin de siècle malaise, and partly as a direct consequence of it, new movements in art, literature, and poetry began to emerge and coalesce in pre-war Germany and Austria with a view to providing alternatives to the stifling determinisms of the positivist-scientistic legacy, on the one hand, and Marxist socialism on the other. (Malik, 354)

Gustav Klimt's faculty painting *Philosophy* stands as an exemplary illustration of the paradigm shift at the turn of the century not only because it marks the artist's first major step away from historicism, but above all because of the outrage the painting evoked. In this essay the inclusion of a scandalous work of modern art and the disappointed expectations of a tradition-oriented society will be compared with the social discourses on the waning power of the Habsburgs as it appears in Robert Musil's unfinished monumental novel *Der Mann ohne Eigenschaften* (*The Man Without Qualities*).

Certainly for the early Klimt, Hans Makart's historicism, celebrated in an almost unsurpassable ecstasy of color, was of fundamental importance. Makart found it important to include as many female figures in his paintings as possible. The fact that these figures presented their bodily charms to the spectator mostly half-naked or reclining provocatively naturally provoked dutiful outrage from the official critics, but it is precisely the erotic sensation which guaranteed record numbers of visitors at Makart exhibitions (see Apke, 77-79).

The death of the 44-year-old Makart in 1884 marked a gradual disillusionment with the costumed dream of the *Gründerzeit* (founding epoch). In the arts, however, Gustav Klimt soon emerged as a successor to Makart. (This is why the Viennese Bourgeoisie was particularly disappointed when he later turned from a Makart-like historicism to modernism.) Already in his early work for the serial publication *Allegories and Emblems,* Klimt had "borrowed several elements of compositional elements and motifs [...] directly from Makart."[7] Klimt, whose work frequently focuses on the female body, follows in the footsteps of his predecessor in his approach to nudity, presenting his nude figures under the guise of allegory, until his faculty paintings. There for the first time in his depictions of women he allows the women to stand for themselves, a move which was partially responsible for the ensuing scandal (see Apke).

In 1883, together with his brother Ernst and Franz Matsch, a fellow student from the *Kunstgewerbeschule*, Klimt founded the "*Künstlercompagnie*" (the artists' company), which produced paintings heavily influenced by Makart's style for public buildings. In Vienna, Ferdinand Fellner (1874-1916) and Hermann Helmer (1849-1919), owners of one of the leading architectural firms in Europe, awarded the group numerous commissions for the interior decoration of theaters throughout the monarchy, including the great curtain for the Reichenberg Theater (today the Liberec in the northern Czech Republic; 1882,1883) and ceiling paintings for the Stadttheater (city theater) in Karlsbad (1886). They did not, however, receive the commission for the City Theater in Brünn (1882) which was also built by Fellner and Helmer. Robert Musil was well-acquainted with the theater in Brünn in his youth and describes it in *The Man Without Qualities*: "In the '80's or 90's there must have been an architect who plunked down such theatrical jewel boxes in most of the larger cities, with every available nook and cranny plastered with decoration and ornamental statues"(*Posthumous Papers,* 1479). Gustav Klimt and his *Künstlercompagnie* had also contributed to the ornamentation. The buildings of the highly regarded architectural firm distinguished themselves with their first-class execution, which fully corresponded to the contemporary taste and aesthetic conceptions of a discerning clientele (see Hans-Christoph Hoffmann).

The first larger commission for the *Künstlercompagnie* for the imperial city Vienna itself was the ceiling painting of the Hermesvilla in the imperial hunting grounds of the Lainzer-Tiergarten. Emperor Franz Joseph had presented the castle to Empress Elisabeth in the hopes of keeping his wife—an avid traveler—more often in Vienna. Together with the renowned history painter Hugo Charlemont and his brother Eduard, the artists' company completed the ceiling installation according to Hans Makart's designs. The artists embodied historicism so flawlessly that their stylistic similarities make it impossible today to ascribe the work to one or the other artist. This work increased the market value of all of the artists involved, and the *Künstlercompagnie* received as their next large commission the staircases of the Viennese Burgtheater, for which they later received the personal recognition of the Emperor Franz Joseph (see Koja). Hugo Charlemont in turn received further commissions and decorated the interior of numerous villas and castles. In this function he was to go down in world literature as van Helmond in *The Man Without Qualities*: "Redecorating old castles was the specialty of the well-known painter van Helmond, whose masterpiece was his daughter Clarisse" (314). Clarisse is the literary incarnation of Charlemont's second daughter, Alice (1885-1939; she died in Vienna's psychiatric hospital am Steinhof), who as Clarisse (the name of her younger sister) was to be exhaustively depicted in *The Man Without Qualities* (see Corino, 293).

Robert Musil met the Charlemont Family, who were originally from Brünn, through Gustav Donath, a childhood friend from his Brünner days. A multi-talented and promising young man, Donath had studied law, music, and philosophy since 1897 in Vienna. In 1901 he was introduced to the Charlemont family, where he met the 16-year-old Alice. Alice was well-aware of her effect on men, something she had been cognizant of since she had been groped as a 10-year-old in the night by a friend of the family, an event which is recounted in detail both in Musil's diary (90), and in *The Man Without Qualities* (318f.). Donath, Alice, and Robert Musil appear to have been close friends in those years; in 1907 Musil was a witness at Donath's wedding and gave the bride a copy of the collected works of Nietzsche as a wedding gift (*Diaries*, 301). After the wedding celebration on the 3 September 1907, Musil wrote the following in the

Charlemont family's guestbook: "Charmed by the sophistication of this house, I am grateful that I was permitted to enjoy the hospitality of a great artist and his dear and brilliant wife."[8]

It is not too great a stretch to assume that in the house of the "great artist" Charlemont, they discussed other artists as well. Perhaps it was in this way that Musil heard anecdotes about Charlemont's collaboration with Klimt on the Hermesvilla and other details about the historicist period of the *Künstlercompagnie*, or about Hugo Charlemont's brother Eduard's collaboration with Hans Makart for the great pageant (see Bernhard, 251-62). Unfortunately, however, there is no evidence in either the published diaries or in Musil's letters to support this theory. Whereas Charlemont (or van Helmond) continued to paint in the tradition of historicism—"Papa painted old-fashioned/musical, as he still does today" (*The Man Without Qualities*, 315)—Klimt, after the death of his brother Ernst in 1892, continued to develop his artistic style. He dissolved the *Künstlercompagnie*, but for the next two years still shared his atelier with Franz Matsch (see Pirchan, 27).

When the ceiling frescos of the great hall of the university (known then as the *Aula*) were to be designed, first Franz Matsch and then Matsch and Klimt together were given the commission. Encircling a grand central panel illustrating the "Victory of Light Over Darkness," four smaller paintings (still large at 4.3 meters high and 3 meters wide) were to depict the four faculties. Around the ceiling itself, Klimt was to provide numerous spandrels with allegories of the diverse academic disciplines of the faculties (*Zweites Programm*; qtd. in Strobl, 159). The entire budget for the project was set at 60,000 guilders, which would be the equivalent of about 400,000 euros today.[9] Allegedly, Matsch and Klimt drew lots, and Klimt was to be responsible for the faculties "Philosophy," "Medicine, and "Jurisprudence," for which he would receive 15,000 gilders. The commission was officially granted on the 6 July 1894, and the installation was to be complete by the end of 1898. But almost at once the ministry intervened in the design; Klimt was instructed to alter certain figures, emphasize certain lines, etc. Eight years later he remembered, "At that time I wanted to resign immediately. Only the intervention of Baron Weckbecker in the Ministry of Education, who negotiated a very reasonable contract which included a clause granting me full artistic freedom convinced me to continue working."[10]

When the Ministry of Education granted Klimt the commission in 1894, they had no way of foreseeing the changes in his style that were to come. In 1897 he left the conservative *Künstlerhaus* and in the same year became one of the founders of the Viennese Secession and its first president. The difference between the *Künstlerhaus* and the Secession could not have been greater. Hermann Bahr noted that in addition to artistic concerns, economic concerns played a role as well. The members of the *Künstlerhaus* refused to exhibit the latest paintings from abroad, because they didn't want to undermine their profit by introducing foreign artists with different styles into Austria. Thus, they clung to an outdated historicism for economic reasons. The Secessionists, on the other hand, wanted to move beyond historicism and to allow new movements into the country and finally break into modernism. They were, according to Bahr, artists, not businessmen (see Bahr, *Secession*, 8; Daviau, 165). Robert Musil also refers to the split within the art world in *fin de siècle* Vienna: "leaving the *Künstlerhaus* for the Secession, one could put 100 years behind one in a single day."[11]

The Faculty Paintings

Musil never mentions the public outrage about the faculty paintings in his published writings, but he certainly would have followed the scandal. As a young engineer and writer living in Brünn he could not have missed it; the reverberations in the media were too great. In addition his father painted as a hobby and was interested in the fine arts; he could take advantage of exhibitions of modern art in the Moravian Kunstverein (art society). In all likelihood he even read the journal of the Secession, "*Ver sacrum*" (Sacred Spring; see Corino, *Bildende Kunst*, 3). The faculty paintings and the scandal surrounding them reflect Viennese culture around 1900 and point to themes that are meticulously illuminated in *The Man Without Qualities*. According to Musil that is hardly surprising; he himself says that the most diverse arts are only different plants from the same soil: "Because they are nothing but different forms of expression by the same individual, diverse art forms, and indeed even objective language, must at some level share common roots. Therefore they must also be mutually translatable and interchangeable."[12]

Philosophy

In 1900, when Gustav Klimt first publicly exhibited his *Philosophy* (see Figure 4-1) as part of the seventh exhibition of the Viennese Secession, his painting not only provoked enormous outrage, but also attracted a record number of visitors—34,000—in less than three months. The painting was a far cry from the familiar idealized allegory of historicism and thus fulfilled neither the expectations of those who had commissioned the work, nor those of the educated Viennese middle class (*Bildungsbürgertum*). The result was a prolonged debate in the diverse newspapers of the monarchy and widespread discussion in the so-called Viennese society. While the depiction of nudity was criticized vociferously, as the following demonstrates, the roots of the scandal lay in the content of the painting—namely in Klimt's attempt to depict life in its totality.

The catalog for the seventh exhibition of the Secession announces and explains the painting shortly and succinctly:

> Philosophy. One of the five allegorical ceiling paintings for the Aula of the University. Left group of figures: Creation, The Fruitful Life, Decay. Right: The Earth, the Mystery of Life. Below, an enlightened figure rising: Knowledge.[13]

The chief problem was that the painting, in contrast to the pronouncement, is simply not a classical allegory. Above all, the ambiguity of the work was subject to great debate. The newspaper *Deutsches Volksblatt* summarized the debate thus:

> In music, Klimt's painting can only be compared to Richard Strauss's *Thus Spoke Zarathustra*. Here as there we witness the failed attempt to explain philosophy. In the one a muddled shimmer of colours, in the other a chaos of tones—both works without clarity.[14]

Indirectly this nationalistic German paper references the philosophy of Nietzsche. Even if he wasn't read, Nietzsche, particularly because of his position as a successor to Schopenhauer was, "somehow in the air": "[W]e may now think that by evoking a mood of almost Schopenhauerian gloom, Klimt had painted a true picture of the spiritual conditions of the day" (see Hamilton, 135). It is ironic that the polemic and harsh critiques leveled against Klimt's faculty paintings often reveal the intentions of the artist better than the rather superficial descriptive tributes of his admirers (see also Vergo, 71).

In the following, I will demonstrate that *Philosophy*, the first of the three great faculty paintings by Gustav Klimt, struck a nerve of the time, sparking a surprisingly vocal and aggressive debate about the validity of such art. The scandal surrounding the faculty paintings encapsulates the many facets of the Kakanian culture that Robert Musil describes in *The Man Without Qualities*. Interesting is that both the novel and the painting claimed to portray the world as a totality, which contemporary critics regarded as megalomaniacal, if not simply insane.

Figure 4-1 Gustav Klimt: Philosophie (Philosophy), 1899/1907 (burnt 1945), (4, 3 meter x 3 meter), black and white reproduction in original size, Leopold Museum, Vienna.

"Novela Total"

The claim to depict the world as a totality conspicuously coincides with the theory of the "*novela* total" by the Peruvian author Mario Vargas Llosa (*1936). Vargas Llosa developed the concept of the "the total novel" by means of an analysis of the Catalonian chivalric romance *Tirant lo Blanc* (*Tirante the White*), written in 1490 by Joanot Martorell. Don Quixote called this work "the best book in the world: here the knights eat, sleep and die in their bed, draw up their last will and testament before they die, and other things as well that are left out in all the other books of this sort" (Cervantes, 60). In other words, the famous knight with the melancholy disposition praises the completeness of the depiction of the life of the "white knight." It is precisely this point which Vargas Llosa emphasizes:

> The medieval romance authors' concept of reality encompasses at a single glance multiple categories of human existence, and in this sense, their notion of literary realism is broader and more encompassing than that of later authors.[15]

Thus the quality of the work arises out of the simultaneous and equally weighted presence of the most diverse aspects of life:

> Such a book about knight errantry, which simultaneously includes fantastic, historic, combative, social, erotic and psychological elements without isolating one particular element or devoting itself exclusively to one, does neither more nor less than represent reality.[16]

It is precisely this simultaneity of reality that Ulrich observes when he acknowledges that his life is unconcerned with the "primitive epic" of conventional narrative, which follows the "celebrated thread of the story" (*The Man Without Qualities*, 708). His life—and "life" and "reading" must be read synonymously here—no longer follows a thread, but rather spreads itself out into an "infinitely interwoven surface" (709). The "overwhelmingly manifold nature of things" no longer finds a place in the unidimensional (708). Vargas Llosa contends the same:

> As a constructed word that conveys the same impression of ambiguity as real life does, it is, as is reality, objectivity and subjectivity, fact and dream, a feat of the understanding and a marvelous apparition. Therein lies its "total realism." (*Fehdebrief*, 138)

This ideal of the novel emerged out of a particular historical situation: out of the late medieval und early modern dissolution of a closed worldview. At the advent of modern history, as at the outset of Viennese modernism, there was an attempt to depict the world in all its aspects in a single work of art. However, the desire to depict the world as it is and not as it should be was considered in both historical moments a subversive act:

> This attempt to depict reality in an impartial way, on all its levels, neither didactic nor typifying, neither pedagogical nor showing people as they should be, but simply as they are—what they believe themselves to be and what they would like to be—was an enormously subversive act because it shattered all kinds of taboos, and eliminated all possible pretense.... There is, it seems to me, a curious connection between the appearance of a great novel and situations of crisis and the dissolution of a society.[17]

The fact that a work of art would be in the position to "eliminate all possible pretense" suggests a certain fragility of the depicted society. Therefore Vargas Llosa believes that the total novel is related to periods of crisis, which is certainly the case in Musil's *The Man Without Qualities*, as well as in Klimt's faculty paintings.

The attempt to apply this theory to the fine arts is certainly legitimate; indeed Vargas Llosa himself asserts that while he based his theory on a novel, it can be applied to all "great art": "There can be no great art without a certain dose of irrationality, for great art is always an expression of human totality."[18] Even the first newspaper critics recognized that Musil's novel encompasses this human totality:

> It (the book) offers a fully complex picture of a society and a country during a set period of time. It encompasses all types from the upper class down to the murderer Moosbrugger, whose life and fate constitute a dark foil—the shadow side of life with all its horrors. It is astounding how realistically Musil's figures retain their intellectual capabilities. Not an organ is missing. The vigor of their thinking is entirely true to life.[19]

It is, however, not only society as a whole that is manifest in the novel, but man himself is plumbed to his conceivable limits. That manifests itself particularly in Musil's idea of the "other condition," a concept which appears very early in Musil's work and is explained in more detail for the first time in an article in 1914 entitled "Anmerkungen zu einer Metapsychik" (Remarks on a Metapsychic) about Walter Rathenau's book, *Zur Mechanik des Geistes* (On the mechanics of the Spirit). With time the concept changed from a "fundamental experience of mysticism" to a unification of all conceivable conditions of being (including incestuous sexual unions).

Robert Musil's "Other Condition"

Together with Agathe, Ulrich succeeds in deepening and holding fast to the fleeting moments of "other thinking." This collective experience of the "other condition" can be seen most clearly in the early drafts of the chapter "Journey into Paradise":

> And they further perceived that the circumscribing powers in them were not lost at all, but in reality inverted, and with them all boundaries had been inverted. They noticed that they had not become mute at all but were speaking, but they were not choosing words but were being chosen by words; no thought stirred in them, but the whole world was full of marvelous thoughts; they thought that they, and things as well, were no longer mutually displacing and repelling hermetic bodies, but opened and allied forms (*The Man Without Qualities*, 1456)."

Thus emerges a reciprocal correspondence between the self and the world which is similarly clarified in Moosbrugger's language thinking, which does not correspond to the logical discourse of society, but is more a kind of "subjectless thinking": "He thought better than the others, because he thought both inside and outside. Thinking went on inside him against his will. He said thoughts were planted in him" (258).[20]

In this same manner the "other condition" means a becoming one with the world; it is a condition in which all boundaries are fluid: "The world appeared to be only the physical manifestation of a certain inner attitude, and the two were interchangeable."[21] Through critical reflection in the "day-bright mysticism," Ulrich comprehends the "other condition" as precisely as possible. Rössner summarizes the "other condition" as follows:

> It turns out to be predominantly a mystical and subjective-affective experience of the world, which lacks a religious component but demonstrates strong parallels to the experience of the primitive, or to certain comparable psychopathological forms. Musil emphasizes that this condition lives on in modern man, that its repression through reason is accompanied by a sense of pain, but that it is experienced as elation when united with rationality.[22]

According to Ulrich, the insanity of reality arises out of the painful repression of the "subjective-affective experience of the world" within the rational discourse of the Enlightenment (1109). He finds the predetermined emotional life of society, with its attendant social indifference and violence, nothing short of insane. In opposition to this Musil, through his "other condition," offers the ideal of a union which will overcome the dualism which marks society.[23]

The society of his time, according to Ulrich, borders on insanity because it is incapable of comprehending certain conditions in their totality. In the same way as "an idiot of a certain degree is not up to forming the concept 'parents' even though he has no trouble with the idea of 'father and mother'" (1101-2), so society lacks the capacity for abstract thought. Just as in a story an orderly sequence of facts is confused with genuine narrative skill (see 709 and 1102), so the entire state of mind of his time is limited to a list of concepts that are linked together with "and." However, this state of mind "of the crudest pattern" prevents one from thinking of the concepts simultaneously; it prohibits one from grasping, sensing, and understanding the world in its totality. That which mankind has in common is, as Ulrich reiterates, a mental condition

> "that cannot be spanned by far-reaching concepts, or refined by distinctions and abstractions, a mental state of the crudest pattern, expressed most clearly in the way it limits itself to the simplest of coordinating conjunctions, the helplessly additive "and," which for those of meager mental capacity replaces more intricate relationships; and it may be said that our world, regardless of its intellectual riches, is in a mental condition akin to idiocy." (1102)

In his large-format faculty paintings Klimt attempted to portray an all-encompassing image of the various states of mind of humanity. These mental states are not connected sequentially with "and," but rather appear, as is usual in a painting, simultaneously and without comment. According to Musil, a society that is incapable of connecting concepts holistically, instead of simply enumerating them, is insane. It is precisely this society which condemned Klimt's painting as insane, because it tried to depict the world as a whole.

Klimt, Musil, and Madness

"Klimt is great artist: a skillful hand, led by a muddled mind."[24] Klimt's body and mind are thus split, crazy, the unnamed author of the article in *Plein-air* implies. When Klimt was recommended for a professorship by the Academy, these innuendos became clearer; in order to prevent Klimt's appointment as a professor, his critics resorted to character assassination. According to Hermann Bahr rumors abounded throughout Vienna: "Klimt has gone crazy," or "He's been in the insane asylum since early this morning" (*Gegen Klimt*, 3ff.).

> His opponents set out to destroy Klimt. Imagining Klimt to be an unstable and sensitive individual, who perhaps—as is often the case with artists when they descend from a blissful ecstasy into exhaustion—felt himself threatened by a vague fear of himself, they calculated that such diabolical rumors would inwardly shatter him. Precipitating a mental breakdown was more comfortable and—something which is always important to us—more congenial than poisoning him.[25]

While Sigmund Freud also had to fight for years against critics who repeatedly sought to prevent his appointment as a university professor, he finally succeeded, and in 1902, the father of psychoanalysis received an associate professorship in neuropathology at the University of Vienna (see Schorske, 181-208). Klimt, in contrast, never became a professor, but he also placed far less value on an appointment than had Freud. The character assassination that was to have relegated the artist to the realm of madness seems to have worked.

At the beginning of the twentieth century, the non-scientific population discussed the boundaries of normality with great intensity and widespread interest. Musil had already thematized the fragility of social norms in his 1905 novel, *The Confusions of Young Törless*:

> Törleß was assailed by a sort of madness that made him experience processes and people as something equivocal: as something which, through the power of some inventor, had been fettered to a simple, explanatory word and which, at the same time, was entirely strange, threatening every second to tear itself loose.[26]

Similar deliberations appear in *The Man Without Qualities*, primarily in the legal discussions concerning Moosbrugger and in the psychological studies that make up part of the Clarisse plot. In addition, the adultery of women and every kind of deviant sexuality is diagnosed as mental illness, a conclusion which would factor Bonadea into this discussion. Particular attention is naturally paid to hysteria as a female illness of the spirit (an illness Ulrich literally experiences first-hand when Gerda has a fit of hysteria in his bed; see chapter 119) which is interpreted as a result of the repression of a sexuality that deviates from the heterosexual norm: "The depiction of neurasthenics and hysterics around 1900 as sexually enervated, because their sexuality could not be expressed and satisfied in the usual way within the marital bed, penetrated into the contemporary discourse of illness" (see Guth, 75).

Musil became acquainted with the phenomenon of hysteria coupled with a singular repression of sexuality in the fall of 1913 in Rome, where he and his wife Martha lived with the Sergi family. Professor Sergi was a famous doctor and a member of the "Societá italiana per il progresso delle scienze." His son Quirino, who was himself a doctor, accompanied Musil on 2 October to the Manicomio in Rome. In his diary Musil exactly describes his visit to the insane asylum, a visit which ultimately appeared, slightly transformed but essentially the same, as chapter 22 in the second volume of *The Man Without Qualities.* Both Quirino and his brother adore their sister, but they keep her like a bird in a cage:

> "We worship her," says Quirino. "I couldn't bear it if she married. I perhaps would kill the man." She is to remain pure. Untouched by life's darkness. He supervises her reading. Keeps her completely naïve in sexual matters. (Musil, *Diaries*, 162)

Musil recognizes in the figure of the adored sister a severe disorder: "Her face is anything but peaceful. As if ravaged by nervous energy from things that have been suppressed. She grimaces when she speaks. Displays an exaggerated, impetuous gaiety […] Frau Croce says she's an idiot." The diagnosis here comes not from the doctors in her own family, but rather from an acquaintance.

In the German-speaking world of 1900, hysteria as a kind of nervous degeneration was considered a female sickness. If a man were affected by hysteria, then it was a feminine man, as the notoriously misogynistic and anti-Semitic philosopher Otto Weininger explained:

> Hysteria is the organic crisis of the organic mendaciousness of women. I won't deny that there are also hysterical men, although this occurs quite rarely; for one of the countless possibilities that exist in the male psyche is to become a woman, and therefore possibly hysterical.[27]

It was thus doubly demeaning when critics implied that Gustav Klimt was an hysteric.

Schopenhauer

In Vienna around 1900, Otto Weininger's misogynistic theories were in vogue and Schopenhauer's misogynistic aphorisms and pessimism were widely acknowledged as indicative of the prevailing atmosphere. His main works, on the other hand, were discussed less (see Vergo). According to Schopenhauer, when we seek to understand the why of existence, we attempt to explain the world by steadfastly relating effects to their causes. He contended that this is most clearly expressed in the principle of sufficient reason, which can be traced in its essence back to Plato. He claimed to have found the most general expression of this idea in the version of the polymath Christian Wolff (1679-1754): "Nihil est sine ratione sufficiente, cur potius sit, quam non sit" (nothing is without reason as to why it is, rather than why it is not). Schopenhauer translated this freely as "Nothing is without reason why it is" ("Nichts ist ohne Grund warum es sei"; 17)

In *The Man Without Qualities* Ulrich makes fun of this causal idea of life that prevents people from looking beyond a series of experiences and seeing their life as a totality: "And although a little 'because' or 'in order that' gets knotted into the thread of life, they generally detest any brooding that goes beyond that" (709). The idea that laws of causality hold the world together is criticized here as far too narrow, and this criticism has been the dominant paradigm at least since the advent of postmodern philosophy.

If one understands so-called post-structuralism thus—that the depiction of a self-contained, closed system of meaning is impossible because systems change constantly—then cultural phenomena as a single entity are neither explicable nor comprehensible. Post-structuralism demonstrates that the structures of a system of meaning cannot exist independent of the subject; instead the subjects themselves create a structure which seems objective to them. However, in so far as the subjects themselves are inherently bound up in these structures, these can never be explained objectively. Post-structuralism is therefore a critique of both the idea of objective knowledge and the critique of a subject which is too sure of itself. It is precisely this disintegration of the subject, this "I," which Musil depicts in *The Man Without Qualities*:

> Probably the dissolution of the anthropocentric point of view, which for such a long time considered man to be at the center of the universe but has been fading away for centuries, has finally arrived at the "I" itself. (159).

A spitefully inclined critique in the *Deutsches Volksblatt* identifies this disintegration of the individual in Klimt's *Philosophy*:

> Blueish-whiteish waves of foam descend. Thicker and thicker, it almost seems as if they were bodies. Forms shimmer, dissipate, and reform. They are bodies, eerily sheathed in a blueish mist of decay.[28]

Lyotard finds in the multi-dimensional logic of the unforeseen and the surprising an alternative to the restrictive rationality of the Enlightenment. At the heart of postmodern thinking stands the idea of an unstable or open system: "Insofar as science is differentiating, it presents in its pragmatics the anti-model of a stable system."[29] This contradicts Schopenhauer's thesis on the "Principle of Sufficient Reason." As the protagonist in a novel of classic modernity, Ulrich once again proves himself a prophet of postmodernism. Accordingly, he modifies Schopenhauer's "Principle of Sufficient Reason" and proclaims a "Principle of Insufficient Cause." Ulrich explains to the banker Leo Fischel: "in our personal lives and in our public-historical lives, everything that happens happens for no good or sufficient reason" (140). One can observe this futile endeavor to find a causal sequence for life's events beautifully illustrated by the despairing figures of mankind in Klimt's *Philosophy*. The figurative "Philosophy" in the foreground is also incapable "of influencing human fate and penetrating the mystery of the phenomenal world" (Vergo, 77). She does not even see humanity; she looks in the other direction.

Although Musil turns against the principle of reason, he continues to avail himself of reason in order to analyze the fate of rationality: "The collapse of reason as a principle does not prevent our recourse to reason as a medium."[30] We can observe similar arguments in the debates around Klimt's faculty paintings. It is disconcerting that after abandoning historicist allegories, Klimt returns again to painting allegories. Beginning with *Nuda Veritas* and proceeding to the faculty paintings and *Tod und Leben* (Death and Life), he repeatedly returns to the form of allegory, but disregards established iconographic tradition:

> If one wanted to assert in no uncertain terms that Klimt's painting is incomprehensible as an allegory, that it possesses neither a decorative nor a coloristic charm, then the story would make sense. This can be proven.[31]

To be sure, the faculty paintings were seen as allegories ("because Klimt should have and must have intended to paint an allegory, since one cannot paint the abstract" [see Bahr, *Gegen Klimt*, 21]), but they were no longer understood as such. Although Klimt uses the form of allegory, he invests these allegories with new content, which can no longer be easily deciphered according to the interpretative formulas of the upper middle class. Rather they represent a personal depiction of the period, which frequently approaches the boundaries of the ineffable and extends and transcends the prevailing discourse of rationality so that "it is rationality itself which is beaten by its own means," as Hans-Georg Pott writes about Musil's novel *Törleß*.[32]

Truth—Truths

A critic in *Plein-Air* touches upon another important point about the representation of philosophy when he writes: "The attempt to visually depict the unexplored had to fail; what we see is a formless, incomprehensible dream world, the exact opposite of all true philosophy."[33] Thus, according to this critic, Klimt does not depict philosophy, but rather its dark side; instead of reason he portrays "the incomprehensible dream world," as had Goya in his famous Caprichio no. 43, *El sueño de la razon produce monstrous* (see figure 4-2)[34]. In Goya, in the best tradition of the Enlightenment, the absence of Reason leads to a wild, "incomprehensible dream world" that the critic of *Plein-air* also discovers in Klimt's *Philosophy*. Whereas in Goya's drawing Reason is conspicuous in its absence, Reason is clearly represented in Klimt in the form of the allegorized figure of Knowledge. This juxtaposition of dream and rationality, the dissolving forms of a directionless humanity, and the clear, piercing look of knowledge is confusing and can only be interpreted with difficulty. The critic seeks in vain for a "true philosophy," for the True, truth itself, seems to have dissolved in this unexplained juxtaposition of the most diverse states of consciousness.

Musil writes in an entry in his diary on the 20 February 1902 about the collapse of the unified worldview of bourgeois liberalism: "There are truths but no truth. Without difficulty I can maintain two fully contradictory things and be correct in both instances. […] See Nietzsche."[35] Musil takes his critique of an absolute truth from Nietzsche, who contends in his *Genealogy of Morals*, "They are far from free spirits, for they still believe in truth …" [36] Suddenly there are many truths in place of one universally valid truth. In Musil, this break with the prevailing, rational worldview, a view influenced by the Enlightenment, leads to a "holistically heightened state of feeling and living,"[37] a condition which, as explained above, Musil calls "the other condition." Klimt's faculty paintings could not have illustrated this condition better. Ludwig Hevesi, a contemporary critic, described *Philosophy* as "Life, eternally flowing, ceaselessly coalescing into forms and then dissipating again."[38]

Not only Musil's "other condition," but also the flowing life in Klimt expand the dominant social norm and displace the line between normality and insanity. Ulrich actually inverts the whole idea of normality and insanity and highlights the collective madness of the prevailing society, which he wants to transcend with his holistic life that unites thought and feeling.[39] Klimt, in his attempt to capture philosophy in a painting, naturally moves as well in the gray zone between reason and madness. As

Figure 4-2 Francisco de Goya: El sueño de la razon produce monstruos (The Sleep of Reason Produces Monsters), 1797/98. From the series Los Caprichos, plate 43, (30 cm x 22 cm), Stadtmuseum Oldenburg.

a critic in the *Montags-Zeitung* (the Monday Paper) polemically observes: the attempt to think in multiple philosophical systems cannot help but lead to madness. The abandonment of an absolute truth, paired with the attempt to unite diverse truths in one "total picture," is nothing other than the depiction of madness:

> In passing we would like to note, that even if we are willing to admit that the individual who has thoroughly studied only the various systems of the German philosophers must perforce slip into a mild madness, nothing forced Klimt to also assail us with his painted insanity.[40]

Whilst the philosopher Nietzsche lay dying in Weimar in a state of mental derangement (he died on 25 August 1900), here philosophy and madness are being thought of together in a completely different way.

The Protest by the Positivistic Professors

For the professors of philosophy at the University of Vienna, the allegorized depiction of philosophy itself was naturally of great interest. Above all they were intrigued by the female figure who appears in the lower center of the picture, who, according to the text of the catalog and sundry interpretations, is meant to symbolize Knowledge or Philosophy. She stares at us out of the picture, eschewing any form of contact with the pillar of humanity or even the sphinx, the mystery of the world, behind her. Thus, Philosophy as pure knowledge can in no way answer the ultimate questions of life; indeed, she barely has anything to do with life in its cycle of birth, flowering, and age.

This critique of knowledge, particularly in the positivistic period of Viennese philosophy, naturally challenged the professors to protest. The rector of the university, Wilhelm Neumann, organized the "Professors' Protest" and pronounced in no uncertain terms that philosophy, "which seeks her source in the exact sciences, does not deserve, particularly at this juncture in history, to be depicted as a nebulous, phantasmagoric entity, an enigmatic sphinx."[41] It is interesting to note here that Professor Neumann takes the sphinx, which is generally interpreted as the mystery of the world, to be an allegory of philosophy, rather than the female head below. Nevertheless, it is clear that he regards philosophy as belonging to the "exact sciences" and dismisses as absurd any depiction that lies outside rational discourse.

One of the most important spokesmen of the opposition against Klimt was the philosopher Friedrich Jodl. In 1880, when Franz Brentano's chair at the University of Vienna was vacated, the faculty recommended

Friedrich Jodl as his successor. (Brentano was a teacher of Musil's doctoral advisor in Berlin, Carl Stumpf.) However, the Ministry rejected the nomination, and the appointment in Vienna went to Ernst Mach, about whom Musil was to write his dissertation. When a professorship opened up, Mach lobbied for Jodl. So finally in 1896, under Baron von Gautsch und the section chief, Wilhelm von Hartel, Jodl received an appointment in Vienna.[42] In April 1896 Jodl wrote a letter to Wilhelm von Hartel, who would become the minister of Education in 1900, and as such would be responsible for the faculty paintings.

> I make no secret of the fact that as a philosopher I do not agree with the church's worldview; I am not a dualist, but a monist, and subscribe to a religion of morals, rather than theism. Furthermore, I am fundamentally convinced that for the philosopher there can be no external authority, regardless of its nature, only that of his inner consciousness, of scientific tradition. [43]

The Minister of Education, Dr. Ritter von Hartel, proved to be liberal and did not resent the anti-religious attitude of the university professor.

Jodl, who became known through his *History of Ethics* (1882-89), clearly argued for progressive ideals and went even further, publicly advocating for the emancipation of women and national education. Jodl had good reason to turn against Klimt, whose "unclear symbolism"[44] must have contradicted his view of philosophy as a matter of reason. With his rejection of Klimt, however, Jodl automatically landed in the conservative camp, whose sham morality compromised Jodl's commitment to freedom in art (see Fellner, 117). In order to differentiate himself from the champions of tradition and the opponents of nudity in art, he took the position that his fight was neither against nakedness nor against free art, but rather against ugly art: "What we object to is not the nakedness in the picture, but the ugliness."[45] This in turn inspired the art history professor Franz Wickhoff to speak in defense of Klimt under the title, "What is ugly?"[46]

Despite the protest of 87 professors, Minister Hartel supported granting Klimt the commission, with the warning: "any work of art that deviates from the heretofore usual forms of expression and strives for individuality will always come up against opposition."[47] The protests which appeared in the newspapers were particularly severe, even though they did little more than repeat the arguments of science:

> Regardless of the fact that the philosophy faculty, whose allegorical depiction the painting attempts, actually concerns itself with truly realistic

> and exact scientific subjects such as history, linguistics, mathematics, etc., modern philosophy is nothing less than mystical-metaphysical daydreaming amidst unsolved mysteries. In contrast, the physiological part of this discipline is ever expanding while the purely theoretical is steadily shrinking. The *ignorabimus* is recognized both in and through this science and constitutes a boundary which one no longer attempts to transcend.[48]

It is precisely this border of not-knowing which "great art," according to Vargas Llosa, attempts to cross and to which "intuition, obsession, madness, and phantasy" belong as much as ideas (Vargas Llosa, *Gegen Wind*, 85). In *Philosophy*, Gustav Klimt presents not a specific philosophical school but rather life in itself (*Das Leben an sich*). Humanity is on display as a pillar of naked bodies which includes every generation, from the tiny baby at the very top to the broken old man at the bottom. Just as there is a chapter in *The Man Without Qualities* entitled "Moosbrugger reflects," one could refer to this pillar of humanity with the somewhat flamboyant title: "Humanity reflects." "If mankind could dream as a whole," Ulrich opines, "that dream would be Moosbrugger" (77). In the case of Klimt's painting, only the unanswerable questions about the meaning of life emerge out of the nebulous ether. The allegorical figure of Knowledge or Science on the lower edge of the painting fails to see mankind's struggle; she looks piercingly out through the painting; perhaps she knows an answer for herself, but most certainly not for the world at large.

This juxtaposition of mankind and science, which remains without comment, is analogous to Musil's observation that in the rationalistic West, art and science mutually exclude each other: "here artistic and scientific thought haven't yet converged. The questions of an intermediate zone between the two remain unresolved."[49] It is scarcely surprising, then, that the attempt to depict the struggle for truth in its entirety was met with incomprehension by the philosophical schools at that time.

Ulrich knows, as well, that the philosophy of his time strictly rejects "mystical-metaphysical daydreaming."[50] The contemporary mathematical-natural scientific form of philosophy holds little meaning for Ulrich; when he abandoned mathematics, it would have been logical to turn to philosophy, but he did not find his new calling in the latter, for this "resembled what he had been doing himself and held no attraction for him" (*The Man Without Qualities*, 44). When he gives up his career as an engineer, he does so primarily because engineers separate their feelings from their intellect and leave their senses underdeveloped. Here emerges the outline of something new: the eternal world of feelings (see Pekar, *Ordnung*, 13). Thus Ulrich desires to overcome the gap between thought and life in favor of a holistic approach; he becomes "the man without qualities." This is not to be understood negatively, but rather means possessing "all of the abilities and qualities favored by his time" (*The Man Without Qualities*, 44), so as not to be associated with one particular world view.

The Border of Madness

Musil does not find it surprising when art causes great commotion, for he believes that although every work of art "disturbs our sense of reality" there is an immediate counterbalance, and thus the "abnormal becomes the new norm, the disturbed reaches a new equilibrium of the soul."[51] Art always operates on the border of abnormality, and it is therefore not particularly surprising that the faculty paintings were seen as an expression of madness or indeed as the expression of a madman. Within the Secession Klimt's works effectively became a "new norm." Musil concludes that the simple fact that art arises out of fantasy means that it falls into the domain of psychiatry:

> To be sure, one is accustomed to finding the effect of a work of art described as an exalted, unburdened state of life; we used to like to call it fantasy, now we call it illusion; but seldom or never does one encounter an analysis of the possibility that this illusion, for all its differences, is analogous to that which is understood as illusion in psychiatry; in other words, a "disorder" in which elements of reality are combined to form an imaginary whole that usurps the "reality value."[52]

Pathologically considered, creativity is therefore a "disorder," exactly what Klimt's critics diagnosed:

> It is impossible to see the painting without thinking of Zola's Novel *L'Oeuvre* and the tragic conclusion in which the ingenious Claude, driven into madness by failure, desires to unite the world and mankind in a painting, and also commits such an act of painted revenge.[53]

The unification of world and humanity, the attempt at a total depiction of reality, can therefore only be undertaken by a madman. Karl Schreder, following the same argument in his negative critique, contends that Klimt went a step too far in *Philosophy*: "Klimt's audacity in his depiction of absolute humanity exceeds all limits."[54] Klimt had violated boundaries in his depiction of naked elderly bodies, humanity floating in cosmic dust, and vague visions which preclude unambiguous interpretation. It is precisely this side of humanity, the uncertain, dream-like quality of life that Vargas Llosa defines as "total realism." He asks: "Is that which people do less real than that which they believe and dream? Are visions, nightmare images, and myths less real than deeds?"[55] The art critic Hevesi, who followed the genesis of the faculty paintings, makes an analogous statement: "Never was a painter more fantastic and at the same time more true to nature."[56]

The Further Fate of the Faculty Paintings

On 11 November 1903, the Ministry's Artistic Advisory Committee visited the Secession exhibition that included Klimt's three faculty paintings together with *Theology* by Franz Matsch, which had been brought specially for the exhibition. It was unanimously determined that an almost insurmountable difference in quality existed between Klimt's paintings and those of Matsch. Contrary to expectations, Klimt's paintings were preferred over the traditional work of Matsch. In order to avoid insulting the latter, however, no decision was made. In March 1905, at a second session chaired by Prof. Dr. Karl, one of the professors who had initiated the petition against *Philosophy*, the commission finally decided to install only the central panel by Matsch and none of the four faculty paintings. Gustav Klimt was outraged, as he had spent ten years working on the project (see Fellner, 117).

On 25 May 1905, Klimt returned the fee of 30,000 Kronen to the Ministry.[57] The industrial tycoon August Lederer placed the necessary funds at Klimt's disposal in exchange for *Philosophy*. Kolo Moser, who had come into money through his marriage to a Mauthner-Markoff, purchased the paintings *Medicine* and *Jurisprudence*.[58] After the owner's death the paintings became the possession of the Österreichischen Galerie (the Austrian Gallery). On 9 May 1945, the very last day of the war, they burned in the fire at Immendorf Castle in lower Austria, where they had been brought for safekeeping. In all probability the fire was set by retreating SS troops who didn't want the castle and the paintings to fall into the hands of the Russian army.

Arnheim's Position

The great man of letters, Arnheim, thinking like a businessman and speaking idealistically, faces the same problem that the conservative Viennese middle class faced when they saw the faculty paintings—namely that artistic quality in the age of modernism does not lend itself to measurement in a closed system, for "because our skeptical contemporaries believe in neither God nor humanity, kings nor morality—unless they believe in all of them indiscriminately, which amounts to the same thing" (*The Man Without Qualities*, 470). Thus Arnheim faces the problem of totality: "everything together" can neither be grasped nor analyzed. One must be able to convey the world in a closed system and have some way of evaluating art. He falls back on a kind of principle from reception-history in that he makes the "greatness of influence" a criterion for his reflections on art. However, that does not solve the problem of determining the quality of the art—what is now considered "great art?" Arnheim avoids giving an answer by confining himself exclusively to the question of the reception of the artwork: "So now whatever counts as great *is* great; but this means that eventually whatever is most loudly hawked as great is also great"(470). This is a remark which was also made in reference to Klimt's faculty paintings. "It seems that [...] the advertising artist who wins is the one who pushes the line between genius and madness most strongly in the latter direction."[59]

Even today, scandal as "advertisement" is not the worst way of propelling art into the media and thus winning the interest of the public and, at best, provoking a vigorous discussion about the nature of art. Thus, as it has been particularly difficult since modernism to properly evaluate contemporary artists, the great man of letters and industrialist Arnheim resorts to a rather cowardly position, namely "that it was a sign of greatness in a man not to be overly critical of his time!"(471). The scandal surrounding Klimt's faculty paintings suggests that the Viennese middle class lacked the necessary sang-froid for such a position. And perhaps that was just as well.

Works Cited

Apke, Bernd. "Der nackte Körper: Verschleierung und Tradition" In *Die nackte Wahrheit. Klimt, Schiele, Kokoschka und andere Skandale*. Edited by Tobias G. Natter and Max Hollein. Munich: Prestel 2005. 77-98.

Arntzen, Helmut. "Varianten des Wahns in Robert Musils Roman *Der Mann ohne Eigenschaften*. Moosbrugger, Clarisse und andere." *Fundamenta Psychiatrica* 3-4 (2003): 89-95.

Bahr, Hermann. *Gegen Klimt. Historisches, Philosophie, Medizin, Goldfische, Fries*. Vienna: J. Eisenstein & Co.: 1903.

—. *Secession*. Vienna: Wiener Verlag, 1900.

Bernhard, Marianne. *Zeitenwende im Kaiserreich. Die Wiener Ringstraße. Architektur und Gesellschaft 1858-1906*. Regensburg: Friedrich Pustet, 1992.

Cervantes Saavedra, Miguel de. *The Adventures of Don Quixote*. Translated by J. M. Cohen. Baltimore, MD: Penguin Books, 1950.

Corino, Karl. *Robert Musil*. Reinbek bei Hamburg: Rowohlt, 2003.

—. "Robert Musil und die bildende Kunst." *Rapial* 3.1 (March 1993): 2-8.

Daviau, Donald G. *Understanding Bahr*. St. Ingbert: Röhrig Universitätsverlag, 2002.

Demkó-Bélanskzky, Marion. "Hans Makarts zeitgenössische Rezeption." In *Festschrift für Alberto Martino*. Edited by Ernst Grabovski, Stefan Kutzenberger, and Philipp Wascher. Berlin: Weidler, forthcoming in 2008.

Fellner, Sabine. *Kunstskandal*. Vienna: Ueberreuter, 1997.

Frodl, Gerbert. "Makart und Klimt." In *Traum und Wirklichkeit—Wien 1870-1930. Ausstellungs-Katalog*. Vienna: Historisches Museum der Stadt, Künstlerhaus, 1985. 48-56.

Guth, Doris. "'Das ist kein Zeichen der Zeit, das ist ein Zeichen der Überspanntheit.' Der Skandal um Gustav Klimts Fakultätsbilder." In *Die nackte Wahrheit. Klimt, Schiele, Kokoschka und andere Skandale*. Edited by Tobias G. Natter and Max Hollein. Munich: Prestel 2005. 67-76.

Hamilton, Georges Heard. *Painting and Sculpture in Europe, 1880-1940*. Harmondsworth, UK: Penguin Books, 1972.

Hesse, Hermann. *Vorwort zu "Sinclairs Notizbook." Gesammelte Werke*, 11. Frankfurt a. M.: Suhrkamp, 1970. 33.

Hevesi, Ludwig. *Acht Jahre Sezession. (März 1897 - Juni 1905). Kritik-Polemik-Chronik*. 1906. Klagenfurt: Ritter, 1984.

Hoffmann, Hans-Christoph. *Die Theaterbauten von Fellner und Helmer*. Munich: Prestel, 1966.

Hofmann, Michael. "Musil und Lyotard: *Der Mann ohne Eigenschaften* und die Postmoderne." *Musil-Forum. Studien zur Literatur der klassischen Moderne* 27 (2001/2002): 150-166.

Jodl, Friedrich. *Geschichte der Ethik*. 2 vols. Stuttgart: Cotta, 1882-89.

Jodl, Margarete. *Friedrich Jodl. Sein Leben und Wirken*. Stuttgart: Cotta, 1920.

Koja, Stephan. "Biographie Gustav Klimts." In *Gustav Klimt – Landschaften*. Edited by Stephan Koja. Munich: Prestel, 2002. 191-210.

Lyotard, Jean-François. *Das postmoderne Wissen. Ein Bericht* Translation of *The Postmodern Condition: A Report on Knowledge* into German by Otto Pfersmann. Vienna: Böhlau, 1986.
Malik, Habib C. *Receiving Søren Kierkegaard. The Early Impact and Transmission of His Thought.* Washington, D.C.: The Catholic University of America Press, 1997.
Musil, Robert. *Briefe, Kommentar, Register.* Reinbek bei Hamburg: Rowohlt, 1981.
—. *Diaries 1899-1941.* Translated by Philip Payne. Edited by Mark Mirsky. New York: Basic Books, 1998.
—. *From the Posthumous Papers.* Translated by Burton Pike. New York: Alfred A. Knopf, Inc. 1995.
—. *Gesammelte Werke in neun Bänden.* Reinbek bei Hamburg: Rowohlt Verlag, 1978.
—. *The Man Without Qualities.* Trans. Sophie Wilkins, ed. Burton Pike. New York: Alfred A. Knopf, Inc., 1995.
—. *Tagebücher.* Reinbek bei Hamburg: Rowohlt, 1983.
Neue Freie Presse, Morgenblatt 28 April 1879.
Nietzsche, Friedrich. *Zur Genealogie der Moral. Sämtliche Werke. Kritische Studienausgabe in 15 Einzelbänden,* 5. Edited by Giorgio Colli and Mazzino Montinari. Munich: DTV, 1980.
Pekar, Thomas. *Ordnung und Möglichkeit: Robert Musils "Möglichkeitssinn" als poetologisches Prinzip.* Oldenburg: Bibliotheks- und Informationssystem der Universität, 1990.
—. *Robert Musil. Zur Einführung.* Hamburg: Junius, 1997.
—. *Die Sprache der Liebe bei Robert Musil.* Munich: Fink, 1989.
Pirchan, Emil. *Gustav Klimt. Ein Künstler aus Wien.* Vienna: Wallishauser, 1942.
Pott, Hans Georg. *Robert Musil.* Munich: Fink, 1984.
Rössner, Michael. *Auf der Suche nach dem verlorenen Paradies.* Frankfurt a. M.: Athenäum Verlag, 1988.
Schmied-Kowarzik, Wolfdietrich. "Vergessene Impulse der Wiener Philosophie um die Jahrhundertwende. Eine philosophiehistorische Skizze wider den main stream verdrängenden Erinnerns." In *Die Wiener Jahrhundertwende. Einflüsse, Umwelt, Wirkungen.* Edited by Jürgen Nautz and Richard Vahrenkamp. Vienna: Böhlau, 1993. 181-201.
Schönert, Jörg. "Gesellschaftliche Modernisierung und Literatur der Moderne." In *Zur Terminologie der Literaturwissenschaft.* Edited by Christian Wagenknecht. Stuttgart: Metzler, 1989. 393-413.

Schopenhauer, Arthur. *Über die vierfache Wurzel des Satzes vom zureichenden Grunde. Werke in zehn Bänden*, 5. Zürich: Diogenes, 1977.

Schorske, Carl E. *Fin-de-Siècle Vienna: Politics and Culture*. New York: Random House, 1981.

Strobl, Alice. "Zu den Fakultätsbildern von Gustav Klimt." *Albertina-Studien* 4 (1964): 138-69.

Thomé, Horst. "Modernität und Bewußtseinswandel in der Zeit des Naturalismus und des Fin de Siècle." In *Naturalismus. Fin de siècle. Expressionismus 1890-1918*. Edited by York-Gothart Mix. Munich: Hanser, 2000. 15-27.

Vargas Llosa, Mario. "Fehdebrief zur Verfechtung der Ehre von Tirant lo Blanc." Translated into German by Fritz Vogelsang. *Neue Rundschau* 101.1 (1990): 124-43.

—. *Gegen Wind und Wetter. Essays.* Translated into German by Elke Wehr. Frankfurt a. M.: Suhrkamp, 1988.

—. *La Novela*. Buenos Aires: América Nueva, 1974.

Vereinigung bildender Künstler Österreichs. *Katalog der VII. Ausstellung der Secession*. Vienna: Secession, 1900.

Vergo, Peter. "Gustav Klimts 'Philosophie' und das Programm der Universitätsgemälde." *Mitteilungen der Österreichischen Galerie* 66/67 (1978/79): 69-100.

Weininger, Otto. *Geschlecht und Charakter*. Vienna: Universitäts-Verlagsbuchhandlung, 1920.

Zweites Programm für die Anordnung der Deckengemälde im Festsaal der Wiener Universität, eingereicht von Franz Matsch. Vienna: Allgemeines Verwaltungsarchiv, 1905.

Notes

[1] "...das Aufblitzen einer Einsicht in die Einheit im Zeichen der Polarität, des Zusammenfallens der Gegensätze" (Hesse, 33; unless otherwise stated, all translations are by Maria Morrison). We will not attempt a more exact definition of the concept of modernity here. For a short and succinct attempt at defining this epoch in the field of literature and literary criticism, see Thomé and Schönert.

[2] "Ich glaube, darüber [über die Fakultätsbilder] müssten bereits Andere urtheilen als Künstler und Publicum, denn das ist pathologisch. Und das Gefährliche daran ist, dass dieser Wahnsinn ansteckend wirkt" [I believe that other critics besides artists and the public would have to judge them (the faculty paintings), because

that's pathological. And the most dangerous thing is that this madness is contagious] (qtd. in Bahr, *Gegen Klimt*, 30).

[3] "Unfaßlich. Lyrisch. Und manches andere" (*Tagebücher*, 208).

[4] Albrecht Dürer's travel journal, which describes the entry of Charles V into Antwerp and his letters to Melanchton, served as a historical model for the pageant. The Makart pageant allegorized the social and economic self-confidence of the middle classes, but above all it served the glorification of the continuity of the imperial family. In *The Man Without Qualities* Diotima searches once in the court library for a contemporary depiction of this parade. She acts on a suggestion by Arnheim: "His Grace had urged Diotima to find out about the famous Makart pageant, which had brought all Austria together in the 1870s in a burst of national fervor; he still had vivid memories of the richly draped carriages, the heavily caparisoned horses, the trumpeters and the pride the people took in their medieval costumes, which lifted them out of their humdrum daily lives" (615). Later Diotima herself, as her contribution to the Parallel Campaign, would design such a parade with the programmatic name "The clans of Austria and Hungary pay homage to internal and external peace" (*From the Posthumous Papers*, 1218).

[5] The approximately 5 x 10 meter painting depicts the "virgin honor guard" in the Emperor's retinue almost completely naked. The painting is made more interesting by rumors that among these virgins Makart included portraits of respected Viennese society women. Over 34,000 visitors saw the painting in the Künstlerhaus—and that in a time in which social interactions were characterized by a high degree of prudishness. For more about the erotic in Makart's work see Demkó-Bélanskzky.

[6] "Wien, unser schönes, fröhliches, kunstsinniges Wien hat sich heute um den Namen der Kaiserstadt, den es mit Stolz trägt, wohl verdient gemacht. Wie festlich, wie herzlich, wie großartig auch die Huldigungen waren, welche diese Woche hindurch dem Kaiserpaare dargebracht wurden: die Huldigung des Wiener Bürgertums hat sie alle übertroffen" (*Neue Freie Presse, Morgenblatt* 28 April 1879: 1).

[7] "einzelne Kompositionselemente und Motive [...] direkt von Makart entlehnt" (Frodl, 51).

[8] "Von der stilvollen Haltung dieses Hauses entzückt, danke ich, daß es mir vergönnt war, die Gastfreundschaft eines großen Künstlers und einer geistvoll liebenswürdigen Hausfrau zu genießen" (*Briefe*, 22; translation by Maria Morrison).

[9] Ms. Christa Magerl from the Österreichischen Institut für Wirtschaftsforschung (The Austrian Institute for Economic Research) was so good as to calculate these figures. The guilders (*Gulden*) were converted first to kronen, then to schillings, then to reichmarks, then again to schillings and finally to euros, taking into account the increase in the consumer price index between 1891 and 2007.

[10] "Ich wollte damals sofort zurücktreten und nur die Vermittlung des Baron Weckbecker im Unterrichtsministerium, der einen sehr vernünftigen Vertrag aufsetzte, welcher einen Passus enthielt, der mir als Künstler vollste Freiheit

einräumte, ließ mich bestimmen, an die Arbeit zu gehen" (Klimt in an interview with Bertha Zukerkandl, qtd. in Strobl, 161).
11 "[M]an konnte an einem Tag hundert Jahre zurücklegen, wenn man aus dem Künstlerhaus in die Sezession ging." Robert Musil, "Wiener Frühjahrsausstellungen" (*Prager Presse* 8 June 1922, in *Werke*, 9:1585).
12 "Die verschiedenen Künste müssen aber miteinander und sogar mit der sachlichen Rede gemeinsam in irgendeiner Tiefe die Wurzel haben, da sie ja nichts als verschiedene Ausdrucksformen des gleichen Menschen sind; sie müssen deshalb auch irgendwie ineinander übersetzbar und durcheinander ersetzbar sein" (*Werke* 8:1149).
13 "Die Philosophie. Eines der fünf allegorischen Deckenbilder für die Aula der Universität. Linke Figurengruppe: das Entstehen, das fruchtbare Sein, das Vergehen. Rechts: Die Weltkugel, das Welträtsel. Unten auftauchend eine erleuchtete Gestalt: das Wissen" (Vereinigung, 7).
14 "Uns ist Klimts Bild musikalisch nur mit Richard Strauss' "Also sprach Zarathustra" vergleichbar. Da wie dort der mißglückte Versuch, Philosophie zu erläutern. Bei dem einen ein Durcheinanderflimmern von Farben, bei dem anderen ein Chaos von Tonmassen, beide Werke ohne Klarheit..." (qtd. in Bahr, *Gegen Klimt*, 18).
15 "Der Wirklichkeitsbegriff der alten Ritterbuchautoren umschließt mit einem einzigen Blick mehrere Kategorien menschlichen Seins, und in diesem Sinne ist ihre Vorstellung vom literarischen Realismus weiter, umfassender als diejenige späterer Autoren" (Vargas Llosa, *Fehdebrief*, 138).
16 "Ein Buch der Rittertaten voller phantastischer historischer, kriegerischer, sozialer, erotischer, psychologischer Komponenten: all dies zugleich darstellend und keines dieser Elemente isoliert oder gar ausschließlich offerierend, nichts mehr und nichts weniger als die Wirklichkeit repräsentierend" (Vargas Llosa, *Fehdebrief*, 138).
17 "Dieser Versuch, die Realität auf allen ihren Ebenen darzustellen, auf ein desinteressierte Weise, nicht didaktisch, nicht exemplifizierend, nicht pädagogisch, nicht zeigend, was die Menschen sein sollen, sondern schlicht, was sie sind, was sie zu sein glauben und sein möchten, das war eine enorm subversive Sache, denn es vernichtete alle möglichen Tabus, löste alle möglichen Vorspielung auf.... Es gibt also, wie mir scheint, eine sehr merkwürdige Verbindung zwischen dem Erscheinen einer großen Romanproduktion und dem Zustand von Krise und Auflösung einer Gesellschaft." (Vargas Llosa, *La Novela*, 37).
18 "Es gibt keine große Kunst ohne eine gewisse Dosis Unvernunft, denn große Kunst drückt stets die menschliche Totalität aus" (Vargas Llosa, *Gegen Wind*, 85).
19 Es [das Buch] gibt ein völlig complexes Bild einer Gesellschaft und eines Landes in einem geschlossenen Zeitraum. Es umfaßt alle Typen von den Spitzen bis hinunter zum Leben und Schicksal des Mörders Moosbrugger, das die dunkle Folie, die Nachtseite mit all ihren Schauern dazu bildet...Erstaunlich wie naturhaft Musils Gestalten auch noch in der geistigen Durschsicht bleiben. Es fehlt ihnen

kein Organ. Die Strenge des Denkens bleibt der Wirklichkeit nichts schuldig" (Efraim Frisch in *Die Frankfurter Zeitung*, qtd. in Corino, 1004).

[20] For more about Moosbrugger's thinking and the "other condition" and their relationship to Lévy-Bruhl and non-European thought, see Michael Rössner, *Auf der Suche nach dem verlorenen Paradies*.

[21] "Die Welt schien nur die Außenseite eines bestimmten inneren Verhaltens zu sein und mit diesem gewechselt werden zu können." (*Der Mann ohne Eigenschaften*, 1664; translation by Maria Morrison).

[22] "[E]r erweist sich dabei als vorwiegend mystisches und subjektiv-affektives Weiterleben, dem die religiöse Komponente fehlt und das starke Parallelen zu dem Erleben der Primitiven, bzw. zu gewissen, damit verglichenen psychopathologischen Formen aufweist. Musil betont, daß dieser Zustand im modernen Menschen weiterlebt, daß seine Verdrängung durch die Ratio schmerzhaft empfunden, seine Vereinigung mit ihr dagegen als Hochgefühl erlebt wird" (Rössner, 94).

[23] For more on splitting and unification in Musil see Pekar, *Die Sprache der Liebe*, 255ff.

[24] "Klimt ist ein großes Talent, eine geschickte Hand, die von einem unklaren Kopfe geleitet werden [sic]" (*Plein-air,* Vienna, 27 March 1901, qtd. in Bahr, *Gegen Klimt*, 52).

[25] Darauf war es nun angelegt: sie rechneten, einen labilen und empfindlichen, vielleicht auch schon, was bei Künstlern, wenn sie aus den seligen Extasen in die Ermattung sinken, nicht selten ist, von einer vagen Angst vor sich selbst bedrohten Menschen, wie sie Klimt sich denken, durch dies teuflische Gerücht so zu verstören, daß er innerlich zerbrechen würde. Bequemer und worauf man doch bei uns immer Wert legt: gemütlicher, als ihn zu vergiften" (Bahr, *Gegen Klimt*, 4).

[26] "Es kam wie eine Tollheit über Törleß, Dinge, Vorgänge und Menschen als etwas Doppelsinniges zu empfinden. Als etwas, das durch die Kraft irgendwelcher Erfinder an ein harmloses, erklärendes Wort gefesselt war, und als etwas ganz Fremdes, das jeden Augenblick sich davon loszureißen drohte" (Musil, *Werke*, 6:64).

[27] Hysterie ist die organische Krisis der organischen Verlogenheit des Weibes. Ich leugne nicht, daß es auch, wenngleich relativ nur recht selten, hysterische Männer gibt: denn eine unter den unendlichen vielen Möglichkeiten, die psychisch im Manne liegen, ist es, zum Weibe, und damit, gegebenfalls, auch hysterisch zu werden" (Weininger, 352). The outbreak of the First World War forced doctors to contend for better or worse with male hysteria. The hysterical collapses of the soldiers threatened to destabilize the army.

[28] "Bläulichweißes Schaumgewoge senkt sich hernieder. Dichter und dichter, fast scheint es, als wären es Körper. Formen erschimmern, lösen sich und ergänzen sich. Körper sind es, spukhaft von bläulichem Verwesungshauche überzogen" (Karl Schreder, *Deutsches Volksblatt* 26 March 1900, qtd. in Bahr, *Gegen Klimt*, 18).

[29] "Insoweit die Wissenschaft differenzierend ist, stellt sie in ihrer Pragmatik das Anti-Modell des stabilen Systems dar" (Lyotard, 185).

[30] "Das Scheitern der Vernunft als Prinzip verhindert nicht den Rückgriff auf die Vernunft als Mittel" (Jean-Louis Poitevin, qtd. in Michael Hofmann, 150).

[31] "Wenn man klipp und klar sagen wollte, daß Klimts Bild als Allegorie unverständlich ist, daß es weder dekorativen noch koloristischen Reiz hat, so hätte die Geschichte einen Sinn. Dies ließe sich beweisen" (E. v. Gayrsperg., Vienna, 25 March 1900, qtd. in Bahr, *Gegen Klimt*, 20). It is worth noting here, that the page of the Vereinigung bildender Künstler Österreichs [Association of Austrian Artists] ("Secession"), in contrast to the absolute pronouncements of the critics, classified their value judgments not as a demonstrable natural law, but rather as personal opinion: "Wir erachten das genannte Werk als eine hervorragende und hocherfreuliche Erscheinung unserer heimischen Kunst" [We regard the aforementioned work as an excellent and highly gratifying embodiment of our native art] (*Illustriertes Wiener Extrablatt*, Vienna, 26 March 26 1900, qtd. in Bahr: *Gegen Klimt*, 21).

[32] "es der Rationalismus selbst ist, der mit den eigenen Mitteln geschlagen ist" (Pott, 23).

[33] "Das Unerforschte sichtbar darzustellen mußte misslingen, und was wir sehen, ist eine formlose unverständliche und [sic] Traumwelt, das gerade Gegenteil aller wahren Philosophie" (12 March 1900, qtd. in Bahr, *Gegen Klimt*, 17).

[34] "The Sleep/dream of reason produces monsters." "Sueño" in Spanish can mean "dream" as well as "sleep." This double meaning allows for several different translations and interpretations. 1) If we translate "sueño" as "sleep," then the sleep of reason gives birth to monsters. Thus if reason is absent, then the ghosts of an old superstition return and govern the individual, who thus loses his freedom. 2) If we translate "sueño" as "dream," then reason is not sleeping but rather dreaming, which means that reason itself gives birth to the monsters. All of the horrors and pitfalls of humanity lurk in each of us; reason must fight against its own unconscious. 3) If we translate "sueño" with "dream of the future, goal," then we find ourselves confronted with Horkheimer and Adorno's question (Dialectic of Enlightenment): why did the Enlightenment, with its rational belief in progress, and which had as its goal a free and responsible humanity, have to end in Auschwitz? This interpretation is also implicit in Goya's multi-layered work.

[35] "Es giebt [sic] Wahrheiten aber keine Wahrheit. Ich kann ganz gut zwei einander völlig entgegengesetzte Dinge behaupten und in beiden Fällen Recht haben [...] Siehe Nietzsche." (*Tagebücher*, 12).

[36] "Das sind noch lange keine freien Geister: denn sie glauben noch an die Wahrheit ..." (Nietzsche, 900).

[37] "ganzheitlich-gesteigerten Gefühls- und Lebenszustand" (see Pekar, *Robert Musil*, 33).

[38] "als ewig fließendes, ununterbrochen zu Formen gerinnendes und wieder zerrinnendes Leben" (Hevesi, 233-34).

[39] See *Der Mann ohne Eigenschaften*, 1021, and Arntzen, 94.

[40] "Nur so nebenbei möchten wir noch bemerken, daß, wenn wir auch gerne zugeben wollen, daß Derjenige, welcher die verschiedenen Systeme auch nur der deutschen Philosophen gründlich studirt [sic!] in einen Zustand gelinden Wahnsinnes gerathen muß, doch nichts Herrn Klimt gezwungen hat, uns nun auch einen gemalten Wahnsinn zu versetzen" (qtd. in Bahr, *Gegen Klimt*, 19).
[41] "...die heute ihre Quellen in den exacten Wissenschaften sucht, gerade in unserer Zeit nicht verdient, als nebelhaftes, phantastischen Gebilde, als rätselhafte Sphinx dargestellt zu werden" (*Neue Freie Presse* 27 March 1900; qtd. in Vergo, 81).
[42] According to the university archives in Vienna, Gustav Donath, Musil's childhood friend and the model for the literary figure of Walter, the husband of Clarisse, completed his orals in philosophy with Professors Friedrich Jodl and Laurenz Müllner. See Schmied-Kowarzik.
[43] "Ich darf kein Hehl daraus machen, daß ich als Philosoph nicht auf dem Boden der kirchlichen Weltsicht stehe, nicht Dualist, sondern Monist bin, nicht den Theismus, sondern die Religion der Moral vertrete, daß ich grundsätzlich der Ansicht bin, für den Philosophen existiere keine wie immer geartete äußere Autorität, sondern nur die innere seines Gewissens, der wissenschaftlichen Tradition" (qtd. in Margarete Jodl, 169-70).
[44] "unklare Symbolik" (Jodl, qtd. in Bahr, *Gegen Klimt*, 23).
[45] "Nicht das Nackte auf dem Bilde, sondern das Häßliche wird von uns angefochten" (*Neue Freie Presse* 28 March 1900; qtd. in Bahr, *Gegen Klimt*, 23).
[46] "Was ist häßlich?" (Prof. Franz Wickhoff's speech is reproduced in Bahr, *Gegen Klimt*, 31ff.).
[47] "...daß jedes Kunstwerk, welches von der bisher üblichen Ausdrucksweise abweicht und nach Individualität strebt, stets auf Widerspruch stoßen wird" (*Illustriertes Wiener Extrablatt* 26 March 1900; qtd. in Bahr, *Gegen Klimt*, 22).
[48] "Ganz abgesehen davon, daß die philosophische Fakultät, deren allegorische Darstellung das Bild beabsichtigt, sich eigentlich mit recht realistischen und exakt wissenschaftlichen Fächern beschäftigt, als da sind: Geschichte, Sprachwissenschaft, Mathematik, u.s.w., ist auch die moderne Philosophie nichts weniger al mystisch-metaphysisches Dahinträumen unter ungelösten Rätseln. Im Gegenteil gewinnt der physiologische Teil dieser Disziplin immer mehr an Ausdehnung, während der rein spekulative immer mehr zusammenschrumpft. Das Ignorabimus ist auch in dieser Wissenschaft—und eben durch diese Wissenschaft—anerkannt und bildet eine Grenze, über die hinauszustreben gar nicht mehr versucht wird" (*Plein-air* 12 March 1900; qtd. in Bahr, *Gegen Klimt*, 16-17).
[49] "künstlerisches und wissenschaftliches Denken berühren sich bei uns noch nicht. Die Fragen einer Mittelzone zwischen beiden bleiben ungelöst." Robert Musil, "Anmerkungen zu einer Metapsychik" (*Werke*, 8:1019).
[50] "mysthisch-metaphysisches Dahinträumen" (*Plein-air* 12 March 1900; qtd. in Bahr, *Gegen Klimt*, 16).

[51] "Gleichgewichtsstörung des Wirklichkeitsbewußtseins ... Abnorme zur neuen Norm, das gestörte zu einem andren Seelengleichgewicht" (*Werke*, 8:1140).
[52] "Man ist zwar gewohnt, die Wirkung des Kunstwerks als einen gehobenen, wohl auch als einen erleichterten Lebenszustand beschrieben zu finden, früher nannte man ihn gern Phantasie und heute Illusion, aber man trifft selten oder nie auf die Auswertung der Möglichkeit, daß diese Illusion bei aller Verschiedenheit eine Analogie zu dem ist, was die Psychiatrie unter einer Illusion versteht; also eine 'Störung', bei der Elemente der Wirklichkeit zu einem unwirklichen Ganzen ergänzt werden, das Wirklichkeitswert usurpiert" (*Werke*, 8:1140).
[53] "Es ist unmöglich das Bild anzusehen, ohne an Zolas Roman 'L'Oeuvre' zu denken, und an den tragischen Schluß, wo der geniale Claude, vom Mißerfolg wahnsinnig geworden, die Welt und die Menschheit in ein Bild vereinigen will, und auch einen solchen gemalten Racheakt verbricht" (*Berliner Lokal-Anzeiger* 25 March 1901; qtd. in Bahr, *Gegen Klimt*, 50).
[54] "Die Kühnheit Klimts in der Darstellung des absolut Menschlichen übersteigt alle Grenzen" (29 March 1901; qtd. in Bahr, *Gegen Klimt*, 56).
[55] "Ist das, was die Menschen tun, weniger real als das, was sie glauben und träumen? Sind die Visionen, Alptraumbilder und Mythen weniger Existent als die Taten?" (Vargas Llosa, *Fehdebrief*,138).
[56] "Nie war ein Maler phantastischer und naturgetreuer zugleich" (Hevesi, 444).
[57] 30,000 Kronen from the year 1905 would buy 100,000 Euros today. Between 1891 and 1905 there was very little inflation. In 1892 the government switched the currency to kronen with 1 gulden equal to 2 Kronen. Thanks to Christa Magerl at the Österreichischen Institut für Wirtschaftsforschung. [Austrian Institute for Economic Research].
[58] A contrast between Gustav Klimt's *Medicine* (1900-1907) and its contemporary reception and the theme of Madness in the Clarisse story in *The Man Without Qualities*, as well as the analysis and reception of "Jurisprudence" (1903-1907) in direct comparison to the depiction of the insane serial killer Moosbrugger will be addressed by the author of this article elsewhere.
[59] "Es scheint, daß [...] derjenige Reklamekünstler gewinnt, der die Grenze zwischen Genie und Wahnsinn nach der letzteren Richtung am kräftigsten verschiebt" (*Montags-Blatt* April 1901; qtd. in Bahr, *Gegen Klimt,* 54).

CHAPTER FOUR

ALBAN BERG'S MUSICAL DEPICTION OF ILLNESS, MADNESS, AND CRIMINALITY IN *WOZZECK*

LYLE BARKHYMER

"Illness, Madness, Criminality." The Modern Austrian Literature and Culture Association (MALCA) chose these insalubrious words as the theme for its annual conference in 2005 at Wake Forest University in North Carolina, USA. Holding in abeyance for the moment thoughts of Sachertorte, "Sisi," and Strauss, one might ask, "What could be more Austrian?" However inappropriate it might be to label the full sweep of a complex culture and its history with these words, there is certainly no difficulty locating within their dark realm the decadence of the fin-de-siècle or the self-mutilation and "frighten the middle class" [Bürgerschreck] penchant of the Viennese Actionists.

When the opera-goer, whether aficionado or scholar, looks at the words "madness and crime," musical motives can play vividly in the mind, and this internally heard music is most likely from Alban Berg's expressionistic operatic oeuvre, from *Wozzeck* and *Lulu.* Based on a presentation at the aforementioned MALCA conference, this essay will be restricted to *Wozzeck,* which the composer worked on in Vienna from 1914 onward until 1922.

The twentieth century after Puccini and Strauss did not add a wealth of material to the standard operatic repertory, and virtually no modernist or progressive works are presented on a regular basis in the major opera houses of the world. But, as a modernist exception in that select company of more frequently heard twentieth-century works, *Wozzeck* has perhaps received the most performances, been most recorded, and most attracted the sustained attention of critics and top-ranking conductors, opera houses, and singers. No other has engaged at length the scholarly minds of thinkers on the level of an Adorno, or challenged the most talented singers from Walter Berry, Dietrich Fischer-Dieskau, and Franz Grundheber onward to a younger generation including great artists such as Falk Struckmann at the Metropolitan Opera, the Stadttheater Basel, and the Vienna Staasoper.

The problem facing anyone writing a relatively short piece on *Wozzeck* is how to focus, what to leave out. In the bibliography of its "Alban Berg" article, *Grove Music* records at least ten substantial, highly respected scholarly sources that focus on *Wozzeck* alone, and a wide field of others that touch upon it. The opera has been the subject of highly regarded scholarly books by George Perle and Douglas Jarman, not to mention Berg's own analysis and description of his opera in a 1929 lecture. The text by Georg Büchner has been studied widely and offers many challenges and interesting paths for comparison and research. These include, for example, establishing a definitive *Urtext,* examining the historical *Woyzeck,* and describing Berg's transformation of Büchner's *Woyzeck* text into his *Wozzeck* libretto. It is no doubt best to leave these considerations to the Germanists, to leave a feminist deconstruction of the text to the feminists, and to leave a study of the opera as drama on the stage to the dramatists, however tempting and fruitful those lines of inquiry might be.

Abandoning the temptations of the foregoing, the music itself remains. This article will be limited to, first, briefly presenting the context of the opera, placing the work in its time and in the composer's output; second, a short general description of *Wozzeck's* unique features; and third, a focused attempt to illustrate the specific musical means that Berg uses to represent illness, madness, and criminality. The audience for this article is neither the practicing musicologist nor the casual reading public, but rather a highly educated, broad, cross-disciplinary group that is interested in Austrian literature and culture and that has some knowledge of the basic elements of music. While examples in musical notation from Berg's full score and piano-vocal score are included for those to whom they may be helpful, the ability to read music is not assumed, and the jargon of the specialist in music theory and music history will be avoided.

Figure 4-1 "Michael Devlin (l.), The Doctor; Falk Struckmann, Wozzeck. By permission of The Metropolitan Opera."

Berg and the Schoenberg School

The early-twentieth-century names Schoenberg, Berg, and Webern become so tightly linked that it is startling to read Alma Mahler's anecdote regarding how Berg wavered between choosing Arnold Schoenberg or the arch-conservative Hans Pfitzner as his composition teacher. Berg is supposed to have told Alma Mahler, the dedicatee of *Wozzeck,* that he became Schoenberg's pupil only because he missed a train to Strasbourg, where he intended to study with Pfitzner (Mahler-Werfel, 25). Pfitzner, of course, later vigorously opposed the Schoenberg School and its music. With regard to Berg's place with Webern in the Schoenberg School—sometimes called the "New Vienna School," the "Second Vienna School," the" Viennese Expressionists," or the "Viennese Atonalists," all designations that are susceptible to challenge on some point—one need only know that he was sometimes flippantly referred to as "the good one." This is a result of his less stringent application of Schoenberg's serial technique and his fondness for textures and chord structures that meet the post-romantic listener half-way. In this regard his music has received wide acceptance in the standard repertory, especially the *Lyric Suite,* the *Violin Concerto*, and *Wozzeck*. The opera *Lulu* has not been performed as often, and its complexity and the difficulty of establishing a definitive version place it outside even the modernist operatic mainstream.

Wozzeck in Context

The creation of *Wozzeck* began with a performance of Georg Büchner's unfinished play *Woyzeck*, misspelled *Wozzeck* and in the text version by Franzòs-Landau, that Berg saw in Vienna in 1914. Inspired and intrigued by the experience, he began work on the piece then, but the full score was not finally ready until 1922. The premier did not take place in Vienna, but rather in Berlin, on December 14, 1925, at the Staatsoper. It was conducted by the young, ambitious, and obviously daring Erich Kleiber, who was also general director [Intendant] of the house and had arranged for the opera to be produced (see Clements).

Except for omitting some scenes and some minor roles, the libretto that Berg created is not complicated and hews almost exactly to the Franzòs-Landau version of the text (Perle, 42). Adorno summarizes it as the "drama of the tortured, paranoid soldier Wozzeck, who avenges the injustices done him by giving vent to his unrestrained nature and murdering his mistress" (*Alban Berg*, 5). One might question whether "paranoid" is an entirely appropriate word. The drama certainly depicts

Wozzeck's hallucinations and further descent into madness and crime, but "paranoid" would imply that the causes and influences are not real, only imagined. The simple soldier Wozzeck, however, suffers severely as the subject of a bizarre medical experiment involving diet, he endures constant denigration and humiliation from his captain, and his jealousy is inflamed by his common-law wife Marie's all-to-real sexual liaison with the Drum Major. Surely Wozzeck's fears and hallucinations have a basis in fact.

The libretto is a spare, economical telling of a bleak tale. In act 1 Berg presents a dramatic exposition in five scenes. Wozzeck, a poor soldier who lives with Marie and has a son with her, is seen shaving his Captain and later with his friend, Andres, in the country cutting sticks and having disturbing visions. In the next scene Marie watches from a window as a parade goes by, led by a handsome drum major. She argues with her neighbor, and then sings her child to sleep with a lullaby. Wozzeck enters, still hallucinating. The fourth scene tells us why Wozzeck is ill: his regimental doctor is keeping him on an experimental diet of only beans in return for three pennies [Kreuzer] a day. In the last scene, the drum major enters Marie's room and she indifferently gives herself to him.

Act 2 is subtitled "Recognitions and Reversal" by Douglas Jarman. In scene 1, Wozzeck comes to Marie's room and sees earrings the Drum Major has given her and becomes suspicious. She makes excuses; he gives her money and leaves. The Captain and the Doctor open the next scene, and Wozzeck comes past, giving them the opportunity to mock him and mention the Drum Major. In the third scene Wozzeck goes to Marie and they argue. He is about to strike her when she presciently cries "Better a knife in me than a hand on me." In scene 4 Wozzeck follows Marie and waits for her while she dances with the Drum Major. An idiot looks on and remarks on the smell of blood. Scene 5 takes place in the guardroom, where the Drum Major taunts Wozzeck and bests him in a fight.

The disaster occurs in act 3. Marie's "Bible Scene" opens the act, as she reads the stories of the adulteress and Mary Magdalene. Next, on a path in the woods Wozzeck sees no way out, he must act. As the moon rises blood-red, he stabs Marie in the neck. Scene 3 is in a tavern, where Margaret sings a folk song. Blood on his arm betrays Wozzeck, and he rushes out to look for the knife before it can be found. In scene 4 Wozzeck stumbles over Marie's body, finds the knife, and throws it into the pond. Thinking that he didn't throw it far enough, he wades into the pond after it and drowns. The Captain and Doctor pass by. The poignant final scene takes place in the street in front of Marie's door on a bright, sunny day. Children are playing there, including her little boy. A child comes running in yelling, "Hey, you, your mother is dead!" All rush out to look at the excitement. Uncomprehending, Marie's child goes on riding his hobby horse, "Hop hop,—hop hop," and follows the others (see Jarman, *Alban Berg*, 35-37).

Table of Scenes

Act One

Wozzeck shaves his captain
Wozzeck cuts wood in countryside, hallucinates
Marie sees Drum Major, sings lullaby, distraught Wozzeck enters
Wozzeck, on diet of beans, examined by doctor
Drum Major comes to Marie's room, she gives herself to him

Act Two

Wozzeck sees earrings from Drum Majors, Marie makes excuses. He gives her money and leaves.
Doctor and Captain mock Wozzeck
Wozzeck argues with Marie
He follows her, waits while she dances
Drum Major mocks Wozzeck, throws him to the ground

Act Three

Marie's "Bible Scene"
Wozzeck stabs Marie to death as the blood-red moon rises
In the tavern, blood on his arm betrays Wozzeck
Wozzeck drowns in pond
Children rush out to see the excitement, Marie's child follows, "Hop hop—hop hop."

Wozzeck and Expressionism

One of the ways in which *Wozzeck* follows some of the trends of expressionism is that it denies the dramatic plot-line structure of eighteenth- and nineteenth-century "number operas" and the three- to five-act narrative structures of romantic opera. As can be seen from the table above, *Wozzeck* presents its characters in a series of tableaux or vignettes, structured in a progressive time-line, to be sure, but not leading dramatically from one to the next. Berg had forerunners in this method of operatic presentation, especially Debussy in *Pelléas et Mélisande* and Mussorgsky in *Boris Godunov.* In this form of operatic drama, the cumulative effect of the vignettes is surprisingly powerful and excavates deep veins of resonant memory in the listener.

Expressionism is a descriptive term that musicology and music criticism have borrowed from other fields, principally from the visual arts and literature, for music that is in some sense a reaction to *impressionism* as represented primarily by works of Claude Debussy and, to a lesser extent, Maurice Ravel. Expressionism is known for exaggerated, unrestrained portrayal of psychic turmoil (think Edvard Munch, *The Scream*) and for its gravitation to the darker, problematic, violent, primordially sexual aspects of the human experience. However, musicology has adopted a more limited concept of expressionism. David Fanning, writing in *Grove Music*, defines it in its most limited application as music of Arnold Schoenberg's "post-tonal pre-12-note output," music that "largely avoids cadence, repetition, sequence, balanced phrases, and reference to formal or procedural models." He admits some works of Schoenberg's pupils Berg and Webern to this tight circle if they consistently exemplify these characteristics.

In this strictly limited sense, *Wozzeck* might not be considered essentially expressionistic music because, as Fanning points out in his article,

> the success of *Wozzeck* from 1925 on helped popularize Expressionism; but that very success was a symptom of the opera's sensational and ultimately consoling aspects, which fall outside the stricter definition of Expressionism.

What aspects of *Wozzeck*, then, in Fanning's words did "help bring expressionism to the attention of the twentieth-century musical public?" If the music sometimes does seem "soothing," particularly when it represents Marie's vacant mental state or her very human maternal feelings for the child, the spare text abounds in the iconic images of violent expressionism. These include Wozzeck's mental precipitous decline into madness, his visions and hallucinations; the bizarre diet and cruelty of the captain and doctor; jealousy, lust and seduction; a blood-red moon; the knife; the misery of the poor; drunkenness; fate and evil; and violent death—both Marie's death at Wozzeck's hand and his subsequent drowning in water that looks like blood.

Formal Structure in *Wozzeck*

Wozzeck is exceptional in the variety and detail of its structural organization, in the extensive use of historic forms from the baroque and classical music traditions, and in the fact that the composer himself has written and lectured about the structure (see Redlich, 311).

Table of Forms in Wozzeck (see Perle, 38-88)

Act One

Scene 1: Baroque Suite
- Prelude
- Pavane
- Gigue
- Gavotte
- Air and Reprise

Scene 2: Rhapsody
Scene 3: Military March, Two-Verse Lullaby
Scene 4: Passacaglia
Scene 5: Quasi-Rondo

Act Two: Symphony in Five Movements

Scene 1: Exposition – Development – Recapitulation
Scene 2: Fantasia (waltz) – Fugue
Scene 3: "Largo," A – B – A
Scene 4: "Scherzo," Ländler and Trio

Act Three: Five Inventions

Scene 1: Invention on a Theme with 7 Variations – Fugue
Scene 2: Invention on Note
Scene 3: Invention on a Rhythm
Scene 4: Invention on a Six-Note Chord
Scene 5: Invention on Continuous 8th note Motion

As Berg himself explained in his 1929 lecture and as has been elucidated by Perle and Jarman (*Alban Berg*, 25), act 1 begins with elements of a Baroque suite of stylized dances, a prelude as the curtain rises followed by pavane, gigue, gavotte, air, and reprise separated by brief cadenzas. Scene 2 introduces a folk-like element in a rhapsody alternating with Andres' "hunting song." A military march is the basis for scene 3 as Marie sees the Drum Major for the first time, and the scene continues with a 2-verse "cradle song" as she lullabies her child to sleep. The very tightly structured form of a passacaglia, an eight-bar theme with 21 variations, shapes scene 4, and in scene 5 we encounter a "quasi-rondo," not as clear-cut as its classical model, but still identifiable as repeating sections that are separated by episodes of contrasting material.

Berg structures the second act using symphonic form, i.e. "A Symphony in Five Movements." Scene 1 includes the exposition, development, and recapitulation of established sonata form. A fantasia with a waltz character leads in scene 2 to a fugue, while the confrontation of Marie and Wozzeck in scene 3 occurs in a symphonic slow movement or "largo" in A B A form. The traditional dance-based movement of a symphony occurs in scene 4 as a scherzo that alternates *Ländler* and waltz ideas with contrasting material referred to as "trio."

Act 3 is called "Five Inventions." An "invention" in musical terms is a short composition that dwells on one idea or a technical problem, and typically is written in counterpoint. Notable is Marie's "Bible Scene," which opens act 3 with an invention on a theme with seven variations, after which follows a brief fugue.

Illness, Madness, and Criminality Depicted by Music

As Wozzeck and his Captain appear in the first scene of the opera, Berg shows in orchestral terms what the text holds in store. The curtain goes up without any preparation at all, and we hear the Captain's motive. Using nine of the possible twelve chromatic notes, the angular shape, staccato articulation, and hectic rhythm are a masterful character study in only two measures.

Ex. 1. Act 1, Ms. 4-5, (English Horn) Captain's Motive[1]

Throughout the opera Berg uses the Wagnerian technique of the "leading motive" [Leitmotiv] to represent both characters and concepts. The motive of the Captain is sharp, hectic, almost manic. It is presented in atonal half-steps, where tonality is denied by presenting each of the possible tones before repeating any, and yet there is an implication of a center or emphasis on one note, the C#/Db. The manic quality of the captain is also depicted by the use of *falsetto* in his vocal line, requiring the singer to produce tones far above the normal male voice range. Rhythm plays a roll as well, with dotted, jerky rhythms and a confusing abundance of duple and triple note values in a variety of tempos. The nasal qualities and biting staccatos of the oboe and English horn are used to good effect in the motive.

The first notes that Wozzeck sings immediately exemplify the beaten-down, dehumanized state that poverty, malnutrition, contempt, and mockery have brought this common soldier to. He leadenly sings to the Captain in a rhythmic motive that will be identified with him throughout the opera. All of the drudgery and humiliation of his life seem wrapped up in this plodding, monotone phrase.

Ex. 2, Rhythm of Wozzeck's Motive

In the scene out in the fields that follows, Wozzeck's mental state has deteriorated markedly. Berg emphasizes this by juxtaposing his comrade Andres' jolly but slightly pushed-out-of-shape hunting song with Wozzeck's outbursts in a singing technique called *Sprechstimme*, first made notorious in Schoenberg's song cycle with chamber orchestra *Pierrot lunaire.*

Ex. 3, Schoenberg, *Pierrot lunaire*

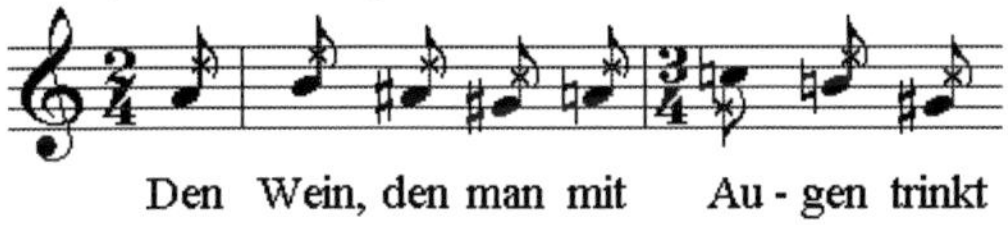

The note-stem is marked with an "x" and the singer is asked to half-sing, half-speak in the pitch-vicinity of that note. Andres is one of the few characters who serve as foils to the characters who represent "illness, madness, and criminality" in the opera. These "healthy" characters tend to be naïve, simple folk, and their music stems from folk and popular music styles. If it were not for the sharps on the last two pitches (Ex. 4), this tune could be any jolly huntsman's tune, or a call played on a hunting horn:

Ex. 4, Act 1, Ms. 213-15 Andres' Song

As Marie hears the military march music in scene 3, a march that is weirdly distorted, and sees the Drum Major for the first time, the seeds of the catastrophe are sown:

Ex. 5, Act 1, Ms. 334-35 Military March

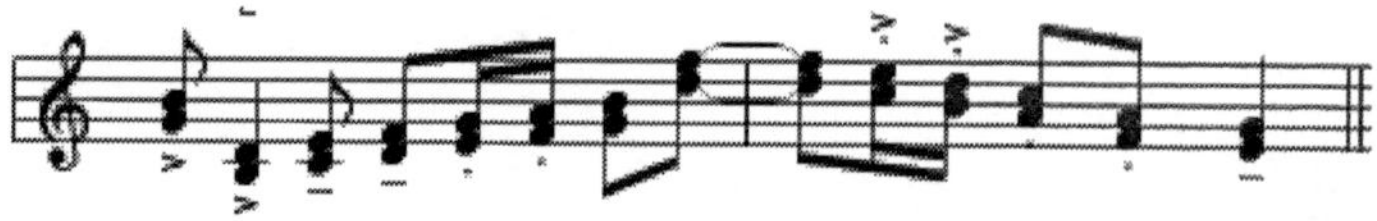

Marie and her neighbor trade spoken insults above the music, rising to a scream of "Whore!" thrown at Marie, who closes her window, and turns to her child. Marie's lullaby is one of the only moments when Berg comes close to an aria in *Wozzeck,* and because of that it is often excerpted in recital. Here Berg uses a musical language and material in which notes move in a way that implies tonal centers:

Ex. 5, Act 1, Ms. 372-73, Marie's Lullaby

This musical language is associated with the humanistic elements in the opera, such as Marie's love for her child, and it stands in opposition to the dissonant, often atonal, and rhythmically complex language associated with the more prevalent expressionistic motifs. The lullaby ends with a masterstroke, as the composer represents Marie's sinking into absent-mindedness by a series of empty chords missing their core middle note:

Ex. 6, Act 1, Ms. 415-16 Marie's Vacant Mind

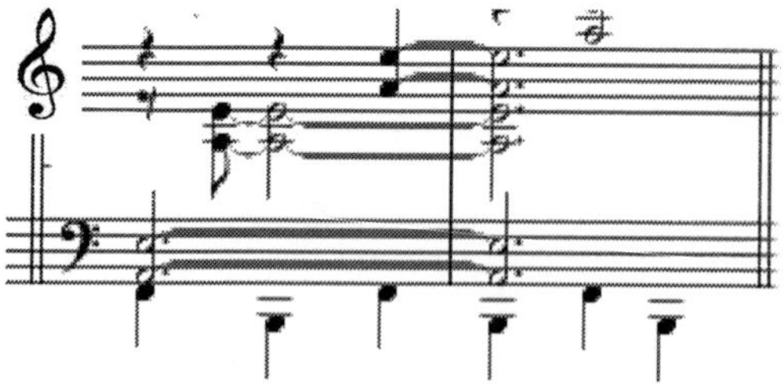

After Wozzeck enters briefly and departs, Marie is alone again with her thoughts and fears. Clashing adjacent notes (major seconds) aptly depict her apprehension:

Ex. 7, Act , Ms 462-463 Marie's Fear

The doctor's cruel and bizarre experiments on Wozzeck and his acquiescence because of his poverty fill the fourth scene. We are kept in a nervous state by the unbalanced and continuously pushing rhythm of the repeated *passacaglia* theme that organizes the scene. This is one of the few places in which Berg made a change in the Büchner text, for where Berg's Doctor is angry because he heard Wozzeck coughing in the street, in the original the Doctor has seen him pissing against a wall and is angry because he will not be able to get a urine sample. In light of everything else that goes on in the opera, this change seems a strange bit of squeamishness, but perhaps it was just too much in 1925.

Scene 1 of act 2 finds the dissonant major seconds used again for Marie's feelings, this time for her irritation as she rebuffs the child who will not sleep and rather cruelly tells him that the bad Gypsies will get him if he does not keep his eyes shut:

Ex. 8, Act 2, Ms. 29-32 Marie's Irritation

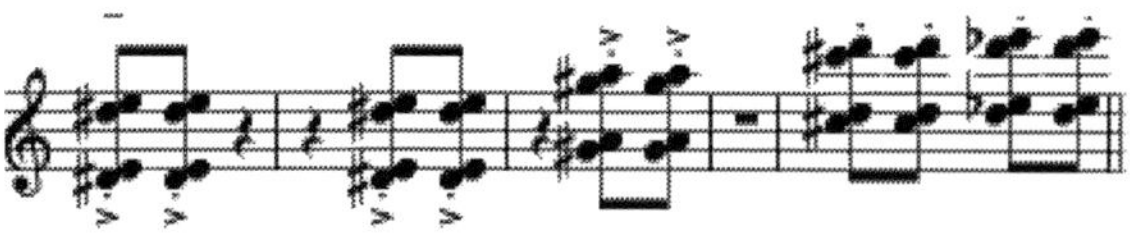

In act 2, scene 2, we hear once again an extreme range and dynamics, as well as tightly knotted chords of close intervals as the Captain complains that the Doctor should not try to scare him, because people have died of fright. Berg then uses the ultimately controlled and craftsman-like compositional process of fugue to illustrate the cruel mockery of Wozzeck at the hands of the Doctor and Captain. A falling line of closely connected half-steps signifies the knife, which first comes to our attention in scene 3 as Marie resists Wozzeck's blow with the prophetic words, "Better a knife in me than a hand on me."

Ex. 9 Act 2, Ms. 395, Knife

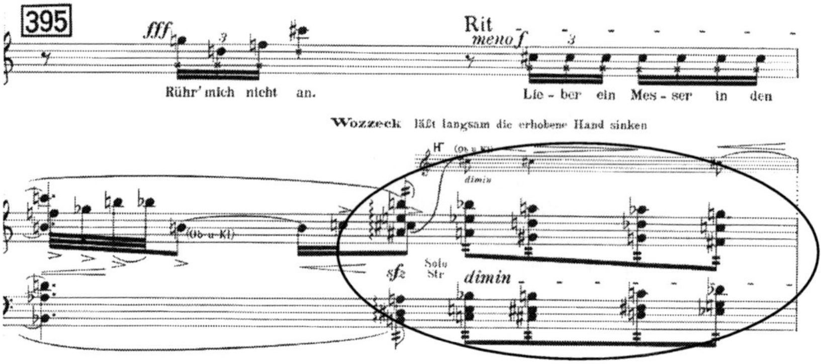

The *Ländler* that follows demonstrates another of Berg's strategies for illustrating Wozzeck's descent. By using familiar genres twisted and punched out of shape, Berg here in the waltz and tavern song drags us into Wozzeck's increasingly demented inner world:

Ex. 10, Act 2, Ms. 481-83 Distorted Waltz

Act 3, "The Catastrophe" in Douglas Jarman's apt designation, begins with a scene in which Marie is reading in her Bible the stories of the adulteress and of Mary Magdalene. Berg again uses *Sprechstimme* expressively and convincingly. The second scene brings the bloody knifing of Marie in the neck by Wozzeck. As rising lines of music mimic the rising blood-red moon, the murder occurs to sounds of extremes range and dynamics and the clashing of adjacent notes (major seconds):

Ex. 11, Act 3, Ms. 103 The Murder

Berg effectively uses the leading motive technique as Marie's dying thoughts of her child fade out simultaneously in her mind and in the child's motives in the orchestra, followed by her "vacant-mindedness" motive from act 1 as her thoughts dwindle into the unconsciousness of death.

The subsequent "Invention on B" is unique in the music repertory, and justly famous. Berg uses two tremendous crescendos separated by the rhythm of tragedy to emphasize the repeated note "B natural" that has already been an ostinato throughout the previous scene.

Ex. 12, Act 3, Ms. 109-21 Invention on the note "B"

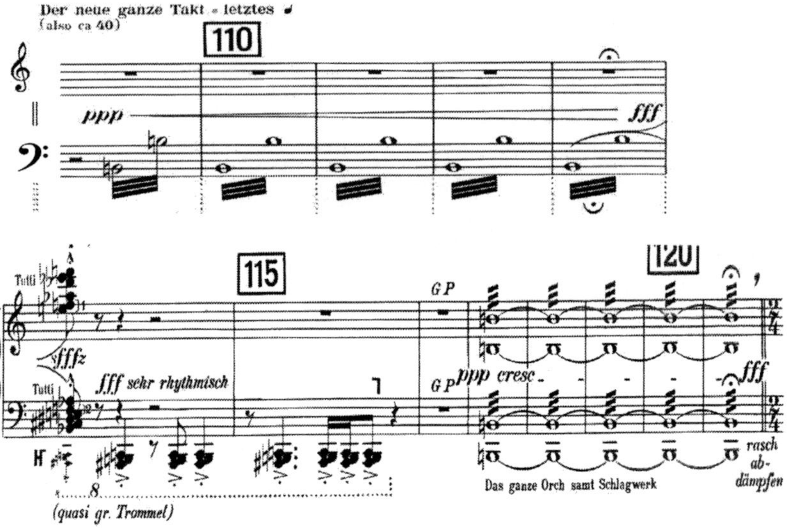

As Wozzeck drags himself next to the tavern, out-of-tune pitches help create the overheated, violent-erotic, and distorted reality of the low-class drinking- and dance-hall. Berg specifically states in the score that the bar piano on stage must be mistuned.

Ex. 13, Act 3, Ms. 122-30, Out-of-tune piano played on stage

Wozzeck's drowning occurs to a slipping, sliding, ascending line of half-steps, and then Berg uses paradoxical juxtaposition once again in the final scene. Children are playing "Ring around the Rosie," a simple children's tune, but once again with insidious distortions. That Marie's child is oblivious to the other children who run gleefully to have a look at his mother's corpse is both poignant and chilling. In this final, heartbreaking scene he sings to his hobby-horse "Hop hop, hop hop, hop hop," and follows the other children off stage to see what the excitement is all about.

Ex. 14, Act 3, Ms. 385 Marie's Child

Berg brings the opera to a close with a shimmer of wavering triplet chords of tri-tones, an interval that defies tonality because it is completely ambiguous. Furthermore, these are supported by blocks of "empty" chords with open fifths, chords that are incomplete because the third note of the scale is missing. This is a musical idea that had closed each of the previous acts, and one that ends the opera with neither satisfaction nor resolution.

Ex. 15, Act 3, Ms. 390 – 392 Indeterminate shimmering chords

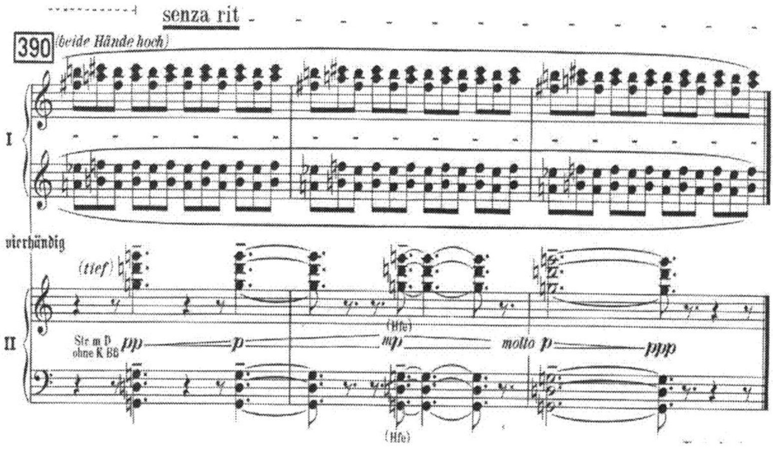

Berg and Atonality

Composing in a way that denies a tonal center is one of the musical means that Berg uses to present "illness, madness, and criminality" in *Wozzeck.* His use of 12-tone technique is brilliant, and not, as George Perle points out, somehow a throwback in the direction of the tonal style of Mahler and others, but rather an advancement into the future. He finds a way to imply tonal centers without using traditional functional harmony, and in this opera he especially succeeds in using a more astringently atonal idiom for expressionistic images and heightens that by contrasting it with other child-like, folk-like, or popular genres. We have also seen the careful organization and the ingenious use of classical structures. The extreme range of his melodies, the devilish complexity of his rhythms, both of these juxtaposed with their opposites, and the inclusion of what Adorno calls Berg's "Viennese-ness" [*Wienertum]*, the *Ländler* and waltz, even the military march, all work their magic to evince the essence of our theme: madness and crime. *Sprechstimme* seems especially apt at moments of emotional extremes, and is especially effective in Marie's "Bible Scene." In lesser hands the painting of meaning by musical direction— an ascending line as the moon rises, a falling line for the knife—might seem banal, but not in Berg's skillful use of the technique. As final examples of Berg's musical means of expression there are the use of distortion through mistuning, and his refusal to use a concluding gesture for the piece.

The reception history of *Wozzeck* is unusual because of its immediate recognition as a masterwork in 1925. With the exception of its suppression as "degenerate art" [entartete Kunst] by the Nazi regime—ultimately a boost to its reputation—*Wozzeck* has continued to grow in esteem along with the whole of Berg's opus. One reason for this must surely be Berg's ingenious and affecting skill at representing madness and crime by musical means.

Works Cited

Adorno, Theodor W. *Alban Berg, Master of the Smallest Link.* Translated by Juliane Brand and Christopher Hailey. Cambridge, UK: Cambridge University Press, 1991.

Adorno, Theodore W., and Alban Berg. *Correspondence 1925-1935.* Edited by Henri Lonitz. Translated by Wieland Hoban. Cambridge, UK: Polity Press, 2005.

Berg, Alban. *Wozzeck, Oper in 3 Akten, Op. 7.* Piano score by Fritz Heinrich Klein. Vienna: Universal Edition, n.d.

—. *Wozzeck, Oper in 3 Akten, Op. 7.* Edited by H. E. Apostel. Vienna: Universal Edition, 1955.

Berg, Erich Alban. *Alban Berg, Leben und Werk in Daten und Bildern.* Frankfurt a. M.: Insel Verlag, 1976.

Clements, Andrew. "Wozzeck." In *Grove Music Online.*

Fanning, David. "Expressionism." In *Grove Music Online.*

Grove Music Online. Edited by L. Macy. http://www.grovemusic.com.

Jarman, Douglas. "Alban Berg." In *Grove Music Online.*

—. *Alban Berg, Wozzeck.* Cambridge, UK: Cambridge University Press, 1989.

—. "Synopsis and Musical Structure." Libretto brochure accompanying *Wozzeck,* Deutsche Grammophon CD423587-1/2, 1987.

Mahler-Werfel, Alma. *Mein Leben.* Frankfurt a. M.: Fischer Taschenbuch Verlag, 1978.

Perle, George. *The Operas of Alban Berg. Vol. 1: Wozzeck.* Berkley: University of California Press, 1980.

Redlich, Hans. *Alban Berg: Versuch einer Würdigung.* Vienna: Universal Edition, 1957.

Notes

[1] Musical examples are from the full score and the piano-vocal score of *Wozzeck* published in Vienna by Universal Edition.

CHAPTER FIVE

"WHAT WOMEN ARE WILL NOT BE KNOWN, UNTIL THEY ARE NO LONGER TOLD WHAT THEY SHOULD BE": ROSA MAYREDER AND THE SO-CALLED "FRAUENFRAGE" IN VIENNESE MODERNITY

SUSANNE HOCHREITER

1. Viennese Modernity

Until far beyond the first half of the past century, female experience in Austria was constricted by very narrowly defined social and gender norms. The discussion of what a woman is intensified and accelerated as of the middle of the nineteenth century. It is symptomatic of the times that attention was given to the contributions by men, while prominent women authors were more or less disregarded. Rosa Mayreder was one of the leading feminists of the *fin de siècle*, who sought to defy and lay bare the predominantly misogynistic world she lived in.

The so-called Viennese Modernity was an era of manifold and important changes in music, art, and literature, as well as in the social fabric and politics of the time, and ranged from the last third of the nineteenth century to the beginning of World War I. During this period Vienna was the multicultural capital of the Habsburg Empire, whose vast borders encompassed more than 50 million nationals. Migrants from all over the empire surged to the metropolis: mainly poor people from the countryside looking for work and full of hope, many of them Jews from the east. Industrialization and fierce capitalism coupled with this wave of migration created intense social tension. The social question and the growing conflicts between the nationalities of the empire were the main challenges that the new modern political parties had to meet. The emperor, Franz Joseph I, seemed—not only retrospectively—more of an obstacle than a solution to all these problems of the multinational territory. Inevitable reforms, such as a reform of electoral law, were implemented much too hesitantly. He insisted on the imperial structure of his dynasty and was, and is, therefore often criticized as one of the "roots" of the crisis (Scheuch, 8).

One of major parties was the Christian Social Party, founded by the notorious mayor of Vienna Karl Lueger. While he managed to change Vienna into a modern and well-organized city, he attracted votes through his anti-Semitic populism. Anti-Semitism at the end of the nineteenth century was a strong engine for the party's rise to a mass movement. The "United Christians," for example, proclaimed a program against Jewish citizens in 1889. They demanded the exclusion of Jewish people from property ownership and from certain professions (officer, judge, teacher). Lueger, a former Liberal, used the existing anti-Semitism for his strategic purposes. The Christian Social Party became a strong partner for Franz Joseph I against the German nationalists, who sought unification with Germany, and against the Labor movement.

In 1888/89 Victor Adler, a Jewish physician, succeeded in unifying the fragmented factions of the Labor movement that suffered from the rigorous anti-socialist laws. When these laws were overruled in 1891, the Social Democratic Worker's Party had a better position and became a strong force for the rights of workers.

Despite the interior political challenges, the conflict of the nationalities was the most dangerous for the empire at the end of the century. No more than a few years later, Europe saw the complete breakdown of the monarchy and a tremendous destruction of lives and culture—with the beginning of World War I in 1914.

At the same time, parallel to these demanding social and political problems, Vienna was the site of many influential scientific findings and inventions, and the home of well-known artists and writers. The philosophers Ernst Mach and Moritz Schlick, the physicist Ludwig Boltzmann, and the physician Theodor Billroth are only a few names that illustrate the concentration of intellectual power in those years. Innovations in architecture and painting are associated with the names Adolf Loos, Otto Wagner, Gustav Klimt, Egon Schiele, and many others.

Sigmund Freud published his groundbreaking work "Die Traumdeutung" in 1899, postdated 1900 to emphasize the importance of his theories for the new century. Although his developing project of psychoanalysis was just getting off the ground at that time, he had important predecessors. His teachers were Theodor Meyning, Richard Krafft-Ebing, and Julius Wagner-Jauregg, the founders of modern psychiatry. Most influential for Freud were Joseph Breuer's studies on hysteria. Breuer used hypnosis to heal his patients, a technique for which Freud developed the alternative method of "free association." The treatment of "Anna O."—a pseudonym for Bertha Pappenheim—provided the basis for the *Studies on Hysteria* which Breuer published together with Freud in 1895. Pappenheim was not only a patient, but is said to be the inventor of the "talking cure" and worked together with Breuer on the model of the so-called cathartic psychotherapy. Her case study provides insights not only into the pioneering days of psychotherapy, but also into the lives of middle-class women in the late nineteenth century. Bertha Pappenheim suffered, like many other girls and women, among them Rosa Mayreder, from the rigid social rules, oppression by her family, and the restriction of her education.

It is not at all incidental that sexologists and psychiatrists at that time worked mainly on female patients. The "dark continent" of femininity had been discovered and was now due to be explored. The metaphoric parallel has its political reality in the colonial activities. The "description of the savage" shows a quite similar pattern of attribution as "the other" of white, middle-class, heterosexual masculinity.

The fundamental principle of the immense volume of texts produced by male philosophers, physicians, sexologists, psychiatrists, and artists concerning "femininity" was the misogynist belief in the physiological inferiority of women. A great many lectures were given, speeches held, books and essays written to uphold an argument that hardly anyone, excepting many women, questioned. The so-called *Frauenfrage* (question of women's rights) was closely linked to the dominant theories of the time; the demands of women for equal rights, for education, for participation in all spheres of public live, and for the freedom of choice in general stood in opposition to the dominant conviction of the female as an illogically thinking, emotional, irresponsible being.

2. Illness, Madness, Criminality: Concepts of Femininity

The gender norm for the middle-class woman was clearly defined: she had her place at home and the right to exist by and for her husband. Her duty was to care for him and the children; her field of work was the household. She was denied the right to individual will, creativity, and even cogitation. At the same time, this ideology of gender reveals what it intends to conceal: the struggle for a place in society, as Waltraud Heindl puts it (21). The place meant here is the position the bourgeoisie had obtained in society and its claim to political relevance.

The fact that women had continued to demand their rights since the Enlightenment and now increased their joint efforts (despite differing opinions) made them dangerous to the dominant patriarchal order. Actually, the living conditions had changed enormously. Demographically, the number of women was disproportionately high, so that for many middle-class women, marriage, the traditional institution of provision, was not accessible anymore. Unlike female workers, for whom it was self-evident and imperative to work (though under terrible conditions), middle-class women could only find employment as governesses and the like (22). Not few middle-class families and unmarried women became impoverished. As a consequence, the women's movement demanded access for women to professional education.

Representatives of the women's movement—regardless of their political wing—were exposed to severe criticism and social sanctions. The term *Entartung* (degeneracy) particularly stands out. Various discourses on illness, madness, and criminality converged in this topic. The debates on gender and culture were strongly brought into correlation with medical and juristic discourses. "Anaemia and neurasthenia" were said to be a sign of the times (Krafft-Ebing, 5). The doctrine of degeneracy for instance advised against "unhealthy" living, which would weaken not only the individual body, but also the body of the nation (*Volkskörper*). Especially an "artificial" urban lifestyle, i.e., bad nutrition and stress in the more and more bustling cities was made responsible for society's weak condition.

The term degeneracy was also used to discredit and marginalize people of lower social classes, handicapped people, and members of different ethnic groups. Hans Gross, the Austrian pioneer of scientific police work and founder of modern criminology, was emphatic on the idea of deporting "gypsies," vagabonds, thieves, etc. into penal colonies. "Degenerates" should be deported to save society's health (Dienes, 18). Not much later, this most inhuman idea was, as we know, implemented in the terror regime of the Nazis. Yet already in the late nineteenth century, illness, madness, criminality, and sexuality were associated in very restricted and restrictive binaries such as good and bad, healthy and ill, sane and insane, male and female.

2.1. Hysteria

The female in middle-class society was principally associated with illness. The most important keyword in this debate and for Western culture as a whole is "hysteria" (von Braun, 11). The word derives from the Greek "hystera," uterus, and since ancient times the phenomenon has been bound to the female body and understood as an expression of femininity in its essence—or better, understood as its nature itself—"*Hysterical is always the other*—and hysterical is particularly the 'other sex,' femininity as difference par excellence."[1] Because there could and cannot be any doubt about it: the "normal" sex is male. Hysteria is the oldest known mental illness and, despite its over 1,000-year medical history, eludes precise definition. It is a "flexible somatic neurosis" (Bronfen, 109) that shows a great variety of symptoms and has therefore been an ideal object of projection for "diagnostic fantasies of physicians" (von Braun, 24).

A dominant theory on hysteria in Christian belief is that this illness was a form of possession. Thus, no longer the "wandering animal" in the woman's body, but the devil himself had to be fought.[2] Christina von Braun sees witch hunts, with their brutal expulsions of "evil," as a consequence of this thinking. They suggested not only an erasure of the woman, but of sexuality in its essence (38). The destruction of sexuality was intended to help overcome the human body and its mortality. The conjunction of disease and its "cure" is a paradox relationship of two hysterias, as von Braun argues: hysteria of the symptoms and hysteria of the clinical pattern. Both saw analogous changes over the centuries and conspicuously adopted similar forms. Hysteria produces, as Joseph Breuer puts it, the paradox of "controlled unconscious" (184): the patients are, unlike those who suffer from epilepsy or schizophrenia, the subject of their illness. "They reverse the heteronomy of the body by acting 'pseudo-logical'" (von Braun, 30). During the historical process of secularization, the source of hysteria moved upwards: from the uterus to the brain. In the nineteenth century, the female body seemed to be fully malleable and ultimately became the therapists' toy. It could finally be stated as scientific "fact," that woman embodied nature and man embodied intellect.

Influenced by Rousseau's ideas, motherhood at that time was the ideal of female normality, seen as women's true nature. Every woman who did not embody the self-sacrificing mother was classified as pathological, abnormal, hysterical (von Braun, 26). After miscarrying, Rosa Mayreder decided not to bear another child. It was a decision against motherhood and against the norms of her time. Mayreder barely mentioned the miscarriage, but she complained about physical discomfort for years. We do not know whether she bemoaned the loss or missed the experience of being a mother, but her essays show that the question of motherhood was part of her theoretical discussion of gender roles. Her position was very clear: she considered it an important achievement of the women's movement that "the so called natural profession of women, motherhood, is no longer seen as the only truth."[3]

2.2. "Degeneracy" ("Entartung")

Because of the aforementioned "natural" disposition of the female body and psyche, women were said to be weak, susceptible to illness, and morally and intellectually inferior. The book *The Woman as Criminal and Prostitute* (1894), by Cesare Lombroso and Gugliemo Ferrero, is an example of the scientific work a few years before substantial progress in psychiatry and the appearance of psychoanalysis. The authors stated that "the female [is] a half criminaloid being of mental inferiority" (qtd. in Wagner, 76). Findings of this sort mirror political and legal decisions, e.g., concerning electoral law and university admission: women were not allowed to study at the university because of "intellectual inferiority," as scientists and philosophers insisted. The allegation that women who were politically engaged were "viragos," thus "degenerate," is another example of a discriminatory practice should a woman leave her assigned place. "Degeneracy" means pathologization, social stigmatization, and criminalization. Nike Wagner comments: "The discussion on degeneracy resulted in the interest in eugenics. [...] Science discovered the criminal at the same time it discovered the woman" (76).

Max Nordau published the first volume of his most famous book, *Entartung* (Degeneracy), in 1892. In 1893 the second volume of this 1,000-page work followed. It was translated into many languages and reprinted several times within a few years and discussed intensely, especially in England and the USA. Nordau was one of the leading Zionists of the German-speaking world. The basic thesis of this book can be found in the foreword, an open letter in which the author answers Cesare Lombroso, who could not have written his studies without Nordau's earlier work (Fischer, 95). Nordau claimed to use Lombroso's methods to examine the field of art and literature because "degenerates are not always criminals, prostitutes, anarchists, and lunatics. They are sometimes writers and artists." He was making an attempt to prove that the whole *fin de siècle* era showed symptoms of degeneration and hysteria, like selfishness, mental debility, and mysticism (104). The solution for this "nuisance," he formulated hatefully, was to slay the "vermin." Without direct reference to Nordau, the Nazis used this language for their propaganda. Nordau's book is more of a polemical pamphlet than a scholarly piece and was rightly criticized. Though he did not discuss the question of gender in detail, Nordau provided a binary model and a vocabulary that fit in with contemporary discourses.

The tremendous success of another book, Otto Weininger's *Geschlecht und Charakter*[4] (*Sex and Character*), an equally unscientific work on the "natural" dichotomy of the sexes and the male superiority, can only be explained by following state of affairs: misogyny was like idolatry and demonization of femininity part of the habitus of thinking of European intelligentsia at the turn of the century (see Wagner, 9). Leading figures such as Arthur Schopenhauer, Friedrich Nietzsche, and Sigmund Freud advanced a misogynist view, and well-known artist and writers such as Oskar Kokoschka, Robert Musil, and Heimito von Doderer read Weininger's book with approval. Also Karl Kraus applauded Weininger (see Schmölzer, 79)—not without emphasizing his adoration for women, but contempt and adoration are just two sides of the same coin.

Illness and madness—especially hysteria—always quickened the interest of scientists, doctors, and philosphers as well as artists and writers—and at no other time as intensely as in the nineteenth century. Although writers such as Hugo von Hofmannsthal, Hermann Bahr, and Arthur Schnitzler were not directly influenced by the new theories, an exchange of ideas, narrative elements, dramatic scenes, and case studies can be observed. Literature and science arose from the same intellectual, social, cultural, and political climate. Arthur Schnitzler's work is the best known example of this process. There are astounding parallels between the work of Schnitzler and Freud, even though one is a writer and the other a doctor. The biographical fact that Schnitzler was also a doctor is certainly of importance. And Freud's essayistic writing is often seen as close to literature. In 1922 Freud wrote a letter to Schnitzler in which he confessed:

> I agonized over the question, why in all these years I never made the attempt to come into personal contact with you and have a conversation with you [...]. The answer to this question contains the confession that seems too intimate. I think I avoided you because of a kind of Doppelgänger timidity. (249)

Freud's impression that Schnitzler learned everything that he himself had found out in his extensive studies by precise observation seems all-too-true. Schnitzler, on the other hand, knew the studies by Charcot and read Freud's works as well. As a doctor he had specialized in hysteria and neurasthenia and was interested in hypnosis, which he used in his medical practice. Even though both Freud and Schnitzler were among the more open-minded and liberal thinkers of their time and showed an interest in the real lives of women, they have frequently been accused of holding misogynist views.

2.3. "Woman Question" ("Frauenfrage")

In this era, everything that pushed for change of the dominant system became a "Frage" (question): the national question, the constitutional question, the social question, the question about women, Jews, and workers. *Meyer's encyclopedia* from 1908 says: "The woman question is how to handle the position of the female within the social organism" (Hausen, 8). The existence of the woman question shows an awareness of an existing disparity between the claims that women raise—legitimate or not—and their actual position. This entry clearly demonstrates the concept of society as male. Every argument here is traced back to "nature": "the social position of the female gender will always be defined by marriage and family," because of the purported different disposition of men and women (9). This thesis sees equality of the sexes as limited by "natural borders."

As Otto Weininger's book represents the essence of the debate, his "provisional" reply to the woman question in "Sex and Character" should not be left unmentioned:

> W [the principle of femininity] has no need and, accordingly, no capacity, for this kind of emancipation. All those women who really strive for emancipation [...] always display many male properties, and the more perceptive observer will always recognize in them some anatomically male characteristics, an approximation to the physical appearance of a man. (*Sex and Character* [2005], 58)

This biologism is a specific modern form of reductionism and is still, as present-day discussions show, the most powerful obstacle to gender equality (see Bock, 40).

Biology is usually used as an argument against women and as an explanation for gender asymmetry. Its paradigm is based on the dichotomy of "female biology" and "male culture." Much costly research has been and is done to verify biological difference between the sexes, but no matter what the results are and will be, they say nothing about cultural concepts of gender and gender relations. They say nothing about social hierarchy and oppression. Detractors of biologistic argumentation in the nineteenth century needed patience, courage, and wit for their intricate mission. Rosa Mayreder was one of them.

3. Rosa Mayreder

Rosa Mayreder was born in 1858 as the eighth daughter of the well-to-do innkeeper of a popular restaurant in Vienna, Franz Obermayer. She suffered early on from the restricted access to education, despite the fact that her father, a politically liberal self-made man, was very anxious to give his sons and daughters the best education. Lessons in painting and piano-playing were allowed. Later, she joined her younger brother in his Latin and Greek lessons. In addition, she attended a young lady's college in the city. Nevertheless, higher education was not part of this arrangement. Almost everything else she learned was self-taught. The 16-year-old was interested in the works of Schopenhauer and Nietzsche, and later she was also fascinated by Richard Wagner's music. By this time she had already gotten to know the works of Goethe and Schiller. Despite her multiple talents, Rosa Mayreder soon realized that she wanted to write. Music and painting would have been acceptable for a "higher daughter"—but writing? She was accused of being a "bluestocking," which was another way of sanctioning "female misbehavior." Not to be a "real" woman meant that she would risk gambling away the only possibility for a good life as it was foreseen for a woman of her class: to marry a man.

Indeed, she did marry. After four years of engagement, she celebrated her wedding with the architect Karl Mayreder in 1881. This marriage was quite happy—despite Rosa's extramarital love affairs—until 1912, when Karl was diagnosed with a mental disease. For a long time she had idealized this relationship as a perfect harmony of two free and equal spirits, even though she fell in love with two other men. But when Karl's depression became worse, she felt her world break down and wrote in her diary: "Our life is destroyed […]" (qtd. in Schmölzer, 188). Her disappointment was of course a very personal one, but was so hard for her to bear because of the intense struggle for the sheer possibility of a partnership between woman and man based on freedom, respect, and equal rights. To live that possibility was important to her as an intellectual woman, as a feminist, and as the daughter of a patriarch who did not care at all about women's rights (except for a good education for his daughters).

Reading her diaries makes it clear how difficult her lifelong conflict with the social norms that she encountered as a girl and as a grown woman was. As an adolescent she wrote: "I suffer awfully. First they tell me the world of antique poetry is paradise […] and then they answer: 'You? You are a broad, you don't need Greek'" (qtd. in Schmölzer, 37). Mayreder's biographer, Hilde Schmölzer, explicates: "The theories being constructed to keep women away from higher education were ridiculous and absurd and show once again that no argument is too silly, when it is necessary to maintain the status quo in power relations" (37). Rosa Mayreder fought against the specters of self-doubt her whole life, but she followed her beliefs. She shed the corset—in the literal and metaphorical sense. She continued painting, but she started to write fiction (novels, dramas, and poems) and scholarly literature.

At the beginning of the 1890s, Mayreder got strongly involved with the women's movement. Together with Auguste Fickert and Marie Lang she founded the "General Austrian Women's Association" (Allgemeiner österreichischer Frauenverein), and from 1893 until 1903 she held the office of vice-president. Her first public speech, in 1894, was about prostitution. In the city hall of Vienna, she argued against conventional concepts of decency and against state control. A few years later, in 1897, she founded an art school for women and girls together with Marianne Hainisch and Olga Prager. One of the most important feminist publications of that time was the magazine *Women's Documents* (*Dokumente der Frauen*), which Mayreder published together with Auguste Fickert and Marie Lang. The first issue appeared in 1899. Although she quit her official activities for the Austrian Women's Association in 1903 to concentrate more on her writing, she continued to concern herself with its work.

One of the most brilliant feminist thinkers, Mayreder wrote remarkable essays on femininity and questions of gender and culture that are still highly inspiring. In 1905 the volume *Zur Kritik der Weiblichkeit* (*A Survey of the Woman Problem*) was published and 18 years later *Geschlecht und Kultur* (*Gender and Culture*). In "Die Tyrannei der Norm" she explains the double standard she was confronted with: "[the progressive individual of female gender] is up against the norm that imperious male natures have defined as female, and is up against the norm that rules as a result of the average female disposition" (83). She was convinced she had a special calling, but she knew very well that transgressing borders demanded an extraordinary effort: "[I]t was clear to me," she remarked, "that I only had the right to trespass beyond the boundaries of feminine duties if I was a 'phenomenon'" (*Das Haus*, 150; Anderson, 261).

4. Femininity and Masculinity: Mayreder's Essays

The essay is not a "female" genre, even if there are claims that it was at least a possibility for women writers who were excluded from studies at academies and universities to express their thoughts. Not many women wrote essays, and when they did, men accused them of improbity or incompetence. A consequence of this situation is that most collections of essays hardly include texts by women. Ludwig Rohner, in his influental collection of German essays, mentions only Ricarda Huch. Marlis Gerhardt, who in the 1990's published a collection of essays by women writers, had serious difficulties filling the volume. That Mayreder's essays are missing from Gerhardt's collection probably has historical reasons. When Rosa Mayreder died in 1938, the Nazis were already in power and her work was soon forgotten, even though she had been a very well-known and important personality. Despite the re-discovery of her texts in the 1980s, her work found a weak reception in Germany. I think she chose this genre not because of any inconvenience, but in accordance with Theodor Adorno's definition of the essay as "critical form par excellence," as a conscious decision for the adequate and sophisticated form of intellectual debate. However, it shall not be left unmentioned that she regarded her fiction as her more accomplished and important work.

Rosa Mayreder sparred intellectually with the leading thinkers of her time. To do this as a woman under the above-mentioned conditions was remarkable. She was not the only feminist theorist or activist to do so. Many others should be named here, including Helene von Druskowitz, Grete Meisel-Hess, Auguste Fickert, and Therese Schlesinger.[5] Mayreder's essayistic work was not only appreciated by her contemporaries, but at times overly praised, as Hanna Schnedl states (23)— praise which overlooked some inconsistencies in her argumentation and, more important, the radical elements in her texts. Mayreder's theory was often seen as a self-help guide by self-critical individuals. In some essays she allows this reception when her conclusions are much more moderate than her in-depth analysis would lead us to expect, but she was certainly not a hesitant feminist; "that would allow us to forget the results of her analysis in favor of her idealistic projections" (Schnedl, 24).

4.1. A Survey of the Woman Question

To discuss even just a few aspects of Mayreder's work in all its complexity is hardly possible in this limited form. I have chosen to concentrate on her first volume, as it is especially this book that has been of interest to feminists in Austria since the 1970s.

In the opening text of the first volume of essays, *Zur Kritik der Weiblichkeit*—"Grundzüge" (Basic Traits)—we find the central arguments that Mayreder's critique is based upon. First of all, she makes clear that the terms commonly used at that time are much too diffuse. She wonders about words like "soul," "mind," "rationality," etc. that refer to divergent concepts of phenomena of the soul and their relation to the body. She makes the usual "method" of generalization in various disciplines, especially psychology of that time, responsible for considerable confusion. When everybody talked about "woman" and "man," what did they mean? Mayreder denies the existence of something like a "metaphysical Realwesen" (real essence). To state "woman" would negate the real differences between women and result in assertions that claim a right to universal validity. Reading literature on this topic generates the impression that "one half of mankind is made into something unknown, dark, mysterious," treated as "fabled creatures" (13).

Mayreder raises important issues. The inevitable problems of conceptuality are of course still unsolved and often cause prejudice because of generalizations. Even though nowadays concepts of identity and self, the question of gender, of sex and sexuality, of ethnicity and culture in general can be discussed in their full complexity on a higher theoretical level, the same (political) mistakes are made, as the present global situation shows (for instance, many people in the so-called Western world today purport to know about the workings of the Islamic world). Mayreder herself cannot avoid similar misjudgments, but an element of the substantial contribution she makes is the effort to discuss terms and to question assumptions.

By listing prevailing and conflicting concepts of femininity, she shows their inconsistency and deconstructs them by confrontation and comparison. No matter who or what—Lombroso and Ferrero or Weininger and Schopenhauer—Mayreder scrutinizes the arguments and counters in a few sentences to show their lack of logic and precision. She noticed the variety of misogynist statements, but refused to go into the pathologizing discourse on femininity, including the use of such terms as "degeneracy" ("Entartung"). The strategy of taking her adversaries seriously was surely an effective method, because she never engaged in bare provocation. On the contrary, she used elegant irony, e.g., when she comments on Schopenhauer's peculiar theory of heredity. In this theory he declares the necessity of reasonable marriage: only men of character and the most intelligent women could guarantee the best progeny. Mayreder thought that this theory was "an example of how a preconceived notion cannot be unsettled by results of observation; because those cases in which character and intellect are not bequeathed to the next generation in perfect completion are so numerous and obvious that even Schopenhauer could not have overlooked them—had he not had his theory" (30).

In the opening essay of the volume, we already find the main arguments against various misogynist positions. Mayreder argues that physiological attributes do not match the ideal to which most of the writings on femininity are geared. The claim that a certain mental and intellectual disposition is based on a gender-specific physique is, as Mayreder explains, not verifiable. She refers to more serious scientific work like the studies by Havelock Ellis (for example, "Man and Woman"). In her opinion, cultural and social factors are responsible for gender characteristics and the individual's development in general. The physiologically most obvious differences concern those bodily features regarding reproduction. For this, Mayreder used the expression "teleological differentiation of sex" (36), but even this cannot be used to define "pure" gender types: "We have seen that in sexual differentiation, it is not possible to establish a natural principle that would necessarily designate a certain character" (41). She gives the following example to prove her argument: while motherliness is classified as the most important feminine trait and any weaker tendency seen as degeneracy, men are not expected to develop a "fatherly psyche" (42).

She comments on single arguments, even the defamatory statements by Lombroso or Weininger, in order to show that their assumptions are completely arbitrary. In this way she makes clear that any notion of "normality" or "anormality" lacks a serious scientific basis and arises from bare prejudice. Attributions of women as being criminal or mad (as in the discourse of hysteria) are an indefensible reduction. Mayreder's position in this respect is unmistakable. Lombroso's claim, for instance, that female gender exists only as complete normality or extreme aberrance is for Mayreder "one of the many arbitrary and unproven allegations that characterize Lombroso's standpoint as entirely subjective" (29). She unmasks scientific thinking of this sort as philistine (42). But she also shows that this thinking has consequences for women's lives. The mixture of superstition and prejudice she criticized effected the social position of women: "Oppression to the point of slavery and glorification to the point of adoration" ("Das Weib," 124). Unlike Helene von Druskowitz in her satire *Pessimistische Kardinalsätze* or Grete Meisel-Hess in her rather aggressive answer to Otto Weininger's book, Mayreder avoided any overly polemic tone or condescension to her adversaries. Meisel-Hess was the best-known contemporary adversary of Weininger and criticized him of being degenerate—despite the fact that he did not use the term for women (see Schnedl, 26).

This first essay also shows a central characteristic of Mayreders's thinking and a topic of many other texts as well. She criticizes the women's movement, particularly its tendency to idealize motherhood and to insist on a fundamental difference of the sexes: "Motherhood may be an obstacle to external equality with men, but as an internal condition, it is just as little a universal criterion of femininity as any other general attribute" ("Grundzüge," 19). The result of the choice between either case—only one criterion or a bundle of characteristics—is the same: a fictitious gender-type is created. The consequence is the establishment of a majority of so-called "normal" and a minority of so-called "abnormal" individuals. Furthermore, she cannot see any valid evidence that certain physiological features are the precondition for a clear differentiation of just two strictly defined sexes. Femininity and masculinity are, for the most part, "mere cultural products, thus neither determinate and self-contained, nor generally applicable" (26). Next, she raises the question of what biological necessity there might be for an essential division of the sexes. Referring to the results of research of that time, thereby using the same data as her opponents, she manages to adduce that it is not possible to verify a natural principle governing sex and gender (41). She explicates here in a few sentences the state-of-the-art of academic discourse nowadays: gender is a social construct. What seems so clear to us now must have been exceedingly difficult to argue at a time when not only misogynist thinkers, but all of society and even representatives of the women's movement claimed a specific, biologically determined femininity and masculinity. The modernity and autonomy of Rosa Mayreder's thinking becomes evident in this example.

Mayreder's criticism of norms and normative concepts of how humans are supposed to be turns against the binary logic that shaped the thinking (not only) of her time. Her theory can be read as a fundamental refusal of ideas which result in social exclusion of people and limitation of basic human rights like the right to education. Opposite categories as normal vs. anormal, sane vs. insane, or righteous vs. criminal cannot signify the complex reality of individual characters and lives. Her pledge for regard of the individual is more than just a consequence of contemporary liberal politics; it is a consistent humanitarian attitude that is able to recognize and respect differences between people.[6]

4.2. "The Man Question"

Mayreder was one of the first to critically discuss the bourgeois concepts of masculinity (see "Von der Männlichkeit" [On Masculinity]). The debate on femininity would not make any sense, she states, if changes in the conditions of male lives are ignored. She considered those changes to be the most important cause for the emergence of the women's movement. In gender studies, research on masculinity even today is quite neglected, compared to the number of books and articles on femininity.

Something is wrong with masculinity: the observation that the idol ("Götterbild") of old cannot be conjured up any longer but is still adored, leads Mayreder to the conclusion that it is especially men who are confronted with a significant disproportion between real life and the dominant norm. Specifically, a kind of "feminization" of masculinity is responsible for individual and social conflict (96). While public and theoretical discourses refer to a strict binary of the active, aggressive, strong-willed man on the one hand and the passive, defensive, weak woman on the other, cultural development brought about a differentiation of masculinity, with the consequence that male "tendencies" in a narrower sense (like martial characteristics) decreased. Once again, she demonstrates that there are no fixed "genders."

Interesting in the context of "illness" and "madness" is Mayreder's following argument: the nervous system of men is said to be more robust than the female one, so calmness and mental balance are seen as male features. But the reality of life in the modern cities of the nineteenth century was an acceleration in all respects that resulted in "overstimulation" and the above-mentioned "neurasthenia" and caused a radical change in the image of masculinity. Mayreder names symptoms of neurasthenia such as depressivity, uncertainty, moodiness. etc.—altogether symptoms that emanate from enervation: "One can observe that the male neurasthenic adopts a type conventionally seen as female, even effeminate" (107). That women might be more susceptible to mental disease and illness is rejected here as a myth of existing gendered concepts. Mayreder argues that certain "symptoms" are not necessarily evidence of an actual disease and that the pathologizing description of the female in general originates from a misogynist fantasy. By contrast, her cultural-historical approach focuses on political, social, and cultural facts.

4.3. Prostitution

One major site of conflict, where all ideas, prejudices, fantasies, and more or less sophisticated theories seem to converge, was the debate on prostitution, an important topic and widely discussed publicly: "sex and crime"—a problem "made" for media and fiction. It was discussed in parliament as well as in newspapers and at events of various caucuses. The popular issue appeared in contemporary literature and was portrayed in such dissimilar books as Felix Salten's *Josefine Mutzenbacher* and Else

Jerusalem's more socially critical novel *Der heilige Skarabäus*. The real situation of prostitutes was of course far from adventurous in any romantic sense.

Prostitution was illegal and penalized by fine or arrest. In 1873, with the so-called "Prostitution Statute," a standardized regulation for "commercial fornication" was established (see Pronay-Stasser, 128). Prostitutes were obligated to register with the authorities, to keep a health-book, to regularly undergo medical examination, and to tolerate oversight by the vice squad. These very rigid governmental measures were taken because of the rising number of illegal prostitutes, and a significant increase in venereal diseases. That men were not obliged to undergo medical examination was an effect of the bourgeois gender order, recognizing women as motherly saint or whore of dangerous sexuality. In 1900 official statistics counted approximately 2,000 officially registered prostitutes. Almost 350 of them suffered from syphilis, but the estimated number of illegal prostitutes and unreported cases was much larger. Josef Schrank, a police doctor and a leading authority in this field, put the real number ten times higher (Schmölzer, 128). It can be assumed that at least 20,000 women were sex workers. They were mainly women of the lower class—servants, actresses, seasonal workers—who tried to supplement their income. And it was the women who were criminalized—not their male "customers."

Karl Kraus, though he did not support the women's movement, still criticized the double standards in public debate. Referring to Karl Marx and his comments on the English middle classes, Kraus claims the validity of Marx's thesis for the "whole capitalistic middle classes": "Bourgeois morals clashed with everyday experience. Everything that morals preach is left by the wayside in real life and belied"—in theory, morality, equal rights for all, protection against rape; in practice, "rampant fornication," an increase in prostitution, general greediness, "in short: practice quite the opposite of theory" (4).

Three years before this comment, Rosa Mayreder again held a speech on prostitution after she had already dedicated her first appearance in public to the same topic. The occasion was a rejected petition concerning rights for prostitutes: exemption from medical examination rules was one major demand. The petitioners were furious—not only because of a four-year delay, but also because of the caustic writing of the parliamentary commission (see Schmölzer, 119). They were accused of incompetence and immorality because women should not be concerned with this issue; they should engage in charity, but not in political activity.

The meeting of the members of the General Austrian Women's Association (AÖFV) took place on February 20, 1897. Vice President Rosa Mayreder expressed her disappointment and resentment: "it is typical for the way in which the representatives of the people put up with the most serious social problems" (see Schmölzer, 119). She again named social misery as a leading cause of prostitution. The struggle against prostitution was, in her opinion, connected to the highest ideals of the women's movement. Even in their own ranks there was no unity: only two other women's organizations agreed to support the AÖFV petition, and some members even resigned because of this affair. Mayreder shared her opinions with other progressive feminists: she understood prostitution as a social and economic problem that could not be solved by berating people's chastity. The argumentation of the Women's Association hit the mark of bourgeois gender politics, which accepted prostitution as a necessary evil and condemned it as a vice at the same time. While feminists today understand that it is impossible to abolish prostitution, it was their explicit aim back then.

It is interesting that despite Mayreder's public engagement, prostitution does not find as much attention in her essays. She writes more about this topic in the second volume of essays. In some comments, an ambivalent attitude becomes visible; for instance, when she writes that "prostitution is no socially approbated way of life and the innate disposition to it represents a more atavistic defect of the individual" ("Frauen und Frauentypen," 162). On the one hand, she clearly sees the social question as the major issue in this regard; on the other hand, she adheres to the idea of "good" and "bad" women, of women with a more primitive character and those with a "developed personality" (Schmölzer, 168). Thus Mayreder identifies two dimensions of gender-roles: the social aspect and a natural disposition. However, this ambivalence certainly does not put her central thesis into question: that a general gender-type does not exist. Respect for the individual—whether it is male or female—and freedom to develop its abilities are of prime importance. At the same time, she is an intellectual middle-class woman with certain ideals (such as harmonious partnership) and not free from prejudice or conventional habits or beliefs. But still there was almost no other writer who discussed concepts of sexuality and the question of sexual desire of middle-class women so openly and seriously—leaving behind the pathologizing and criminalizing discourse of her time. This is part of Rosa Mayreder's rich intellectual legacy.

5. Writing and Losses

Though Mayreder's argumentation is systematic and solid and respectful of other thinkers, she is radical in her verbalization and some of her demands: she sees the education of middle-class girls and younger women as a tool to simply discipline them; to her, prostitution is a paradigm of sexual, economic, and emotional exploitation of women; the coercion of social roles prevents individual self-determination. The ideal she aims for is a synthesis of the "sexes": absolute masculinity or absolute femininity do not exist. That this ideal is connected to an elitist concept that privileges "gifted" individuals who outclass average men and women is a problematic aspect of her theory. Despite the clear refusal of biological definitions of gender, she maintained a belief in a regulatory power of nature. She came into conflict with the convictions of social reformers and socialists with this position (see Schmölzer, 168).

Mayreder's second volume of essays was published 18 years later—much later than she had planned. In the foreword she writes: "Not only more than 15 years have passed—the most harrowing incidents have disrupted my inner and outer life [...]" (7). The editor, Eva Geber, describes the divide between the first and the second volume in terms of content: Mayreder retracted her ideal of androgyny, no longer sustained the differentiation of biological sex and social gender, and introduced references to motherhood. Formulations became more unwieldy and complicated, and the freshness of *Kritik der Weiblichkeit* was missing," but Geber also explains that this change was the consequence of dashed hopes and lost happiness ("Der Verlust," 321). What she calls "civilization" and her expectation of true humane "culture" diverges immensely in view of the brute force and millions dead in World War I. She tried to set an anchor against the resignation she and the general public felt, but the invocation of a "world-healing motherliness" she conceptualized was very difficult for her (322). In *Sex and Culture* she turned once again against Otto Weininger and criticized the old metaphysics of "female" and "male" virtues (see Kubes-Hoffmann, "Etwas," 132). Mayreder unmasked the general verdicts on women ("the broad") that hardly concealed the misogyny of their authors as male fantasies. Her conclusion was: "What women are will not be known until they are no longer told what they should be."

6. Rosa Mayreder Today

Rosa Mayreder and her work are still an insider tip. When Hanna Schnedl published the first selection of essays in 1982, a Mayreder-renaissance seemed promising. The reprint of the complete volumes of essays in 1998 was a substantial improvement for the reception of her thinking, but the distance between the initial publication of her essays and the reprint shows that the discussion of Mayreder's analysis and theories was not very lively at any time, except among some feminist academics whose writings enable us to learn about her and to continue the debate on her ideas today. Scholars that deserve mention are above all Hanna Schnedl(-Bubenicek), Harriet Anderson, Hilde Schmölzer, and also Eva Geber, who edited and annotated *Zur Kritik der Weiblichkeit* and *Geschlecht und Kultur*. Several students and junior researchers have also dealt with Mayreder's thinking, but although there are some recently published articles, the scholarly production on Mayreder taken as a whole is limited. "Ariadne," a special collection of literature on women's and gender studies of the Austrian National Library, counts only 22 articles on Rosa Mayreder between 1955 and 2004. Although her work is considered more radical than Simone de Beauvoir's "The Second Sex" from 1949, the latter was an outstanding success, finding inexhaustible reception, and is still regarded as *the* theoretical introduction to the modern women's movement (see Kubes-Hofmann, "Etwas," 136). One reason for this is the disruption of discourse that was caused by National Socialism. The other possible reason evinced by Eva Geber is that the radicalness of Mayreder's thinking was not understood; the reception of her essays shows that only selected aspects (like the relevance of love) were noticed ("Rosa Mayreder," 268).

In view of this situation, the initiative by Ursula Kubes-Hofmann is of great importance for the succession of Rosa Mayreder and the continuation of her work. Kubes-Hofmann founded the "Rosa Mayreder College" (RMC) in Vienna in 1999, an educational establishment for the advancement of women in the fields of art, science, and education. It is an institute that offers academic training courses with an international orientation. RMC is also a site for experimental forms of mediation and presentation. Its motto is "Against the tyranny of the norm" ("Wider die Tyrannei der Norm")—quoting the title of an essay by Rosa Mayreder. Kubes-Hofmann describes the eponym of her institution as follows:

> Her whole life, Rosa Mayreder stood up for the reduction of political power structures and hierarchies, against bourgeois double standards, for women's rights, for political education and enlightenment. This is the

> reason the college was named after her: to bear this pioneer ("Grenzgängerin") of modernity in remembrance and to set anti-normative concepts against the "dark times" [Hannah Arendt] of our days. ("Wer war Rosa Mayreder?")

Acknowledgement

Many thanks to Monique A. Göschl for her support and assistance with translation.

Works Cited

Adorno, Theodor W. "Der Essay als Form." In Rohner, *Deutsche Essays*, 61-83.

Anderson, Harriet. "Rosa Mayreder." In *Major Figures of Turn-of-the-Century Austrian Literature*. Edited by Donald G. Daviau. Riverside, CA: Ariadne, 1991. 259-290.

Bock, Gisela. "Historische Frauenforschung: Fragestellungen und Perspektiven." In Hausen, *Frauen suchen ihre Geschichte*, 22-60.

Breuer, Joseph, and Sigmund Freud. 1895. *Studien über Hysterie*. Frankfurt a. M.: Fischer, 1970.

Bronfen, Elisabeth. *Das verknotete Subjekt. Hysterie in der Moderne*. Berlin: Volk und Welt, 1998.

Dienes, Gerhard M. "Der Mann Moses und die Folter der Maschine." In *Die Gesetze des Vaters. Hans Gross. Otto Gross. Sigmund Freud. Franz Kafka*. Edited by Gerhard Dienes and Ralf Rother. Vienna: Böhlau, 2003. 14-36.

Druskowitz, Helene von. *Der Mann als logische und sittliche Unmöglichkeit und als Fluch der Welt. Pessimistische Kardinalsätze*. 1903. Freiburg i. Br.: Kore, 1988.

Fischer, Jens Malte. "Dekadenz und Entartung. Max Nordau als Kritiker des Fin de siècle." In *Fin de Siècle. Zu Literatur und Kunst der Jahrhundertwende*. Edited by Roger Bauer et al. Frankfurt a. M.: Vittorio Klostermann, 1977. 93-111.

Freud, Sigmund. *Briefe 1873-1939*. Edited by Ernst L. Freud. Frankfurt a. M.: Fischer, 1960.

Geber, Eva. "Rosa Mayreder: Visionäre Theoretikerin des Feminismus." In Mayreder, *Zur Kritik der Weiblichkeit*, 261-274.

—. "Der Verlust der Hoffnung." In Mayreder, *Geschlecht und Kultur*, 321-330.

Gerhardt, Marlies, ed. *Essays berühmter Frauen*. Frankfurt a. M.: Insel, 1997.

Hausen, Karin. Introduction. *Frauen suchen ihre Geschichte. Historische Studien zum 19. u. 20. Jahrhundert*. Edited by Karin Hausen. Munich: Beck, 1983. 7-20.

Heindl, Waltraud. "Frauenbild und Frauenbildung in der Wiener Moderne." In *Die Frauen der Wiener Moderne*. Edited by Lisa Fischer and Emil Brix. Vienna: Verlag für Geschichte und Politik, 1997. 21-33.

Krafft-Ebing, Richard von. *Über Nervosität*. Graz: Leuschner & Lubensky, 1884.

Kraus, Karl. "Das Ende einer Komödie." *Die Fackel* 42 (1900): 4-10.

Kubes-Hofmann, Ursula. "Etwas an der Männlichkeit ist nicht in Ordnung. Intellektuelle Frauen am Beispiel Helene von Druskowitz und Rosa Mayreder." In *Die Frauen der Wiener Moderne*. Edited by Lisa Fischer. Vienna: Verlag für Geschichte und Politik, 1997. 124-136.

—. "Wer war Rosa Mayreder?" <http://www.rmc.ac.at/rmwar.html>. (accessed January 30, 2007)

Mayreder, Rosa. Foreword. 1923. *Geschlecht und Kultur*. Edited by Eva Geber. Vienna: Mandelbaum, 1998. 7-10.

—. "Frauen und Frauentypen." In Mayreder, *Zur Kritik der Weiblichkeit*, pp. 139-164.

—. "Grundzüge." In Mayreder, *Zur Kritik der Weiblichkeit*, pp. 12-47.

—. *Das Haus in der Landskrongasse. Jugenderinnerungen*. Edited by Eva Geber. Vienna: Mandelbaum. 1998.

—. "Mutterschaft und doppelte Moral." *Zur Kritik der Weiblichkeit. Essays*. Edited by Hanna Schnedl. Munich: Frauenoffensive, 1982. 46-51.

—. "Die Tyrannei der Norm." In Mayreder, *Zur Kritik der Weiblichkeit*, pp. 79-92.

—. "Von der Männlichkeit." In Mayreder, *Zur Kritik der Weiblichkeit*, pp. 93-123.

—. "Das Weib als Dame." In Mayreder, *Zur Kritik der Weiblichkeit*, pp. 124-138.

—. *Zur Kritik der Weiblichkeit. Essays*. 1905. Edited by Eva Geber. Vienna: Mandelbaum, 1998.

Meisel-Hess, Grete. *Weiberhass und Weiberverachtung*. Vienna: Perles, 1904.

Pronay-Strasser, Inge. "Von Ornithologen und Grashupferinnen. Bemerkungen zur Sexualität um 1900." In *"Glücklich ist, wer vergisst*

...?" Das andere Wien um 1900. Edited by Hubert Ch. Ehalt, Gernot Heiß, and Hannes Stekl. Vienna: Böhlau, 1986. pp. 113-132.

Rohner, Ludwig, ed. *Deutsche Essays. Prosa aus zwei Jahrhunderten*. Neuwied: Luchterhand, 1968.

Scheuch, Manfred. *Österreich im 20. Jahrhundert. Von der Monarchie zur Zweiten Republik*. Vienna: Verlag Christian Brandstätter, 2000.

Schlesinger, Therese. *Die Frau im 19. Jahrhundert*. Berlin: Verlag Aufklärung, 1902.

Schmölzer, Hilde. *Rosa Mayreder. Ein Leben zwischen Utopie und Wirklichkeit*. Vienna: Promedia 2002.

Schnedl, Hanna. "Rosa Mayreder. Eine Sympathisantin des Lebendigen." *Zur Kritik der Weiblichkeit. Essays*. Edited by Hanna Schnedl. Munich: Frauenoffensive, 1982. 9-32.

von Braun, Christina. *NICHT ICH. Logik. Lüge. Libido*. Frankfurt a. M.: Neue Kritik, 1999.

Wagner, Nike. *Geist und Geschlecht. Karl Kraus und die Erotik der Wiener Moderne*. Frankfurt a. M.: Suhrkamp, 1987.

Weininger, Otto. *Geschlecht und Charakter. Eine prinzipielle Untersuchung*. Im Anhang: Weiningers Tagebuch, Briefe August Strindbergs sowie Beiträge aus heutiger Sicht von Annegret Stopczyk, Giesela Dischner und Roberto Calasso. Munich: Matthes & Seitz, 1997.

—. *Sex and Character. An Investigation of Fundamental Principles*. Edited by Daniel Steuer with Laura Marcus. Bloomington: Indiana University Press, 2005.

Notes

[1] Braun, 24. That a male hysteria is also known—"le petit mal du Grand Mâle"—does not challenge the paradigm.

[2] In ancient times, the uterus was believed to be an animal that wandered through women's bodies.

[3] Mayreder, "Mutterschaft und doppelte Moral," 46; my translation here and throughout unless otherwise noted.

[4] In the years from 1903 to 1947, 28 editions were printed. The book was even reprinted recently, in 1997.

[5] Auguste Fickert published numerous articles in *Dokumente der Frauen* and *Neues Frauenleben*, which she edited. For the other women mentioned here, see my bibliography.

[6] In this respect Rosa Mayreder seems to be close to the utilitarian ideas of John Stuart Mill and Jeremy Bentham. Ursula Kubes-Hofmann points out the influence of Franz Müller-Lyer's sociological work and his concept of social individualism.

CHAPTER SIX

LUNACY AND THE LAW: MELA HARTWIG'S *THE CRIME* AND *THE FANTASTICAL PARAGRAPH*

SARAH PAINITZ

> "Why do you throw your body in front of my feet, so that I always have to stumble over you?"
> —Mela Hartwig, *The Crime* (1927)

I. Hartwig's Excesses

Mela Hartwig's fictional world is full of crazy women: one believes herself in love with her father, another is moonstruck and has monthly visions that result in a phantom pregnancy, a third is driven to compulsive self-deprecating confessions, while yet another, mute, wildly contorts her body as an instrument of language.[1] These crazy women don't sit well with many critics and reviewers of Hartwig's work. "The hideous erotic desires and delusions of a brain sullied by muck-minded psychoanalysis," deems one review about her first book, the collection *Ecstasies (Ekstasen)*, in 1928.[2] In part, this type of reaction is due to the topics Hartwig openly and unabashedly deals with in her texts: female sexuality and desire, the beauty ideal, incest, rape, abortion – topics which were certainly controversial in the early twentieth century. But even in today's more open climate, Hartwig's work frequently arouses contradictory reactions – an indication of the difficulty many critics have in dealing with her female characters, for it is not only the explosive issues raised in the texts, but also the way in which the protagonists are portrayed, that leaves many readers uncomfortable. Reviews of Hartwig's novel *Am I A Superfluous Human Being? (Bin ich ein überflüßiger Mensch?)*, for example, which was written in 1931 and published posthumously in 2001, describe the book as "just as touching as it is repelling," as being simultaneously "painful," "extraordinary and gruesome, … alluring and disgusting, a book of great shame and shamelessness, tantalizing, unforgettable, although one would like to forget it."[3] Mela Hartwig just doesn't let herself be categorized. Her texts, oscillating between obscurity, cult, and rediscovery, continue to be controversial almost eighty years after they were first published.

But there is method to the madness portrayed in Hartwig's works, for it is through hysteria, visions, dreams, and lunacy – all manifested through the female body – that her protagonists attempt to construct an identity of their own. In so doing, they circumvent and transgress logic and reason, disrupting the binary oppositions by which Western culture determines its social relations. The social function of hierarchical oppositions has been, of course, debated and criticized by feminist theorists since the 1970s. Luce Irigaray, for example, calls on women "to question the systems and to show how we can deconstruct them …. to reject all the great systems of opposition on which our culture is constructed."[4] Women must, according to Irigaray, by

> repeating/interpreting the way in which, within discourse, the feminine finds itself defined as lack, deficiency, or as imitation and negative image of the subject … signify that with respect to this logic a *disruptive excess* is possible on the feminine side.[5]

It is precisely this disruptive excess that Hartwig puts to use in her texts as early as 1927, when she first appeared on the Viennese literary scene with her award-winning novella *The Crime (Das Verbrechen)*, subsequently published in the collection *Ecstasies*.[6] The four protagonists of the collection's novellas, which I briefly characterized in the opening of this essay, are women who, in their attempts at identity-formation, cause ruptures and breaks in the structures of patriarchal society. By the very act of aspiring to a self-identity that does not conform to social norms, they constitute an imminent and dangerous threat to the dominant powers. The title of the collection clearly marks them as outside the bounds of logic and reason.[7] The novellas themselves outline the two different realms in which the female characters and their male counterparts move. The men, as representatives of the psychoanalytical, medical, judicial, and clerical discourses, are in positions of power and authority. The women, excluded from these discourses, lack not only power, but also legitimacy.

While questions of law and order – one of the pillars of modern societies – are addressed in all four novellas of *Ecstasies*, they play an especially prominent role in the first two, *The Crime* and *The Fantastical Paragraph (Der phantastiche Paragraph)*. Both texts question how society defines criminal behavior and assigns guilt. Their protagonists counter the social imposition of seemingly arbitrary legal structures by seeking alternatives in the irrational and imaginary – alternatives which, however, prove unachievable in the end. In both texts, the legal system is interwoven with the medical discourse, both on a physical and psychological level. Male representatives of the authoritative social structures diagnose the female protagonists' psychic or physical ailments and subject them to various "treatments": In *The Crime*, the father figure, a psychiatrist, performs psychoanalysis on his daughter Agnes against her will; in *The Fantastical Paragraph*, various representatives of the medical and legal professions diagnose Sabine Seltsam as hysteric, pregnant, and an abortionist, regardless of whether any of these designations are actually true or not. In their desperate struggle against the rigid logic of the medical and legal discourses, both Agnes and Sabine challenge their authority by expressing the fantastical and irrational through their bodies.

II. Freud's Crime

Perhaps representative of the way in which Hartwig has frequently been misunderstood, the above quoted review exhibits an utter misreading of her novella *The Crime*. What the reviewer identifies as the "desires and delusions of a brain sullied by muck-minded psychoanalysis" comprises in fact a critique of Freudian psychoanalysis. Agnes, the female protagonist, is mentally tortured by her sadistic father, a psychiatrist, who has developed the theory that Agnes is in love with him and desires an incestuous sexual relationship with him.[8] The opening of the story places the reader in the middle of an already full-fledged confrontation between father and daughter. Agnes, apparently in shock over her father's diagnosis of her psychological state, has locked herself in her room and has remained there for the past three days "in a state of half-consciousness": "Darkness glued shut the windows, gummed up her eyes, rolled shadows and a chaos of meaningless sounds over her bed … the colorless walls of her darkened room pressed closer and closer upon her, like a grave."[9] Fleeing from her father and his accusations, Agnes, helpless and barely conscious of her surroundings, seeks refuge in her cave-like room. Indeed, the description of Agnes as completely passive and unable to see, and her room as steeped in darkness and senseless noise, are reminiscent of a fetus in the mother's womb. As such, she is protected from the outside world and her father. At the same time, however, the text equates her feeling of the walls closing in with a grave. As womb and grave, the room simultaneously represents birth and death, the beginning and the end.

The room's double meaning is complicated further when, on the fourth day, her father has the door to Agnes's room broken down. The force of his entry seems tantamount to a physical violation:[10] "On the fourth day the door was broken open and in the midst of the bright daylight her father stood before her blinded eyes."[11] For Freud, "Zimmer" ("room"), is symbolic for "Frauenzimmer" ("woman");[12] the various entrances to a room thus take on another level of meaning and the father's forced entry into Agnes's room can be understood as a metaphorical rape.[13] In forcing the door open the father allows blinding light into the room and he immediately commands that the windows be opened. In playing up the dichotomies light/dark, day/night, and their traditional alignment with "male" and "female" characteristics, Hartwig taps into and exploits those very oppositions for her critique of binary thought, for here the liberating light of reason does not bring freedom or release or truth, but rather oppression. As the father begins his interrogation of Agnes, it becomes clear that he not only intends to shed light into her room, but also onto her psyche, analyzing and explaining the instinctual drives of Agnes's unconscious. He counters Agnes's passivity, apparent even in the syntax of the prose, with aggression and confrontation. Light, logic, and analysis are the weapons of the father: "Agnes felt vaguely that the bright, sober daylight gave him the advantage, that it favored his dispassion."[14] Thus, a battle begins, a battle Agnes is doomed to lose from the beginning.

In her description of the conflict, Hartwig aligns the visual sense with masculine rationality. While her father employs logic to illuminate and explain his daughter's psyche, Agnes's lack of understanding is symbolized by her frequent inability to see clearly, as well as by her obstructed or impaired vision. In addition to her gummed-up eyes in the opening scene, Agnes's eyes are described as "blinded," "blank-eyed," "veiled," "closed," and "overtired … they could no longer take in an image."[15] Whereas her father sees, understands, and argues based on logic, Agnes's comprehension is "vague;" she is "undecided," "tentative," and "staggers … dazedly;" her behavior is "like under hypnosis," "as if sleepwalking," "groping," and "only mechanical."[16] In contrast to her father, Agnes takes in her surroundings and makes sense of the world around her through sensual perception. Her mode of being in the world is defined through her physical body rather than her mind.[17]

Agnes's father, combining within his person both paternal and psychoanalytic power, is in a doubly reinforced position of authority over his daughter. Agnes is completely helpless, for her resistance and denial must be read, according to Freudian theory, as reinforcement of the validity of the diagnosis. For Freud, the patient's initial rejection of the analyst's diagnosis is merely indicative of the repression that has taken place in the patient's psyche.[18] Because the patient is incapable of maintaining objectivity, Freud asserts that she is not to be believed. If the analyst ignores the patient's protests and presses on, "the first evidence soon begins to appear that in such a case 'No' signifies the desired 'Yes.'"[19] By placing all the power into the hands of the analyst, Freud ensures that he will always be in the right. For Agnes, this means that there is no way out as she becomes the victim of psychoanalytic discourse.

This novella forms Hartwig's reaction to and criticism of Freud's theories on female sexuality, which he laid out in three essays, "Some Psychical Consequences of the Anatomical Distinction Between the Sexes" (1925), "Female Sexuality" (1931), and "Femininity" (1932), part of the *New Introductory Lectures on Psycho-Analysis.*[20] Although Freudian theory enjoyed wide-spread reception by the 1920s, Hartwig's mode of criticizing the tenets of psychoanalysis through its own methodologies is rather unusual at this time. In his essays, Freud consistently discusses the sexual development of girls in contrast to – and in deviation from – that of boys. He bases his theories of female sexuality on the male model, assuming "that the little girl is a little man,"[21] despite the fact that the resulting explanations are rather "circuitous,"[22] as Freud himself admits. In order to become a woman the girl must overcome two obstacles that the boy is spared: first, her leading genital zone must change from the clitoris to the vagina; second, her love object must switch from her mother to her father. It is the second of these transitions that Freud is most concerned with and he invests much in his explanation.

In short, the little girl enters into the castration complex when she makes the discovery that the little boy has a penis and she has nothing. Envious of the boy's penis, she gradually learns to accept her lack and thus her own inferiority. She gives up clitoral masturbation, which indicates her becoming more passive, and acquires increasing hatred toward her mother, the original love object. These developments ultimately allow the girl to turn toward her father as her new, and rightful, love object. Thus, while the boy's Oedipus complex ends with the castration complex, the situation is reversed for the girl: for her, the Oedipus complex is initiated by the castration complex.

The road to "normal" womanhood is a difficult one and it seems almost inevitable that the young woman will not come away from it unscathed: her penis envy "will leave ineradicable traces on [her] development and the formation of [her] character,"[23] including feelings of inferiority. Her Oedipus complex, which is difficult for her to overcome and can reach far into adulthood, has among its consequences a weakened super-ego:

> In these circumstances the formation of the super-ego must suffer; it cannot attain the strength and independence which give it its cultural significance, and feminists are not pleased when we point out to them the effects of this factor upon the average feminine character.[24]

These effects include increased narcissism, vanity, shame, an inferior sense of justice, envy and jealousy, fewer social interests, and a decreased capability of controlling her urges. Thus, woman's character is determined by her anatomy as Freud attributes these supposed characteristics to her "difficult" sexual development.[25]

If we now return to Agnes's supposed sexual attraction to her father in *The Crime*, we recognize that, following Freud, her sexual development has been incomplete and unsuccessful. She has been unable to overcome her Oedipus complex and is still, like the little girl, in love with her father. Agnes's father, in his diagnosis that his daughter is in love with him and desires a sexual relationship with him, subscribes to Freud's theories of female sexuality completely and unquestioningly. In her portrayal of the father-daughter conflict, then, Hartwig illustrates how Freud's theories might play out in two individuals' lives. She takes the abstract psychoanalytic theories and builds on them, following them consistently to their extreme. In this sense, the story represents that which Freud left unsaid – the logical consequences of his theories.

In his position as psychiatrist, her father views Agnes's supposed psychic conflict as a psychological phenomenon, calling it "a harmless, everyday affair,"[26] thereby trivializing and generalizing the situation Agnes finds herself in. For him, Agnes is the case study for his theory. In his urge to analyze, he denies her even her own subjectivity: "You do not have the right to make a primitive erotic conflict, to which all humans are subjected, into a personal question of being and not being," and accuses her of claiming "an ordinary physiological phenomenon as a singular fate."[27] In response to her father's theorizing, Agnes personalizes his abstract analysis by transforming the psychic into the physical, thereby reclaiming her subjectivity and individuality on a tangible level: "It's as if you beat me,"[28] she says in response to his verbal abuse. The psychological pain Agnes suffers at the hands of her father is converted into physical pain. In an extraordinarily vivid image she equates her father's analysis with a physical dissection:

> I am lying on the dissection table. You cut open my abdomen and rummage with bloody hands in my bowels, you cut my heart out of my breast, stuff it into my mouth like a gag so that I cannot scream, for I am still alive, and I choke on my own heart until I suffocate. You scrape my brain out of my skull as if it were a miscarriage and fill the empty space with your semen.[29]

Although the analysis her father performs functions purely on a linguistic level, with his words as his scalpel, Agnes perceives it as physical violence. In her description, she sees herself lying on the dissection table, utterly passive but still alive. Her father, in cutting her heart out of her chest, removes that part of her which represents her emotions, thereby denying their validity. He proceeds to stuff her heart into her mouth like a gag, so that Agnes chokes on her own emotions and cannot scream, preventing her from articulating herself and depriving her of speech. And in making her speechless he causes her death. He then scrapes her brain out of her skull – inhibiting her intellectual existence – and fills up the empty, mind-less space with his semen, thus sexualizing her and reducing her to solely procreative purposes. In this powerful passage, Hartwig creates a disturbing image of the position of women in patriarchal society: deprived of language and without a voice, denied either an emotional or intellectual existence, and reduced to an empty sexual vessel.

As the narrative progresses, Agnes's body seems to gain more power over her behavior, which is becoming increasingly erratic. She begins to realize "that her body controls her will," as it shuts off her "ability to think" and her "consciousness."[30] She increasingly seeks her father's approval and becomes more dependent on him, a process which culminates with her dancing naked in front of him, begging him to touch and kiss her. In this scene of complete subjugation, Agnes's body acts out her psychic and mental submission: "Her blood had made its last stand, her body had undertaken to wage this battle to the end."[31] Now acting as though she really were in love with her father, Agnes's behavior seems to affirm his diagnosis. Her father's assertion earlier in the text that "a theory is a prison for the believers and fate for the nonbelievers," is here confirmed by Agnes's own actions.[32] The theory is inescapable, regardless of whether or not it is actually true or even believed. For Agnes, theory becomes destiny when she begins to behave exactly according to her father's diagnosis. Which came first – Agnes's behavior or her father's theory of that behavior – can no longer be determined.

Still trapped in the prison of her father's theory after the humiliation of offering herself to him and being rejected, Agnes, now desperate, breaks into her father's poison cabinet with the intent to kill herself. It is at this moment that her father once again violently bursts into her room. In his belief that Agnes stole the poison from his cabinet not to commit suicide but to kill him, he, for the first time, miscalculates the situation. Just as he had implanted his own theories about Agnes's psychic condition into her mind, he now suggests to her that she might be able to rid herself of his grip by killing him. Ironically, the technique of suggestion which had tipped the power-scale in his favor is the very impetus for his own demise. He is so completely certain of his power over Agnes that, in an apparent act of hubris, he gives her a revolver. He is convinced that she is too weak to use it against him.

But the act of giving Agnes the revolver, the quintessential phallic symbol, is equivalent to handing over his authority.[33] Once Agnes is in possession of the revolver, she slowly gains more power, becomes more aware and conscious of her position, and begins to exploit it. The tables have turned: Agnes becomes stronger while her father physically withers away, loses control, and lives in constant fear for his life. It is not only the revolver and the realization that Agnes might actually use it that gnaw away at his strength, but also Agnes's other weapon, her body. Through his theory, her father had reduced Agnes to her body, turned her into a "physiological phenomenon,"[34] and made her anatomy her destiny. Now, she turns that very body against him, casting it against his rationality, until it becomes an obstacle for him: "Why do you throw your body in front of my feet, so that I always have to stumble over you?" he exclaims frantically.[35] In the final scene he in desperation offers to castrate himself in exchange for his life – a castration which already occurred symbolically at the moment in which he threw the revolver into Agnes's lap.[36]

The end of the story places Agnes in an ambiguous situation. Having moved into a position of power through the possession of the revolver-phallus, she can either kill her father, taking on the masculine role – an alternative that remains within the logic of patriarchal society – or she can let her father live, thus remaining in the role of the victim. Agnes kills her father, and with this act of liberation, she believes, "now my life begins."[37] Through this act, she challenges the psychoanalytic order, transgressing and subverting the power structures she has been subjected to rather than succumbing to them. Psychoanalytic law, however, is underwritten and enforced by the institutions of law and order implemented by society. Thus, the doctor examining her father's body strictly instructs Agnes in response to her exclamation, "now it is over .... In a few moments the police will be here."[38] In the end, although Agnes has dared to commit this act of personal liberation, it offers no escape from the social structures within which she has been caught since the beginning. Indeed, her symbolic liberation will result in her physical incarceration. Thus, the story demonstrates that a true alternative to patriarchy does not exist, and that even this act of liberation remains inscribed within the boundaries of social norms. Nevertheless, there is a clear sense of hope and optimism in the defiance of Agnes's last words: "Quietly, confidently, almost jubilantly, Agnes repeated: 'My life begins!'"[39]

The end of the text calls into question how society defines criminal behavior and prosecutes it, a concern that figures even more prominently in *The Fantastical Paragraph.* The crime alluded to in the title of the novella refers simultaneously to the crime Agnes commits when she kills her father and to the father's psychological torture of his daughter. Indeed, it is this crime of the father's that necessitates his murder. However, only Agnes's crime will be prosecuted, for her behavior is socially condemned, while there are no laws against what her father did. Although Agnes identifies his behavior as "violation of the mind," and "a crime," her father correctly responds, "There is no law that prohibits [violation of the mind]."[40] In denouncing such socially accepted criminal behavior, Hartwig anticipates Ingeborg Bachmann's notion of a kind of fascism that pervades all social interactions:[41]

> Fascism .... does not begin with the first bombs that are thrown .... It begins with the relationships between people. Fascism is the first thing in the relationship between a man and a woman, and I have tried to say ... here in this society there is always war.[42]

The end of *The Crime*, then, formulates Hartwig's indictment of society. The abuse and torture to which the father subjects his daughter is only reflective of a society in which such behavior is tolerated.

III. The Lunacy of the Law

Despite vast differences in their circumstances and stories, the protagonists of the two novellas *The Crime* and *The Fantastical Paragraph* find themselves in similar situations in that both are caught within a system from which they cannot escape and which ultimately leads to their incarceration – their removal from society. In *The Fantastical Paragraph*, Hartwig criticizes the laws criminalizing abortion, as well as the judicial system in general, by demonstrating the paradoxical relationship between the law and the body. The protagonist of this story is Sabine Seltsam, a medical student, who, after a mysterious nightly visitation – whether it is a dream, a hallucination, or an actual event remains unclear – believes that she is pregnant. The narration culminates when Sabine is put on trial for abortion even though she was never pregnant to begin with.

Both *The Crime* and *The Fantastical Paragraph* capitalize on the ambivalence of whether or not the experiences the protagonists undergo are real. For Agnes, the question of whether her love and sexual desire for her father is real, imagined or suggested is, in the end, immaterial, for the theory *becomes* reality, and the theoretical and abstract are made manifest; they become evident on Agnes's body and are acted out by her. This is also the case in *The Fantastical Paragraph*, in which fantastical and imaginary events become reality for the protagonist. Sabine suffers from a strange condition:

> For three nights of every month, as the moon became full, Sabine lost all control over herself and wallowed in somnambulistic raptures. It always overcame her suddenly, like an illness, heating her prudish, infertile imagination like a fever until the usual measure of things fantastically displaced itself, every gesture revealing its most secret meaning, and her simple heart became addicted to miracles.[43]

Sabine is moonstruck, and for three nights every month the full moon exerts such power over her that she loses all control of herself. This passage illustrates how the physical and mental components of her condition are inextricably interwoven. Her "Mondsucht" ("somnambulism") is like an illness; it is likened to a fever that infects her fantasy – "her prudish, infertile imagination" – making it, as we shall see, fertile, until the normal, ordinary measure of things becomes "wunderlich verrückt" ("fantastically displaced"): "ver-rückt" in a material sense, meaning displaced, as well as on a psychological level, meaning crazy, insane.

Sabine here is marked by illness: physical illness, as she suffers from consumption, and mental illness, or at least instability, as her "somnambulism" points directly toward a condition of lunacy, defined by the OED as "intermittent insanity such as was formerly supposed to be brought about by the changes of the moon."[44] That the mental and physical components of Sabine's affliction are connected with each other is expressed in the idea of addiction ("Sucht"). Her "Schwindsucht" ("consumption") and "Mondsucht" ("somnambulism") make her "*wunder*süchtig" ("wonder-addicted"), they leave her longing for a miraculous or wondrous adventure.

Sabine's somnambulism manifests itself in distinctly physical, even sexual terms, because it enables her to live out her repressed sexual desires:

> overwhelmed, she [closed] her eyes until she lost all consciousness, sank backwards onto her bed, her lips opened in desire, her legs spread while softly and warmly, out of the force of her belief and desire, unending lust seeped achingly and benevolently into her womb …[45]

In this apparent state of sexual ecstasy, Sabine, overwhelmed and no longer conscious of her surroundings, has clearly lost control of herself. Although this experience manifests itself physically and is acted out in Sabine's body, it is apparent from this passage that this encounter is taking place in her imagination, as the words "out of the force of her belief and desire" indicate. It is through the power of her belief and desire that Sabine creates this sexual encounter.

While asleep immediately after this mysterious event, Sabine receives a dream-like message that she will bear a child.[46] At first skeptical and unsure of what actually happened, she eventually makes a conscious decision to believe in her "miracle": "I will overcome the dream and bear a child," she asserts.[47] Thus, a fantastical event that has taken place in Sabine's imagination, triggered by her strange somnambulism, becomes for her a reality, as she starts to experience the physical effects of pregnancy: she ceases to menstruate, her sense of taste and smell become excruciatingly sensitive, she is often overwhelmed by nausea and fainting spells, and craves unusual foods. It is at this point, confronted with the physical reactions of her phantom pregnancy, that the apparent reality of her situation begins to scare her and she has second thoughts. But now it is too late; the miracle she had wished for can no longer be undone. "One cannot trifle with reality …. Reality is dangerous," Sabine concludes as her body gains "absolute power" over her.[48] By allowing such imaginary and fantastical events to have concrete manifestations and real consequences, Hartwig makes it impossible for her protagonist as well as for the reader to clearly differentiate between what is real and what is imagined, enabling her to break down the dichotomy between reality and illusion. In Hartwig's texts, reality is not absolute – "Reality … was only a different measure of things, shared by all …"[49] – it only happens to be the one way we all agree to look at things. Sabine's offence, then, is that she decides to look at things from a different perspective.

Now convinced that she is indeed expecting a child, Sabine desperately tries to find a way to end her pregnancy. She seeks out a social worker, doctor, and midwife, but none are willing to help her. Finally, she acquires an unidentified drug, but takes too much, and on the brink of losing consciousness she realizes: "The horror sat in my brain, not under my heart …. I was not pregnant, truly, I was not pregnant."[50] She is taken to a hospital and eventually recovers, but charges are brought against her for abortion.[51] That she was never actually pregnant seems to be utterly immaterial, since the fact that she sought an abortion is taken as proof of her guilt. Sabine doesn't stand a chance against the legal system that now takes control of her life, for she is caught within the abstract reasoning and rhetoric of the law that asserts her guilt regardless of the circumstances, regardless even of whether or not she has done anything wrong.

The paradoxical relationship between the law and the body that the story demonstrates is already captured within the title. The "fantastical paragraph" is the law criminalizing abortion, a law which intrudes into a woman's body with the purpose of regulating and controlling it. This intrusion is vividly depicted when Sabine feels as though she is being physically violated by the letter of the law creeping into her body: "Paragraphs crept, she felt, into her empty eye sockets, nested in her skull …. The dead letter of the law triumphed over life."[52] Language, as the mode of execution of the law, and death stand in opposition to the body and life. The entire text, mirroring the title, sets the law as the dominant, authoritative discourse defined by logic and reason in opposition to the body, the imaginative, fantastical, and irrational – the subversive alternative which the legal system refuses to recognize.

Indeed, Hartwig literalizes judicial discourse and makes it physically manifest as abuse. When the law, by making reproduction a matter of jurisprudence, intrudes into Sabine's body intent on regulating and subjugating it, when the law physically violates her body in a humiliating search and brutal beating she suffers at the hands of the police, the violence inherent in the law is experienced physically by Sabine. The dissection and analysis of evidence that are part of the judicial process – acts that usually take place in the realm of language – are transposed into the physical, displayed in the body, thereby exposing their inherent brutality.

But what the law desires to achieve – regulation of the body – proves to be impossible. Hartwig demonstrates throughout the text how the body, seemingly taking on a life of its own, evades the rule of the law. The "fantastical" of the title therefore refers not only to the realm of the imaginary which is so prominent throughout the story, but it also characterizes the "paragraph," the law itself, as ludicrous, thereby inverting the traditional hierarchy between the two realms. This paradox is brought to the foreground when the judge asserts: "Justice has no imagination."[53] But Sabine contradicts him; the law, she claims, "has no medical, no psychological imagination. But it has a different, excessive imagination. It sees facts instead of illness, facts instead of need, facts instead of lunacy."[54] The law, precisely through its unrelenting claim of objectivity and its refusal to take individual circumstances into consideration, takes the fact-based discourse of logic and reason to its extreme and ceases to be humane. When the only thing the legal system recognizes is facts, it begins to lose touch with reality.

Indeed, a strict division between the real and the imagined, the rational and the irrational, normalcy and madness, is precisely what Hartwig undermines. The boundaries between these categories which we think of as binary oppositions are actually blurred to the extent that they can no longer be differentiated. In the end, the male representatives of the legal system lose control of themselves during the increasingly ludicrous trial. Here, the narration culminates when the realm of the law and the realm of the body collide with each other in a judicial and sexual climax.[55] The judge "turned pale," "stammered … in bewilderment," and "shrieked … hysterically," the prosecutor "fell into a frenzy" and "panted."[56] Finally, at the height of excitation, the judge pronounces the guilty verdict: "At that moment the judge lunged across the table spitting his 'Guilty' into [Sabine's] face."[57] It is the only possible reaction for a court which cannot recognize the fantastical as valid, because such an acknowledgement would undermine its own authority. The court pronounces this verdict in order to uphold its power in spite of its realization that the realm of the irrational threatens to reveal the hypocrisy of the law. Indeed, each of the justices

> understood in his withered heart that this woman had superceded the boundaries of reality …. The mask of justice fell from their slack faces, the law books of a decaying justice crumbled into paragraphs and dust in their hands.[58]

The transgression of reality of which the court officials so suddenly become aware is in danger of unraveling the very fabric of legal justice. The guilty verdict thus serves to reinforce the structure of the judicial system. At that moment Sabine recognizes just how volatile and unstable the law has become and "that only the frenzied death throes of a harried judiciary could bring forth this desperate admission of its arbitrariness and that she was herself a victim in whom the victor already began."[59] The prosecutor's final words, "That is revolution,"[60] thus ring true: the subversively revolutionary realm of the fantastic is threatening to unravel the logic and reason that hold together a decrepit judicial system.

Like Agnes in *The Crime*, Sabine cannot, in the end, escape the oppressive social structures in which she is caught. Since there is no escape from society, there is also no escape from the judicial system that is part and parcel of the social fabric. An alternative simply does not yet exist.

But despite the fact that Sabine is found guilty by the court, the end of the novella is carefully, almost subversively, optimistic. Although the legal system has won another victory with Sabine's incarceration, the last lines of the text are clearly indicative of a utopian hope for a better future. In recognizing her own situation as "a victim in whom the victor already began," Sabine negates the same oppositional categories that are responsible for her fate. Thus, she can simultaneously be victim and victor.

Dividing the world into guilty and innocent, victim and perpetrator is precisely what the legal system depends upon in order to function. Hartwig shows how these categories, rather than being in opposition to each other, are actually two ends of a continuum where clear boundaries do not exist. Indistinguishable from each other, they have lost their purpose as guidelines of how to live in modern society. By revealing the inadequacy of such divisions as the rational and the irrational, reason and lunacy, the law and the body, Hartwig deconstructs the logic of binary oppositions that continue to shape our world.

Works Cited

Bachmann, Ingeborg. *Wir müssen wahre Sätze finden: Gespräche und Interviews*. Ed. Christine Koschel and Inge von Weidenbaum. Munich: Piper, 1983.

Baruch, Elaine Hoffman, and Lucienne J. Serrano. *Women Analyze Women in France, England, and the United States*. New York: New York University Press, 1988.

Fraisl, Bettina. *Körper und Text: (De-)Konstruktionen von "Weiblichkeit" und Leiblichkeit bei Mela Hartwig*. Vienna: Passagen, 2002.

—. "Wer hat Angst vor Mela Hartwig? Stürmische Texte; Stürmische Reaktionen." *Schreibkraft* 7 (2002): 37-40.

Freud, Sigmund. *The Standard Edition of the Complete Psychological Works of Sigmund Freud*. 24 vols. Trans. James Strachey. London: Hogarth Press, 1953.

Hartwig, Mela. *Bin ich ein überflüßiger Mensch?* Graz: Droschl, 2001.

—. *Ekstasen*. Frankfurt/Main: Ullstein, 1992.

Irigaray, Luce. *This Sex Which is Not One*. Ithaca, NY: Cornell University Press, 1985.

Kernmayer, Hildegard. "Ekstasen oder Das Andere der Vernunft: Mela Hartwigs Kritik an der 'rationalistischen Moderne.'" In *Über den Dächern von Graz ist Liesl wahrhaftig: Eine Stadtgeschichte der Grazer Frauen*. Ed. Carmen Unterholzer. Vienna: Wiener Frauenverlag, 1996: 166-187.

Moi, Toril. *Sexual/Textual Politics: Feminist Literary Theory*. London: Routledge, 1985.

Schmid-Bortenschlager, Sigrid. "Exil und literarische Produktion: Das Beispiel Mela Hartwig." In *Keine Klage über England? Deutsche und österreichische Exilerfahrungen in Großbritannien 1933-1945*. Ed. Charmian Brinson et al. Munich: Iudicium, 1998: 88-99.

—. "Der zerbrochene Spiegel: Weibliche Kritik der Psychoanalyse in Mela Hartwigs Novellen." *Modern Austrian Literature* 12.3/4 (1979): 77-95.

Spreitzer, Brigitte. *Texturen: Die österreichische Moderne der Frauen*. Vienna: Passagen, 1999.

Vollmer, Hartmut. *Liebes(ver)lust: Existenzsuche und Beziehungen von Männern und Frauen in deutschsprachigen Romanen der zwanziger Jahre; Erzählte Krisen – Krisen des Erzählens*. Oldenburg: Igel, 1998.

Wedekind, Franz. *Lulu: Erdgeist, Die Büchse der Pandora*. Stuttgart: Reclam, 1989.

Notes

[1] The four protagonists of, respectively, *Das Verbrechen*, *Der phantatische Paragraph*, *Aufzeichnungen einer Häßlichen*, and *Die Hexe*, the four novellas that comprise Hartwig's collection *Ekstasen*.

[2] "Scheußliche Wunsch- und Wahn-Erotika eines durch Psychoanalyse verjauchten Gehirnes." Quoted in Hartmut Vollmer, *Liebes(ver)lust: Existenzsuche und Beziehungen von Männern und Frauen in deutschsprachigen Romanen der zwanziger Jahre; Erzählte Krisen – Krisen des Erzählens* (Oldenburg: Igel, 1998), 254. Unless otherwise noted, all translations are my own.

[3] "ebenso berührend[] wie zurückweisend[]," "schmerzhaft," "außerordentlich[] und grauenhaft[], … anlockend und widerlich, ein Buch der großen Scham und der Schamlosigkeit, aufreizend, unvergessbar, obwohl man es gern vergessen … möchte." Quoted in Bettina Fraisl, "Wer hat Angst vor Mela Hartwig? Stürmische Texte; Stürmische Reaktionen," *Schreibkraft* 7 (2002): 40.

[4] Elaine Hoffman Baruch and Lucienne J. Serrano, *Women Analyze Women in France, England, and the United States* (New York: New York University Press, 1988), 159.

[5] Luce Irigaray, *This Sex Which is Not One* (Ithaca: Cornell University Press, 1985), 78.

[6] In 1927 Hartwig entered a literary competition carried out by *Die Literarische Welt* with her novella *Das Verbrechen*, which was chosen by Alfred Döblin as one of the award-winning prose texts. With the support of Döblin and Stefan Zweig,

she was subsequently taken under contract by the renowned Zsolnay-Verlag as its first Austrian woman writer.

7 Ecstasy, from the Greek *ex*, "outside," and *histēmi*, "place." See Toril Moi, *Sexual/Textual Politics: Feminist Literary Theory* (London: Routledge, 1985), 136. Hartwig had originally suggested the title *Besessene*. See, for example, Sigrid Schmid-Bortenschlager, "Exil und literarische Produktion: Das Beispiel Mela Hartwig," in *Keine Klage über England? Deutsche und österreichische Exilerfahrungen in Großbritannien 1933-1945*, ed. Charmian Brinson et al. (Munich: Iudicium, 1998), 89. While *Besessene* adequately describes the protagonists, *Ekstasen* is particularly fitting as it indicates the women's position as outsiders not only on an individual, but also on a social level.

8 The striking similarities between *Das Verbrechen* and Freud's analysis of the hysteric Dora in "Fragment of an Analysis of a Case of Hysteria" have been pointed out by Kernmayer and Spreitzer. See Hildegard Kernmayer, "Ekstasen oder Das Andere der Vernunft: Mela Hartwigs Kritik an der 'rationalistischen Moderne,'" in *Über den Dächern von Graz ist Liesl wahrhaftig: Eine Stadtgeschichte der Grazer Frauen*, ed. Carmen Unterholzer (Vienna: Wiener Frauenverlag, 1996), 170; Brigitte Spreitzer, *Texturen: Die österreichische Moderne der Frauen* (Vienna: Passagen, 1999), 186. In his psychoanalysis of Dora, Freud reaches the conclusion that she is in love with her own father. See Sigmund Freud, *The Standard Edition of the Complete Psychological Works of Sigmund Freud*, vol. 7, trans. James Strachey (London: Hogarth Press, 1953), 56. All subsequent quotations are from this edition and noted by volume number.

9 "in einem Dämmerzustand des Bewußtseins": "Dunkelheit verkleisterte die Fenster, verklebte ihre Augen, wälzte Schatten und ein Chaos von Geräuschen ohne Sinn über ihr Bett … die farblosen Wände ihres verfinsterten Zimmers drängten sich immer enger um sie zusammen, wie ein Grab." Mela Hartwig, *Ekstasen* (Frankfurt/Main: Ullstein, 1992), 7.

10 See also Bettina Fraisl, *Körper und Text: (De-)Konstruktionen von "Weiblichkeit" und Leiblichkeit bei Mela Hartwig* (Vienna: Passagen, 2002), 171.

11 "Am vierten Tag wurde die Tür aufgebrochen, und mitten in der Helle des hereinstürzenden Tages stand ihr Vater vor ihren geblendeten Augen" (Hartwig, 7).

12 "Frauenzimmer," as noted in Strachey's translation, literally means "women's apartment" and is a slightly derogatory term for "woman" (Freud, vol. 4, 214).

13 "Rooms in dreams are usually women; if the various ways in and out of them are represented, this interpretation is scarcely open to doubt. In this connection interest in whether the room is open or locked is easily intelligible" (Freud, vol. 5, 354; see also vol. 7, 67).

14 "Agnes fühlte unbestimmt, daß das helle, nüchterne Licht des Tages ihn in den Vorteil setzte, daß es seine Sachlichkeit begünstigte" (Hartwig, 9).

15 "geblendet" (ibid., 7), "blicklos" (ibid.), "verschleiert" (ibid., 22), "geschlossen" (ibid., 21), "übermüdet[] … konnten [sie] kein Bild mehr aufnehmen" (ibid.).

16 "unbestimmt" (ibid., 14), "unschlüssig" (ibid., 18), "zögert" (ibid.), "taumelte … betäubt" (ibid., 24), "[w]ie unter Hypnose" (ibid., 20),

"[s]chlafwandlerisch" (ibid., 21), "tastend" (ibid.), "nur mehr mechanisch" (ibid., 24).

[17] See also Fraisl, *Körper*, 167. In *Der phantastische Paragraph*, Hartwig similarly endows her protagonist with thought patterns that are far from logic and reason. Rather, thoughts seem to fall into her mind accidentally, and, like Agnes, she perceives her surroundings physically rather than processing them through rational thought.

[18] "The 'No' uttered by a patient after a repressed thought has been presented to his conscious perception for the first time does no more than register the existence of a repression and its severity; it acts, as it were, as a gauge of the repression's strength" (Freud, vol. 7, 58).

[19] Ibid., 59.

[20] By 1927, when Hartwig wrote *Das Verbrechen*, Freud had only published one of these essays; however, he had set the groundwork for his theories on sexuality with his 1905 *Three Essays on the Theory of Sexuality*. By the time he published "Some Psychical Consequences" in 1925, his ideas were firmly established and did not change with subsequent publications. Indeed, the three essays basically repeat the same conclusions, evident even in some instances of Freud's wording.

[21] Freud, vol. 22, 118.

[22] Freud, vol. 21, 230.

[23] Freud, vol. 22, 125.

[24] Ibid., 129.

[25] "After all, the anatomical distinction [between the sexes] *must* express itself in psychical consequences" (Ibid., 124, my emphasis).

[26] "eine harmlose, alltägliche Angelegenheit" (Hartwig, 9).

[27] "Du hast nicht das Recht, einen primitiven erotischen Konflikt, dem alle Menschen unterworfen sind, zu einer persönlichen Frage um Sein und Nichtsein aufzuwerfen" (ibid., 16), "ein gangbares physiologisches Phänomen als Einzelschicksal" (ibid., 11).

[28] "Es ist, als ob du mich schlügst" (ibid.).

[29] "Ich liege auf dem Seziertisch. Du schneidest mir die Bauchdecke auf und wühlst mit blutigen Händen in meinen Gedärmen, du schneidest mir das Herz aus der Brust, stopfst es mir in den Mund wie einen Knebel, damit ich nicht schreien kann, denn ich lebe ja noch, und ich würge an meinem eigenen Herzen, bis ich daran ersticke. Du kratzt mir das Gehirn aus dem Schädel wie eine Frühgeburt und füllst den Hohlraum mit deinem Samen an" (ibid., 11-12).

[30] "daß ihr Körper über ihren Willen verfügte" (ibid., 32), "Denkkraft" (ibid., 29), "Bewußtsein" (ibid.).

[31] "Ihr Blut hatte seinen letzten Einsatz gemacht, ihr Körper hatte es übernommen, diesen Kampf zu Ende zu führen" (ibid., 43).

[32] "Eine Theorie ist ein Kerker für die Gläubigen und Schicksal für die Ungläubigen" (ibid., 14).

[33] Schmid-Bortenschlager has pointed out how this move on behalf of the father corresponds to Freud's account of female sexual development. See "Der

zerbrochene Spiegel: Weibliche Kritik der Psychoanalyse in Mela Hartwigs Novellen," *Modern Austrian Literature* 12.3/4 (1979): 82.
[34] "physiologisches Phänomen" (Hartwig, 11).
[35] "Warum wirfst du mir deinen Körper vor die Füße, daß ich immer über dich straucheln muß?" (ibid., 51).
[36] The ending recalls Wedekind's *Erdgeist*. Some aspects of Hartwig's novel *Das Weib ist ein Nichts* are also reminiscent of Wedekind's drama, most notably the new names and identities each lover bestows upon the female protagonist. As numerous scholars have noted, Hartwig had occasion to study *Erdgeist* in depth when she played the role of Lulu during her acting career.
[37] "Jetzt beginnt mein Leben" (ibid., 54).
[38] "Jetzt ist es zu Ende .... In wenigen Augenblicken wird die Polizei hier sein" (ibid.).
[39] "Leise, zuversichtlich, beinahe jubelnd, wiederholt Agnes: 'Mein Leben beginnt!'" (ibid.).
[40] "Notzucht im Geiste" (ibid., 24), "ein Verbrechen" (ibid.), "Es gibt kein Gesetz, das [Notzucht im Geiste] verhindert" (ibid.).
[41] Similarities in style and subject matter between Hartwig and later Austrian women writers, such as Ingeborg Bachmann, Elfriede Jelinek, and Ilse Aichinger, can easily be discerned. It is highly unlikely that these later authors were aware of Hartwig, whose career was cut short when she was forced to emigrate to London in 1938. Unable to continue publishing, Hartwig's work was quickly forgotten despite her early successes. For further information on Hartwig's life and career see Fraisl, *Körper*.
[42] "der Faschismus .... fängt nicht an mit den ersten Bomben, die geworfen werden .... Er fängt an in Beziehungen zwischen Menschen. Der Faschismus ist das erste in der Beziehung zwischen einem Mann und einer Frau, und ich habe versucht zu sagen ... hier in dieser Gesellschaft ist immer Krieg." Ingeborg Bachmann, *Wir müssen wahre Sätze finden: Gespräche und Interviews*, eds. Christine Koschel and Inge von Weidenbaum (Munich: Piper, 1983), 144. The similarities between *Das Verbrechen* and Bachmann's fragmentary novel *Der Fall Franza*, in which a young woman is made the object of psychological study by her husband, a psychiatrist, has been pointed out repeatedly, for example by Fraisl in *Körper*.
[43] "Drei Nächte in jedem Monat, während der Mond sich vollendete, verlor Sabine jede Herrschaft über sich und schwelgte in somnambulen Verzückungen. Das kam immer jäh, wie Krankheit, über sie, erhitzte wie Fieber ihre spröde, unfruchtbare Phantasie, bis sich ihr das gewohnte Maß der Dinge wunderlich verrückte, jede Gebärde ihren geheimsten Sinn entblößte und ihr schlichtes Herz wundersüchtig wurde" (Hartwig, 55).
[44] The moon and its phases have been, of course, traditionally associated with the female. Indeed, Sabine's "lunacy" might be understood as figuratively referring to her menstrual cycle.
[45] "sie [schloß] überwältigt die Augen, bis sie jede Besinnung verlor, hintüber auf ihr Bett sank, mit begehrlich geöffneten Lippen, die Beine gespreizt, während

weich und warm aus der Gewalt ihres Glaubens und ihrer Lust unendliche Wollust schmerzhaft und gütig in ihren Schoß einsickerte …" (ibid., 56).
[46] The obvious allusion to the Immaculate Conception is made even before the story proper, in the heading "Unbefleckte Empfängnis" (ibid., 55).
[47] "Ich bezwinge den Traum und gebäre ein Kind" (ibid., 61).
[48] "Die Wirklichkeit läßt nicht mit sich spaßen …. Die Wirklichkeit ist gefährlich" (ibid., 63), "unumschränkte Gewalt" (ibid., 62).
[49] "Die Wirklichkeit … war nur ein anderes, allen gemeinsames Maß der Dinge …" (ibid., 59).
[50] "Das Grauen saß mir im Gehirn, nicht unterm Herzen …. Ich war nicht schwanger, wahrhaftig, ich war nicht schwanger" (ibid., 86).
[51] The paragraph the story refers to is § 144. Passed into law in 1803, it made abortion a felony until 1927, when it became a misdemeanor until the law was abolished in 1975. Activists began to demand the legalization of abortion in the early 1920s.
[52] "Paragraphen krochen ihr, spürte sie, in die leeren Augenhöhlen, nisteten in ihrem Schädel …. Der tote Buchstabe des Gesetzes triumphierte über das lebendige Leben" (ibid., 93).
[53] "Die Justiz hat keine Phantasie" (ibid., 108).
[54] "hat keine medizinische, sie hat keine psychologische Phantasie. Aber sie hat eine andere, ausschweifende Phantasie. Sie sieht Tatbestände statt Krankheit, Tatbestände statt Not, Tatbestände statt Irrsinn" (ibid.).
[55] Fraisl successfully demonstrates how the proceedings during Sabine's trial are equated with sexual arousal and climax. See *Körper*, 180-81.
[56] "erbleichte," "stotterte … fassungslos," "kreischte … hysterisch," "geriet in Ekstase," "keuchte" (Hartwig, 124-25).
[57] "Da bäumte sich der Vorsitzende quer über den Tisch und spie [Sabine] sein 'Schuldig' ins Gesicht" (ibid., 126).
[58] "begriff in seinem ausgetrockneten Herzen, daß diese Frau die Grenzen der Wirklichkeit übersprungen hatte …. Die Maske der Gerechtigkeit fiel ihnen vom erschlafften Gesicht, das Gesetzbuch einer verwesenden Gerechtigkeit zerfiel ihnen unter den Händen in Paragraphen und Staub" (ibid.).
[59] "Da erkannte Sabine, daß nur ein rasender Todeskampf einer bedrängten Justiz dieses verzweifelte Bekenntnis zur Willkür erpressen konnte und daß sie selbst ein Opfer war, in dem schon der Sieger begann" (ibid., 126-27).
[60] "Das ist Revolution" (ibid., 127).

CHAPTER SEVEN

PROSTITUTION AND SEX TRAFFICKING OF WOMEN IN AUSTRIA: THE LEGALITIES AND ILLEGALITIES OF THE SEX TRADE[1]

LESLEY BART

The issues surrounding legal and illegal prostitution and how they relate to the growing problem of trafficking in women in Austria and around the world has become a growing concern among human rights activists, governing bodies, and scholars. One particular group that has addressed this issue is the international feminist community, composed of scholars, activists, social workers, and sex workers themselves. In this essay, I will address the debate between pro-prostitution and anti-prostitution feminists, specifically each perspective's theoretical positions and their recommendations for addressing prostitution in a pragmatic manner. In addition is an examination the overlapping issues of prostitution and trafficking in Austria and their relationship to each other.

I have chosen to define legal prostitution, illegal prostitution, and trafficking of women for sexual exploitation as different categories within the sex work industry. The definitions are not entirely concrete as sex trafficking is a sub-category within illegal prostitution. Additionally, anti-prostitution feminists often address all forms of prostitution and sex trafficking as forms of sexual exploitation.[2] I define legal prostitution as the sale of sexual services for money by a prostitute to a john.[3] Legal prostitutes adhere to prostitution laws of their country of residence, in this case Austria. Prostitution is legal to some extent in all of Austria; however the exact laws vary from province to province.[4] The general laws established by the Austrian government (*Legal Agenda*) stipulate that

(a) Prostitutes must work on a self-employed basis;
(b) Prostitutes must have a temporary or permanent residence permit;

(c) Prostitutes in certain provinces must register with the district authority in Vienna;

(d) Prostitutes must undergo weekly health checks and a mandatory HIV test every three months;

(e) Provinces apply their own restrictions as to where and what time of day prostitutes can work;

(f) In some provinces prostitutes can only work in an officially approved brothel;

(g) Prostitutes have to pay taxes.

Illegal prostitution includes all other forms of prostitution that are not legally sanctioned. This includes unregistered sex workers who continue to work, prostitutes who exchange sex for non-monetary compensation (drugs, etc.), as well as illegally trafficked women working as sex workers. For this paper I focus on female prostitution, but illegal prostitution would also encompass children under the age of fourteen, and unregistered male prostitutes.

For the definitions of trafficking in women for the purposes of sexual exploitation I refer to the definitions established by the United Nations Convention against Transnational Organized Crime:

> "Trafficking in persons" shall mean the recruitment, transportation, transfer, harboring or receipt of persons, by means of the threat or use of force or other forms of coercion, of abduction, of fraud, of deception, of abuse of power or of a position of vulnerability, or of the giving or receiving of payments or benefits to achieve the consent of a person having control over another person, for the purpose of exploitation. Exploitation shall include, at a minimum, the exploitation of the prostitution of others or other forms of sexual exploitation, involuntary labour or services, slavery or practices similar to slavery, servitude. ("Protocol to Prevent")

I will be specifically addressing trafficking of women for the purposes of sexual exploitation, although migrant trafficking of women in the broader sense will also be addressed as it relates to the sex trade industry.

The case of legalized prostitution in Austria and the implications it has regarding trafficking are interesting for many reasons. Austria's central location within the European continent has made it possible for traffickers to transport women from several Eastern European countries into the country very easily. In 2004 the US Bureau of Democracy, Human Rights, and Labor reported:

> The country [Austria] was particularly attractive to traffickers because of its geographic location and because citizens of the Czech Republic,

> Slovakia, Hungary, Romania, and Bulgaria did not need visas to enter the country. Most trafficked women were brought to the country with promises of unskilled jobs such as nannies or waitresses. Upon arrival, they were coerced into prostitution. According to police, there also were cases of women who knowingly entered the country to work as prostitutes, but who then were forced into dependency akin to slavery. Most victims were in the country illegally and feared being turned in to authorities and deported. Traffickers usually retained victims' official documents, including passports, to maintain control over them. Victims of trafficking reported being subjected to threats and physical violence. A major deterrent to victim cooperation was widespread fear of retribution, both in the country and in the victims' countries of origin. (*Country Reports*)

Austria has essentially become a gateway between the East and West for sex trafficking. The US Bureau of Democracy report cites that most traffickers are citizens involved in organized crime, although the number of foreign nationals involved in the trade is increasing. In considering the issues of legal and illegal prostitution we must recognize the significance of migration. While some women involved in legal prostitution in Austria are indeed Austrian, an overwhelming majority of those involved in legal and illegal prostitution are migrants. According to Luzenir Caixeta, coordinator of the Autonomous Centre for and from Migrant Women (MAIZ), nearly 90% of all current Austrian sex workers are migrant women.

One of the complications in examining prostitution in any area of the world is how to accurately assess how prevalent the prostitution industry is. Legalization has allowed authorities to account for the total number of registered sex workers, but the number of illegal sex workers and women who are victims of trafficking is more difficult to assess. The reliable information we do have about sex trafficking has come from various publications by non-government organizations (NGOs) such as the International Organization for Migration (IOM), Autonomous Centre for and from Migrant Women (MAIZ), and the Coalition Against Trafficking In Women International (CATW).

The increasing problem of sex trafficking suggests that illegal prostitution is becoming a serious issue around the world. The increasing number of trafficked women accounts for an overall increase, but legalization itself has been argued to be an explanation for the increase in illegal prostitution. Advocates against legalization such as the Coalition Against Trafficking in Women cite examples such as Victoria, Australia, where legalization of prostitution has led to an increase in the number of brothels the majority of which do not have licenses and are therefore illegal.[5] The CATW also argues that decriminalization in the Netherlands, which includes the requirement for sex workers to register, has increased illegal prostitution. The organization discerns that "legalization or decriminalization of the sex industry cannot erase the stigma of prostitution but, instead, makes women more vulnerable to abuse because they must register and lose their anonymity" (Raymond). Because women have to go through such lengthy means to obtain a legal permit to become a legal sex worker, many do not even bother.

When discussing prostitution and sex trafficking within the context of feminist theories, we must first make distinctions where they are necessary as the connection between trafficking and the existing forms of prostitution are disputed among scholars holding anti-prostitution and pro-prostitution feminist positions. Anti-prostitution feminists support ending prostitution as an occupation and trade. Feminist scholars such as Catherine MacKinnon and Andrea Dworkin, argue that prostitution is an outcome of patriarchal hierarchy and a function of woman's duty, as a subordinate to man, to serve his sexual urges and reaffirm his power.[6] Such scholars argue that whether or not an individual finds a sexual act or behavior liberating does not change the nature of objectification, abuse, and subordination as a whole. Janice Raymond and Melissa Farley have conducted research on prostitution and sex trafficking for the Coalition Against Trafficking Women (CATW) and have been two of the key leaders in the anti-prostitution movement. Their numerous studies and reports have advocated eliminating prostitution as an occupation for women, especially racial minorities and economically challenged and migrant women and children. These feminists support their stance by citing the uncalculated amounts of psychological and physical harm that has been inflicted on prostitutes.[7] Anti-prostitution activists have focused a great deal of attention on the increasing global problem of sex trafficking and sex tourism. Anti-prostitution scholars and activists take a very strong stand on ensuring women and children's human rights and realizing gender equality through ending prostitution. Researchers and activists Monica O'Connor and Grainne Healy directly address the disservice that pro-prostitution activists have inflicted upon the public's understanding of prostitution:

> The pro-prostitution lobby use the language of sexual liberalism to promote the idea of a women's freedom to choose what to do with her own body and that those opposing legislation are denying women the right to sell their own bodies. *One cannot have the right to violation. One only has the right to be free from violatio*n. (12; emphasis added)

The pro-prostitution stance argues for the decriminalization and legalization of prostitution. In distinguishing these two models scholar Laurie Schrage explains that, "'Legalization' refers to an intermediate approach that regards prostitution as inevitable, but in need of special social controls and regulation," whereas "'decriminalization' refers to the repeal of all laws that criminalize the action of taking money for sex." Pro-prostitution feminists such as sexologist Carol Queen and feminist author Inga Muscio argue that women should be allowed to sell sex just as one would sell any other service, and argue that true equality for women would mean sexual self-determination, using their sexuality in any way they see fit without political, moral, and, feminist ideological judgment.[8] Pro-prostitution feminists criticize the anti-prostitution stance for denying women's agency in assuming that every sex worker has been coerced into prostitution. Scholars such as Priscilla Alexander have argued that anti-prostitution feminists overemphasize the link between trafficking and prostitution to "present prostitutes as passive bodies, victims who must be rescued" to bolster their side of the debate (see Alexander, 90).

These scholars cite the fact that the criminalization of prostitution has only served to punish sex workers and does little to stop traffickers, pimps, or johns, and argue that by decriminalizing and legalizing prostitution, women will be less susceptible to violence, abuse, and financial exploitation (see St. James). Inga Muscio promotes not only the acceptance of prostitution but demands respect for the occupation as well. In her book entitled *Cunt*, Muscio states that "Without honoring Whores, we cannot truly understand and transcend the dynamics of violence, destruction, and ignorance fostered in our cuntfearing society. The fact that some women are considered 'bad' is a puritanically based value judgment that reinforces a fatal division between women" (91). Muscio recognizes the ideological shift from what she calls puritanical to a sex-positive view of women and their right to be sexual in every way possible. The anti-prostitution position has been criticized as being "puritanical" for other reasons as well, mainly that anti-prostitution feminists are aligning themselves too closely with the conservative right in their disapproval of more radical sexual practices (see Walkowitz).

Both sides of the prostitution/sex work debate make valid and convincing cases. Despite their differences, both sides have women's interests in mind. Both pro- and anti-prostitution have run organizations that support sex workers' rights, provide legal consultation, alternatives to sex work, and support for those trying to leave or still involved in prostitution.[9] In the increasingly globalized, sexualized, and consumer-driven world in which we live, prostitution will never be eliminated.

However, turning over control to patriarchal government systems will not ensure the safety and well-being of sex workers. The case of prostitution and sex trafficking in Austria reveals the complexities of how we address sex work and legalization. Both anti- and pro-prostitution evaluations lack a comprehensive soluton for dealing with global prostitution.

Janice G. Raymond, of the Coalition Against Trafficking in Women (CATW), states,

> Legalization was supposed to get prostituted women off the street. Many women don't want to register and undergo health checks, as required by law. . . so legalization often drives them into street prostitution. And many women choose street prostitution because they want to avoid being controlled and exploited by the new sex "businessmen." ("10 Reasons")

This argument seems to hold true in the case of Austrian sex workers. Despite the variation in law by province, most areas have laws that demand work- and residence-permits, registration with the police, mandatory weekly health checks, and restricted times and areas within the city where one can work (*Legal Agenda*). These restrictions demand a great amount of extra time, effort, and sometimes money from prostitutes which, not surprisingly, ends in women not registering and gaining legal status. And if, as Raymond argues, these restrictions do more to benefit the "businessmen," the brothel and bar owners and johns, than the women, prostitutes have even less incentive since the measures do little to afford them any political or financial gain. Governments that establish these laws certainly have more interest in legalization versus decriminalization, purely for reasons such as collecting taxes and still maintaining some legal control over sex workers.

Even some pro-prostitution feminists argue that legalization is not the answer. Margo St. James, a leader of the fight for sex worker rights in the United States, argues,

> The effect of criminalization is that clients are guaranteed a turnover and a variety, which is what they want. When the police are licensing, they don't give licenses to anyone with a prostitution record. Communities that hope that licensing bawdyhouses will get whores off the street have a false hope because the people with a record aren't allowed to get a license or get off the street. (81-82)

Pro-prostitution feminists like St. James argue for decriminalization rather than legalization of sex work. Decriminalization, as opposed to abolition or legalization, allows women to continue working with the fewest risks and restrictions.

Health checks and legal recognition seem to be beneficial, but under a patriarchal capitalist system in which sex work is viewed as morally reprehensible, these women have gained few clear advantages.[10] The moral biases of those who work within the system (police officers, courts, judges, etc.) have great impact even if someone is legally guaranteed equal and fair representation. An example of this injustice may be as simple as whether a prostitute is legally entitled to payment. As the group Amnesty for Women asserts, "A prostitute is entitled to receive payment from the client. This means, in legal terms, that she can go to court to claim her money. Nevertheless, a still-valid judgment exists stating that the contract between a prostitute and a client contravenes public morality and is thus null and void" (see Shrage). These situations make it clear that the ideals of legalization are not a reality, for prostitutes still live in a world where commonly held morals stigmatize them and disadvantage them legally and financially.

Sex trafficking and migration as they relate to the prostitution industry are a particular concern when analyzing the sex work trade in Austria. As discussed earlier, Austria's location between Western Europe and several economically-challenged Eastern European countries dramatically affects the illegal prostitution industry. Women, especially racial and ethnic minorities and women from economically-disadvantaged countries, are particularly disadvantaged and discriminated against in the world market. These non-Western migrant women are left with fewer choices than women of the Western world and their migrant male counterparts.

Migrant women face the most discrimination in job placement and employment compared to men (see Tiuriukanova, 99). Migrant work is overwhelmingly gender-segregated, with women being placed in the "entertainment industry" (primarily as dancers and sex workers), the service industry, or are employed as "domestic help", whereas men are placed in manual-labor positions (97). Scholar Elana Tiuriukanova claims that the "low status of migrant labor has a subjective manifestation," that is to say, "based on the fact that women are usually employed in non-prestigious, often socially demeaning jobs, the society forms a negative, stigmatized image of women-migrants" (100). Women suffer discrimination and stigmatization via the global job market and placement in the employment arena, as well as in the context of societies' views and treatment of them as a result of this discriminatory employment segregation. This discrimination and vulnerability is amplified for trafficked women, who are often held in exploitive situations where some or all of their already meager earnings are taken by pimps or traffickers as "fees." It is the feminization of poverty, the inherent discrimination against women in the workforce and the increasing number of women represented among the working poor, combined with the feminization of migration, that places these women in extremely exploitive scenarios that become difficult or impossible to escape. Luzenir Caixeta notes that the requirements for migrant women working in Austria create a "dependency relationship" between brothel owners and managers which is also exploitive. Because of the rigorous requirements for migrant women working in the sex industry, they are dependent on and vulnerable to those they work for, allowing brothel owners the freedom to exploit and manipulate the situation.

It is important to recognize that trafficking of women differs from other forms of migrant work: "The countries of destination generally treat the victim as offenders and proceed to their immediate expulsion. Arrest in the course of a police check is likely to lead to the woman being deported forthwith, and thus being unable to give evidence in court against the traffickers" (Galiana, 18). Courts tend to favor the traffickers rather than the victims revealed by the fact that punishment for trafficking is exceptionally low; in Austria the penalty for traffickers ranges from 6 months to 10 years in prison (35-37). This claim is supported by the US Bureau of Democracy report:

> The Government provided temporary residence to trafficking victims who were prepared to testify or who intended to file civil law claims. However, victims still rarely agreed to testify, due to fear of retribution. Temporary residency status allowed victims to stay in the country only during a trial. There were no provisions allowing victims of trafficking to remain in the country following their testimony; virtually all victims were repatriated. (US Dept. of State)

Trafficked women trying to escape the industry are granted little assistance by the Austrian government. These women face dual-stigmatization, as illegal migrants and illegal sex workers, which deters them from seeking assistance. NGOs, such as the Coalitional Against Trafficking in Women, seek to not only do research on the issue of human trafficking, but also provide legal assistance.

It is important to note the criminal reality of prostitution and trafficking, especially when considering legalization and the role of the state in affairs such as prostitution. Recent researchers and scholars alike agree with the consensus position that "[trafficking in women] represents the third largest source of profit to [global] organized crime, after drugs and arms.[11] One must recognize that when we address prostitution, legal or illegal, we inherently address trafficking in women as well. The criminal nature of such an industry has affected the sex work industry of Europe in a very direct way. According to the International Organization for Migration (IOM), "There are reports that Western brothel keepers find themselves under increasing pressure from organized gangs based in the CEEC [central and eastern European countries] countries to hire eastern European women."[12]

The issues surrounding prostitution are much more complex than the mere question of "Should we or should we not legalize?" When we consider the complex issues of criminality of the legal and illegal sex industries and exploitation of women, it becomes clear that prostitution and sex trafficking are not just loosely connected industries, but are increasingly becoming dependent upon one another. One organization that has attempted to address the needs of sex workers and trafficked women is MAIZ, an Austrian "organization by and for migrant women," whose purpose is assisting "migrant women ... as well as refugees, asylum seekers, and migrant women working in the sex trade" (Autonomes Integrationszentrum). MAIZ presents an interesting combination of assisting migrant women in developing careers outside of exploitive industries like the sex trade while arguing for the de-stigmatization of sex work. It is clear when examining MAIZ's key principles that empowerment and diversity are key goals of the organization. Statements within their principles include "We support subjects—not clients or objects" and "[we] demand the right for sexual self-determination." More direct statements include the "demand for the recognition of prostitution as sex work," implying the reality that sex work, despite political or ideological definition, is an occupation. Organizations like MAIZ are desperately needed to address the dire situation that many sex workers face from a global rather than a limited local perspective. Despite any particular country's laws regarding prostitution's legality, prostitution exists and will continue to, and organizations independent of any economic and political interests need to be assisting and representing these women.

In examining Austria's prostitution situation, it can be concluded that neither legalization nor abolition of prostitution can effectively address the needs of sex workers. Abolition will only serve to place more prostitutes in jail, diminishing any chance they have of finding opportunities outside of the prostitution industry. Legalization ensures the women with previous criminal offenses for prostitution are not provided licenses, leaving them excluded from legal protections and services. Legalization provides the benefit of services such as weekly health checks and some legal protections, but comes with the cost of increased restrictions on women that limit the ability of sex workers to earn a living in their newly legalized profession.

The legalization of the prostitution industry has made it easier for trafficking to go unnoticed once migrant women reach their countries of destination. The legalization of prostitution in Austria has affected a population of women who are overwhelmingly migrants. Along side the legal aspects of how we deal with prostitution, we must address the weighty moral and ideological dilemmas inherent in the problem if we are going to deal with prostitution in a practical way. How governments and human rights groups approach the issue of prostitution and trafficking will be decided by the ideological assumption they make about women's human rights and gender equality, as well as how these groups deal with the demand for prostitution and the economic impoverishment of certain populations. The feminist perspectives discussed have been some of the first to offer any form of support for sex workers, but each group's long-term goals and agendas are very different. The debate between attempted elimination or acceptance of sex work, women's right to sell or men's right to buy, and women's right to leave or the promotion of a legitimate career are all issues which rely on a knowledgeable and informed discourse among feminist activists, NGOs, and governing bodies which is taking place with regard to the cultural context in which these decisions are being made.

Works Cited

Autonomes Integrationszentrum von & für Migrantinnen. "About MAIZ." Autonomes Integrationszentrum von & für Migrantinnen. <http://www.maiz.at>. Accessed March 21, 2006.

Caixeta, Luzenir. "Everything Under Control (?!): Regulation, Stress Factors, and Health consequences of Prostitution in Austria." *Research for Sex Work* 6 (2003): <http://nswp.org/pdf/R4SW-06.PDF>.

Farley, Melissa. "'Bad for the Body, Bad for the Heart': Prostitution Harms Women Even If Legalized or Decriminalized." *Violence Against Women* 10 (2004): 1087-1125.

Farley, Melissa, and Jacqueline Lynne. "Prostitution of Indigenous Women: Sex Inequality and the Colonization of Canada's First Nations Women." *Fourth World Journal* 6.1 (2005): 1-29.

Farley, Melissa, Isin Baral, Merab Kiremire, and Ufuk Sezgin. "Prostitution in Five Countries: Violence and Post-Traumatic Stress Disorder." *Feminism & Psychology* 8 (1998): 405-26.

Galiana, Carmen. "Trafficking in Women." *European Parliament* (2000). <http://www.europarl.eu.int/workingpapers/libe/pdf/109_en.pdf>.

Hughes, Donna M., Laura Joy Sporcic, Nadine Z. Mendelsohn, and Vanessa Chirgwin. *The Factbook on Global Sexual Exploitation* (1999). *Coalition Against Trafficking in Women.* <http://www.catwinternational.org/factbook/Austria.php>.

Humm, Maggie. *The Dictionary of Feminist Theory.* Columbus: Ohio State University Press, 1995.

International Organization for Migration. *Trafficking in Women to Austria for Sexual Exploitation.* International Organization for Migration and the Office of the Austrian Minister for Women's Affairs, 1995.

Kelly, Elizabeth. "Journeys of Jeopardy: A Review of Research on Trafficking in Women and Children in Europe." *IOM Migration Research Series* 11 (2002), http://www.iom.int/documents/publication/en/mrs_11_2002.pdf.

Legal Agenda for Migrant Prostitutes and Trafficked Women on the Internet, 2005. Amnesty for Women. http://www.femmigration.net/countires/austria.html. (accessed February 27, 2005).

Muscio, Inga. *Cunt: A Declaration of Independence.* Emeryville, CA: Seal Press, 2002.

O'Connor, Monica and Grainne Healy. *The Links Between Prostitution and Sex Trafficking: A Briefing Handbook.* Coalition Against Trafficking in Women, 2005.

Alexander, Priscilla. "Feminism, Sex Workers, and Human Rights." *Whores and Other Feminists.* Ed. Jill Nagle. New York: Routledge, 1997. 83-97.

Raymond, Janice G. "10 Reasons for Not Legalizing Prostitution and a Legal Response to the Demand for Prostitution." *Coalition Against Trafficking in Women* (2003), http://action.web.ca/home/catw/readingroom.shtml?x=32972.

—. *Report to the United Nations Special Rapporteur on Violence Against Women: Prostitution and Trafficking*. Coalition Against Trafficking in Women, 1995.

Sadoghi, Alice. *Offene Rechtsfragen zur Prostitution in entwicklungsgeschichtlicher Perspektive.* Linzer Schriften zur Frauenforschung 30. Ed. Ursula Flossmann. Linz: Trauer, 2005.

Shrage, Laurie, "Feminist Perspectives on Sex Markets." *The Stanford Encyclopedia of Philosophy* (2004), http://plato.stanford.edu/entries/feminist-sex-markets/.

St. James, Margo. "The Reclamation of Whores." *Good Girls/ Bad Girls.* Ed. Laurie Bell. Toronto: The Women's Press, 1987. 81-7.

Tiuriukanova, Elana. "Female Labor Migration Trends and Human Trafficking: Policy Recommendations." *Human Traffic and Transnational Crime.* Ed. Sally Stoecker and Louise Shelley. Lanham, MD: Rowman & Littlefields Publishers, Inc., 2005.

Tong, Rosemarie Putnam. *Feminist Thought.* Boulder, CO: Westview Press, 1998.

United Nations. "Protocol to Prevent, Suppress and Punish Trafficking in Persons, Especially Women and Children." United Nations Convention Against Transnational Organized Crime, 2000.

US Department of State. *Country Reports on Human Rights Practices 2004: Austria.* Bureau of Democracy, Human Rights, and Labor (2005), http://www.state.gov/g/drl/rls/hrrpt/2004/41669.htm.

Walkowitz, Judith. "The Politics of Prostitution." *Feminism and Sexuality.* Ed. Stevi Jackson and Sue Scott. New York: Columbia University Press, 1996. 288-96.

Notes

[1] Lesley Bart's and Lorely French's essays are a result of a collaborative effort regarding the issue of prostitution and sex trafficking of women in Austria. The project is inspired by two different approaches to the topic, namely Lesley's as a sociologist and Lorely's as a literary scholar, and by recent developments in Austrian politics and literature regarding sex trafficking. Austrian media reports in 2005 revealed the alleged involvement of politician Gerhard Roder, one time candidate for the house of representatives in Lower Austria and then press spokesperson for the National Parliament president Andreas Khol, in a sex trafficking scandal. Police investigations into the criminal activities of a Viennese escort service engaged in exploiting minors identified Roder's voice in a call to the traffickers on August 4, 2004. Transcripts of that call have Roder requesting information on the availability and specialties of specific women. Roder, who once stressed "the protection of women" ["Frauenschutz"] as a major part of his political agenda, and who once brought a petition in front of the National Parliament asking for stricter punishments for sex crimes against children, claimed his calls were part of his own private investigation into the sex ring. Strangely, he had informed neither his boss Khol nor the police about such. Since then, he has been dismissed from his position under Khol. The recorded conversations between the men soliciting the women and the traffickers have become the subject of a recent piece by Elfriede Jelinek called "Über Tiere." (The authors thank Professor Hubert Lengauer at the Universität Klagenfurt for this reference.) The first part of

---

Jelinek's piece was published in *Falter* on 13 January 2006 (Elfriede Jelinek, "Über die Tiere," *Falter* 13 January 2006: 8-10, 12) and the complete text is now on Jelinek's website: Elfriede Jelinek, "Über die Tiere," http://www.elfriedejelinek.com/. Accessed October 30, 2006.

Three months before these telephone calls and a year and a half before Jelinek's piece, Marlene Streeruwitz's novel *Jessica, 30.* had appeared in bookstores and immediately became a bestseller in Austria. Among other issues related to gender roles, relationships, and sexuality, the book deals with an Austrian politician's involvement in a prostitution ring of Eastern European women. While the shared timing of these two events is most certainly a coincidence, one cannot ignore the heightened significance that such criminal activities in the sex trade industry, as played out in political reality and literary fiction, have for Austrian society and culture. Lesley Bart's paper will first examine the realities of sex trafficking and prostitution from distinctly feminist and sociological perspectives, providing definitions and background material on the legal codes and feminist theoretical approaches to the topic. Lorely French's subsequent paper will investigate the ways in which Streeruwitz lays the framework for evaluating the cultural forces that lead more to the exploitation of women in the sex trade than to their empowerment.

[2] I use the terms "sex work" and "prostitution" interchangeably. The term 'sex workers' is an encompassing term for erotic dancers, performers in pornography, and prostitutes, however my use of the term refers exclusively to prostitution throughout this essay.

[3] Prostitution industry term for a man who procures sex from a prostitute.

[4] In the provinces of Upper Austria, Salzburg, Carinthia, Tyrol, Vorarlberg, Burgenland, and Styria, for example, prostitution is allowed only in bordellos that have been approved by the district in which they are located. The irony of the law is that in Vorarlberg it is not possible to receive a legal permit to operate a bordello. In Styria and Burgenland, prostitution may also occur in a private residence, with a so-called "house call" [Hausbesuch]. In Vienna and Lower Austria prostitution is allowed in public places (with certain local restrictions, such as not around churches, cemeteries, hospitals, schools, children's playgrounds, youth centers, etc.) as well as with "house calls." Another difference between provinces is that in Styria, Lower Austria, Burgenland, Vorarlberg, and Carinthia the age for legalized prostitution is nineteen, whereas the age for the national laws is fourteen (see Sadoghi, 62-63).

[5] Mary Sullivan and Sheila Jeffrey, *Legalizing Prostitution is Not the Answer: the Example of Victoria, Australia*, (Australia and USA: Coalition Against Trafficking in Women), qtd. in Raymond.

[6] MacKinnon and Dworkin are two of the most well-known anti-pornography and ant-prostitution scholars in the United States. They gained notoriety after a controversial 1992 case, R. v. Butler, in which the Canadian Supreme Court ruled against Donald Victor Butler, the owner of a pornography shop, and charged him with the distribution of "obscene" material. A brief written by MacKinnon and

Dworkin was heavily cited, and the case's ruling secured a victory for anti-pornography feminists.

[7] In an extensive study across five countries, Farley et. al interviewed 475 prostitutes, including women, men, and transgender persons, finding that "73 percent reported physical assault in prostitution, 62 percent reported having been raped since entering prostitution, [and] 67 percent met criteria for a diagnosis of PTSD [post-traumatic stress disorder]."

[8] The pro-prostitution position is held primarily by pro-sex or sex-positive feminists, although it should be noted that the positions on prostitution vary greatly among sex-positive feminists. The notion of sex-positive feminism came about as a reaction to the tendency of feminists to internalize the notion of sex as shameful.

[9] In the United States, organizations such as WHISPER (Women Hurt in Systems of Prostitution Engaged in Revolt) and COYOTE (Call Off Your Old Tired Ethics) exist. MAIZ (Autonomes Integrationszentrum von & für Migrantinnen) is an Austrian equivalent which will be discussed later in the text.

[10] "In Austria, prostitution has historically been perceived as morally reprehensible, as implied in the terminology from the eighteenth century onwards, whereby legal codes were established. Prostitution was termed a 'commercial sexual offence' ['gewerbliche Unzucht'] and 'unchastity against nature' ['Unkeuschheit wider der Natur']" (see Sadoghi 7-52 for a history of the legal language and codes.

[11] Congressional Research Service, *Trafficking_in Women and Children: The US and International Response* (Washington: Library of Congress, 2002), qtd. in Kelly.

[12] IOM Migration Information Programme (May 1995) qtd. in Galiana, 11.

CHAPTER EIGHT

PROSTITUTION AND SEX TRAFFICKING OF WOMEN IN AUSTRIA: THE LEGALITIES AND ILLEGALITIES OF THE SEX TRADE MEET MARLENE STREERUWITZ'S JESSICA

LORELY FRENCH

Marlene Streeruwitz's novel *Jessica, 30.* appeared just some three months before politician Gerhard Roder, one-time candidate for the provincial parliament in Lower Austria and then press spokesperson for the National Parliament president Andreas Khol, was telephoning sex traffickers in Vienna on August 4, 2004, to request information on the availability and specialties of specific women.[1] The novel's protagonist, Jessica Somner, has studied German literature and philosophy in Vienna and cultural studies in Berlin and is now living in Vienna. She is overqualified for many jobs and works as a freelance journalist at a women's magazine. Her lover is Gerhard Hollitzer, who is married, has two children, and works as the "State Secretary for Future and Development Issues" for the conservative Austrian People's Party, the "ÖVP."[2] During a late-night/early morning visit from Hollitzer, after he has sat through a long session during which the ÖVP has tried to build a coalition with the Greens[3], Jessica finds herself confronted with the following admission from him:

> And sometimes, you know, I find whores more interesting, and they would scratch your eyes out if you were to tell them that we exploit them. They understand quite a bit more about freedom than you all with your daintiness, and these women—these women really work for their money. They really have to work for their money, you know. A real life, you all will never accomplish this. You neither. You also still live off your Papa.[4]

In expressing his preference for women who earn their money through sexual favors over those like Jessica who have pursued career goals through academe, Hollitzer draws clear lines between the body and the mind and their relationship to productivity and non-productivity, and to independence and dependence. His assertions provoke many questions: Is work by women most productive and independent and thus most valid when it involves the body? Will women never be able to earn a "decent" living with their minds? Will they always be dependent on Papa, that is, on a patriarchal system that adheres to certain "laws of the father," if they do pursue a life of the mind?

What precedes and follows Hollitzer's observations here in the second section of the novel is important. Readers have heard Jessica's inner thoughts from the beginning of the evening as she has been sitting and waiting for Hollitzer to arrive. We know she has been out to undress him (in more ways than one, as will be explained later) for his treatment of her friend Mia, whom he has sexually abused, although he does not yet know that Jessica knows what he has done. Jessica questions who the "real Hollitzer" is. Is he the man who comes to her apartment to eat his sweet-and-sour pork and drink his white wine? Or is he the man whom her friend Mia has accused of holding her in bondage for two weeks, tying her to her bed and giving her only water to drink? When Hollitzer does finally arrive, he wants to have sex with Jessica, who does not immediately comply. Instead, she decides to perform oral sex on him, during which he receives a phone call from his wife. While talking with his wife about the political meetings of the day, he forces Jessica to continue her act to the (his) climax by holding onto her head and hair. This humiliating blow (pun intended!) incites Jessica to destroy her lover's political career through revealing his involvement in a prostitution ring, called the Panhans, which has arranged for Eastern European women to grant sexual favors to politicians at their so-called seminars. This is the subject of the third and last chapter of the novel, in which Jessica is on the airplane to Hamburg to tell her story to the editor of the German magazine *Stern*.

In this essay I wish to analyze some of the most significant intertextual references and reexaminations of cultural icons that are at work in *Jessica, 30.* within the context of sex trafficking of women in Austria and the above questions regarding the dichotomous split between the body and the mind. Lesley Bart presents in this volume a sociological perspective on the current situation regarding the sex trade in Austria and the possible causal relationship between legalized prostitution and the increase in trafficking in recent years. Streeruwitz, through Jessica's inner monologue, lays the framework for evaluating the cultural forces that form roots for that relationship, namely those that lead more to the exploitation of women in the sex trade than to their empowerment. Analysis of some of Jessica's references unveils her in the process of realizing those cultural forces that have done more harm than good to women's bodies and sexuality, including a literary canon that portrays limited options for women, media conglomerates that project unrealistic images of women, a consumer society that buys into the objectification of women's bodies, and a politician who admits to admiring the work of prostitutes over that of well-educated women.

The intertextuality, repetitions, and deconstructions of gendered worlds in Streeruwitz's novel stem from her own openness about her feminism and about the ways in which feminist theory intersects with the postmodern.[5] To be sure, scholars have recognized the adroit way in which Streeruwitz combines postmodernism and feminism in her prose works. Likewise, Streeruwitz has never denied this mutual affiliation in her theoretical essays. Postmodernism in her dramatic and prose works comes to be defined as her questioning "the concept of a coherent and autonomous self," as Britta Kallin writes in her analysis of Streeruwitz's novel *Afterworld* (*Nachwelt*; 337). Streeruwitz herself sees postmodernism as allowing her simultaneously to defy those who interpret the movement as only deconstructive and discursive and to engage feminist perspectives that she finds have little acceptance in modernity. In her Frankfurt lectures on poetics she contends:

> And all the amazement about how in the postmodern everything is allowed to exist only as a process and discursively is an attack from the pre-modern. An attack of the direct patriarchy of religions and nationalism. . . . A non-patriarchal poetics needs to concern itself with decolonization.[6]

Writing from a feminist literary perspective would mean focusing on a viewpoint that is different from that championed by the patriarchal culture. Again in her Frankfurt lectures she writes:

> Only when both sides [the masculine and feminine] dare to break into an Other can freedom from oppression and oppressing begin. And. We know that the oppressed know more than the oppressors. Have to know more. For this reason it would be necessary to begin listening to women.[7]

Comments about Streeruwitz's particular brand of postmodernism have almost always arisen in conjunction with analysis of the particular aesthetics that she has consistently adopted in all her other prose works. Her novels and essays usually contain a proliferation of periods and short sentences, a major aesthetic maneuver in a style that deliberately distances the reader through indirect speech full of the subjunctive form. Language thereby becomes an obvious mediating device between character and reader.[8] Full stops serve as "a type of estranging device," as Alyson Fiddler has pointed out (70). They portray what Helga Schreckenberger has analyzed as, and what Streeruwitz herself calls, "A poetics of the banal. A poetics of silence."[9] Such poetics occur, to cite remarks from Fiddler again, in a "distanced and non-natural manner" (70). In contrast to this alienating style in Streeruwitz's earlier prose works, Jessica's language in the later novel is not mediated, but rather comes at the reader full force from her inner monologues. There is almost no punctuation, and there are no full stops (except in the middle dialogic part). Instead, the prose style runs on and on. Jessica, to be sure, is not silent, at least not in the thoughts to which the reader is privy. We have to listen to her.

In other words, while postmodernism and feminism may define the style and content of Streeruwitz's earlier works and certainly are pertinent on a number of levels to *Jessica, 30.*, there are both new and old forces at work in the 2004 novel that complicate the applicability of these two theoretical perspectives as we know them. Already the title of the novel represents a drastic departure from her previous prose works. Gone are protagonists' names that evoke images of well-known cultural figures, such as Helene in *Seductions* [*Verführungen*], Margaret in *Afterworld* [*Nachwelt*], and Madeline in *Party Girl*. Even without knowing Jessica's age, her name alone conjures up a more youthful time when names with lighter sounds such as Jennifer and Julia were popular. Still more remarkable about these surface aesthetics is the insertion of the comma between Jessica's name and her age. Rarely has Streeruwitz used any punctuation except the period, the"strangulation mark" ["Würgemal"], as she once labeled the most characteristic feature of her prose.[10] In *Jessica, 30.*, a period ends the title, but the comma places the possibility of "strangulation" in question. Instead, the comma suggests a welcomed, even healthy rupture in Jessica's life, a time when she may pause to reflect on the ways in which her identity is or is not dependent on her age.

On the surface the stream-of -consciousness style is, of course, not new to literature. In fact, one critic has dubbed Jessica "the Miss Else of the 'Golf Generation" (Streitler). The former refers to Arthur Schnitzler's short story *Fräulein Else*, written also in an inner-monologue style from the vantage point of Miss Else, who must show her naked body to the disgusting Dorsday in order to gain money for her father and save him from financial ruin. Unable to face the humiliation into which her nakedness has forced her, she ends her own life. The latter reference is to the bestseller by Florian Illies, characterizing the generation born between the years of 1965 and 1975 as one that grew up being transported around in Volkswagen Golfs, having playrooms filled with Playmobil figures, and, being the first generation to confront the outgrowth of HIV and AIDS, engaging only in *Blümchensex*, or "weak sex."[11] As we shall see, Jessica ultimately fits neither of these molds.

Hence, although the inner monologue is not new to literature, the portrayal of Jessica's continual thoughts as she is constantly jogging and driving through Vienna in the first part and then flying to Hamburg in the final chapter embodies a new aesthetic method for Streeruwitz to address how mind and body movements are inseparable. Almost always on the go, Jessica contemplates the body as a wonderful machine—"what a wonderful little machine, the body, when everything runs well and nothing else exists"[12]—while she simultaneously prepares the reader for her ensuing exposé on media and literary images. Through the constant reflections of the inner monologue, the machine-like motions of the physical body work in tandem with the mental capacities.

Jessica thus becomes a spokesperson for a newer generation of women, one born into what many feminist theorists have come to identify as a "Third-Wave Generation."[13] To understand what this so-called Third-Wave Generation thinks about body image, sexuality, pornography, prostitution, and sex trafficking, the scholar must turn less toward the writings of earlier feminists such as Susan Brownmiller, Robin Morgan, Andrea Dworkin, and Catherine MacKinnon and more towards recent popular writings that reflect a younger generation, such as Eve Ensler's *Vagina Monologues*, Jennifer Baumgardner and Amy Richards's *Manifesta: Young Women, Feminism, and the Future*, and Inge Muscio's *Cunt*, to which Lesley Bart previously referred. These works portray how the feminist movement has taught women to value their bodies as sources of empowerment and not disgrace. That empowerment, however, holds contradictions, as Ariel Levy asserts in the recently published *Female Chauvinist Pigs: Women and the Rise of Raunch Culture*. The term "raunch culture" depicts the recent fascination among younger women with casual sex, with strippers and sex workers, and with midriff-displaying, cleavage-showing, "skanky" fashion, actions many women boast make them view sex "like one of the guys." Being "one of the guys," however, according to Levy, only serves to denigrate women. In such a world of gendered opposites, sex stays a commodity and human behavior remains divided into the two camps of "like a man" or "like a woman," whereby the former becomes the goal to which women must aspire. In other words, according to Levy:

> Even if you are a woman who achieves the ultimate and becomes like a man, you will still always be like a woman. And as long as womanhood is thought of as something to escape from, something less than manhood, you will be thought less of, too. (112)

The move toward a more sex-positive generation and the danger that efforts to "be like a man" may hold for younger women are important background to consider in Jessica's case and in her ultimate discovery of Hollitzer's political sex ring. Hollitzer, for one, refers several times to Jessica and her generational cohort as "ihr jungen Frauen," calling attention to her position in a generation that talks differently, that has lost its sense of the romantic, and that doesn't know what it wants regarding gender expectations.[14] On the top of the list of concerns for the younger generation, according to those writing as Third-Wave-Generation feminists, are issues of sexual health, eating disorders, and body image.[15]

These, too, are Jessica's main concerns, at least at first. At the beginning of the novel, we see the ways in which she has bought into the "Beauty Myth," as described by Naomi Wolf in her book of the same title. At the center of Jessica's thoughts are reflections, to the point of obsession, on body images and their relation to sexuality. As she jogs in Vienna in the first scene, she judges others and herself superficially, albeit to a point of being humorous and ironic for the reader. Running, for example, is not exhilarating for her; she has no upbeat thoughts on how the exercise will lead to better health and fitness. Rather, she is plagued with guilty feelings for having consumed her favorite ice cream, maple walnut, late the night before: "but why still eat then, why stuff oneself and then when one is already no longer size 36, and size 38 the absolute limit, one should not be any larger, no way."[16] She constantly tries to rationalize what she sees as her odd eating habits, as well as her personal life now that she has turned thirty. As her friends and family constantly remind her that her "biological clock" has begun to tick, Jessica envisions "fucking as a basic right."[17] She laments the narrow options for a fulfilling career with a mass-market magazine while telling herself that her body is too old for the usual day jobs: "waitressing isn't possible any more, my dear, there are many more enthusiastic people than you who can do that much better, and you don't look young enough anymore for such jobs, you'll never get them anymore, my dear."[18] She reexamines her life in her apartment, shared with other women who are controlling and envious; her missed opportunity with her previous boyfriend, Harti, who is now a doctor with good earnings; her relationship to her mother, who taught her so much and whom Jessica now believes is the only person really interested in her; her fashion choices as real "fashion statements" (68); and her thoughts about her boss, Claudia, who has "5 orgasms in one meeting and thus can stay calm" (74).

Connected with thoughts about her own life come those of media personalities and stars, such as Ostwalt Kolle, the German journalist and commentator on sexual issues (15, 29); the author of the "Sextipps" column every Sunday in the *Krone-Zeitung* (84, 86); Dawson's Creek, the popular TV series from the late 1990s on teen sexuality (125, 190); Kylie Monogue, the Australian supermodel (126); and Angelina Jolie, sex symbol and tabloid star (230). In her sarcastic personal comments on public figures Jessica spares few key Austrian politicians as well. Among others are Susanne Riess-Passer, Vice-Chancellor until 2002 of the conservative FPÖ (Freedom Party of Austria), who represents to Jessica the epitome of superficiality:

> Riess-Passer has an insanely high judgement regarding competency, competency of superficiality, and we of the Post-*Brigitte* [a magazine oriented mostly towards women over thirty-five] generations, we can make something out of every guy, "you only have to make the effort."[19]

Federal Chancellor Wolfgang Schüssel is "this puppet chancellor" ("dieser Kasperlkanzer"; 121), the eternal politician whose entrenchment has made political change impossible: "Mr. Schüssel is still in politics, he has only done politics, he has always participated in politics; what we have today, he has participated in and how then should he get us out of it."[20] Federal President Thomas Klestil receives mention in the context of "die Klestil-Women," his mistresses, who became tabloid stars in Austria (79). About finance minister Karl-Heinz Grasser Jessica asks: "Do you think he even knows what prostitution is? He comes across so fishy to me, so truly cold fishy."[21]

The pervasive presence of political figures within the literary text continually reminds readers of the on-going questions regarding legal and illegal prostitution and the increasing problem of sex trafficking of women in Austria as enumerated in Lesley Bart's essay. Interestingly and ironically, even the names of two prominent clients of the Viennese escort service implicated in the scandal in August 2004 receive mention. The first is American reparations lawyer Ed Fagan, who represented Holocaust victims in lawsuits against the Swiss government and also represented victims in the mountain railway disaster in Kaprun, Austria, in November 2000. Jessica sees him as unaware of cultural differences between the United States and Austria, a theme that surfaces throughout the novel: "Gerhard would also say that Mr. Fagan will soon be instructed that he is in Austria and not in America, and that a different kind of wind blows here."[22] And second, "the Khol" ("der Khol") comes up in conversation between Jessica and Gerhard—yes, the same Andreas Khol who unbeknownst to Jessica was ringing up the leaders of the sex-trafficking rings while she jogged through Vienna; here he is criticized for his long-wind sermons: "he can't get enough of such appearances, because he can preach his sermons. He is sadistic then, you can't imagine it. It's like in school when the teacher says the same thing every hour."[23]

In contemplating the lives of these well-known people, Jessica becomes intent on connecting or not connecting her own lifestyle with those of the beautiful and famous. The TV series *Sex and the City* acts as an initial reference point for her. For those familiar with this show, this should come as no surprise. Take, for example, the first episode, which premiered on June 6, 1998. At Miranda's thirty-something birthday party, her friends Carrie and Samantha and Miranda herself decide to start having sex "like men," or at least like how they see men having sex, namely, without feeling. Carrie, played by Sarah Jessica Parker (one cannot help but wonder whether she was Jessica's namesake), agrees to try the idea out first on her ex-boyfriend. To her surprise, he does not mind being used as a sex object, causing the deconstruction of all kinds of gender stereotypes.

Jessica obviously sees herself in the model of the successful, independent women in *Sex and the City*, and indeed she is, as a single, well-educated, working woman, by far the most independent of Streeruwitz's protagonists. That independence implies that Jessica possesses a strong sense of her own sexuality, but it also means she must face contradictions. The attempt of the *Sex and the City* protagonists to have sex "like a man" evokes the work of Ariel Levy again, the author of *Female Chauvinist Pigs*, who analyzes *Sex and the City* as exerting a tremendous amount of cultural power in its presentation of "a complete lifestyle package—what to wear, where to eat, when to drink (always), who to have sex with—for the high-end, urban liberated woman" (174). As in Jessica's world, "the truly defining pursuit of [the *Sex and the City* protagonists'] world wasn't sex so much as it was consumption" (172). Through this constantly moving protagonist and her prose, the reader is swept up in Jessica's alternating fascination with and questioning of women selling their bodies and of men talking about women selling their bodies.[24]

Yet according to Jessica's thoughts, modern media alone cannot account for the possible causal connection between the portrayal of sexuality as a commodity and sexual encounters that often end, to quote from Levy, "with someone feeling like a conqueror and someone feeling compromised" (174). Years of literary texts, too, which, as we shall see in Jessica's analysis of these texts, portray male figures in dominant roles and female figures in submissive roles, have contributed significantly to this connection between conqueror and compromised. This relationship depicting men in power over women is very much akin to the possible relationship that Lesley Bart has observed between legalized prostitution and the increase in sex trafficking. Jessica as a Germanist loves to read, although within the mind/body split that Hollitzer has laid out for her, she also has guilty feelings about others discovering this passion of hers. She admits her guilt at the possibility of people spying in through her uncovered window as she sits and reads on the couch and drinks a glass of wine: "yesterday one could have seen me reading for 4 hours."[25] Another time she expresses nostalgia for days when she could sit and read all day out of enjoyment, a pleasure that her studies have threatened to squelch:

> and to spend the whole day on the back porch, and read, what a pleasure, only reading, oh, I want that to continue, this greedy reading, that happens only at the beginning, that gets lost, that is like children's drawings, this eagerness, that gets lost, and academic studies didn't bring it back, actually I would have thought, you study German literature and the pleasure of reading would become more exquisite.[26]

Here Jessica's guilty feelings and her wish for the days when reading was not linked to studies that squelch the pleasure hark back to the difficulties of combining the life of the mind with a socially acceptable career. She shows signs of having internalized the belief that the life of the mind is non-productive. Moreover, her voracious reading patterns suggest an interesting parallel between reading as desire engendering guilt and sex as desire engendering guilt, not to mention the idealized, initial excitement of first encounters, whether sexual or literary, and the destruction of pleasure through experience and expertise. These emotions play into the banalization of "casual sex" to which Levy alludes.[27]

Still, Jessica obviously takes great pleasure in analyzing literature and applying it to real life. What works then serve to guide her in her pursuit of truth? Works by the American writer Charles Bukowski and the French writer Michel Houllebecq represent late-twentieth- and early twenty-first-century literature by men that provokes Jessica to perceive interconnections between consumerism, violence, sex, and gender relations. Early in the novel there is the reference to a story by Bukowski, an author whom readers have described as "wild and weird . . . a madman, a recluse, a lover . . . tender, vicious . . . ."[28] At one point Jessica contemplates creating a series of articles to present to her boss, Claudia, at the women's magazine, a series not very unlike *Sex and the City*, "an 'Everything-About Sex'-Series, 'More Than Everything About Sex' and what the human consumer has to do with sex,"[29] not a story as would appear in *Cosmopolitan*, not "glamorous masturbation,"[30] but how "it is" from a women's perspective, a story that men most likely would not read, she laments. Then she comes to Bukowski: "with Bukowski there is this story that he has to come, while a whore works his dick, and he doesn't want to and still he has to come and is totally embarrassed about it and that's exactly what it's about."[31] The story could come from Bukowski's enormous repertoire of stories about men's sexual relations with women, stories that readers find "come pounding out of his violent and depraved life . . . horrible and holy" (see book cover). What most preoccupies Jessica, however, is whether she should show the story to her friend Katrin and what her reaction would be. Would she believe it all because the writer is a man? Would she believe that a woman could write that way?

> Katrin will have to read that sometime, what Mr. Bukowski has invented there, and whether he's lying, or will she read that from a man and accept it and consider women stronger, or does she not consider women so exposed, sexually organic.[32]

For Jessica, the fascination of connecting the images that we have in our minds of how sex is with possible renditions of how reality really is drives us to devour the cultural literature that we love. We all want to know what it's like, thinks Jessica, in intertextual references that follow not too far on the heels of Bukowski, namely to Michel Houellebecq, of whom she thinks subsequently:

> that's why Houellebecq has such sales numbers, because he describes exactly how it is to sleep with whores and then everyone else would be able to go there and would already know how it is and what he has to feel, how it feels, how it must be[33]

Houellebecq is best-known for his novels that graphically, honestly, and often ironically portray one man's rather perverted view of sexuality. In his 2001 work *Platforme: Au milieu du monde,* to which Jessica refers later, he follows the main character, Michel Renault, a modern-day Meursault-like character from Camus's *L'Etranger*, who shows little emotion when his father dies at the beginning of the novel, and who lives a life as a civil servant devoid of close friendships, pleasures, and fulfilling sexual relationships. Instead, he finds solace in prepared dinners, visits to massage parlors, pornography, and masturbation. On a group holiday to

Thailand he meets Valerie, with whom he later takes up a relationship when they return to Paris. At one point Valerie wants to know: "What have Thai girls got that Western women don't?" (89). Michel answers that Western men don't feel appreciated by Western women. The typical Thai woman "would be happy to find someone who simply does his job and hopes to come home to a pleasant family life after work. Most Western women do not want such a boring husband. . . . As Western women do not appreciate men . . . as they do not value traditional family life, marriage is not the right thing for them" (89-90). For Michel, the downfall of male/female relationships lies in the fact that women are becoming more like men.

Valerie and Michel engage in some very kinky sex acts together, such as visiting an S&M parlor, participating in ménages à quatre, and making love on the streets. They eventually begin a sex-tourist venture in Thailand which ends in disaster when Islamic fundamentalists bomb one of the hotels in protest against the immoral Western behavior happening there. Valerie dies in the explosion. In contemplating their relationship after her death, Michel realizes that she has really been his greatest love. Jessica, however, fails to be moved by his love and remarks: "even in 'Platform' the love of one's life has to appear, and that's the reason this book scares me so much."[34]

Other authors who enter Jessica's thoughts are more canonical, and yet the underlying portrayal of the man as conqueror and the woman as compromised still remains. Henry James's *Daisy Miller*, for example, receives mention, the story of the American girl whom the Europeans find too flirtatious, lively, and unsophisticated (46). The implication at the conclusion of the story is that Daisy's death was surely deserved in the end. By wandering around late at night alone with an Italian man in the Rome Colosseum, she contracted what was most likely malaria from the insects that bred in the marshes. The implication is that her open sexuality led to her demise. The American narrator, however, may feel as if he conquered in the end, as her admission that she was not engaged to marry the Italian suggested that she really did have eyes for the American suitor.

In addition to the compromised Daisy, at least twice Jessica mentions Hedda Gabler and her own "Hedda-Gabler-Feeling" inspired by Ibsen's play.[35] Hedda is the strong-willed, independent protagonist who sees suicide as her only escape from a life bound to sexual favors to a man she does not love. In the play Judge Brack knows Hedda's secret of having been privy to the downfall of her former lover, Lövborg, by supplying the pistols with which he shot the real love of his life and himself. In knowing that Judge Brack knows about her indirect role as accomplice, and in knowing that he will try to blackmail her into giving him "pleasure in life," Hedda implies that she cannot bear the thought of indulging the judge while he holds the secret above her head. Thus, she decides to shoot herself with her husband's pistol.

Austrian literature does not get spared in Jessica's ruminations either. When talking about her previous boyfriend, Alfred, who admitted to her on a trip to Venice that he did not want to sleep with her anymore, she compares his way of talking to her to the female characters in a Musil play, most likely the academic gushers in *Die Schwärmer*: "he talked like one of the women characters in this Musil piece, a person finding himself."[36] Alfred's actions and words also remind her of Schnitzler's *Anatol*, which for Jessica represents the epitome of male-controlled love trysts, albeit humorous and witty. Ironically, Jessica equates the scene in Venice to "the last scene in 'Anatol,' when he walks around so melancholically on the patio."[37]

All these tragic female and male figures lead Jessica to assert: "the most beautiful heroes of novels are those invented by women."[38] Surprisingly, however, Jessica hardly talks at all about any of these "most beautiful heroes" or heroines, nor much about the female authors who have created them. With a passion for detective novels, she mentions writers such as Marcia Muller and Sue Grafton, creators of the strong female detectives Sharon McCone and Kinsey Millhone, respectively. As for other women writers, there is the passing reference to Ingeborg Bachmann's personal relationships and the power she exerted in refusing sexual advances: "I understand the stories about Bachman, how it's whispered around that she didn't let anyone really."[39] But there is no mention of any of Bachmann's literary figures, nor those of her Austrian colleagues, such as Elfriede Jelinek, Marlene Haushofer, Ilse Aichinger, Christine Lavant, or even Streeruwitz herself. The silence is deafening. Perhaps here, too, it is difficult to find positive role models. This silence appears to belong again to what Helga Schreckenberger has analyzed in Seductions (*Verführungen*) and Lisa's Love (*Lisas Liebe*), and what Streeruwitz herself has coined as "the poetics of silence."[40] Moreover, with respect to the feminist theoretical underpinnings that mark Streeruwitz's works, the silence seems like a tacit lament about the absence and powerlessness of women relative to their male counterparts, even in the literary field. Given the pervasive intertwining of the literary with the political in the novel, in focusing her thoughts mainly on male authors, Jessica implicitly calls for an incrimination of the men involved in prostitution, not the women. This incrimination would support a viable solution to the burgeoning sex trade which Lesley Bart has mentioned, namely tighter regulations and penalties for the men who control the women and brothels.

The barrage of literary images has caused Jessica to contemplate her options in life and to evaluate her own personal and public situation more keenly.[41] The constant interplay between the personal and political in the novel harkens back to one of the founding adages of Second Wave Feminists, namely, that the personal is political. In the middle, more dialogic section of the novel, the personal body does really become political, yet the added twist is that the political turns personal as well. Thus, an analysis of exactly what occurs during Hollitzer's late-night visit to Jessica is important. First, the two talk about the nature of relationships, including comments on the ways in which the private and the public intersect, or not, in Austrian culture, especially in contrast to American ways. Jessica, who has always been careful to draw the drapes when they make out on the living room couch so as not to jeopardize Hollitzer's career and turn their private affair into a political scandal, is surprised that Gerhard has allowed his chauffeur just to drop him off at her door: "I am still amazed that everything is not stricter. In no other country could you get away so easily from your bodyguards."[42] To this, Hollitzer points out the freedom that Austrian politicians have in relation to the United States and England:

> "That's Austria! That is one of the advantages in Austria. . . ."
> "Dear!! We're not in America. I mean, nothing goes totally unnoticed. But how should it be. Do you think that really interests anybody? OK, since the Klestil-stories it's gotten a little rougher here. . . . Thank God we don't have these women's organizations here, which set up such pursuits as in England. We have it better. Here we have more freedom. You don't worry. You don't have anything to lose!"[43]

The Austrian politician thinks he can escape the threat of having the personal turn political and the political turn personal. Little does he know the impossibility of this maneuver.

The layers of the personal go deeper as Jessica continues to have her own private thoughts that comment on, and often contradict what she tells Hollitzer in their dialogue. When Hollitzer begins to move too quickly in his sexual forays, she asks him to slow down:

> "That with the falling all over each other, that only happens in the beginning. When you know each other a little bit. I find it nicer when one takes one's time. I've always thought that it really only begins when one isn't in such a hurry."[44]

Then privately she thinks, "and when he holds me like this from behind, that's OK, because I don't have to smell him and if it's enough for him to touch me."[45] And then later she questions her own motives: "and you can't sleep with a man whom you can't stand the smell of because he's eaten cheese sausages."[46] While the reader is able to see the irony in these explanatory statements and to liken them to a Woody Allen movie in which the characters say one thing to each other, but the subtitles project inner erotic thoughts, there is more than just an irony between character and reader at work here. Jessica shows herself trying to take control of the situation. In maintaining her humor she attempts to hold sovereignty over the situation, yet shows her capacity for human vulnerability as well, especially where the erotic is involved.

In a simple twist of fate, Hollitzer is the one who finds himself in the vulnerable position of being undressed. After gently telling Jessica to go to sleep on the couch, he slips into the bathroom and returns naked. "Shit, he's undressed," exclaims Jessica to herself. "'Oh. I thought I'd make myself comfortable," states Hollitzer. The reader discerns what happens afterwards only through reading Jessica's private thoughts, „'What are you doing, my love, joking, Jessica, joking, and take him into your hand, you can't just let this thing flap around.'"[47] Again, she attempts to have the upper hand (!) in the situation. As the scene progresses (or regresses, depending on your point of view), rather than allow him to penetrate her, she decides to perform oral sex. Hollitzer reacts at first rather defensively, aware of what he fears is his own helplessness: "Why don't you get undressed? That's unfair. You sit enthroned over me and I am totally helpless. No. O yes. Please go on and yes, I say yes already."[48] The irony of this situation lies not only in the switch in the usual gendered positions. In his nakedness, Hollitzer, and not Jessica, ends up being the "Miss Else" of the novel, to draw on previously mentioned intertextual references, exposing his vulnerability for all the world to see, for, after all, he did not insist that Jessica pull the drapes.

In the end of the second chapter, after Hollitzer has humiliated her during the oral sex scene, he makes an effort at reconciliation by offering to satisfy her sexually. Jessica says "no," but her inner thoughts admit that she doesn't know if she means "no." As Hollitzer begins to stroke her with his hand in an attempt to arouse her, she tells him "no": "You, Gerhard, I think I have to sleep now, really, I can't now, that is, that is not now,"[49] but she thinks to herself:

> and actually I would like to, actually, how is that, I don't want to at all, I can't want that, there is such a stream, such a dark stream, from the navel to some kind of deep place and following that I could do it now and what

> that means, how did this masochism come to me, why would that absolutely please me and dirty me in such a way that I would be content, that would be like a kind of order to me and "Come on, leave it, now is not the right time, really, I don't want to!"[50]

Still, he accepts the "no" and leaves. Hence, the scene ends in personal humiliation for Jessica, but in public humiliation for Gerhard.

Until this point in the novel, there has been no mention of the prostitution ring in which Hollitzer and other politicians have participated, the so-called Panhans, involving trafficking in women from Eastern Europe. Jessica has not known about its existence or the politicians' participation. Only in the third and final chapter do the details surface. On the plane on her way to report the Panhans story to a German journalist from *Stern*, Jessica contemplates the possible impact of her reporting the story. In her thoughts the sexual violence, consumerism, and political hypocrisy that connect the personal, the political, and the literary merge. She envisions a Broadway theater piece about Monica Lewinsky and Bill Clinton, forging an ultimate link between making love and making war, not avoiding, of course, her last chance to reflect again on Schnitzler's *Anatol*:

> but the Broadway play is surely being written right now, the meeting between the two [Monica and Bill], that would be an Anatol without the melancholy, but with a war, like the guy who bombed Iraq a little, so that everyone can look over there, the war that was still outstanding for Anatol, but the latest wars have brought about sexual repression again, with this war now, prudishness has come back, it is an outlet, it is a relief for the nightly need to function in bed, the men are hitting back and taking revenge out on the dating system and double-dating, where everyone learns right away when someone doesn't get his dick up and in America the young men are the most scared that they won't get a woman, that happens long before the career wishes, and then they would rather go to war than on a date, where they have to prove themselves, and then they are traumatized enough to be allowed to have problems[51]

What begins as speculations about a new literary piece turns into an exposé on the ways in which war and violence have become the means to compensate for men's feelings of inadequacy. Subsequently, Jessica's literary knowledge leads her to observe the reading material of the other passengers, which grounds inhumane actions in consumer capitalism: "they are reading Dickens to find out how to transform a society into a real achievement-oriented society."[52]

In bringing the illegal sex trafficking affair to the press, Jessica chooses her battle carefully. As a literary scholar, she realizes that she needs hard evidence. She reviews that evidence many times over, as in the following passage:

> I have the piece of evidence from the party, I have the dates. . . ; I have the interview with Vera [one of the prositutes], I have photos of the apartment in Panhans, we know when and where the women were picked up, where they were taken, how long they were there, when they went away, how many there were, and it is clear that they were there for these seminars because the party paid the security service for the transportation[53]

She does not have such proof in the case of Hollitzer's abuse against Mia, just one person's word against the other's. Her own humiliating sexual incident becomes murky when defining exactly what sex and rape are. Paragraph 201 in Austrian law sees rape as violence that robs personal freedom or that is harmful to life and limb through engaging in or enduring sexual intercourse or an act equivalent to sexual intercourse.[54] Is fellatio "sexual intercourse or an act equivalent to sexual intercourse?" Or, to put it in American English: Is it sex? Did he have sex with this woman? On top of this gray area in defining sex lies the question as to the extent to which Jessica was "forced," a complication drawn from the fact that rape in a marriage was first made illegal in Austria in 1989, thus also questioning the notion of date rape. Did Jessica, in admitting her own "masochism" at wanting to have sex after her humiliation, consequently make it difficult for her to argue that she had been coerced?

The bondage of her friend Mia has shown Jessica that Hollitzer is capable of violence against women, and it is for this reason that she wants to bring the story of the illegal sex trafficking ring to the media. The final irony is that the media are in Germany, not Austria. Jessica may harbor the need for revenge or redress after her own personal, sexual humiliation. Her exposure of the illegal prostitution ring, however, indicates her own recognition that she must move away from the self-absorption that characterized her initial reflections while jogging. She thereby progresses on to acknowledge a political reality that involves many women who may not be able to find complete justice in Austria. In fact, she insists on her own "prohibition against revenge" ("Racheverbot"; 183). By the end of the novel, she has transitioned on from the social norms of beauty that faced her at the beginning to an awareness of those norms as forces that lead more to the exploitation of women, such as those in the sex trade, than to their empowerment.

Through a keen sense of literary and media figures that have formed cultural images of women, Jessica comes to understand the limited options that women have had in confronting those norms. She refuses to remain like the passive women subjected to the violence in Bukowski's and Houellebecq's stories. Luckily, she does not meet the fate of Miss Else, Daisy Miller, Hedda Gabler, or Valerie. Jessica does not have to end her own life, unable to cope with the consequences of her nakedness, symbolic or real. In having the undressed politician Hollitzer stand in front of (and lie beneath) a fully clothed Jessica, Streeruwitz exerts a sarcastic critique not only on the political body and on body politics, but also on a society whose aesthetics have bowed to obsessions over beauty, functionality, and consumerism. From her observations of media images and literary scenarios, she knows the forces she must combat. Ultimately, Jessica shows that the life of the body cannot exist without the life of the mind.

Works Cited

Baumgardner, Jennifer, and Amy Richards. *Manifesta: Young Women, Feminism, and the Future*. New York: Farrar, Straus, and Giroux, 2000.

BKA/RIS Bundesrecht. BGBl. Nr. 60/1974 zuletzt geändert durch BGBl. I Nr. 15/2004. "Vergewaltigung." Gesetzsnummer 10002296, Dokumentnummer NOR40050386. <http://www.ris.bka.gv.at>. Accessed on 15 January 2007.

Bukowski, Charles. *Tales of Ordinary Madness*. San Francisco, CA: City Lights Books, 1983.

Butler, Judith. "Contingent Foundations: Feminism and the Question of 'Postmodernism.'" In Butler and Scott, 3-21.

Butler, Judith, and Joan W. Scott, eds. *Feminists Theorize the Political*. New York: Routledge, 1992.

Ensler, Eve. *The Vagina Monologues*. New York: Villard Books/Random House, 1998.

—. *Die Vagina-Monologe*. Translated by Peter Staatsmann and Bettina Schültke. Hamburg: Nautilus, 1999.

Fiddler, Allyson. "Modernist or Postmodernist? The Absurd Question in Marlene Streeruwitz." In *Centre Stage: Contemporary Drama in Austria*. Edited by Frank Finlay and Ralf Jeutter. Amsterdam: Rodopi, 1999. 57-72.

Houellebecq, Michel. *Platform*. Translated by Frank Wynne. New York: Alfred A. Knopf, 2003.

Hutcheon, Linda. *A Poetics of Postmodernism. History, Theory, Fiction.* New York: Routledge, 1988.

Huyssen, Andreas, and Klaus R. Scherpe, eds. *Postmoderne: Zeichen eines kulturellen Wandels*. Reinbek bei Hamburg: Rowohlt, 1997.

Ibsen, Henrik. *Hedda Gabler. The Collected Works of Henrik Ibsen*, 10. New York: Charles Scribner's Sons, 1914. 1-185.

James, Henry. *Daisy Miller*. New York: Modern Library, 2002.

Jameson, Fredric. *Postmodernism, or, The Cultural Logic of Late Capitalism*. Durham, NC: Duke University Press, 1991.

Kallin, Britta. "Marlene Streeruwitz's *Nachwelt* as Feminist Postmodern Biography." *German Quarterly* 78 (2005): 337-56.

Kedveš, Alexandra. "'Geheimnisvoll. Vorwurfsvoll. Aber zusammenhängend.' Marlene Streeruwitz' Romane, Frauengeschichten, Männersprache." *Marlene Streeruwitz. Text und Kritik* 164 (Oct. 2004): 19-36.

Levy, Ariel. *Female Chauvinist Pigs: Women and the Rise of Raunch Culture*. New York: Free Press, 2005.

Moser, Gerda E. "Die Romantik ist die Schwester der Pornographie. Jelineks *Lust*, Marlene Streeruwitz' *Jessica, 30* und Vergleichbares aus der Populärkultur." In *"Klug und stark, schön und erotisch:" Idyllen und Ideologien des Glücks in der Literatur und in anderen Medien.* Edited by Gerda E. Moser, Katharina Herzmansky, and Friedbert Aspetsberger. Innsbruck: Studien Verlag, 2006. 187-209.

Muscio, Inga. *Cunt: A Declaration of Independence*. New York: Seal Press, 2002.

"Oberösterreich: Sorge um Verblassen der 'grünen Handschrift.'" *Standard* 28 October 2005. <http://derstandard.at/?url=/?id=2223092>. Accessed 15 January 2007.

Schnitzler, Arthur. *Anatol*. Stuttgart: Reclam, 1979.

Schreckenberger, Helga. "Die 'Poetik des Banalen' in Marlene Streeruwitz' Romanen *Verführungen* und *Lisas Liebe*." *Modern Austrian Literature* 31.3/4 (1998): 135-47.

Streeruwitz, Marlene. "Ich schreibe vor allem gegen, nicht *für* etwas. Interview with Willy Riemer and Sigrid Berka." *German Quarterly* 71.1 (1997): 47-60.

—. *Können. Mögen. Dürfen. Sollen. Wollen. Müssen. Lassen*. Frankfurt a. M.: Suhrkamp, 1998.

—. *Jessica, 30. Roman*. Frankfurt a. M.: S. Fischer, 2004.

—. *Sein. Und Schein. Und Erscheinen. Tübinger Poetikvorlesungen.* Frankfurt a. M.: Suhrkamp, 1997.

Streitler, Nicole Katja. "Marlene Streeruwitz: *Jessica, 30.*" <http://www.literaturhaus.at/buch/buch/rez/streeruwitz-Jessica30/> 29 June 2004. Accessed 26 March 2005.

Wappis, Bernhard. *„Darüber spricht man(n) nicht . . .!": Magersucht und Bulimie bei Männern*. Norderstedt: Books on Demand, 2005.

Weimann, Robert, and Hans U. Gumbrecht, eds. *Postmoderne—Globale Differenz*. Frankfurt a. M.: Suhrkamp, 1991.

Wolf, Naomi. *The Beauty Myth: How Images of Beauty Are Used Against Women*. New York: Doubleday, 1991.

Notes

[1] See endnote 1 in Lesley Bart's essay in this volume.

[2] Hollitzer's title in the novel is "ÖVP Staatssekretär für Zukunfts- und Entwicklungsfragen." The ÖVP (Österreichische Volkspartei) is a real party in Austria, but the title is fictitious.

[3] Such a coalition is not a fiction, but was actually under discussion in 2003, and one did come to fruition in Oberösterreich (see "Oberösterreich").

[4] "'Und manchmal, weißt du, da finde ich Huren interessanter und die würden dir die Augen auskratzen, wenn du ihnen sagen würdest, dass wir sie ausbeuten. Die verstehen von Freiheit um einiges mehr, als ihr da so in eurer Verspieltheit und diese Frauen, diese Frauen arbeiten wirklich, für ihr Geld. Die müssen wirklich für ihr Geld arbeiten, weißt du. Ein wirkliches Leben, das schafft ihr doch alle nicht. Du doch auch nicht. Du lebst doch auch noch vom Papa'" (166).

[5] I cannot possibly do justice here to all the scholarship written on feminism and postmodernism. The following provide good introductions to postmodern theories: Hutcheon, Huyssen and Scherpe, Jameson, and Weimann and Gumbrecht. For the relationship between postmodernism and feminism see Butler and Scott, and especially Butler's essay in that same volume.

[6] "Und jede Verwunderung darüber, daß es sich in der Postmoderne nur prozeßhaft und diskursiv leben läßt, ist ein Angriff aus der Vormoderne. Ein Angriff der direkten Patriarchate der Religionen und des Nationalismus. . . . Es muß in einer nicht patriarchalen Poetik um Entkolonialsierung gehen" (*Können*, 22).

[7] "Erst wenn von beiden Seiten [der männlichen und der weiblichen] der Aufbruch in ein Anderes gewagt wird, kann Freiheit von Unterdrückung und Unterdrücken beginnen. Und. Wir wissen, daß die Unterdrückten mehr wissen als die Unterdrücker. Mehr wissen müssen. Aus diesem Grund wäre es notwendig zu beginnen, den Frauen zuzuhören" (26).

[8] "Driven by the necessity to describe the unspeakable, I have found silence, pause, the period as strangulation mark as artistic means and the citation as a means of escape, and thus to help the unspeakable surface" ["Ich habe durch die Notwendigkeit des Akts der Beschreibung eines Unsagbaren im Ausdruck zu

Kunstmitteln wie Stille, Pause, dem Punkt als Würgemal und dem Zitat als Fluchtmittel gefunden, um damit dem Unsagbaren zur Erscheinung zu verhelfen"] (*Sein.Und Schein*, 48).

[9] "Eine Poetik des Banalen. Eine Poetik des Schweigens" (*Sein. Und Schein*, 71).

[10] See endnote 8 above. In reference to Streeruwitz's first novel, Alexandra Kedveš writes: "*Seductions* worked with a personal female narrator who looked back retrospectively, conversations were recounted in indirect speech full of subjunctives, and thus from the beginning the narrative situation created distance and displayed language as a negotiating and negotiated strategy" ["*Verführungen* arbeitete mit einer rückblickenden personalen Erzählerin, Gespräche wurden in der indirekten Rede voller Konjunktive wiedergegeben, und so schuf die Erzählsituation von vornherein Distanz und stellte die Sprache als vermittelnde und vermittelte Strategie aus"] (33-34).

[11] The term "Blümchensex" is a variation on the more commonly used word "Blümchenkaffee," originally characterizing coffee that is so weak that one can see through it to the little flowers imprinted at the bottom of the coffee cup.

[12] "was für ein wunderbares Maschinchen, der Körper, wenn alles so läuft und nichts anderes existiert" (10).

[13] Feminists in most Western countries now distinguish between three major eras: a so-called "First Wave," occurring in the latter half of the eighteenth century and the beginning of the nineteenth century, which battled for the vote and then later equal rights amendments and treatises in politics; a later "Second Wave," beginning in the 1960s, which attempted to establish reproductive freedom, job equity, and equality in matters that affected personal lives, such as family care and childcare; and now, most recently, the "Third Wave." This brief description, of course, does not reflect all the complexities and diversities in feminist theories for each of these eras. It also does not take into account much overlap in concerns, especially between the Second and Third Waves. For more information see especially Baumgardner and Richards.

[14] "'You young women have such a way of talking about that!'" ["'Ihr jungen Frauen habt schon eine Art darüber zu reden!'"] (153-54); "'. . . and yes, I am a piggish stoneage monster, but you young women, you all have to decide what you want'" ["'. . . und ja, ich bin ein schweinisches Steinzeitmonster, aber ihr jungen Frauen, ihr müsst euch halt auch einmal entscheiden, wie ihr es wollt'"] (162). "'Oh, there is the accusation again that we are not romantic. That we don't know any more what romanticism is. That we don't have any more romantic stories. But I'll tell you something, I prefer having no romantic stories and because of that I can say what I would like and what not, and beforehand and not afterwards, like here'" ["'Ah, das ist wieder der Vorwurf, dass wir nicht romantisch sind. Dass wir gar nicht mehr wissen, was Romantik ist. Dass wir gar keine romantischen Geschichten mehr haben. Aber ich sage dir etwas, ich habe lieber keine romantischen Geschichten und dafür kann ich immer sagen, was ich möchte und was nicht, und zwar vorher und nicht danach, so wie hier'" (158). For a discussion of the interaction between the romantic, the erotic, and the pornographic in *Jessica, 30.* within the context of cultural studies, see Moser.

[15] Baumgardner and Richards, 21. The concentration on the body for the newer generation of feminists began largely with Naomi Wolf's *The Beauty Myth* (1991). This study began then to incite women to look more positively at their natural bodies, a movement that found resonance through Eve Ensler's play *The Vagina Monologues* (translated shortly thereafter into German and reaching a wide audience in both Germany and Austria) and Inga Muscio's book *Cunt.* Issues such as anorexia and bulima began to occupy studies of women and, more recently, men. For an insightful study of the latter in Austria, see Wappis's recent study, which includes an extensive bibliography of research on eating disorders in men and women.
[16] "aber warum dann noch essen, warum in sich hineinstopfen und doch ohnehin schon keine Größe 36 mehr und Größe 38 die absolute Grenze, mehr darf es nicht werden, auf keinen Fall. . . " (12).
[17] "das Ficken als Grundrecht" (51).
[18] "kellnern geht nicht mehr, meine Liebe, da gibt es viele Eifrigere als dich, die das viel besser können, und du schaust nicht mehr jung genug aus, für solche Jobs, die kriegst du gar nicht mehr, meine Liebe . . ." (79).
[19] "die Riess-Passer hat eine irrsinnig hohe Beurteilung bei der Kompetenz, die Kompetenz an der Oberfläche und wir Post-Brigitte Generationen, wir können ja aus jedem Typ etwas machen, you only have to make the effort" (43).
[20] "der Herr Schüssel ist jetzt schon immer in der Politik, der hat doch nur Politik gemacht, der hat immer Politik mitgemacht, das, was wir heute haben, das hat der mitgemacht und wieso soll der uns jetzt herausholen" (50).
[21] "Glaubst du, der weiß überhaupt, was Prostitution ist? Mir kommt der so fischig vor, so richtig kalt fischig" (146).
[22] "und der Gerhard würde ja auch sagen, dass man dem Herrn Fagan schon noch beibringen wird, dass er in Österreich und nicht in Amerika ist, und dass hier ein anderer Wind weht" (112).
[23] "der kann von solchen Auftritten gar nicht genug kriegen, da kann er seine Predigten halten. Der ist da sadistisch, das kannst du dir nicht vorstellen. Das ist wie in der Schule dieser Lehrer, der jede Stunde dasselbe erzählt" (156).
[24] Levy's further discussion of *Sex and the City* is relevant to my analysis of *Jessica, 30.* here: "Little by little, the show became less about women having 'sex like men' and more about the characters trying to negotiate their independence as they pursued intimacy with lovers, husbands, children, and each other" (171). "The ethos of the show was all about women getting themselves the best and the most, sexually and materially. They were unapologetically selfish, and civic-mindedness was scoffed at" (173). "[T]he fantasy Manhattan of *Sex and the City* was a sphere in which sex was just another commodity, something to be acquired rather than shared, so sexual encounters often ended with someone feeling like a conqueror and someone feeling compromised" (174). "*Sex and the City* was great entertainment, but it was a flawed guide to empowerment, which is how many women viewed it" (175-76).
[25] "gestern hätte man mich 4 Stunden lang lesen sehen können" (13).

[26] "und den ganzen Tag auf der Veranda nach hinten hinaus, und lesen, was für ein Vergnügen, nur lesen, ach, ich wollte, das ginge noch, dieses gierige Lesen, das geht wohl nur am Anfang, das geht verloren, das ist wie die Kinderzeichnungen, dieser Eifer, das verliert sich, und das Studium hat da nichts zurückgebracht, eigentlich hätte ich mir das gedacht, du studierst Germanistik und das Lesevergnügen wird noch erlesener" (198-99).
[27] I thank Rebecca Thomas for this insightful observation.
[28] Quoted from the book cover of *Tales of Ordinary Madness*.
[29] "eine 'Alles über Sex'-Serie, 'Mehr als alles über Sex' und was der Menschenfresser mit Sex zu tun hat (9-10).
[30] "glamouröses Onanieren" (11).
[31] "bei Bukowski gibt es doch diese Geschichte, dass er kommen muss, während eine Hure seinen Schwanz bearbeitet und er will gar nicht und muss doch kommen und geniert sich fürchterlich dafür und genau darum geht es" (11).
[32] "das muss die Katrin einmal lesen, was der Herr Bukowski da erfunden hat und ob der auch lügt oder liest sie das von einem Mann und akzeptiert es und Frauen hält sie für stärker, oder hält sie Frauen für nicht so ausgeliefert, geschlechtsorganisch" (11).
[33] "deshalb hat der Houellebecq solche Verkaufszahlen, weil er genau beschreibt, wie das ist, mit Huren zu schlafen und dann jeder auch hingehen könnte und schon wüsste, wie das geht, und was er fühlen muss, wie es sich anfühlen muss, wie es sein muss" (22).
[34] "sogar in 'Plattform' muss ja die große Liebe auftreten, und deswegen macht mir ein solches Buch Angst" (98).
[35] "Hedda-Gabler-Gefühl" (47, 62).
[36] "er hat geredet wie eine von den Frauenfiguren aus diesem Musil-Stück, ein Selbstfinder" (225)
[37] "die letzte Szene vom 'Anatol', wenn er so wehmütig auf der Terasse herumwandert" (59).
[38] "die schönsten Romanhelden sind doch die von Frauen erfundenen" (13).
[39] "ich verstehe die Geschichten von der Bachmann, die sie so herumflüstern, dass sie niemanden richtig gelassen hätte," (184). The language here is interesting and hard to translate. The implication could be one of a woman who is able to tease men sexually without letting them go further. Also suggested is the idea that Bachmann had it in her power to let the man have sex with her. Regarding works by Ingeborg Bachmann, another possible intertextual connection that warrants mentioning is Bachmann's story "Das dreißigste Jahr," whose title bears a strong resemblance to *Jessica, 30*. Both are also about aging, but Bachmann's protagonist is a man who meets a worse fate than Streeruwitz's Jessica. I thank Professor Hubert Lengauer for this reference.
[40] See endnote 9.
[41] It would be impossible to analyze all the intertextual connections in this novel. Other authors who surface are Dostoyevsky, Carson McCullers, and D. H. Lawrence.

[42] "'Mich wundert das ohnehin, dass das alles nicht strikter ist. In keinem andern Land könntest du deinen bodyguards so leicht entkommen'" (137-38).
[43] "'Das ist eben Österreich. Das ist einer der Vorteile von Österreich. . . .'"
"'Schatzl! Wir sind ja nicht in Amerika. Ich meine, ganz unbemerkt bleibt nichts. Aber was soll schon sein. Glaubst du das interessiert jemanden? Gut, seit den Klestil-Geschichten, da geht es rauer her. . . . Wir haben hier Gott sei Dank nicht diese Frauenvereine, die solche Verfolgungsjagden anzetteln wie in England. Da geht es uns schon besser. Da haben wir hier mehr Freiheit. Du machst dir doch keine Sorgen. Du hast doch nichts zu verlieren!'" (138)
[44] "'Das mit dem Übereinanderherfallen, das geht doch nur ganz am Anfang. Wenn man sich dann ein bisschen kennt. Ich finde es schöner, wenn man sich Zeit lassen kann dafür. Ich habe geglaubt, dass es dann erst richtig anfängt, wenn man es nicht mehr so eilig hat'" (140).
[45] "und wenn er mich so von hinten hält, das geht, da muss ich ihn nicht riechen und wenn es ihm reicht, dass er mich berührt," (140*)*.
[46] "und du kannst nicht mit einem Mann schlafen, den du nicht riechen kannst, weil er Käsekrainer gegessen hat" (142).
[47] "shit, der hat sich ausgezogen.. . . 'Ach. Ich dachte, ich mache es mir bequem.'. . . was machst du jetzt, meine Liebe, scherzen, Jessica, scherzen, und nimm ihn in die Hand, man kann dieses Ding nicht so herumflappen lassen" (143).
[48] "'Warum ziehst du dich nicht aus. Das ist unfair. Du thronst da über mir und ich bin vollkommen hilflos. Nein. O ja. Bitte, mach das weiter und ja, ich sage ja schon'" (147).
[49] "'Du, Gerhard, ich glaube, ich muss jetzt schlafen, wirklich, ich kann jetzt nicht, das ist, das ist jetzt nicht…'" (173).
[50] "und eigentlich wollte ich, eigentlich, wie kommt das, ich will doch gar nicht, ich kann das nicht wollen und doch, es gibt so einen Strom, so einen dunklen Strom, vom Nabel weg in irgendeine Tiefe und dem folgend könnte ich es jetzt machen und was bedeutet das, wie ist dieser Masochismus in mich hineingekommen, wieso würde mir das absolut gefallen und mich in so einer Art beschmutzen, mit der ich immer zufrieden wäre, das wäre wie ein, wie eine Art Orden wäre mir das und 'Komm, lass das, jetzt ist nicht der richtige Zeitpunkt, wirklich, ich möchte nicht!'" (173).
[51] "aber das Broadwaystück wird sicher gerade geschrieben, das Treffen zwischen den beiden, das wäre dann ein Anatol ohne die Wehmut, dafür mit einem Krieg, wie der den Irak ein bisserl bombardiert hat, damit alle dorthin schauen, der Krieg, der für den Anatol noch ausständig war, aber die letzten Kriege haben die sexuelle Repression wieder instand gesetzt, mit diesem Krieg jetzt, da wird die Prüderie zurückgeholt, der ist ein Ventil wieder, der ist die Entlastung vom nächtlichen Funktionierenmüssen im Bett, damit schlagen die Männer wieder zurück und rächen sich für das dating system und das doubledating, wo jeder gleich erfährt, wenn einer den Schwanz nicht hochkriegt und in Amerika haben die jungen Männer am meisten Angst, dass sie keine Frau kriegen werden, das steht noch lange vor den Karrierewünschen, und da gehen sie lieber in den Krieg, als zu

einem date, wo sie es wieder beweisen müssen, und dann sind sie traumatisiert genug, Schwierigkeiten haben zu dürfen, . . ." (224-25).

[52] "die lesen doch Dickens, damit sie sich informieren, wie man die Gesellschaft wieder in eine echte Leistungsgemeinschaft verwandeln kann" (247-48).

[53] "ich habe den Beleg von der Partei, ich habe die Daten . . .; ich habe das Interview mit der Vera, ich habe Fotos von dem Appartement im Panhans, wir wissen wann und wo die Frauen abgeholt worden sind, wohin sie gebracht wurden, wie lange sie da waren, wann sie wieder weggingen, wie viele es waren, und es ist klar, dass sie für diese Seminare da waren, weil die Partei den Sicherheitsdienst für die Transporte bezahlt hat . . ." (236).

[54] "Vornahme oder Duldung des Beischlafes oder einer dem Beischlaf gleichzusetzenden geschlechtlichen Handlung." The key word here is "Beischlaf," which literally means "sleep together." The law against rape reads: "Whoever forces a person with violence, through the withdrawal of personal freedom or through threatening with present danger for body and life to engage in or endure sexual intercourse or an act equivalent to sexual intercourse is subject to punishment with a prison sentence of six months to ten years" ["Wer eine Person mit Gewalt, durch Entziehung der persönlichen Freiheit oder durch Drohung mit gegenwärtiger Gefahr für Leib oder Leben zur Vornahme oder Duldung des Beischlafes oder einer dem Beischlaf gleichzusetzenden geschlechtlichen Handlung nötigt, ist mit Freiheitsstrafe von sechs Monaten bis zu zehn Jahren zu bestrafen"] (see BKA/RIS).

CHAPTER NINE

PATTERNS OF REPRESENTING MADNESS IN AUSTRIAN FICTION

GEOFFREY C. HOWES

One of the achievements that has resulted from the rising awareness of madness since the publication of Michel Foucault's *Madness and Civilization* (1961; English 1965) has been the effort to reestablish the dignity of the mad, and their right to civic respect and self-determination.[1] The deinstitutionalization movement that started in the fifties, however, removed many of the afflicted from the grim conditions of the mental hospital or closed institution only to place them in a precarious freedom too often lacking in sufficient care, monitoring, and social assistance.[2]

The recognition of the mad as individuals has not yet been fully extended to their role as members of society, and even if the official repression of the mad through law and medicine has seemingly been relaxed, we have not come to terms with the fact that madness itself, and not just our institutions, removes those afflicted from our midst. Those labeled "mentally ill" are not simply (and perhaps heroically) unreasonable and unconventional, as the anti-psychiatric movement would have it;[3] for complex endogenous and exogenous reasons, they lack certain neurological abilities to participate in the elaborate arrangement of fictions that allows our societies to function. Even if these fictions include fear and abuse of the mentally ill, these are just as much reactions to as causes of the fundamental break with society that afflicts the mad. And even if society's functioning usually falls short of what we would wish, involuntary banishment from it is rarely better than participation in it.

The intellectual liberation of madness championed by Foucault and others was an antidote to the excesses of reason that were manifested in the expansion of state power in the Western European states, the medicalization of human experience, and the mechanization of life and death that reached its pinnacle in German National Socialism. On the other hand, this liberation from the domination and limitations of reason romanticized madness and conscripted it into service in a philosophical war that was often waged far away from the daily lives of those afflicted with mental illness.

Foucault, for example, after his epochal historical account of the taming of madness by the powers of law and medicine, concludes *Madness and Civilization* by connecting madness and modern art, by discovering the moment in which art struggles with madness and "seems to drown in the world, to reveal its non-sense," concluding that "by the madness that interrupts it, a work of art opens a void, a moment of silence, a question without answer, provokes a breach without reconciliation where the world is forced to question itself" (Foucault 288). This questioning comes because the mere reason and science of the world cannot contain, and therefore cannot subjugate or explain, the vastness of the non-world opened by the art of certain modern figures who confronted madness in their works and lives: the world that "sought to measure and justify madness through psychology must justify itself before madness, since it measures itself by the excess of works like those of Nietzsche, of Van Gogh, of Artaud" (289).

For Foucault, literature is a prime place where the confrontation between madness and reason, or madness and power, occurs. But in reading literature, we must be careful not to let our descriptive discourses, those informed for example by psychology or psychiatry, subsume this confrontation within what Shoshana Felman calls the "trap" of rhetoric (Felman 30). Working in Foucault's slipstream, Felman proposes in *Writing and Madness* (1978; trl. 1985) a theory of rhetoric as a form of reading that is "rethought, reformulated as the blind *repetition*, the performative enactment of the *rhetoric* of the text (and not of its meaning)" (31). Like Foucault, Felman is interested in "the vanishing point of the uninterpretable toward which the effort of interpretation heads, but where it falls apart" (Felman 32). Interpretation must enact, not explain, this disintegration. Bringing psychology into the process as an explanatory system only mistakes madness for something that can be intellectually domesticated. Rather than attempting to tame it, Felman argues, reading must follow madness as far as it can into what can no longer be articulated.

As banal as it may seem given the heady stakes of Foucault's philosophico-aesthetic gigantomachia and Felman's "madness of rhetoric" (32), what gets lost here is the daily struggle of the mad, the fact that *they* must justify themselves before the *world*. It is an exploitation of the suffering of the mad to make their struggle into a model, a metaphor really, for an intellectual adventure. Mimicking madness in order to experience its power (as Felman suggests) may challenge reason, but it does not reproduce the experience of madness, for madness is not only mental and social, it is also organic.[4] For those whom madness excludes from emotional, economic, and social intercourse with their fellow human beings, it is small comfort that the world as constituted in our limited systems suffers from philosophical inferiority to the "void," the "fundamental absence of language" that marks madness (Foucault 287). The absence of language may be a source of philosophical triumph, but is also a source of nameless suffering for human beings who are meant to act socially but cannot.

In light of this, this essay will take a step back into the meaning of texts while not losing sight of the "vanishing point of the uninterpretable." I will proceed from the assumption that the fictional texts to be examined are not primarily enactments of madness, but representations of it that can afford significant knowledge about how the mad deal with and are dealt with by society. Hence I will view the "vanishing point of the unintepretable" not as a "textual act" (Felman 32) per se, but as a recurring *motif* in Austrian fiction. A striking number of Austrian fictional texts have explored the relationship between the "normal" and the "mad" as a social phenomenon, in terms of the non-clinical interaction of the mad and their fellow human beings. Many of these texts explore the philosophical possibilities of madness by following the madperson to the vanishing point, only to find that the potential triumph of philosophy in fact becomes a tragic loss of humanity, if humanity is defined simply as the ability to interact meaningfully with one's fellow humans. In three texts I have selected for their representative richness, Robert Musil's *The Man without Qualities*, Norbert Gstrein's *Someone*, and Ingeborg Bachmann's *The Book of Franza*, we see that the void, the silence that madness opens up, is at once an indictment of society and, as a loss of society for the mad person, a terrible incursion of the inhuman.

Where Such Ailments are Endemic

In Ingeborg Bachmann's novel fragment *The Book of Franza* (1966-67; trl. 1999), the protagonist's brother Martin Ranner has returned on a hunch to their childhood home in southern Austria in search of his sister Franziska (Franza), who has telegraphed him for help, but not told him where she is. He discovers her in mental turmoil, alternating between an urgently laid-out plan to escape Austria, and the depths of catalepsy. What she says and how she acts make no sense to him, but it finally dawns on him what her problem might be:

> Yet she wasn't quite right, was she? He couldn't believe this was the first he thought of this, and he began to think about the immediate family and all of the distant relatives. In the immediate family there had been no mental illness, which was hard to believe in a country in which such ailments were endemic. But that's how it was, yet despite such reassurance, what Franza said was crazy, namely what she had done or thought she had done, and conjured up. (Bachmann, *The Book of Franza* 31).

The fictional character Martin Ranner repeats a common stereotype of Austria: that it is a country with a high incidence of mental illness. He can hardly believe that his family has escaped this supposed pandemic unscathed, and perhaps it hasn't: in spite of his hopeful probabilistic assessment, according to the evidence before his own eyes, his sister, or at least her behavior, is "crazy."

The stereotype of Austria as a breeding ground for madness appears as well in a more humorous form—although the Bachmann text is droll in its own way—in Anton Kuh's "The Lunatics of Görz," a tale of the First World War published in 1931. The narrator states: "In those days the city of Görz (Gorizia) still belonged to Austria. As a consequence, there was a madhouse there" (Kuh 127).[5] The ensuing story does not explain the natural connection between Austria and madness. Was it the schizoid political and cultural situation of an Austrian-Italian-Slovenian city like Gorizia? Was it an outlandish neurosis that arose from German Austria's domination of local ethnic groups? Was it the dislodged existence of the German-Austrians themselves, who ruled so many places where they did not precisely belong? Whatever the correlation may be, Kuh assumes that his readers will get the joke.

At the same time he reveals something about Austrian attitudes toward the mad. The story tells how a sergeant is given the mission of evacuating the local madhouse, since the Austrians are losing the city to the Italian enemy. When he arrives at the asylum, a gendarme greets him: "Yes, yes, I know, you're here to pick up the lunatics" (128). The word translated here as "lunatic," *Narr*, is a colloquial, pejorative, but somehow still euphemistic German word that means both "fool" and "madman." Spoken with an Austrian accent, the "a" in "Narr" sounds more like an "o." Kuh's narrator observes:

> When an Austrian says *Narr*, a mocking 'o' softens the chalk-white terror of the 'a.' This is not encouraging to the sergeant, who hears only the two jarring 'r's'. (Kuh 128)

This one word, then, contains two related but varied reactions to the mad: fear and contempt. The sergeant hears the fearsome "r," but there is also the mitigating, condescending "o," which suggests mockery but thereby allays fear and thus humanizes the word, moving the *Narr* slightly toward the speaker's own level. Contempt breeds familiarity.

This familiarity turns up again later in the story. After the inmates have been moved to a military barracks, they suddenly and uncharacteristically fall silent. The sergeant and the gendarme peer into the darkened barracks. The gendarme clears his throat, but then thinks better of it:

> "Say," he whispers to the sergeant, 'maybe you better talk to 'em, since you've known 'em longer ..."
> The sergeant steps in front of the barracks and apostrophizes the darkness.
> "Lunatics! ... Good evening!"
> The form of address sounds sharp, the greeting sounds warm." (Kuh 131)

The word "Narren"("lunatics") once again contains fear and contempt, expressed also in the sharpness of this "title," but the rather stilted "good evening" also conveys *warmth*, possibly even *respect*. When the sergeant gets no reply from within the dark barracks, he modulates from formality to familiarity: "Second address (milder): 'Hey, folks ... you guys already asleep?'" (131). The Austrian diminutive "Leuteln" ("folks") and the Austrian familiar second-person plural form "schlaft's" ("you guys asleep?") remove the advantages of rank and even soften up the border of sanity in order to address the "fools" as fellow human beings. At the same time, however, the abrupt shift to the familiar address can have a belittling effect, by demoting the addressee from respected status.

In this gamut from decorum to intimacy one can hear a mix of attitudes: besides fear and disdain, it expresses a degree of forbearance, even tolerance. Buffered not only by their polite formulas for social interaction (to some foreigners perhaps overly polite), but also tempered by the *Gemütlichkeit* (warmth, coziness) that issues from the gentle edges of the language, Austrians can express distance and cordiality at the same time.

This corresponds to a more general cultural pattern that combines strictness with amiability, something witnessed, for example, when a bureaucrat ironically lets on that he too is merely a victim of the bureaucracy, or when a waitress breaks through her dutiful routine to share a wry aside on the passing scene. This irony, with its dose of "we're all human after all," and "there but for the grace of God go I," permits an influx of the unexpected, the irrational, or even the extravagant into daily discourse. It is the enduring baroque wink of Austrian culture, which has never totally surrendered to the menace of reason identified by Foucault.

Perhaps Austrians believe there is more madness in their midst because this breach between how things are supposed to be and how they actually are allows them to see madness better, and to see it not only as radically other than the "normal," not only as the antithesis of reason, but as a common human phenomenon.

At this point the reader may protest that Austrians are just as able as any other culture to ostracize marginal groups such as the mad, and that confusing a subtle linguistic defense mechanism with tolerance is an exaggeration. It is true that Austrians, like other groups, can be intolerant, bigoted, moralizing, and sanctimonious. This essay, however, proposes to buttress the claims made on the basis of the Bachmann and Kuh texts—that Austrians see their culture as particularly prone to madness, and that Austrian culture is correspondingly curious about and at times even tolerant of madness—with further examples of the literary exploration of the interaction between the sane and the mad, and of the border traffic between the two. Looking at sympathetic but non-clinical responses to madness in fictional texts, it is hoped, will contribute to an understanding of the complexities of madness within Austrian culture.

Patrons and Clients

The texts mentioned, like a number of other Austrian fictional texts, are marked by a pattern of human—and narrative—relationships in which a character takes a personal, non-professional interest in another character who is afflicted with madness. These relationships create dramatic tensions that move plots along, but they are also important for their ontological implications. Whereas normally the perception of the mad is relegated to professional accounts (the rhetoric of psychology, psychiatry, and sociology) or popular stereotypes (the rhetoric of social exclusion), the fictional text is able to present madness at the intersection of predetermined rhetorical systems, and within the complexity of social interaction. Fiction need not assume the clinical perspective; it can create other points of view, the perspectives of persons who spend time with the mad not out of professional considerations, but because the mad are their relatives, friends, or associates, their would-be peers. The interest shown is thus not specifically medical or therapeutic, but more generally human, sometimes philosophical, and possibly even humane. For the purposes of this study, I will call literary figures who take such a an amateur interest in the mad *patrons*, and their protégés I will call *clients*.

Just as the relationships between these fictional patrons and clients are themselves not without paradoxes and ironies, so too is the use of these words potentially problematic, not least because of their implications of power and gender. But it is precisely such difficulties in the fictional representations of the partnerships that make these words pertinent. The *Oxford English Dictionary* defines "patron" in the first place as a "person standing in a role of oversight, protection, or sponsorship to another." The word, of course, ultimately derives from the Latin *pater*, "father," and its historical meaning has variously been "master," "patron saint," "protector," "advocate," "employer," and "benefactor." A thesaurus further yields the synonyms "supporter," and "fan," and this last, colloquial sense is not the least appropriate of the word's connotations. As will be seen, however, the less-positive connotations of "paternalistic" and "patronizing" often fit particular cases as well. The most important synonym of "patron" for present purposes is probably "advocate," that is, one who "pleads, intercedes, or speaks for, or in behalf of, another; a pleader, intercessor, defender" (*Oxford English Dictionary*). While not all of the patrons in this study are as active as this implies, fiction also admits of internal pleas and unspoken intercessions, and sometimes the advocacy implicit in the act of narration creates a patron-client relationship between a narrator and a character.

"Client," from Latin *cluere*, "to hear," probably originally meant "'one who is at the call of' his patron" ("client," *Oxford English Dictionary*). In Roman antiquity, the "client" was a plebeian who was "under the patronage of a patrician, in this relation called a 'patron.'" All subsequent and modern meanings of this pair of terms derive from the Roman social structure, and "client" is thus the natural counterpart to "patron."

A significant impetus for using this set of complements comes from one of the works under discussion, *The Man without Qualities*, in which the protagonist Ulrich takes an interest in the notorious murderer Moosbrugger. (Ulrich's interest is philosophically related to Foucault's interest in madness as the edge of the scope of reason.) Ulrich is present at the closing session of Moosbrugger's trial. After the court has convicted the accused man and sentenced him to death, Ulrich falls into a reverie on the trial's implications:

> Ulrich came back to reality only when "that miserable clown of a lawyer," as Moosbrugger ungratefully referred to him during the trial, announced that he would appeal to have the verdict set aside on grounds of some detail or other, while his towering client was led away. (Musil, *The Man without Qualities* 77)

The 1995 English translation does not render an important detail of this passage, for in the German original the narrator ascribes Moosbrugger as a client to both his lawyer *and* Ulrich; the phrase "ihrer beider riesiger Klient" (Musil, *Der Mann ohne Eigenschaften* 76) means "their *shared* towering client." Musil hence opens up the meaning of "client" (and by implication, "advocate" or "patron") in the direction I have tried to suggest, that is, to mean the object of a non-professional but lively interest that is, for all its good intentions, marked by a difference in power resulting from the social weakness conditioned in part by the mental state of the "client." Thus, Musil's patron-client association of Ulrich and Moosbrugger is both an inspiration for, and one pattern of, the heuristic use of the terms in this study.

Another model for the patron-client relationship is presented by the narrator and the title character in Franz Grillparzer's novella *The Poor Fiddler*, published in the 1840s.[6] The narrator, a semi-autobiographical figure, is drawn to the street musician Jakob by two things that set the fiddler apart from the gaggle of other beggars: his destitution in spite of his apparent middle-class background, and the bizarre music that he plays on his violin. These awake what the narrator calls his "anthropological appetite," an attitude that is in part a distancing mechanism to keep the very object of his interest—the old man's otherness—from coming too close to his sense of his own self, since he is also an isolated artist. At times the narrator is rather rude and thoughtless toward the fiddler—the patron is often quite patronizing—yet it is his interest in him, his patronage of him, that brings out Jakob's story in the first place. I include Grillparzer's novella among narratives of madness because Jakob, while in no way psychotic, displays symptoms of an autism-spectrum disorder like Asperger's Syndrome and of obsessive-compulsive behavior, which have isolated him from society at large.

Regarding another source for the patron-client model, Arthur Schnitzler's "Flight into Darkness" (1931), it is less fitting to speak of a patron than to note two characters who might have become, indeed perhaps should have become, patrons to Robert, a mentally unstable public official who returns to Vienna from a rest cure to try to reestablish himself personally and professionally. The two men who are in the best position to keep him from his violent end—he murders his brother and then commits suicide when his paranoia completely overcomes him—are his brother Otto (his eventual victim), who is a distinguished professor of psychiatry, and his lifelong friend Dr. Leinbach, who is a general practitioner. Otto's stern moral judgment of his brother keeps him from seeing the actual nature and extent of his affliction until it is too late. And although

Leinbach doesn't seem to take Robert seriously (in fact, he envies him his therapeutic "vacation"), at the end of the narrative it is he who regrets, in a private journal, that Robert's life story will be written off under the inadequate diagnosis of "paranoia," with no attention to the "unsettling complexity of individual cases" (Schnitzler 98) [7]

These two professionals who might beneficially combine their clinical and personal insights, but instead allow them to interfere with each other, are instances of failed patronage, of good intentions gone wrong. As his intimates, neither Otto nor Leinbach can accept that Robert is beyond the pale; as long as his afflictions are viewed as symptoms of immaturity or overwork, they seem manageable. Indeed, it is their personal relationship with the "client" that prevents them from seeing beyond the familiar into the uncanny world of Robert's madness.

In this case, it is the narrator who is ultimately Robert's patron, because he is empathetic enough to try to understand Robert's world from the inside, but objective enough to portray it unsentimentally in its social context. What the fictional text is able to do that its characters in this case cannot do is to combine both empathy and objectivity. It can show madness in its social context, in the interactions of patrons and clients, without resorting to the clinical diagnosis that is at once enlightening and, in its diminishing of an individual to a category, reductive.

Robert Musil: *The Man without Qualities*

The significance of Ulrich's interest in the apparently schizophrenic Moosbrugger was touched on above with regard to the patron-client relationship. Ulrich is not Moosbrugger's only patron, and Moosbrugger is not Ulrich's only client. The narrator of the novel, though often aligned with Ulrich's point of view, is a further patron, distinct from Ulrich the observer, for he imagines the vicissitudes of Moosbrugger's life. Ulrich, furthermore, is also a patron of Clarisse, the wife of his boyhood friend Walter. He gives her a set of Nietzsche's works for her birthday, which fuel the fire of her emergent schizophrenia. (Perhaps they have something of the philosophically radical effect envisioned by Foucault.) Clarisse, sensing the kinship between her condition and the murderer's, also becomes a champion, a sort of patron, of Moosbrugger's. As for Ulrich, his intellectual affinity, sexual attraction, and slightly amused irony vis-à-vis Clarisse combine into a form of patronage that simultaneously takes her mental extravagances seriously and looks down on them from the rationalist's perch.

The central conceit of the satire in *The Man without Qualities* is the so-called "Parallel Campaign," a celebration of the seventieth anniversary of Emperor Franz Josef's coronation planned for 1918 to "parallel" the thirtieth anniversary of the Prussian Emperor's ascent to the throne. Ulrich is secretary to the committee that is looking for a unifying "Austrian idea" as a theme for the observance. Clarisse proposes the outlandish idea that Moosbrugger should be the symbol of Austria. In order to appease Clarisse (and also out of his curiosity about Moosbrugger), Ulrich arranges a visit to the insane asylum. This allows Musil to explore the institutional world of the mad as a complement to Clarisse's madness, which can be seen as a form of (Foucauldian?) intellectual adventure, a quest on which her patron Ulrich accompanies her.

This intellectual exploration, a tour of the asylum with the intention of allowing Clarisse to meet Moosbrugger, fails in at least two ways. First, because their host is called away, the visitors never do make it to see Moosbrugger. And second, seeing the mad produces no philosophical breakthroughs for Clarisse or, for that matter, Ulrich. To be sure, Clarisse responds strongly to some of the patients she meets, but these responses end in solipsistic fantasy and not in communication. Seeing those who are similarly afflicted only reinforces Clarisse's idiosyncratic whims. It does not lead to any sort of Nietzschean epiphany, even if she is

> mulling over some of her pet ideas. Nietzsche: "Is there a pessimism of strength? … Perhaps madness is not necessarily a symptom of degeneracy." She was not thinking this in so many words, but she remembered it as a whole; her thoughts had compressed it all into a tiny packet, admirably fitted to the smallest space, like a burglar's tool. (Musil, *The Man without Qualities* 1063)

Clarisse has arrived at the "vanishing point of the uninterpretable" (Felman), but this means that she moves further away from any possibility of communication, either with normal society or with her new "friends" the mad. One patient who seems to be waving to her turns out to think she is a man (which she finds flattering), and then identifies her as "the seventh son" (1072). Just as she wants the man to be a significant figure in her mental constructs, she has become one in his, but these are separate and completely private worlds.

Clarisse's other patron, the narrator, interprets the disappointment that Clarisse feels when madness turns out not to afford the intellectual excitement it promises: "Hell is not interesting, it is terrifying" (1070). This is because, unless it has been humanized as by Dante, Hell promises "an inexorable change for the worse, impervious to any attempt to reverse it," which has the "fascination of an abyss." Musil continues: "Insane asylums are also like that. They are poorhouses. They have something of hell's lack of imagination" (1070). Confronting this lack of interest and imagination, even Clarisse "suffered a faint disappointment, which stemmed from some vague expectation implanted by her upbringing" (1070).

Ultimately, then, Ulrich's patronage of Moosbrugger, along with the narrator's, dwindles when Moosbrugger, awaiting the results of an appeal, is swallowed up by the workings of the legal system and the insane asylum. The client, like Robert in "Flight into Darkness," has crossed the line to where the patron cannot follow him. Ulrich's patronage of Clarisse is likewise fruitless. After the asylum tour, she is "absent-minded and quiet" (1078). Ulrich feels the need to apologize for not having protected her from the worst of the inmates, but decides "it was probably best to say no more about it" (1078). As has been seen, Clarisse's patronage of Moosbrugger also dissolves into disappointment and silence. Like so much of Musil's novel, his treatment of madness, while rich in insights and precise and imaginative portraits, resembles the narrative arc of the novel's first chapter with its apt title "From which, remarkably enough, nothing develops."

Musil also explores the intellectual possibilities of madness by showing the limits of clinical management and legal definitions. One chapter, for instance, is titled "To the Legal Mind, Insanity is an All-or-Nothing Proposition" (583), or, to translate it more literally, "For Legal Thinkers There is no Such Thing as a Half-Crazy Person." This is the satirical and socially critical movement of his novel: our attempts to deal with madness are hampered by fundamental epistemological inadequacies. But with his portrayals of the subtleties of Moosbrugger and Clarisse and their inner development and social interactions, Musil goes beyond a social critique and concomitant romantic rescue of madness. His epistemological precision does not allow him to turn the account of Ulrich's patronage of these two madpersons into a story with a decisive outcome. For this indecision, not only human institutions are at fault. Madness itself withdraws the clients from their patrons, and all their good intentions end in both intellectual and narrative uncertainty.

Norbert Gstrein: *Someone*

Someone by Norbert Gstrein (1988) is a narrative of madness in provincial Austria. Set in a village in Tyrol dependent on ski tourism for its modest prosperity, it tells the story of Jakob, who, as he grows into adulthood, descends into madness, most likely a form of schizophrenia. Jakob's primary patron is the unnamed narrator, his brother, who is one of a group of people who are waiting for the police to come and arrest Jakob after he has apparently murdered his on-again, off-again girlfriend Hanna.

The narrator tries to reconstruct when and how Jakob's afflictions began. He has only "memories" to work with. "But what do they explain, if you are not a dreamer or like the village, which flippantly knows it all after the fact?" (Gstrein 12).[8] Here the narrator positions himself precisely between a dreamer's irrationalism and the common sense of his fellow villagers. Assuming this middle ground, he becomes his brother's patron. Faced with Jakob's mental and social collapse, he cannot accept a diagnosis of madness either as romantic individualism or as a truism that closes the case rather than opening it. The narrator opens the case just as it is closing from the common-sense village point of view. He wants to know who his brother actually is, and how things came to this end.

In this he resembles the narrator in *The Poor Fiddler*, who would like to figure out how that other Jakob, a well-educated middle-class man, has landed among the mendicants. But Gstrein's narrator is distinguished in two important ways from Grillparzer's: as the client's brother, he has a direct personal interest, and he was a witness to most of Jakob's stories. He cannot distance himself through some "anthropological appetite," and as the teller of the tale, he inhabits both the frame story and the internal narrative.

Since Jakob the fiddler is the narrator of his own story, Grillparzer's narrator is an audience and perhaps a filter. But Gstrein's Jakob is in no position to narrate his own life, and so his brother must reconstruct it from fragments of memory and the testimony of others. The frame story—the meeting in the kitchen, waiting for the police—becomes something like a trial, not of Jakob, but of his family and neighbors and their roles in Jakob's life and sufferings:

> Those are stories, and we could tell stories, straight into the stillness of the kitchen, where we have been sitting since early morning, asked by Mother for our support, and we could recall again and again the old anecdotes heard on one occasion or another, and not find a beginning, clueless, relying only on conjectures that easily turn out to be wrong. We say Jakob, and mean our brother and we could begin anywhere, just start telling how he drank up his cocoa in one swig or left a little bit of it and immediately reached for his notebooks and books; we could tell about walking to school together, how he ran after them crying, the time they didn't wait for him, and complained later to Mother or maybe Father, if he was willing to listen to him … . (13)

It is not so much the distance from the client (as in Grillparzer's *Fiddler*) as his closeness to him (as in Schnitzler's "Flight") that creates the difficulty of narrating "how he got that way." In the passage quoted, Jakob's patron-brother not only reflects on the technical difficulty of using narrative to reconstruct a life, he launches immediately into the problem itself, remembering moments that seemed to set Jakob apart from those around him. He tells these stories in one long sentence, but their syntactic connection does not create a connection of meaning. These memories lead to a perhaps surprising question: "Did he have a hard time?" (14).

This question establishes both the method of the text—questioning—and its theme: Jakob's hard times. What they mean, and what event or circumstance led to other events and circumstances, becomes a narrative problem, and since a story should classically have a beginning, middle, and end, Jakob's patron wonders how and where to begin. After his first set of memories he says:

> We could begin with that, or we could first tell how he didn't have to help out with the work in the inn, even at an age when we had long been helping out by washing the dishes, or fetching bottles from the cellar and taking the empties back. (15)

This second beginning then becomes a second false start. After telling how their father had freed Jakob of any duties, and how he became enraged at Jakob's clumsiness, the narrator starts again for the third time:

> Sometime before or after that, that's how we could begin, in that summer when we discovered the fox holes, the weather was always nice, and they spent whole days outside, tirelessly crawling into the narrow cracks in the rock and sitting during the hot hours in the shade between the huge boulders that were piled on each other as if from another time. (15)

Here we also encounter a curious flickering in the narrator's perspective. At times he says "we," meaning not only the group in the kitchen at the time of narration, but also himself and his brothers or the other kids in the past. At other times he says "they," as if he were remembering from a third-person perspective.

This technique not only approximates the fluid perspective of memory, it shows the narrator as someone who was at times an observer and at times a participant. The pronoun switches in the first sentence of the passage just quoted, from "we" who found the foxholes, to "they" who spent whole days outdoors. In a later sentence, this shift occurs again, in the other direction:

> Their games grew more serious, they were real Indians and the stories we told ourselves were more real than the life down there in the village, which might as well have been a thousand miles away and didn't have anything to do with them anymore, with its guests that tirelessly climbed one peak after another. (16)

The shift from "we" to "them" here, and once more in the same paragraph, seems to depend on whether the narrator is including himself in the remembered image or not. This may have to do with the vividness of the memory, but it also has to do with the degree of the narrator's involvement then and the degree of involvement he is willing or unwilling to acknowledge now:

> The hours in the forest remained their secret, and we knew that we would never talk about how Hanna undid her dress and let us reach into her panties, between her legs, where there was nothing, and even today we laugh at Jakob, who then chickened out and only watched while they took off their pants and, standing next to each other, urinated in a wide arc over the cliff. (16)

It is significant that the narrator as a member of "we" is able to keep the implied rule of silence about their sexual initiation with Hanna, yet is ready "even today" to laugh about Jakob, who "chickened out."

Our narrator is unreliable, not because he wishes to suppress information, but because his own role in the story is ambiguous. He is sometimes part of "us" and sometimes an observer of "them," at which moments he assumes his client's perspective and "speaks for or in behalf of" him. It seems that he has to identify both with the "majority culture" and with the "other" to pursue the answer to his own question about his client: "Did he have a hard time?" (14).

At one point the narrator gains the insight that Jakob's isolation is as much self-produced as it is an ostracism,[9] that it is part of a feedback system in which Jakob's difference provokes rejection (especially by his father) and rejection drives him further away from normal society. The difference between the abstract desire to be with others and the actual, tormenting reality of being in society is expressed when the narrator imagines his brother alone at school:

> Sometimes he would have liked to have someone in the room, but when he thought about it, every wish immediately crashed to pieces on definite images of someone or someone else or anybody at all. (21)

Here the narrator-patron begins to understand his client's madness. Reality and the compromises it demands are too acute for Jakob's sensibilities. The demands of simply interacting with others put too much strain on him. He is at the vanishing point of the uninterpretable. Like Musil's narratives of madness, Gstrein's narrative is, by the very nature of its object, incapable of going beyond this vanishing point. Jakob fits Arno Gruen's sociological characterization of schizophrenics: "They dissociate themselves from the outer world as a means of staying in touch with their own world of inner feelings and with the potential for autonomy contained in that world" (Gruen 12). But this autonomy inevitably clashes with the outer world's rules.

When Jakob's condition goes from chronic to acute to violent crisis, the narrator, his patron, must reconstruct Jakob's world of inner feelings with the clues supplied by "stories" and "old anecdotes." This reconstruction sheds some light on Jakob's madness, but it is like Dr. Leinbach's journal entry in "Flight into Darkness": too little and too late for Jakob. The narrative as a whole, however, represents from a non-clinical perspective Jakob's gradual vanishing as both a social and a private phenomenon.

Ingeborg Bachmann: *The Book of Franza*

As was noted above in the section on the position of madness in Austrian culture, in Ingeborg Bachmann's *The Book of Franza* Martin Ranner responds to an incoherent telegram from his sister Franza by looking for her first in Vienna and then in their hometown in southern Austria. Franza has fled from her husband Jordan, a prominent psychiatrist, because she discovers that he has turned her into one of his "cases." Already mentally unstable, she is pushed by this breach of trust deeper into madness. Martin's interest in his sister makes him into her patron: like Ulrich with Clarisse, he is trying to understand the irrational behavior of someone close to him. Like the narrator in Gstrein's story and Otto in Schnitzler's, he is the brother of his client—his family relation is what creates his interest.

Martin is willing to cross professional, epistemological, and even legal boundaries in order to help his sister, and he is one of the patrons with the least self-interest in his inquiry into his client's madness. Professionally, Martin is a geologist, and he uses geological concepts to reconstruct what has happened with his sister. In this regard, he is like Ulrich in *The Man without Qualities*, who is also a scientist (a mathematician), but who wants to see if he can apply the precision of his scientific method to ethical problems. Martin approaches his sister and their relationship by applying his geological understanding metaphorically:

> Someone like Franza was such a fossil that she had to live constantly amid a sense of magic and marvel. Martin knew no magic, for he was content to be like the painter who said that before he painted a picture of a landscape … he first had to know its geology. That was well put. And before Martin could know something of his sister and complete a portrait of her, he needed to find out just what kind of ground she stood upon. (Bachmann, *The Book of Franza*, 48).

He decides he is basically familiar with the "terrain," but he needs to know

> what had been covered or had shifted, what had migrated, what had formed folds, and what hanging walls had remained stable. For geology had wonderful words. Hanging walls. And what kind of geological inclusions still existed inside her person? Why had something gone wrong and what could have disturbed her so? (48-49)

His quest thus resembles that of Jakob's patron in *Someone*—he needs to find out what went wrong, but he is more clever than Otto and Leinbach in Schnitzler's text, for he is able to cross the borders of his personal and professional lives in order to seek answers. He is able to imagine his sister in terms that are deeply meaningful to him, yet flexible enough to be turned into metaphor. This will to live in imagination, to use language as tool of discovery and not mere communication, is a step in the direction of Utopia that one finds again and again in Bachmann's texts. But again and again, the utopian impulse is thwarted by the violence deeply rooted in European culture. It is this culture that Franza is trying to escape, first internally through madness, and then physically, geographically, and historically through a flight into Egypt.

When Martin finds Franza, she seems to be cycling rapidly between deep depression and manic energy. If I "diagnose" Franza as having bipolar illness, it is not in order to shut the book on her case (like the common sense of Gstrein's villagers) but to understand her condition as pathological. By taking this step, we can see Bachmann's narrative not only as an indictment of psychiatry and patriarchy, but also as an indictment of how these systems subjugate those with mental illness. The problem is not simply, as antipsychiatry would have it, that Jordan has made Franza mentally ill by labeling her that way. The problem is also that Western society is cruel to the socially weak, including the mad. I argue that Bachmann draws a precise picture of a particular case of bipolar illness, but my use of this term is not meant to foreclose judgment. It is meant to show one source of Franza's sufferings, not to "define" her as Jordan does, "in conjunction with the latest point of view" (68). What Martin refers to as Franza's need for "magic and marvel" is related to her manic phases, and it is this extravagance that removes her from society at large. As Gstrein's story indicates, the mad person's loss of social position results from a complex feedback system of behavior on both sides.

One problem with terms like "bipolar illness" within our Western cultural contexts is that they both remove agency and imply culpability. I would ask the reader to suspend such judgments; Franza is represented neither as without free will nor as solely responsible for her difficulties. Franza diagnoses herself as not having been mad (70), but starting with her childhood at the end of the war, there is evidence in the text for her growing inability to function in normal society. While she is married to Jordan, she meets Ödön Csobadi, with whom she can share the imaginative manic and melancholy depressive phases, although this temporary harmony is also disturbed by the intrusion of reality in the form of Jordan. It seems that precisely the social weakness of her fantastic mental world is the vulnerability that attracts Jordan to her as a wife to be dominated and a case to be observed and controlled.

When Franza discovers that Jordan has been keeping notes on her as a "case," this triggers her worst episode of depression yet. When she recovers from this phase, her manic energy allows her to take control of the situation and force Martin to change his vacation plans to go Egypt, leaving his girlfriend behind and taking Franza, who has forged a visa in her passport just for this purpose. When manic, Franza is able to reclaim agency and try to use her madness, as it were, to escape her madness.

What Bachmann does differently from the other texts is to reverse the patron-client relationship in the course of the narrative, making the older sister Franza into the patron of her younger brother Martin as she schemes to remove herself from the scene of her suffering, Europe. As her client, Martin is introduced into the world of madness in a direct way that, in the texts under discussion, only Clarisse has experienced. In terms of narrative perspective, we are taken from the third-person point of view of the "normal" person, who seeks to interpret mad behavior in intelligible terms, to the first-person point of view of the "mad" person, who seeks to interpret normal behavior in the imaginative terms her madness has opened up for her.

After the "hometown" episodes, we get the exposition for Franza's crisis in the second section, "Jordanian Time." The final part of the novel treats the "Egyptian Darkness," a reference ultimately to Franza's death.

As Clarisse does with Ulrich in *The Man without Qualities*, Franza gets Martin to take her to the "asylum." From Franza's point of view—the book moves into a first-person narrative—the desert is described as an "immense sanatorium," but also, in terms that recall Musil's language about Moosbrugger's asylum, "the immense and inescapable purgatory." "Like an institution, it had engulfed them" (89).[10]

When she and Martin arrive in Egypt, Franza takes on the role of tour guide. Franza believes that getting away from Europe will cure her, but she finds that the oppressive powers she associates with European male society exist in the other world of Egypt as well. Although she does begin to recover in Egypt, she sees a madwoman being kept on a leash and beaten by her husband, she encounters a former Nazi physician, and she sees how even in ancient Egypt the memory of the female Pharaoh Hatshepsut was obliterated. Here Bachmann identifies the difference between Franza's sort of madness and the "madness of normality" that Arno Gruen describes. While Franza goes to great lengths to preserve the inner integrity of her emotional life, the world around her has sacrificed its own integrity, a loss that avenges itself in the form of violence (for instance, the long-term, methodical violence of Jordan's supposed therapy). In spite of Franza's self-sponsorship, her taking herself on as a client, she ultimately succumbs to depression and suicidality. Her patronage, like that of Grillparzer's narrator, like the patronage of Ulrich, Clarisse, and Gstrein's narrator, ultimately fails, as madness takes her beyond the pale.

Franza's client after she has turned the tables, Martin, is in the same position as the reader when the Egyptian story is over. He takes the story she has created into the world and tries to relate the lessons of its madness to his daily life. He sees images of Egypt on television, but "as he tried to match up the images with those he remembered, it simply didn't work" (144). Although Franza's patronage of Martin led him into the asylum on a voyage of discovery, like Musil's visitors, he cannot evoke the experience in words. "Hell is not interesting, it is terrible." The statistical details of northern Africa Martin shares with his friends reveal nothing of "what had happened. How all consuming it was" (145). Like the mad persons in all of the narratives discussed here, Franza has disappeared across the "vanishing point of the uninterpretable." "The Egyptian darkness, after all, is absolute" (146).

In this sampling of Austrian fictional texts I have described a set of patterns and variations on these patterns that show an Austrian cultural propensity to treat the question of madness with a certain openness and sensitivity, even as it indicts Austrian society for its intentional and unintentional cruelties to the mad. Furthermore, by using fiction to augment our clinical and historical understanding of madness, a number of significant Austrian authors guide us along the path between what Gstrein's narrator calls the "dreamers" and the ready-made knowledge of the "village, which flippantly knows it all after the fact" (12), between the philosophical cooptation and the clinical subjugation of madness and the mad. In each case, the efforts of the patrons end tragically, in the absolute loss of the client to madness. These fictions combine humane interest in the other with scrupulous precision to bring new inflections to our picture of the mad and the role of madness in Austrian culture. And like the patrons they represent, these fictions are fallible: their pictures are fragments, their conclusions are open. But each one brings us a step closer to understanding the complex collision of individual and culture that madness provokes.

Works Cited

Bachmann, Ingeborg. *The Book of Franza* and *Requiem for Fanny Goldmann*. Translated from the German and with an Introduction by Peter Filkins. Evanston, IL: Northwestern University Press, 1999.

—. *Das Buch Franza. Das "Todesarten"-Projekt in Einzelausgaben*. Ed. Monika Albrecht and Dirk Göttsche. Taschenbuchausgabe. Munich: Piper, 1998.

Felman, Shoshana. *Writing and Madness*. Ithaca: Cornell University Press, 1985.

Foucault, Michel. *Madness and Civilization*. New York: Random House, 1965. Vintage Books Edition 1988.

Grillparzer, Franz. *The Poor Fiddler*. Translated by Alexander and Elizabeth Henderson. Introduction by Ivar Ivask. New York: Ungar, 1967.

Gruen, Arno. *The Insanity of Normality. Realism as Sickness: Toward Understanding Human Destructiveness*. Translated from the German by Hildegarde and Hunter Hannum. New York: Grove Weidenfeld, 1992.

Gstrein, Norbert. *Einer*. Frankfurt am Main: Suhrkamp, 1988.

Haug, H. J. and W. Rössler, "Deinstitutionalization of psychiatric patients in central Europe," *European Archives of Psychiatry and Clinical Neuroscience* (1999) 249 (3):115-22.

Kuh, Anton. "Die Narren von Görz." In *Der unsterbliche Österreicher*. Edited and with a foreword by Ulrich N. Schulenberg, 126-32. Vienna: Erhard Löcker, 2001.

Musil, Robert. *The Man without Qualities*. Translated by Sophie Wilkins. New York: Alfred A. Knopf, 1995.

—. *Der Mann ohne Eigenschaften. Gesammelte Werke*, volume 1. Ed. Adolf Frisé. Reinbek bei Hamburg: Rowohlt, 1978.

Schnitzler, Arthur. "Flight into Darkness." In *Desire and Delusion. Three Novellas*. Selected and Translated from the German by Margret Schaefer, 3-98. Chicago: Ivan R. Dee, 2003.

Szasz, Thomas. *Liberation By Oppression: A Comparative Study of Slavery and Psychiatry*. New Brunswick NJ: Transaction Books, 2002.

—. *The Myth of Mental Illness: Foundations of a Theory of Personal Conduct*. New York: Harper & Row, 1960.

Torrey, E. Fuller. *Out of the Shadows: Confronting America's Mental Illness Crisis*. New York: John Wiley & Sons, 1997.

Notes

[1] Foucault's book is one of the most visible of a great number of works of the last fifty years that examine the cultural and historical position of madness. Other authors who have drawn attention to the question are Thomas Szasz, Roy Porter, and Sander Gilman.

[2] See, for example, Torrey, *Out of the Shadows*, which describes how the prison system has largely assumed the care of the mentally ill in the widespread absence of adequate community mental health care, which had been envisioned as the substitute for institutionalization. In Europe, deinstitutionalization has taken place at varying rates, with Italy leading the way. Germany has rapidly deinstitutionalized, while in Austria the process was comparatively delayed, but experienced an increase in the 1990s. Europe is seeing problems similar to those in the US, but on a lesser scale. See Haug and Rössler, "Deinstitutionalization."

[3] Anti-psychiatry is most closely associated with Thomas Szasz, a Hungarian-born US psychiatrist who has written a series of books asserting that mental illness is an invention of the psychiatric profession that medicalizes unconventional human behavior and labels it pathological. See for example the fundamental book *The Myth of Mental Illness: Foundations of a Theory of Personal Conduct* (New York: Harper & Row, 1960) and *Liberation By Oppression: A Comparative Study of Slavery and Psychiatry* (New Brunswick NJ: Transaction Books, 2002).

[4] It would go beyond the scope of this paper to provide a basic argument for the organic component of major mental illness. Suffice it to say that recent work in psychiatry and neurology has made great progress in discovering the chemical, neurological, and genetic influences on mental illness. My argument here mainly shifts attention from the etiology of mental illness to its social effects, while making the fundamental assumption that the authors discussed describe madness in inductive terms based on observation. These descriptions therefore do not exclude

the involvement of organic factors, even though the authors wrote before this research was available.

[5] English translations of Kuh's text by Geoffrey C. Howes.

[6] I would like to thank Peter Rosei for suggesting *The Poor Fiddler* as a text to be examined in the context of mental illness, a connection that in my experience is not always obvious to readers.

[7] I would like to thank Andrew Wisely for suggesting I look into "Flight into Darkness" for my project.

[8] English translations of Gstrein's text by Geoffrey C. Howes.

[9] Gstrein, *Einer*, 21.

[10] In the original, this sentence is more direct, employing metaphor rather than simile. A close translation, also preserving the relative sobriety of the original, would be "The institution had assumed them." ("Die Anstalt hatte sie aufgenommen."; Bachmann, *Das Buch Franza*, 90.)

CHAPTER TEN

THEATER AS THERAPY IN THE ASYLUM AT MAUER-ÖHLING: THE *FIN DE SIÈCLE* REALIZATION OF A ROMANTIC DREAM?

JULIE M JOHNSON

On July 2, 1902, the opening ceremony was held for a new state asylum for psychiatric care at Mauer-Öhling in Lower Austria. This ceremony, which was attended by Emperor Franz Joseph, was held in a theater situated in a large green park-like space surrounded by a forest (Koller-Glück, 8). The new asylum was made up of forty individual buildings housing different types of patients, long- and short-term, men and women, and even children with developmental disabilities.[1] Among the buildings in the complex were a separate kitchen facility, an administration building, and the theater building where the ceremony was held, but this was not just any theater: not only was it purpose-built for a new insane asylum, it was also one that converted the altar area of a church into a stage by covering it with a rolling wall (fig. 10-1). The subject of this essay is this theater and how it was used. This theater was not the only theater built for insane asylums at this time, but it was the most active, eventually forming its own in-house theater company, the House-Theater and Variety Company (*Haus-Theater und Varieté Gesellschaft*; 1908).

Figure 10-1 Carlo Boog, Interior of church/theater at Mauer-Öhling, 1903, in "Die Kaiser Franz Josephs Landes-Heil-und Pflegeanstalt in Mauer-Öhling," *Der Architekt* 9:1 (1903):95-98. Photo: author.

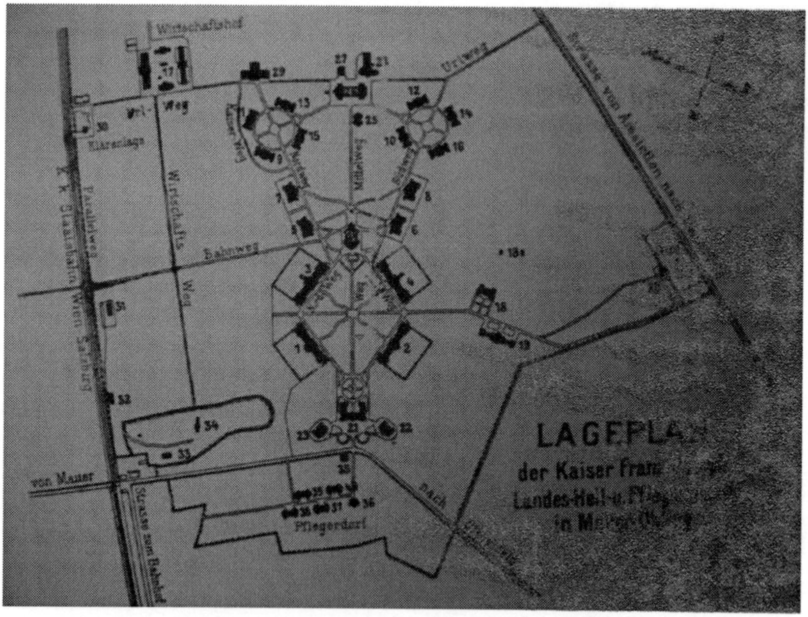

Figure 10-2 Plan of Mauer-Öhling, in "Die Kaiser Franz Josephs Landes-Heil-und Pflegeanstalt in Mauer-Öhling," *Der Architekt* 9:1 (1903):95-98. Photo: author

Although Mauer-Öhling was not actually replacing the Fool's Tower (*Narrenturm*), a round, panopticon-like building which had been built in 1784 by Josef II and nicknamed the *Guglhupf* (Austrian cake), the buildings were compared in the publicity for the new asylum; where patients had once been mistreated in dark cells in Joseph II's *Narrenturm*, now they would be treated humanely, with the best medical care.[2] Mauer-Öhling was the first state-run insane asylum in Lower Austria devoted to the no-restraint system. By comparison, photographs of patients shackled in cells in the old *Narrenturm* were (re)created with actors, to produce visually stunning evidence of the emergence from the dark ages of psychiatric care. Even when the *Narrenturm* was new and modern, one psychiatrist had recommended that a care facility be situated on a large, expansive, and airy green space, with rolling hills, alongside a stream, for their soothing effects on the psyche (Reil, 459). It was none other than Johann Christian Reil (1759-1813), who was considered the "German Pinel" and acknowledged to be the "father of modern care for the insane."[3] In his famous 1803 book, *Rhapsodies on the Application of Psychotherapy to Mental Disturbances*, Reil had also recommended the building of free-standing theaters in asylums, for which he had a particular psychiatric use in mind—a cure through playing roles (209). But by the time the theater was built for Mauer-Öhling, most medical doctors doubted that the otherwise venerated Reil was serious in his recommendation for theater as therapy, so far had psychiatry wandered from Reil's Romantic frame of reference. During the nineteenth century, most of the medical profession had turned toward somatic causes and cures for psychiatric disease (see Shorter). Indeed, Michel Foucault points out that when Freud invented his "talking cure," placing a new emphasis on the psyche, he was really returning to the Romantic period of psychiatry (198).

Why would theater facilities be built for state-run asylums when medical opinion had turned against theater as therapy? Why in particular would Mauer-Öhling have such an active theater group? I have argued elsewhere that the *architecture* of the theater at Steinhof, a state psychiatric institution built in Vienna in 1907, invokes a specifically Austrian and Baroque theatrical tradition. Here, however, I will be focusing not on the symbolic invocations of architecture, but the actual use of its space, with a consideration of the atypical example of performances at Mauer-Öhling, which had the most active in-house theater program of all the asylum theaters and even reviewed performances with critiques of the players in its in-house newspaper.

By the turn of the century, a dire need for more humane psychiatric and medical care was perceived in Austria, not necessarily due to an increase in insanity relative to the population, but rather because new discoveries in neurology led to increased and more varied diagnoses.[4] The biggest problem that had plagued state asylums in Austro-Hungary before was legal: only violent patients could be housed in psychiatric facilities; the non-violent would simply be placed in the poor-house.[5] Once the law was changed, the building of new asylums commenced throughout the Monarchy. The new asylum at Mauer-Öhling was meant to incorporate all of the latest in medical developments and to serve a large population of patients—short- and long-term, as well as a new colony (which involved placing non-violent patients as laborers with local farm families, under the oversight of the asylum doctor). For the planning of Mauer-Öhling, two administrators were sent out on an expedition to tour the asylums of Germany. They returned with the recommendation that these three kinds of care (long- and short-term and colony) be offered under one institutional umbrella, and that the centralized facilities (church, kitchen, theater, administration), would not only be shared, but one administrator with medical expertise would direct them all.[6]

(INDENT)At Mauer-Öhling, the building authorities decided to build in the pavilion style, which was associated with the latest ideas in healthcare. The corridor system of hospitals was now out of favor, having been replaced by the pavilion system in new building schemes. It was already in use in Germany where the officials had toured buildings, and they praised them for allowing in more sunlight and fresh air and incorporating large green spaces. This was not simply common-sense therapy for mental health, where patients might exercise in privacy and enjoy the outdoors; the latest ideas and discoveries in medicine called for a new, more therapeutic architecture that would allow air to circulate. The bacillus of tuberculosis had been discovered, and the pavilion style answered the need for more fresh air, with sunning porches, plenty of windows, space between buildings, and park-like grounds (see Colomina). The idea was to get as far away as possible from the dark corridors of older hospitals, where little sun and air could penetrate.

Figure 10-3 Front and back views of church/theater at Mauer-Öhling, 1903, in "Die Kaiser Franz Josephs Landes-Heil-und Pflegeanstalt in Mauer-Öhling," *Der Architekt* 9:1 (1903):95. Photo: author.

Figure 10-4 Carlo Boog, Altar of church at Mauer-Öhling, in "Die Kaiser Franz Josephs Landes-Heil-und Pflegeanstalt in Mauer-Öhling," *Der Architekt* 9:1 (1903):95-98. Photo: author

Like new asylums, new hospitals designed for tuberculosis also followed the pavilion-style plan, most of which included administration, kitchen, church, and theater buildings lined up on a central axis, with women patients on one side and men on the other. Mauer-Öhling's own plan was designed around such a central axis (fig. 10-2). One architect/doctor team explained that a sanatorium for tuberculosis should give its patients the feeling of a "friendly vacation" in a "comfortable pension." Of their surroundings, they wrote, "patients should not be reminded, except for the warnings from their doctors, that they are in a grave battle with one of the worst enemies of humankind, a battle with the bacillus of tuberculosis" (Hinterberger, 10). The pavilion style lent itself to this "friendly vacation" feeling: as one commentator wrote of the new asylum at Mauer-Öhling, "In place of the huge cell-like building complexes are fun pavilions with verandas where patients enjoy the greatest freedom possible."[7] The pavilion style of asylum building should be viewed in the larger context of sanatorium building of the time.[8]

Mauer-Öhling had no bars on its large glass windows, the ceilings were high, and an effect of light airiness predominated. The administration, church, and theater buildings were decorated with Rococo-Jugendstil elements (fig. 10-3). The church/theater remains to this day a beautifully restored example of Jugendstil architecture (fig. 10-4). Mauer-Öhling's state-appointed architect, Carlo Boog (1854-1905), not only experimented with the new style of art nouveau, but also with the architectural footprint of one of the central buildings. The rare combination church-and-theater building at the heart of Mauer-Öhling combined the sacred and profane in a convertible building. The altar of the Jugendstil church that he designed had a rolling wooden wall that could cover the chapel to create a stage for secular performances (fig. 10-1).

Boog's project was published in *Der Architekt*, a journal for professional architects, with photographs of the interior and exterior of the theater/church along with a description of the entire asylum (figs. 10-1-4).[9] Boog also used his engineering expertise to experiment with new materials.[10] He started to use concrete slabs, for example, for his foundations while building the asylum at Mauer-Öhling, saving both time and money. He even made exterior ornaments out of poured concrete, rather than employing the traditional time-consuming method of hand-carving stone (Koller-Glück, 16).[11] For this he was rewarded with the job of overseeing and planning the next new asylum at Steinhof. He even built the first villa out of concrete, his own summer family home, which he called "Betonia" (loosely translated as Concretia).[12] If Boog had not died suddenly in 1905 of a heart attack, he would have been the architect of record at Steinhof (except for Otto Wagner's church), which has a free-standing theater at its center (completed in 1907).

Once the pavilion style took hold of the imaginations of planners and architects involved in psychiatric care, it was not long before these were being built throughout not only the Austro-Hungarian empire, but also the Americas. I cannot give a precise inventory here, but to call the asylum building activity a "boom" would be accurate. Of the ten pavilion-style asylums that were built in the Austro-Hungarian Monarchy between the years 1883 and 1910, roughly half had separate entertainment or social gathering buildings. These were Troppau (1889), Mauer-Öhling (1902), Steinhof (1907), Kremsier (1908), and Bohnitz bei Prag (1910) (Hofmokl, Schlöss). Of these Austro-Hungarian state institutions, only Troppau had in common with Mauer-Öhling the unusual building type of the convertible church space, but Troppau did not add a stage for theater performances until 1909.

Surprisingly, architects had less influence over asylum building than the asylum directors, who were also typically doctors. One doctor, who wished to remain anonymous, complained that these "mammoth institutions were popping up like mushrooms," each looking just like the other, with buildings clustered around a Gathering House (*Versammlungshaus*). The pavilion plan, he complained, had two disadvantages: the doctor had to bundle up against the cold to make his rounds, and his approach could be seen by the orderlies. He proposed that a barrack system would be better suited for some institutions, and a hospital-type plan better for patients and doctors ("Zum Bau").[13] But he was unique in his dissent. Asylum directors were generally enthusiastic about the pavilion plan; they exchanged ideas on asylums and the care of patients via lecture circuits and journal articles, often consulting with other asylum directors during on-site visits. The weekly *Psychiatrische Wochenschrift* provided an illustrated forum where photographs, plans, and descriptions of new asylums were reproduced. This newspaper helped to establish a community of German-speaking asylum planners that existed across large geographical expanses throughout the Austro-Hungarian Empire and Germany.

The quick publicity given to new buildings helps to explain why one type would become so influential so quickly. Another way in which ideas circulated was the student-teacher relationship among medical professionals. C. W. F. Roller, for example, thought the pavilion or cottage system was ideal but unattainably expensive when he wrote a book about the ideal asylum in 1838 (*Grundsätze*). Roller had been the director at Illenau and Pforzheim and also wrote a comprehensive book documenting the hospitals for the insane in the German-speaking world (*Psychiatrische*

Zeitfragen, 1874). By the time his students were directing asylums—and he trained so many that Dieter Jetter has called him the teacher of all the asylum doctors of the world[14]—the pavilion plan had become financially feasible. At Emmendingen, outside of Freiburg, an asylum opened in September 1889 that was built according to Roller's recommendations: it was a village-like compound, with porter houses flanking an entrance and a social-gathering house (*Gesellschaftshaus*).[15] Emmendingen provided a model for the asylum at Troppau, which, like Mauer-Öhling, would eventually have a combination church/theater.[16]

But the inclusion of a separate social-gathering house did not necessarily indicate a nod toward theater; in fact, Roller was himself entirely against theater as therapy, although he considered festivities important and the use of music in them quite necessary (see Hofmokl). Roller therefore included a large community space, which was needed to accommodate everyone at dances and large gatherings. But he did not include a theater in his architectural plans, noting,

> To allow the insane to study roles is always difficult and therefore a theater for insane asylums fully unnecessary. Even attending dramas can arouse feelings and passions that one would have better pacified. In no way can this means be considered effective. (qtd. in Ferentschik, 14)

In 1907, after several asylums had been built, including the just-opened Steinhof, Gustav Kolb recommended that theaters be combined with other spaces to be multi-functional, because there tended to be so many separate buildings in the pavilion system. He recommended not only combining church and theater, but also a gym, school, library, and separate game-room for the caretakers into one building type, the Gathering Building (*Versammlungsgebäude*; Kolb, 235-36).

Within this larger architectural context and historical overview of an evolving building type (with its several names), one might simply view the theater at Mauer-Öhling as part of a widespread tendency to include gathering spaces and theaters in asylums that provided long-term care, bringing an end to a story of what seems like a curiosity, given the famous episode in the history of asylums at Charenton. I refer to the residency of the Marquis de Sade, who famously staged theatrical performances at Charenton for Parisians, who would visit the psychiatric hospital to gawk and laugh at the spectacle of inmates performing.[17] If theaters were part of the typical plan, one would think they were somehow connected to medical recommendations, given the tendency for medical doctors to become very closely involved in the planning and dissemination of architectural plans. But a review of medical discourse reveals that theater was shunned as therapy by the time the theaters were being built—and not just by Roller and his many students. Nor do the theaters I consider here have a history of spectacular performances held for outsiders (like Charenton did for Parisians), nor did they have a history of performing classical or traditional dramas that might engage an audience's intellect or feelings.

A journalist writing for the Viennese *Neue Freie Presse* explained how theater might function therapeutically in the new institutions for psychiatric care:

> With endless patience the doctors try to create order in the confused brain, by slowly redirecting patients away from their imaginary ideas to ordinary everyday thinking. Their principle is that their patients should above all forget about themselves and their delusions, and their means to this end consists of work and distraction through entertainment; especially beneficial are presentations of selected dramatic and musical arts.

This description of theater as therapy was written by a journalist for a lay public and was part of the publicity to make insane asylums appear beneficent rather than horrific. It was not an example of the latest medical opinion, unless one reads a special emphasis into the words *SELECTED dramatic and musical arts*. The selection was indeed narrow, tending toward variety acts and skits. Overall, the dramatic presentations at Mauer-Öhling were inspired by vaudeville, cabaret, and the genre of the *Posse*, popular comedic farces peopled with stock characters and simple plots. These farces are associated with Nestroy, the Volkstheater and summer street-theater revivals today. Such "low" genres of theater arts were not selected for state-run insane asylums because of a sense of class distinctions, but rather because of a long-standing ambivalence towards theater in the psychiatric profession.

The ambivalence toward theater did not exist in the nascent discipline of psychiatry, as mentioned above. Johann Christian Reil, the "German Pinel," had posited that theater could provide instantaneous cures for patients. He proposed, therefore, that each asylum should have its own theater, with all the necessary apparatus, masks, machines, and decorations to create complete illusions in the patient, who would act in roles rather than merely observe as a traditional spectator. Reil suggested that such theaters could be turned into prisons, lion's dens, places of execution, and operating rooms (209). To support his theoretical assertions, Reil cited Pinel's story of the festival of the holy handkerchief of Besançon, which was basically a colorful exorcism performed in an amphitheater, complete with music, cannons, and priests in ceremonial garb. Reil understood it not as a religious act so much as a dramatic ritual that actually cured some of the patients (211). He enthused that through dramatic illusionism, "Don Quixotes would turn into knights, imagined pregnancies would be lightened of their burdens, and rueful sinners happily relieved of their sins" (209).

Later psychiatrists perceived Reil's experiments as torture, risible, or simply inadvisable. Even those who recommended theater in general found his ideas unbelievable. Otto Snell, for example, was entirely in favor of presentations for entertainment purposes, particularly magic shows and concerts, noting in his 1897 book that Reil had recommended using them too. Snell remarked, however, that Reil had had the "incredible" idea that one should write one's own dramas for the insane asylum in order to (quoting Reil) "make each crazy person's ideas laughable to himself."[18] Even as early as 1829, Nostitz u. Janckendorf, who designed the model asylum for its time at Sonnenstein in Saxony, simply thought Reil was not serious in his recommendations for theater (340; also cited at length in Ferentschik, 15).

But he was: Reil's intent was based on a Romantic notion of the self in which the self becomes a "stage upon which, with or without consciousness, the self functions as a representing power" (Thiher, 172). By placing Reil's ideas in a Romantic, anti-Kantian context, literary historian Allen Thiher explains the logic behind them:

> Madness creates an inner metaphysical theater to which the self is an unwilling spectator, when not a willing participant therein. Or madness can produce the disjuncture between the self as spectator and the irrational representations in which the self is an actor. Madness is much like a dream [...]. Madness is representation; therefore, Reil thought that theater could be a form of therapy. By acting roles or watching theatrical representations, the mad should experience alternative representations that were designed to capture their attention and bring them back to reason. (172)

Thiher has uncovered a nexus of ideas about the self that began with Romanticism and have found their way to us again via Freud, who, after all, based some of his cases on stories by Romantic authors (E. T. A. Hoffmann in particular). Hoffmann, for example, had read both Reil and Pinel, and used their texts ironically in his stories (Thiher, 190). Thiher further notes that psychiatry and litearature both represent the self as "a space described by allegory" (182), but that "after romanticism, nineteenth-century medicine usually preferred scalpels to allegories" (194). As the nineteenth century wore on, more and more doctors denounced theater as therapy, but Reil's ideas were taken seriously early in the century.

In 1823, C. L. Klose, a doctor and professor at Breslau, recommended that German doctors take note of the experiment at Charenton, and that theaters be built in German asylums (Klose, 32-34). He was the most sympathetic toward Reil's theater cures, and for him the most important question was whether to choose roles that matched the problems and character of the patient or that went against them. The acting was better in the former case, but Klose thought it might be more therapeutic to do the latter. He recommended assigning a role that had no other purpose than to place the patient in another sphere of "psychic activity" ("geistige Thätigkeit") than he normally moved in, so that he got used to playing a dramatic role, and then moving him to the opposite of his insanity. It was important, he noted, to keep away patient-spectators who might find fodder for their own insanity in the performance. A. F. Schweigger, who was neither an asylum director nor a doctor but a botanist, wrote sympathetically of Charenton's experiment with theater, but he was more interested in the effects on the spectator than the actors. He noted that there were problems inherent in producing theater with patients: it was difficult to get them to concentrate, it took them too long to learn lines, and there was an uncontrolled aspect to the performances (26; qtd. in Klose, 32).

By the end of the nineteenth century, one of the most important tenets of care for the insane was to never engage in fantasy, to never argue with a patient, but to simply and calmly exhibit reason, and, where possible, to distract the patient through light activities (sewing, billiards, bowling, cards, or even unpaid labor). The primary reason was that patients could remember what doctors said to them, even after they returned to a state of reason (Henne, 110; Snell, 20). There was also a tendency to reject the imagination and narrative in favor of studying exterior facts (math) or simpler occupations. Music was allowed, for it was abstract. Drawing and painting were allowed, especially for paying patients in the sanatoria. By 1845 Ernst Freiherr von Feuchtersleben (1806-1849) had declared that Reil's ideas were useless "theatrical gimmicks."[19] He found the use of ghosts and tricks undignified, although he was in favor of selected entertainments if carefully chosen. He warned, however, that entertainment could have a negative effect on patients who gave way to their imaginations, and that one might even stir up new problems that one could not treat.[20]

By mid-century the tide had turned completely against theater as therapy; there was now opposition to even allowing patients to read dramatic works as literature. In 1847 Carl Maass, who was generally an advocate of light entertainments and occupational therapy, advised against any kind of drama whatsoever. He noted that dramatic works usually failed to have the effect that their authors intended: simply reading Schiller's *Don Carlos* upset one patient as much as attending a theatrical production of Shakespearean drama. The best results, he argued, came from purposeful study of physics and mathematical writings.[21] The use of theater that would touch a spectator or actor deeply was entirely a Romantic experiment.

Lively discussion about theater continued throughout the nineteenth century, many doctors finding reasons to exclude it from asylum life. Several doctors cited a famous episode about a patient who became enraged by a dramatic performance and cut off the head of the asylum doctor, but this incident most likely occurred in England.[22] In 1858 Bruno Schön, the asylum priest for the Lower Austrian Insane Asylum, then located in the ninth district in Vienna (Brünnlfeld), explained why theater was problematic:

> We consider balls and concerts part of psychiatric therapy, but not theater. Why not? The insane is no longer himself, but another person, the actor not himself but plays the role of another, that is, places himself in another personality, which goes against the psychiatric goal of healing, which consists of nothing other than bringing the patient back to himself through somatic and psychic means. The mentally ill or insane actor not only gains nothing but also risks losing himself even more.... The majority of mentally ill spectators gain nothing, even when a drama is carefully chosen; one patient may benefit while ten others are harmed. (Schön, 3:206; also qtd. at length in Ferentschik, 214)

There was no theater in asylums in Austria until the 1880s. The documentation for performances in Lower Austrian asylums has been assembled by Klaus Ferentschik: from August 1886 until December 1914 there were 191 theater performances, 47 in-house productions with patients or employees on stage, 132 guest performances by theater groups, and twelve puppet or marionnette shows. Mauer-Öhling had the most in-house productions (23), while Steinhof had only six, half of which were repeat showings. Most of the guest performances took place at Kierling-Gugging (44), with the fewest at Steinhof, which had no puppet shows at all (Ferentschik, 227).

Mauer-Öhling's active theater troupe and its in-house newspaper were therefore unique to the asylum landscape. The editor of the house newspaper (*Anstaltszeitung)*, Dr. E. Holub, declared that theater as therapy was just as beneficial as occupational therapy. He thought it followed that new asylums were more likely to add theaters, or *Festsaalgebäude*, because of this.[23] Similar commentary on the existence of theater buildings in the asylum-planning literature began to appear around this time (close to 1910), but the emphasis was on theater as a part of the educational programming and light entertainment. Even at Mauer-Öhling, which had the most active and creative theater ensemble of all the asylums, the idea of theater as therapy had nothing at all to do with Reil's notion of theater being used to perform psychic interventions. Rather, the programs were oriented toward using theater as education and occupational therapy.

Mauer-Öhling became the leader in theater productions because its director, Josef Starlinger, was an advocate. He wrote articles and delivered lectures for fellow asylum directors, championing the effects of having an active and regular entertainment program that went beyond the usual Christmas and Carnival (*Fasching*) celebrations. Starlinger connected an active theater and entertainment program, along with occupational therapy, to the "socialization and civilization of the insane asylum" (Bresler, 69). An important part of the programming for Starlinger was that it was announced a month in advance in the asylum newspaper, allowing patients to anticipate the events (see Starlinger). During a typical season at Mauer-Öhling the following events were staged: a slide lecture about exotic plants, which reportedly drew murmurs of admiration from the audience, and a black family dancing performance that drew "the liveliest interest of the patients" (such events were combined with interludes filled by the institutional orchestra or raffles for prizes). Also on offer were an "amusing kinometograph, with dances, mishaps on honeymoon trips, and adventures of a distracted professor," as described by the institution's newspaper. One member of the community wrote and directed a children's play, "Snow White," which was shown to the children at Mauer-Öhling, who reportedly watched quietly for two hours. The players were a mix of children from the institution and employees' children.[24] In February 1907 two one-act plays were performed: "Clever Jacob" and "The Geizhammel Company"; also presented was "The Kilometer Eater," "The Governess, Light Comedy in one Scene," and "The Fools, Light Comedy in Two Scenes." The players were sometimes the children of the employees who had repeatedly appeared on the stage. The editor praised the performance for its smooth and natural qualities, as well as for being "Posse-like."[25]

By 1908 a troupe was formed and farces were performed regularly. The House Theater und Variety Company (*Haus-Theater- und Varieté-Gesellschaft*) led by Mr. Bayer debuted with its first evening of theater in 1908. He often chose farces from the current Vienna programs, as noted by the editor of the house newspaper. For this first official theatrical debut, a one-act play, "Fourteen Days under Arrest. Farce with Songs," by Friedrich Rotter, and "Whose Child is It?" a sketch by Richard von Kanna, were performed. In 1908 Heinrich Bayer also directed the New Year's Eve show, with songs, comical scenes, and farces.[26] The ingredients were present at Mauer-Öhling for an enthusiastic participation in the theater from the top (Starlinger) down.

Because the theater programming was primarily oriented toward education and entertainment purposes, the theater reviews in the house newspaper typically followed two formats: one was a general advice column to players (how to be more natural on stage), and the other was a general form of theater criticism that might appear in a Viennese newspaper, singling out laudable performances with descriptive words. For the advice column format, the educator in the editor, Dr. E. Holub, can be sensed in an early review, as he doles advice out to the players. While acknowledging the "personal charm" that amateur plays have, and praising the players, he also warned them to avoid "declamatory speech in their conversational tone."[27] He proposed that roles should be matched as closely as possible to each player's physique and character, which would allow the play to unfold naturally. In a later review, he noted the progress the players were making—they were more self-possessed and natural, and making fewer mistakes. He declared some performances to be "perfect," and ended with this advice:

> Each player must completely give himself over to the role in order to find the correct movement, emotion, and attitude, to avoid all exaggerations. Real people and real life must be expressed on stage, not cardboard cutouts and marionettes. The natural performance … captivates the spectator.[28]

He treated the performances as a kind of labor, the learned labor of acting. There was nothing to suggest that the performers themselves are entering into a psychological space, but rather they were, through saying lines and participating in this community endeavor, occupying themselves and learning how to say theatrical lines naturally. His criticism also points out that this was an amateur or community theater, not one in which a spectator might experience the deep dramatic, emotionally cathartic experiences associated with performances of the Burgtheater. The genres chosen for these performances (one-acts, farces) were suitable for the intended "therapy." The aim was, as in professional theater, to capture the attention of the spectator; because of the amateur performances, there was no worry about performances causing these particular spectators to further lose their sense of reality.

For an example of the second kind of criticism, the teacher in the editor (Holub) is again evident, for he ended the season by mentioning players by name and the types or roles they played. The last theater presentation of the season, held on 7 May 1908, was chosen from the programs of the Viennese theaters especially for Mauer-Öhling, according to Holub, who noted that the performance included something for everyone.[29] He declared it to be well-studied and carried out as directed by Heinrich Bayer, and singled out individual performances, from a "lovable country waitress" to

> Mr. Kogler, who was funny in all his comic roles, [and] drew extra applause for his pratfalls, Mr. Ettl, who was an exquisite hen-pecked husband and spent aristocrat.... Everyone played with enthusiasm, and Miss Peireder especially, with her slim and neat stage appearance ... promises to be a second star of the stage.[30]

Holub had compared the theater activities to occupational therapy, which was all the rage in the medical community, declaring it was just as beneficial (see Starlinger). But the players were primarily employees, nurses, and the children of employees, with only the occasional patient participating. The occupational therapy that Holub envisioned was still minimal. But there was another aspect to the therapy that was beneficial for asylums, and this was described by Georg Ilberg, who also noted that only a very few patients acted in the productions at asylums, which depended heavily on the enthusiasm of the personnel and their families.

In his 1904 book on insane asylums, Ilberg mentioned with interest the combination theater/church at Mauer-Öhling, but restricted most of his remarks to his knowledge of the theater at Gross Schweidnitz, which had a similar church/theater. Theater was therapeutic, explained Ilberg, because it was a stimulation that patients in the audience enjoyed, that calmed them down, and that could be used as a reward for labor or to keep hysterical symptoms in check. Events were staged once a month at Gross Schweidnitz where, Ilberg declared, "all slumbering talents had been awakened."[31] Theater was part of a larger program of occupations for Ilberg, who was an advocate of education at asylums. He had been affiliated with the asylum at Sonnenstein, which had seven educators, and when he realized this was the exception rather than the norm, he wrote an essay recommending that all asylums hire education specialists in 1908. In his essay, Ilberg described the role of the teacher: taking care of the library, helping patients choose literature, practicing languages with the educated patients, organizing games of billiards and card games, directing music for the church, organizing concerts, theater, dance and costume parties, and casting plays and dramatic readings from patient, administrator, and orderly populations. The teacher organized field trips, walks in the country or to restaurants, and got to know the patients quite well. Because of the level of education of the teachers, they could follow the doctor's point of view and also have a distinct psychotherapeutic role to play with some patients ("Der Lehrer"). Within a year of that essay, Mauer-Öhling hired a new educator, Franz Schindler. The editor of the house newspaper pointed out that with this new hire, Mauer-Öhling was making a huge step in following the example of the insane asylums of Saxony, where teachers had long been employed.[32] The teacher would provide organization and order, using theater as a reward within the no-restraint system there.

At Mauer-Öhling theater was therapeutic in the way that architecture was considered to be therapeutic. The new architecture of the Jugendstil insane asylum suggested a life of freedom and lightheartedness for patients, who were occupied rather than schackled. The medical community agreed that the no-restraint system required constant occupation of mind and body to create order in the insane asylum. If theater was therapeutic as occupational therapy, it was only one option among many in the no-restraint life at the asylum. It was not a therapy of psychic cures as Reil had imagined it might be, but part of civilization and order, creating an environment with a community for both long- and short-term patients. This was certainly Starlinger's position. Theater was associated with education in asylum culture, and there was no attempt to delve into the psyche of the actors or spectators as Reil had tried to do. By the time Reil's fantasy of a theater building had materialized, the medical community did not take his theatrical therapy seriously, so the farce, with its stock characters and plots, was deemed appropriate. That it could actually be a subversive genre politically mattered not a bit. It was an accepted part of mainstream Austrian culture and therefore woven into its institutions with ease by an enthusiastic lover of the theater, as long as no troubles ensued (plays were always carefully selected).[33]

The fact that theaters were actually built for several of these new institutions demonstrates how much theater was a part of culture at the time. But it takes more than a building to make theater. Steinhof's free-standing theater was rarely used. Mauer-Öhling had the most creative and active theater program because the right conditions were present: the enthusiasm of individuals like Heinrich Bayer and the support of the director, Josef Starlinger, made Mauer-Öhling a very special place where theater arts would be incorporated into an educational program for patients.[34] In this story, then, the threads of material fact (actual buildings), medical opinion, and ephemeral performances (sometimes reviewed in the institutional newspaper) hardly weave together into a unified pattern. Taken together, however, fact can be sorted from fiction: the architecture of *fin- de-siècle* asylum theaters would have met every wish that Reil ever had as far as the building and theatrical apparatus went. But his 1803 fantasy of theatrical cures had little relationship to the therapeutic reality that was practiced a century later within those beautiful theaters. The occupational therapy of theater at the *fin de siècle* was intended to bring spectators and actors outside themselves instead of closer to the mirror of representation within the psyche that Reil had envisioned.

Works Cited

Apfelter, Irene. *Zwischen Humanitären Bemühen und Sozial-disziplinierung: Psychiatrische Therapien in deutschen und österreichischen Irrenanstalten in der ersten Hälfte des 19. Jahrhunderts*. MA Thesis, University of Vienna, 1999.

Bernhard, Thomas. *Wittgenstein's Nephew: A Friendship*. Translated by David McLintock. New York: Alfred A Knopf, 1989.

Boog, Carlo. *Zur Sicherheit des Lebens in den Theatern mit besonderer Berücksichtigung der Theaterbrände*. Vienna: Lehmann & Wentzel, 1882.

Bresler, Johannes. *Ausgewählte Kapitel der Verwaltung öffentlicher Irrenanstalten.* Halle a.S.: Marhold, 1910

Colomina, Beatriz. "Krankheit als Metapher in der modernen Architektur/The Medical Body in Modern Architecture." *Daidalos: Architektur, Kunst, Kultur* 64 (1997):60-71.

Ferentschik, Klaus. *Theater im Tollhaus*. Diss. University of Vienna, 1994.

Foucault, Michel. *Madness and Civilization*. Translated by Richard Howard. New York: Random House, 1965.

Henne, Hugo. *Über Geistesstörungen und Irrenanstalten. Zur Aufklärung für Aerzte und gebildete Laien*. St. Gallen: Scheitlin und Zollikofer, 1865.

Hinterberger, Dr. A. F., Freiherr von Krauss. "Bemerkungen und Erläuterungen zu einem Projekte einer Heilanstalt für Tuberkulose." *Der Architekt* 9:1 (1903): 5-10.

Hofmokl, Eugen. *Heilanstalten in Österreich.* Vienna: Holder, 1913.

Ilberg, Georg. *Irrenanstalten, Idioten- u. Epileptikeranstalten*. Jena: Gustav Fischer, 1904.

—. "Der Lehrer an der Heil- und Pflegeanstalt." *Psychiatrisch-Neurologische Wochenschrift* 20 (7 August 1909): 169-71.

Jetter, Dieter. *Grundzüge der Geschichte des Irrenhauses*. Darmstadt: Wissenschaftliche Buchgesellschaft, 1981.
Johnson, Julie M. "Asylums and Theaters: The Incompetent Spectator and the Baroque Ideal." Association of Art Historians Annual Conference, Nottingham, UK, April 2004.
"Die Kaiser Franz Josephs Landes-Heil-und Pflegeanstalt in Mauer-Öhling." *Der Architekt* 9:1 (1903): 40-42; 95-98.
—. *Festschrift niederösterreichisches Landesausschusse* 1902.
Klose, C. L. *Beiträge zur Klinik und Staatsarzneiwissenschaft*. Leipzig: Kummer, 1823.
Kolb, Gustav. *Sammel-Atlas fur den Bau von Irrenanstalten*. Halle a. d. S.: Marhold, 1907.
Koller-Glück, Elisabeth *Carlo von Boog und Mauer-Öhling*. St. Pölten-Vienna: Verlag niederösterreichisches Pressehaus, 1988.
Maass, C. *Practische Seelenheilkunde nebst Grundbedingungen einer guten Irren-, Heil- und Pflegeanstalt*. Vienna: P. Rohrmann'sche Hofbuchlandlung, 1847.
Mauer-Öhlinger Anstaltszeitung Feb. 1907-October 1909.
Neue Freie Presse. "Die neuen Landesheil- und Pflegeanstalten." 6 October 1907.
Nostitz und Janckendorf, Gottlob Adolf Ernst von. *Beschreibung der Konigl. Sachsischen Heil- und Verpflegungsanstalt Sonnenstein*. Dresden: Walther, 1829.
Psychiatrische Wochenschrift 1:1 (1 May 1899): 1-13 ("Johann Christian Reil").
Reil, Johann Christian. *Rhapsodieen über die Anwendung der psychischen Curmethode auf Geisteszerrüttungen*. Halle a. d. S.: Curtsche Buchhandlung, 1803.
Roller, Christian F. W. *Grundsätze für Errichtung neuer Irrenanstalten insbesondere der Heil- und Pflegeanstalt bei Achern im Grossherzogthum Baden*. Karlsruhe: Muller, 1838.
—. *Psychiatrische Zeitfragen aus dem Gebiet der Irrenfürsorge in und ausser den Anstalten und ihren Beziehungen zum staatlichen und gesellschaftlichen Leben*. Berlin: Reimer, 1874.
Schlöss, Heinrich. *Die Irrenpflege in Österreich in Wort und Bild.* Halle a. d. S.: Marhold, 1912.
Schön, Bruno. "Notizen über die k.k. Irrenheil- und Pflegeanstalt." *Humoristiche Pillen gegen üble Laune, Melancholie und dergleichen Grillen*. Vienna: Prandel und Mayer, 1858.
Schweigger, A. F. *Über Kranken- und Armen-Anstalten zu Paris*. Bayreuth, 1809.

Shorter, Edward. "Private Clinics in Central Europe, 1850-1933." *Social History of Medicine* 3.3 (1990): 159-95.
Showalter, Elaine. *The Female Malady: Women, Madness, and English Culture, 1830-1980*. New York: Pantheon Books, 1985.
Snell, Otto. *Grundzüge der Irrenpflege für Studirende und Aerzte*. Berlin: Reimer, 1897.
Starlinger, Josef. "Zum Ausbau des Anstaltswesens." *Psychiatrisch-Neurologische Wochenschrift* 16 (10 July 1909): 139-41.
Thiher, Allen. *Revels in Madness: Insanity in Medicine and Literature*. Ann Arbor: The University of Michigan Press, 1999.
West, Shearer. *Fin de Siècle*. New York: The Overlook Press, 1994.
Wolf, Peter. "Am Steinhof spielt das Personal Theater." *Die Presse* 13 December 1959.
"Zum Bau der Irrenanstalten. Von einem Anstaltsarzt." *Psychiatrish-Neurologische Wochenschrift* 7 (9 May 1908): 53-55.

Notes

[1] Criminally insane patients were not housed at Mauer-Öhling.
[2] The *Narrenturm* was abandoned as an insane asylum in 1853 and is now a museum for pathological anatomy.
[3] "Johann Christian Reil,"*Psychiatrische Wochenschrift* 1.1 (1 May 1899): 1-13.
[4] The idea that more people were nervous and insane was widespread and took its more exaggerated form in theories of degeneration, like Max Nordau's (see West).
[5] *Die Kaiser Franz Joseph-Landes-Heil- und Pflege-Anstalt in Mauer-Öhling.* Festschrift niederösterreichisches Landesausschusse 1902: 9 (Law from February 17, 1864).
[6] Leopold Steiner, who was also involved in the planning of Steinhof, and Fedor Gerényi went on the trip ("Die Kaiser Franz Joseph-Landes Heil- und Pflegeanstalt in Mauer-Öhling," *Das Österreichische Sanitätswesen*, 14.42: 463).
[7] "An Stelle der großen, kerkerartigen Gebäudekomplexe sind lustige, mit Veranden versehene Pavillonbauten getreten, in welchen sich die Kranken der größten Freiheit erfreuen und zur Ablenkung von ihren Wahnideen in den verschiedensten Arten beschäftigt werden" ("Zur modernen Irrenpflege," *Österreichs Illustrierte Zeitung* 16:1 (7 October 1906): 27).
[8] Steinhof, the most famous psychiatric facility built in the pavilion style was, in fact, partially converted to a facility for treating tuberculosis, and was the hospital where Thomas Bernhard spent time (see Bernhard).
[9] "Die Kaiser Franz Josephs-Landes-Heil-und Pflegeanstalt in Mauer-Öhling," *Der Architekt* 9:1 (1903): 40-42; 95-98.
[10] Boog also wrote a very thoughtful book about preventing the spread of fires in theaters, with special recommendations to architects for allowing proper exits to spectators (see Boog).

[11] Boog came under the projected budget by 4,700,000 Kronen.
[12] Villa "Betonia" had a swimming pool, bowling alley, tennis court and ice cellar—all made of concrete (Koller-Glück, 33-35).
[13] That he wrote his article anonymously was entirely atypical for this journal and suggests how alone he was in his opinion, at least for the public of the journal.
[14] "Für fast zwei Jahrzehnte wurde Roller der Lehrer der Irrenärtzte der Welt." Dieter Jetter, *Grundzüge der Geschichte des Irrenhauses* (Darmstadt: Wissenschaftliche Buchgesellschaft, 1981), 41.
[15] See www.zfp-emmendingen-de, accessed March 7, 2005.
[16] Emmendingen had been worked on in Baden by the architect Waldemar Osterloff; that asylum was planned by Dr. Schule, who had been a protégé of Christian Roller (see Hofmokl).
[17] The Marquis de Sade interned there from 1801-1814, and took part in the theatrical presentations.
[18] "Schon Reil (1803) hat die Einführung von Concerten und Theateraufführungen in die Irrenanstalten vorgeschlagen, hatte dabei aber den wunderlichen Gedanken, man solle "eigen Schauspiele fürs Tollhaus" schreiben und darin "jeden Narren seine eigenen Thorheiten lächerlich machen lassen" (81).
[19] "theatralischen Gaukeleien" (350, as cited in Apfelter, 62). Feuchtersleben is credited with coming up with the term "psychosis."
[20] "Und man leicht in den Fall kommen könnte, Geister heraufzubeschwören, die man nicht zu bändigen im Stande wäre" (357, qtd. in Apfelter, 67).
[21] "Ich habe diess an einem Zöglinge der hiesigen Irrenanstalt nur zu deutlich gesehen. Schiller's Don Carlos hat den armen Mann ebenso krankhaft erregt als Shakespeare's Dramen: Digitalis und Nitrum mussten das unzweckmässig angefachte Feuer wieder dämpfen. Zweckmässig eingetheiltes Studium mathematischer Schriften, Physik und andere zweckmässige Geistes-Thätigkeit, die die krankhaft gesteigerte Einbildungskraft nicht in Anspruch nimmt, lassen die beste Wirkung erwarten" (Maass, 91).
[22] This episode is described in the German literature without a specific reference to the place, but Elaine Showalter identifies a similar anecdote at the Fisherton Asylum for the criminally insane, in which an actor's recitation of a murder scene from Hamlet upset the inmates, especially one who cut off his doctor's head and kicked it about the garden (38).
[23] "[E]s ist in der modernen Anstalt ebenso ein Mittel zur Ablenkung wie Koerperliche Arbeit oder Beschäftigung und muss somit direct zu den Heilmitteln gezählt werden gleich diesen. In Verfolgung dieses Zweckes sehen wir auch in der modernen Anstalt ein neues Gebäude auftauchen, dass den früheren Anstalten entweder überhaupt fehlte oder das nur in dem einen oder anderen ganz unzulänglichen grosseren Raume repräsentiert wurde, es ist dies das sogenannte Festsaalgebäude" *Mauer-Öhlinger Anstaltszeitung* 2:17 (1 February 1908):1.
[24] *Mauer-Öhlinger Anstaltszeitung* 1:5 (1 February1907):3.
[25] "Recht possierlich war ein mundartlicher Vortrag "Die Streitenden" der flott und naturlich gegeben wurde." *Mauer-Öhlinger Anstaltszeitung* 1:12 (1 September 1907):4.

[26] *Mauer-Öhlinger Anstaltszeitung* 3:26 (1 November 1908):4.

[27] "Dilettanten-Vorstellung haben immer auch einen persönlichen Reiz, der sonstige kleine Mangel gerne übersehen lasst. Übrigens Zeigen sich bei mehreren sehr gute Ansatze und ist namentlich ihre Naturlichkeit im Spiele hervorzuheben. Das Deklamatorische, Predigerhafte soll im Konversationstone nie zum Vorschein kommen. Die Rolle soll deshalb dem eigenen Leib und Charakter möglichst angepasst sein, dann wird das Spiel sich von selbst natürlich gestalten."*Mauer-Öhlinger Anstaltszeitung* 1:7 (1 April 1907):4.

[28] "Haltung und Szenen werden immer ungezwungener und natürlicher und die Sprachfehler verlieren sich immer mehr. Einzelne Darstellungen waren schon vollig tadellos. Der Darsteller muß sich ganz seiner Rolle hingeben, um die richtige Bewegung, Gemütslage und Haltung zu finden, und alle Ubertreibung vermeiden, so nicht eine störende Komik entstehen.....Wirkliche Menschen und wirkliches Leben mußen auf der Bühne zum Ausdrucke kommen, nicht Standbilder und Marionetten. Die natürliche Darstellung packt am meisten, weil sie den Zuschauer am leichtesten gefangen nimmt und mitfortreißt." *Mauer-Öhlinger Anstaltszeitung* 3:27 (1 December 1908):3.

[29] "jenem Erheiterung, diesem Gesang; Salonstück und Bauernstück ... Ohrenschmaus durch köstliche Couplets-Vorträge." *Mauer-Öhling Anstaltszeitung* 2:21 (1 June1908):4.

[30] "ein anmutiges Bräutchen und ländliche, liebliche Kellnerin, eine kernige handfest Wirtin, eine originelle Drechslermeisterin, forsch und schneidig im Auftreten als plötzlich Reichgewordene, Herr Kogler, in allen Rollen als Komiker ganz besonders hervorragend, erzwant geradezu Beifallsturme durch seine zwerchfellerschutternde Komik, Herr Ettl, ein köstlicher Pantoffelheld und verlebeter Aristokrat, Herr Berger, als Geselle und Holzknecht gleich gut...sie alle waren allen Lagen, ob Salon, oder Bauernstuck gerecht, spielten mit Eifer und man kann wohl auch sagen, mit ganz hervorragender Routine, so dass das Gesammtspiel ein vorzügliches zu nennen war. Frl. Peireder besonders, mit ihrer netten, schlanken Bühnenerscheinung, als Wirtin Schneidig und kurz angebunden, verspricht ein zweiter Stern der Bühne zu werden." *Ibid.*

[31] "alle schlummernden Talente sind aufgestobert worden" (*Irrenanstalten*, 408).

[32] *Mauer-Öhling Anstaltszeitung* 4:37 (1 October 1909):3.

[33] Heinrich Bayer was identified as the director of the theater troupe in several reviews.

[34] In relatively recent times, the theater at Steinhof staged plays with the personnel as actors, the patients as spectators. The rare events are documented in its theater archive with programs and newspaper clippings (for example, see Wolf). The theater at Steinhof has also been used as a venue during the Wiener Festwochen.

CHAPTER ELEVEN

LEGITIMATING STRANGENESS: ART, LABOUR, AND THE ASYLUM IN FIN DE SIÈCLE VIENNA

LUKE HEIGHTON

> What Clarisse saw, to her astonishment, was a sketch for a large composition, the drawing sure and accomplished, entirely sensible, in spirit even commonplace, with many figures perspectively involved with each other in a large room the details of which were executed with the painful correctness, the schoolmasterly sanity, of something straight from the National Academy... "We've no time for you today," Dr. Friedenthal told him. Turning to Clarisse, he summed up his criticism in the words: "He's not schizophrenic, but I'm afraid he's the only artist we have at the moment. Schizophrenics are often splendid artists, absolutely modern, absolutely modern." "And insane?" Clarisse queried. "Why not?" Dr. Friedenthal mournfully retorted.
> —Robert Musil[1]

> A new mystery sings in your bones. Cultivate your legitimate strangeness.
> —René Char[2]

The episode from Robert Musil's *The Man Without Qualities*, quoted above, describes an encounter between a madman and one of the novel's chief protagonists, Clarisse, as she attempts to visit the insane murderer Moosbrugger in an asylum just outside Vienna. It is, needless to say, a scene written not entirely in earnest, though we should not make the mistake of thinking Musil's intentions anything but deadly serious. The very act of ironising the scene, in fact, points towards some measure of ineluctable belief on the part if its author: the belief that creativity, subjectivity and madness are somehow inextricably intertwined, perhaps nowhere more so than in the truly modern work of art and in Viennese modernity. So certain is Musil, indeed, that he is prepared to cast his belief into doubt, if only for it to re-emerge from this metaphorical cloud of unknowing all the more compelling. Such a process, I contend, constitutes an important aspect of the theoretical work behind Musil's own creative endeavours, and the idea of the work within art will form the central organising concept for this discussion. We do not even know whom, if anyone, Musil had in mind when he thrust Clarisse into the asylum to be confronted, first, not by a criminal but by "a cheerful, fat painter."[3] Had he wished to find such examples close to home he would not have been lacking in source material, for in both 1898 and 1908 Vienna was host to two exhibitions featuring works of artistic creation produced by mentally ill patients from Lower Austria's principle psychiatric hospitals. Intriguingly, each was held to coincide with the 50th and 60th anniversaries, respectively, of the accession of Emperor Franz Joseph I. An overview and analysis of each will form an important part of this essay, paying particularly close attention to the points at which the work of art and the art of work intersected or overlapped within the nineteenth century Austrian asylum.

Equally prominent, however, will be a consideration of the work of one individual, the manic-depressive painter Josef Karl Raedler (1844-1917). Raedler's work, despite his being interned at one of Lower Austria's most famous long-term psychiatric facilities throughout the period under consideration, was shown at neither–indeed it has only come to (limited) prominence in the past forty years or so, after more than 400 of his paintings, drawing and writings were discovered in a heap of rubbish by a nurse at the still extant Mauer-Öhling psychiatric hospital a few hours from Vienna. Shortly afterwards the "collection," as it has henceforth been referred to, was transferred to Dr. Leo Navratil, a pioneer in the field of art therapy for the mentally ill, at Vienna's Gugging asylum. Navaratil acquired roughly a hundred of these works, which were eventually donated to the Lower Austrian Provincial Museum, whilst writing a singularly informative, albeit largely psycho-biographical, study of their creator. Raedler's work was first shown to the general public in 1994, since which date his work has become collectible. Today it is principally through the efforts of New York's Galerie St. Etienne and its Director, Jane Kallir–a prominent scholar of Austrian and German Expressionism as well as of outsider and self-taught art in her own right–that Raedler's international reputation has grown. Raedler's work, it will be shown, provides a valuable correlative and counterpart to both the patient art exhibitions of 1898 and 1908, and to those questions regarding the nature of creativity and the work of art that so fascinated Robert Musil.

Towards the end of the nineteenth century, numerous studies on the art of the mentally ill began to appear. These purported to discuss the etiology of the art of the insane as opposed to their historical depiction in art. In the event it proved harder to draw clear lines of distinction between the two groups than was generally assumed, not least because the art of the insane's at times "autobiographical" nature, the mad artists' (not uncommon) awareness of both art history and its usefulness in his or her own self-presentation, tempered only by their subsumption beneath the socially-conferred trope of psychological infirmity, threatened to collapse the hitherto self-sustaining borders which existed between "inside" and "outside" forms of representation. Ever since the art of the insane emerged as a distinct area of study, it has laboured under the burden of having somehow to reconcile to the demands of this "insider/outsider" dichotomy, dependent always on conventional art-historical authority for its status as art, whilst at the same time steadfastly resisting easy assimilation into art's historical narrative. It is thus extremely difficult to locate with any certainty the madman's place in such a narrative, just as, even as our reading of "outsider" art in all its forms becomes ever more subtle and differentiated, it becomes harder to situate the art of the insane within either artistic or clinical-medical discourses, much less to evaluate its historical importance within them. The better to avoid further confusion, two contrasting–albeit highly complimentary and by no means mutually exclusive–approaches have grown up, as exemplified by the work of two important scholars within the field, Sander Gilman and, latterly, Jane Kromm. One the one hand, at any given historical point the art of the insane is definitively not read against art history in general, but is instead seen as but one type of artistic production occurring within a specific social, cultural and historical context, albeit with much to say to us which is of relevance beyond such limited confines. This, perhaps, is preferable when attempting to approach the work of patients themselves. Sander Gilman—to name but one of the most well known recent commentators within the field—makes explicit his view that this interest was fired principally by a growing contemporary conviction that the uniqueness of the individual was derived from some greater, overwhelming force, such as madness; a conviction which itself had its roots in the German Romantic tradition. In contrast, the view of the insane given in the majority of visual sources discussed by Jane Kromm in her extremely valuable study *The Art of Frenzy: Public Madness in the Visual Culture of Europe, 1500-1850* is derived from without, demonstrating how less attention has been paid historically to madness' hermeneutic potential than to its heuristic relevance within successive discourses on social reform.[4] In Kromm's work the mad are discussed primarily in relation to the manner in which they were represented by others–undifferentiated, highly objectivized–rather than via the more complex means through which they might construct their own identity through visual media. Nevertheless, neither approach can be entirely separated from the other, for within the historical process of social and psychiatric reform lay the seed from which differentiation and the recognition of individual patients' subjectivity could grow. Within this parallel process creativity, and, more specifically, the creativity of the mentally ill played an important role, for "with the reform of the asylums in the early nineteenth century," Gilman argues,

> . . . and the parallel literary glorification of the mad as those solely possessing true insight (in the writings of Romantics such as E. T. A. Hoffmann), attention is thrown for the first time on the artistic production of the insane. For if the creative are mad, must not the corollary also be true, that the mad are creative?[5]

Gilman goes on to cite a number of these works, from the great reformer Philippe Pinel's brief mentioning of the art of the insane in his 1801 textbook of psychiatry, to Pliny Earle's essay 'The Poetry of Insanity' (1845), to those most famous studies–Walter Morgenthaler's study of the Swiss patient-artist Adolf Wöllfli (1921), and Hans Prinzhorn's essay *Das bildnerische Schaffen der Gesiteskranken* (1919), which became the basis for his seminal monographical work, the *Bildnerei der Geisteskranken* (1922).[6] Gilman's own *Seeing the Insane* (1982), sets itself a similar task to that of Kromm, albeit extending the scope of his study into the latter part of the twentieth century.[7] His, Kromm argues, is an approach which, whilst enormously valuable, is broadly consistent with that of his nineteenth and early twentieth century predecessors: a detailed description of individual or works or the graphic practices of significant individuals or institutions, followed by the author's diagnosis of the image as an example of a specific malady, albeit more critically and within a given cultural context.[8] Yet it is Gilman's capacity both to read his subject matter within the whole of these contexts, perceptively interpolate the whole range of contemporary discourse within a given period, whilst at the same time being able to intelligently and provocatively extrapolate beyond these critical boundaries, delineating the art and the image of the insane as a site of inquiry rather than mere prognostication which makes his work qualitatively different from his 19th century predecessors.

If, in the 19th century, there appears to have been a gradual movement from the literary towards the pictorial as the principle site of inquiry in both art and literature as the century progresses, this was a development mirrored, as it were, by the way in which technological developments–namely, the increasingly widespread use of the camera–allowed psychiatric clinicians not merely to embellish their accounts of the symptomology of mental illness with the occasional photographic image, but to make those images (one thinks particularly of the French neurologist Jean-Martin Charcot (1825-1893), though the X-ray, too, was discovered in 1895 by the German physicist Wilhlem Röntgen), a crucial aspect of their initial diagnosis. This could not have happened, however, had not the focus already shifted some way away from the body of the patient as a spectacular, superficial manifestation of some unknown and unknowable malignant influence, and towards a regard for, and a confidence in the body as the extension of and a visual index to nosologically identifiable physiological processes.

Such a move went hand-in-hand with the materialist tendencies of much nineteenth-century academic medicine, implied not just in the primacy of the factually observable in clinical psychiatric diagnosis, but also by the existence of a growing body of evidence pointing towards a profound diversity of visual forms through which psychiatric illness manifested itself. Paradoxically, perhaps, it was this determinist emphasis on the internal, mechanistic causes of mental disorder that led to a re-evaluation of *looking* as a means of clinical (indeed critical) investigation of its outward signs. Looking itself became to some degree a participatory, albeit highly subjective, speculative and specular act. Only by seeing through the eyes of the insane, by attempting to perceive the world as they did, was it thought possible to trace an etymological path back to the root cause of the disease. "Art," it can be argued, offered a way to do just that. In this way the methodological processes of art history were reproduced within the field of medicine, at least in so far as each attempted to discern the internal "truth" within the object of their attention.

There is another reason why the medical profession should have given increased import to the non-verbal utterances of their patients. For, Gilman reminds us, in the 1860s and early 1870s it was in art in which the most visible and controversial experimentation was taking place.

> Art became the appropriate vehicle for experimentation, just as poetry had been some four decades earlier. Thus the central questions asked of the creativity of the insane both pre-selected that medium in which experimentation was then taking place, and imposed upon the products of the insane the ideology of the avant-garde. By the end of the nineteenth century, the *art of the insane* represented not only the lost world of childhood but also the utopia (or distopia), of aesthetic experimentation.[9]

In fin de siècle Vienna there obtained a number of parallels, and a number of points of contact between contemporary discourses within the visual arts, literature, medicine and psychiatry. In part this was rooted in a greater awareness of the considerable philosophical questions raised by post-Darwinian, post-Nietzschean modernity's unravelling not just of their respective disciplinary methodologies, but of the fundamental precepts upon which those methodologies and associated interpretive systems were founded. It was as if the boundaries between them were beginning to dissolve, one by one, and in their place it was necessary to construct new approaches, new forms, new sciences which might better define man's relationship both to a changing world and to the changes he felt in himself.

"Objects," wrote Ludwig Wittgenstein "contain the possibility of all states of affairs . . . Only if there are objects can there be a fixed form of the world."[10] Thus, objects, no less the art object, can be accorded a fundamentally important role in the ways in which we reflect on ourselves and society, and through which we are in turn reflected. In doing so, however, Wittgenstein also emphasised that such apparent fixedness necessarily carries with it certain tensions; namely the possibility of the changing, the variable, and therefore the unknowable, expressed as form.[11] Wittgenstein suggests that such objects hold the key to determining what is and what is not real, what is factually observable and what is not. And yet in doing so he dares to suggest that that which is not observable as fact is no less a part of the landscape of reality; that reality is as much defined by its negatives, its non-existences, appearing perhaps, nonsensical and counter-intuitive, as it is by those things which are not. If the object represents something akin, as Franz Marc put it a year before, to a "negligible echo" of man, which "makes the thought specific, and banal," might we therefore suggest that, after Wittgenstein, the very banality of objects might lead us back their imaginative inception?[12] How we interpret such "banal" objects depends on what they are, who produced them, how they were produced, how they present themselves or are exhibited as objects to be considered, and–perhaps most of all–what we expect such objects to communicate. Do they, as Wittgenstein suggests, express something static, bound by historical circumstance and epistemological conviction? Yet cannot those same objects shed light on the shifting dynamics of that particular context as a whole?

The *Irrenpflege*–literally, "Care of the Insane"–exhibitions of 1898 and 1908 were to a considerable degree the products of not only of medical and psychiatric discourses current in Vienna at the time, but of contemporary political and ideological discourses also. This essay will seek to place the exhibitions of 1898 and 1908 with the context of a broader critical examination, current at the time, not only of the psychiatric patient's relationship to the society from which they were excluded, but also in relation to the strategies employed by both clinical psychiatric professionals and politicians (at a local and municipal level), to define the relationship which existed–at least as a possibility–between the asylum itself and that same society. Further, I hope to show that the exhibition strategies employed by psychiatrists and political bodies alike were as much influenced by the rubric and rhetoric of contemporary exhibition practices as they were by the narratival necessities of their own clinical/socio-political objectives. And I shall discuss the ways in which the patient art contained within the *Irrenpflege* exhibitions of 1898 and 1908 was deployed in order or shore those ambitions. Crucially, however, that same art contained within it the possibility of something which, though not entirely unaccounted for by psychiatric professionals in particular, gave a form and a voice to something which has not yet achieved the historical. Patient artists were thus able to (re)introduce their own subjectivity into the discourses conduced on their behalf.

The Jubilee and *Irrenpflege* Exhibitions of 1898

The Jubilee Exhibition of 1898 was organised first and foremost by the Lower Austrian Provincial Committee, under which was the Regional Economic Committee and the Lower Austrian Provincial Trade Association, which together formed the Exhibition Commission. In the lyrical pangyric which was the foreword to the official catalogue the Exhibition Commission attempted to set out the motivation behind the proposed festivities; namely, the spectacularly high regard in which, on the eve of his fiftieth anniversary as monarch, the Emperor Franz Joseph was still held. The exhibition was, then, somewhat of an attempt to simultaneously amalgamate and gloss over the various well-known contradictions bedevilling the Habsburg Empire so publicly. Framing the problem as if it were really a question of how best to do justice to the aims and achievements of the monarchy throughout the Empire, the committee sought to explain how the structure of the exhibition as a whole would go some way to countering the perception that both the Empire, and Austria, was riven by internal strife, insurmountable regionalism and social exclusion. In so doing, they also hoped to recapture some of the incomparable national optimism– even pride–which, they asserted, had been in evidence during Vienna's hosting of the 1873 World's Fair. What better way to do so than by having trade, production, technological and industrial advancement form the central organising principle behind the show? The same principle might best be articulated through those aspects of everyday modern life least in dispute, and therefore most capable of fashioning some sort of reconciliation, however uneasy. Anxiety was to be refashioned into an expression, albeit a somewhat qualified one, of confidence. The Jubilee Exhibition offered Austria an opportunity to show the world how such an event should be conceived and executed, though the Committee struggled to find a form for the Jubilee Exhibition which would prove sufficiently inclusive and representative whilst not becoming too bloated or too expensive, and which would distinguish itself from previous, similar events.[13] One thing, however, remained clear: the exhibition should transcend factional party interests, and in so doing not only conform to the traditional rubric of large-scale national and international exhibitions, but surpass it. Such an exhibition, it was hoped, would serve as a useful preparation for the forthcoming World Exposition Paris in three years' time. This last was made clear in a passage highlighting the considerable pessimism associated with such exhibitions across Europe and the world–a feeling, it was argued, in part attributable to the world-wide economic downturn, but which was as much attributable to their ubiquity and the over-blown rhetoric that so often accompanied them. The Jubilee Exhibition, would, it was emphasised, require something of a leap of faith, especially if factional politics and a lack of preparedness conspired to instil a sense of "exhibition fatigue" as well as a greater pessimism amongst potential participants and visitors alike.[14] Occupying a place of special prominence amongst the Jubilee Exhibition's many pavilions, each dedicated to one or another aspect modern, industrialised, increasingly consumer-driven Viennese life was the Welfare Exhibition, which sought to draw attention to the many public services and social provisions offered by the city and province's municipal and social authorities. To that end, the Welfare Exhibition was divided in several sections, each denoting a specific aspect of progressive governmental responsibility. Amongst these, however, one stood out. It was that devoted to the care of the insane, the *Irrenpflegeausstellung*, or "Exhibition of the care of the insane."

> Here, more than anywhere else in contemporary society, can one behold the rich reservoirs of compassion and cooperation, the unsurpassed quality of the work carried out by so many committed to the fight against the ravages of nature, against poverty, misery, sickness and insanity, and dedicated to their cure, their alleviation, and their reduction.[15]

The *Irrenpflege* exhibition, as we shall refer to it, was located in the largest of the seven exhibition spaces within the Wohlfahrts [welfare] pavilion, immediately to the right of the main entrance.[16] It ran from the 7th May until the 1st October 1898, from ten in the morning until late afternoon. Entrance was general admission ticket, which also afforded access to the Jubilee exhibition as a whole.[17] Several prominent individuals had been deputised to acquire the objects that would appear in the section for the Lower Austrian Government's presentation on the work done by its many "Cure and Care Institutes for the Mentally Ill."[18] Among these men were Lower Austrian Regional Sanitation Inspector Fedor Gerenyi, member of the Commission and in charge of works relating to public health and welfare care institutions;[19] and Professor Heinrich Obersteiner, who was responsible for gathering material relating to both public and private psychiatric institutions.[20] Subsequently, the governor of Lower Austria, Joseph Freiherr von Gudenus established a provisional Exhibition Committee, which was in turn granted a budget of 5000Fl for the installation of the exhibition and another 3000Fl for the Wohlfahrtsausstellung [Welfare Exhibition] by the provincial government. It was decided conclusively that the exhibition should include a collection of items fully representative of all the public health and welfare services, and of the autonomous regional administrations and individual institutions within Austria. The task of coordinating such an impressive undertaking was then handed over to the Provisional Committee's Chair, Leopold Steiner, second to whom was the administrative director of the region's health institutions, Fedor Gerenyi. Thus it was Gerenyi who acted as official head of the exhibition.[21] Part of Gerenyi's brief was to describe in plain terms the complex local, regional and national governmental structures which, to the general public, had hitherto remained obscure. Once again, the report stressed that many of the methods of treatment currently used in several of Lower Austrian institutions were not yet employed as commonly as they ought to be. This, it was felt, was because of a hostility on the part of the public, government and the institutions themselves. Nowhere was this more the case than in the field of psychiatric care. What was needed was a greater, better dialogue between doctors, civil servants and Vienna's regional psychiatric hospitals, which would in turn be reflected in the quality of the exhibition. For that reason, contributions from all the relevant institutions as to design of the exhibition were encouraged, and delegates from all the institutions falling under the aegis of the Lower Austrian Government were to be welcomed. As to the personnel responsible for the *Irrenpflege* section of the exhibition, in addition to the aforementioned Steiner and Gerenyi, one Dr. Starlinger, then a junior doctor at Kierling-Gugging, was put in charge of works by psychiatric patients.[22]

According to the author of the foreword to the official Wohlfahrtsausstellung catalogue, the motivation behind the exhibition was to present to the public a picture of both communal and private welfare provisions put in place during the Kaiser's reign.[23] The catalogue thus provided an extensive overview of the changes in Austria's health and welfare provision over a much greater period, from the founding of the general hospital in 1784, to the closure of the Narrenturm, or "Fools' Tower" in 1869, and the eagerly awaited opening of the new *k. k. Jubiläums- Landes- Heil- und Pflegeanstalt für Geisteskranke* [Imperial and Royal Provincial Cure and Care Institute for the Mentally Ill] at Mauer-Öhling. The *Irrenpflegeausstellung* conformed to just such a progressive narrative. Indeed, as the commentator for one commemorative publication, the *Pracht-Album*, made clear, it played a crucial role in sustaining that narrative.

Shortly after the Jubilee Exhibition's opening, the Lower Austrian Provincial Committee published its own report on it. The report traced the Welfare Exhibition from its inception to its eventual realisation.[24] It described in greater detail how, in the spring of 1897, a committee of health-care and social service experts in the field had been formed with a view to participation in the celebration to take place in the summer of the following year. Rather than functioning independently of the Austrian state apparatus, the organisation was committed to working alongside it in a bid to provide a general picture of the changes which had taken place in welfare provision over the fifty years of the Kaiser's reign. A secondary, though equally important objective was to raise awareness within both the public and private sector of the new directions, new initiatives and new efforts which, it was felt, not only could but should be introduced into existing practice. By these means the potential of care institutions could be fully exploited, and it was therefore decided that the exhibition should be structured in as openly didactic a fashion as possible.[25] What followed in the report was an extensive documentary on how the exhibition actually shaped up, a tour through the various displays the content of which differs little from that described in the official Welfare Exhibition catalogue. We do learn, however, that the exhibition pavilion itself was constructed in a 'classical' style, including a triumphal arch – symbol of the victory of progress over ignorance. The room in which the *Irrenpflege* exhibition took place measured 26m x 10m, the total area covered by the exhibition amounting to 383.75 square meters, and that four separate large display walls or units were constructed to increase the surface area available. These were arranged in the center of the room, and it was intended that the visitor should walk through and around them, moving through the room in clockwise fashion, entering through one set of doors and leaving through another. This was a deliberate strategy on behalf of the organising committee, intended to ensure that even the most casual visitor was at least required to walk through the entire exhibition before they could get out, encountering the items and displays specially designated to receive the most attention along his or her way.[26] Four friezes by the academic sculptor Othmar Schimkowitz were commissioned, called respectively *Sickness – Francis in Assisi*; *Madness – Saul and David*; *Maternity – the Repentant Madonna*, and *Infirmity - The Good Samaritan*. Schimkowitz, like the better-known Gustav Klimt, was a prominent Secessionist, and designed a number of statues for Otto Wagner's church in the Lower Austrian asylum „am Steinhof." Unlike Klimt, whose trio of allegorical images intended for the University–*Philosophy, Medicine* and *Jurisprudence*–would attract such critical and official opprobrium when they were finally presented to the public in 1907, Schimkowitz appears not to have deviated at all, either figuratively or intellectually, from what was expected of him. In avoiding such notoriety, however–indeed in courting respectability instead –Schimkowitz also avoided achieving the same level of fame, patronage and, ultimately, collectability as his more risqué counterpart.

Upon entering the porticus one first of all encountered a display by Dr. Karl Kosterlitz, showing each of the autonomous institutions featured and explaining both their respective functions, their relationships to one another and to the administrative center. Immediately opposite that was a pictographic installation describing the history and development of each. Inside the exhibition hall itself one then saw a table, on which were laid out several articles–pathological samples, patients' report books and forms of physical restraints used on patients from the present to the 1850s. Further on were to be found charts and diagrams which attempted to break down and categorise the various forms of disorder from which an individual might suffer, their possible causes and treatments. Opposite were a number of models of asylums; the Narrenturm, by Hans Vicovsky, (a profession model-maker from Vienna);[27] the asylum at Ybbs (by postal assistant Josef Schindlöcker of St. Pölten); those of Vienna and Klosterneuburg (by the Viennese sculptor Josef Gilgen); Kierling-Gugging (Laurenz Moder, sculptor in Vienna); a mechanical, electrified model of an isolation cell in the Vienna Psychiatric Hospital produced by Anton Tenzer; and, finally, a model of a pigsty made by an anonymous inmate of the Langenlois asylum.[28]

The rear middle wall of the hall was given over to a detailed excursus on the physical handling of the insane. This included a life-size mock-up of a cell from the old Fools' Tower, complete with an original door and window. In the cell could be found a life-size wax figure of a patient, wearing an iron belt and cuffs, a wooden gag in his mouth, as was frequently the case during the previous century.[29] Also present was an original restraining chair, strapped into which was another wax figure wearing yet more diverse types of restraint. This, it was explained, had been common practice at the Ybbs asylum up until 1842. There followed numerous pieces intended as accurate representations of *modern* psychiatric care.[30] There was also, however, what they described as an excellent model of the new wing for "ruhige," or calm patients at Kierling-Gugging, complete with soundproofed rooms, the facilities for more manic and/or dangerous individuals, the bath- and washrooms, dormitories and dayrooms. In particular, attention was drawn towards the model of plans for the new asylum at Mauer-Öhling, its opening timed to coincide with the Emperor's 50th jubilee which, it was reported, proved the high point of the exhibition for His Majesty.[31] A 150 square meter diorama of the separate, pavilion-style "colonial" buildings at Kierling-Gugging covered an entire wall of the exhibition room. It was painted by one Rudolf Weber of the atelier of the Royal Opera painter Brioschi, and consisted in paintings and wax sculptures depicting patients going about their daily work–work, it was to be understood, integral to the running of the asylum. Nearby were three more wax figures of patients made by patients. The artfulness of these, the committee reported, resonated particularly well with female visitors to the exhibition.[32] Next came a display of scientific apparatus and examples of anatomical abnormalities associated with nervous ailments prepared by a Dr. Sickinger of the Vienna Pathological-Anatomical Institute. This section of the display concluded with a demonstration of the ways in which patients might harm themselves or take their own lives, and the objects with which they did so. In this respect there was an element of the performative, or at least of the dramatic, to the exhibition which the official catalogue failed to mention, but which the Provincial Committee report felt deserved attention.[33] Nearby was a selection of paintings by an unnamed inmate of the Vienna Psychiatric Hospital, „einem Geisteskranken Maler"–a mad painter–chief amongst which was a work entitled *Pinel descends into Paris' Salpêtrière to remove the chains from the mad*, after Robert Fleury's work of 1876.[34] This was all that was mentioned regarding the patients' artistic or craft-based involvement in the exhibition, however it is hard to deny that patient art played a key, if not a dominant role in the *Irrenpflege* exhibition of 1898.

1908: Mauer-Öhling

A central feature of the exhibition so far discussed has been the keen emphasis placed by its organisers not only on the rhetoric of reform, but also of sustainability. With very few exceptions, patients' contributions to the *Irrenpflege* exhibition of 1898 appeared only because they supported the aims and objectives of those responsible for its organisation. Yet the objects included were, seemingly, unclassifiable even to those who had selected them. Paintings *were* openly referred to as works of art, but the great majority of objects occupied a space somewhere between art and crafts. Whilst it is very often as impossible to deduce the exact circumstances in which a piece was created, as it is the motivation behind its creation, in many instances they *were* spoken of directly as products of the workshop, the sewing room, or even the land itself. "Art," therefore, and the economy of its production, had a role to play in the economy of the asylum; literally–in terms of its day-to-day running; figuratively–in so far as it could be employed in service of a particular discourse; and, lastly, as an expression of the fundamental inscrutability of mental illness itself. In the nineteenth century asylum the boundaries between work and the work of art were therefore blurred to a considerable degree, and it is in part this act of blurring, coupled with the contingent act of re-viewing and reclassification with which this section is concerned. Madness therefore began to occupy a space previously thought the province of aesthetics, a space in which art, morality and mental illness collide.

Conformity to and assimilation of group norms played an important part in the rehabilitation of psychiatric patients throughout Europe, founded on the utilitarian belief that, if properly provided for, even the insane individual was capable of responding positively to those forms of treatment which appeared, almost self-evidentially, beneficial both to themselves and the community. Two points stand out: Firstly, that the discipline and self-control required for artistic accomplishment was an important characteristic of moral therapy as a whole. Secondly, that the "arts" were viewed as appealing to the more refined sensibilities of patients. Art, in so far as it is the product of discipline, is understood as capable both of apprehending and advancing the aesthetic sensibilities of the patient, whose capacity for self-restraint increased through his or her contact with art. Art therefore served a mediatory function (as distraction from the pathological idea) and a managerial one (as benefiting the general economy of the asylum). It partook of a reflexive strategy according to which the psychological and physical characteristics of madness were made apparent to the patient himself.

In Vienna, as elsewhere, patients were seen as individuals, certainly, but also in a more general sense: as reflective of a condition, an illness, or a type. As such, they must be *seen* to be treated, as this reassures those in whose care they are placed, society at large, and, potentially, the patients themselves, that neither one is irredeemable. It was also important that the patient should produce something, artistic or otherwise–that they should work–for although the products of their labour bear the formal, conceptual and perceptual marks of their insanity and of the constant presence, the continued possibility, of sanity. Although this model does not account for those individuals whose work was carried out furtively, in secret, for no-one's gaze but their own, nor does it serve those whose art was simply dismissed, and whose reflexivity was thus directed entirely inwards, nevertheless, it is possible that ideas such as discipline and self-restraint might enable us to enter more fully into the "spirit" of individual artworks, as we learn to detect discrete disciplinary regimes and "refined" schemata falling outside the bounds of both traditional aesthetic and "pathological" appreciation. That which strives most to achieve the condition of normality is itself revealed as anything but by that selfsame effort. The prominence of work–which is inherently normative–in the moral and therapeutic discourse of the asylum is beset by the same implacable contradiction: The mad are asked to prove that they are not mad, or at least to fashion themselves as individuals capable of overcoming their madness by demonstrating their ability to work as they might otherwise do, though their very presence in the asylum is an acknowledgement of the fact that, according to "objective" standards of the world outside, they cannot. Yet in another sense they are impelled to mock society, its moral code, and the liberal doctrine of self-improvement and self-advancement, by doing exactly as it decrees in abjection, and from a position of absolute powerlessness.

The therapeutic value of work was one echoed by Dr. Josef Starlinger who in 1908 wrote a lead article for the newsletter of institution of which he was now Director, the *Mauer-Oehling Anstalts-Zeitung*,[35] Starlinger unambiguously linked the work performed by the patients to the continued economic and administrative wellbeing of the hospital itself, whilst at the same time taking the opportunity to offer a few clues as to the content of the following month's Jubilee Exhibition [Jubilaeumsausstellung], which was very much framed by the notion of "Arbeitstherapie": work therapy.[36] Mauer-Öhling's Jubilee Exhibition of July 1908 was conceived less as the kind of exhibition one associates with present-day Gugging, and more in keeping with, for example, the Jubiläumsausstellung of 1898. Starlinger's article gave relatively little space to a discussion of the arts, as compared with a preponderance of space, print and prestige to all that the recent advances in scientific knowledge, industrial innovation and material production had to offer the psychiatric profession. Yet in conjoining work and the spirit in such a fashion Starlinger was not doing something particularly unusual for the time. Much parodied as it might have been Schiller's phrase, "the burger's pride is his work" did indeed ring true.[37] Instead, the Director of Mauer-Öhling can be seen to have taken account of a number of his principal obligations as director of the institution, transmitting that same message to the patients for whom he was responsible.[38] With the exhibition of 1908, Mauer-Öhling was better able to present itself to the public, the press and assembled local dignitaries – including Fedor Gerenyi – clinical specialists and assorted beneficiaries not only as viable, but as "normal." Once again, this time in his preface to the special, commemorative Exhibition edition of the *Mauer-Oehling Anstalts-Zeiting* [Mauer-Öhling Institution Newspaper], Starlinger's concern is to stress not only the efficacy of the treatment programmes available at the asylum, but also the sustainability of the community itself. The form and the content of the exhibition, along with its demonstrable concern for the integration of the asylum into the small community in Lower Austria from which it took its name, provide us with a key to understanding one of the most significant founding principles behind the institution itself: that it should, in so far as was possible, mirror, and in doing so endorse, the social and economic structure of the world beyond its walls, whilst simultaneously stressing the interdependence between, and the institution's dependence on, that very world.

The exhibition received notices in two Viennese newspapers, one in the *Kronen Zeitung* and a longer review in the *Neues Wiener Journal*, in which, once again, the importance of Arbeitstherapie was made explicit. The article praised what the reviewer regarded as

> . . . one of the strangest and most wonderful of exhibitions one can imagine. One can hardly believe that these items, handicrafts of all kinds, all forms of art. These testaments to the last remains of creative strength, artistic sense, and the spirit of invention are wonderful.[39]

Less clear-cut amongst these assorted "Curiosa," as Starlinger collectively named them, were the paintings and portraits, the latter mostly produced and submitted by a "Herrn Krenn" (also responsible for the theatre decorations)–some thirty of them in total.[40] Unfortunately, only such works as a Herr Lancidelli's watercolors, *Hermann's Battle*, *A Walk Through the Prater*, *The Birth Of Venus*, and *The Adoration of the Madonna*, are named or spoken of in any detail.[41] Lancidelli, indeed, was one of those awarded the gold prize of 10 Kronen for his efforts. The term "Curiosa" is itself interesting, used both to stand in for and to encompass a variety of other classificatory terms–arts and crafts, book-binding, wood-cutting, glass-working–and, apparently, painting.

In what, one hopes, will go on to be regarded as a hugely important investigation into the relationships which exist between art, schizophrenia and modernity, Louis A. Sass writes,

> Only with [that] which we do not readily understand are we in need of theory; and theory works mainly by analogy, a 'seeing-as' that uses something we think we do understand as a model for comprehending less intelligible things.[42]

In addition to Starlinger's, one other account of the exhibition at Mauer-Öhling appeared in the professional journal *Psychiatrisch-Neurologisch Wochenschrift* on 26th September 1908, written by one of his senior colleagues at the institution, Dr. D. Stelzer. Once again, Stelzer began by making the connection with the Kaiser's 50th anniversary explicit. Once again, having done so the author of the report went on to stress that the aim of the exhibition was to showcase the advantages and opportunities bestowed on the asylum population, and by implication the financial advantages to the taxpayer, of modern work [Arbeits-], or "Job" [Beschäftigungs-] therapy.[43] He pointed, unambiguously, to the propaganda value of the exhibition, which he believed would go some way to convincing certain sceptical circles within the public at large that the asylum was both a viable and a successful place of treatment and care.[44] He then went on to provide for his readership a brief descriptive tour of the exhibition. All the works shown, he wrote, were produced by patients, male and female, between 1st April 1907 and 31st March 1908, over what amounted to a total of 174, 275 work days, involving almost 60% of all the patients–both those who were confined within the asylum and the Familienpflege–under supervision.[45] Arranged by category and laid out either on tables along the edges of the corridors, the center of the patients' day room and the two rooms adjoining it, in the niches in the walls or stacked in pyramids in the middle of the floor, were the same example of patients' handiwork to which Starlinger referred. But these were only an antecedent to the exhibition itself, which began, Stelzer writes, with a very large number of hats made a patient suffering from chronic depression. Next came a great pyramidal display of water-tanks, barrels and buckets made by another patient who, having until relatively recently been extremely difficult to control, had, by virtue of his labours become a peaceful, hard-working member of the asylum community.[46] Nearby were several chess-pieces, napkin rings and puppets made by an episodically former metalworker who had transferred the skills he had learned from his previous life into the medium of wood. Meanwhile, hanging along the length of one wall was a large fishing net, under it a hammock. This was either a re-creation of something used by one maniac both to prevent his ideas from escaping and to catch his rage, or it was an installation of the same by that individual to represent his desire do to be able to do so. Unfortunately Stelzer gives us no information besides its basic description and supposed function

Dotted throughout the exhibition were copious examples of what might more easily have been recognised as patient art–oil paintings and watercolors, drawings, and a number of busts and other sculptures made from clay or plaster. Like Starlinger, Stelzer gives particular prominence to one "paranoiac-melancholy academic painter," presumably Lancidelli or Krenn, although from the pictures we have of the exhibition it seems their work was but a small proportion of that on offer.[47] In one particular case, Stelzer also informs us of a patient who, having first sketched the figure of a man in paper went on to reproduce it first as a meter-high clay statue, and then another out of plaster. This figure, it seems, provides Stelzer with the bridge he needs to his discussion of the "Curiosa." "Naturally," he writes, "no such exhibition in an insane asylum would be complete without them."[48] There are, too, strange, unsettling [zerfahrene] drawings, unusual puppets and 'mad' costumes. Yet, either in spite or because of their strangeness Stelzer is clearly at as least as fascinated –and moved–by these items as he is disturbed by them. The author offers us nothing by way of explanation or interpretation, but he does convey the sense that these items were somehow not altogether different from those which constituted the rest of the show, and were therefore in some way representative of another, less regulated, more individual and expressive side of asylum life which was valued equally.

Contrary to those examples of patient art shown in 1898, the "Curiosa" shown in 1908 implicitly recognise a contradiction inherent in the asylum's public face as opposed to its private life, allowing the patients the right to some form of self expression beyond that which served to articulate the form and function of "official" asylum culture. Rather than being created by clandestine individuals working in isolation, without encouragement or provision, the works shown were very much sanctioned and approved of, albeit not necessarily understood. Stelzer does not pretend, even to an audience of his medical peers, to be able, or even to desire to interpret these works, let alone to attribute to them a psychiatric or psychoanalytic cause or meaning. Rather he places them firmly within the context of asylum life as a whole, and is content to let the individual define him or herself outside the limits of institutional rhetoric. This suggests a dramatic change in attitude even from 1898, when the artistic production of patients was chiefly valued for its ability to help sustain a progressive master narrative. Perhaps, then, this is an example of how unreason or the irrational could exist alongside, or protrude into the rational, without radically challenging it. Inarticulate as madness might be it could nonetheless be articulated, its presence made perceptible. Madness therefore retained a capacity to evoke the fugitive, the inarticulable, the irrational and the unthinkable located at the margins of reason as the shadow of the "real," and to give them form. Here we see unreason being given its place within reason, offering the latter a depth and a meaning without which it appeared arid. Far from challenging the authority of reason, therefore, unreason is conceived as something with the potential to restore to the rational world that which it is in danger of losing and without which its liberal-progressive ideals remain dangerously abstracted from the life of art and of the soul. This is not a flight away from madness, but rather madness' return to its rightful place inside reality.

Arguably the key feature of the 1908 exhibition, and that which–in spite of its lack of a political sponsor beyond the provincial authority comparable to that of 1898–differentiates it most clearly from its earlier counterpart, is the focus given to those works, those practices, even, which lay outside a given ideological narrative or established clinical approach to the care of the insane. The attention paid by both Starlinger and Stelzer to the presence of the "Curiosa" at the Mauer-Öhling exhibition gives us a clue as to how art within the asylum gradually liberated itself from the confines of official discourse and somewhat spectatorial culture, and indeed came to be recognised as valuable for its own and the individual patient's sake. In each case, the exhibitions suffered from a lack of explanation, a lack of contextualisation, with regard to those works less easily classifiable. By 1908, such works were considered both necessary and desirable. They provided something more than any polemic or any show of statistics ever could, and therefore gave the visitor both a truer and a more human account of the Viennese asylum, its aims and its inhabitants, even whilst it failed to enunciate each as clearly as its directors might have liked. Nor should it escape our attention that, ten years after the first exhibition of its type, items such as the "Curiosa" were, as Stelzer tells us, an expected element of such an endeavour. What had Stelzer seen, or what did he know, which could have led him to this surprising conclusion? Certainly my research has not uncovered anything directly comparable to the *Irrenpflege* exhibitions in the intervening period that might have led to such a conclusion. Stelzer's claim, though, supports the belief that something fundamental had changed, that the public's conception of the asylum and of the insane and their works had altered dramatically, that it was no longer feasible, perhaps not even desirable, to "cure" the mentally ill. This change in expectations was expressed through the medium of art.

Josef Karl Raedler

Although we know comparatively little about a great many of the works shown in the *Irrenpflege* exhibitions of 1898 and 1908, we know a good deal more about one artist whose name did not feature in the *Mauer-Oehling Anstalts-Zeitung* report-cum-catalogue, and whose work seemingly was not shown; Josef Karl Raedler. Raedler was a patient at Mauer-Öhling from 11th August 1905 until his death in 1917. He was initially diagnosed as suffering from "circular psychosis with manic tendencies," and later on with "secondary dementia." Raedler's work offers us evidence of a deeply personal art practice quite different from which is otherwise described as having taken place at Mauer-Öhling. Raedler saw himself as an artist, a writer and philosopher and was, it appears, moved by that same combination of creativity and necessity more commonly associated with the artist, reminiscent more of the genuinely vocational rather than the merely therapeutic.

Raedler began to paint before entering the Mauer-Öhling asylum, whilst he was a patient at the Vienna Psychiatric Hospital. There his subject matter comprised mainly portraits. At Mauer-Öhling, however, a far greater range of scenes were presented to him, and found their way into his work accordingly. He began to paint group scenes, social gatherings and events, and to capture images from the daily workings of the hospital–the workshop, the bathhouse, the dayroom, and–particularly–the physical environment of the hospital, especially its extensive wooded grounds. Much is made both of the geometry of the painted surface itself and of the built environment, though Raedler is also seen to integrate abstract geometric elements into the pictures themselves where to do so allows the viewer to comprehend more than one scene simultaneously, and where, perhaps, he feels it necessary to add a sort of meta-textual element to the work in order for each of its constituent parts to be properly understood.

Several of his works incorporate a substantial body of text. These are sometimes legible, though just as often they are not. Dr. Leo Navratil–former director of Vienna's Gugging asylum, a pioneer as much in the field of Outsider Art and the closest Raedler has to a biographer–has devoted considerable attention to these texts and their relationship to the images upon which they appear. Sometimes they refer simply to the identity of the sitter, though it is unclear as to whether, as with the group portraits, the image was constructed "live," from memory, or as a combination of both. People's faces, each carefully individuated, are invariably turned to meet the viewer's gaze directly, somewhat expressionlessly. It is by no means certain whether all the portraits refer to real people, real scenes, or an amalgamation of the real and the imagined. Highly colorful and often featuring some kind of floral motif, it seems likely that Raedler's compositional style was heavily influenced by his previous career as a porcelain decorator. Sometimes descriptive, sometimes taking the form of a poem, essay, or stream of consciousness, sometimes little more than extended word-play, Navratil concludes that, to our eyes at least, much of Raedler's output is meaningless, banal, silly, repetitive. Despite this, and in addition to snippets of personal biography, certain themes recur: his pacifist convictions; his self-confessed debt to (and occasional exceeding of) the achievements of Schiller and Goethe and his imaginary travels across the globe. Raedler also believed–though we have no evidence to prove the case one way or the other–that the doctors at the Mauer-Oehling treated him unjustly. Still, Navratil suggests, one wonders as to whether to Raedler these writings represented something positive, perhaps even showing some sort of internal development invisible to our eyes, or whether they are in fact as repetitious, as static, as unreal or as unproductive as they appear: in one, not atypical case, Raedler's elaborate, concentric decoration of the borders of the paper threatens to overwhelm the images which it frames–an image which is in fact a text, the lines on which it is written heavily ruled, divided, colored, or with the paper left bare where one would expect color to appear.

Precisely deciphering Raedler's schematic intentions is perhaps impossible. This does not mean that they did not exist, that there was no such plan, no formal, textual or intertextual logic, no sense in which compositional details were tailored to fit the artist's own sense of style or his purely aesthetic satisfaction, however psychotic. We cannot, then, deny that their creation owes a great deal to a conscious economy of effort, irrespective of what one might regard as their artistic failure. As Derrida reminds us "madness is what by essence cannot be said, [for ultimately] what is a language that would not be one of reason in general?" And yet, both art and language can be said to embody the process of normalisation, "that is, sense, in every sense of the word."[49] If we are to begin to understand the art of Joseph Karl Raedler and others like him we need, therefore, to acknowledge the discipline and self-restraint at work within them, serving both as corollary and corrective to their less stable, "unreasonable" elements. Only then might we be able to enter more fully into the "spirit" of individual artworks, as we learn to detect discrete disciplinary regimes and "refined" schemata falling outside the bounds of both traditional aesthetic and pathological appreciation. The normal and pathological are no more mutually exclusive than are creativity and genius. Nor can they be characterized as poles within a singularity, now together, now apart. As Foucault put it, a conjoined deciphering of the normal and the non-normal will never reduce the meaning between them.[50]

For Musil, the distinctions between science and the individual, between the "ratioid" and the "non-ratioid" lay at the basis of his distinction between morality and ethics. Musil believed that neither ethics nor aesthetics can be submitted to rational systemisation and law without fundamental distortion. Indeed he includes ethics in the realm of the non-ratioid, whose "facts consist of experiences which are not known to scientists in the necessary multiplicity and variety, since empirical thought "naturally narrows the spirit."[51] In Musil's thought, David Luft tells us, the creative individual, the poet or "Dichter" replaces the philosopher, just as the creative person replaces the normal, moral human being. The "Dichter" speaks on behalf of the exception in an unstable world with unstable values.[52] The Poet meanwhile, stands as that human being in whom "the desperate isolation of the individual in the world and among people comes most strongly to the surface."[53] In an article written in 1910, Musil contended that art "not only ought to portray the immoral and the repugnant, but may also love them." In fact, the representation of perversity was central to the ethical task of art: "In truth," he wrote,

> There is no perversity which would not have as its correlative health and morality, as it were. This presumes that for all the elements of which it is composed there are analogies in the soul that live virtuously in other people.[54]

Crucially, however, Musil was not arguing that the insane artist should be accorded a special place within the cultural field. He was not advocating an art in which the language of feelings, of the 'non-ratioid' took preference over the intellect. Rather he was concerned with effecting a more flexible use of intellect, in turn engendering a more creative, co-optive, and critical tension with reality in the service of pathos than was generally in use. As for the language of feelings, he declared, it "is conservative, even when the feeling is not."[55] For Musil, the emblematic "man without qualities" represents both a mad, nightmare embodiment of humanity's moral, ethical, spiritual and aesthetic confusion, and at the same time a perfectly perversely ideal type, open to all possibilities. In stressing his antipathy towards intellectual homogeneity, Musil anticipated, or rather foreshadowed, one of the key elements in George Bataille's development of his theory of the General Economy: namely, that in so far as heterogeneity exists as a "splitoff" structure of the homogenous, it is for the same reason all the more encompassing, including everything which results from unproductive expenditure–be it in terms of capital, social production, or intellectual exchange. For Bataille, "The homogenous" does not recognise the homogenous as such, and in this it performs much the same operation as that of the conscious upon the unconscious."[56] It the implacable homogeneity of Raedler's approach which, perversely, signals the extent of its difference from the normative and which makes visible its very peculiarity, but in seeking to suppress their essential abnormality differences he simultaneously risks rendering the work itself mute. Similarly, the point at which Raedler's paintings become most concrete, most coherent, and most "legible" to us, is the same point at which they become least visible as works of art.

The idea that the insane, the autistic, and the mentally ill are little more than 'rendering machines' incapable of artistic expression, incapable of accumulating any intrinsic creative awareness of past work against which to measure current creations, is one which has been in currency since long before the end of the nineteenth century and the beginning of the twentieth. Refuting the theory is not easy, since there are undeniably a variety of examples attesting to it. In the first instance, however, one can and must be able to distinguish between works of unequal complexity, to say nothing of the thorny question of technique/style. Not all works by such people are equally complex; and, as Lyle Rexer remarks, "not all savants are created equal," though he stops short, as indeed do most writers on 'Outsider Art,' of offering the alternative, sufficiently critical, aesthetic theory which is required if we are ever to escape the clutches of those biologically reductive, psychoanalytic, or all-too romantic interpretations which have so far prevailed.[57] Yet he does remind us that,

> Only modern art has explicitly assumed the tragic burden of isolated self-consciousness and a temporality that hurtles us forward into the unknown. Earlier art and most sacred art sees the world as more static, and human consciousness as only one of its elements. The fact that the 'vision' and technique of artists with [for example] autism does not seem to change or expand in range or depth means that their relationship to the world is not changing. Is that relationship incomplete? Certainly. Is the self behind it incomplete, limited? Perhaps. But the self as expressed in art is not some

> discrete thing but only the gestures that embody it, the traces it leaves behind. The repertoire of gestures can be rich and varied or narrow and repetitive, but the validity of the gesture cannot be dismissed.[58]

The self, however, is not a complete or discrete thing however manifold the forms of its expression. Moreover, the very repetition to which Rexer refers not only plays a vital part in constituting the incomplete self, but has found a role of singular importance within contemporary art, with its abiding post-Duchampian interest in abstraction, seriality, reproduction, reduction, recombination and reiteration. Thus the accusation, if that is the right word, that artists like Josef Karl Raedler are in some sense indistinguishable from another because they are, ultimately, indistinguishable from themselves, is to sidestep a proper evaluation of their work. Raedler exists to us only through his work, *as* his work. In a sense, then, he is reducible to his art and it to him. However, the work itself cannot be understood without reference to its creator, and we only know what we think Raedler wants to tell us. He is essential to it, and it, so far as we can say, him *in essence*. In so far as Raedler is only ever the subject of, or the guiding hand behind his paintings, he himself is very much at *their* disposal: it is the image and not author which is realised, and which is at the root of our fascination with him. He exists, but is unrealisable. His subjective viability is inherent in the work–indeed it is dependent on it– but at the risk of displacing the work itself, and vice versa. Thus we are witness not simply to a system of endless repetition, denying the possibility of expression, but to of one of endless substitution and re-creation which constitutes its own back-and-forth dynamic, admirably resistant to the meaning-creating machine of interpretation. This is itself fundamentally expressive, as when Musil describes expressionism as that which turns its back on mere appearances, in harmonious alliance with a tendency toward the abstract, the non-purposive, anti-productive, independent, and *un*-viable, though never truly divorced from each.[59]

This same divorce from reality, known also as *l'art pour l'art*, is extremely problematic. "What is ideological in the principle of *l'art pour l'art*," Adorno writes, "does not have as its locus the energetic antithesis of art to the empirical world, but rather the abstractness and facile character of this antithesis."[60] Madness, like art, is subject to a double language, "a matrix of language that, strictly speaking, says nothing. The fold of the spoken which is an absence of work."[61] This, then, is the tautology from which the work of art as an expression of something other than itself, is logically impossible, since whatever is produced only refers back to an original madness: the all-encompassing sign for that which arises from the unspeakable. In the art of the insane we come face to face with an economy of both uncontainable excess, and incomprehensible–or uncomprehending–deficiency.

Notes

[1] Robert Musil, *The Man Without Qualities*, trans. Eithne Wilkins and Ernst Kaiser, London: Panther Press, 1968, vol. 3, 378-9. Unless otherwise noted, all translations are my own.
[2] From Char's "Partage formel," in *Poèmes et prose choisis*. Cited in Jean Khalfa's introduction to Michel Foucault's *History of Madness*, ed. Jean Khalfa, trans. Jonathan Murphy and Jean Khalfa, London and New York: Routledge, 2006, xxxvi.
[3] Musil, *The Man Without Qualities*, (1968), vol. 3, 378.
[4] Jane Kromm, *The Art of Frenzy: Public Madness in the Visual Culture of Europe, 1500-1850*, London: Continuum, 2003, passim.
[5] Sander Gilman, "The Mad Man as Artist: Medicine, History and Degenerate Art," *Journal of Contemporary History*, Vol. 20, No. 4, (October 1985), 577-78.
[6] Ibid., 577-78.
[7] Sander Gilman, *Seeing the Insane*, Lincoln and London: University of Nebraska Press, 1996.
[8] Kromm, *Studies in the Iconography of Madness*, PhD dissertation, Emory University, 1984, iii. To the above list of works on the iconography of the insane, Kromm adds those by the Salpêtrière clinicians Jean-Martin Charcot and Paul Richer, in Paris: *Les dèmoniaques dans l'art* (1887) and *Les difformes et les maladies dans l'art* (1889); Richer's *L'art et médecine* (1902); and another Salpêtrière doctor, Henri Meige's contributions on art to Charcot's hugely influential and long running periodical, the *Iconographie de la Salpêtrière*. See also Sander Gilman's study of nineteenth century Scottish psychiatrist and photographer Hugh W. Diamond, *The Face of Madness: Hugh W. Diamond and the Origin of Psychiatric Photography*, New York and London: Brunner-Routledge, 1976.
[9] Gilman, *Medicine, History and Degenerate Art*, 580-1. My emphasis.
[10] Ludwig Wittgenstein, *Tractatus Logico-Philosophicus* (1921), trans. C.K. Ogden, London and New York: Routledge, 2002, 35 ¶2.02; 37 ¶2.026.
[11] Ibid., 37 ¶2.0271.
[12] Franz Marc, *Briefe, Aufzeichnungen und Aphorismen*, 1920.
[13] Ibid., 2.
[14] Ibid., 3.
[15] Ernst Keiter in *Pracht-Album der Jubiläums-Ausstellung Wien, 1898*, ed. Julius Laurencic (Vienna, 1898), 9.
[16] *Pracht-Album*, 104. The Committee was presided over by Dr. Anton Löw, who, alongside Richard von Kraft-Ebing had founded the Purkersdorf Sanatorium for nervous ailments in 1890.

[17] Ibid., 104. These cost 40 Kroner on weekdays and 30 Kroner Wednesdays, Sunday and holidays. Military servicemen were only required to pay 20 Kroner, and children 10. Tickets for the entire duration of the Jubiläumsaustellung cost 15 Gulden.

[18] „Heil- und Pflegeanstalten für Geisteskranke."

[19] Gerenyi was a notable reformist in areas of public health, who would go on to play a major role in the Mauer-Öhling exhibition of 1908.

[20] *Pracht-Album*, 14. Obersteiner was Director of the private sanatorium at Ober-Döbling, Vienna. Obersteiner sent work eleven patients from Ober-Döbling to Hans Prinzhorn, in Heidelberg, which would become the basis for what is now the Prinzhorn Collection. Of these, however, only the work of two such patient-artists – Frau Gr. and Frau St. – has received much attention. They, along with works by an Oskar Herzberg, a patient of a Dr. Paul Schilder at Vienna's University Psychiatric Clinic, are discussed at greater length in Bettina Brand-Clausen, *Irre ist Weiblich* (Heidelberg: Wunderhorn, 2004), and *Beyond Reason: Art and Psychosis. Works from the Prinzhorn Collection*, ex. cat. (London: Hayward Gallery, 1996). According to the introduction to the *Pracht Album*, Löw, Gerenyi and Obersteiner were each scheduled to produce articles for a collection intended to be published by the Wohlfahrtsausstellungs Commission in the autumn of 1898, which my research is yet to uncover. Further, the publication would have, and perhaps did include an essay by Bertha Zuckerkandl entitled *Kunst und Gewerbe*. Bertha was the wife of the great anatomist Emil Zuckerkandl and sister-in-law to the famous businessman and art collector Viktor Zuckerkandl, who in 1902 purchased the Purkersdorf sanatorium, a private institution not far from Vienna. Bertha, however, was herself a highly respected art and cultural critic, and an admirer of the work of Josef Hoffmann, whom Viktor eventually commissioned to design the new building at Purkersdorf, and for which it is now chiefly known. Work on the building began in 1904. See Leslie Topp, "The Purkersdorf Sanatorium and the Appearance of Science," in her *Architecture and Truth in Fin-de-Siècle Vienna*, Cambridge: Cambridge University Press, 2004, 63-94. Also listed amongst the volume's contributors was a young Felix Salten, who was to write a piece on theatre. Salten (1869-1945), found fame in 1902 for his moving obituary of Emile Zola, before beginning his career as a novelist in 1910. He was a member of the modernist literary group known as "Jung Wien," whose members included Peter Altenberg, Hermann Bahr, Richard Beer-Hofmann, Hugo von Hofmannsthal, Arthur Schnitzler, Stefan Zweig, and, for a time, Karl Kraus.

[21] „Die Betheiligung des Landesausschussreferates für Gesundheitswesen und Wohltätigkeitsanstalten an der Jubiläimsausstellung Wien 1898," in *Bericht des niederösterrecihischen Landesausschuses über seine Amtwirksamkeit vom 1. Juli 1897 bis 30 Juni 1898*, B.VI, 414.

[22] Ibid., 415.

[23] „[E]in Bild der communalen und privaten Wohlfahrtseinrichtung....welche in Oesterreich während der 50jährigen Regierungszeit unseres Kaisers geschaffen wurden und bestehen." Exhibition catalogue *Jubiläums-Ausstellung Wien 1898*.

Oesterreichische Wohlfahrts-Ausstellung, Vienna: Verlag des Präsidium des Oesterreichischen Wohlfahrts-Ausstellung, 1898, 1.

[24] *Bericht des niederösterrecihischen Landesausschuses*, 414-420.

[25] Ibid., 414.

[26] Ibid., 416.

[27] The same model can presently be found in the Nieder-österreichisches Landesmuseum, St. Pölten, Lower Austria.

[28] *Bericht des niederösterrecihischen Landesausschuses*, 416-417.

[29] „[W]ie im vorigen Jahrhunderte in der Irrenbehandlung verwendet wurden," ibid., 417.

[30] Ibid., 417.

[31] Ibid., 417.

[32] Ibid., 418. Though the authors of the Provincial Committee's report were willing to admit that the inclusion of an iron restraining bed was perhaps not quite in-keeping with the image they were attempting to convey.

[33] One possible interpretation of such a disparity is that the Lower Austrian Provincial Committee took a different view on how best to publicise their exhibition, one whose tone–not shirking from, indeed to some degree revelling in the more gruesome aspects of institutional life as was–was at odds with the more conservative Jubilee Committee.

[34] This painting, I contend, and the other, unnamed paintings displayed alongside it, were the work of one "Herrn Lancidelli," for, although the connection was not at the time made explicit–a painting of the same name was included in the 1908 Mauer-Öhling Jubilee Exhibition. This seems all the more likely given Starlinger's close involvement with the 1898 exhibition and the fact that by 1908 he had been appointed head of the Mauer-Öhling asylum, which itself included a number of works by Lancidelli. For a more detailed discussion of Fleury's original see Kromm, *Art of Frenzy*, passim, and Foucault, *History of Madness* (2006), 452.

[35] *Mauer-Oehling Anstalts-Zeitung*, (June, 1908), 1-2.

[36] Ibid, 1-2 also: „N.Oe. Landes-Heil-und Pflegeanstalten fuer Geistes- und Nervenkranke "am Steinhof" in Wien, XIII," in *Die Irrenpflege in Oesterreich in Wort und Bild* (Halle: Carl Marhold Verlagsbuchhandlung, 1912), 178-88; *Kronen Zeitung* (3rd July, 1908), 2.; *Neues Wiener Journal*, (3rd July, 1908), 4.

[37] Cited in Peter Gay, "The Problematic Gospel of Work,' *Schnitzler's Century: The Making of Middle Class Culture 1815-1914*, London: Allen Lane, 2001, 192-93.

[38] *Statut fuer die N.Oe. Landes- Heil- und Pflege-anstalten fuer Geistes- und Nervenkranke "am Steinhof" in Wien, XIII*, Vienna: Verlag des Landesausschusses des Erherzogtumes Oesterreich unter der Enns, 1907.

[39] „[E]ine der eigenartigen und bewundeswerten Austellungen, die sich man denken kann. Man glaubt es kaum, das diese Erzeugnisse des Handwerks aller Art, des Kunstgewerbes und der bildenden Kunst, von Geistsumnachteten herruehren. Wie wundervoll sind diese letzten Reste schaffender Kraft kuenstlerischen Sinnes und des Erfindergeistes." *Neues Wiener Journal* (5th July, 1908), 13.

[40] *Mauer-Oehling Anstalts-Zeitung* (July, 1908), 5.

[41] Ibid., 5.
[42] Louis A. Sass, *Madness and Modernity: Insanity in the Light of Modern Art, Literature and Thought*, Cambridge, Mass.: Harvard University Press, 1994, 11.
[43] *Psychiatrisch-Neurologisch Wochenschrift*, 27 (26th September 1908), 217.
[44] Ibid., 217.
[45] „Familienpflege" was the collective name given to patients considered both safe and able enough to re-enter the community, though not well enough to be released entirely, who were allowed to live with local families, working as domestic help or however the household saw fit. It was the household's responsibility to look after such individuals, in return for which they would in turn receive a modest stipend from the psychiatric institution in question. This was a the fairly common practice in Austria and Germany, at least amongst its more progressive, reform-oriented local authorities. Gerenyi especially showed considerable interest in it, and published several articles on the subject. For further discussion on the history on psychiatric internment in Austria including both Mauer-Öhling and am Steinhof, see Gerenyi's "Les Progress de L'assistance des aliénés dans la Basse Autrich depuis 1902," presented at the II Congres International de l'assistance des aliénés, Milan, September 1906 (Bologna: Stabilimento Poligrafia Emiliano, 1907), 1-11; „Irrenpflege und Verwaltung," in the proceedings of *Die Dritter internationaler Kongress fuer Irrenfuersorge in Wien vom 7.-11. October 1908*, Vienna: Franz Doll Verlag, 1909, 1-14.
[46] *Psychiatrisch-Neurologisch Wochenschrift*, 218.
[47] Ibid., 219-20.
[48] Ibid., 220. My emphasis.
[49] Jacques Derrida, *Writing and Difference*, trans. A. Bass, London: Routledge, 2001, 34.
[50] And yet, as Foucault remarks: ". . . they are always infinitely close to one another, just as is close to something possible the possibility that founds it; the continuity of meaning between the work and madness is possible only on the basis on the enigma of the same which permits the absoluteness of the rupture to appear" Michel Foucault, "Le 'non' du pere," *Critique*, March 1962, 207-8.
[51] Robert Musil, „Erlebnisse." Cited in David S. Luft, *Robert Musil and the Crisis of European Culture, 1880-1942*, Berkeley, Los Angeles, London: University of California Press, 1980, 164.
[52] Luft, 164.
[53] Musil „Skizze," 784. Cited in Luft, 165.
[54] Cit. Luft, 104.
[55] Musil, „Buecher und Literatur," (1926); Luft, 168
[56] Eleanor Kaufman, *The Delirium of Praise: Bataille, Blanchot, Deleuze, Foucault, Klossowski*, Baltimore and London: Johns Hopkins University Press, 2001, 120.
[57] Lyle Rexer, *How to Look at Outsider Art*, New York: Harry N. Abrams Inc., 2005, 66.
[58] Ibid., 69.

[59] C.f. Theordore Adorno, *Aesthetic Theory*, ed. Gretl Adoro and Rolf Tiedemann, trans. and intro. Robert Hullot-Kentor, London: Continuum, 2002, 318: "The element of repetition in play is the afterimage of unfree labour, just as sports....is reminiscent of practical activities and continually fulfils the function of habituating people to the demands of praxis." "Part of the rage," Adorno remarks, "against hermetic works [of art] is that they also shatter the comprehensibility of traditional works. It holds true in general that the works sanctioned by tradition and public opinion as being well understood withdraw behind their galvanised surface and become completely incomprehensible; those manifestly incomprehensible works that emphasise their enigmaticalness [sic] are potentially the most comprehensible."

[60] Adorno, *Aesthetic Theory*, 237.

[61] Michel Foucault, 'La Folie, l'absence d'oeuvre' (1964). Quoted in Eleanor Kaufman, *The Delirium of Praise*, 63.

CHAPTER TWELVE

THE SIGNIFICANCE OF THE ASYLUM GUGGING IN GERHARD ROTH'S *ARCHIVES OF SILENCE* AND *THE LABYRINTH*

PAMELA S. SAUR

Like prisons, mental hospitals engender several types of fear: fear of individuals too destructive or delusional to be free in society, fear of the great power of the institutional authorities, power accompanied by possible misdiagnosis, maltreatment, or abuse, and in some of us, too, fear of ourselves, our own potential for guilt, mental disturbance, and confinement. In an apparently autobiographical passage in the novel *The Investigating Officer* (1988), the fifth volume of his seven-part cycle of interrelated novels *The Archives of Silence* (1980-1991), contemporary Austrian writer Gerhard Roth, born in 1942, recalls such self-doubts amid other speculations when, at age thirteen, he came across a textbook on the treatment of nervous disorders in his physician father's library.[1] He imagined that he had all the symptoms he read about, and had to hide his illness, fearing the straitjacket and rubber cells he read about. As a boy in Graz, he also saw or heard of several neighbors and relatives, some violent, some suicidal, taken away to be hospitalized locally in Feldhof or in Steinhof in Vienna. Watching one neighbor, an exhibitionist, taken away, he recalls thinking,

> How did the asylum know of his existence? I admit I was afraid of him, but even more fear came over me when strange men appeared, obviously with complete knowledge of the situation, and took him away with them (46).[2]

Young Roth pondered whether insanity is fantasy, imbecility, or a survival mechanism; later he is both attracted and repelled by his own secret, if fleeting, wish to be hospitalized. He thought to himself, "In there I would be allowed to be the way I really am" (49).[3]

In addition to these salient early experiences with mental illness, through both books and real encounters, Gerhard Roth as a young man also became involved with artistic mental patients at the Austrian asylum Gugging, near Vienna (see Figure 12-1), whose patients in the House of Artists pavilion have produced widely acclaimed art and creative writing for several decades; current works are displayed and marketed on a web page. At age 23 Roth was profoundly affected by books on schizophrenia and art and schizophrenia and language by Leo Navratil, founder of the successful artistic project at Gugging. Navratil began the project for diagnostic purposes, but over time the art and literature produced by his patients became recognized, and much of it has been judged meritorious by professionals and knowledgable patrons.

For many years after first visiting the asylum, Roth returned to visit the patients and help promote their art. Not surprisingly, he was especially interested in a fellow writer there, patient Ernst Herbeck. Roth made countless visits to Herbeck and promoted his works, giving recitations of his poetry in Vienna and Berlin after his death. Roth, always concerned with problems of individuals, especially the powerless struggling to express themselves, sympathized with Herbeck's frustrated communication, for a cleft palate made his speech very difficult to understand. Roth was also fascinated by many of the paintings produced at Gugging, particularly the eccentric religious creations of August Walla. According to Johann Feilacher, who interviewed Roth about Gugging in 1995, he admired the mental patients' genuine, individual creativity, uninfluenced by any outside influence, whether financial concerns, social norms, or artistic trends or traditions. Feilacher points out the relevance of Roth's own distrust of authority in his home area, Styria, Austria:

> The absolute rule of the [Nazi] fascistic system of government, as well the power of the Roman Catholic Church, under whose influence every life in rural Styria had been controlled, left deep marks on Gerhard Roth. He found in the drawings, paintings, and poems the individualism that he had been yearning for. (57)[4]

Figure 12-1 Group Portrait of the Artists of Gugging in front of the "House of Artists". *Museum Gugging.* Photo courtesy of Museum Gugging.

Although his complex works cannot be labeled as treating any single subject, the legacy of the Nazi era is mentioned frequently and pointedly enough to designate him as one of the German and Austrian postwar writers whose works confront the Nazi legacy and the many issues it involves; this confrontation is known as *Vergangenheitsbewältigung*, or "coming to terms with the past." In Roth's fiction the reader can assume that the historical reality of the Nazi rule and the ideology of his parents' generation is always implied as an aspect, but not the entire significance, of Roth's general presentation of individuals facing societal authority.[5] Roth's experiences with Gugging patients had profound effects on his writing in general, in particular on the two major works in which he writes directly about the Gugging asylum, *The Archives of Silence* cycle and the 2005 novel *The Labyrinth*. For Roth and his readers, the institution brings together the themes of mental illness, creativity, individual expression, and individuals versus authority, as well as linking fiction to reality, both in Roth's life and in his native Austria, in the present and as haunted by the Nazi past and other traces of history.

Within the tapestry of diverse interwoven texts and images comprising *The Archives of Silence*, Roth chose to tell the world about Gugging in overtly factual, non-fictional segments of *A Journey into the Interior of Vienna* (1991), the seventh and last volume of the *Archives* cycle, ironically modeled on a travel guide, but emphasizing ugly and disturbing facets of the city rather than diverting tourist attractions. The reality of Gugging is emphasized by labeled photographs of the psychiatrist, Leo Navratil, August Walling and other patients, and by an essay, "The House of Sleeping Rationality" peppered with facts—dates, names, visual details—and impressions given by an observant narrator. Roth manipulates the reader's reactions to this objective portrayal, however, by comments in the essay and by the context into which he sets the photographs. Photographs of the mental patients are accompanied by other pictures representing society's control and treatment of outsiders, such as scenes of a homeless shelter and a prison; others feature eerie aspects of society's functions of cataloging and displaying—images from judicial archives, the pathological-anatomical museum, bones in a royal crypt, and a theater in which animals were tortured and killed for entertainment.

In this lurid context, society's enjoyment of the confined patients' artwork seems more macabre than inspiring, as it first seems in theory. The collection of photographs, like the essays and the book's title, emphasizes not only forgotten and powerless people, but death and disturbing underground realms containing dark secrets. More specifically, the murderous rule of the Nazi era is evoked. Featured in the volume's gallery of photographs are images of a Jewish cemetery and a synagogue which, according to its caption, was destroyed by Nazi mobs during the infamous "Crystal Night" of November 9-10, 1938, named for the gleaming fragments of broken windows of Jewish businesses and homes. Also portrayed is another real person, the Viennese Jew Karl Berger, a survivor and eyewitness to the Holocaust (or Shoah) in Austria. Berger is the protagonist and narrator of the factual sixth volume of *The Archives, The Story of Darkness* (1991).

Roth's essay on Gugging accompanying these photographs begins with a description of a colorful mural near the entrance, "Paradise," by August

Walling, which anticipates the title of Roth's 2005 novel set in Gugging, *The Labyrinth*: "In labyrinthian fashion, human beings and nature are tangled together with one another in peaceful strangeness" (32).[66] The suggestion of peacefulness here, and the appealing notion that mental patients have the opportunity for creativity, productivity, and recognition in art, are dramatically undermined by the next sentence:

> Not far away in the park there is a memorial plaque commemorating around a thousand murdered residents of the Gugging asylum who fell victim to the National Socialist project [to eliminate], "lives unworthy of living." (32). [7]

This ghastly detail, that a thousand patients were murdered by state authorities at the facility in a relatively recent era, haunts and colors Roth's presentation of Gugging as an institution of creativity: one cannot help but wonder if anyone belongs in a place where such a thing could and did actually happen.

Mentions of the horrors of the Nazi era throughout Roth's work remind us that brutality and violence could and did happen in "free" Austria outside such institutions as well. It is well-known that Roth has often spoken of both Austrian society's and his own parents' silence over the Third Reich era; Roth told one interviewer, for example, "Nazism is the greatest taboo. Austria, for example, is a realm of silence. And the son generation continues to reproduce that silence [on this subject]" (qtd. in Barlt, 311).[8] Without a doubt, silence about the horrible realities of Nazi crimes and Austrian complicity in them is a major aspect of the "silence" referred to in the cycle's title; yet readers are prevented from a simplistic, unitary interpretation of the title or the cycle by its complex structure and diverse, interrelated subject matters and messages.

Well over seven hundred pages long, the novel *Everyday Death* (1984) is the centerpiece and core of *The Archives*, its third volume. Here the reader encounters a pair of boyhood friends, Jenner and Lindner. Alois Jenner, a lawyer and serial killer, later becomes the guardian of Franz Lindner, whose years-long silence, his unexplained muteness, and his institutionalization are related to fear that he will become another of Jenner's victims because he knows of his guilt. Long sections of the novel are identified as creations of Lindner while a patient in the Feldhof asylum, including drawings, diary entries, aphorisms, meditations, memories, and fantasies, his style ranging from realistic and mundane to wildly surrealistic. A collection of sixty-six fairy tales is included. They are said to have been compiled by Lindner masquerading as a double to the Brothers Grimm through creation of an imaginary brother. The tales are labeled as "Gathered by the Brothers Franz and Franz Lindner" (611).[9] The fairy tales recall the connection between mental illness and creativity represented by Gugging. Like the idea of paintings created by mental patients, the very idea of fairy tales written by mental patients has a unique appeal:

> The idea is fascinating, for it conjures up a special entrance to a new world of fiction, fantasy, and truth, unknown terrains, unexplored areas of thought and perception, emotion and experience, and possibly access to new kinds of secret beauty and supremely honest, unrestrained truth. . . The imagination of both the insane person and the anonymous or collective author of a fairy tale is very free, released from the bonds of rationality, causality, and logic, from all rules of thought or narration . . . (Saur, "Guiltless Confessions, 172)

The subject of asylums in Roth's fiction is an aspect of his general presentation of insanity itself, of course, which is a rather vast field within his oeuvre. As explicated in a lengthy study of *The Archives. The Austrian Mind*, by Matthias Auer, a critical assessment of the subject in the cycle of novels involves several dimensions. On the one hand, one must plumb extensive fictional psychiatric histories: collecting and assembling clues, which are fragmentary, difficult to interpret, and sometimes contradictory, to the psychiatric history, diagnosis, and etiology of Franz Lindner's mental condition (including such questions as causes of his muteness, his flight into insanity, his quests for both alternative better worlds and his own authentic identity through self-expression in behavior, fantasy, or art) as well as the minds of the other characters. On the other hand, this specific task is related to more general questions about societal constraints and norms, and societal as well as individual pathology. Auer explicates Lindner's reversed role, not as patient, but as diagnostician of his rural Austrian village:

> Lindner, the outsider and self-appointed chronicler of his rural homeland, proves to be a sharp observer and analyst of human patterns of behavior, an ethnologist who, within the domain of his studies, comprehends diverse manifestations of the exercise of power as well as physical and psychological use of violence as characteristics of individual as well as collective behavior. (127-28)[10]

As Auer explains, Lindner's traumatic experiences are rooted not only in his family, but in the pathology of society itself, in his father's dual victimization and guilt during and after World War II, and in common Austrian experiences of the recent past. Auer says of Lindner's village,

"The war, that maintains a haunting presence in the people's heads after it is over, becomes . . . a symbol of a barbaric world that has gone out of its traces."[11]

Auer discusses the portrait of Austrian village life found in the first volume of *The Archives, The Quiet Ocean.* In this novel an urban physician moves to a rural area where he finds a great deal of poverty, sickness, and suffering, domestic violence, and cruel, brutal treatment of less powerful beings, including animals, women, the young, and outsiders. The priest is ineffectual, education and medical care lacking. The experience leads to his suicide, his body discovered by Lindner. Auer points out that Roth's emphasis on the superior insights of Lindner, always a marginal character in his community and later a mute mental patient, is but one way in which Gerhard Roth critiques not only Austrian society and Austrian psychiatric institutions, but the psychiatric profession in general. Even before the more direct exploration of psychiatry's limitation in *The Labyrinth,* Auer pointed out that the *Archives* cycle qualifed Roth as one of a host of contributors to a wide interdisciplinary and international movement critiquing psychiatric oppression of individuals, and the power of the profession, seated in questionable social orders:

> The diagnosis given here, that psychosis reflects the inhumanity of the social order and schizophrenia is to be understood as the expression of a socially created self-alienation, conforms to the theses of the so-called "anti-psychiatry" movement that, across the world, has provided fuel and recognition of such views since the early 1960s. . . . (149)[12]

Auer notes that one of the pioneers of this movement was the influential modern philosopher Michel Foucault, author of *Madness and Civilization* (1961).

A study by Uwe Schütte makes explicit connections between the literary techniques Roth employs in *Everyday Death* and the art produced at Gugging. He asserts that Roth was "emulating" rather than "simulating" schizophrenic texts. He brings up the tradition, promoted in the writings of the French painter Jean Dubuffet (1901-1985), of "art brut" or "raw art," also sometimes labeled primitive or outsider art, to which the Gugging movement belongs. Dubuffet critiques the conformity of "cultural" or "museum" art of professional artists in Western culture, as well as its creation in pursuit of fame and profit, saying that "art thrives in its healthiest form among . . . ordinary people, because [it is] practiced without applause or profit, for the maker's own delight" (qtd. in Thévoz 1968, 7). Three essential features of art brut have been identified:

> First, the makers of Art Brut are outsiders, mentally and/or socially. Second, their work is conceived and produced outside the field of "fine arts" . . . it is also conceived without any regard for the usual recipients of works of art, or indeed . . . any recipient at all. Third, the subjects, techniques and systems of figuration have little connection with those handed down by tradition or current in the fashionable art of the day; they stem rather from personal invention. (Thévoz 1968, 9-10)

Of course Gerhard Roth is a professional and commercial writer and not a mental patient. However, his efforts to understand this branch of art and model his writing after it are effective. Uwe Schütte asserts: "In fact, the correspondences between art brut in the visual arts and the novel *Everyday Death* are evident to such an extent that one could designate the novel heuristically as a novel brut" (92).[13]

In addition to the generalized and theoretical freedom and imperviousness to outside influence that Roth admired in the Gugging artists, this strikingly original montage novel displays specific techniques in common with the art brut movement. For example, in the novel Lindner exhibits "graphomania" or "the compulsive need to convey his fantastic inner world through detailed descriptions" which Schütte identifies as "a typical feature of psychopathological writing" (165).[14] Among the "primitive" features Schütte identifies in *Everyday Death* are its chaotic form, its status as a "work in progress" without a decisive beginning or end, its mixtures of realism and fantasy, and the inclusion of magical rather than logical or scientific causes. More specifically, the sentences themselves, reflective of "free association," break free not only from the laws of rationality, but also from grammatical rules of sentence and paragraph construction. The creative freedom, innovation, and open form of the novel may be likened to many twentieth-century art forms, including non-representational art, twelve-tone music, concrete poetry, and Theater of the Absurd. Schütte adds a comment on Lindner's role in the fairy tale segment of the volume:

> Just as Roth gave, so to speak, a voice to insanity through the figure of Lindner, so too does Lindner in turn give a voice to his fellow residents of the asylum in order to prevent their stories from disappearing. (182)[15]

The fourth volume of *The Archives* is *At the Precipice* (1986), also largely "authored" by Franz Lindner, the mental patient. Two lengthy segments are titled "The Autobiography of Franz Lindner" and "From Lindner's Papers." Readers interpreting texts written by mental patients are likely to be intrigued, but they cannot tell if the texts should be considered therapeutic self-expression, akin to couch narratives told to a psychiatrist, creative works that have nothing to do with the author's mental condition, fantasies the author believes to be literally true, possibly including violent or bizarre impulses that may be acted upon, humorous texts—Lindner identifies himself as "The Humorist Franz Lindner" at one point (56)—or deceptive pieces in which the author wishes to mislead the reader about his or her mental condition or factual situation. Appreciated as literary texts in their own right, of course, like the paintings created by Gugging patients or any other artists, the mental condition or intentions of the creator would be regarded by many readers to be of little or no relevance. *At the Precipice* contains a good deal of information on the life stories of Lindner, Jenner, and the examining officer Sonnenberg, central in the volume to follow, threads of story line that must be assembled by the reader from fragments found throughout many of Roth's novels. For our purposes, references to asylums are pertinent; here, such passages offer, like Gugging paintings, surrealistic visual images. In the opening of the book's first chapter, "Franz Lindner: Self-Portrait in the Shaving Mirror," the patient-narrator tells us,

> Here in the asylum there are out-of-tune pianos on which lizards play children's songs. The fire-cloud over the asylum harbors angels made of glowing sandstone . . . The residents differ from people living in freedom in that instead of blood coursing through their veins they have monsters who, when they are in the mood, tell the most desolate and improbable fairy tales. (15)[16]

The segment "Asylum" reads, in its entirety:

> The murderers and thieves were driven into a yellow snail's shell. When they came up to the top they were told to go back. But they were not allowed to leave the snail's shell but instead were made to go back up to the top and then back again, as long as it took for them to go crazy. (56)[17]

Irrational and strange as these passages seem to be, they have meaning: the first segment points to the creative potential of patients to see and transmit fantastic images and to create extraordinary fairy tales, the second to the patients' potential for criminal guilt and to the coercive power of the institution, here described as either incomprehensible or as actually causing and requiring insanity.

A long passage set inside the asylum is devoted not to the patient Lindner, but to a judicial official, the examining officer Sonnenberg, who visits Lindner while investigating the crimes of which Jenner is accused, but fails to establish communication with him. Sonnenberg, who will reappear as the central character of the next volume in the *Archive, The Examining Officer*, and again as a patient in *The Labyrinth*, provides one important connection between judicial and medical institutions. In *The Examining Officer* the reader enters the world of his violent and disturbing hallucinations, some of which imply that he may be the perpetrator of the very murders he investigates. Despite his disorientation and possible guilt, Sonnenberg longs for truth and justice; one of his missions is to prove that Lindner is right in accusing Jenner of murders. He provides the reader with grim insights into the judicial system from the inside, revealing how painful and disturbing his chosen profession is; perhaps its frustrating involvement in the world of crime and society's response to it has led him into insanity and crime himself. In several passages, Sonnenberg reflects directly on the oppressive authorities he represents, and on the links between prisons and asylums. When he visits an asylum to intervew Lindner, he is quite uneasy. He shocks both himself and a psychiatrist he is addressing by referring to the patients as "prisoners"(106). Shown through a building for the criminally insane, he reflects:

> Sonnenberg regarded prisons and asylums less as sadistic products of society than as the expression of helpless and habitual self-defense. . . . Sonnenberg had to act every day. His profession did not allow him to regard things from a distance and dissect them. He stood in the middle of life . . . and had to try to make judgments. (107)[18]

Similar thoughts are revealed in the first chapter of *The Examining Officer*, which opens with one of his horrifying cases, a fourteen-year-old boy who has killed his father and wounded his mother; the matter-of-fact way it is narrated suggests that it is nothing more than a routine case in Sonnenberg's day-to-day professional life. The author/narrator comments directly on psychiatry in its judicial role:

> The competency hearings before the courts show how helpless psychiatrists are whenever their insights are taken as anything but speculation. Today psychiatrists and psychologists are mere tools of the state. They bestow on the state the ability to lock people up and they are called on to advise the state which institutions to choose, asylums or prisons. (13) [19]

During Sonnenberg's investigation of the murders of which Alois Jenner is accused, he tries to locate a document about Lindner's whereabouts. Suddenly, a wave of revulsion comes over him as he faces one of the tools of his own trade, a mass of legal documents. Symbolic of bureaucratic "red tape," documents are both a means of exerting state authority through categorizing and labeling individuals and pronouncing judgment on them, and through providing records of evidence and, ultimately, truth. The document about Lindner is a mere scrap of information, but it leads him to more documents that overwhelm him:

> Besides that there was a bundle of documents lying on the table, with new charges, suspicions, determinations . . . the documents themselves didn't make Sonnenberg sick, but rather the fact that they continued to appear, never stopping, and they never made any difference in anything. (155)[20]

As Sonnenberg's paranoia and delusional state worsen, an insight is given into some of the many barriers that make truth and communication so difficult to achieve:

> Maybe a new philosophy will emerge, maybe in asylums or hospitals or prisons, for only despairing people recognize the fraud that exists all around them and is an unremovable part of language because language is constructed to resist self-betrayal, just as everything in nature is developed, first and foremost, for preserving the self—even thinking. (171-72)[21]

Despite such grim and hopeless passages, this assertion of the will to self-preservation and honest self-expression is found throughout Roth's fiction. The idea expressed here that language is a tool in this cause reminds the reader of Franz Lindner's self-imposed silence; his knowledge of his childhood friend Jenner's murders makes honest self-expression dangerous; his artistic creation of pictures of Jenner's murders in the context of the asylum is coded enough that it cannot provide real judicial evidence that would put Lindner's life in danger.

Although aspects of his experiences at Gugging resonate throughout *The Archives,* it was not until 2005—four other relatively conventional novels later, over a decade after publication of the *Archives* cycle, and thirty years after his first involvement with the famous artistic asylum—that Gerhard Roth published a novel explicitly about Gugging, *The Labyrinth*. The provocative title recalls the title of the second book of *Everyday Death*, "Reports from the Labyrinth." As the first segment of that book is "Seven Never Sent Letters from the Asylum," the word can be taken as referring to an asylum. However, the other sections—"The Creation," "The Frozen Paradise," and "The Age of Time,"—are fantasies, delusions, or stories authored by Lindner while a patient. Certainly the labyrinth could refer to his mind. Moreover, the novel *The Labyrinth* is based on a real event in Vienna in 1995, a mysterious fire that broke out in the ancient city's imperial castle complex, the Hofburg, a major tourist attraction and literally an architectural labyrinth of interconnected rooms and corridors with diverse purposes, from apartments to offices, to libraries and exhibits, to catacombs of storage areas. Even setting aside the intricate contexts of Roth's interrelated novels, the Hofburg represents labyrinths of historical events and objects, and hidden secrets from both the Imperial Habsburg past and the more recent era when the Nazis ruled Vienna and the Hofburg as its seat of power. In *The Labyrinth* Lindner is now a resident in the House of Artists at Gugging. The novel develops earlier stories and ideas from *The Archives* while adding new insights and literary functions involving mental hospitals in general, as well as specific details about a fictionalized Gugging and its unique artistic mission.

Much shorter than the earlier, seven-volume cycle, and even several hundred pages shorter than its central novel, *Everyday Death*, Roth's "Gugging novel" is necessarily less complex, but it is hardly simple, and it employs similar montage techniques to unite different types of texts and pictures, as well as shifting points of view. The complexity and mystery of the "labyrinth" evoked in its title point to typical Rothean issues involving questionable legal and medical authorities, societal oppression of individuals, and the continued presence of the Nazi legacy. In addition, the image of the labyrinth as a puzzle or trap with no beginning or end also suggests the novel's links, through common characters, to the *Archives* cycle, and finally to new mysteries in the new novel. On the surface the novel seems more like Roth's relatively unified and conventional mystery novels published in the intervening years; however, the book's opening crime mystery concerning whether the mental patient Philip Stourzh set fire to the Hofburg and broke into his doctor's apartment gives way to numerous levels of confusion. Often the reader does not know who is narrating sections of the book.

Although the novel can certainly be read independently, the full significance of the asylum Gugging in *The Labyrinth* can only be assessed in the context of its links to the earlier novels *Everyday Death*, *At the Precipice*, and *The Investigating Officer*, which feature the same characters, Jenner, Lindner, and Sonnenberg. The novels are linked not only by these characters and their stories, but by their common concern with asylums both as story settings and as sources of provocative moral, social, and artistic questions. In many ways *The Labyrinth* is a sequel to the earlier cycle. Among its new directions is a new emphasis on the perspective of medical personnel and of literary authority in the person of "The Writer," a persona described as physically very much like Roth himself.

The Labyrinth opens with these words, "My name is Heinrich Pollanzy. As a psychiatrist and head of the Gugging asylum I am accustomed to hearing strange life stories and viewpoints" (9).[22] This passage, a type of traditional literary frame device, establishes the doctor, already invested with diagnostic and administrative authority over patients deprived of their freedom, as a narrator, an authority on literary truth. This role is undermined even as it is asserted, however. The psychiatrist is accustomed to hearing strange (possibly delusional) life stories and opinions from people classified as mentally ill; his statement that he "hears" them falls quite short of asserting that he is confident in his ability to interpret them or judge their veracity. More doubt in the doctor's profession is encouraged by the next sentence introducing a main literary character: "My former patient and current patient-care assistant, Phillip Stourzh, I have known for more than fifteen years" (15).[23]

Stourzh does not present an inspiring case of a patient whose cure was so successful that he became a mental health professional himself, for the patient is still a patient as well as assistant. He has merged the roles rather than progressed from one to the other. Passages following reveal that the doctor, after so many years of acquaintance, does not know a great deal about the patient, and, indeed, a central issue of the book will be the doctor's suspicion that the patient has set the Hofburg on fire. Thus, to the problems of medical diagnosis, reliability of literary narrative, and reliability of mental patients' narratives are added the problems of criminal investigation and psychiatric responsibility for foreseeing or preventing patients' crimes.

Pollanzy and Stourzh represent and link society's authority to judge and treat or confine criminals and mentally ill individuals, seen in the twin institutions of mental hospitals and prisons; the psychiatrist's responsibility is ultimately judicial as well as medical, and society relies on him as a source of truth. The sensational and bestseller-worthy event, the Hofburg fire, not only merges fiction and non-fiction, but brings in nationalism and history. The pride of the cultural center, Vienna, former capital of the Austro-Hungarian Empire, is represented by the Hofburg; and Austrians are well aware of the fact that Hitler greeted cheering crowds from one of its balconies when Austria was annexed to the Third Reich in 1938.

Events from Stourzh's life story also present difficult questions and ethical dilemmas. He is first introduced as a patient with seizures (later alleged to be feigned) from being shot in the head by his father, presumably by accident. The medical consensus was that the bullet was too risky to remove; the patient had also forgotten being shot. Stourzh developed pyromania as a teenager, according to the doctor-narrator "not in connection with his shot to the head." He adds, "I consider Philipp's obsessive condition to be to a much greater extent the result of repressed hatred for his own family" (10). The boy had set fire to his father's rare-stamp business out of hatred for his family rooted in revulsion that his grandfather, according to legal and accepted procedures during the Nazi era, had taken over the apartment and stamp-store of a Jewish family that was evicted and very probably put to death. His father, who happens to share Hitler's first name, Adolf, had hushed up his son's arson. This detail in a sense "justifies" the boy's development of pyromania as well as associates his doctor, as an Austrian official, with the earlier Nazi authorities. The doctor also points out another aspect of his profession that is mentioned regularly in the novel: the function patients serve as objects of study needed to advance medical careers. It is mentioned that many medical researchers have seen x-ray images of the lodged bullet. Also, while introducing Stourzh, Dr. Pollanzy comments, "At that time I was taking notes about Philipp for an article in a professional psychiatric journal" (11).[24]

We next learn that Stourzh requests to serve as an assistant in the House of Artists. The narrating psychiatrist explains and praises the unit and its inventor, here named Neumann, and the fulfillment and recognition he has brought the creative patients. The reader notes as well that the advantage is mutual; Dr. Neumann is a published scholar of art history as well as a psychiatrist. Neumann accepts Stourzh's offer, motivated not solely by concern for his welfare, but also by interest in him as a case study in amnesia. Both doctors are motivated, at least in part, by the same secret desire to use him, without his full knowledge, as a "case study" to advance their careers.

The first chapter of the book introduces Franz Lindner, now a patient in the House of Artists, and describes his drawings of fires and murders. Dr. Pollanzy presents Lindner's belief that his lawyer and guardian, Jenner, is a murderer as an illusion. Neither he nor Dr. Neumann places any credence in Jenner's crimes; however, the reader of *The Archives* knows better, and the reader who has seen the film version of *Everyday Death* has "seen" Jenner commit these crimes and "heard" the "mute" man say one word, "no."[25] The Jenner/Lindner situation calls into question the wisdom of both medical and judicial authorities; it also represents peculiar functions a mental hospital might serve: as a place for a powerful criminal to warehouse a witness to a crime, or a haven for a threatened witness. Lindner's decades-long refusal to speak is a mechanism, whether shrewd or crazy, to protect his own life from his violent "friend." A reader with knowledge of Roth's earlier creations has more knowledge of Lindner than the psychiatrists. Such a reader might well speculate that Stourzh's seizures and amnesia were similar defenses, conscious or unconscious, against real threats. A somewhat negative light is also cast on the aims and motivations of psychiatry by frequent references throughout the novel to the psychiatrists' interest in their own career advancement.

Guilt, mental illness, and the limits of medical knowledge are brought together in the fire in the Hofburg, which Dr. Pollanzy, not insignificantly one of the few privileged residents of the building, suspects was set by his patient, as dangerous as he is difficult to diagnose and treat. The doctor recalls that he had told Stourzh about the Nazi killings of patients at Gugging, caused by deliberate starvation. He concludes that Stourzh blames him for apathy regarding Nazi crimes, thinking, "For him the Hofburg must have actually been a symbol for my intellectual attitude, even more so because I lived there in an apartment I had more or less inherited" (51).[26] The doctor had moved into the apartment of his father, a museum curator. His "inherited" apartment there associated him with privilege and power and general, and with Austrian authorities and history in particular. After the fire, Stourzh admits himself as a patient to the House of Artists where he works, like Lindner fleeing from judicial authorities. Another connection between mental illness and criminality, the asylum and the prison, is made through the character Sonnenberg. In this book he is a patient of Dr. Pollanzy's, his schizophrenic tendencies controlled by drugs—thus in a state between sanity and insanity. Like Lindner, he believes that Jenner is a murderer, but he never was able to collect enough proof to convict him. His life mission ends in failure as he cannot vindicate Lindner by bringing Jenner to justice.

The book *The Labyrinth* contains several passages explicating the positive, creative side of mental illness as expressed by an authority in each domain: "The Writer" and the psychiatrist Pollanzy. When the doctor meets the writer, he has the following thoughts:

> "The Writer" seemed to me at that time to be a spy who in the service of normality was traveling to the land of insanity. Presumably he would ask me about Lindner, but how ought I to answer him? I was overtired and suddenly began to wish for insanity myself. . . . Sometimes I envied the insane their condition, wishing for a madness that could perhaps let me better understand the universe, that might unveil to me its secret in a stone, an ice flower, or a fingernail as in the strokes of color and cracks of pigment in a painting. . . . And I see, moreover, in most mad people religious human beings. . . . The world is a trap that lures us with deceptive glimmers of beauty. What we seek are narcosis and visions. What we possess is cages and imprisonment. . . . I am convinced as well that the love between men and women is nothing other than the substance out of

which insanity is made. (89-91)[27]

A discussion of the creative dimension of insanity is found in "The Writer," the first chapter of the section of the novel, titled "Insanity" (Book IV). Its insights, however, are undermined by an introduction attesting either to his incompetence or to the impossibility of his task, for the writer begins by revealing that he has been collecting notes for a book on insanity for over thirty years and is still in the research stage of the project! Thus, like Sonnenberg's judicial and Pollanzy's medical career, his literary profession is portrayed as falling far short of any mission to achieve truth and enlightenment, improvement of human lives, or fulfillment to the professional himself. Just as a trip to a medical congress is but one of a swirl of confused adventures of the patients and doctors in the novel, the research of the writer seems pointless and trivial, a never-ending process of paperwork like the paperwork that overwhelmed Sonnenberg on a visit to the asylum. "The Writer" lists some of the hundreds of interviews and books he has consulted during his years of study, yet, ridiculously enough, he has not yet started to write. He explains,

> I have not yet begun writing my study, for which I first have to work through the enormous amount of material that has accumulated. For this material I have rented a whole apartment, the Insanity Archives Apartment, which I first have to get organized. . . . I have to keep adding new aspects of the subject all the time. (299-300)[28]

This passage is a rare touch of out-and-out humor for Roth. By implication it satirizes the study of mental illness, as well as his own books on the subject and the efforts of readers and critics to understand them. In the passage, the profession of the writer and researcher has obviously taken on a life of its own, divorced from its supposed purposes, and a parallel can be drawn with several medical and judicial careers in Roth's fiction. Within his account of his research procedures, however, "The Writer" unveils some conclusions he has already drawn, ironically before he has entered the labyrinth of endless research. Eloquently enough, he goes on to link insanity to the human impulses toward religion, art, even the discoveries of science and innovations in politics. Undermined as it is by the image of the apartment full of jumbled papers representing thirty years of unfulfilled research, this chapter nevertheless presents significant discussions of creativity and art, as in this key passage:

> In this connection I came to the phenomenon of the transformation of reality in art. . . . In art there exists from the beginning the intention to make the portrayed reality more suggestive than the so-called everyday world. Even writing verses is a renouncing of so-called reality, as much as is inventing incomprehensible worlds or splitting apart and distorting time and phenomena. I recognized the general yearning for insanity, for extending the perceptible, tracing the unknown as far as the fantastic, that becomes reality through art and religion. (301-02)[29]

Gugging in particular and asylums in general function in Gerhard Roth's fiction as both intriguing story elements and theoretical constructs; his still-developing body of books and films is a labyrinth of interrelated mysteries, stories, and ideas. Many characters and events appear in several places, sometimes clarifying previous material, sometimes offering alterrnative possibilities. The asylum Gugging is a fictional place, a real place, and a realm of artistic creation, just as the semi-real persona "The Writer" is both author of and a character in the stories he is creating. As in his previous work, Roth's newest novel reveals inadequacies and oppression in medical and judicial institutions and explores the vast world of human thought and behavior, especially the "abnormal" realms of mental deviance, criminal behavior, and artistic creativity. Roth's works contain indictments of social institutions in general, and, in the case of his native Austria as complicit with the Nazi regime, an undeniable historical fact concerning Gugging and many other still-existing Austrian institutions.

The ideas and artistic techniques in *The Labyrinth* and Roth's other creations pose challenges for critics, but the reader can also enjoy them without pondering their implications, but rather for the many sensational elements that would be suspenseful and entertaining in a contemporary thriller in book or movie form. A mystery about the famous, intriguing Hofburg being set afire! A psychiatrist fearful that his patient set the fire and that he may follow him home and attack him! A female medical professional who sleeps with a patient and asks him to kill her colleague and lover! In Roth's world of ideas corrupt, even criminal officials, patients with feigned symptoms hiding in asylums in their own witness-protection programs, the problematic haunting of Nazi crimes in contemporary society and families, complicated connections between mental abnormality, artistic creativity, and ecstatic religious experiences—they all cry out for serious attention. In an entertaining mystery movie, they would not; surprises such as murderous magistrates or lawyers, or patients with more insight than their psychiatrists, would be enjoyed as fiction and verbal art, not necessarily generalized into commentary about society and its institutions.

A review of *The Labyrinth* by Hans Jürgen Heinrichs emphasizes a salient aspect of the novel that makes the reader of ideas in the book uncertain about interpreting it as a guide to the author's theories about what is true, just as it makes the book challenging to enjoy as an entertaining mystery novel. The title and sub-title of the review are revealing: "The Multiplied Psychiatrist: Who Is Writing in Whose Name? Gerhard Roth's fascinating game of confusion of characters in the labyrinth of an insane mind." The identity of characters, particularly narrators, is confusing in all six books of the novel. As Heinrichs writes,

> The complexity of the novel becomes more intricate with each of the six "books" (or major chapters.) Always in the background is the question: Who is the author of the text one is reading at a given time? Who is writing in whose name?

In this passage, Heinrichs goes so far as to suggest that Dr. Pollanzy and Philipp Stourz "are different aspects of the same person" (75).[30] He points out the confusing fact that a portion of the text apparently by Pollanzy or Stourzh is later identified as written by Franz Lindner, although we are told that he burned it and it was retrieved by someone else. Heinrichs concludes, "In reality the characters are perspectives, shapes, and forms of a single overarching persona" (75).[31] Although the book has no conventional plot line, Heinrichs does identify an orderly structure in its two halves:

> . . . Books One through Three form an extended exposition; the following books present the dissolution of the figures into heteronyms of one figure—more accurately one idea, the idea of insanity, in which the conscious mind no longer has any power over images of the subconscious. (76)[32]

This description of a work of art in which the unconscious is uninfluenced by the conscious mind recalls Roth's praise of the Gugging patients' art as likewise uninfluenced by artistic trends or models, or indeed any outside influences, whether from society or other individuals. In *The Labyrinth* Roth explores insanity as a subject matter, employing the literary technique of interweaving fragments of stories infused with mystery and uncertainty, and authored by numerous possible "real" or "unreal" narrators. Such a novel has much in common with the artistic creations of the patients in Gugging's House of Artists.

In the related works *The Archives of Silence* and *The Labyrinth*, Gerhard Roth has created a complex, fascinating, and frustrating montage of fiction and non-fiction, autobiography and fantasy, memorable characters, sensational stories, and provocative webs of ideas, combined in organizational structures that magnify their complexity. Contradictions, connections, and omissions make these ideas, like the stories with which they are interwoven, virtually impossible to extract and summarize; attempts to do so can meet with only partial success. The inclusion of drawings and photographs, as well as numerous images created through words, add an additional complication, a visual dimension. The challenging task of explicating these eight books does indeed resemble moving about in a labyrinth—not a labyrinth that is a maze of wrong turns with a defined goal, whether treasure chest or way out, but a labyrinth that offers numerous richly rewarding paths, a labyrinth that is also a kaleidoscope and a hall of mirrors. Different experiences are provided by the same path in the labyrinth depending upon where one has already been. As one moves through verbal paths, one also sees images not arranged in rows on the walls, but projected onto each other, moving and shifting, reflecting, refracting, and ever-changing. Opening the door marked "Gugging" is one fruitful way to gain access to a good number of the halls, for it leads us to many significant aspects of the stories and ideas.

Gugging unites fiction and non-fiction, word and image; it represents numerous aspects of such central Rothean subjects as artistic creativity, individual expression versus societal oppression, and the limitations of judicial, medical, and literary professions. Gugging is also a real place, with an appealingly humane artistic-medical mission that represents not only a unique achievement of Roth's native Austria, but also the horrifying history of patients murdered by state authority during the Nazi era. We readers might be tempted to speculate that the setting of these eight books is the author's mind, or perhaps the world itself, but the specific place called Gugging calls us back from such abstractions and reminds us not only of the specific visual and concrete elements of these books, but also of the fact that they are not merely about humankind, the mind, and the universe, but also about a real place called Austria.

Works Cited

Auer, Matthias. *Der österreichische Kopf .Gerhard Roths Zyklus"Die Archive des Schweigens" als literarisches Psycho-Analyse der Alpenrepublik.*. Herdecke: GCA-Verlag, 1999.

Bartl, Marianne. "Die Inspiration der Bilder: Zur Biographie Gerhard Roths." In *Gerhard Roth*. Edited by Marianne Bartl and Christian Ehetrieber. Graz: Droschl, 1995. 325-43.

Feilacher, Johann. "Gerhard Roths Auseinandersetzung mit den Künstlern aus Gugging." *Text und Kritik* 128 (1995): 56-60.

Heinrichs, Hans Jürgen. "Der vervielfachte Psychiater: Wer schreibt in wessen Namen? Gerhard Roths faszinierendes Personenverwirrspiel im Labyrinth des wahnhaften Sinns." *Österreichische Literatur 2005. Ein Pressespiegel* 65 (2006): 75-76. First published in *Der Rundschau*, Frankfurt a. M., 2 March 2005.

Roth, Gerhard. *Am Abgrund*. Frankfurt a. M.: Fischer Taschenbuch Verlag, 1994.

—. *Die Geschichte der Dunkelheit*. Frankfurt a. M.: Fischer Taschenbuch Verlag, 1994.

—. *Im tiefen Österreich*. Frankfurt am Main: Fischer Taschenbuch Verlag, 1994.

—. *Das Labyrinth*. Frankfurt a. M.: Fischer, 2005.

—. *Landläufiger Tod*. Frankfurt a. M.: Fischer Taschenbuch Verlag, 1994.

—. *Eine Reise in das Innere von Wien. Essays*. Frankfurt a. M.: Fischer Taschenbuch Verlag, 1994.

—. *Der Untersuchungsrichter*. Frankfurt a. M.: Fischer Taschenbuch Verlag, 1992.

Saur, Pamela S. "A Concentrated Honey: Gerhard Roth's Film "Landläufiger Tod." *Modern Austrian Literature* 32.4 (1999): 222-32.

—."Gerhard Roths *Die Archive des Schweigens*: A New Genre." *Modern Austrian Literature* 31.3/4 (1998): 89-102.

—. "Guiltless Confessions in Gerhard Roth's *Archives of Silence*." In *The Fiction of the I: Contemporary Austrian Writers and Autobiography*. Edited by Nicholas J. Meyerhofer. Riverside, CA: Ariadne, 1999. 164-83.

Schütte, Uwe. *Auf der Spur der Vergessenen—Gerhard Roth und seine Archive des Schweigens*. Vienna: Böhlau, 1997.

Tevóz, Michel. *Art Brut*. New York: Rizzoli, 1976.

Notes

[1] References to *The Archives of Silence* (*Die Archive des Schweigens*) are to the 1992-1994 edition published in Frankfurt a. M. by Fischer Taschenbuch Verlag. The volumes (1-7) are listed below with their original publication dates: (1) *Im*

Tiefen Österreich (In Deepest Austria, 1990); (2) *Der Stille Ozean* (1980; translated into English by Helga Schreckenberger and Jacqueline Vansant as *The Quiet Ocean* [Riverside, CA: Ariadne, 1993]); (3) *Landläufiger Tod* (Everyday Death, 1984); (4) *Am Abgrund* (At the Precipice, 1986); (5) *Der Untersuchungsrichter* (The Investigating Officer, 1988); (6) *Die Geschichte der Dunkelheit* (1991; translated into English by Helga Schreckenberger and Jacqueline Vansant as *The Story of Darkness* [Riverside: Ariadne, 1999]); and (7) *Eine Reise in das Innere von Wien: Essays* (A Journey into the Interior of Vienna, 1991).

[2] The English translations of quotations are my own unless otherwise indicated. The original German passages will be given in endnotes, the first to follow: "Woher wußte das Irrenhaus von seiner Existenz? Ich gebe zu, ich fürchtete mich vor ihm, aber noch mehr Furcht flößte mir ein, daß plötzlich fremde Männer erschienen und ihn mit sich nahmen, offerbar in voller Kenntnis der Sachlage."

[3] "Dort dürfte ich sein, wie ich bin, redete ich mir ein."

[4] "Die absolutischen Systeme faschistischer Regierungen sowie die Macht der römisch-katholischen Kirche, unter deren Einfluß jegliches Leben in der ländlichen Steiermark kontrolliert wurde, hinterließ auch bei Gerhard Roth tiefe Spuren. Er fand in den Zeichnungen, Malereien und Gedichten jenen Individualismus, nach dem er sich gesehnt hatte."

[5] It is generally believed that Austrian writers have had less of a voice in this movement of *Vergangenheitsbewältigung* than Germans, due to the widespread view, promoted by the United States after World War II, that Austria was an innocent "victim of Nazi aggression" rather than a country with significant support for the Nazi party. Famous German authors representing this movement include Heinrich Böll, Günther Grass, and Wolfgang Borchert.

[6] "Labyrinthisch intereinanderverschlungen sind Mensch und Natur in friedlicher Fremdheit vereint.

[7] "Nicht weit davon findet man im Park eine Gedenktafel, die an die rund tausend Ermordeten der Gugginger Anstalt erinnert, welche dem Unternehmen 'Lebensunwertes Leben' der Nationalsozialisten zum Opfer gefallen sind."

[8] "Der Nationalsozialismus ist das größte Tabu. Österreich, zum Beispiel, ist ein Reich des Schweigens. Und die Söhne reproduzieren das Schweigen weiter."

[9] "Ausgezeichnet von den Gebrüdern Franz und Franz Lindner."

[10] "Lindner, der Außenseiter und selbsternannte Chronist seiner ländlichen Heimat, erweist sich als scharfer Beobacher und Analytiker menschlicher Verhaltensweisen, als Ethnologe, der im Rahmen seiner Studien unterschiedliche Manifestationen der Machtausübung sowie physicher und psychischer Gewaltanwendungen als Charakteristika individuellen wie kollektiven Verhaltes begreift."

[11] "Der Krieg, der über sein Ende hinaus in die Köpfen der Menschen weiterspukt, geriert sich . . . als Sinnbild einer barbarischen Welt, die aus den Fugen geraten ist."

[12] "Der hier gestellte Diagnose, daß die Psychose die Inhumanität der sozialen Ordnung reflektiert und die Schizophrenie als Ausdruck gesellschaftlich bedingten Selbstentfremdung zu verstehen ist, deckt sich mit den Thesen der sogenannte

Anti-Psychiatrie, die seit den frühen 60er Jahren weltweit für Aufsehen und Zündstoff sorgte . . . ."

[13] "In der Tat sind die Korrespondenzen zwischen der *art brut* und dem *Landläufiger Tod* derart evident, daß man das Buch heuristisch als einen *roman brut* bezeichnen könnte."

[14] " . . . Graphomanie, d. h. das zwanghafte Bedürfnis, seine phantastische Innenwelt durch detaillierte Niederschrift mitzuteilen, ist ein typisches Kennzeichen psychopathologischen Schreibens."

[15] "Gab Roth sozusagen in der Figur Lindners dem Wahnsinn eine Stimme, so leiht wiederum Lindner in den Märchen seinen Anstaltsgenossen die Feder, um ihre Erzählungen vor dem Verschwinden zu bewahren."

[16] "Hier in der Anstalt gibt es ein verstimmtes Klavier, auf dem Eidechsen Kinderweisen spielen. . . Die Feuerwolke über der Anstalt beherbergt Engel aus glühenden Sandstein. . . . Die Insassen unterscheiden sich von den Menschen in der Freiheit dadurch, daß anstelle von Blut Molche in ihren Adern kreisen, soferne sie bei Laune sind—die wüstesten und unwahrscheinlichsten Märchen erzählen."

[17] "In ein gelbes Schneckenhaus trieb man die Mörder und Diebe. Als sie an der Spitze angekommen waren, hieß man sie zurück, so lange bis sie verrückt waren."

[18] "Sonnenberg betrachtete auch die Gefängnisse und Irrenhäuser weniger als sadistische Auswüchse einer Gesellschaft, sondern vielmehr als den Ausdruck hilfloser und gewohnter Notwehr. . . . Sonnenberg mußte täglich handeln. Sein Beruf gestattete es ihm nicht, die Dinge aus der Entfernung zu betrachten und zu sezieren, er stand im Leben, . . . und mußte versuchen, Urteile zu finden."

[19] "Die Unzurechnungsfähigkeitsdebatte vor den Gerichten zeigt, wie hilflos die Psychiater sind, wenn ihre Erkenntnisse jeweils auf etwas anderem beruhen als Spekulation. Heute sind Psychiatrie und Psychologie etwas für den Staat, sie sollen ihm die Befugnis erteilen einzusperren, und sie sollen ihm beraten, welche Anstalten in Frage kommen, Irrenhaus oder Kriminal."

[20] "Außerdem lag ein Bündel Akten auf dem Tisch mit neuen Anklagen, Verdächtigungen, Feststellungen . . . nicht die Akten machten Sonnenberg krank, sondern daß sie unaufhörlich erschienen, ohne daß sich jemals etwas änderte."

[21] "Vielleicht muß eine neue Philosophie erst entstehen, vielleicht in Irrenhäusern, in Gefängnissen oder in Hospitälern, denn nur die verzweifelten Menschen erkennen den *Schwindel*, der um sie herum stattfindet und unausrottbar in der Sprache steckt, weil die Sprache *gegen den Selbstverrat gebaut ist*, wie alles andere in der Natur zuerst für die *Selbstbehauptung* entwickelt ist—auch das Denken."

[22] "Mein Name ist Heinrich Pollanzy. Als Psychiater und Leiter der Anstalt Gugging bin ich es gewohnt, seltsame Lebensläufe und Ansichten zu hören."

[23] "Meinen Ehemaligen Patienten und und heutigen Pflegegehilfen Philipp Stourzh kenne ich seit mehr als fünfzehn Jahren.

[24] "Ich machte damals Notizen über Phillip für einen Artikel in einer psychiatrischen Fachzeitschrift."

[25] Gerhard Roth himself collaborated on the film, directed by Michael Schottenberg and produced by ORF, Österreichische Rundfunk (Austrian

Broadcasting) in 1991. Despite this evidence of authenticity, the stories in the film version in some aspects contradict their literary versions (see Saur, "A Concentrated Honey").

[26] "Die Hofburg mußte für ihn geradezu ein Symbol für meine geistige Haltung sein, noch dazu wo ich in ihr wohnte und diese Wohnung gewissermaßen geerbt hatte."

[27] "Der Schriftsteller kam mir damals wie ein Spion vor, der im Auftrag der Normalität in das Land des Wahnsinns reiste. Vermutlich würde er mich über Lindner ausfragen, aber was sollte ich ihm antworten? Ich war übermächtigt und empfand plötzlich selbst den Wunsch nach Wahnsinn. . . . Manchmal beneide ich die Wahnsinnigen um den Wahnsinn, einen Wahn, der mich vielleicht das Universum besser begreifen ließe, der mir in einem Stein, ein einer Eisblume oder in einem Fingernagel sein Geheimnis enthüllte wie in den Farbstrichen und Pigmentsprüngen eines Gemäldes. . . (Ich sehe nebenbei gesagt in den meisten Wahnsinnigen religiöse Menschen.) . . . Die Welt ist eine Falle, die uns mit Irrlichtern der Schönheit lockt. Was wir suchen, sind Betäubungen und Visionen. Was wir besitzen, sind der Käfig und Gefangenschaft. . . . Ich bin auch davon überzeugt, daß die Liebe zwischen den Geschlechtern nichts anderes ist als die Substanz, aus der der Wahn besteht."

[28] "Ich habe noch nicht mit der Niederschrift meiner Arbeit begonnen, da ich zuerst das ungeheure Material aufarbeiten muß, das sich angesammelt hat. Für dieses Material habe ich eine eigene Wohnung gemietet, die Wahnsinns-Archiv-Wohnung, in der ich aber erst dabei bin, eine Ordnung hineinzubringen . . . es kommen immer neue und neue Aspekte hinzu."

[29] "Dabei stieß ich auf das Phänomen der Veränderung der Wirklichkeit in der Kunst. . . . In der Kunst besteht von Anfang an die Absicht, die dargestellte Wirklichkeit suggestiver zu gestalten als die sogenannte alltägliche. Schon in Versen zu dichten . . . ist eine Absage an die sogenannte Wirklichkeit, genauso wie unfaßbare Ereignisse zu erfinden und die Zersplitterung und Deformierung der Zeit und der Erscheinungen. Ich erkannte die allgemeine Sehnsucht nach Verrückung, nach Ausdehnung des Wahrnehmbaren, Entdeckung des Unbekannten bis hin zum Phantastischen, das durch die Kunst und die Religion Wirklichkeit wird. . . ."

[30] "Die Komplexität des Romans wird mit jedem der sechs 'Bücher' (oder Großkapitel) in sich verschachtelter. Hinter allem steht die Frage: Wer ist der Verfasser des jeweils gerade Gelesenen? Wer schreibt in wessen Namen? . . . [Dr. Pollanzy und Philipp Stourzh] . . . sind Ausgestaltungen einer Person. . ."

[31] "In Wirklichkeit sind die Personen Perspektivierungen, Gestalten und Formen einer Über - Figur."

[32] " . . . die Bücher Eins bis Drei bilden eine großangelegte Exposition, die folgenden Bücher sind die Einlösungen der Figuren also Heteronyme einer Figur, richtiger: eine Idee, der Idee des Wahnsinns, in dem das Bewusstsein keine Macht mehr über die unbewussten Bilder hat."

CHAPTER THIRTEEN

EXCESSES OF VIOLENCE IN AN APOCALYPTIC MOOD: NAZI ATROCITIES IN THE FINAL PHASE OF THE WAR—AND THEIR PRESENCE/ABSENCE IN PUBLIC MEMORY AND LITERATURE

WINFRIED R. GARSCHA

In the spring of 1945, Adolf Hitler's "Greater German Reich" was in its death throes. German and Austrian cities lay in rubble, millions of German and Austrian soldiers and civilians were streaming westward to escape the wrath of the Red Army, and German and Austrian broadcasting stations dollfully played selections from Richard Wagner's Ring Cycle to evoke the Twilight of the Gods (Götterdämmerung). The collapse of the Reich was also accompanied by the transference of power from Berlin to the province leaders ("Gauleiter"), who—as Homeland Defense Commisars ("Reichsverteidigungskommissare")—suddenly received absolute authority in non-military issues. Where there was no more communication with the administrative center of the Gau, a district leader ("Kreisleiter") of the Nazi party could also be installed as "Reichsverteidigungskommissar." The impending collapse of the Reich brought hope to the surviving victims of Nazi persecution, particularly the handful of Jews who had managed to survive Hitler's Final Solution. For many, however, this hope of liberation was forlorn. Instead, in March and April 1945 fleeing guards, soldiers, and, on occasion, civilians paused long enough to inflict a final series of atrocities. This article deals with crimes against humanity in this final phase of the war—atrocities which occurred everywhere during the collapse of the Nazi regime but most appallingly in the eastern regions of the Reich, i.e., also in the eastern parts of Austria.1

Calling these atrocities "excesses in an apocalyptic mood" is an interpretation referring to the conduct and attitude of many perpetrators, who, convinced that the defeat of the regime marked the end of their own world, succumbed to an "after us, the deluge" mentality. Susanne Uslu-Pauer, who recently published a study about the punishment of those crimes by Austrian courts, categorizes these crimes as atrocities emenating from extermination fury ("Vernichtungswut") and slavish obedience ("Kadavergehorsam"). The difference between these atrocities and the crimes committed in earlier years was not the degree, but the public nature of cruelty. Before, with a few exceptions, the most atrocious crimes had been committed behind the walls of concentration camps or somewhere in the East and were not witnessed by ordinary German civilians. One of the execeptions happened in Upper Austria, in February 1945, around Mauthausen. Some five hundred Soviet P.O.W.s who had managed to escape from the concentration camp were chased down and slain by both SS and ordinary people of the Mühlviertel district in what came to termed the Mühlviertler Hasenjagd ("Mühlviertel Rabbit Hunt"). This gruesome experience lasted several days, and nearly all the prisoners were killed, with only a few Austrian peasants daring to show compassion and save some of the escapees by hiding them in hovels or barns.2

The most important difference, however, was that earlier Nazi crimes in the camps and prisons and rear areas of the Eastern front were committed by perpetrators acting as executioners of a regime still in power. The crimes of the final phase of the war were committed by people acting as if they had orders. A comparison between the "Mühlviertler Hasenjagd" and similar atrocities in parts of eastern Austria (Lower Austria, Styria, and the Burgenland) two months later highlights this difference. Even the civilians who took part in the chase of the Russian soldiers in February 1945 were ordered to do so by regular authorities, the police and the mayors of the villages, and nobody was allowed to kill on one's own account. The corpses had to be collected and were brought back to the Mauthausen concentration camp. But in April and May 1945, when thousands of Hungarian Jews and other camp inmates were driven over the roads and through the villages of eastern Austria, no superior authority forced the accompanying guards or their entourage to murder or abuse the prisoners or, for that matter, hindered them from doing so. During the "Mühlviertler Hasenjagd" there was one single order, emanating from a central authority: to bring back, dead or alive, the escaped prisoners. But during the death marches the guards acted on their own authority inflicting harm and killing their prisoners at will.3

There are other significant differences between the experiences in the final phase of the war and the earlier ones. By March/April 1945 the overwhelming majority of the German "Volksgemeinschaft" viewed the end of the war with a mixture of hope and panic: hope because the end of the war had to mean an end to Allied bombings and an end to Gestapo terror (in that order); panic because Joseph Goebbels' Propaganda Ministry told people that they had to expect the worst when the Russian troops arrived. As many Reich citizens knew or at least had heard rumors of what German soldiers had done in Soviet Russia, they had good reason to believe Goebbels and fear the bloody revenge to come. There were also Nazi diehards, however, whose faith in Hitler and National Socialism remained unbroken. These stalwarts hoped that a diplomatic master stroke by the Führer and/or a combination of new weapons ("Wunderwaffen")—jet planes, ballistic missles (the so-called V2 rocket), and advanced submarines—would save the Nazi regime. Either because of or in spite of the apocalyptic scenario surrounding them, these ardent Nazis were willing to commit any cruelty to prevent "rash" surrender by a "defeatists."

This mixture of hopes and fears was particularly complicated in what the Nazis styled as the "Ostmark." An unknown but growing portion of the populace living in those provinces of the Reich which had been Austria before the Anschluss in March 1938 expected the restoration of Austrian statehood and—as "Austrians" (and therefore "the first victims" of "Hitlerite aggression," as the Allies had put it in the Moscow Declaration on Austria in November 1943)—a more lenient treatment than the Germans by the victorious Allies. But almost none of them was ready to take a risk in order to contribute to the restoration of Austria as an independent nation, although the Allies had also declared at Moscow that they would take into account Austria's own contribution in the struggle against Nazism. There was also the question of Austrian opponents of the regime. For those few who had been active in clandestine resistance circles or had managed to hide themselves—like Jews living in the underground ("U-Boote" or "submarines")—the end of the war meant simply liberation. Their concern was to avoid last minute mistakes that would betray them when the hour of deliverance was at hand. Similar thoughts motivated P.O.W.s, slave laborers, and concentration camp inmates, but with one added difference. Their fear was not the arrival of the Russians, but that their guards might kill them before the Allied soldiers arrived.

As it turned out, these latter fears were all too justified, for potential behavior on the part of guards and other perpetrators ran a volatile gamut of possibilities. Some earlier perpetrators simply shed their uniforms and attempted to drift into the civilian population. Others, bizarrely, tried to change sides at the last minute, to make undone what they had done, either by aiding persecuted people or at least by pretending to feel sympathy for all those who had been oppressed by the regime. Others swiftly dispatched presumed witnesses of the crimes in order to prevent legal retribution after the war. Finally, still others continued to commit ignominious crimes against prisoners, ill-treating, insulting, humiliating, and in some cases killing them, mostly by beating them to death or by torturing them and then shooting them as a pretended "coup de grâce."

Whereas the first, second, and to some extent even third pattern of behavior seemed reasonable, the fourth one made no sense whatsoever and yet was the most widespread. The end of the nightmare was to come in only a few days—in many cases the Red Army was already so close to the scene of the crime that both victims and perpetrators could hear the Soviet artillery—but there remained hundreds of eye-witnesses to these killings. The fear was that after the liberation, these survivors would be able to testify to the mistreatment they had suffered at the hands of their guards. It is therefore sensible that the perpetrators would seek to silence the witnesses to their crimes in the final days. Their fears were born out when hundreds of surviving victims reported to the police what they had lived through and identified their perpetrators. It was not by chance that a large number of the trials held before Austrian courts in the immediate post-war period dealt with the excesses of violence in the final phase of the war.

Thanks to the research of Claudia Kuretsidis-Haider, co-director of the Austrian Research Center for Post-war Trials, it is possible to demonstrate this fourth pattern of behavior with the example of the village Engerau, a suburb of the Slovakian capital Bratislava. 4 In November 1944 some two thousand Jewish men who had escaped deportation to Auschwitz were brought from Budapest to Engerau to dig anti-tank ditches and foundation for pillboxes for the "Southeast Wall" (Südostwall), a fortified zone protecting eastern Austria from the approaching Red Army. In Engerau they were confined in filthy stables and barns of the local population, with inadequate medical facilities and poor nutrition. Around five hundred of these Jews died of disease or were slain by their guards, most whom were members of the Vienna Brown Shirts (Sturmabteilung or SA).

On 29 March 1945, the night before Good Friday, the camp was evacuated after Soviet troops reached Bratislava. Those unable to march were shot on the spot, and the remaining 1,200 men had to march from Engerau to Deutsch-Altenburg on the Danube, a small town in Lower Austria, where two ships waited to take the prisoners to Mauthausen. Although the distance between Engerau and Deutsch-Altenburg was only about ten miles, the exhausted men needed the whole night to reach their destination, and more than a hundred Jews were shot before the march had ended. After the war some of the survivors testified against the perpetrators. A Viennese doctor, an Auschwitz survivor who helped Hungarian Jews return home, collected evidence against the perpetrators, and beginning in August 1945, a series of six "Engerau Trials," lasting until 1954, took place in Vienna. Legal proceedings were instituted against more than seventy suspects, twenty were indicted, and nine of them received the death sentence and were executed.

Court records show that many of the accused explained their crimes as simple fulfilment of their duties. They insisted that they had to push those weak, starved people westwards, and they were convinced that this was impossible without forcing them by humiliating and beating them individually. None of them admitted committing murder, although many were convicted of having shot dead one or more wounded men. They justified the killing as a kind of relief for prisoners who had already been ill-treated—by "others," of course—in such a way that it was likely they would die within a few hours. For all of these Nazi storm troopers it went without saying that the only remedy for a wounded prisoner was not medical treatment, but a "coup de grâce."

Engerau is only one case in this "last chapter" of the Holocaust. 5 There are many similar incidents, mostly involving Hungarian Jews deployed as forced labor, that transpired either in Austria or along the Austro-Hungarian border. All those cases followed the same pattern: starvation and ill-treatment in camps or hastily improvised shelters during the winter 1944-45; the exhausting and ultimately killing work of digging ditches for the Southeast Wall; the shooting of 50, 100 or 200 prisoners before the evacuation marches started; and the killing of hundreds more during the marches toward the already overcrowded concentration camp at Mauthausen. The total number of victims from the camps along the Southeast Wall and during the death marches is unknown, but on the basis of calculations by survivor organizations after the war, Austrian historians estimate that 23,000 is not an overstatement.6

These gruesome events from the last days of the war have belatedly attracted the attention of scholars. In the 1980s and early 1990s, the Hungarian historian, Szabolcs Szita, used eye witness accounts and Hungarian and Austrian documents to reconstruct the ordeal of Hungarian Jews along the Southeast Wall. During the last fifteen years Austrian historians have also taken up the investigation. Eleonore Lappin has expanded upon Szabolcs Szita's work with her work on death marches in Austria and, with Susanne Uslu-Pauer and Manfred Wieninger, on the overall fate of Hungarian Jewish forced laborers in Lower Austria. Claudia Kuretsidis-Haider has thoroughly analyzed the "Engerau Trials" in a recently published study. The political scientist, Eva Holpfer, and the the historians, Harald Strassl and Wolfgang Vosko, have independently explored the implications of two particularly shocking crimes in the Burgenland from the final phase of the war. The first occurred in the village of Deutsch-Schützen, where a leader of the Hitler-Jugend commanded boys of the local Nazi youth organization to assist an SS murder squad. The second took place in the small town of Rechnitz, where on the night of March 24/25, 1945, some 180 Hungarian Jews were compelled to dig their own graves and were then murdered by guests from a neighboring castle. One of the last massacres in Austria, which took place on the Prebichl pass between Styria and Upper Austria on 7 April 1945, is the subject of a volume edited by Heimo Halbrainer and Christian Ehetreiber. Finally, at the University of Vienna in the 1990s, Professor Gerhard Jagschitz encouraged students to work with court documents7, some of them wrote masters theses about the massacres at the end of the war (see Jagschitz/Neugebauer and Achenbach/Szorger)8.

Some of these scholarly works affected the public memory and stimulated local grassroots activities, often sponsored by schools. Whereas 1995, at the fiftieth anniversary, there was hardly any public acknowledgment of those events, in 2005 there were commemoration events in several towns and villages in the eastern parts of Austria where most of the atrocities had occurred in 1945. Since 2000 Claudia Kuretsidis-Haider has been organizing a kind of annual pilgrimage which starts at the monument for the murdered Hungarian Jews in the cemetery of Petržalka (the Slovakian name for Engerau) and traces the route of the 1945 death march.

There is hardly any piece of literature which deals directly with these events of the last days of Nazi rule in Austria, although Nazi crimes play an important role in contemporary Austrian literature. One of the rare exceptions is a novel by Johannes Mario Simmel, *Wir heißen euch hoffen* (1980), but the author does not write about the mass violence during the death marches. His topic is an example of individual violence, the killing of two members of a resistance group at the University of Vienna by a professor after they tried to prevent the destruction of an electron microscope during the last days of the war.

What writers and filmmakers are interested in is the dealing with those events. One of the best movies is *Totschweigen*9 about the above-mentioned case of Rechnitz10. In this town Nazi networks had a strong influence even after the war. An eye-witness who was ready to give evidence before the court was murdered, and since then, older people have been afraid to tell "strangers" what they experienced in 1945. *Totschweigen* is more than a documentary: in documenting the failed search for the mass grave it depicts the obstinate refusal of the local population to remember—fueled either by fear of or by complicity with the murderers.

There are movies, novels and short stories, some of them real masterpieces[11], which all have the same background: A person (or a whole village, as depicted in the movie *Der Himbeerpflücker* [*The Raspberry Picker*], starring Helmut Qualtinger[12]) refuses to remember a crime that had happened during the Nazi period, in most cases at the end of the war, but it is always memory and not the event itself the author is interested in. In some cases the plot is transferred to within the family[13].

Maybe there is a kind of obsession, which Austrian contemporary writers share with many of their readers, and that is not the Nazi period as such but the repression of the Nazi period in public memory, the dealing with—or better: the impunity of—Nazi crimes after 1945.

For an archivist and historian who is convinced that arts and literature can play a prominent role in understanding historical events, especially when psychological problems arise, it is regrettable that the outbreaks of unrestrained violence in the last days and weeks of Nazi rule have not been tackled by writers and movie-makers. Court records contain thousands of pages of interrogations of the perpetrators, and these documents await not only historical and psychological research, but also use as an inspiration for film and literature.

Post scriptum

In March and April 2007 the city theater of Klagenfurt performed the play *Jedem das Seine* [*To Each to His Own*], by Silke Hassler and Peter Turrini, the first artistic treatment of the horror that Hungarian Jews experienced in Austria in 1945. And, as Hassler said in an interview, "an important source was the records of the post-war trials for so called 'final phase crimes'; there we learned a lot about perpetrators and victims" (see Mottinger). Hassler and Turrini call it a "people's operetta." On their death march to Mauthausen a group of Jews—among them some musicians from Budapest—are abandoned by their guards and left in a barn, where they come into contact with the local population. A few peasants try to help them, while others are convinced that they have to die and are ready to do what their guards had failed to do. Meanwhile the Jews and their local helpers begin to hold rehearsals for a performance of Wiener Blut, the famous operetta by Johann Strauss. But Roland Neuwirth, a composer of modern, artistic Viennese folk songs, transforms the Viennese waltz to a danse macabre. The critic for the Viennese newspaper Die Presse wrote:

"Schubert's 'Schöne Müllerin' is quoted en passant, this paradigmatic forboding of death with its cruel cradle-songs. The song ends badly: 'My sweetheart loves hunting so much,' sings the tenor, and outside the barn one can hear the shots of the hunters, and the torches have already been lit" (see Mayer).14

There is no happy ending: fanatical Nazis set fire to the barn, and no one survives.

Works Cited

Achenbach, Michael, and Dieter Szorger. "Der Einsatz ungarischer Juden am Südostwall im Abschnitt Niederdonau 1944/45." Masters thesis, University of Vienna, 1996.

Declaration on Austria, issued by the governments of the United Kingdom, the Soviet Union and the United States of America, Moscow, 30 October 1943 <http://www.yale.edu/lawweb/avalon/wwii/moscow.htm>

Gerlach, Christian, and Götz Aly. *Das letzte Kapitel. Der Mord an den ungarischen Juden*. Stuttgart: Deutsche Verlags Anstalt, 2002.

Halbrainer, Heimo, and Christian Ehetreiber, eds. *Todesmarsch Eisenstraße 1945. Terror, Handlungsspielräume, Erinnerung. Menschliches Handeln unter Zwangsbedingungen*. Graz: Clio, 2005.

Hasenjagd: Vor lauter Feigheit gibt es kein Erbarmen. Andreas Gruber, dir. 1994.

Henisch, Peter. *Die kleine Figur meines Vaters*. Wien: Langen Mueller, 1975.

"Der Himbeerpflücker." Erich Neuberg, dir. Fritz Hochwälder, script. 1965.

Holpfer, Eva. "Der Umgang der burgenländischen Nachkriegsgesellschaft mit NS-Verbrechen bis 1955 am Beispiel der wegen der Massaker von Deutsch-Schützen und Rechnitz geführten Volksgerichtsprozesse." Masters thesis, University of Vienna, 1998.

Jagschitz, Gerhard, and Wolfgang Neugebauer, eds. *Stein, 6. April 1945. Das Urteil des Volksgerichts Wien (August 1946) gegen die Verantwortlichen des Massakers im Zuchthaus Stein*. Vienna: Bundesministerium für Justiz/Dokumentationsarchiv des österreichischen Widerstandes, 1995. 152-62.

Jedem das Seine. Eine Volksoperette. Silke Hassler and Peter Turrini, text. Roland Neuwirth, music. First performance 8 March 2007, Stadttheater Klagenfurt.

Kohl, Walter. *Auch auf dich wartet eine Mutter. Die Familie Langthaler inmitten der "Mühlviertler Hasenjagd."* Grünbach bei Freistadt: Verlag Franz Steinmaßl, 2005.

Kuretsidis-Haider, Claudia. *"'Das Volk sitzt zu Gericht'. Österreichische Justiz und NS-Verbrechen am Beispiel der Engerau-Prozesse 1945–1954*. Innsbruck: StudienVerlag, 2006.

Lappin, Eleonore. "Die Ahndung von NS-Gewaltverbrechen im Zuge der Todesmärsche ungarischer Juden durch die Steiermark." In *Keine "Abrechnung". NS-Verbrechen, Justiz und Gesellschaft in Europa nach 1945*, edited by Claudia Kuretsidis-Haider and Winfried Garscha. Leipzig/Vienna: Akademische Verlagsanstalt/Dokumentationsarchiv des österreichischen Widerstandes, 1998). 32-53.

—. "The Death Marches of Hungarian Jews through Austria in the Spring of 1945." *Yad Vashem Studies* 27 (2000): 203-42.

—. "Rechnitz gedenkt der Opfer der NS-Herrschaft." *Jahrbuch des Dokumentationsarchivs des österreichischen Widerstandes* 1992: 50-70.

Lappin, Eleonore, Susanne Uslu-Pauer, and Manfred Wieninger. *Ungarisch-jüdische Zwangsarbeiter(innen) in Niederösterreich 1944/45*. St. Pölten: NÖ Institut für Landeskunde, 2006.

Mayer, Norbert. "Das böse Wiener Blut." *Die Presse* (Vienna) 10 March 2007.

Mottinger, Michaela. "Eine traumhafte Geschichte vom Tod." Interview with Silke Hassler and Peter Turrini. *Kurier* (Vienna), 25 February 2007.

Pollack, Martin. *Der Tote im Bunker. Bericht über meinen Vater*. Vienna: Zsolnay, 2004.

Reichart, Elisabeth. *Februarschatten*. Vienna: Verlag der Österreichischen Staatsdruckerei, 1984.

Rizy, Helmut. *Hasenjagd im Mühlviertel. Roman einer Gegend*. Weitra: Bibliothek der Provinz, 1995.

Rüter, Christiaan Frederik, and Dick de Mildt, eds. *Justiz und NS-Verbrechen. Die Deutschen Strafverfahren wegen NS-Tötungsverbrechen*, 40 vols. Amsterdam/Munich: Amsterdam University Press/K. G. Saur Verlag, 1966- .

Simmel, Johannes Mario. *Wir heißen euch hoffen*. Ascona: Droemer Knaur Verlag, 1980.

Strassl, Harald, and Wolfgang Vosko. "Das Schicksal ungarisch-jüdischer Zwangsarbeiter am Beispiel des Südostwallbaues 1944/45 im Bezirk Oberwart unter besonderer Berücksichtigung der Massenverbrechen

bei Rechnitz und Deutsch-Schützen." Masters thesis, University of Vienna, 1999.
Szita, Szabolcs. "The Forced Labour of Hungarian Jews at the Fortification of the Western Border Regions of Hungary, 1944-1945." In *Studies on the Holocaust in Hungary*, edited by Randolph L. Braham. New York: Columbia University Press, 1990. 175-93.
—. *Holocaust az Alpok Elött* (Holocaust at the foot of the Alps). Györ: Szabo Kalman, 1983.
—. *Verschleppt, verhungert, vernichtet. Die Deportation von ungarischen Juden auf das Gebiet des annektierten Österreich 1944-1945*. Preface by György Konrad. Vienna: Eichbauer-Verlag, 1999.
"Totschweigen." Margareta Heinrich and Eduard Erne, dirs. 1994.
Uslu-Pauer, Susanne. "'Vernichtungswut und Kadavergehorsam'—Strafrechtliche Verfolgung von Endphaseverbrechen durch österreichische Volks- und Geschworenengerichte." In *Holocaust und NS-Kriegsverbrechen vor Gericht: Der Fall Österreich*, edited by Thomas Albrich, Winfried R. Garscha, and Martin F. Polaschek. Innsbruck: StudienVerlag, 2006. 279-304.
Yad Vashem Report of the Jewish "Historische Dokumentation," 19 November 1951; Yad Vashem archive N° 015/36.

Notes

[1] For this kind of Nazi crimes the Dutch law professor C. F. Rüter coined the term "Final phase crimes" ("Endphaseverbrechen"). Cf. Rüter/de Mildt.

[2] Cf. Kohl, *Auch auf dich wartet eine Mutter. Die Familie Langthaler inmitten der "Mühlviertler Hasenjagd."* Because the escaped prisoners were hunted like rabbits, the action was called "Mühlviertler Hasenjagd," and it has been the subject of two novels—Elisabeth Reichart's *Februarschatten* (1984) and Helmut Rizy's *Hasenjagd im Mühlviertel. Roman einer Gegend* (1995)—and of a movie directed by Andreas Gruber, *Hasenjagd: Vor lauter Feigheit gibt es kein Erbarmen* (1994).

[3] The situation resembled the first days of the Nazi regime in Austria, in March 1938, when the new Nazi police authorities tolerated the public humiliation of Jews and the looting and/or confiscating of their apartments by Nazi and non-Nazi individuals for almost a week before they intervened and stopped the pogrom and replaced it by anti-Jewish laws and decrees.

[4] Under Habsburg rule the official (Hungarian) name of this village—on the River Danube, opposite Bratislava/Preßburg/Pozsony—was Pozsonyligetfalu. After the foundation of Czechoslovakia in 1918 the village (under the name Petržalka) became part of Slovakia, but the local population continued to call it Engerau.

[5] Christian Gerlach and Götz Aly in *Das letzte Kapitel. Der Mord an den ungarischeJuden*. Stuttgart: Deutsche Verlags Anstalt, 2002, call the whole experience of the Hungarian Jews—from the confinement and deportation of some 700,000 of them to the extermination camp of Auschwitz-Birkenau in April, May, and June 1944 until the last "death marches" in April-May 1945—the "last chapter" of the Holocaust.

[6] Report of the Jewish "Historische Dokumentation," 19 November 1951; Yad Vashem archive N° 015/36. See also Eleonore Lappin, "The Death Marches of Hungarian Jews through Austria in the Spring of 1945." In March 2007 in reports about the premiere of the play *Jedem das Seine* in Klagenfurt, Austrian newspapers suggested the number of 80,000 victims of the "death marches" through Austria in spring 1945, which is an exaggeration.

[7] A result of these research seminars for advanced students was a chronology of the massacre in the penitentiary of Stein on the Danube and its surroundings on April 6th and 7th 1945 by six of Professor Jagschitz' students in: Gerhard Jagschitz and Wolfgang Neugebauer (eds.), *Stein, 6. April 1945. Das Urteil des Volksgerichts Wien (August 1946) gegen die Verantwortlichen des Massakers im Zuchthaus Stein*. Vienna: Bundesministerium für Justiz/Dokumentationsarchiv des österreichischen Widerstandes (1995), pp. 152-162.

[8] E.g. Michael Achenbach and Dieter Szorger, Der Einsatz ungarischer Juden am Südostwall im Abschnitt Niederdonau 1944/45. University of Vienna master thesis (1996).

[9] English title: "Walls of Silence" (1994). Directors: Margareta Heinrich and Eduard Erne.

[10] A first study of the murders in Rechnitz in 1945 and the difficulty in locating the mass grave was published by Eleonore Lappin, "Rechnitz gedenkt der Opfer der NS-Herrschaft" (1992).

[11] E.g. Hans Lebert, *Die Wolfshaut* (1960; in 2005 the novel was broadcast in a radio-play version); Thomas Bernhard, *Frost* (1963); Gerhard Fritsch, *Fasching* (1967). Worth mentioning among more recent works is "Lanz" by Andreas Weber (2004).

[12] "Der Himbeerpflücker" (1965). Director: Erich Neuberg. Script: Fritz Hochwälder.

[13] E.g. Peter Henisch, Die kleine Figur meines Vaters (1975). This is true, to a certain extent, also for Martin Pollack, Der Tote im Bunker. Bericht über meinen Vater (2004).

[14] "En passant wird Schuberts 'Schöne Müllerin' zitiert, dieses Paradigma der Todesahnung mit seinen grausamen Wiegenliedern. Das Lied, es geht böse aus. 'Mein Schatz hat's Jagen so gern' singt der Tenor, und draußen vor dem Stadel hört man bereits die Schüsse der Jäger, die Brandfackeln liegen bereit."

CHAPTER FOURTEEN

TERRORISTS, FREEDOM FIGHTERS, ACTIVISTS AND FOUNDING FATHERS: THE HISTORICAL REVISION OF THE 1960S BOMBING CAMPAIGN IN THE SOUTH TYROL

GEORG GROTE

In memoriam Antony E. Alcock (1936-2006)

"I Turchi oggi hanno occupato Firenze!"[1] - The Turks have annexed Florence today! This is how solicitor Sandro Canestrini, acting for the South Tyrolean defendants at the 1963 trials in Milan, opened his defense, shocking both the judge and those in the auditorium. Briefly relishing the silence he created within the chamber, he then continued to explain that this was a joke, but that the scenario was nevertheless extremely similar to the one the German South Tyroleans experienced after both World War I and World War II when they had to accept that they were ruled by Italy. Canestrini's surprising statement was aimed at the Italian public and press who were present at the trials in Milan, as he wanted to create some understanding in Italy for the living conditions of the German South Tyroleans, a people largely unknown to most Italians. Only in 1961, when the political situation erupted into violence, did Italians become aware that everything was not well in the Northern border region of their country. Then, all that was perceived in Italy was the destruction caused by the bomb attacks—and they were seen as seemingly mindless terrorist attacks. Therefore Canestrini continued his statement by saying that by forcing the German South Tyroleans to live in Italy (and attempting to Italianize the German-speaking majority in the province), the Italians had created a dualism in society that was hard for the native German South Tyroleans to tolerate.

The Historical Situation

South Tyrol, an area in the Dolomites in northern Italy, was inhabited by mainly German-speaking mountain folk whose fate was to have become the victims of a World War I agreement between Italy and the Western Allies. When the war ended in 1918, Italy was granted this part of the Southern Alps as a reward for its support of the Allies' war efforts. South Tyrol had formerly belonged to Austria. The German-speaking population of South Tyrol was exposed to a rigid policy of Italianization under Mussolini and so longed for reunification with the old fatherland. Hitler's access to power in Germany in 1933 promised an end to suppression, yet Hitler sacrificed the South Tyroleans to his friendship with Mussolini. In 1939 the South Tyroleans were presented with the option to leave their homeland and gain German citizenship or to stay and accept Italian citizenship—an awful quandary and an issue that caused major rifts in German South Tyrolean society for the duration of the war.[2]

Politically as well as economically post World War II South Tyrol was anything but a cozy homeland for the German-speaking South Tyroleans. First, they still suffered from the political and social fallout that the fascist regimes in both Berlin and Rome had inflicted on them during the "Option" period (see Grote, "Gehen oder Bleiben?); second, they faced an uncertain future in Italy as their hopes for political and cultural autonomy had been dashed by the Allied decision to return South Tyrol to Italy unconditionally.[3] The Gruber-deGasperi agreement of 1946 had come about through Allied pressure on Italy to grant the South Tyroleans some kind of autonomy, yet the ensuing creation of the Autonomous Region Trentino-Alto Adige in 1947 proved to be little else but a strategic move by the Italians: they had shown some movement on the issue and thus satisfied the Western Allies, but had amalgamated German-speaking South Tyrol with purely Italian Trentino. Italy therefore retained control over South Tyrol as 200,000 South Tyroleans were never going to win any vote in the regional parliament in Trento over 500,000 Italians. The aspirations of South Tyroleans to any kind of autonomy were thus skilfully dissipated.[4]

The fusion of Trento and South Tyrol in 1947 by deGasperi revealed the tactical considerations behind the Gruber–deGasperi agreement on the Italian side. This new situation meant that the German South Tyroleans were now completely exposed to an Italian policy that in the 1940s and 50s bore close resemblance to the fascist measures of the 1920s and 30s.[5] These measures did not instill any confidence in the German-speaking South Tyroleans that Italy was serious about granting them any kind of autonomy, political or cultural. However, it was the planned and promoted immigration of Southern Italian workers to the industrial zone in Bolzano that annoyed the South Tyroleans most. Canon Michael Gamper, editor of German South Tyrol's newspaper *Dolomiten*, expressed his people's anger when in October 1953 he wrote:

> The deliberate infiltration of our people continues unabated. Many tens of thousand of Italians from the Southern provinces have immigrated, while, at the same time, the return of some tens of thousands of our fellow country people has been made impossible. The percentage of our native population is thus diminishing annually compared to the uncanny swelling of immigrant figures. It is a simple mathematical task to predict the time when we will be the minority, not just within the region that has been created to majorize us, but within the closer boundaries of our native land where we will then become a defenseless minority. All this within an area, which only a short while ago only bore 3% Italians of the overall population. Since 1945 we South Tyroleans have been on a death march and all we can hope for is a last minute rescue action.[6]

In his article Gamper articulated the fear which would trigger the political unrest in the late 1950s and early 1960s: Italy's 51% policy, the planned immigration of thousands of Italian workers to South Tyrol while many native South Tyroleans were still abroad as a result of the war or forced to emigrate as they were deliberately denied jobs in Italian-dominated industry, trade, and public administration. The protective power Austria ("Schutzmacht Österreich") was of little help in this situation.[7]

The symbol of this policy was Italy's social housing program, which aimed at eradicating the slum-like developments on the outskirts of major Italian cities including Bolzano—featuring makeshift houses built by immigrants from the South—by introducing a point system favouring the poorest. While it was undoubtedly a reasonable idea to grant these workers proper living space, it meant that native German-speaking South Tyroleans who would often have endured poor living standards, too, were not entitled to these new flats. 1960s political activist Sepp Mitterhofer describes the local perception of this Italian scheme as follows:

> Poor men from the South of the state arrived in droves at Bolzano station and they carried their few belongings in cardboard boxes to the dismal shanty-towns where they were housed. After some weeks, however, they would be given brand new apartments in the newly built public housing complexes, because they were entitled to new housing as they had amassed sufficient points on the social housing list more quickly than any native South Tyrolean because they had lived in the shanty towns. Some time

> later they would then be followed by the rest of their entire families and even their parents and grandparents.[8]

Social housing thus symbolized Italian oppression and forced immigration and was regarded as a provocation of the native Germans (see Mitterhofer and Obwegs, 62; Widmann, 344), especially when it transpired that Guiseppe Togni, minister of public works, in 1957 sent a telegram to the lord mayor of Bolzano, Giorgio Pasquali, in which he announced that the population of Bolzano was to rise from 83,000 to 150,000 during the coming 30 years. This increase could never have been realized through an increase in the birthrate of the existing population of Bolzano, and it thus meant a massively increased immigration from the South (Widmann, 430). The political representation of the German-speaking population, the Südtiroler Volkspartei (SVP), proved to be without influence in this situation and could only protest verbally. The SVP's new chairman, Silvius Magnago, voiced the German population's unease when he said: "We cannot help the impression that this is nationalistic policy, all the more so as the housing problem is much more acute in other Italian cities than it is in Bolzano, where the government nevertheless spends more billions on public housing than in those other cities. And not even 10% of public housing has been allocated to South Tyroleans."[9] The *Dolomiten* prophesied that Bolzano was going to drown in a sea of Italians (10 May 1957), while the SVP decided in 1959 to withdraw its delegates from the regional parliament in Trento. This hardening of the political situation corresponded with a polarization and radicalization of the South Tyrolean population, both Italian and German. The Germans had been particularly enraged about the Italian treatment of the "Pfunderer Buam" in August 1956.[10] German South Tyrol was in mourning about the fact that half a dozen young men had to spend years behind bars because they wanted to highlight the plight of the South Tyrolean people and because they chose to do so employing illegal means.[11]

The reaction to the trial of the Pfunderer Buam was unequivocal in South Tyrol, and the SVP was hoping to mobilize the population through events such as the mass demonstration of Sigmundskron in November 1957, when some 35,000 South Tyroleans claimed their right to self-determination and requested an end of the regional autonomy with Trento. The *Dolomiten* in its commentary had praised the peaceful character of the demonstration; however, the paper had also pointed out that the mood in the country was explosive, so Rome should listen to South Tyrolean demands when drafting new legislation and policies. Otherwise, the paper concluded, the pot which had been simmering for a long time might actually boil over.[12]

How explosive the atmosphere in the country had become was made clear by the numerous Italian counter-demonstrations in which the German South Tyrolean claim for self-determination was refuted. The Italian politician Andrea Mitolo encouraged his fellow citizens to counter attacks, and the political party Giovine Italia demanded the abolition of the Paris agreement of 1946, which, at least on paper, ascribed some autonomy to the German South Tyroleans. Italian radical voices now argued that the Italians in South Tyrol needed protection themselves as they had become a minority in an area dominated by the German South Tyroleans. Verbal and public hostilities between the two groups were succeeded by the "Feuernacht," the night of fires, on June 11/12, 1961, when the "Befreiungsausschuss Südtirol" (BAS), the resistance movement, managed to blow up 37 electricity pylons, 19 of them in the greater Bolzano area. The BAS aimed to target the industrial zone and particularly the electrically heated aluminum furnaces, which would have been irreparably damaged had the plan succeeded. Even though the infrastructural targets of the attacks were not fully met, the "Feuernacht" resulted in the immediate creation of global interest in the conflict, which was a major success for the BAS. However, one bomb accidently killed an Italian street worker who had tried to defuse it, and this was a major PR desaster for the BAS. Politically, things began to move much more rapidly after June 1961: in October the Italian minister for the interior, Scelba, inaugurated the council of 19 (11 Italians, 8 South Tyroleans) which began to hammer out a compromise for South Tyrol—the beginnings of the second autonomy status, known as the "Paket," the package of 1969.

The Italian press, voicing the opinion of Italian politicians and the wider Italian public, dismissed the attacks as sheer terrorism and indiscriminately called all those involved in them "dinamitardi e terroristi," a view that prevails to this day. On 12 June 1961, the *Dolomiten*, voice of German South Tyrol, called the attacks a violation of the traditional Heart of Jesus celebrations of that night and accused the activists of un-Christian and near communist behavior, an accusation that was considered wholly unfair by the members of the BAS. The wider German South Tyrolean public remained silent or even distanced itself from the attacks. Initially, the SVP denounced the events of the "Feuernacht" sharply and accused the activists of torpedoing the political process. It took the party chairman Silvius Magnago until 1976 to express some form of sympathy for those who committed the violent acts when he admitted that these had been "politically explicable and humanly understandable" and that they had "contributed significantly to achieve a better autonomy for South Tyrol" (see Steininger, *Südtirol im 20. Jh.*, 491).

The "Feuernacht" in South Tyrol's Public Discourse

In the decades following the bombings of the early 1960s there was no public discussion of their significance within the South-Tirolean population. Historians dealt with the issue in passing, while the political situation for the German South Tyroleans remained unclear (see Ermacora, Gatterer, Drechsler, Stadlmayr, and Volgger). It was only after 1992—the full implementation by Italy of the 1969 "Paket" and the ensuing Austro-Italian UN declaration that their quarrels over Südtirol had come to an end—that the public taboo prohibiting any discussion of the violence of that period was overcome. The first to do so were Elisabeth Baumgartner, Gerhard Mumelter, and Hans Mayr in their publication *Feuernacht. Südtirols Bombenjahre. Ein zeitgeschichtliches Lesebuch* (Night of Fire. South Tyrol's Years of Bombings. A Contemporary Reader), which opened the public debate in 1992.[13]

This first real engagement with the difficult issue in a politically sensitive time was careful in its editorial style, provided many pictures and statements from both sides of the linguistic divide, and attempted to approach the polarising issue from various different views. It was Baumgartner, Mumelter, and Mayr's aim "to begin a public discussion. After three decades of silence it is time that the public deals with this issue, it is time that questions are answered and that positions are taken."[14]

The same period saw the release of Felix Mitterer's four-part docudrama *Verkaufte Heimat. Bombenjahre, (Lost Homeland)* part 3 of which, *Bombenjahre*, deals with the bombing campaign. Mitterer's production managed to reach a wide audience in Germany, Austria, and South Tyrol. He depicts the protagonists of the early 1960s and their struggle in a way symptomatic for the treatment of the *Bombenjahre* in 1994: his heroes are riddled with self-doubt, troubled by what they feel they must do to save their *Heimat*. This series reflected the *Zeitgeist* in South Tyrol in the same way that more recent publications document the change in perception. These recent publications paved the way for a six-part documentary on the bomb attacks of 1961, which RAI Bolzano broadcast in the autumn of 2005. Through *Bombenjahre* the authors Helmut Lechthaler and Christoph Franceschini managed to reopen a public discussion about the effect of these violent attacks on the political process.

The New "National Library"

The academic debate about the effect of violence has often been characterized by wishful thinking and idealist approaches, while the public discourse is characterized by a rehabilitation of the "men and women" of 1961, and this process resembles historical phenomena of the early twentieth century—that is, those phases in the existence of small states that, after achieving national independence, resort to writing their own history in the light of what has been achieved. Yet modern-day South Tyrol is not a newly founded nation state, but a strong autonomous province within the "resident state" of Italy. However, on investigating the relevant publications of the past number of years in South Tyrol that deal with the period of the early 1960s, one discovers that the 1960s "terrorists" have been cast as public icons. This mythmaking is the foundation for the new South Tyrolean "national library"—a corpus of publicly accepted printed histories of the South Tyrolean struggle. As the topic of the "Bombenjahre" has been in the realm of the South Tyrolean public for a number of years, it has provided sufficient interest to sustain a number of publications, both academic, such as Rolf Steininger's 1999 three-volume publication *Südtirol zwischen Diplomatie und Terror* (South Tyrol between Diplomacy and Terrorism)[15], and non-academic, these mainly of a biographical nature. Most of these publications are more than just memorial accounts of the past in that they place the activists and their individual destinies of the violent era in the 1960s in the wider context of South Tyrolean history of the twentieth century. This new literature clearly reflects South Tyroleans' strong regional self-confidence, which is based on the wide-reaching constitutional autonomy of the Autonomous Province of Bolzano. A close look at the relevant publications will support this observation.

The traditionally undisputed founding father of South Tyrolean autonomy has always been Silvius Magnago. He led the SVP from 1957 to 1989 and served as South Tyrolean "Landeshauptmann." He oversaw and influenced the transition of South Tyrol from being an underprivileged and poor backwater to the wealthiest and politically most independent region of modern Italy. Gottfried Solderer's publication *Silvius Magnago. Eine Biographie Südtirols* (Silvius Magnago. A South Tyrolean Biography, 1996) is a literary monument to a man who is synonymous with the South Tyrol success. In this massive production Solderer creates a human image of Magnago, often a larger-than-life personality enshrouded in the mist of cool professional political distance, an image widely accepted by the South Tyrolean public.

Recently new biographies of the more controversial activists of 1961 have been published which are now rivaling the towering Magnago and his significance for the autonomy process. These (mainly) men come from a different background from Magnago; they were farmers, shopkeepers, students, and, above all, family men. It is the families and the women behind the activists whose roles have now also been honored in recent publications. A more detailed analytical look at the most significant of these publications reveals modern South Tyrol's changed perception of the events and activists of 1961:

The year 2000 saw the publication of Josef Fontana and Hans Mayr's biography of Sepp Kerschbaumer, *Eine Biographie* (A Biography). Fontana and Mayr were fellow-activists of Kerschbaumer, who ranks (in the company of Luis Amplatz and Georg Klotz) among the three icons of the South Tyrolean "liberation movement." Mayr, Fontana, and Kerschbaumer were members of the BAS who were arrested and interned by the Italian police in 1961 and are thus witnesses of the violent struggle of their former fellow-fighter. This makes for an intimate, well-informed, but at the same time biased interpretation of Kerschbaumer, because his struggle was their struggle, and an evaluation of his actions is a justification of their involvement in the violent activities. This proximity to Kerschbaumer makes for a problematic publication and a curious interpretation of his character: Mayr and Fontana do not spend much time on the evolution of the human being that Kerschbaumer was, from shop owner and family man to political activist/terrorist; instead they produce an image of him through the "benefit of hindsight," through the focus of the BAS-activist and sentenced prison inmate. Kerschbaumer is thus not shown as acting in his time and developing along the general *Zeitgeist*, but his life and actions are evaluated from the perspective of 2000, which makes for a regrettably shallow and two-dimensional characterization.[16]

Numerous passages of the publication suggest that the authors' interest in Kerschbaumer is primarily not historical but contemporary in that his legacy for today's South Tyrol is being emphasized. This becomes obvious in passages of the text where Kerschbaumer's altruism (28), his philanthropy (25), and his extraordinary tolerance (27) are mentioned, all of which were exceptional even "in the context of today." This allusion, which serves no purpose in a historical interpretation of Kerschbaumer, reveals the authors' strong personal involvement in the subject: they belong to the generation of South Tyroleans who accepted significant personal risks for their participation in the armed struggle and who paid the price and served time in Italian jails. This generation tends to evaluate the achievements in the living standards in South Tyrol since the 1980s more critically: they equate the current wealth with materialism, complacency, and political lethargy. Kerschbaumer symbolizes the opposite: he is passionate in supporting fellow-citizens (84), he demonstrates "exemplary civic courage" (101), he declares himself singularly responsible for the attacks of 1961 in the Milan bomb trials in order to protect his fellow-accused (145, 147), and he looks after his fellow inmates in Verona jail "like a father" (207).

Fontana and Mayr repeatedly stress Kerschbaumer's strong Catholic beliefs and his exceptional care for other human beings (28), but they fail to give plausible and specific reasons for his turning to violence against Italian installations. Instead they draw a general image of post-World War II South Tyrol, they describe minutely the injusticies of the first autonomy status of 1947, and they emphasize the threats of Italian immigration to South Tyrol and the Italian government's 51% majorisation policy. Their interpretation of the period creates an image of heightening tensions in South Tyrol's mixed society in the early 1950s, epitomized in Gamper's article in the *Dolomiten* in October 1953.

Gamper's phrase, the "death march of the South Tyroleans" prompted Sepp Kerschbaumer to press the SVP leadership into a more decisive stance against the Italian government and its representatitves in South Tyrol. Consequently, he supported strongly the new style of leadership under Silvius Magnago after the internal party revolution in the SVP in 1957. Magnago disappointed Kerschbaumer, too, in his speech at the Sigmundskron mass gathering as he remained very moderate and attempted to quell the public anger. Kerschbaumer then took individual action and wrote leaflets in order to politically mobilize the South Tyroleans by encouraging them to take action against Italian cultural oppression. These pamphlets were signed "Befreiungsausschuss Südtirol BAS" and spread among the population. He also displayed great personal courage when he flew the Tyrolean flag from the church steeple in Frangart in February 1957 and was subsequently arrested and sentenced to 10 days in prison. Actions such as these mobilized the public somewhat and for the following number of weeks Tyrolean flags appeared in inaccessible yet very visible places. Moreover, civic disobedience now had a name and a symbolic figure in Sepp Kerschbaumer. His political struggle continued when he stepped down from his post as SVP "Ortsobmann" (local chairperson of the SVP) "to protect the party" (Fontana and Mayr, 75), and in particular when he began a 15-day hunger strike after the "Pfunderer Buam" were sentenced in what was widely perceived as an unjust trial. His letters from jail to the Italian prime minister Amintore Fanfani, president Giovanni Gronchi, and minister of justice Guido

Gonella remained unanswered. Kerschbaumer concluded that political circumstances in South Tyrol could only be changed if more radical steps were taken: "in short, we need dynamite" ("...kurz gesagt: Dynamit"; Fontana and Mayr, 101).

This was the watershed in Kerschbaumer's political biography. He emerged from being a very Catholic, courageous, and disappointed South Tyrolean citizen who was driven by the political events to become an activist who remained faithful to his Christian beliefs but employed violent means to improve the future of his fellow-citizens. Fontana and Mayr fail to investigate the political alternative represented by Silvius Magnago. They present Kerschbaumer as someone who was forced to become a "dinamitardi." From then on things moved swiftly: Kerschbaumer created an active organization, linked up with North Tyrolean sympathizers who would become instrumental in procuring dynamite, and fell out with its leaders, especially Wolfgang Pfaundler. The groups differed significantly in their strategic considerations which, according to the authors, were based on their different individual mentalities (117). Pfaundler and Kerschbaumer's diverging views relate to the question of whether the violent struggle should be limited to attacks against installations representing Italian supremacy, or whether it should be extended to guerilla warfare and focus on human targets, i.e. carabinieri, soldiers, and Italian representatives.

Kerschbaumer favoured the fight against installations, and the authors of his biography support this view strongly. After all, they were members of his group, and a struggle against the symbols of oppression is easier to justify to today's readership than guerilla warfare.[17] In their text Josef Fontana and Hans Mayr created an image of Sepp Kerschbaumer that was easy to contextualize in a peaceful society at the turn of the millennium. Kerschbaumer's ethics, his courage, and his initially peaceful struggle conform to today's ethics, and he thus turns into a modern unitarian figure representing South Tyrol's struggle for cultural independence from Italy. Few will disagree with his moderate anti-Italianism—focused against Italian policies but never against individual Italians—and Fontana and Mayr use the opportunity to ascribe anti-Germanism to Italian policies and Italian demonstrations in Bolzano even though it has been shown repeatedly by historians that at the root of the controversial Italian policies against South Tyrol lay the fear of a separation of the Italian state.[18]

Kerschbaumer, however, remains an icon. His letters from jail are described as the "poetry of a virtuous heart" (Fontana and Mayr, 169), his altruism is praised, culminating in the comment of an unknown Italian who calls Kerschbaumer a saint (169). His funeral (he died of a heart attack in a Verona jail in 1964) turns into a religious pilgrimage—a third Sigmundskron(216). Fontana and Mayr claim that Sepp Kerschbaumer was a unitarian figure, in both his views and in his conduct. He was opposed to division and disintegration. He worked for peace and justice, for unity and cohesion in pursuing a common goal (223). The Sepp Kerschbaumer that Fontana and Mayr create is designed to be an idol for the reader of the year 2000. Their biography is not true to the historical Kerschbaumer, but to their desired Kerschbaumer legacy, which, in turn, would include them as members of Kerschbaumer's group. Kerschbaumer's entry into South Tyrolean history was as a political activist who corresponded only to modern moral categories and who acted only with the full backing of the entire German South Tyrolean population.

The year 2000 also saw the publication of another significant book on the same issue; Sepp Mitterhofer and Günther Obwegs titled their monograph programmatically *"...Es blieb kein anderer Weg..." Zeitzeugenberichte und Dokumente aus dem Südtiroler Freiheitskampf* (There was no other way… Eyewitness Reports and Documents from the South Tyrolean Struggle for Freedom). In the book's preface the authors and editors declared that their publication served two functions: first, they wanted to preserve the events of the past for future generations and explain their history to the young generation, and second, they intended to put an end to the "litany of lies which has enshrouded the 1960s struggle for freedom and instead tell the truth" (13). Therefore the authors indicate clearly that their publication was bridging the void between the past and the present and that the violent phase of the South Tyrolean struggle for autonomy was going to be used for the political debate of the present.

According to the title—*"Es blieb kein anderer Weg..."* (There was no other way…)—the South Tyrolean struggle is seen as self defense ("Notwehr," 45), and all the individual essays collected in this book support this interpretation of the events. The contributors are well-known activists such as Hans Stieler, Sepp Mitterhofer, Luis Steinegger, and Luis Gutmann, but there are also contributions by some of the women of the resistance movement, such as Maria Mitterhofer, Rosa Klotz, and Midl von Sölder. All contributions are similar in their justification of the bomb attacks as the only possible protest of an otherwise powerless German population.

Hans Stieler, leader of the so-called Stieler Group, which became famous at the end of the 1950s, paved the way for this discourse of justifications by describing in detail the political situation of post-World War II South Tyrol: Italy remains fascist, the SVP betrays "our homes"

(Mitterhofer and Obwegs, 26), dispossession of German property and emigration of South Tyroleans and a massive influx of Italian workers created an atmosphere of bitterness and gloom (27). This was the environment that brought the Stieler Group to life in 1955. Its members were gravely concerned for the future of their *Heimatland*, and in order to highlight the plight of the people they created home-made devices and used them to warn "our politicians to become harder in their negotiations" for a wider-reaching independence from Italy. In his contribution Stieler sees a strong connection between the Italian negotiation strategy of dragging its feet and the ensuing attacks, because injustice creates resistance, and resistance is yet another form of negotiation between the oppressors and the oppressed (34).

It is the collective Italian suppression after the bomb attacks and the ensuing torture of those arrested which is addressed by all contributors. Thus it is not the violent deeds of the activists which are the focus of this publication—these are merely mentioned in one short sub-clause—but the acts of torture that the Carabinieri inflict on their victims. Mitterhofer repeatedly stresses the isolation of the South Tyroleans that forced innocent citizens into using violence as a means of protest as they did not want to remain idle in the face of genocide (45). Furthermore, they were Catholic—if disappointed by their church and their bishop (78)—and consequently anti-Communist (46). This presents Mitterhofer and Obwegs's freedom fighters as individuals who are embedded in the societal consensus of past and present-day South Tyrol and whose deeds in the 1960s are therefore deemed acceptable even by modern standards. The fighters, to all intents and purposes terrorists, are portrayed as being fellows of Sepp Kerschbaumer and his pacifist views as he employed violence only against inanimate objects, not human beings. Kerschbaumer has been accepted as a genuine freedom fighter by most South Tyroleans since the 1960s, and their portrayal of other, less pacifist activists seeks to link them closely to Kerschbaumer in order to have them participate in his legacy. Mitterhofer and Obwegs quote Rosa Klotz, wife of the most notorious guerilla fighter of that era, Georg Klotz, who claims that Klotz and Kerschbaumer had solemnly declared that they would devote themselves to liberate South Tyrol.[19]

Mitterhofer and Obwegs consider it important to create in their book an image of a German-speaking South Tyrolean society which is united in its rejection of Italian supremacy (even though the initial response of contemporary South Tyroleans suggests otherwise): the leaders of the active resistance against the Italians are thus the leaders of contemporary South Tyrolean society and, as a group, feature characteristics worthy of leadership, and Kerschbaumer is deeply religious, unflinchingly Christian in his beliefs (219) and strongly connected to his Heimat. He is a philantropist (221), the father figure of the resistance, and open to Austrian foreign minister Bruno Kreisky's encouragement to "Do something!" ("Tut's was!"; 226), thus accepting Austrian involvement in his patriotic struggle. Luis Amplatz is seen as a man of great political wisdom, who is among the first South Tyroleans to see through Italian plans to marginalize the German population (201). South Tyrolean resistance—"self-defense against an unjust system" ("Notwehr gegen ein Unrechtsregime"; 270)—is thus similar to contemporary colonial struggles, where rules and laws have to be violated in order to achieve an overarching ideal of liberation. Luis Gutmann summarizes it thus: "While we violated Italian law we obtained the moral justice."[20]

In summary Mitterhofer's publication is an attempt to justifiy the violent past. Violence is portrayed as a phenomenon which has to be understood in its contemporary context and which can then be morally justified. If the reader accepts this reading, he/she will see the protagonists as heroes of an ethnic and national struggle. Obviously, this interpretation is not necessarily historically authentic, but motivated by political strategy: Mitterhofer and Obwegs strongly criticize current attempts by the SVP to harmonize the relationship between the Italian and German people in South Tyrol (346), and any attempt to find compromises—such as in the hotly debated issue of the recognition of Italian road signs—is being labeled "rape." Other comments, such as Mitterhofer's negative opinion of mixed marriages between Germans and Italians, clearly mark him a representative of a South Tyrolean liberation movement that has remained loyal to the principles of a cultural "apartheid"—principles that thankfully become increasingly irrelevant to modern-day South Tyrol.

Mitterhofer's attempts to morally justify the guerilla fighters Amplatz and Klotz paved the way for Eva Klotz to publish the biography of her father, *Georg Klotz. Freiheitskämpfer für die Einheit Tirols* (Georg Klotz. Freedom Fighter for the Unity of Tyrol) in 2002, where she tells the story of the freedom fighter partly from her own perspective as the daughter, partly from a third-person narrator's point of view. Her perspective changes often and suddenly, which makes the book quite difficult to read, but she also allows the reader insights into the family life of a freedom fighter. These sequences place her publication in the genre of memory literature, but, at the same time, it is overtly political in its message.

Eva Klotz paints a picture of her father as a hero, a tragic hero admittedly, who bears all the hallmarks of the hero in a classic Greek tragedy: he is a freedom fighter who pursues his path of violent activism even though this creates huge hardship for him and his family of six. And he is a hero in many ways: a hero who lives the rough life out in the mountains because South Tyrolean civilization equals persecution and betrayal; a hero who emigrates to Austria and suffers badly from home sickness and repeatedly returns to South Tyrol illegally to see his farmstead and his family; a hero who survives an assassination attack but dies from the disintegration of his own body; and finally a tragic hero because his ideal of the armed resistance to liberate South Tyrol becomes anachronistic and outdated after the "Paket" of 1969. He remains an outcast, outliving his old comrades Sepp Kerschbaumer, Kurt Welser, and Luis Amplatz, and experiencing real loneliness as he feels that even the Tyrolean people do not support him any longer (Klotz, 308).

The way in which Eva describes her father suggests an attempt to socially rehabilitate her hero: Georg Klotz. While throughout the book he remains the lone wolf who adheres to nothing but his very strong principles, Eva attributes many human characteristics to her father which take away some of his proverbial remoteness as a human being. He appears almost fragile and tender in some passages, and it is this tenderness and fragility that are supposed to facilitate modern South Tyrol's easier access to the complex Klotz. She describes him as a military strategist (73), calls him the symbol of Italian defeat (152), a knightly and tough warrior (123, 104), but at the same time compassionate, caring, and full of sympathy (78). He is not an adventurer, but a liberation fighter who devotes his service entirely to his country in order to achieve South Tyrolean self-determination.

His daughter's characterization turns Klotz into a larger-than-life epic hero with humane traits. He is being morally rehabilitated despite all his tragic aspects, as his fight is described as valuable (from a military point of view). Eva Klotz maintains that the government in Rome was considering ceding South Tyrol to Austria (206) as Italy obviously could not win the fight again the resurgents. She simultaneously draws a picture of the military struggle in which her father figures as a lonesome fighter, who, as a result of his actions, is forced to watch his family live isolated from the wider South Tyrolean population. She describes how her mother, Rosa, attempts to meet her husband in hiding and how she cannot even trust her neighbors (147, 149). The SVP as the political representative of the German South Tyroleans was equally disappointing and did little to support the freedom fighters as they were exposed to systematic police torture (103). On the contrary, Klotz claims that the SVP rejected the attacks and welcomed the condemning of Amplatz and Klotz to exile (179). Klotz had to endure lasting separation from his family, loneliness, and home-sickness (308). His personal fight for South Tyrolean freedom only ends with the SVP's agreement to the "Paket" in 1969 and its gradual implementation in the early 1970s (319). It is then that he seeks reconciliation with the Italian authorities, who reject his advances. He is thus forced to live his life away from his beloved South Tyrol, makes a modest living as a forest worker in Northern Tyrol and dwells in a small mountain hut, away from the "materialistic life" in the valleys (327). To his very end in 1976 he is convinced that his struggle for South Tyrol was successful in that he stemmed the tide of Italian immigration (342). Eva Klotz's portrayal of her father bears all the characteristics of a Greek hero's epos (236); he is larger-than-life (243), a hero who can only be brought down through conspiracy and intrigue (177, 181, 248). Even his physical decay and his chronic stomach pains are attributed to his bitterness about Austria, which let him down in his mission, and not to his chain-smoking (314).

In *Zersprengtes Leben. Frauen in den Südtiroler Bombenjahren* (Scattered Lives. Women in the South Tyrolean Years of Bombings), published in 2003, Astrid Kofler chose an altogether different angle of interpretation of the South Tyrolean years of violence. Her publication is impressive through multiperspectivity and the mixture of social history, politics, and psychology as she presents various different women and their recollections of the period in question. The selection of women she includes in her volume is not discriminatory in any way, coming as they do from all walks of life and all political factions to present their accounts of family life of recriminations and suppression in the bombing era. None of the women interviewed—Rosa Klotz, Anna Amplatz, Pia Widmann, Maya Mayr, and Rosa Gutmann to name but a few—raise the question of guilt, justice, or injustice. As victims of the political circumstances they present a forum of experiences and background information. All of them have their (political) views, but these come second to recollections of a very personal nature, whose common denominator is basically: our family lives were "blown up" because our fate was determined by our husbands (80).

Nevertheless, Kofler's interviewees reiterate the issues which turned the men of the early 1960s into military activists: cultural suppression (219), financial problems due to the preferential treatment of Italians on the job market (34, 117), and political repression (248), but the emphasis is certainly on the practical side of this struggle—the struggle to master the challenges of everyday life—often with several children—without their men. "Everyday life did not leave us women any time for despair,"[21] while their children suffered from being ostracized in school (89), and they knew that the political establishment would not help out either (77). The story of the activists' women of the early 1960s is a story of isolation (236) and betrayal within and without the family framework (242) despite occasional moments of solidarity (186, 290). It is impressive to learn about the women's courage in this time of stress: Midl von Sölder challenges the prison priest in the confession box (32), Maya Mayr swallows explosive capsules in order to get them past the Italian border controls (254), and Rosa Klotz becomes the Mother Courage of the South Tyrolean liberation struggle (216). Christl Kerschbaumer summarizes the book when she says that "history was not and is still not amusing—it left traces in all families."[22] Astrid Kofler refrains from a political judgment on the 1960s; instead she gives those contemporaries who had not been heard before a public voice and thus contributes greatly to a better understanding of the period of the "Bombenjahre" and the effect on the people and families behind the activists.

The last of the biographies which have been published in the last few years is Günter Obwegs's biography of Luis Amplatz, *Ein Leben für Tirol* (A Life for Tyrol, 2004). Besides Kerschbaumer and Klotz, Amplatz was the third in the triumvirat of icons of the South Tyrolean struggle for independence from Italy in the 1960s. He is known for having been a man who embraced life and remained an idealist to the very day of his assassination by the Italian agent Christian Kerbler in the Brunner Mahder, high above the Passeier valley in 1964. This character is a dream for any biographer: he is three-dimensional, full of life, a family man who embraced tradition and folklore and who had a great sense of humour. However, Obwegs manages to present him in a lifeless, two-dimensional, and superficial way. Amplatz degenerates into a vehicle of Obwegs's anti-Italianism, which obscures the figure of the historical Amplatz. The author's intentions become apparent as early as in the preface of the book, which is described as a "legacy of the South Tyrolean struggle for freedom"[23] when he characterizes contemporary Italy: "To Italy, which had not rid itself of the spirit of fascism, Amplatz became the most dangerous terrorist.[24] This Luis Amplatz, Obwegs continues, is a person with a "happy-go-lucky mind" ("… sonnigem Charakter"; 22) who from an early age had been a true rebel and resistance fighter as he was first arrested by the Carabinieri at the age of 15. He allegedly threatened to slit an Italian's belly with a penknife, a threat that Amplatz would never have carried out as Obwegs assures his readers (18).

Amplatz joined the militant resistance movement because he felt he was pushed into it as he had to obey the *Zeitgeist*: "Today's people, who are wealthy, may struggle to understand, but what was done then was done because of desperation which was visible and tangible everywhere."[25] This presentation does very little to bring Luis Amplatz to life and represents little else but a black and white view of the situation in South Tyrol, where a fascist Italian state (24) full of torturing policemen ("Foltercarbinieri"; 96) meets a family man who, even at the young age of 19, in 1945 reveals his political sophistication when he predicts that "politics and talk alone will not change this state."[26] Obwegs uses Amplatz as a vehicle for his own political views and does not pay proper tribute to the historical person.

Finally, in November 2005 a book was published that closes the circle of new interpretations of the "Bombenjahre" in South Tyrol in the early 1960s. Hans-Karl Peterlini wrote *Südtiroler Bombenjahre. Von Blut und Tränen zum Happy End?* (South Tyrolean Years of Bombings. From Blood and Tears towards a Happy End?), a publication that sees itself as the legitimate successor to the *Feuernacht* of 1992. This becomes obvious in its preface, where Peterlini states that this book has "included all the literature and created a provisional conclusion."[27] And this is exactly what he has done; he presents a new interpretation of the era to a modern audience. It is a compendium that redefines the "Bombenjahre" and presents it in the context of the millennium. However, Peterlini does more, presenting his own eyewitnesses and new interviews and therefore coming to new historical conclusions. The timing of his publication was excellent as he could avail himself of the findings and reinterpretations of Mayr, Fontana, Obwegs, and Kofler and include those in his overall view of the period. Thus his book is a logical continuation, or rather a reinterpretation of the *Feuernacht* of 1992.

In so doing, Peterlini does not revolutionize the view of the era, but he contextualizes the fates of the main protagonists and presents them to an audience which is far removed from the situation of the 1960s—today's South Tyroleans, and particularly its young generation, to whom material poverty and political repression are alien. Peterlini had to face critical voices in South Tyrol and beyond, who claimed that his book contained nothing new, but the counter-argument is that every generation rewrites history to explain its own present. This is what he does best: he reinterprets the violent years in the 1960s in their own right but from the perspective of a modern South Tyrolean. He takes into account the successfully executed South Tyrolean autonomy, the new "Europaregion Tirol-Südtirol/Alto Adige-Trentino", which is changing the structures of political power in the Alpine region as we speak, and acknowledges the massive changes in modern Europe, too.

Terrorism and Historiography

These monographs are different in presentation, academic, and popular approach, and in the strength of their political/social messages. However, there are a number of similarities among them, and these parallels originate in what I would like to term "accepted parameters of resistance against Italy." All of these authors emphasize strongly the political and social injustices of the Italian administration towards the German-speaking South Tyroleans. They mention the notorious social-housing issue, and all of them attribute major significance to Canon Gamper's 1953 article in the paper *Dolomiten* in which he coined the term "death march of the South Tyroleans," the number-one programmatic slogan for the following two decades. This article served as a catalyst for a frustrated South Tyrolean public which was in a process, slow though gathering momentum, of becoming politically astute and demanding. The Sigmundskron mass gathering of November 1957 was inconceivable without Gamper's polarizing slogan, and so was the "palace revolution" within the SVP. Other issues which all the authors agree were vital steps towards June 1961 were the trial versus the "Pfunderer Buam" and the early bomb blasts against the Mussolini memorial, the so-called "Aluminum Duce" in Waidbruck in January 1961.

The most important similarity of all these publications is the fact that they—all in their own way—ascribe current political significance to the 1960s activists/terrorists. This political role, however, is more than a historical role: it is a contemporary political function. Taking the historical figures out of the strictly historical context and relating them to modern South Tyrol means that they are no longer seen as the terrorists of the past, but that they have found a new place in South Tyrol's collective memory and contribute to modern South Tyrol's collective identity. It would appear that the interpretations of Kerschbaumer and others serve to cohese the way South Tyrolean history is to be understood by today's German South Tyroleans, and this in a contemporary political climate in which current political debates threaten to overshadow the achievements of the women and men of the 1960s.

These monographs represent modern South Tyrol's changed perception of the 1960s. They also manage to bridge the past and the present by ascribing to the protagonists of the 1960s a significant role in and for contemporary society. They therefore become part of the foundation myth of the modern "regional state South Tyrol," which is in fact not a state at all, but an autonomous region of Italy. It is part of such a "nationalist" interpretation of history to attempt to create a national history, that is in this case, a generally accepted interpretation of German South Tyroleans' history. This version of history is naturally different from the North Tyrolean view, the Italian South Tyroleans' view of the same period, and certainly most different from a purely Italian version. This new interpretation of South Tyrolean history creates the image of an independent and autonomous South Tyrolean history in the second half of the twentieth century, even though South Tyrol has been embedded in the Italian state. This "separate history" finds its contemporary international recognition in the current wide-reaching autonomy of the Province of Bolzano and in the political and economic strength of the region within the (loose) framework of the Italian state.[28]

Interest in the phenomenon of terrorism in South Tyrol in the early 1960s has been renewed in the region. While the historical facts have long been established, their evaluation has become open to reinterpretation. Whether one describes the women and men involved in the "Bombenjahre" as terrorists, freedom fighters, revolutionaries, rebels, liberators, criminals, or, most neutrally, as (military) activists, depends on one's own allegiance to either ethnic group in South Tyrol and on one's own moral views. This shows that "terrorism" is a relative term embedded in a specific culture. It is used by the victims, those not belonging to the particular culture that facilitates terrorist acts. Terrorists never call themselves terrorists, and members of the culture under attack will never call them anything but terrorists. If cultural and societal parameters change, as in the case of South Tyrol during the last 40 years, then (one time) terrorists may be renamed freedom fighters or founding fathers by the ensuing generations reaping the harvest of past violence.

It is the very nature of terrorism to be a minority opposition movement, however, if this movement becomes mainstream in a given society one-time terrorists may transmute (posthumously) into trailblazers of the new societal order. Their once illegal and outlawed actions may become part of the foundation myth of this new society and its legal framework, the state. Their violent actions become somewhat vindicated because their illegality under an old and injust order is overshadowed by the moral right for change to a new and just system of law and order. The integrity of the terrorists is thus restored, as seen in the case of South Tyrol.

The German South Tyrolean interpretation of the violent era of the early 1960 has changed considerably as the emergence of a "national literature" exemplifies, (while Italians still refer to them as "dinamitardi e terroristi"). This change in interpretation of Kerschbaumer and others came about as South Tyrol enjoys a far-reaching cultural, political and economic autonomy within Italy, and this autonomy serves as an institutional framework similar to that of a state. In short: the struggle for autonomy has been successful, and terrorists of the 1960s mutate into founding fathers of this autonomy. This new interpretation is, however, modestly expressed in the modern historical literature of Südtirol in order not to alienate Italians within and outside the province as it still remains part of the Italian federal state, however loosely attached.

Works Cited

Alcock, Antony E. *The History of the South Tyrol Question*. London: Michael Joseph, 1970.

—. *The South Tyrol Autonomy*. Bolzano: Südtiroler Landesamt, 2001.

Baumgartner, Elisabeth, Hans Mayr, and Gerhard Mumelter. *Feuernacht. Südtirols Bombenjahre.* Bolzano: Raetia, 1992.

Dolomiten. Tagblatt der Südtiroler. (Daily newspaper of the German-speaking South Tyroleans, relevant issues in this context: October 28, 1953, May 10, 1957, November 18,1957, January 2, 1958.

Drechsler, Robert, ed. *Sepp Kerschbaumer. Ein Leben für Südtirol.* Vienna: Drechsler, 1965

Ermacora, Felix. *Südtirol und das Vaterland Österreich.* Vienna: Amalthea, 1984.

Fontana, Josef, and Hans Mayr. *Sepp Kerschbaumer. Eine Biographie.* Bolzano: Raetia, 2000.

Franceschini, Christoph. "Kampf um Südtirol." *Profil.* Jg.22/1991, issues 47-50.

Gamper, Michael. "Bemerkungen zu einem Kommentar." *Dolomiten* 28 October 1953: page 1.

Gatterer, Claus: *Im Kampf gegen Rom, Bürger, Minderheiten und Autonomien in Italien*, Wien, Frankfurt, Zürich 1968

Grote, Georg. "Gehen oder Bleiben?—Die Identitätskrise der deutschsprachigen Südtiroler in Optanten- und Dableibergedichten der Optionszeit, 1939-1943." *Modern Austrian Literature* 37.1/2 (2004): 47-70.

—. "Vielsprachigkeit in Südtirol—Modell für Europa oder Kapitulation vor der Geschichte?" *Acta Germanica, Jahrbuch des Germanistenverbandes im südlichen Afrika* 33 (2005): 69-80.

Janke, Peter, ed. *Terrorism and Democracy*. London: Macmillan, 1992.

Klotz, Eva. *Georg Klotz. Freiheitskämpfer für die Einheit Tirols*. Vienna: Molden, 2002.

Kofler, Astrid. *Zersprengtes Leben. Frauen in den Südtiroler Bombenjahren*. Bolzano: Raetia, 2003.
Leidlmair, Adolf. *Bevölkerung und Wirtschaft in Südtirol*. Innsbruck: Wagner, 1958.
Lechthaler, Helmut and Christoph Franceschini. *Bombenjahre*. 6-part TV production, RAI Bolzano, 2005.
Lill, Rudolf. *Südtirol in der Zeit des Nationalismus*. Konstanz, UVK, 2002.
Meyerhofer, Nicholas J., and Karl E. Webb. *Felix Mitterer. A Critical Introduction*. Riverside, CA: Ariadne Press, 1995.
Mitterer, Felix. *Verkaufte Heimat. Bombenjahre*. Innsbruck: Haymon, 1994.
Mitterhofer, Sepp, and Günter Obwegs. *"Es blieb kein anderer Weg." Zeitzeugenberichte und Dokumente aus dem Südtiroler Freiheitskampf*. Merano: Arkadia, 2000.
Obwegs, Günther. *Luis Amplatz. Ein Leben für Tirol*. Bolzano: Athesia, 2004.
Pan, Christoph. *Die Südtiroler Wirtschafts- und Sozialstruktur von 1910-1961*. Bolzano: Südtiroler Wirtschafts und Sozialinstitut, 1963.
Peterlini, Hans Karl. *Südtiroler Bombenjahre. Von Blut und Tränen zum Happy End?* Bolzano: Raetia, 2005.
Solderer, Gottfried. *Silvius Magnago. Eine Biographie Südtirols*. Bolzano: Raetia, 1996.
Stadlmayer, Viktoria. *Kein Kleingeld im Länderschacher. Südtirol, Triest und Alcide Degasperi 1945/1946*. Innsbruck: Wagner, 2002.
—. "Südtirols Weg." In *Südtirol, Eine Frage des europäischen Gewissens*. Edited by Franz Huter. Munich: Oldenbourg, 1965
Steininger, Rolf. *Südtirol im 20.Jahrhundert*. Vienna: Studienverlag, 1997.
—. *Südtirol zwischen Diplomatie und Terror. 1947-1969*. 3 Vols. Bolzano: Veröffentlichung des Südtiroler Landesarchivs, 1999.
Volgger, Friedl: *Mit Südtirol am Scheideweg*, Innsbruck 1984
Widmann, Franz. *Es stand nicht gut um Südtirol. 1945-1972. Von der Resignation zur Selbstbehauptung*. Bolzano: Raetia, 1998.

Notes

[1] Interview with Sandro Canestrini, in *Bilder aus Südtirol*, broadcast by 3sat on October 6, 2006. Report by Josef Ebner, ORF Tirol 2006

[2] The Hitler-Mussolini agreement of 1939 and the defeat of Germany and Austria in World War II, (while at the same time Italy had managed to change sides in 1943), led to a deep division of the remaining German-speaking population in South Tyrol—many thousands had actually moved to the Reich during the war—and to the situation that none of the Allies would speak up for the South Tyroleans. They were generally—and unjustifyably—regarded as collaborators of Nazi Germany.

[3] The Allied decision in May 1946, which stipulated that South Tyrol remained with Italy, was met with widespread resentment and resulted in spontaneous protests all over the country. This decision was taken against the background of geopolitical consideration as the Western War Allies feared that Austria was drifting into the Communist camp. Their insistence on the Brenner border guaranteed the energy supply for the Northern Italian industrial compounds near Milan and Turin generated by the hydroelectric power stations in South Tyrol. Moreover, the Allies argued that Italy had been fighting on the Allied side since 1943, while Austria remained hostile until the total collapse of Nazi Germany in May 1945. After the war, Italy's importance in the strategic alliance against Stalin's communist empire was immediately recognized while Austria political reliability, first under Allied control and then sworn into neutrality, was far from certain. This preferable treatment in the South Tyrol issue was counterbalanced by the Western Allies' desire for Italian reassurances that they enable the return of those South Tyroleans who had opted to leave Italy in the Option period—an issue Italy only most reluctantly agreed to as it had hoped to get rid of the problems with the native Germans for good.

[4] Italy bowed to Allied pressure and allowed the South Tyroleans back into Italy (they had to give up their German nationality and become Italian), but by now the South Tyroleans were bitterly divided into those who went and those who stayed during the Option. This was the scenario in which the Austrian foreign minister Karl Gruber attempted to negotiate a deal with the Italian foreign minister Alcide deGasperi which would guarantee the South Tyroleans some kind of autonomy. However, the so called Gruber—deGasperi agreement which was signed in 1946, was little else but a declaration of good will by two foreign ministers: There was no political force that would oversee the implementation of the autonomy, and the agreement was no more that a gentlemen's agreement as it was not ratified by either government and thus no international contract. Yet it was the most Austria could do for the South Tyrolean people.

[5] New and revived legislation originating in the Mussolini era aimed at excluding German South Tyroleans from even the lowest levels of public service and forced the German language out of all office communication, even between German-speaking public servants (Steininger, *Südtirol im 20. Jh.*, 476). In 1953 the government reintroduced a law abandoned since 1847 that stipulated that changes of ownership of property had to be sanctioned by military authorities (as South Tyrol was redefined a sensitive border region). Various other laws targeted the cultural heritage of the German South Tyroleans, such as the one ratified in 1955,

which prohibited Italian citizens to give their children anything but Italian Christian names, this, of course, hit the German South Tyroleans hardest. Finally, Rome reintroduced a fascist law which facilitated the dispossession of German South Tyrolean properties.

[6] "Die gewollte Unterwanderung unseres Volkes [geht] unaufhaltsam weiter. … Zu vielen Zehntausenden sind nach 1945 und nach Abschluss des Pariser Vertrages Italiener aus den südlichen Provinzen eingewandert, während zur gleichen Zeit die Rückkehr von einigen Zehntausenden unserer umgesiedelten Landsleute unterbunden wurde. Von Jahr zu Jahr sinkt so der Prozentsatz der einheimischen Bevölkerung steil ab gegenüber dem unheimlichen Anschwellen der Einwanderer. Fast mit mathematischer Sicherheit können wir den Zeitpunkt errechnen, zu dem wir nicht bloss innerhalb der zu unserer Majorisierung geschaffenen Region, sondern auch innerhalb der engeren Landesgrenzen eine wehrlose Minderheit bilden werden. Dies in einem Raume, in dem noch vor kurzem die Italiener nur 3% der Gesamtbevölkerung ausgemacht hatten. Es ist ein Todesmarsch, auf dem wir Südtiroler seit 1945 uns befinden, wenn nicht noch in letzter Stunde Rettung kommt."

[7] Austria, which regarded itself as a protective power monitoring the welfare of the South Tyroleans, tried repeatedly to raise the problems in South tyrol with the Italian government, but Italian politicians declared the South Tyrol to be an entirely domestic Italian issue. This tactic was working for some time, but as soon as Austria received its full diplomatic potency in the "Staatsvertrag" of 1955, it fulfilled the duty of protective power by pressing the issue harder. Finally, as the Italian position remained unmoved, Austria brought the South Tyrol issue to the United Nations general assembly in 1960, even though this did not bring any relief to the situation of the German South Tyroleans.

[8] "Scharenweise und fast täglich kamen arme Männer mit ihren Habseligkeiten im Pappkarton vom Süden des Staatsgebietes am Bolzanoer Bahnhof an und wurden in armseligen Baracken untergebracht. Nach einigen Wochen erhielten sie aber schon eine neue Wohnung in den staatlich gebauten Volkswohnbauten, weil sie durch das schlechte Barackenlager immer mehr Punkte bekamen als die Südtiroler. Nach einigen Monaten holten sie dann ihre Familien samt Grosseltern nach." (Mitterhofer and Obwegs, 37).

[9] "Wir können uns … des Eindrucks nicht erwehren, dass man Politik betreibt, und nicht zuletzt nationalistische. Dies umso mehr, weil in anderen Städten Italiens grössere Wohnungsnot als in Bolzano herrscht, die Regierung aber im Verhältnis in Bolzano mehr Milliarden für den Wohnungsbau ausgeworfen hat als in jenen anderen Städten. Dazu kommt, dass von den mit Staatsmitteln in Südtirol gebauten Wohnungen nicht einmal zehn Prozent an die Südtiroler gegangen sind" (Widmann, 366).

[10] On August 18 of that year the Italian policeman Raimondo Falqui was found dead beside a footbridge in the Pustertal after he had been involved in a fistfight with some local men in a public inn the night before. Even though the circumstances of his death have never been found out, seven young men from the

area were accused of his murder and sentenced for up to eight years in prison. As a response a group of young men under the leadership of Hans Stieler committed a first wave of "six relatively innocent" bomb attacks in late 1956 and early 1957 while the *Dolomiten* publicly supported the eight young men (see Widmann, 298).

11 "...dass ein halbes Dutzend junger Menschen Jahre hinter Kerkermauern verbringen muss, weil sie die Welt auf die Not des Südtiroler Volkes aufmerksam machen wollten und dabei zu ungesetzlichen Mitteln griffen" (*Dolomiten*, 2 January 1958).

12 "[...[sollten auch dort gehört werden, wo über italienische Südtirolpolitik entschieden und offenbar geglaubt wird, man müsse hier noch weiter einheizen. Sonst kann es geschehen, dass der Kessel, der bisher nur brodelte, einmal auch überkocht. Was in niemandes Interesse ware, am wenigsten im italienischen" (*Dolomiten*, 18 November 1957).

13 At the same time Christoph Franceschini completed his MA thesis with Rolf Steininger at the Institut für Zeitgeschichte in Innsbruck which, unfortunately, has not been published to date. However, excerpts were published in the Austrian periodical *Profil* in 1991.

14 "[...] mit diesem Buch Diskussionen auszulösen. Nach drei Jahrzehnten Schweigen ist es höchst an der Zeit, dass sich eine breitere Öffentlichkeit des Themas annimmt, dass Fragen beantwortet und Positionen geklärt werden" (preface, XI)

15 "... a publication so extensive that is thus accessible only to experts," Lill, p.8.

16 A case in point is the historical introduction, which focuses on Kerschbaumer's emergence as an activist: Kerschbaumer joined the SVP in 1946 and stepped down from his post as Ortsobmann (party chairman) of Frangart in 1958—this very significant phase in his life is summarized in one short paragraph which concludes: "Sie [the SVP] war und blieb [...] seine politische Heimat" (The SVP remained his political home [21]). This is factually wrong—Kerschbaumer left his post because of the massive divergence in strategy with the SVP leadership—and stylistically most regrettable, because Fontana and Mayr rob themselves of the unique opportunity to draw an analytical picture of Kerschbaumer's character in the era 1946-1958, which forms the basis of his later actions. Similarly regrettable in its superficiality is the chapter "Kerschbaumer und die Italiener" (Kerschbaumer and the Italians), where the authors write: "Er hatte [...] einen heiligen Zorn auf das offizielle Italien, gleichzeitig aber griff er italienischen Zuzüglern unter die Arme, wenn sie in Not waren. Er unterschied nämlich streng zwischen den Menschen und der Politik. Das wird von allen, die ihn kannten, herausgestellt" (He nourished a holy rage towards the offical Italy. At the same he helped Italian immigrants when they needed help. He sharply distinguished between people and politics. Everybody who knew him, emphasized this fact. [25]). This comment is unnecessary; it is a shortcut in interpreting Kerschbaumer which originates not in his time, but in the present. A few pages on, Kerschbaumer as leader of the BAS is being described as such: "Diese tolerante Haltung im Hause des Chefs der Südtiroler Untergrundbewegung war aber im damaligen Südtirol gewiss nicht die

Regel und hätte auch heute noch Vorbildcharakter" (This tolerance in the home of the South Tyrolean separatist movement was unusual in contemporary South Tyrol and would even be exemplary today. [27]).

[17] Nevertheless, they are careful not to come down too hard on the other group and its most prominent members, Wolfgang Pfaundler, Georg Klotz, and Luis Amplatz, as they describe the relationship between the two groups as a "Nebeneinander, nicht Miteinander" (a parallel struggle, not a unified one [103]), yet at the same time it is not a "Gegeneinander" (fight against each other) either.

[18] At the same time the Trient Carabinieri trials of 1963 would lend themselves for anti-Italian polemics, but here Fontana and Mayr remain moderate in their criticism of events which are clearly in the past and which have, thanks to the dynamics of the autonomy process of the 1970s and 80s, become history.

[19] This was in "1959 or 1960" and they had done this in the presence of "an embroidered pillow featuring the Tyrolean eagle" (Mitterhofer and Obwegs, 163).

[20] "Wir brachen italienisches Recht, hatten aber das moralische Recht auf unserer Seite"; 110.

[21] "Der Alltag ließ uns Frauen keine Zeit zum Verzweifeln"; 82.

[22] "…die Geschichte war und ist nicht lustig—sie hinterließ Spuren in allen Familien"; 212.

[23] "Vermächtnis des Südtiroler Freiheitskampfes"; 9.

[24] "Für den italienischen Staat, der die Geisteshaltung des Faschismus noch nicht abgelegt hatte, galt Luis Amplatz bald als der gefährlichste Terrorist"; 9.

[25] "Es mag heute für Menschen des Wohlstandes unverständlich klingen, aber das, was damals getan wurde, wurde aus Not getan. Eine Not, die man überall sehen und begreifen konnte"; 27.

[26] "Mit Politik und Reden allein ist diesem Staat nicht beizukommen"; 31.

[27] "…alle Literatur miteinbezogen und ein vorläufiges Gesamtbild erstellt"; Preface.

[28] The revised interpretations of the activists of the 1960s is a process similar to many small national states' literary and historical reinterpretation of their own past after achieving national independence from imperialist nations.

CHAPTER FIFTEEN

A QUESTION OF JUSTICE? PETER HANDKE AND THE HAGUE TRIBUNAL

THEODORE FIEDLER

At 65 Peter Handke is one of the most prominent—and prolific—authors writing in German today. He is also one of the most controversial. While this is nothing new, the nature of the controversy surrounding his work has changed considerably since he first gained prominence as the *enfant terrible* of German letters in the spring and summer of 1966. Then he had polemicized against the "impotent description" of his literary elders at an April meeting of established authors and critics known as *Group 47* [*Gruppe 47*] at Princeton University, and his anti-play, *Offending the Audience* [*Publikumsbeschimpfung*], had its rousing premiere in June under Claus Peymann's direction at the Frankfurt Theater at the Tower [Theater am Turm]. During this same period his experimental first novel, *The Hornets* [*Die Hornissen*], appeared with Suhrkamp, the leading literary publisher of the day, adding to his reputation as a major, if difficult, new writer despite its critical reception. While this anti-novel models an alternative mode of description, a fragmented plot, and the linguistic skepticism that underlies both, it also allusively constructs a rural Austrian setting reminiscent of Handke's origins, where German and Slovenian place-names and the two languages intermingle (74, 112). In his 1972 memoir about his mother's life (b. 1920) and her death by suicide on 20 November 1971, *A Sorrow Beyond Dreams* [*Wunschloses Unglück*], Handke situates her life and death in the Austrian state of Carinthia and especially the small town of Griffin, some forty kilometers east of the capital of Klagenfurt, where both languages were spoken and most of his mother's life and his own childhood and youth unfolded. In the memoir he duly identifies the Slovenian ethnic background of his maternal grandfather (13) and refers in passing to his mother's fluency in the language (49), but he treats mainstream Austrian culture and politics as the shaping matrix of his mother's life as well as his own. The male protagonists of his fiction of these years, the unnamed narrator of *Short Letter, Long Farewell* [*Der kurze Brief zum langen Abschied* (1972)] and Gregor Keuschnig, press attaché at the Austrian embassy in Paris in *The Hour of True Feeling* [*Die Stunde der wahren Empfindung* (1974)], are similarly identified with mainstream Austria. Nonetheless both free themselves from it in their separate ways, and Keuschnig's name alludes to a Slovenian heritage.

Just when Handke developed a serious and sustained interest in Slovenia and his Slovenian heritage is a matter of conjecture. Perhaps he did so as early as his work on *Slow Homecoming* [*Langsame Heimkehr* (1979)], a short novel whose Central European protagonist, geologist Valentin Sorger, leaves North America behind as the work closes. There is also evidence of a transforming experience in the karst region, above Trieste, in August 1978.[1] In any case we do know that once he had moved with his then ten-year-old daughter from Paris to Salzburg in 1979, where he lived for the next eight years while she attended school, Handke pursued an interest in things Slovenian by learning the language systematically and then translating several Slovenian literary texts by Austro-Slovenian authors into German.[2] As early as 1983 he was at work on *Repetition* [*Die Wiederholung* (1986)], a retrospective travel novel set in Carinthia and Slovenia that draws on his own youth and his mother's family history, especially his maternal uncle Gregor's schooling in and identification with Slovenia. In the end it establishes something of a dual Austrian and Slovenian identity for its young protagonist, Filip Kobal, and perhaps reestablishes it for the middle-aged Kobal who recalls his earlier life and travel.

Given his own primary engagement with Slovenia within the formerly socialist federation of Yugoslavia, it came as something of a surprise when Handke, in July 1991, published an essay highly critical of Slovenia's declaration of independence from Yugoslavia on 25 June 1991.[3] Taking Slovenian intellectuals to task for their ostensibly imported "Western" assumptions about "Central Europe" (18) and the "disintegration" of Yugoslavia (20), he argued that even the Serbian revocation of the autonomy of the province of Kosovo did not justify what he saw as an act of political betrayal and a breach of international law (22-23). In the face of fundamental conflicts within the Yugoslavian federation he angrily invoked the founding pathos and legitimacy of the country's experience of injustice at the hands first of Austria prior to and during World War I and then Greater Germany during World War II as primary and binding (25). Needless to say, Handke's essay did not sit well with his Slovenian counterparts. More than a year later he conceded in an interview that some aspects of it had been too idealistic.[4] Perhaps for this reason and the fact that the brief war between the new Republic of Slovenia and the Yugoslavian Peoples Army in late June and early July 1991 did not involve the killing and displacement of civilian populations, Handke's initial intervention in the Yugoslavian wars of the 1990s did not embroil him in ongoing controversy.[5]

The same cannot be said of his later interventions. In January 1996 his polemically framed travel narrative *A Journey to the Rivers: Justice for Serbia* [*Eine winterliche Reise zu den Flüssen Donau, Save, Morawa und Drina oder Gerechtigkeit für Serbien*] appeared in two weekend editions of the liberal *Süddeutsche Zeitung*. During the next four months Handke gave a series of readings from it that took him from Hamburg to Priština, underscoring the importance he attached to it. By mid-year the text had appeared in book form in German and Serbo-Croatian, followed in 1997 by its English translation.[6] Since then Handke has published two more travel narratives, two essays, and a play setting forth what some of his readers saw and see as uncritical pro-Serbian views on the bloody unraveling of Yugoslavia during the 1990s and its aftermath.[7] In varying combinations these publications exhibit the following features: outraged polemics against Western intellectuals, journalists, media, governments, and institutions; a reliance on insinuating questions, on conceptual and rhetorical analyses, cultural criticism, the narration of direct experience, and the selective use of recent Yugoslavian history in arguing his positions; and a concerted effort to give ordinary ethnic Serbs, especially refugees, a voice in the Western discourse on Yugoslavia.

In his most recent publications in this vein, *Around the Great Tribunal* [*Rund um das Große Tribunal* (2002/03)] and *The Tablas of Daimiel: Roundabout Testimony on the Trial of Slobodan Milošević* [*Die Tablas von Daimiel. Ein Umwegzeugenbericht zum Prozess gegen Slobodan Milošević* (2005/06)], Handke has focused his attention on the International Criminal Tribunal for the Former Yugoslavia. He construes the topic broadly to include the Tribunal's legitimacy and funding, its material presence and surroundings in The Hague, its day-to-day workings and procedures, the self-understanding of its judges and prosecutors, its witnesses, the presence and role of journalists and the media, and its ostensible partisan ties to NATO.

Handke's assessment of the Tribunal as a judicial institution ranges from a categorical denial of its legitimacy to a begrudging acknowledgment of some of its work. Significantly, traditional notions of national sovereignty, the importance of local (and continental European) judicial traditions, and narrow constructions of valid evidence play a crucial role in that assessment. But he is also critical of the Tribunal's failure to indict NATO officials for alleged war crimes committed during the alliance's bombing war during Spring 1999 against the Federal Republic of Yugoslavia (Serbia and Montenegro) over that country's policies toward Kosovo. The same criteria understandably inform his related consideration of the charges that the Tribunal's two longest-serving chief prosecutors, Louise Arbour and Carla del Ponte, Arbour's successor, brought against Slobodan Milošević.[8] These range from the initial indictment of 24 May 1999 that charged him and four associates with crimes against humanity and violations of the laws or customs of war in dealing with Kosovo to the indictment of 22 November 2001 that charged him with genocide, crimes against humanity, grave breaches of the Geneva Conventions, and violations of the laws or customs of war during the war in Bosnia.[9]

Well before focusing on the Tribunal in his essays of 2002 and 2005, Handke had presented it in a less than favorable light. In *A Journey to the Rivers*, for example, he had pointed to what he saw as a continuum between the failure of the Western media to report on Serb victims of the wars in Croatia and Bosnia and the Tribunal's then current (late 1995) listing of suspects of war crimes by ethnicity:

> And doesn't the number just published by the International [Tribunal] of those suspected of war crimes in the Yugoslavian war fit that pattern? Forty-seven (47) Serbs, eight (8) Croats, and one (1) Muslim are said to be sought, perhaps, by those in The Hague—as if for this side too, for form's sake, one is needed, a token war criminal, as otherwise a token [Good Samaritan].[10] (19-20)

In *Addendum to A Journey to the Rivers* [*Sommerlicher Nachtrag zu einer winterlichen Reise* (1996)], written a half-year later after a visit to Višegrad and Srebrenica in eastern Bosnia, Handke recalls meeting the Serbs of Višegrad who had gathered on a Sunday at the Orthodox cemetery to mourn their war dead and then opened their minds and hearts to him and his Serb traveling companions. Serving as their mouthpiece, he articulated their perception (and no doubt his own) of the Tribunal as a superimposed institution serving political ends:

> The politicians over in Belgrade have betrayed us, but what else could they do. A small people such as ours can no longer exercise self-determination. And who determines them? Determines? Who has them in hand? In their fist? Under their thumb? And such power and arbitrariness, and not the law, is what gives shape to the legal system imposed by those who have the upper hand. Trials, yes! But then of people from all three warring

> parties simultaneously, and not of a Serb to begin with—the attention of the world is especially drawn to such an accused, who on top of it is the first, and that will shape perception and warp history even more! (213)

In a final aside on the Tribunal in the same text, Handke refers to it as the International Security Council Tribunal [Internationaler Sicherheitsratsgerichtshof], an instance of thinly veiled sarcasm based on its founding by the UN Security Council in resolutions of 22 February and 25 May 1993. He finds fault with the Tribunal here for its handling of an unidentified terminally ill Bosnian Serb general whom it had "put in one of its cells" in this state of ill health and had then released a few days before his death without any proceedings, "simply to die, lenient—leniency from whom?—and still under indictment as a war criminal" (244).[11]

Several years later, following his first observation of the Tribunal's workings in March 1998, Handke gave a rather more ominous account of it in his *Travel in the Dugout Canoe or The Play for the Film about the War* [*Die Fahrt im Einbaum oder Das Stück zum Film vom Krieg*], a work for the theater that appeared in bookstores shortly after the start of the war over Kosovo in March 1999 and then, the day before that war came to an end, had its premiere on June 9 at the Burgtheater in Vienna, one of the leading theaters in the German-speaking countries. In the play the Tribunal is closely identified with the Three Internationals, Handke's relentless caricatures of ostensibly typical international (=Western) journalists whom the play as a whole portrays as the root of all evil and ultimately holds responsible for the wars in Croatia and Bosnia. More precisely, it is the First International, loosely based on Lawrence Weschler, a staff writer for *The New Yorker* whose pieces on the Hague Tribunal and the aftermath of the wars in Croatia and Bosnia began to appear there in November 1995, who embraces the Tribunal and its necessary punitive role in restoring peace. After self-importantly proclaiming his knowledge of the region and its languages and his familiarity with some of the major players among the warring factions, but also with the daily life of its ordinary inhabitants, the First International expounds on just what he knows about the wars and what needs to be done:

> The matter is clear. First, the guilty are known. Second, those who have been accused—no matter whether they have a sense of their guilt or even know that they are among the accused—are to be captured—no matter how, whether in the course of giving blood in a mobile blood unit borrowed as a pretext from the International Red Cross or, if they have the gall to go skiing, picking berries, or swimming like harmless nobodies, to

> be hauled on a hook from the ski run, the woods or the lake by one of our NYT helicopters! Third, no peace without punishment of those known to be guilty by means of our IPACC—. (62-63)

When asked to decipher the acronym, the First International quickly obliges—"International Peace and Criminal Court" (63)—and then proceeds to recount the story of one of the Tribunal's suspects who had been shot while resisting arrest as a warning to all who would defy this international institution (63-64).

In a similar vein Handke uses the Second International, gendered as a woman, to ridicule unwittingly Louise Arbour, the Canadian jurist who replaced Richard Goldstone as the Tribunal's chief prosecutor in October 1996 and served until September 1999, by having her focus in exaggerated admiration on the unnamed Arbour's appearance, progressive self-understanding, literary knowledge, multi-ethnic roots, personal gestures, and outgoing nature:

> The red suit jacket of the newly chosen prosecutor causes her pale Canadian complexion to glow. She wants to be the voice of the victims. With her throaty laugh she reveals how good it feels to know oneself on the side of goodness. She knows all of Brecht and is proud of her Irish-Spanish grandmother. As if she wanted to grasp her precious words out of the air, she forms every sentence with her hands and gazes inward with her deep-set eyes. In the room with the low ceiling from which a bare light bulb dangles she raises her rich alto voice: "Because I've come as a friend, I have to speak German with you!" (68-69)

In order to implicate an entire profession in the reach of his ridicule Handke has the Second International then turn to the audience and proudly proclaim of her words, "Common effort of the Intercontinental War Correspondents' office 'Text Without Borders!'" (69). It goes almost without saying that the intended incriminating allusion is to the progressive international association of journalists *Reporters without Borders*.

In more than one respect Handke has continued to write about the Tribunal in the same vein, though clearly in greater detail and at greater length, in his essays of 2002 and 2005. Especially in the first of these, commissioned by the editor of the weekend *Magazin* of the *Süddeutsche Zeitung* as a report on the trial of Slobodan Milošević and published under the title "And Who Will Free Me of My Prejudice?" ["Und wer nimmt mir mein Vorurteil?"] as the centerpiece of the *Magazin* of 4 October 2002,[12] one of Handke's intentions in writing the piece appears to have been to discredit the Tribunal at every opportunity. Significantly, at a crucial juncture in the opening argument of his essay, which serves to frame the Tribunal as an integral part of an upside-down world, a long-established figure of cultural criticism, he is not above misrepresenting a text to fit this purpose. I am thinking here of his use and abuse of Lawrence Weschler's thoughtful, if at times self-important, essay "Inventing Peace," published in *The New Yorker* on 20 November 1995.[13]

Weschler wrote the essay shortly after observing preliminary hearings that led months later to the Tribunal's first full trial, that of Dusko Tadic, a Bosnian Serb who was arrested in Germany in February 1994 on suspicion of having committed crimes punishable under German law at the Omarska Camp near Prijedor in northwestern Bosnia.[14] He was then extradited to detention at the Hague Tribunal on 24 April 1995 following his indictment there on 13 February 1995 on charges of grave breaches of the Geneva conventions, violations of the laws or customs of war, and crimes against humanity. In the opening paragraphs of his essay Weschler records part of a conversation he had at lunch with Antonio Cassese, the Italian jurist who was named the first President of the Tribunal and in this role served as head of its then panel of eleven judges. Among other gruesome stories related to him by Cassese Weschler recalls "'some of the tales about Tadic himself, how in addition to the various rapes and murders he's accused of, he is alleged to have supervised the torture and torments of a particular group of Muslim prisoners, at one point forcing one of his charges to emasculate another—*with his teeth*. The one fellow died, and the guy who bit him went mad.'"[15] Asked by Weschler how he himself kept from going mad while being "regularly obliged to gaze into such an appalling abyss," Cassese is said to have responded with a smile, "'Ah [...] You see, as often as possible I make my way over to the Mauritshuis museum, in the center of town, so as to spend a little time with the Vermeers.'" The only other statement Weschler attributes to Cassese is the latter's view that Vermeer's paintings "radiate 'a centeredness, a peacefulness, a serenity'" (56-57).

Weschler then spends much of the rest of the essay exploring his own "intuition as to the true extent of Vermeer's achievement," an intuition premised on the fact that

> when Vermeer was painting these images, which for us have become the very emblem of peacefulness and serenity, *all Europe was Bosnia* (or had only just been): awash in incredibly vicious wars of religious persecution and proto-nationalist formation. [...] Holland, to the extent that it ever existed, was of relatively recent provenance, and even then under the continual threat of being overwhelmed once again. (57)

Given the "conspicuous exclusion" of such themes from his paintings, he argues, "Vermeer can be seen, amid the horrors of his age, to have been asserting or inventing the very idea of peace" (59). As a corollary of this view, he goes on to argue that Vermeer intended the figures in his paintings, especially the women, "not to be seen as merely a type, a trope, an allegory. If she is standing in for anything, she is standing in for the condition of being a unique individual human being, worthy of our own individual response" (62).

Weschler contrasts this conception of the individual with the one he sees at work in the Yugoslavian wars in Croatia and Bosnia-Herzegovina:

> [T]he entire Yugoslavian debacle has been taking place in a context wherein the Other, even one's own neighbor, is suddenly being experienced no longer as a subject like oneself but as an instance, a type, a vile expletive: a Serb, a Croat, a Turk, and as such, preordained for an ages-old, inevitable fate.

As Weschler is quick to add, "such a construction has to be as assiduously 'invented' as its obverse: people who have been living in relative peace for decades have to be goaded into seeing one another, once again, in this manner" (62). To illustrate his point, he draws on the work of Dutch journalist Alfred van Cleef, who chronicled the resistance of a Bosnian village to the nationalistic harangues emanating from Belgrade and Zagreb television until a carload of militiamen appeared one day to execute an individual whose father had killed an uncle of one of the militiamen during the partisan conflicts of 1941-1945. Weschler relates this state of affairs to the moral universe of epic poetry in which vengeance for past wrongs becomes part of a seemingly never-ending cycle of violence (62-63). Returning then once more to Vermeer, clearly not a painter in this epic tradition, Weschler sees in his life's work, within its historical moment, "a heroic, extended attempt to steer his (and his viewers') way clear of such a depersonalizing approach to experiencing one's fellow human beings." He then links this "project" to that of the Tribunal itself via a conversation he had with Richard Goldstone, the South African jurist who was then chief prosecutor for both the Tribunal for the former Yugoslavia and the parallel one established for Rwanda after the 1994 genocide there. In Goldstone's view

> "interethnic violence usually gets stoked by specific individuals intent on immediate political or material advantage, who then call forth the legacies of earlier and previously unaddressed grievances [...] and it is they, not the group as a whole, who need to be held to account, through a fair and

> meticulously detailed presentation and evaluation of evidence, precisely so that the next time around no one will be able to claim that all Serbs did this, or all Croats or all Hutus—so that people are able to see how it is specific individuals in their communities who are continually endeavoring to manipulate them in their fashion. I really believe this is the only way the cycle can be broken." (64)

It is within this conceptualization of the Tribunal's mission that Weschler draws out the analogy between Vermeer's project, accomplished with the aid of a camera obscura, and the goals of the "various lawyers and judges" of the Tribunal, outfitted with their equivalent of the camera obscura, a high-tech legal chamber. Reversing the positive focus on the individual in Vermeer's painting, Weschler notes how the automated camera that scans the room also captures the defendant Tadic, first in a medium shot and then in a close-up, as "a quite specific individual" facing allegations on the basis of his autonomous free agency (64).

In recapitulating Weschler's essay, Handke mentions neither Weschler nor Cassese by name but, as part of his rhetorical strategy, stereotypes them as "the journalist" and "the star judge." In a related move he has the journalist present the "world judiciary" of the Tribunal, yet another pejorative term, "not just as a community of heroes but also one of artists" (18), though there is no basis for this caricature in the text beyond Weschler's careless use of the epithet "heroic" to describe Vermeer's efforts in implicitly opposing the epic tradition. Instead of having Weschler and Cassese converse informally over lunch, he has them do so "during an elegant dinner at an Italian restaurant" (18), reinforcing his contention that we are dealing with privilege rather than justice. Handke furthermore considerably embellishes what Weschler's Cassese had to say. Instead of merely keeping himself sane by going to see the Vermeers in the Mauritshuis as often as possible, Handke's judge visits the museum to observe "the paintings of the old Dutch masters in order to recover from the atrocities at issue in the trials, to keep a counter-world in view, to gather strength for his judgments. And to this end he would spend most of his time in front of the paintings of Vermeer van Delft, the *Letter Reader* in her chamber, *The View of Delft*" (19). Weschler's Cassese however says none of these things. Instead it is Weschler himself who names and deals at length with Vermeer's paintings, in particular *The View of Delft* and *Head of a Young Girl* that hang across the room from one another in the Mauritshuis. As already noted, it is also Weschler, using Richard Goldstone's conceptualization of the mission of the Tribunal, a mission Handke simply ignores, who draws out the analogy between Vermeer's efforts at "inventing peace" and those of the Tribunal. Moreover, he does not restrict these efforts to the activity of the judges, "rendering justice, passing judgment, convicting" (19), as Handke would have it, but anchors them in the common work of the Tribunal's various participants, including judges, prosecutors, and lawyers for the defense, all using the resources of their high-tech legal chamber, "the improbably calm site for a similar effort at transmutation" (64).[16]

Handke's misrepresentation of Weschler's Tribunal essay, especially troubling in view of his own moralizing about the lack of ethics among journalists, sets the stage for a series of polemical attacks and asides that allow him to conclude the opening frame of his own essay with the assertion that the upside-down world he has just revealed has already become the new everyday reality of the contemporary world. It is a state of affairs he sees embodied in Carla del Ponte's declared intention to "make history" with the trial of Slobodan Milošević (24). We are of course not given the context in which she made this remark, which would allow us to make sense of it and assess its import. Instead Handke expects his readers to carry forward his characterization of her as an illegitimate "star prosecutor" of the same ilk as Weschler's Tribunal judges and their evolving counterparts in the world of television and film. He advances this view of her on the basis of her being featured in a "monumental color photo" in the *Süddeutsche Zeitung* at the beginning of June 2002 receiving the Westphalian Peace Prize along with a separately recognized youth group. Most incriminating, as a strategically placed "(sic)" suggests, is the fact that this prize was awarded by the Economic Society for Westphalia and Lippe.[17] But del Ponte's acceptance of the prize as "an incentive" to pursue her work at the Tribunal—"'The perpetrators have to be punished, we owe that to the victims'" (20-21)—seems no less damning. Such utterances, after all, entail that she is speaking "in the name of the world" (21), and in Handke's eyes it is precisely this "world" that is suspect, just as he insists that the Tribunal's judges are partisan because they are in the pay of the "world community." In keeping with this fact, he asserts, they never execute the responsibilities of their office against this "community (European Union, NATO, USA, etc.) but instead do so exclusively against the now almost voiceless remainder of the rest of the world" (22).

Handke bridges the two polemical references to Carla del Ponte with an array of negative characterizations of other undeserving prize recipients who in his view exemplify the newly normative upside-down everyday reality he deplores. While he mentions none of them by name, they are identifiable as the literary critic Marcel Reich-Ranicki, philosopher Jürgen Habermas, financier and political reform philanthropist George Soros, French journalist Florence Hartmann, whose "prize" is to have been named spokeswoman for the Office of the Prosecutor of the Hague Tribunal, the organization *Doctors without Borders*, awarded the Nobel Peace Prize in 1999, and Bernard Kouchner, a cofounder of that organization in 1971. Contrary to Handke's assertion, Kouchner was no longer a member of *Doctors without Borders* when he was named UN High Commissioner for Kosovo in June 1999, the "prize" for which he is included in this gallery of the undeserving.

Of particular interest in the present context are the charges Handke levels against *Doctors without Borders* and, appended to his denigration of Kouchner, his discussion of the destruction of public statuary in Priština following the end of the war over Kosovo. As Handke would have it, *Doctors without Borders*, an otherwise laudable organization, crossed two borders too many, both in violation of the Hippocratic Oath. In the months leading up to the war over Kosovo it had "repeatedly announced, amplified again and again by Western European headlines, that there was 'Terror in the Middle of Europe. Already 60,000 victims of Serb Leader Milošević in Kosovo!' and thus, clearly partisan, helped to prepare the bombing runs" (23). What is wrong with this picture? For starters there is no compelling logic to Handke's charge that, by going public with its concerns about the situation in Kosovo, *Doctors without Borders* had both abandoned its commitment to help everyone in need in the region and become complicit in NATO's arguably ill-conceived response to the Yugoslavian government's well-documented brutal policy of repression of what had become an armed and violent opposition movement in Kosovo.[18] But his polemical representation of that organization's publicizing what its volunteers (and those of other non-governmental organizations such as Human Rights Watch) experienced in Kosovo in the course of 1998 does serve to divert attention away from what was actually going on there at the time. At the very least it suggests that the organization's concerns were greatly exaggerated and in effect treats these concerns as irrelevant.

Handke's loosely related discussion of the postwar destruction of public statuary in Priština similarly conceals more than it reveals. In noting that the first statues to come down were those memorializing "two great South Slavic poets of the nineteenth century" rather than those of the old-guard Yugoslavian communists Josip Broz Tito and Edvard Kardelj, he laments the fact that the few Western correspondents who reported on these events failed to elaborate on the identity of the less well-known figures (24). The poets in question are Petar II Petrovic Njegoš (1813-1851), who was also a key political and religious leader of Montenegro, and Vuk Karadžić (1787-1864), linguistic reformer and collector of Serbian folk literature. Yet Handke himself fails to report that both Njegoš and Karadžić, whatever their achievements, were also ardent Serb nationalists in their day whose major works such as *The Mountain Wreath* [*Gorski Vijenac*, 1847] or *Serbian Folk Songs* [*Srpske Narodne Pjesme*, 1814-1866] contain exclusionary conceptions of Serb identity that lend themselves to destructive instrumentalization in another time.[19] Since Tito and Kardelj were in power when Kosovo was granted autonomous status in 1974 as part of a reform of the federal constitution of the Socialist Federal Republic of Yugoslavia, a status that was revoked by various means under Milošević's leadership in 1989, it is hardly surprising that their statues were not among the first to be destroyed by Kosovar nationalists in 1999.[20]

With its polemical opening frame in place, Handke spends a good deal of the remainder of his essay (24-52) recalling and interweaving diverse aspects of his several visits to the Hague Tribunal and its environs. In an abrupt shift from polemics to description readers are given the name and street location of the prison in which the Tribunal's indicted prisoners are held and then receive a tour of the upscale neighborhood in coastal Scheveningen on the northern edge of The Hague where the prison is located as well as of the less appealing Scheveningen promenade (24-28). Passing references to Milošević's indictment in May 1999, misstated here (25) but correctly stated later (34), and his extradition "by his own state" (25) to the jurisdiction of the Tribunal keep readers connected to the primary occasion for the essay.

In the following segment of the essay (29-34) Handke recalls his initial visit to observe the Tribunal in March 1998. The twin foci of this segment are an older Bosnian Serb forest ranger who had been detained with other Serb civilians at the Čelebići Prison Camp within the predominantly Muslim municipality of Konjic (the Camp existed from late May to December 1992) and the Tribunal's prosecution of four Bosnian Muslims for grave breaches of the Geneva conventions and violations of the laws and customs of war in connection with the treatment of those held at the Camp.[21] Both the Bosnian Serb forest ranger, whose leg had been doused with gasoline and set on fire at the Camp by one of the four defendants in the case, and the case itself assume exemplary status in Handke's augmented presentation of his recollection. What Handke finds memorable about the forest ranger's testimony on the first day he observed the trial is less the instances of physical cruelty the man recounted than the spatial disorientation he experienced in the process of being transported and forced to march for days on end through the "mountain forests of Southeast Bosnia" to the camp, this despite his familiarity with the area.[22] As Handke assures his readers in a deliberately evenhanded aside, "all of the ethnic groups of this region went through this following the outbreak of the war in April 92" (30).

Handke's presentation of the Čelebići Prison Camp and the Tribunal's prosecution of four of its personnel likewise stresses the similarity of this camp to those established by the Serbs at Trnopolje, Keraterm, and Omarska in keeping with his established position that all sides in the Yugoslavian wars through the mid-90s were equally responsible for and victimized by what happened. As he notes, "the testimonies of the victims are absolutely identical down to the hair, the skin, the ribs, and other bones. The only difference is that almost nothing of the acts of violence and torture in Čelebići became known" (29). His presentation of the outcome of the Tribunal's trial of the four Bosnian Muslims accused of war crimes and related offences at the Čelebići Prison Camp not only signals his agreement with the verdicts that were handed down but also points toward their implications for the trial against Milošević:

> Of the four accused in the Čelebići trial three were found guilty in November 1998. All three were individuals with responsibility for the Camp. The fourth went free: he was the commander of Muslim forces in the Čelebići area [Zejnil Delalic], and it couldn't be proved that he knew of the abuses and murders in the Camp, let alone that he had planned and organized them. The highest sentences were given to the immediate perpetrators, the guard (who had poured the gasoline) [Esad Landzo] and his immediate superior, the deputy commander [Hazim Delic]. The camp commander himself [Zdravko Mucic], found "not guilty" of the murders but only of infractions of the laws of war, received by far the lightest sentence. Alija Izetbegovic, then president of Bosnia and commander-in-chief of the army, a position in a chain of command and planning, was not even taken into account by the Tribunal. (That this almost—almost—makes sense given the specific Balkan circumstances as opposed to, say, those in Germany, etc., more about that later by way of suggestion in reference to the trial of Slobodan Milošević. Small fish? Given the Balkans, weren't and aren't as a rule the small fish, the regional and village capos and their henchmen, the big fish? "Chain of command," where?). (32-33)

While Handke's affirmation of the Tribunal's findings in the case of the Čelebići Prison Camp is rather unexpected given his earlier polemics against the Tribunal, the real surprise is his invoking of "Balkan circumstances" as an explanatory category of significance. A decade earlier, in his angry critique of the Slovenian declaration of independence, he had emphatically dismissed the relevance of this category in general and castigated Milan Kundera for employing it against Serbia in a defense of Slovenia's move (17).

The pause in his critical treatment of the Tribunal is short-lived as Handke moves on to report directly on Slobodan Milošević's appearance before it, in February as well as June 2002. En route he finds fault with the external setting of the Tribunal in what he presents as an inhospitable no-man's-land, then with the close-up photographic portraits of its judges hanging in the stairwell leading up to the trial chambers (34-35).[23] Once he has taken his readers to the observers' area for Trial Chamber No. 1, he recalls being distracted from "direct and immediate viewing" of the actual trial proceedings by the two television monitors located in the upper front corners of that space and insinuatingly questions who might have been responsible for the camera angle and the frequency with which the accused appeared in close-up shots (36). Milošević, who, as he reminds us, had chosen to defend himself, is presented in his initial recollection of his June 2002 visit to the Tribunal as someone who appears "almost alone," as constantly yawning due to the lack of air in the trial chamber, as someone showing "signs of near-exhaustion"—this as an implicit contrast to the "contemporary" journalistic representations of him as a "'defiant pug'" and "'beefy apparatchik'" (37-38).

Recalling the one day in February 2002 that he was allowed to observe the Milošević trial shortly after it had begun, Handke initially quotes snatches, presumably on the basis of the trial transcript, of the defendant's ongoing naming and further identification of the individual victims of the euphemistically termed collateral damage of NATO's air war against Yugoslavia. He then switches to quoting from Milošević's more general remarks toward the end of that day:

> "That bombardment was the worst crime in Novi Pazar since Novi Pazar belongs to Yugoslavia"; "in Yugoslavia America's national interest was more important to Americans than Yugoslavia's national interest"; "there were no negotiations in Rambouillet: Albanians and Serbs never met there face to face"; "Clinton, with his genocide against the Serbs, supported by a tired and sleepy Europe, has ruined the third millennium"; "the Yugoslavian Peoples Army has never collaborated with paramilitary formations. There is an official order on the issue in keeping with the Geneva Convention. All documents are here, read them, shame on you"; "the idea of a Greater Serbia, in contrast to that of a Greater Albania, has never existed. It was part of Austro-Hungarian propaganda, already since 1816, at the Congress of Vienna, with Serbia's gaining of independence after 400 years of Turkish rule—the phantom of a greater Serbia: the wind will blow it away." (40)

It is difficult to tell whether Handke is in agreement with all of these statements, but the utterances themselves respond directly or indirectly to at least some of the charges that Louise Arbour, the Tribunal's chief prosecutor, had brought against Milošević and four of his ruling associates on 24 May 1999.

Having given Milošević his due, as it were, Handke moves on to an expanded account of his visit to the Tribunal in early June 2002 by focusing on two witnesses for the prosecution. One of them is identified only as a young American from New York and a member of the organization Human Rights Watch who was then writing a book about postcommunist Albania. Although Handke does not make the connection for his readers, it can be inferred from the testimony he reports that the individual in question, Fred Abrahams, had been called as a prosecution witness because he had helped to author *Humanitarian Law Violations in Kosovo*, the October 1998 report of Human Rights Watch dealing with the deteriorating situation in Kosovo. Having already prejudiced his readers against Human Rights Watch by depicting a man he identifies as its spokesman as an epiphenomenon of Western journalism, a notion he reinforces with a hand-drawn headless caricature (42), Handke treats Abrahams himself with thinly veiled irony by using his own words to focus attention on his "partisan" advocacy despite his self-understanding as an objective researcher:

> Already in the year before the war against Yugoslavia he had published an article in the *Herald Tribune* in which he had called on the Tribunal to indict Milošević. In doing so he had certainly not wanted to engage in politics: the appeal had been a "conclusion of our field research" (as a rule he used "we" instead of "I"). "The facts led us to this conclusion . . ." He was a researcher; there were fifty footnotes in his report with field interviews; and even if none of the interviewees "had seen the killing directly," we were nonetheless able "to reconstruct the instances." "Our" press releases are also based on field research. (43)

When asked if his organization had also looked into the accusations of crimes of war against NATO, his reply is no less ironically presented:

> Yes, and the report had been critical: the bombs and other "resolute actions" had certainly done "damage," and the fragmentation bombs, for example, those on the civilian center of Nis, deserved "further investigation," but "we didn't collect enough evidence that the killing of the civilian population, whether in Aleksinac [one of the sites mentioned by Milošević in February] or elsewhere, had occurred intentionally"—thus no genocide—"while for the killing of the Albanian population in Kosovo,

> a clear outcome of our field research, there was evidence of the coordination and also the integration of the paramilitary forces into the supreme command. We strive for objectivity, and our strongest argument in this regard is our work. We have a high professional standard and have always worked together with Serbian organizations, such as the Belgrade Center of Human Rights, that is similarly highly professional. We never set ourselves against the Serbian people or nation. And when we establish expulsion and genocide, we are not legal experts but field researchers who draw conclusions. (44)

The one point of this witness's testimony that Handke allows to stand unchallenged is his response to the question whether he could describe the Drenica region in Kosovo where he had done most of his field research: "'Drenica is a hilly region'" (45).[24]

Handke is a good deal more charitable toward the other witness whose testimony he records here, a young Kosovar who survived an attack of Serbian government forces on the village of Račak in January 1999 in which "more than 30 people" were killed. This incident, as Handke puts it parenthetically, for once without a trace of irony, "led in February to Rambouillet and in March to the bombing war" (45). "The witness," as Handke goes on to note with an undertone of irony, "was noticeably outraged about the fact that Serbian authorities had fired on his village, perhaps more than about the death of his uncle who had bled to death at his side from police bullets; 'Something like this just can't be.'" Yet the irony returns full-force as Handke continues his account of the young man's testimony:

> And it was clear to him who was responsible for the whole thing, who had personally arranged it: his former president, Slobodan Milošević, toward whom he pointed again and again by raising his chin. "The whole world knows that, the truth is the truth. (45-46)

Having made his point by connecting the young Kosovar's inference of Milošević's guilt from the immediate incident he had witnessed to "world" opinion in this matter, Handke returns to an empathetic mode of reporting his testimony, in the process implicitly criticizing the presiding judge and the prosecution for not letting him have his say:

> It came across as completely unrehearsed that the young man offered to tell the trial chamber not only the names and dates of every single one of the dead but also their stories; he felt compelled to make public the life history of the victims—only he was immediately cut off, even by the prosecution, it "wasn't necessary," and besides there was no time for it. (46)

As if to reinforce his critique of such an approach to justice, Handke largely turns away from the Tribunal as such in the remainder of his essay (47-69) to relate a number of stories that he clearly regards as relevant to the trial he is covering. The initial focus of the first of these stories is a group of Kosovars from Račak, including the young man whose testimony he sketches in the essay, who happened to be staying in the same beach-front hotel in which he had taken a room. Like the Bosnian Serb forest ranger he had observed at the Čelebići Prison Camp trial in 1998, the four older members of this group, who appear similarly displaced from their village environment, were wearing new suits, presumably bought for the occasion of their appearance as witnesses at the Tribunal. The only thing that distinguishes them from the forest ranger, whom Handke prefers to think of as a "long-serving forest laborer" (30), are the traditional round caps that signal their separate ethnic identity. He then focuses on the oldest member of the group whom he had mistakenly identified as the likely primary witness. What Handke observes, with as much fascination as the forest ranger had elicited from him four years earlier (cf. 31 and 48), is a man who stands apart from his sociable fellow Kosovars in behavior and demeanor, and it is his story that he relates: "He did not speak a word the entire time. He did not smile nor change his expression" (48). In the midst of celebration following a round of testimony by the young Kosovar he remains detached: "On a chair moved slightly aside he sat slightly turned away with a slightly lowered head. I have never seen someone that absent" (51). While this "Albanian villager" appears lost on the beach at the North Sea, he strikes Handke as more "earthly" than the masses of locals pursuing leisure sports there who appear to have come from another solar system (49). Little wonder that at the end of his essay Handke imagines this authentic Kosovar villager together with the equally compelling Bosnian Serb forest ranger qua laborer as ideal local specialists assisting the flawed Tribunal, "people who have in their blood, heart, and gut what the Balkans were and are, who know what precisely the 'small fish,' the all-powerful local capos (the small fish as the big ones) are responsible for" (69).

Handke's remaining stories each build to a moral of their own. On 23 May 1997 a Criminal Law Chamber of the Bavarian Supreme Court found the Bosnian Serb Novislav Djajic guilty of being an accessory to fourteen counts of murder and one count of attempted murder in connection with the execution of fourteen Bosnian Muslim men on the bridge across the Drina at Brod near the district capital of Foča the evening of 22 June 1992. Djajic had been arrested in Munich in January 1996 and initially charged with being an accessory to genocide after the lone survivor of the massacre and his former next-door neighbor, Esad Mujanovic, reported him to the police. Handke's version of the events of that evening is ostensibly based on his reading of "the trial transcripts after the fact" (53) and on Djajic's own oral and written accounts. In Handke's version Djajic was part of a military escort which was to bring "more than a dozen young Muslim men from the village of Trnovaće" across the Drina to the nearby city of Foča, where they were to be interned. The order to do so had come from the regional Serbian-Yugoslavian military commander in Foča in anticipation of a reprisal attack on the Muslim residents of the village following an ambush near it earlier in the day in which several Serb residents of the village had died. Once the group

> came onto the bridge a car stopped on the other side. Masked men got out, with submachine guns. One of them then opened fire without hesitation. Those dead on the spot were thrown into the Drina. Just one of the Muslims survived by jumping, wounded, into the river, submerging himself and fighting his way downstream to the enclave of Gorazde. The masked killers had immediately thrown the bodies over the railing and driven off again. (52-53)[25]

Handke supplements this account by noting that the two groups of young men from the village, the Muslims and their Serb military escort, had mingled and were conversing along the way: "In seeing the masked men on the other end of the bridge, they all fell silent and scattered. The only one who then spoke was the masked killer who berated his victims while he 'mowed them down'" (54). Standing in the middle of the bridge with the rest of the military escort, Djajic, as he told Handke, had finally looked away from the killing into the still-light evening sky and was overcome by an epiphany of his innocence (54). Handke then goes on to quote at length from Djajic's written account of the evening in an unpublished memoir about his role in the war. The passage culminates in a religiously grounded rejection of the world and its injustice: "The bridge smelled of death. In my nostrils I sensed the final breath of these murdered innocent people. I struck the pavement with my gun. 'Cursed be the world and what I have to bear!' I swore" (56). "Was he thus done justice in being put away for years and years by the judiciary," Handke asks rhetorically in anticipation of the larger point of this story:

> For where in the world were there judges, journalists, court psychologists who would believe such a story, who would be able to do something with such a story, for whom such a story would make sense, for whom such a story would have the force of evidence? Isn't nowadays the only valid language that of journalists and others who condemn in advance, and don't

> almost all writers assiduously imitate these schemata that render everything disastrous? What were the facts of the case? What was the guilt of Novislav Djajic? (56)

Although I cannot give a full account of them here, there are major discrepancies between Handke's account of the evening and that presented in the Bavarian Criminal Law Chamber's lengthy justification of its verdict, an account based primarily on the testimony of Esad Mujanovic but also on Djajic's own pretrial statements to the police, an investigative judge, and a court-appointed expert.[26] The crucial discrepancy is that the two men who emerged from the car at the other end of the bridge were not only not masked but wore uniforms and acted in concert with at least one member of the Serb military escort who, at the blinking of a spotlight, ordered the Muslim men to line up on the left side of the bridge with their backs to the railing once they had reached its middle. They complied, and members of the Serb military escort formed a semicircle across from them and were joined by the two men from the car. One of these men, identified as Mladen Lazarevic, a local Serb soldier who was known to Djajic (82), then fired a short burst killing the first of the Muslims instantly. While he berated a second Muslim for not throwing the body into the Drina, Mujanovic jumped over the railing into the Drina. Thereafter Lazarevic and military policemen standing next to Djajic in the semicircle (75) fired the shots killing the remaining Muslims. Because Djajic had initially held back before joining the semicircle, the Criminal Law Chamber concluded that he had been unaware of the regionally coordinated plan involving the Yugoslavian army to kill the fifteen Muslim men not just in revenge for the ambush but as part of a larger strategy of "ethnic cleansing" of all Muslims from the region.[27] The fact that he had nonetheless joined the circle after it had become clear to him that the men were to be killed, thus helping to keep the intended victims from fleeing and making their killing possible, led to his conviction on the reduced charge of accessory to murder and attempted murder (39-41). Handke's concluding assertion that the "German court has at least determined that the masked killers were irregulars or paramilitary agents who had come from nearby Montenegro" (57) is categorically at odds with the findings of that court. The Tribunal's related attribution of the massacre on the Drina bridge to the "'Serb army'" in one of its publications, which his assertion is intended to negate, is indeed very much in keeping with those findings given the various collaborating elements that constituted the Serb army in Foča at the time.

Handke's two remaining stories are less problematical but also warrant critical scrutiny. In one he recalls an apparent terrorist attack in spring 1996 on a bistro owned by a Montenegrin Serb couple in the Kosovo village of Dečani near the Serb Orthodox monastery of the same name. Several patrons and a Kosovar employee died in the attack, which was carried out at night by disguised gunmen with the help of a brief local power blackout. Handke learned of this incident soon after it occurred because he stopped at the bistro following a visit to the monastery that June.[28] While letting his readers know that he had resisted his hosts' efforts to implicate their Kosovar neighbors as complicit in the incident, he does note that when he was taking leave from the couple in front of their bistro, he felt he was being deliberately overlooked by Kosovars passing in the street or standing across the way. His recollection six years later while writing his essay leads to a series of rhetorical questions: "Which ethnic group in Kosovo excluded and is excluding which ethnic group? Didn't allow it? Didn't allow it to get close? Didn't allow it to be?" (59). The problem with this snapshot approach to the most recent history of these two groups is that it focuses on a single moment in time as defining Kosovar/Serb relations. In doing so it conveniently elides sixteen conflicted years—following Tito's death in 1980—of these relations. These years included increasingly nationalistic propaganda directed by Serbian intellectuals and media against the Kosovar majority that had benefitted from the constitutional changes of 1974, Serbia's revocation of Kosovo's status as an autonomous province during 1989 and 1990, and thereafter its increasingly arbitrary and violent repression of Kosovars in the years leading up to 1996. At that time radical Kosovar nationalists with a Diaspora base of support first engaged anonymously in random acts of violence against Serb institutions, officials, and individuals both Serb and Kosovar. These acts were decidedly out of step with the politics of nonviolent resistance that Ibrahim Rugova and the Democratic League of Kosovo had pursued since late 1989 with the support of most Kosovars.[29]

Handke draws a related misleading moral from his final story about the decline of the French newspaper *Liberation* from an emancipatory journal countering prejudice into an "exemplary business selling prejudice" (60) in connection with the destruction of Yugoslavia. One of his cases-in-point is an article that appeared during NATO's bombing war against the Republic of Yugoslavia juxtaposing a Serb policeman and a Kosovar poet living in France who had grown up together as playmates in a Kosovo village. The article's point, he argues, is to present the juxtaposed men as typical of the two ethnic groups. It leads him to ask whether the "world" is aware of how many policemen in Kosovo from both ethnic groups had been killed before the war began (61-62). The issue Handke raises is certainly relevant, but without contextualization it gets his readers no closer to the truth of the matter than the article he decries. Serbia's increasingly hegemonic and repressive policies toward the Kosovar majority, especially from 1988 onward, preceded and prepared the ground for the emergence of the Kosovo Liberation Army and its strategy of targeting the police, other Serb officials, and their Kosovar "collaborators" as symbols of Serbian hegemony. As Noel Malcolm and others have argued, Serbia's overreaction to KLA provocation from early 1998 onward then served to transform the little-known KLA into a broader movement with local support and leadership.[30]

In the final pages of his essay Handke suggests readings bearing on the Yugoslavian wars of the 1990s, attacks German foreign minister Joschka Fischer for identifying doubters of the Serbian "horseshoe plan" to expel Kosovars from Kosovo as revisionists in the tradition of those who deny the Holocaust, laments the flourishing of conspiracy theories on the political left, and offers another gallery of portraits of prominent individuals he detests. His ambivalence toward the Tribunal itself finds expression in the penultimate paragraph: "No question. The crimes in the Balkans, committed this way or that, within the region or at desks (writing—?) abroad, have to be expiated whether 'we owe this to the victims' or not. But how? But where? And by whom?" (68). His related description of the Tribunal's panel of three judges trying the Milošević case as appearing to lack the appropriate judicial experience as well as closer knowledge of the former Yugoslavia for their task, and a prosecutor whose gestures ostensibly recall those of television actors and whose knowledge of "Balkan circumstances" is based on having been a tour guide for a time in Belgrade, leaves little doubt that he finds them all inadequate. To compensate Handke imagines adding "lay judges" such as the Serb forest ranger, the Račak villager, and the Montenegrin innkeepers to the process, "people who have in their blood, heart, and gut what the Balkans were and are, who know what precisely the 'small fish,' the all-powerful local capos (the small fish as the big ones) are responsible for" (69). Despite its poetic appeal, this notion not only remains a utopian construction but also diverts attention from the role that Serbian state power and planning played in the decade leading up to and during the nearly three months of the war over Kosovo, not to mention their role in the earlier wars in Croatia and Bosnia.

In mid-2005 Handke published a second essay on the Hague Tribunal, this time in the journal *Literaturen*. Its enigmatic title, *The Tablas of Daimiel: Roundabout Testimony on the Trial of Slobodan Milošević*, links a natural phenomenon in Spain to the trial of Slobodan Milošević and thus hints at the "roundabout testimony" that Handke's German neologism *Umwegzeugenbericht* promises. The immediate occasion for Handke's second essay was his inclusion in a list of more than 1600 potential witnesses for the defense that Milošević and his legal advisors had drawn up and the Tribunal made public in June 2004 (7).[31] Less than a page into the essay Handke emphatically states his decision not to serve as a witness at the Tribunal. He then spends much of the opening third of his essay elaborating on this decision without explicitly listing the reasons for it beyond his rather attenuated "initial and, objectively viewed, perhaps deciding reason," namely that the Tribunal has "no legal basis whatsoever" (12).[32] Two factors appear to have confirmed him in his decision. One was the request from Milošević's interim defense counsel asking him to serve as an "expert witness," which would have required him to combine analysis and opinion and thus become "partisan" (15-16). The other was the appeal, within the Tribunal's established procedures for the review of decisions and judgments by its Appeals Chamber, that led to a reversal of the decision of the judges hearing the Milošević case that he could no longer defend himself because of illness. Instead of seeing this successful appeal as evidence that the workings of the Tribunal are indeed subject to effective internal review and thus anything but arbitrary and beyond control as he insists elsewhere ("Scrutinized by whom? Responsible to whom?" [19]), Handke grouses about the fact that the overruled judges were allowed to continue hearing the case and coyly asks whether such "pronounced appeal procedures" didn't reinforce his sense of the "senselessness, the mere tokenism, and even the harmfulness" that serving as a witness would entail (16).

In pursuing the "self-clarification" (22) of his decision not to testify, Handke offers a conception of all courts as "more or less [a] theater of consciousness" (18), a term derived from his account of the self-contained, ritualized process his own rationalizations follow in wrongly finding someone "guilty." Leaving aside the question of its validity, Handke's notion, when applied to the Tribunal, allows him to make convenient distinctions. On the one hand there are the Tribunal's second and third trial chambers that are "less" like his self-description, that go about their work having "facts und legal states of affairs that stand in an immediate relationship to the accused testified about, investigated, questioned" (20). On the other there is its central trial chamber, reserved for its most important indictees such as Milošević and "more" like his theater of consciousness, scrutinized by and responsible to no one. Indeed, Handke ridicules it as the New Great World Theater, as the judicial embodiment of his theater of consciousness at its worst:

> The more comprehensive and manifold the jurisdiction of a court, the more liminally transgressive, translocal, "international," the more detached from

> society it presents itself, from any society, the more self-contained and ritualized it is as a quasi-state power beyond nation states, even doing without their principle of the separation of powers. Scrutinized by whom? Responsible to whom? (19)

Using a series of rhetorical questions to effect a transition, Handke concedes that with the passing of the years since his observations of the court something may have changed about the Tribunal's structure that he had just "encircled and more sketched than described" (22). Reflecting on his first essay, he notes that the Tribunal's "self-celebration and metaphorical self-founding" may have disappeared.[33] "But something else has taken their place," he continues, "at least in the so-called major trials in which a general attribution of guilt is at issue without the individual accused having been physically violent personally or having been present at the scene of the crime or even in its vicinity" (24). That "something else" is the legal construct of a "joint criminal enterprise." In the case of Milošević this construct was indeed integral, at least in their amended versions, to all three of the overall indictments brought against him in connection with the wars in Croatia, Bosnia, and Kosovo, including the specific indictment of genocide with regard to the mass killing of Bosnian Muslim men and boys in Srebrenica in July 1995.[34]

It is the last of these indictments that Handke finds most at issue: "By supposedly having a 'Greater Serbia' as his goal, [Milošević] is held to have ultimate responsibility for the genocide in Srebrenica in 1995 even without giving a specific order, indeed, even without knowing about the massacres beyond Serbian borders" (24). The refusal of two of the three judges hearing the case to dismiss the charge of genocide due to a lack of evidence on the grounds that it had been proven that Milošević had control over those immediately responsible on the other side of the Drina leads Handke to see the trial chamber as "partisan," as having reached a judgment before hearing from the witnesses for the defense (25). It also leads to his use of the French judicial concept *intime conviction* to declare his own "innermost conviction" that the Tribunal in the form of its central trial chamber is "worthless—that, no matter how much formal justice it dispenses, it is wrong from the start, its foundation, its origin, and remains wrong" (30). He further declares it to be his inner conviction that Milošević is "'not guilty as charged'" (31). As evidence he adduces a "minute and, for all I care, laughable detail at the start of the trial that convinced me on the spot. I saw, yes, saw that it stood for the whole" (31). Handke ties his epiphany to Milošević's one-sentence response to the charge that, while he may not have aided and abetted the killing und expulsion of the Muslim population of the gorges and mountains of

Bosnia, he had failed to prevent these crimes through stringent presidential orders from Belgrade: "Whoever was of the opinion that a Bosnian Serb taking territory or simply 'a Bosnian Serb policeman' (I remember that expression verbatim) would allow him, M., 'to order him to do something,' had no idea about a policeman beyond the Drina in Bosnia." What had impressed him even more than these words was the tone with which Milošević had uttered them: instead of an angry rejection of the charge, a "sad bafflement accompanied by the hint of a shaking of his head at such insinuation or at least ignorance concerning local Balkan power relations" (33).

Handke's "inner conviction" matches his uncritical account of his meeting with Milošević in his underground office in the Tribunal's prison at the request and in the presence of one of his three legal advisors from Belgrade: "All morning long he discussed in front of me those two events that, after the Yugoslavian wars of secession broke out from 1991 onward, were then interpreted after the fact as if Milošević had brought on, instigated, sparked these wars" (36). The first of the events led to Milošević's oft-quoted remark to Kosovo Serbs who had been organized to demonstrate their presence and voice their grievances at his meeting of 24 April 1987 with local Serb representatives and Kosovar leaders in the House of Culture in the symbolically charged locale of Kosovo Polje. Nearby was the site of the intensely mythologized battle of 1389 that in modern Serb identity construction has been construed as a Serb victory in defeat. In historical reality, however, it was not only indecisive in outcome but also pitted Ottoman Turks and their local vassals, including some Serbs, against a coalition of ethnically diverse local forces led by Serb Tsar Lazar.[35] At the April 1987 event the mainly ethnic Albanian police used batons to keep Serb protesters from forcing their way into the overcrowded meeting hall in the House of Culture. In a moment captured on Serbian television, Milošević told the crowd outside, "No one is allowed to beat you," before giving an impassioned speech in the meeting hall invoking local Serb traditions and hegemony over Kosovo.[36] The second event centered on Milošević's address at the 600th anniversary of the battle on the Field of Blackbirds on 28 June 1989. Handke quotes one sentence of the address, apparently from memory: "Today we have other battles ahead of us" ("Heute haben wir andere Kämpfe vor uns," 37). He then insists that the context of the speech made clear that the battles referred to had nothing to do with weapons and war. Yet the immediate context of this statement near the end of Milošević's speech explicitly leaves open the possibility that these "other battles" might indeed turn into armed struggle:

> Six centuries later there are again battles ahead of us. These are not armed battles that we have to work through, though such battles, too, are not to be ruled out. But independently of which battles are ahead of us, they cannot be won without decisiveness, bravery, and self-sacrifice, thus not without the good qualities that were also demonstrated in the past on the Kosovo battlefield.[37]

In bringing the account of his meeting with Milošević to a close, Handke does offer a critical glimpse of the man reacting to his calling him a "tragic person," an appellation that Milošević appears at the very least to have found off-putting and that clearly contradicted his self-understanding. The awkward moment gives Handke an opportunity to distance himself from his interlocutor *and* articulate his own theory about the Yugoslavian wars of the 1990s:

> Nonetheless, had I not encountered his incomprehension, I would have gladly explained myself, as follows: that in the Balkans at the start of the 1990s an infernal machine got started which, from inside, from the individual republics, regions, valleys, and gorges, was not to be stopped, not by any power, any person, any individual—but that, before it got started, could have been steered from outside, and only from outside—and was no doubt also steered from there, but precisely in an infernal sense—and then, once the machine was started, it was steered ever more from outside, in a one-sided, partisan manner, und thus completely on a course to hell, in the best (best) case infernally clueless—and, in the best case clueless (perhaps to the credit of the Tribunal), continues to be so steered for "at least there is now peace in the Balkans"—peace thus?—and that this infernal machine, set in motion internally and steered from outside, could only produce those who are guilty, of whom internally, entirely different than externally, there is also one or the other (not all! not many!) who is tragically guilty, unable to escape becoming guilty this way or that—tragic figures who have nothing to do with the "tragic" by nature and stature, unsuited by origin and history as protagonists of a tragedy—tragedies of essentially nontragic human beings—a rather novel, yet unresearched tragic state? The Tribunal will do the research? Or at least take this tragic state into account? (41-42)

Whatever one might make of Handke's metaphorical musings about the genesis and course of the wars and their particular tragic character, historically and culturally shaped and locally invested human agency that could and did make choices with consequences throughout the troubled 1980s and 1990s in Yugoslavia is not a part of them.

At the start of the final third of his essay Handke feels compelled to continue his "unuseable" testimony: "The less useable, the better. The less it has to do, obviously or immediately, with indictment or defense, the more I feel compelled" (44). His testimony assumes the form of four discrete travel narratives, three of which nonetheless do in fact bear more or less obviously and immediately on the Tribunal. In the first of these (44-48) he retells the story of his visit to Priština and Dečani in late spring 1996 already contained in his first essay on the Tribunal. This time, however, it also includes segments on his reading in Priština from *A Journey to the Rivers* and a stroll through the desolate, predominantly Serb center of the city and the lively ethnic Albanian quarters spreading away from it in all directions. As before, only more so, the stress falls on the manifestations of an isolated Serb presence in the form of the three-word phrase "We aren't alone" in Cyrillic letters on sheets hung here and there from windows in tenement housing. And as before, only more elaborated, he recalls the passive aggressive indifference of Kosovars to his presence outside the bistro in Dečani that had been targeted by terrorists. This time, however, he also adds a pointed commentary: "But why do I see, no, already saw there and then, in such thousand-eyed registering and being declared not present, an action in the midst of total passivity, symbolic, an action, the anticipation of an action? An action already in its anticipation, as it were, a magical acting. I too in a state of paranoia, ostensibly driven by it like all of Serbia" (48).

Handke's second travel narrative (48-52) recounts his trip of January 2003 to the Srebrenica area where he once again met a number of local Serbs. This time, so he maintains, they were finally able to tell him their story:

> "We were *not* organized at the start of the war. The first dead were ours, in Skelani, then in the other Serb villages, in Podravanje, in Krnici, in Ratkovici, in Zalaze. The Muslims under their commander Naser Oric systematically destroyed all villages. We Serbs already fled Srebrenica in May 1992, primarily to Bratunac, near the Drina. We first organized ourselves after the attack in January 1993 on the village of Kravica. Like all the villages in the vicinity it was not defended, and thus Oric's people could capture it and kill almost all of its inhabitants, well over a hundred. And even then, after January 16, we organized ourselves exclusively as soldiers of the Republika Srpska, no JNA (=Yugoslavian Peoples Army) for us, 'samo srpske vojske!' The organization began only out of necessity, and that's how our army first came into being. With an army before January 1993 the massacre of Kravica could never have come about, and also not all the massacred Serb villages in 1992!" (And then the dark fury sentence:) "Had we [...] had the power in February 1993 when we first heard of Kravica, we would have extinguished all of Srebrenica." And why such a determined assertion of miserable Srebrenica by the Muslim war

> party? […] Because after the fall of Višegrad, the center of East Bosnian Muslims, Srebrenica became their great symbol. It had to become and remain Muslim. And in the villages they killed all Serbs including women and children, our side however after the fall of S. exclusively soldiers. What is genocide? (49-50)

The story that Handke's informants told him is at the very least selective and in part simply fabricated. From the start of hostilities in Eastern Bosnia in April 1992, Srebrenica was targeted for the same ethnic cleansing of non-Serbs that was effectively implemented early on in the nearby municipalities of Bratunac and Zvornik, both more strategically located on major transportation routes at or near bridges across the Drina linking Bosnia and Serbia. Thus Serb militias based in Bratunac, a mere 10 kilometers away, issued an ultimatum to the Muslim residents of Srebrenica to turn in their weapons by the morning of April 18 or face attack:

> The Muslims knew from refugees what had taken place in Zvornik and Bratunac, and many took cover in the densely forested hills surrounding the town. Determined to avoid the grim fate of their fellow Muslims, they held on to the few weapons they had. After the expiry of the ultimatum, Arkan's Tigers and other militias entered Srebrenica and started looting and killing elderly Muslims who had stayed behind. […] On 20 April, two days after the occupation of Srebrenica, Orić and a group of men descended from the hills and attacked the Serbs, killing several. That day, Orić was elected as commander of the territorial defense. […] In early May, the Serbs stepped up their attempts to establish control over the Srebrenica area. The JNA [Yugoslavian Peoples Army] shelled the Muslim villages, and the militias tried to enter them with infantry. The "mopping up" operations were carried out by a coalition of paramilitaries from Serbia and a militia composed of Serbs from Srebrenica and Bratunac. The leader of these local Serbs was Goran Zekić, a judge and a local SDS politician. On 8 May, after two days of gun battles, Zekić was ambushed and killed. His death proved to be the start of a mass exodus of Serbs from Srebrenica to Bratunac. The Muslims had won control of the town, but the Serbs exacted a terrible revenge for their defeat: in the Bratunac football stadium they executed scores of male Muslim prisoners.[38]

The surprise attack by a large Muslim force on the village of Kravica on the morning of 7 January 1993—Christmas morning in the Serb Orthodox calendar—also assumes a different aspect if, as the same source claims, there were 400 Serb soldiers defending it because of its strategic location west of Bratunac: "The fighting was ferocious, but at the end of the day the Muslims drove out the Serbs. Over 100 Serb soldiers and civilians were reputedly killed."[39] Such facts are no doubt of little consequence to the mother still mourning her son killed in the fighting ten years earlier, a woman whom Handke encountered during his related visit to Kravica in January 2003 (51), but they would seem to warrant more attention by Handke himself in his efforts to set the record on massacres straight.

Handke's third and longest travel narrative (53-59) recalls his visits to two locations in Serbia where Serb refugees from the wars of the 1990s were housed in former hotels. It is the only one of the four in which he is not pressing a political agenda. His differentiated account of the two sets of refugees, the one from Kosovo, the other from various parts of Bosnia and Croatia, gives one a first-hand impression of the difficult daily lives of these refugees in their cramped quarters, of their attitudes, adaptations, and, at least in some instances, aspirations for a new life, frequently with relatives abroad. It is of course the young who are most likely to achieve this new life, and Handke concludes this segment with a strongly affirmative description of the work of a young artist whose fellow refugees had concurred in his use of the former dance hall of the hotel to pursue his painting in oils.

Handke's final travel narrative brings us to the furthest reach of his roundabout testimony, the Tablas of Daimiel, oval-shaped stretches of the river Guadiana located some 150 kilometers south of Madrid near the town of Daimiel in the region of La Mancha. Because of its limestone bed, the river disappears and reappears at various intervals. The upper run of the river had once been spring-fed by "eyes," small pools of water rising from the Mancha plain. It had been part of an abundant ecosystem supporting a diversified, self-sufficient economy in which hunting, fishing, various forms of agriculture supported by sustainable irrigation, and basket-weaving had had their place. But the introduction of corn as a monoculture, a move "demanded from outside," had led local private landowners to drain the river's ground and spring water "'for economic reasons'" without regard for the region as a whole: "The result: a drying up of the entire upper run of the river, the collapse of the underground natural water channels and their subsequent blockage due to the rotting peat that plugged up all the underground pores and to the clay and loam seeping in, and that irreversibly" (62). In his account of the experience, Handke becomes aware of this state of affairs only after the local driver whom he supposedly hired to take him to see what no longer exists explains to him why it is no longer there. It is hard to imagine that someone like Handke, who takes pride in his many travels on foot, would not have walked the eleven kilometers in question. In any case, someone local is needed to draw out the moral of a story with allegorical overtones:

"As he told me the story of their destruction [that of the Tablas] there had been, as part of his depiction of their earlier state, an affection, indeed something loving about it (no longing or 'nostalgia'), but what dominated, especially in his curtness, was the bitterest anger, wrath. 'Something has been taken from me. And not just from me: from us" (63).

These could easily be Handke's own words about Yugoslavia, spoken to and on behalf of an imagined community of readers, and it is hardly surprising that in the text of his narrative he then "involuntarily" asks the driver about Yugoslavia. We learn nothing more than that the driver shows himself "informed," but that characterization becomes the occasion for a closing attack on his "otherwise informed countryman," Javier Solana, the Spanish Secretary General of NATO at the time of the bombing war over Kosovo. The attack, in short, is an instance of Handke's own "bitterest anger, wrath" over the demise of Yugoslavia.

Works Cited

Abbott, Scott. "Handke's Yugoslavia Work." *The Works of Peter Handke: International Perspectives*. Edited by David N. Coury and Frank Pilipp. Riverside, CA: Ariadne, 2005. 359-86.

Abrahams, Fred. "My Testimony against Milosevic." <http://www.crimesofwar.org/onnews/news-milosevic3.html>.

Bayerisches Oberstes Landesgericht. *Urteil*. http://www.haguejusticeportal.net/Docs/NLP/Germany/Djajic_Urteil_23-5-1997.pdf.

Cleef, Alfred van. *De Verloren Wereld van de Familie Berberovic*. Amsterdam: Meulenhoff, 1994.

Danner, Allison Marsten, and Jenny S. Martinez. "Guilty Associations: Joint Criminal Enterprise, Command Responsibility, and the Development of International Criminal Law." *California Law Review* 93 (2005): 75-170.

Deichmann, Thomas, ed. *Noch einmal für Jugoslawien: Peter Handke*. Frankfurt a. M.: Suhrkamp, 1999.

Handke, Peter. *Abschied vom Neunten Land. Eine winterliche Reise zu den Flüssen Donau, Save, Morawa und Drina oder Gerechtigkeit für Serbien. Sommerlicher Nachtrag zu einer winterlichen Reise*. Frankfurt a. M.: Suhrkamp, 1998.

—. *Die Angst des Tormanns beim Elfmeter*. Frankfurt a. M.: Suhrkamp, 1972.

—. *Die Fahrt im Einbaum oder Das Stück zum Film vom Krieg*. Frankfurt a. M.: Suhrkamp, 1999.

—. *Gestern unterwegs: Aufzeichnungen November 1987 bis Juli 1990.* Salzburg: Jung und Jung, 2005.
—. *Die Hornissen.* Frankfurt a. M.: Suhrkamp, 1977.
—. *A Journey to the Rivers: Justice for Serbia.* Translated by Scott Abbott. New York: Viking, 1997.
—. *Der kurze Brief zum langen Abschied.* Frankfurt a. M.: Suhrkamp, 1974.
—. *Langsame Heimkehr.* Frankfurt a. M.: Suhrkamp, 1984.
—. *Noch einmal vom Neunten Land. Peter Handke im Gespräch mit Jože Horvat.* Klagenfurt: Wieser, 1993.
—. *Publikumsbeschimpfung.* Frankfurt a. M.: Suhrkamp, 1966.
—. "Rede zur Eröffnung der Belgrader Buchmesse am 21. Oktober 1997." In Deichmann, *Noch einmal*, 266-71.
—. *Rund um das Große Tribunal.* Frankfurt a. M.: Suhrkamp, 2003.
—. *Die Stunde der wahren Empfindung.* Frankfurt a. M.: Suhrkamp, 1978.
—. *Die Tablas von Daimiel: Ein Umwegzeugenbericht zum Prozess gegen Slobodan Milošević.* Frankfurt a. M.: Suhrkamp, 2006.
—. *Unter Tränen fragend: Nachträgliche Aufzeichnungen von zwei Jugoslawien-Durchquerungen im Krieg, März und April 1999.* Frankfurt a. M.: Suhrkamp, 2000.
—. *Die Wiederholung.* Frankfurt a. M.: Suhrkamp, 1992.
—. *Wunschloses Unglück.* Frankfurt a. M.: Suhrkamp, 1974.
Honig, Jan Willem, and Norbert Both. *Srebrenica:Record of a War Crime.* New York: Penguin, 1977.
Hukanović, Rezak. *The Tenth Circle of Hell: A Memoir of Life in the Death Camps of Bosnia.* Translated by Colleen London and Midhat Ridjanović and edited from the original by Ammiel Alcalay. London: Abacus, 1998.
Human Rights Watch, *Humanitarian Law Violations in Kosovo.* New York: Human Rights Watch, <http://hrw.org/doc/?t=pubs1998>.
Ignatieff, Michael. *Virtual War: Kosovo and Beyond.* New York: Metropolitan Books/Henry Holt, 2000.
Ingrao, Charles, ed. *The Scholars' Initiative: Confronting the Yugoslav Controversies.* <www.cla.purdue.edu/si>.
International Criminal Tribunal for the Former Yugoslavia. *Basic Legal Documents: Report of the Secretary-General Pursuant to Paragraph 2 of Security Council Resolution 808 (1993).* <http://www.un.org/icty/legaldoc-e/index.htm>.
—. *Cases and Judgments.* http://www.un.org/icty/cases-e/index-e.htm.
Januš, Gustav. *Gedichte 1962-1983.* Translated by Peter Handke. Klagenfurt: Wieser, 1983.

Judah, Tim. *Kosovo: War and Revenge*. 2nd ed. New Haven, CT: Yale UP, 2002.

—. *The Serbs: History, Myth, and the Destruction of Yugoslavia*. 2nd ed. New Haven, CT: Yale UP, 2000.

Lauer, Reinhard. "Das Wüten der Mythen." *Das jugoslawische Desaster: Historische, sprachliche und ideologische Hintergründe*. Edited by Reinhard Lauer and Werner Lehfeldt. Wiesbaden: Harrasowitz, 1995. 107-48.

Laughland, John. *Travesty: The Trial of Slobodan Milošević and the Corruption of International Justice*. London: Pluto, 2007.

Lipuš, Florjan. *Der Zögling Tjaž*. Translated by Peter Handke and Helga Mračnikar. Klagenfurt: Wieser, 1981.

Malcolm, Noel. *Kosovo: A Short History*. 2nd ed. London: Pan Books, 2002.

Milošević, Slobodan. "Rede auf dem Amselfeld vom 28. Juni 1989." http://www.die-kommenden.net/dk/bn-ai/gerechtigkeit_fuer_slobodan_milosevic.htm.

Pervanic, Kemal. *The Killing Days: My Journey through the Bosnian War*. London: Blake, 1999.

"Peter Handke." <http://en.wikipedia.org/wiki/Peter_Handke>.

Silber, Laura, and Allan Little. *The Death of Yugoslavia*. Rev. ed. London: Penguin, 1996.

Weschler, Lawrence. "High Noon at Twin Peaks." *The New Yorker*, 18 August 1997: 28-35.

—. "Inventing Peace." *The New Yorker*, 20 November 1995: 56-64.

—. "Revising Serbia." *The New York Times* 6 April 1997.

———. *Vermeer in Bosnia*. New York: Vintage, 2005.

Zülch, Tilman, ed. *Die Angst des Dichters vor der Wirklichkeit: 16 Antworten auf Peter Handkes Winterreise nach Serbien*. Göttingen: Steidl, 1996.

Notes

[1] While underway in Slovenia ten years later Handke noted in his diary *Yesterday Underway* [*Gestern Unterwegs*], "With the karst (August 1978) my New Life began—it's just that I can't realize it beyond writing, walking, looking (2 Sept. 1988)" (220). The formulation "New Life" is presumably an allusion to Dante's *Vita nova*.

[2] Handke's initial translation, done together with Helga Mračnikar, was the novel *Der Zögling Tjaž*, by Flojan Lipuš, published in 1981. His translation of Gustav Januš's *Gedichte 1962-1983* appeared two years later.

[3] The essay "Dreamer's Farewell to the Ninth Land. A Reality That Has Passed: Remembering Slovenia" ["Abschied des Träumers vom Neunten Land. Eine Wirklichkiet, die vergangen ist: Erinnerung an Slowenien"] first appeared in the *Süddeutsche Zeitung* on 27/28 July 1991. It then appeared later that year as a Suhrkamp volume illustrated with facsimiles from Handke's notebooks dealing with Slovenia. Finally it appeared without its lengthy subtitle and the illustrations as the first essay in the 1998 collection *Abschied des Träumers* that includes his two polemically charged travel narratives of 1976 on the Yugoslavian wars to that point. Page references in this paper are to the 1998 version.

[4] See the title interview in *The Ninth Land Once More* [*Noch einmal vom Neunten Land*], esp. 99-100. The very title of this volume, which also includes two interviews that the Slovenian cultural journalist Jože Horvat had conducted with Handke in Salzburg in 1987 and in Lipica, Slovenia, in 1988, suggests that Handke and his well-subsidized Austro-Slovenian publisher, Lojze Wieser, were interested in overcoming the negative reaction to which the essay had led.

[5] Under the general editorship of Purdue University historian Charles Ingrao, specialists on Yugoslavia, including scholars from all the former Yugoslavian republics, have collaborated on a comprehensive history of the Yugoslavian wars of the 1990s. While two of the eleven topics are still in preparation, the rest of this informative project, *The Scholars' Initiative: Confronting the Yugoslav Controversies*, is currently available at <www.cla.purdue.edu/si>. At the end of 2008 a book version of this project, *Confronting the Yugoslav Controversies: A Scholars' Initiative*, edited by Ingrao and Thomas Emmert will be published jointly by Purdue University Press and the US Institute of Peace Press. For the record, there were a total of four wars starting with the "ten-day" war between Slovenia and the Yugoslavian Peoples Army that began on 27 July 1991. The second war, between Croatia and Serbia and fought entirely on the territory of the Republic of Croatia, began in earnest in July 1991 and continued intermittently amid multiple ceasefires until November 1995. The third war, fought entirely on the territory of the Republic of Bosnia-Herzegovina, began in earnest in early April 1992 and continued until November 1995. It involved major interventions from Croatia and Serbia and for a period in 1993 pitted Croatian and Muslim forces against each other instead of jointly against Serb forces. The fourth war between NATO and the Republic of Yugoslavia took place from 24 March to 10 June 1999 over the issue of Serbia's repressive responses during 1998 and early 1999 to the actions of the Kosovo Liberation Army.

[6] Even before the essay appeared as a book in German, a collection of sixteen critical responses by a diplomat, a filmmaker, a human rights activist, and writers and journalists from Bosnia, Croatia, England, France, Germany, and Serbia had appeared under the title *The Poet's Anxiety in the Face of Reality* [*Die Angst des Dichters vor der Wirklichkeit*], a play on the title of Handke's *The Goalie's Anxiety at the Penalty Kick* [*Die Angst des Tormanns beim Elfmeter* (1970)]. Three years

later Thomas Deichmann edited the volume titled *Noch einmal für Jugoslawien: Peter Handke*, and the individual contributions largely defend Handke's position. Indeed, the volume includes several interviews with Handke as well as his "Address on the Opening of the Belgrade Book Fair on 21 October 1997" ["Rede zur Eröffnung der Belgrader Buchmesse am 21. Oktober 1997"], in which he anticipates the notion of "tragic guilt" in conjunction with the Yugoslavian wars that he later sees in Milošević (167). For a critical response in English to *A Journey to the Rivers* on its publication, see Lawrence Weschler's review "Revising Serbia." Scott Abbott, the translator of that volume, has recently published the scholarly article "Handke's Yugoslavia Work" defending Handke's "critical dialectics."

[7] Handke sparked yet another round of controversy by attending and speaking briefly in German and Serbian at the funeral of Slobodan Milošević in Požarevac, Serbia, on 18 March 2006. An English translation of his remarks in Serbian, based on a letter he wrote to the French daily *Nouvel Observateur*, is consistent with previous articulations of his solidarity with Yugoslavia (still consisting of Serbia and Montenegro at the time of funeral), Serbia, and Milošević: "The world, the so-called world, knows everything about Yugoslavia, Serbia. The world, the so-called world, knows everything about Slobodan Milošević. The so-called world knows the truth. This is why the so-called world is absent today, and not only today, and not only here. I don't know the truth. But I look. I listen. I feel. I remember. That is why I am here today, close to Yugoslavia, close to Serbia, close to Slobodan Milošević" (<http://en.wikipedia.org/wiki/Peter_Handke>). Further discussion of these remarks and their multifaceted reception in France and Germany is beyond the scope of this paper.

[8] In *Virtual War*, a book that takes a critical look at the war over Kosovo and the lukewarm commitment of Western governments to human rights in the course of the Yugoslavian wars, Michael Ignatieff addresses the issue of Louise Arbour's alleged collusion with NATO governments in bringing about the indictment of Slobodan Milošević. He concludes that, using the growing leverage of her office, she was given some intelligence information that made the indictment possible but brought the indictment itself against the wishes of key figures in the US foreign policy establishment in order to forestall a "Houdini-like diplomatic escape by Milosevic" (125).

[9] The texts of the indictments of Slobodan Milošević, including that related to the war in Croatia, and their multiple modifications can be found under his name at <http://www.un.org/icty/cases-e/index-e.htm>.

[10] The words in square brackets in this passage are my emendations of the published English translation of *A Journey to the Rivers* by Scott Abbott. Handke's use of the German term *Internationaler Gerichtshof* here and in the sequel publication that I quote below in my own translation in the absence of an existing English translation refers to the International Criminal Tribunal for the Former Yugoslavia and not, as Abbott mistakenly assumes, to the International Court of Justice. The latter, also located in the Hague, deals with disputes between states rather than the crimes of individuals in the area of international humanitarian law.

[11] The general in question was presumably Djordje Djukic, who at the time of his indictment by the Tribunal on 29 February 1996 held the rank of Lieutenant General in both the Bosnian Serb Army and the Yugoslavian Army. During the war in Bosnia and at the time of his arrest he served as a member of the main staff of the Bosnian Serb Army and as assistant commander for Logistics to Ratko Mladic. He was initially indicted for a crime against humanity and a violation of the laws and customs of war in connection with the shelling of the civilian population of Sarajevo. Had he been in better health, other indictments might well have followed since he played a central role in coordinating Serbian and Bosnian Serb military actions. He was given a health release on 24 April and died 18 May 1996. For greater detail see <http://www.un.org/icty/cases-e/index-e.htm> under Djukic.

[12] Page references are to the German text published in book form in 2003 as *Rund um das Große Tribunal*. This version includes a segment on the war-related trial of Bosnian Serb Novislav Djajic in a Bavarian court in 1997 and the account of a visit to the Kosovo town of Dečani west of Priština in June 1996 (52-59) that were not included in the original publication of the essay.

[13] An expanded version of the essay appears as the title essay of Weschler's book *Vermeer in Bosnia*. Page references in this paper are to the original publication of the essay.

[14] For two distinct accounts of the Omarska camp by survivors see Kemal Pervanic, *The Killing Days. My Journey through the Bosnian War*, and Rezak Hukanovic, *The Tenth Circle of Hell: A Memoir of Life in the Death Camps of Bosnia*.

[15] Handke incorporates this story in an utterance of his Second International in *Travel in the Dugout Canoe* (67). Although he does not challenge the veracity of the story, he does use it to imply that journalists covering the war relied on such stories to make their living by having his character turn to the audience and note, "Such stories were my daily bread."

[16] In "High Noon at Twin Peaks," written nearly two years later following a visit to the Republika Srpska during summer 1997, Weschler notes in a far less optimistic vein that, at the time of his visit, the Tribunal's intention to help bring about a lasting peace in the former Yugoslavia was not recognized among Bosnian Serbs despite their impoverishment at the hands of those indicted: "It has been lost on no one that many of those indicted in The Hague emerged from the war as the leading mafiosi or security or political figures in the new order, whereupon they took to feasting on their own. One might think that, among the victims of their current depredations, this would have lent credence to the tribunal's charges, but just the opposite has tended to occur. The indictments get portrayed as an aspersion against all Serbs—an especially ironic charge, since the tribunal has repeatedly insisted that it is endeavoring to establish individual culpability precisely as a way of dispelling imputations of collective guilt. That message is clearly not getting through. Even more chillingly, the indictments are repeatedly cast as a potential threat to each and every individual Serb" (32). In the ten years that have passed since Weschler's second piece was published, almost all of the then indicted

Bosnian Serbs, as well as former Yugoslavians from the other ethnic groups, have been brought to trial. Whether this has led to a change in the way Bosnian Serbs perceive the Tribunal I am not in a position to judge. The unfortunate exceptions continue to be the former civilian and military leaders of the Bosnian Serbs, Radovan Karadzic and Ratko Mladic, the latter of whom continued to receive his military pension as recently as 2006 and is almost certainly being protected by the Serbian military.

[17] According to its Web site (<http://www.wirtschaft-westfalen.de/>) the Economic Society awards the prize, established in 1998 on the 350th anniversary of the Peace of Westphalia, "in recognition of individuals who have dedicated themselves to European integration and peaceful coexistence in the world. In a second category the prize is awarded youth or youth groups who through their actions have become a model for conciliation and peace."

[18] For a detailed and, in my view, nonpartisan report on the criminal actions of Yugoslavian government forces *and* those of the Kosovo Liberation Army from February to early September 1998, see the October 1998 report of Human Rights Watch, *Humanitarian Law Violations in Kosovo*, available in printed form and online at http://hrw.org/doc/?t=pubs1998. It is summarized at that site as follows: "This report documents serious breaches of international humanitarian law, the rules of war, committed in Kosovo from February to early September 1998. The vast majority of these abuses were committed by Yugoslav government forces of the Serbian special police (MUP) and the Yugoslav Army (VJ). Under the command of Yugoslav President Slobodan Miloševic, government troops have committed extrajudicial executions and other unlawful killings, systematically destroyed civilian property, and attacked humanitarian aid workers, all of which are violations of the rules of war. The Albanian insurgency, known as the Kosova Liberation Army (KLA, or UÇK in Albanian), has also violated the laws of war by such actions as the taking of civilian hostages and by summary executions. Although on a lesser scale than the government abuses, these too are violations of international standards, and should be condemned."

[19] See, e.g., Reinhard Lauer, "Das Wüten der Mythen," especially his discussion of the myth of the Serbian Prince Marko (130-39).

[20] These means included the use of tanks and armored cars in front of the Kosovo Assembly building in Priština on 23 March 1989, the day of a decisive vote on the autonomy issue. For an account of the revocation of the autonomy of Kosovo in the larger context of Kosovar-Serbian relations see the chapter "Kosovo after the Death of Tito: 1981-1997" in Malcolm, *Kosovo: A Short History*, 334-56. In this paper, following the practice of Tim Judah in *Kosovo: War and Revenge* (xix) , I use the term Kosovar to refer to the ethnic Albanian residents of Kosovo in order to distinguish them from Albanians resident in Albania itself.

[21] The text of the indictment of Zejnil Delalic, Zdravko Mucic, Hazim Delic, and Esad Landzo and the judgments rendered in their case can be found under any of their names at <http://www.un.org/icty/cases-e/index-e.htm>.

[22] Since Handke mistakenly places the Čelebići Camp southeast of Sarajevo "in the vicinity of Foča near the 'border' with Montenegro" (29), it is probable that he is

far too expansive in his characterization of the area at issue. In fact, as the indictment of the Čelebići Prison Camp personnel makes clear, the Camp was located in a former compound of the Yugoslavian Peoples Army in the village of Čelebići on the periphery of Konjic, to the southwest of Sarajevo.

[23] As of November 2005, when I spent a week observing the trials in progress at the Tribunal, the practice of hanging judges' portraits in the stairwell leading up to the trial chambers had been discontinued.

[24] For Abrahams' own view of his testimony against Milošević and his thoughts about the Tribunal, see "My Testimony against Milošević" <http://www.crimesofwar.org/onnews/news-Milošević3.html>. The same site contains links to the transcripts of the Milošević trial on June 3 and 4, the days Abrahams testified. The transcript for June 4 includes the testimony of Argron Mehmeti, the unnamed young Kosovar from Račak whom Handke treats next. Abrahams' commentary includes a revealing reference to the "protected" witness who refused to testify on June 3, a refusal that Handke noted in his essay without indicating what was at issue (43, 51). According to Abrahams, the man in question had transported Kosovars killed by Serbian forces to a site in Serbia and feared for his life if he were to testify to that fact. This would explain his utterance that he had "already suffered enough."

[25] The same version of the incident underlies an extended exchange between two characters in the play *Travel in the Dugout Canoe* (48-52) about a well-meaning bystander who tries to mediate conflict between his ethnically polarized neighbors but fails when "strangers, militia and killers from far away, intervene" (49) and war breaks out. In the actual incident, however, the "militia and killers" were not strangers but local Bosnian Serbs working in concert with the Yugoslavian Peoples Army.

[26] Except for page 99, the 133-page verdict is available at <http://www.haguejusticeportal.net/Docs/NLP/Germany/Djajic_Urteil_23-5-1997.pdf>. The events of 22 June 1992 and Djajic's role in them are presented on 31-41, but the next fifty-seven pages examine and evaluate the available evidence, including Djajic's pretrial statements, and are no less important to a full understanding of the case. Djajic did not testify at the trial itself. His former Muslim neighbors who testified at the trial did see him as more of a fellow traveler than an aggressive perpetrator, but one who did wear a uniform and carry weapons.

[27] As a listing of their names and birth years makes clear (32-33), the fifteen men came from six families and ranged in age from 22 to 67. Eight of the fifteen men were older than forty and thus well beyond the age of "young men," a term that Handke uses repeatedly to describe the group. The number of men taken into custody that evening is consistent with the threat of the local military commander, identified by the Bavarian court as a man named Vukovic, to kill five Muslims for every Serb killed in acts of resistance (27). The threat had been uttered in April at a time when all Muslim men in the village were placed under house arrest, and it was Vukovic who gave the specific order to take the fifteen Muslim villagers into custody the evening of 22 June 1992. It appears likely that this local commander is Zoran Vukovic, who was initially indicted by the Hague Tribunal on 26 June 1996

along with seven other Bosnian Serbs from the Foča area for the torture and rape of Muslim girls and women. In the indictment he is identified as a subcommander of the military police and a paramilitary leader in Foča. Although never implicated in the incident on the Drina bridge, he was eventually brought to trial at the Hague Tribunal, found guilty of multiple counts of torture and rape, and received a sentence of twelve years in prison on 12 June 2002.

[28] In his first essay on the Tribunal he noted that the attack had occurred "several weeks ago" (58) and dates his trip to the monastery in "early summer" (57). In retelling the story in his second essay (see note 30), he dates his presence in Kosovo to "late spring 1996" and the attack on the bistro as having occurred "three months earlier." He also links it to two similar attacks that same night resulting in five deaths overall, attacks with which, as he notes ironically, "the Albanian freedom fighters gave their first concerted signal" (47).

[29] Judah, *Kosovo: War and Revenge*, gives a detailed and nuanced account of the history of Kosovar/Serbian relations, especially from 1945 onward, and in the process deals with the many factors leading to the war over Kosovo. In his introduction Judah presents his overall perspective on the war: "The idea of this book is to follow the conflict from its origins, especially in the 1980s and 1990s, to the immediate aftermath of the NATO bombing campaign. It is also to show how this was, to a great extent, a war of human error. That is to say that, of course with the benefit of hindsight, we can now see just how haphazard were the steps that led to war. How all of the leading actors, in Serbia and in the West, made mistake after mistake, hoping that somehow everything would be all right in the end. Of course, it was not to be" (xxvi).

[30] In his "Preface to the Second Edition" of *Kosovo: A Short History*, Malcomb notes that "in the two years up to mid-January 1998, the KLA claimed to have killed five policemen, five other Serbian officials, and eleven Albanian 'collaborators' with the Serbian regime. Other European countries had experienced similar small-scale campaigns of politically motivated violence, and had dealt with them using normal police methods. But the response of the Serbian authorities in this case was hugely disproportionate; and it was the nature of this response which, more than anything else, pushed Kosovo into war" (xxx).

[31] Page references to the essay are to the book version published by Suhrkamp in late 2006.

[32] The legal basis for the establishment of an international tribunal "for the prosecution of persons responsible for the serious violations of international humanitarian law committed on the territory of the former Yugoslavia since 1991" is discussed in some detail in Part I of the *Report of the Secretary-General [of the United Nations] Pursuant to Paragraph 2 of Security Council Resolution 808 (1993)* presented to the Security Council on 3 May 1993. The text of Part I as well as that of the entire *Report* is available at <http://www.un.org/icty/legaldoc-e/index.htm>. The crux of the argument is set forth in the following paragraphs:

> 22. In the light of the disadvantages of the treaty approach in this particular case and of the need indicated in resolution 808 (1993) for an effective and expeditious implementation of the decision to establish an international

tribunal, the Secretary-General believes that the International Tribunal should be established by a decision of the Security Council on the basis of Chapter VII of the Charter of the United Nations. Such a decision would constitute a measure to maintain or restore international peace and security, following the requisite determination of the existence of a threat to the peace, breach of the peace or act of aggression.
23. This approach would have the advantage of being expeditious and of being immediately effective as all States would be under a binding obligation to take whatever action is required to carry out a decision taken as an enforcement measure under Chapter VII.
24. In the particular case of the former Yugoslavia, the Secretary-General believes that the establishment of the International Tribunal by means of a Chapter VII decision would be legally justified, both in terms of the object and purpose of the decision, as indicated in the preceding paragraphs, and of past Security Council practice.28. In this particular case, the Security Council would be establishing, as an enforcement measure under Chapter VII, a subsidiary organ within the terms of Article 29 of the Charter, but one of a judicial nature. This organ would, of course, have to perform its functions independently of political considerations; it would not be subject to the authority or control of the Security Council with regard to the performance of its judicial functions. As an enforcement measure under Chapter VII, however, the life span of the international tribunal would be linked to the restoration and maintenance of international peace and security in the territory of the former Yugoslavia, and Security Council decisions related thereto.

A secondary claim that Handke advances against the legality of the Tribunal is that its judicial power "was transferred to it from the very beginning by those forces and powers that in the wars and above all in the last of the wars, the NATO bombardment of the 'Federal Republic of Yugoslavia,' were partisan; and that as a consequence also the Tribunal, paid for by one of the warring parties—and parallel groups of parties—, is itself partisan from the start, through and through, already in its origin" (30). While such impassioned argumentation may at first blush seem persuasive, it elides the fact that Russia and China, not to mention a host of other non-NATO countries, were members of the UN Security Council when it passed the resolution authorizing the establishment of the Tribunal in May 1993.

[33] As I have argued above, Handke's polemically motivated misrepresentation of Lawrence Weschler's essay on the Tribunal led in his first essay to a skewed view of that body, its then presiding President, Antonio Cassese, and Weschler himself. Thus Handke's description of the workings of the Tribunal in its "lesser" chambers in the second essay (20) is readily compatible with Weschler's early description, except for the latter's inclusion of technology, of how the Tribunal worked on the case of Dusko Tadic.

[34] Handke is not alone in raising concerns about the use of the concept "joint criminal enterprise" (JCE) as a basis for indictments before the Tribunal. In "Guilty Associations: Joint Criminal Enterprise, Command Responsibility, and the

Development of International Criminal Law," American legal scholars Allison Danner and Jenny Martinez note its growing importance at the Tribunal since its first explicit use in an indictment on 25 June 2001: "Of the forty-two indictments filed between that date and January 1, 2004, twenty-seven (64%) rely explicitly on JCE. Furthermore, as we discuss in the context of transitional [justice] trials, JCE is now used by international prosecutors as the method of choice for targeting senior military and political leaders. Slobodan Milošević, for example, stands accused of participating in three massive JCEs" (107). Danner and Martinez discuss the two liability doctrines of joint criminal enterprise and command responsibility in relation to the three legal traditions they see informing contemporary international criminal law: domestic criminal law, international human rights law, and transitional justice. They summarize their suggestions for reform in the use of these two liability doctrines as follows: "We suggest that international judges should ensure that JCE adheres more closely to the criminal law culpability principle, that command responsibility continue to do so, and that international prosecutors should not forego command responsibility in preference to JCE. These shifts in law and practice will enhance the legitimacy of the international criminal trials and better instantiate the goals of the human rights and the transitional justice models" (149-50).

[35] See Tim Judah, *The Serbs*, 29-34, for an overview of the battle, its participants, and its less-than-dramatic consequences in its day.

[36] In Serbo-Croatian Milošević said, "Niko ne sme da vas bije." Handke's German translation, "Niemand soll euch mehr schlagen!" (37), adds a time frame and uses the modal *sollen* instead of *dürfen*. The sentence is rendered somewhat differently in the BBC documentary *The Death of Yugoslavia* and the accompanying book of the same title by Silber and Little. In the book it reads, "No one should dare to beat you" (37). It adds a dramatic moment allowed by the Serbian infinitive *smite*, but one that in combination with "should" is clearly overstated, especially in the further amplified subtitle of the BBC documentary version: "No one shall ever dare beat you again." Neither Handke nor John Laughland (*Travesty: The Trial of Slobodan Milošević*), who rightly disputes the translation in the BBC documentary on the basis of Milošević's correction of it at his trial ("No one should beat you") but wrongly dismisses the nationalistic implications of the remark (129) given its charged context, mention the related speech that Milošević gave to those assembled inside the meeting nor the strongly affirmative reaction of the Serbs inside and outside the meeting hall to what they heard. Instead of being calmed down, as Laughland would have it, the crowd outside began to chant "Slobo, Slobo!" According to Miroslav Šolević, a local Serb leader who had helped to organize the protest, "'This sentence enthroned him as a tsar'" (Silber/Little, 38). For a longer excerpt of the speech see Judah, *Kosovo*, 53. I am indebted to Mark Lauersdorf, University of Kentucky, and Mira Miladinovic Zalaznik, University of Ljubljana, for helping me with the accurate rendering of Milošević's seemingly simple utterance into English and German respectively.

[37] Since I do not have access to the original Serbo-Croatian text, I have translated the passage from a German Web site that presents itself as supporting justice for

Slobodan Milošević and goes out of its way to correct misleading German translations: <http://www.die-kommenden.net/dk/bn-ai/gerechtigkeit_fuer_slobodan_Milošević.htm>. Judah (*Kosovo*, 56) offers a compatible translation of part of the same passage taken from Silber and Little, *Death*, 72. However, both Judah and Silber and Little fail to address the multifaceted rhetoric of the Milošević speech. Its many thinly veiled appeals to Serb nationalism based on the recent revocation of the autonomy of the provinces of Kosovo and Vojvodina as well as the Kosovo battle myth itself are coupled with invocations of progressive multiculturalism and shared prosperity among all the peoples of Yugoslavia. Though it clearly eludes both Handke and Laughland (*Travesty*, 128) the speech's carefully calculated duality presumably was not lost on Milošević's Yugoslavian listeners, especially the Slovenians who had openly opposed the revocation of Kosovo's autonomy and those Kosovars who had begun losing their jobs as a result of that revocaton.

[38] Honig/Both, *Srebrenica: Record of a War Crime*, 77-78.

[39] Honig/Both, *Srebrenica*, 81. The authors and Handke's local informants do agree on a crucial issue: "Between May 1992 and January 1993 forces from Srebrenica attacked and destroyed scores of Serb villages. The attacks outraged the Serbs. A great deal of the animosity towards the men of Srebrenica stems from this period" (79).

CHAPTER SIXTEEN

MADNESS ON A GRAND SCALE: PORTRAYAL OF TERRORISM IN AUSTRIAN LITERATURE AFTER 9/11

GÜNTER HAIKA

"so now I have a life. a real life."[1]

With this realization, Austrian born writer Kathrin Röggla opens her book about the terror attacks on the World Trade Center. Does it take an act of terrorism to get a life? Does one have to witness the atrocities of international terrorism, to have a life? Or should one ask: What is "a life"? What is "a real life" in the early 21st century?

While it will not be possible to answer these questions, this essay will attempt to answer a seemingly much simpler question: How did Austrian literature react to the terror acts of the new millennium? Has the most recent world history – and the history this essay will refer to could well be called a history of madness – been noticed by Austrian writers? And if so: How can a gross attack become the subject of a literary project?

To answer the second set of questions, it seems that Austrian writers and Austrian literature in the late 20th and early 21st centuries have been too busy still working on WWII to ever incorporate too many international historic events. In Austria, *Vergangenheitsbewältigung*, the coming to terms with WWII and Austrian involvement in it in particular, has been present since the late 1940s, refueled by the Waldheim affair in the 1980s, and this 60-year old topic still lingers on, as if not allowing for any rivaling political or historical issues in Austrian literature. The terror attacks of the early 21st century are no exception; however, there are at least two works in which two Austrian writers address 9/11 directly or indirectly, a book of essays and a story.[2] Both of these texts show, in very different ways, how mad – if madness be defined as what is outside the norm – the world has become after September 11, or, rather, how the norms have changed since then, giving what used to be the unusual a new status.

Aforementioned Kathrin Röggla was a witness to the terror attacks of 9/11 in New York; she lived only about a kilometer (just over half a mile) away from the World Trade Center. Her book *really ground zero* cannot be identified in the classical terminology of literature. It is neither a fictitious story, nor an essay, nor a diary. Rather, it is all of the above and none; but it is, most likely, not important to establish its literary "status" in the context of this essay. Discussing it will therefore concentrate on the essence of the text, a rather spontaneous account of New York and the USA, which came out as early as December, 2001.

Paulus Hochgatterer is a writer and child psychiatrist in Vienna. The plot of his fictional story *Eine kurze Geschichte vom Fliegenfischen* of 2003 tells the events of a day three psychiatrists take off to go fly fishing; it is a birthday present to one of them. Like most of Hochgatterer's prose before that, it thrives on its precise language and intriguing use of violence both in the reality of the book and in the fantasies of the protagonists. Consequently, the book was mainly discussed as a well written story about a strange day off for three psychiatrists. However, this strange day happens to be Sept 11, 2001, and this should not be taken as a pure coincidence; the book will be read here for the first time as a parable on the events of 9/11.

An Eyewitness Account

Salzburg born writer Kathrin Röggla was spending a year in New York on a German grant when terror hit the city. Immediately after the events, she set out to investigate the feelings and emotions New Yorkers harbored, and probably also to re-establish her own views after this experience. She tried to approach the horrors in a collection of texts she thus compiled – they may be called essays, short stories, diary entries; or simply notes. Journalistic or sensationalist style is far from her, though, and this has led some reviewers to call these 22 texts "detached". However, one must take into account that these texts were written in Manhattan, at the time when the events described happened; they are a rather immediate response or reaction to what Röggla witnessed, and although they may sound detached to a casual reader, they rather show shock and disbelief at first, just like many other accounts we have from these days; later, when they portray the American reaction, they betray the author's astonishment and another form of disbelief,. One huge difference between Röggla's texts and other texts from commentators is that Röggla mostly tries – not always successfully – not to sound judgmental or biased; another difference is that she writes from a European perspective, which means that her texts add to other texts about 9/11 and its aftermath the element of surprise about the American way to deal with the horrors, both on private and political levels. It is this different perspective which mostly accounts for failure to remain detached and unbiased. Most of all, though, Röggla is a writer of literature, her art uses words, and if one reads her texts carefully, one can see how difficult it must have been to find the appropriate words to say what she says in the way that she says it. Sometimes, she references photographs, which are included in the book, as if words fail to describe, and she resorts to images. The photography contained in the book is unusual; the lack of credit given for these images suggests that these, too, are by the author, and this is confirmed in passages where she alludes to herself taking pictures of the scenes on the street, or of the TV screen. She also mentions sound recordings she made, and occasionally quotes from sound recordings of interviews she made. So it is obvious that, like a journalist, Röggla used both visual and audio recordings of the scenes; she used these to confirm what she saw live, before she wrote about it. There is some journalistic approach, but this method of course can also help to achieve the "detachment" which would be lacking from a purely immediate, emotional approach.

The 22 texts are numbered, like chapters, and appear to be in chronological order as far as the events they talk about are concerned. But, referencing the aforementioned photographs and sound recordings, Röggla explicitly brings in the element of reviewing the situations, which may indicate that it is not necessarily the order the texts were written; and of course, reviewing also implies deliberation and afterthought. Still, she writes from the perspective of a witness who collects impressions of other witnesses and commentators, which are then being commented on. It should also be mentioned that Röggla always uses only lower case, and this is therefore not the attempt of the author to "miniaturize" the terror, as Christoph Bartmann speculated in his book review.[3]

The immediate reaction to the airplane strikes is, as quoted in the beginning of this essay, a very personal one. It is the witness's own life which becomes ascertained through the shock of the realization that she is near the scene of the terror attacks, near the crime scene, near the events that dominate world wide media attention.[4] This proximity is important; in text 3, Röggla explains that the flood of photographs shown of the scenes of the World Trade Center offer no routes to navigate, and she, like other witnesses, approach Ground Zero "to ensure themselves of their apperception"[5]. But following right away are observations confirming the approach of the Americans as something unusual to the eyes of a European observer. Text 4, with its English title "waving flags", comments on the spontaneous signs of American pride, such as an outbreak of patriotism, in which flags are shown, but also how the terrors are readily exploited by both political and religious leaders.

> and naturally on tv, there is also this reverend jerry falwell, a high ranking baptist, who holds the liberal forces of the country partially guilty for tuesday's terror acts; those, who want to legalize abortion, those, who claim rights for gay people, and those who banned prayer from schools, in short: those 'who have tried to secularize america.'[6]

The mingling of religious and political jargon happens everywhere, Röggla diagnoses, but she also warns that in some cases, this mingling stems from carefully planned motivations: "mr. bush's act, e.g., to almost break into tears in front of the camera [...] should be reviewed under psychological rather than religious aspects."[7] And also the next text, "mr. speaker", betrays her European astonishment, witnessing for the first time American political rituals and parliamentary procedure - a rather meaningless ceremonial affair, as can be concluded from the way Röggla remembers the tv broadcasts. For five pages, Röggla quotes – interspersed with some commentary – from the meeting of the Congress on Friday, September 14, in which "herr bush" should be given 40 billion US dollars for a military counteraction. "– gentlemen, the time is expired, the gentleman from california! / – mr. speaker, i am pleased to yield one minute to the gentleman from virginia, mr. davis. / – the gentleman from virginia is recognized for one minute."[8] In her commentary, Röggla finds it particularly noteworthy that these rituals never directly address the people in general, or the President, but an interim instance, the Speaker, and she concludes that this is "a ritual which i, with my central european apperception, would like to call juridical and religiously motivated."[9] It may not be readily obvious for an American reader who is used to the rituals Röggla rewrites in great detail here, why Röggla spends so much time on reporting them, and why she deems them "religiously motivated". The interest comes from the strange, even exotic of the procedures, for a spectator from Central Europe, where political debates are less formalized and do not follow traditions so much; in fact, the only European country known for its ritualized form of parliamentary debate is Great Britain, and their procedures are not well known in other parts of Europe, either. But the way Röggla reports the American procedures, they indeed resemble christian religious rites: they are litanies, hierarchically structured, and they are performed by an almost exclusive male group of representatives; the sequence in which she presents them – and she gives no indication that she may have deviated from the actual sequence – is reminiscent of a procession or a conduct.

It may be worth noting here that throughout the book, Röggla refers to George W. Bush as "mr. bush" or "herr bush", and she only uses "mr. president" or "president bush" when she is quoting other sources. While this may be common practice in some American press, such as the New York Times, it would not be identified as such by central European readers. Over here in Europe, this would certainly be seen as a message, and as an expression of the author's political opinions.

These political views of the author begin to play a bigger role soon, when the book turns to its main focus. As mentioned before, the book is much more about the "following" than about September 11. The shock about the actual attacks is only discussed in the first texts; it is soon replaced with the astonishment of the European witness to American reactions, and while it starts with the criticism of the rituals, it quickly moves on to the reactions which were not given full media attention. She talks to intellectuals in Greenwich Village, and learns from a literature professor that the problem of the political left in the USA lies in the fact that they are among the elites, but do not hold positions of power.[10] But she also sees a spontaneous protest of high school students mounting a sign for peace, and learns from a parent that "all the people who are sane are against the war."[11] While she shows this peace protest together with a peace march as rather rare, she is aware that in Europe, peace demonstrations are more frequent. Here again, it is quite obvious that the differences between American and European ideas are a major focal point of the book; different political ideas, and, as said, the different importance of the role of the political left in particular. Röggla then searches and finds exponents of American left-wing policies, or liberalism. For example, she talks to Eliot Weinberger, an essayist and author who, in the aftermath of 9/11, wrote about the "invention of the enemy," as Röggla cites. In this text, she quotes some of Weinberger's statements in the original, but leaves no doubt that she sympathizes with them, e.g. when Weinberger makes it clear that in actual legislature, terrorism is a "'criminal and not a military activity, and it is always a scenario of disaster when the military replaces the police.'" She goes on to include his views on the fate of the victims of the terror attacks, who are exploited by politicians, and whose ethical status have changed, as they are no longer seen as 'murder victims, they will now be portrayed, by both sides, as having died for a cause. by avenging their death with more death, bush and cheney and rumsfeld and rice and powell are murdering the identities and, above all, the innocence of our own dead as they murder abroad.'[12]

While these viewpoints of an American are quite similar to those that were frequently found in the European discussion at the time, Weinberger's statements were only distributed privately in the USA, because, according to himself, the left – i.e. the opposition to practically all governments in the US, as even the Democrats have backed the president – are given no room to publish, have no voice, and only a few (Susan Sontag and Edward Said are named explicitly) could publish freely in American papers such as the New York Times. One of the reasons for this situation Weinberger sees in the non-existence of feature pages in American print media.[13]

While Röggla met with Weinberger personally and quotes him extensively, she is equally impressed by another intellectual whom she only saw on TV, Norman Solomon, a syndicated journalist from the left side of the spectrum who was given time on the C-SPAN morning show on TV on October 15, answering questions of mostly aggressive, right-wing populist callers; at least it is this group of callers that Röggla gives most room in her account of this show. Text 12 is given Solomon's name, and Röggla quotes some of his answers to callers; thought provoking statements which in Röggla's view raise a certain doubt in the reader if they did get through to the callers. Röggla uses this episode as another piece of evidence that the voice of the left is not heard in the USA.

While it becomes quite obvious that Röggla regrets the wallflowery existence of liberal intellectualism in the USA, she then also reports her disappointment with a European intellectual. Text 18, one of the thematically wider reaching texts, and hence fittingly called "an expansion of spatial strategies"[14], talks among other issues about a lecture given by Jacques Derrida, and her surprise that he talks about forgiveness, the shoah, the Merchant of Venice and the term mercy, but never addresses the recent events. With that, she does not just mean 9/11, but also the war in Afghanistan, which at the time of Derrida's lecture had already begun.[15] Here Röggla's report must acknowledge that the European liberals set no example for dealing with the horrors, either. Rather, Derrida focuses his lecture on the planned topic. This is a disappointment for Röggla, but to her surprise it is not so disappointing for many in the audience, who after the lecture remember how charmingly Derrida apologized for his poor English rather than debate the content of his speech, and who seem to be proud that America was currently bombing Afghanistan. But, as the lecture took place in seminar room 405 of New York University, Röggla states that there, "it may well always circle around terminology, as is appropriate for the location."[16] Röggla could not have expressed her frustration and disgust with some of American academia, who remained uncritical to their country's actions overseas, any more clearly.

Returning the focus of her texts to the official USA, Röggla finds the lack of information given to the media by politicians appalling – an entire text called "secret america"[17] is only quoting the spokesman of the State Department, Mr. Boucher, saying nothing concrete, only what he cannot say to the press – yet in phone calls with her friends in Berlin, Röggla learns about parallels in Germany, how Fischer and Schröder and Schily similarly stonewall the press.[18] This is another disappointment for her trust that there was more outspokenness in Europe. But Röggla realizes that the "open society", although mentioned in an inflammatory way, is currently being "protected by being abolished"[19]. Here, obviously, she addresses one of the main changes of society and policies after 9/11: the loss of freedom under the pretence of its protection. This backdoor for totalitarianism opens through a lack of historic memory; and it is in a text discussing and reflecting an evening at the movies, watching David Lynch's *Mulholland Drive*, that brings Röggla to the realization that the most American aspect of the film is that it shows the "continued ignorance of a historic view," and America can be seen as the "country of the self-perpetuating ahistoric, the continued blocking out of the historical picture."[20]

Not surprisingly after the disparate experiences recorded and mostly reported with a negative undertone in texts 1 through 21, the concluding text 22, entitled "coffee to go", brings no real conclusion, but rather, perplexity. Röggla looks back at what she now calls a "heap of authenticity," and she does not know what caused her to compile this heap[21], or how she would get her bearings through it all. It seems that she shrank from facing the task of structuring the texts, and that she decided to pass this task on to her readers. She does write down a few findings and impressions, the most revealing of which is her "new light on pynchon – his absurdities close in on the term 'american daily life' at lightning speed!"[22] At the end, resignation is all that is left: "– but there is no such thing as an overview. / – so what."[23]

While she may not have given her readers an overview, she did, even with structural imbalance, explain through her own confusion how disparate the ideas before and after 9/11 have become, and how a group of leaders have abused the terror events to promote their ideas of control. The behavior of the politicians, the official reactions, the unanimous, bipartisan support for the President, and the willingness to follow his doctrines blindly, the lack of freedom for the political left to publish, and finally, the measures to cut back the rights that freedom-seeking people on both sides of the Atlantic fought for for centuries in the name of a new, protective freedom ... this is "really" ground zero in Röggla's book.

So why does Kathrin Röggla have a life now, a real life? While *really ground zero* never really provides an explanation for its opening statement, it could be fair to conclude that Röggla expresses a typical Central-European trauma here, i.e., the traumatic experience of Germans and Austrians born after WWII, who, as children, invariably had their questions about life and its meaning and hardship answered by the those who had experienced the war with statements such as: "You have not lived in the hard times, you weren't even born, you do not know anything", and sometimes followed by "and just pray you'll never have to live in such times" – a somewhat dismissive statement, but commonly spoken in a conciliatory tone. This accusation of not knowing because not having been around was, unfortunately, often abused by the older generation, those who had witnessed the war, to protect their war history. "You weren't around, you cannot talk about these things", was a common phrase to brush aside attempts of the younger generation to question their parents' and grandparents' involvement in the war; it was their way to not discuss their guilt. In Austria, the aforementioned Waldheim affair of 1986 gave a vivid example for the denial of an entire generation to talk about their guilt, when it was no other than the former UN Secretary General and Austrian presidential candidate and then President who stated: "I did only what was my duty", denying any personal responsibility and unwilling to understand the problematic of this attitude. It opened a new discussion, in which Austria's role in WWII was re-defined; for the first time, history as we understand it today was discussed in schools – and Röggla was a 15-year old high school student then.

Having been near this catastrophe, Röggla now has been through such really tough days; in the eyes of the European war generation, she now has a life, a real life. 9/11 may indeed be the defining incident for the early 21st century; the moment which, for future generations, will become the traumatic experience they did not share with their parents, and by the lack of which they will "not have a real life", like Röggla's generation "lacked" the WWII experience in Austria and Germany. But, as Röggla's "following" shows, the mostly uncritical acceptance of America's reaction to 9/11 – starting a war in Afghanistan (and in Iraq, but of course, this happened after Röggla published her book) – may become the truth to hide for those that lived through 9/11, when they will have to answer the questions of those who were born afterwards. Will they also say: "We only did our duty", as Röggla seems to suggest by drawing the parallel with Germany? Historically, Ground Zero might thus become the American equivalent of the German "Stunde Null", a term meaning the moment where entirely new causalities begin, which in post-war Germany has widely been defined as the time of capitulation after WWII.

A quite normal day: September 11, 2001

> When we meet, we know nothing about what is going to happen on this day, neither about that thing with the World Trade Center not that Julian was going to fall in the giant hogweed and then into the river. The weather is quite different from what we imagined, that we know.[24]

This opening paragraph of Paulus Hochgatterer's 2003 story *Eine kurze Geschichte vom Fliegenfischen* immediately links the story with September 11 Paulus Hochgatterer may not be well known outside of Austria and the German-speaking world, yet he is among the most remarkable and most highly acclaimed Austrian authors of our time. Remarkable not only because of his skills as a writer, but also because for him, writing is but a "second identity"[25], his other profession being a child psychiatrist. Therefore it is not surprising that most of his books deal with the world in a rather unusual way, his protagonists are often outsiders who defy any norms – not just in the sense of strange or peculiar, but in clinically defined terms – or they are, as in this book, representatives of the medical trade. The choice of his subjects and themes, and his competence in medical topics, has frequently led to misunderstandings among some readers, who tend to read his short stories as real accounts of his cases. The apparent reality of Hochgatterer's stories is furthered by his penchant to give them a well-defined historical reference of some sort. Like in the first sentence of this story, quoted above, it is not exact dates he provides, but references. These are often taken from the sports scene, a world-cup soccer game between Brazil and France (in *Carreta Carreta*, 1999) or a formula-1 grand prix race in Silverstone (in *Wildwasser*, 1997). Although all these references define the exact time and background of the story, they are marginal for the plot. For the understanding of the stories, it is totally irrelevant if the readers identify these background markers correctly or not. However, the reference in *Eine kurze Geschichte vom Fliegenfischen* is clearly more than just a casual time marker, and consequently, Hochgatterer makes sure this reference is understood by his readers. Unlike other texts by Hochgatterer, September 11 is not just mentioned as "that thing with the World Trade Center" at the beginning, but the story comes back to the tragic events of this day at the end, again, not outspokenly, but hinted at: "'You won't believe what happened'"[26]. This seems to indicate that unlike in his other books, a reading of *Eine kurze Geschichte vom Fliegenfischen* must not disregard the historical context of the story. The following discussion of the text will point out several more instances throughout the story which indicate a relation with the terror attacks in the USA; and that therefore, an interpretation of the text with regards to the events in New York and Washington, D.C., is not only possible, but necessary. Strangely, five years after the book was published, it seems that no similar interpretations have been offered before.[27]

Hochgatterer's text will here be understood as an attempt to deal with the events of this day in a work of fiction. It should be made clear from the beginning that the text itself does not openly invite this reading, or state any connection with the terrors in New York directly, other than the date. On the other hand, it would be all too easy to dismiss its historic dating as an account to answer the question: "Where were you when the twin towers came down?" But just like the three psychiatrists in the story search for hidden meanings in apparently normal behavior and constantly analyze everyone and everything, if the text itself is searched for hidden statements about the events in the USA on September 11, a few remarkable things can be revealed. Ultimately, the story could be read as a paraphrase of madness and how to deal with it: a day in the life of three psychiatrists, quite mad in itself, could be the spitting image of madness of a grander scale – the madness that led to the loss of almost 3000 lives in New York and Washington, D.C. on Sept 11, 2001.

Eine kurze Geschichte vom Fliegenfischen is the tale of three psychiatrists who take the day off on September 11, 2001, to go out fly fishing. They are friends, at least in common parlance; but the reader learns quickly that their friendship is undermined by distrust, suspicion, and jealousy – both on personal and professional levels. Or, maybe, their friendship is strengthened by their rivalries, as they tie them together. In a way, their friendship is no better or worse than what most friendships commonly are, and the term friends applied to them is a first warning that many, if not all terms in this book need to be investigated for their true, often hidden meaning.

The story fluctuates between the real and the imagined worlds of the narrator, one of the three psychiatrists and most likely not a reliable source. The fishing trip to the Alps south of Vienna is a birthday present for the narrator, who tells the story of this day as a wild mixture of events, fantasies, daydreams, and alternate histories.

Three psychiatrists: Robert Bauer, standing 2.01m tall, known and referred to as "der Ire", the Irishman[28], who has left the psychiatric hospital recently after disagreeing with its administrators; Julian is the director of a clinic for young psychotics, and is introduced as "someone who always feels threatened"[29]; and the narrator, nicknamed "Mesmer" by the Irishman because of his training in hypnosis, in his own account an "imaging neurotic without a camera"[30], meet at 8:30 – in local time, about the same time that the first indications that American Airlines flight 11 was being hijacked became known –, and pack their equipment into the car of the Irishman. It is the oldest car, and nobody knows exactly why it is this car they are taking. While the narrator brags about his new Canadian rod, the Irishman laughs, but it is a mischievous, filthy laughter. In fact, "Only psychoanalysts can laugh so filthy in that way."[31] In the car, the topic of their conversations quickly shifts to wind energy and Neo-Nazis, upon which Julian asks his companions not to discuss politics today. But even without talking about Nazis, an undertone of violence can hardly be overheard. As they stop to get breakfast, and park the car, the Irishman half blocks a handicapped parking zone, which reminds the narrator of his own tendencies to do so, but he puts the thought aside: "sometimes the ill simply wins."[32] At the turnstile into the restaurant, the Irishman and the narrator debate whether to tear it out or blow it up, and Julian scolds their aggressiveness. This first imagination of violence is a prelude to what is to follow, and "the ill" (das Böse) is already introduced as a potential, albeit occasional winner; even in a seemingly harmless fishing expedition; throughout the story, parallels between everyday's evil and evil on a grander, exceptional scale, are hinted at.

In the restaurant, their young waitress inspires their sexual imaginations and fantasies with her semi-transparent blouse and her lanugo; they begin to discuss the validity and reality of imagination. The Irishman takes the most radical position; he denies the validity of arguing whether something is true or not true, and calls imagination "a rather indicative matter. […] An Imagination has a higher content of reality than the simple acting out of alternatives."[33] It is immediately obvious to them that they all harbor erotic fantasies about the girl, and they work out a common daydream in which they invite her to go fishing with them, agreeing that she should wear a copper-red eiderdown jacket. They feed her from the flat palm of their hands, as if she were a horse; they put streamers in her earlobes replacing her pearl earrings; and lastly they shear lanugo from her forearms and make bait from it. In other words, they imagine human parts, being re-used.

As they continue their trip, they turn their minds to the task ahead, and it is revealed that the Irishman is not only the best fly fisher among them, but also the one who never kills the fish, because "to him, killing fish is probably something like bonking female clients."[34] On the other hand, the Irishman declares that hitting his former boss at the hospital would pass as something like vandalism before the law, because, as he says, some people have no soul, and hurting them is only damage to property.

When they reach their destination, the Salza river[35], they handle their fishing equipment with the utmost care. All the while talking about people they know from the psychiatric ward, they put on their gear. The Irishman wears a blue windbreaker; he thinks that with it, fish would not see him, because he would be indistinguishable from the sky from their perspective. Incidentally, looking up to the sky from now on becomes an often used perspective in the story.

As they start fishing, the imagery of the story evokes many parallels to the attack on the World Trade Center; these will be emphasized here. The narrator, who is passionate about but not very good at fishing, finds his concentration interrupted by fantasies of the waitress, who he sees at his side and in the forest and in the brook. In one of his fantasies, the narrator sees a cliff with niches, from where kingfishers shoot down like blue-green flashes. (90) Although the three have divided the brook between them, they occasionally cross each others' paths. Once when all three meet, Julian, with a helping hand from the Irishman, lands a big samlet. While the Irishman releases the hook and prepares to put the fish back in the water, Julian kills it with three big hits on the head with a metal rod. As the fish dies, the Irishman is furious. From the course of events, the reader could estimate that it is early afternoon by now, here in central Europe, which is about the time when in New York, the first plane hit the World Trade Center.

Julian pulls a knife and readies himself to disembowel the fish, but the tall Irishman is already over him; fists clenched, he has "a glance like a God."[36] Julian grabs the fish and sprints away the best he can, hobbling wildly – he has a semi-stiff knee after a botched surgery. The Irishman pursues him. Julian takes a turn into high plants, stumbles, and head-dives into the plants. It is acanthus, hogweed, and Julian breaks out in painful pustules immediately, his hands and face scarred with bright red swellings. It is no relief to him when the narrator later tells him that acanthus effectively burns the skin, but it reminds the reader of the fires in New York. The Irishman picks up the fish and helps Julian up, and while Julian tries to cool his face and hands off in the brook, the Irishman begins to disembowel the fish for him. As the narrator and the Irishman continue fishing, Julian stands in the middle of the river, under the cliff where he imagined the kingfishers earlier, but now small commercial figurines of Virgin Mary are in the niches, with rosaries in their folded hands, and the narrator sees all these figures plummeting head forward into the brook, as if they were on a chain, banging in the water – a strong parallel to people jumping of the WTC, likely with a prayer. Of course, the image of alike-looking, alike-acting figurines could also express religious fanaticism of the terrorists, or religious fanaticism in a more general sense, given that many Christian symbols are evoked.[37] In this sense, it might even be speculated that Hochgatterer alludes to the strong ties of religion and politics in the United States; to the blind following of the masses to their religious leaders, whatever religion or denomination they might be.

Julian slips and falls backwards, goes underwater, and in the narrator's fantasies, he, rather than helping him, casts his bait so that the swimmer floats right over Julian in the water, and he tells himself to later ask him if the reports on how fishing lines look to fish are correct. He imagines how Julian's wife Susanne and his two children will react to his death, his son Richard not knowing if he should grief or be happy there is one person less to tell him what not to do; a shock reaction after the unexpected demise of the father. The narrator's fantasies then shift to the girl again, and lastly, he finds himself fishing side by side with the Irishman. While they are not sure about Julian's whereabouts, they make no effort to look for him, and the reader is left wondering whether Julian is indeed dead or not – like the families and friends of many a victim were uncertain about the fate of their missing people. But as if nothing happened, the Irishman and the narrator keep fishing and talking about psychology and fish as phallic symbols, and only when they finally get back to the car it is revealed to the reader that Julian is alive and his burns are healing.

They stop in a country inn on the way home, when the Irishman remembers to call home. Mobile phones do not work in this valley – mobile phones were not working in the US on 9/11 –, so he goes outside to a public phone. When he comes back,

> he gives a strange impression. He shakes his head incessantly and is pallid; on the other hand, he is obviously taking great pains to suppress his laughter. 'You won't believe what happend', he says, 'you won't believe it.'[38]

Returning to both the laughter – is it again this mischievous, filthy laughter of a psychiatrist on the Irishman? – and the debate about the credibility of reality, and without concretely mentioning what happened, the author hints at the shock and disbelief people all over the world felt when the collapse of the twin towers was not only reported, but televised live. The speechlessness that befell the world in the hours after the attack is similar to the "phenomenon of incapacity to form emotional metaphors,", a subject they discussed at lengths earlier in the story.[39] When it became evident, with the crash of United Airlines 175, the second plane to hit the World Trade Center, that it was no accident but a terror attack, most viewers were aware right away that this event would have a lasting impact, it would change the world, and change the way we see and interpret the world. This realization caused the speechlessness; the feeling of relative safety and security had ended in this moment, and not only for Americans.

This being, by its title, a book about fishing, it naturally also talks about fish, and sometimes draws parallels between fish and people. When the narrator misses a fish, the Irishman persuades him to cast at the same spot again. This leads to a debate if this were indeed the best strategy. Since the fish did not feel the snap, the Irishman argues, it will come back, because it did not hurt. When the narrator calls this a rather weak and unreasonable argument, the Irishman counters: "why should fish be more reasonable than humans"[40], and the narrator finds this rather plausible. The lack of human reason is, of course, a link to the events in the USA. It has been said that no known interpretation has indicated the connections between the day fishing and the terror attacks of the same day. Therefore, passages where the parallels between the fishing disaster and the terror attacks become obvious include should be debated.

On several occasions in the book, the three protagonists discuss what constitutes certainty these days. While there is a consensus that certainty may not necessarily be an asset ("Some people source their certainty mainly in the steadiness of their misery"[41]), it is also made clear that people need certainty of their experience, and that they need to assure themselves of their experience particularly in times like ours, when change occurs "exponentially" faster than ever before[42], and the changes evoked by 9/11 are definitely among the fastest ever. They do, as it is concluded, "by learning to accept the speed of change itself as ascertained experience"[43]. It is noteworthy that these theories on change and experience are not the result of the discussions of the psychiatrists, but are accredited to Marlene, a philosopher, who is the Irishman's wife (who, invariably, the narrator has sexual desires for). Although the book has been criticized for its masculinity, and many reported quotes of the wives of the three men reinforce gender roles – the narrator wife, Lea, is remembered to have called fly fishing “nothing else but masculine group masturbating”[44] –, one must not overlook that one of the most important suggestions how to deal with change comes from a woman, and a philosopher rather than psychologist or psychiatrist.

In the aftermath of 9/11, commentators referenced the symbolism in targeting the WTC as a symbol for American and Jewish imperialism and wealth. But we should not forget that, of course, the WTC, as all skyscrapers, was also a phallic symbol. Florian Rötzer called this symbolism one of the main causes for the phenomenon that the fall of the towers drew more public attention than the attack on the Pentagon, the true symbol of US power.[45] Phallus symbols are also discussed between the protagonists, especially the Irishman and the narrator while Julian is missing. They explain that fish are phallic symbols and as such representatives of male sexual power. Here, there is a resemblance to Julian’s killing of the fish and the attack on the United States again. Julian takes three strikes on the head of the samlet, just as three planes flew into the symbols of American power; two into the World Trade Center, one in the Pentagon.

From a hospital ward psychiatrist’s perspective, trapped in their psychiatric clinic and the world within, the abnormal takes center stage, one sees everyone as a case, and it is quite unusual to accept rationality and relative sanity as the norm. Of course, “normal life is sick enough”[46]; but the Irishman has left the hospital, and he experienced how

> the moment you take your leave from the hospital to establish a practice privately, perspectives change; how you find yourself suddenly confronted with the fact that there is a high degree of sanity in the world; and how you have to learn to cope with this phenomenon.[47] […]

From his slightly more worldly perspective, the Irishman calls the most dangerous threat to all thinking humans stupidity and teamwork, and this combination could equally be identified as the underlying source of the terror acts of 9/11, or terror acts in general:

> Stupidity alone, i.e. this blend of cerebral inability and arrogance, is difficult enough to bear. But when it comes in a pack, and someone calls all this teamwork and markets it as a special achievement, so that one needs not deal with the tragedy of the matter, you can only get up and go.[48]

Protected within a group, stupidity, defined as a combination of mental deficiency and arrogance, and their – sometimes tragic – accomplishments no longer have to be questioned. It seems that Paulus Hochgatterer here wants to give his assessment of the minds of the terrorists, and how their teamwork protects the individual from any need to rationalize the deeds, and from any feeling of guilt. To enhance the statement about stupidity, the car radio simultaneously plays a song in which Tom Waits sings about Captain Ahab. If it were merely a reference to a story about the pursuit of a hated enemy, which eventually also kills the pursuer – like the terrorists were flying into their own death –, it would already be a strong commentary. However, this 1974 Tom Waits' song *Shiver me Timber* begins, fittingly, with the lines: "I'm leavin' my fam'ly / leavin' all my friends / my body's at home / but my heart's in the wind / where the clouds are like headlines / on a new front page sky". Clouds of smoke were pictured under the headlines after 9/11, of course, and the sky over Manhattan was on front pages all over the globe. Combining the Irishman's ideas on stupidity and teamwork with this song, Hochgatterer, who frequently mentions Waits' songs in his texts, gives a hint as to how his book could or should be read. Incidentally, for a music connoisseur like Hochgatterer referencing "Ahab" in a pop song may also evoke thoughts of the 1962 Ray Stevens' song "Ahab the Arab", establishing the geopolitical origin of the terrorists.[49] The conclusion that, facing stupidity in groups, one can only get up and leave, is, of course, unsatisfactory; yet, what other solutions are there?

The end of aforementioned quotation might well be representative for the intention of the entire book. Although there is, as was explained above, strong evidence that the author meant the book to be understood as a parable to the events of 9/11, it is rather hard to exactly define Hochgatterer's position. On the one hand, his book, read in this fashion, is the only literary text by an Austrian writer that tries to deal with the events of September 2001 with the means of literature as art. On the other hand, the disguise of most of these political and historical references leaves the reader with the – possibly more comfortable – option to overlook this reading. In this way, Hochgatterer's story follows closely the path of much earlier politically connected Austrian short stories such as Ilse Aichinger's *Spiegelgeschichte* and Marlen Haushofer's *Wir töten Stella*, which, while referencing in their days recent, uncomfortable Austrian politics, also offered their readers the comfortable choice to overlook these references and read the stories as works of pure art.

Hochgatterer's story returns to normalcy at the end, as far as the protagonists are concerned; the potential horror scenario is resolved peacefully when Julian re-appears, and when the three friends finally sit at the restaurant, their friendship seems neither weakened nor strengthened by the events of the day. Fitting this ending into the terror scenario is a stimulating exercise which could lead to shocking realizations. As quoted before, the Irishman announces the news to his friends, introducing it "you won't believe what happened", and suppresses his laughter. He is aware of what has happened in New York and Washington, yet his contradictory reactions – obvious shock in his face, but hardly concealed laughter – reflect the reactions to the terror attacks world wide. While the majority is shocked and "pallid", the suppressed laughter of those who welcome the fact that the world's only remaining superpower has been struck, is clearly audible. But looking at the reactions of his two companions, it should be understood that it may be implied, but is not made clear whether the Irishman actually does tell them what they will not believe, before their reactions are reported. With this ambiguity in mind, the reactions of the two others are quite interesting. Julian simply states: "Yeah, sometimes, weird things happen"[50], which of course could be an encouragement for the Irishman to continue and break the news, but, if it were following the already told news, this statement is surprisingly succinct. The narrator, hearing or awaiting the news, envisions the peaceful meeting of a grayling and bait, which end the story, fittingly, in the spirit of fly fishing. Had the news not been revealed, this could simply show total disinterest. After hearing about the terror attacks, it could be a vision of peace, of changed standards, or a continuation of the vision of the praying statues falling into the river. But it could also show disinterest or at least indifference, as well. Such indifference may even be justified. After all, these people are psychiatrists who deal with the norm and its deviations, and who in their work must frequently re-define the term normalcy. Even under the impression of these acts of terror, normalcy still exists; the norms are still valid. We may still dream of the marriage of fish and bait. Horrific events such as outbursts of international terrorism or personal violence (as in Colombine or Virginia Tech) are the exception still, although by the way media attention goes to the latter, we may come to think it were the other way round.

Two different authors, two very different approaches to 9/11 in form of a literary text. While Röggla's 2001 book never leaves a doubt about its purpose, Hochgatterer's 2003 story is cryptic and can be read quite differently. Röggla's uneasyness in the final chapter mirrors the situation two months after the attacks; Hochgatterer ends his book in an uncomforting equilibrium of commotion and calm. While Röggla extends the madness of 9/11 to its aftermath, Hochgatterer's imagery stays mainly with the attacks on America.

The two texts may not represent the one and only answer to the problem of dealing with such horrors and the underlying madness with the means of literature, but they are worthwhile and worthy attempts. While Röggla reveals some qualms about the success of her project both for herself and for potential readers, Hochgatterer never commented on interpretations which ignored the connections to 9/11. Both seem to understand that their texts are only, and can be only convergences, not conclusions.

Works Cited

Aichinger, Ilse. *Spiegelgeschichte*. Wien, 1949.

Bartmann, Christoph. rev. of Hochgatterer, Paulus. *Eine kurze Geschichte vom Fliegenfischen* for *Süddeutsche Zeitung* (online at: http://www.buecher.de/w1100485sz3596156467#product_slot_4, accessed Spring, 2007)

Lacour, Eva. rev. of Hochgatterer, Paulus. *Eine kurze Geschichte vom Fliegenfischen* (http://www.rezensionen.ch/buchbesprechungen/eine_kurze_geschichte_vom_fliegenfischen/3216306763.html, accessed Spring, 2007)

Gollner, Helmut. rev. of Hochgatterer, Paulus. *Eine kurze Geschichte vom Fliegenfischen* (online at: http://www.biblio.at/rezensionen/details.php3?mednr%5B0%5D=luk2004461&anzahl=1 and: http://www.kulturundsprache.at/service/Buchrezensionen/Buchrezensionen2004.shtml#hochgatterer, both accessed Spring, 2007)

Gollner, Helmut. *Die Wahrheit lügen. Die Renaissance des Erzählens in der jungen österreichischen Literatur*, Wien-Innsbruck-Bozen: Studien Verlag 2005.

Haushofer, Marlen. *Wir töten Stella*. Wien, 1958.

Hochgatterer, Paulus. *Eine kurze Geschichte vom Fliegenfischen.* Wien: Deuticke 2003.

—. *Die Süße des Lebens*. Wien: Deuticke im Zolnay-Verlag 2006.

—. *Wildwasser*. Wien: Deuticke 1997.

Moser, Samuel rev. of Hochgatterer, Paulus. *Eine kurze Geschichte vom Fliegenfischen* for *NZZ*, Zürich: (http://www.lyrikwelt.de/rezensionen/fliegenfischen-r.htm, accessed Spring, 2007)

Röggla, Kathrin. *really ground zero. 11. september und folgendes.* Frankfurt am Main: Fischer, 2001.

Rötzer, Florian. *Phallische Hochhäuser*. In *Telepolis*, Sept 26, 2003. (online at: http://www.heise.de/tp/r4/artikel/15/15722/1.html, accessed Spring, 2007)

Stevens, Ray. *Ahab the Arab*. First released on *1,837 Seconds of Humor*, 1962.

Streeruwitz, Marlene. *Entfernung*. Frankfurt am Main: Fischer 2006.

Thuswaldner, Anton. rev. of Hochgatterer, Paulus. *Eine kurze Geschichte vom Fliegenfischen* for *Die Presse*, Wien, (http://www.lyrikwelt.de/rezensionen/fliegenfischen-r.htm, accessed Spring, 2007)

Waits, Tom. *Shiver me Timber*. First released on *The Heart of Saturday Night*, Elektra/Asylum Records, 1974.

Zauner, Anne. rev. of Hochgatterer, Paulus. *Eine kurze Geschichte vom Fliegenfischen* (http://www.literaturhaus.at/buch/buch/rez/hochgatterer_fliegenfischen/)

Notes

[1] "jetzt habe ich also ein leben. ein wirkliches.": Kathrin Röggla: *really ground zero. 11. september und folgendes.* Frankfurt am Main, Fischer 2001, pg 6. (really ground zero. Sept 11 and the aftermath; untranslated. All translations in this article by G. Haika) As in most of her work, Röggla uses only small caps throughout the book, and this usage is reflected in the translations.

[2] Marlene Streeruwitz' novel *Entfernung* (Frankfurt am Main: Fischer 2006) uses the terror attacks on the London underground on July 7th, 2005 as a background. While terror is not necessarily the main drive of the book, it serves as a means to identify madness in today's lives.

[3] Christoph Bartmann's book review from the Süddeutsche Zeitung was read online at: http://www.buecher.de/w1100485sz3596156467#product_slot_4

[4] Later in this essay, there will be an attempt to explain this ascertainment, and the opening sentence of the book, from the perspective of Röggla's generation.

[5] "durch all diese medienbilder müssten wir zu fuß gehen, aber das wäre ein zu weiter weg, das schafft man nicht, also bewegt man sich besser runter ins gebiet, um sich seiner wahrnehmung zu versichern." (*really ground zero*, 18f.)

[6] "und natürlich gibt es im fernsehen auch jenen reverend jerry falwell, einen hochrangigen baptisten, der die liberalen kräfte des landes an dem terrorakt vom dienstag für mitschuldig erklärt: die, die abtreibung legalisieren wollen, die, die rechte für schwule einfordern und die, die gebete aus den schulen vertrieben hätten, kurz:. 'those that have tried to secularize america.'" (*really ground zero*, 28)

[7] "mr. bushs aktion beispielsweise, vor laufender kamera beinahe in tränen auszubrechen [...], sollte weniger unter religiösen als unter psychologischen aspekten betrachtet werden." (*really ground zero*, 29)
[8] *really ground zero*, 32
[9] "ein ritual, das ich mit meiner mitteleuropäischen wahrnehmung als juristisch und religiös besetzt bezeichnen würde." (*really ground zero*, 31)
[10] See *really ground zero*, 36.
[11] *really ground zero*, 38.
[12] *really ground zero*, 49.
[13] Röggla quotes Weinberger indirectly, saying "es gäbe [sic!] ja auch kein feuilleton!" (*really ground zero*, 50)
[14] "eine ausdehnung räumlicher strategien" (*really ground zero*, 79)
[15] "ich weiß nicht, warum ich gedacht habe, dass derrida irgendetwas sagen würde zum krieg, oder zur situation. ich wusste ja gar nicht, was er machen würde, es hieß nur: 'derrida spricht.' dass er eine ganz normale vorlesung hält zum begriff der 'forgiveness' und über die shoah, den 'kaufmann von venedig' und den begriff der gnade, erscheint mir komisch." (*really ground zero*, 85f.)
[16] "und dann kann es auch immer im kreis um begriffe gehen, wie es sich ziemt für den ort." (*really ground zero*, 86)
[17] "geheimamerika" (*really ground zero*, 68)
[18] *really ground zero*, 84
[19] "der inflationär verwendete begriff der 'open society', die es zu schützen gilt, indem man sie abschafft" (*really ground zero*, 94)
[20] "das ist wohl das amerikanischste an dem film, versteht man amerika als das land der sich perpetuierenden ahistorik, der fortgesetzten ausblendung eines geschichtlichen blicks" (*really ground zero*, 80)
[21] "was also hat mich da hineingetrieben, in diesen haufen authentizität." (*really ground zero*, 108) note that she does not put a question mark behind the question.
[22] "mein neues licht auf pynchon – seine absurditäten bewegen sich mit höllentempo auf den begriff 'amerikanischer alltag' zu!" (*really ground zero*, 108f.)
[23] "– aber überblick gibt's doch nicht. / – ach was." (*really ground zero*, 109)
[24] "Als wir uns treffen, wissen wir nichts von dem, was an diesem Tag passieren soll, weder von der Sache mit dem World Trade Center noch davon, dass Julian in der Bärenklau fallen wird und dann in den Fluss. Das Wetter ist anders, als wir es uns vorgestellt haben, das wissen wir." (*Fliegenfischen*, 9)
[25] In an interview with Helmut Gollner, Hochgatterer himself used the phrase "second identity – zweite Identität" to describe his situation as a writer. – rf: Helmut Gollner, *Die Wahrheit lügen. Die Renaissance des Erzählens in der jungen österreichischen Literatur*, Wien-Innsbruck-Bozen: Studien Verlag 2005, p. 41.
[26] "'Ihr werdet nicht glauben, was passiert ist'" (*Fliegenfischen*, 112)
[27] Critical and scholarly discussions of Paulus Hochgatterer have been scarce and seem to focus on his "Kinder- und Jugendbücher" and him as a writer of such books; only recently, with the huge success of his 2006 crime novel – with crucial historical background – *Die Süße des Lebens* (which also earned the author the

German "Krimipreis" for 2007), more attention is given to his other works. The book reviews of *Fliegenfischen* such as Eva Lacour's (http://www.rezensionen.ch/buchbesprechungen/eine_kurze_geschichte_vom_fliegenfischen/3216306763.html), Anne Zauner's (http://www.literaturhaus.at/buch/buch/rez/hochgatterer_fliegenfischen/), or Helmut Gollner's (http://www.biblio.at/rezensionen/details.php3?mednr%5B0%5D=luk2004461&anzahl=1 in Literatur und Kritik, and http://www.kulturundsprache.at/service/Buchrezensionen/Buchrezensionen2004.shtml#hochgatterer), Anton Thuswaldner for *Die Presse*, Wien, and Samuel Moser for *NZZ*, Zürich, (both on http://www.lyrikwelt.de/rezensionen/fliegenfischen-r.htm) focus on the masculinity of the text, and the near-tragic ending; the date of the events is only mentioned as a marginal issue.

[28] Please note that in the German original, the pun on "der Irre", the madman, is more obvious than a possible reference to the Irish in general.

[29] "Er ist jemand, der sich ständig bedroht fühlt. " (*Fliegenfischen*, 10)

[30] "Abbildungsneurotiker ohne Kamera" (*Fliegenfischen*, 106)

[31] "Nur Psychoanalytiker können auf diese Weise dreckig lachen." (Fliegenfischen, 10)

[32] "manchmal schlägt einfach das Böse durch." (*Fliegenfischen*, 27)

[33] "eine ziemlich indikativische Angelegenheit. [...] Eine Vorstellung besitzt einen höheren Realitätsgehalt als das bloße Durchspielen von Möglichkeiten." (*Fliegenfischen*, 31)

[34] "Fische umbringen für ihn vermutlich so etwas ist wie Klientinnen vögeln." (*Fliegenfischen*, 50)

[35] Some reviewers from the other German speaking countries concluded from the name of the river that the excursion took them to the Salzburg. However, the river is located south-west of Vienna, which explains the route they are taking.

[36] "einen Blick wie ein Gott." (*Fliegenfischen*, 93)

[37] This is of course not hinting that Hochgatterer alludes to other books inspired by 9/11, such as Sam Harris' *The End of Faith*, in Harris' case obviously as it was published later than *Fliegenfischen.*

[38] "macht er einen komischen Eindruck. Er schüttelt unablässig den Kopf und ist blass, andererseits hat er sichtlich Mühe, das Lachen zu unterdrücken. 'Ihr werdet nicht glauben, was passiert ist', sagt er, 'ihr werdet es nicht glauben.' " (*Fliegenfischen* 112)

[39] "Phänomen der Unfähigkeit, emotionale Metaphern zu bilden." (*Fliegenfischen*, 84f)

[40] "warum sollten Fische vernünftiger sein als Menschen" (*Fliegenfischen*, 89)

[41] "Manche Menschen beziehen ihre Sicherheit vorwiegend aus dem Gleichbleiben ihres Elends." (*Fliegenfischen*, 17)

[42] "wie die Menschen in Zeiten exponentieller Veränderungsbeschleunigung etwas wie Erfahrungssicherheit gewinnen können"(*Fliegenfischen*, 53)

[43] "indem sie lernen, das Tempo der Veränderung selbst als sichere Erfahrung zu verbuchen" (*Fliegenfischen*, 53)

[44] "nichts anderes als männliches Rudelmasturbieren" (*Fliegenfischen*, 105)

[45] Florian Rötzer: *Phallische Hochhäuser*. In *Telepolis*, Sept 26, 2003. (http://www.heise.de/tp/r4/artikel/15/15722/1.html, accessed Spring, 2007)

[46] "das normale Leben ist krank genug" (*Fliegenfischen*, 42)

[47] "wie sich in dem Augenblick, in dem man dem Spital den Rücken kehrt, um sich niederzulassen, die Perspektiven verschieben, wie man sich plötzlich damit konfrontiert sieht, dass es da ein hohes Maß an Gesundheit in der Welt gibt, und wie man den Umgang mit diesem Phänomen erst lernen muss. " (*Fliegenfischen*, 106f.)

[48] "Dummheit allein, also diese Mischung aus cerebralem Unvermögen und Arroganz, ist schwierig genug zu ertragen. Aber wenn sie im Rudel auftritt und man das Ganze dann Teamarbeit nennt und als besondere Errungenschaft verkauft, um sich mit der Tragik der Sache nicht auseinander setzen zu müssen, kann man nur aufstehen und gehen." (*Fliegenfischen*, 44f.)

[49] Although this song is not referenced in the text, "Fatima" is referred to later on (p.98), and Fatima is the name of a courtesan of the emir and Ahab's lover in the song, described as the "swingingest grade A number one US choice dancer" in the harem. Incidentally, *Ahab the Arab* was also covered by Kinky Friedman, who after 9/11 pursued a political career as an independent candidate in Texas.

[50] "Ja, manchmal passieren eigenartige Dinge" (*Fliegenfischen*, 112)

CHAPTER SEVENTEEN

WAR CRIMES, TERROR AND THE MADNESS OF WAR: THE REPRESENTATION OF MADNESS AND CRIMINALITY IN TEXTS BY ELIAS AND VEZA CANETTI IN THE CONTEXT OF THEIR EXPERIENCES IN VIENNA AND LONDON

DAGMAR C. G. LORENZ

Elias and Veza Canetti's novels *Auto-da-Fé* (*Die Blendung*, 1935) and *The Tortoises* (*Die Schildkröten*, 1999) were written under the impression of the victories of National Socialism in Germany and the progress of Austro-Fascism until the annexation of Austria.[1] In the late 1920s and early 1930s there had been increasing fascist influences on Austrian civil society that had formed in the postwar era under Social Democratic leadership. After the bloody unrests in 1927 the democratic structures of Viennese society eroded, and the way was paved towards the ecclesiastical regime, the "Ständestaat." From the outside, National Socialist Germany undermined the Austrian republic. After their rise to power in 1933 the Nazis had established their power in Germany by means of mass arrests, kidnappings, torture, and murder, first tolerated and eventually legalized. The legal establishment, law enforcement, and the professions, notably the medical profession, underwent a reorientation with the result that erstwhile legal practices became criminalized and acts that had been considered crimes were sanctioned.[2]

The Nazis' persecution of their political opponents and their racist anti-Semitism were of particular concern to the Jewish authors Veza and Elias Canetti. They were associated with the Austrian Left and had close ties to the Marxists Ernst Fischer and Ruth von Mayenburg. Their fiction written in the 1930s raises concerns about the subversion of the legal code and law enforcement, and notions of sanity. Their major novels are set in Vienna. Elias Canetti's *Auto-da-Fé* first appeared in Vienna in 1935. Because of the antiliberal and anti-Jewish climate in Austria and the ban of books written by Jewish authors in Germany, the novel had no immediate reception to speak of. Dagmar Barnow believes that the topic of *Auto-da-Fé,* the "destructiveness of the petty bourgeoisie," may have contributed to its failure at the time. Only when in 1963 the German publishing company Hanser undertook a new edition did the novel receive the acclaim it was due. Veza Canetti wrote *The Tortoises* (*Die Schildkröten*) in exile in England and completed it in 1939. The war prevented its publication at the time, and it did not appear until 1999, thirty years after the author's death. The two novels provide detailed social portraits and impressions of the atmosphere in Austria's capital. In shocking clarity they reveal a pervasive corruption and confusion in different social strata, and they uncover barely suppressed asocial and criminal tendencies. *Auto-da-Fé* describes how these tendencies are acted out with impunity in the absence of moral standards and a collective conscience. *The Tortoises*, set a few years later, reveals how formerly criminalized behavior is becoming the norm and anti-social and criminal individuals are taking charge, empowered by the "brown revolution." When Veza Canetti's protagonists flee the city crime rules supreme. Both Canettis also address the themes of insanity and pathology. In the case of Elias Canetti's protagonist Peter Kien insanity wins out; the scholar burns his entire library and himself along with it. In Veza Canetti's novel the insanity of National Socialism culminates in the burning of the temples on November 9/10, 1938, and the ensuing destruction of the entire Jewish community. The collective has gone mad, but the Jewish refugees witness the chaos with increasing clarity.

Elias Canetti's *Auto-da-Fé* portrays a society made up of individuals lacking a sense of responsibility and a vision of the larger context. Each character is caught up in his or her idiosyncratic world. There are no authorities to turn to, there is no one who has the authority to keep transgressions in check. Worse yet, authority figures such as doctors, policemen, and fathers are indifferent, absent, or are part of the criminal milieu. One such example is the caretaker and former policeman Benedikt Pfaff, who tortures his wife to death and keeps his daughter as a sex slave. He ends up protecting the woman who steals the property of the protagonist (Canetti 1981, 282-283). The representatives of the bourgeoisie such as the scholar and bibliophile Kien facilitate socio-pathological and criminal activities since they have withdrawn into their ivory tower and ignore of the problematic developments around them. The psychiatrist Georges Kien, the protagonist's brother, lives in Paris, but when he is called upon to aid his brother, he turns out to be no less insane than the people he treats.[3] *Auto-da-Fé* paints a panorama of dysfunctionality and the absence of moral, humanitarian, and medical norms. This society appears like a volcano whose outbreak is imminent.

Veza Canetti's *The Tortoises* is informed by the author's first-hand experience of the Nazi invasion. What was left of the rule of law in Austria in Elias Canetti's *Auto-da-Fé* has now collapsed and chaos has erupted. Veza Canetti had been a contributor of the Social Democratic *Arbeiter-Zeitung*, where she had published literary texts under different pseudonyms until the unrests of February 1934. After the victory of the rightwing forces this publication venue was closed to her and likeminded intellectuals (Schedel 2005).[4] *The Tortoises* examines how in the early days of the German occupation criminal elements avail themselves of all the new opportunities available to them. She traces how the victors establish their regime, take charge, and enable Austrian opportunists to do the same. Similar to Elias Canetti, Veza examines criminality on the individual and collective level in connection with mental and emotional aberrations. Most of all, however, she is interested in the large-scale crimes perpetrated against the Jews. She also shows the effects of this outrage on the mental and physical state of victims such as her protagonists Eva, Andreas, and Werner Kain and their friends.

In his study *The End of Modernism. Elias Canetti's Auto-da-Fé* William C. Donahue argues that *Auto-da-Fé* undertakes a critical analysis of interwar culture and its, as Canetti believed, dead-end ideologies including Freudianism, Marxism, misogyny, and anti-Semitism, all of which failed to successfully address the disasters of the 1930s and 1940s.[5] The panorama of deranged characters in *Auto-da-Fé* functions like a mirror Canetti holds up to his readers. The alienated scholars Peter and Georges Kien, the brutal Benedikt Pfaff, the dwarf Fischerle, a monomaniacal pimp, and the primitive Therese represent different delusions that keep the individual in his or her isolation. Paranoia and the inability to communicate plague Canetti's characters and make them incapable of participating in any form of communal life.

Elias Canetti's extreme characters and his pessimism notwithstanding, it is obvious that *Auto-da-Fé* and Veza Canetti's *The Tortoises* are products of a different time and experience. His novel focuses on the increasing fragmentation of Viennese society and the lack of a public and cultural sphere in the late interwar period. With its hyperbolic style and exaggerated figures the novel reveals that there is neither a common reference system nor a cultural consensus. The cataclysmic last chapter, "The Red Cock" (457-464) is perhaps inspired by the Nazi book burnings.

Peter Kien, who has gone completely insane, sets his library aflame believing that his books are his allies. From a post-Shoah point of view, this chapter seems like an ominous preview of what the future holds in store.

Veza Canetti's novel *The Tortoises* deals with the traumatic changes between March 12, 1938, when Austria ceased to exist, and she and Elias escaped in November 1938—according to official documents, the Canettis departed on November 19 (Schedel 2005, 196). Veza Canetti's novel sheds light on the mentality change after the Nazi invasion and the ratification of the Nuremberg Laws. Many passages describe in graphic terms the escalating abuse of the Jewish population at the hands of German Nazis and Viennese non-Jews. Her particular situation as a disabled woman—she had been missing her left arm since childhood—and her "Jewish" appearance—she had black hair and a dark complexion—put her in double jeopardy. In *The Tortoises* she articulates her plight through the character of Eva Kain. Like Veza Canetti, also Eva experiences a visible physical decline as a result of the terror against Jews.

> As she moved on, her face lifted, without her volition, to the sky, as if striving upwards with longing. New features showed in that face, a new sorrow cut hard lines across it, cutting through the soft shadows. It must have been a beautiful face. When she lowered her head once again, her dark hair fell across it. (V. Canetti 2001a, 3)[6]

Eva Kain, like Veza Canetti, begins to display symptoms of depression and worry. However, what those around her consider her paranoia, turns out to be justified concerns. Her fear and heightened vigilance are caused by real dangers. In the end Eva turns out to have the appropriate reaction to the abnormal situation. Tragically, the atrocities of the November pogrom prove her right. As was already the case in Elias Canetti's *Auto-da-Fé* also in Veza Canetti's novel fire, in her case the inferno of the Jewish temples, signals the cataclysm followed by a fast decline. In *Auto-da-Fé* the tragedy concerns an individual person: the mad scholar Kien perishes in his library. In the chapter "The Great Fire" in *The Tortoises* (168-179) it is a collective tragedy: the entire Jewish community is being destroyed in what seems a sadistic orgy in a fundamentally insane system:

> Anyone who does not toe the line is impoverished and wretched and is well and truly tormented and stomped down (V. Canetti 2001a, 177)

The chapter "The Great Fire" opens with the news about the pogrom November 9/10. The horrors of that day are filtered through the perceptions and reactions of the Jewish protagonists. Through the arrests of friends and family members, also those who then had considered themselves safe until then, the characters realize the unwelcome truth that they must leave Vienna. The "great fire" ends their hopes of staying and weathering the excesses brought on by the regime change. Eva Kain had realized early on that her "Jewish" looks made her a target for the Nazis and their collaborators, but her blonde carefree friend Hilde had considered herself so much smarter than the Nazis—and safe.

The painful severing of the emotional ties that bind Eva to her beloved city and the trauma of being driven out of her home and having to embark on a journey into the unknown leave Veza Canetti's protagonist virtually paralyzed. Her exotic looks—one of the many traits she shares with the author—placed her at risk earlier than other, less easily identified characters. A comment of Eva to Andreas reveals the irrationality of the persecution based on appearance, and the debilitating effect the race based discrimination has on the victims:

> Because you are not affected by these glances. Because your features happen to be Slavic and your eyes light in color. But as for me—people suddenly hate me, so much that I hate myself," she admitted with vehemence. She walks past a German woman and wishes she could sink to her knees and cry out, accusing heaven and earth. One is black, and all around is blackness. (V. Canetti 2001a, 8)

At the beginning of the novel, it seems like an exaggeration to the blond and blue-eyed Andreas when Eva asserts: "You have to leave the country, Kain" (V. Canetti 2001a, 6). In her Cassandra role, Eva finds herself in a double-bind: Her love of Vienna is as strong as her pain of having to escape. Her grief seems more intense and devastating than that of her companions. Only Andreas's brother, Werner, whose appearance, like Eva's, corresponds to the Jewish stereotypes propagated by the Nazis, is equally attached to his Vienna. His affection for the city robs him of his common sense:

> Werner, who [. . .] will never believe that he has been totally deprived of all rights. That he is a foreigner, an *untermensch* [subhuman], a thief, an exploiter, a molester of children—worse than all that since he 'non-Aryan.' Even though he was the first to be dismissed from his institute because his nose crooks just a tiny bit downwards. He still cannot believe that there really is such a thing as this Führer. (V. Canetti 2001a, 17)

The feelings Eva and Werner have for their hometown may be especially strong precisely because they cannot 'pass' as non-Jews, which leaves them without options. In the end, however, the options Andreas and Hilde thought they had turn out to be illusionary as well. All Jews have become prisoners in Vienna.

During their final days in Vienna, the Canettis had been evicted from their Grinzing apartment and rented a room in a pension in Döbling. Only with difficulty did they secure visas to France, from where they moved on to London (Schedel 2005, 196). *The Tortoises* provides vivid impressions of the uncertainty while waiting for the visa as mass arrests take place and survival becomes a matter of chance. No longer are Eva and Andreas protected by the law: the Storm Trooper Baldur Pilz and his wife, both vulgar petty bourgeois, came and took their home. The character's first name, Baldur, calls to mind Baldur von Schirach, a high-ranking member of the "Sturm Abteilung" (SA, Brownshirts) and "Leader" of the German youth, who in August 1940 was appointed Governor of Vienna. Eva and Andreas take refuge in a small city apartment with Werner and a conservative Jew by the name of Felberbaum. The little group forms a make-shift community whose very composition attests to the fact that Jews have lost their rights as individuals. Under the Nazi regime they no longer can associate with whom they want and live there they like. The Kains, assimilated intellectuals and academics, are thrown in with Felberbaum because in the eyes of the new authorities all Jews are the same. The humiliating experiences the Kains undergo during their last days in Vienna culminate in Werner's arrest and murder in Buchenwald. This atrocity, committed against a law-abiding Austrian patriot, reveals the Nazis's fanaticism and indifference to human rights. Ironically, Werner is arrested because his brother Andreas is not at home when the "brownshirts" come for him (V. Canetti 2001a, 195). To them Werner looks like the Jewish intellectual they are searching for, and they take him into custody. There is no due process. Storm Troopers rather than the police arrest Werner without a warrant and without identifying themselves or him; without ado he is taken to Buchenwald and murdered. This episode reveals that the rule of law has been abolished. It explains why educated persons in 20th century Europe such as Werner, Andreas, and Hilde found it impossible to take the Nazis at their word.

Compared to Germany the changes in Austria took place abruptly and immediately. Veza Canetti's Jewish characters express their shock in different ways. The young wealthy Hilde attempts to save her friends—she does not seem to think she is in danger—through strategies that the readers recognize as misguided. She tries to procure an airplane for their envisioned escape. To this end she tries to bribe the Nazi Pilz, but she fails to understand that the powerful SA-man can take all of her family's possessions at will. Hilde has not understood that the rules of capitalism no longer apply to Jews—Jews have lost their property rights. Only when her father is arrested, does Hilde realize that she, too, is powerless, and that the distasteful Nazi has merely toyed with her. Likewise, Werner Kain refuses to acknowledge that the Nazis consider him an enemy, a foreigner, and a miscreant. In his disbelief, he fails to take precautions that might have saved his life. Like his brother, also Andreas blends out the cruel world around him. In order to cope with his powerlessness, he helps creatures even more exposed and despised than him. He collects tortoises that an Austrian businessman marks with a swastika and sells as novelty items. Helping these animals is Andreas's strategy of coping with the atrocities perpetrated against human beings. During a discussion of the ongoing November pogrom and the burning temples he proclaims, deflecting from himself and his family:

> I am pained by what happens to everything that I can still recognize as living. If someone burns a swastika into the tortoise's shell, that sets *me* afire. Not to mention the torture it is exposed to when someone removes its shell. (V. Canetti 2001a, 188)

In Austria the racist Nuremberg laws which it had taken approximately two years to formalize and enact—from 1933 to 1935—took effect after the annexation. Encouraged by the anti-Semitic regime Austrians eagerly contributed to the destruction of the Jewish community and committed acts of cruelty that had widespread public approval. Ruth Beckermann characterizes the violence during the first days after the invasion as an "orgiastic pogrom."[7] The Canettis, even though they had moved from Vienna's strongly Jewish Leopoldstadt to the suburb of Grinzing, soon felt the effects of the upheavals. Beckermann notes that in Austria the first disappointment about National Socialism became manifest when the Nazi government started to regulate the disposition of Jewish-owned property (Beckermann 1989, 56). Veza Canetti describes in *The Tortoises* how the powerful Storm Trooper Baldur Pilz terrorizes her protagonists—while robbing them of their home he makes sexual advances to Eva and Hilde. When the women do not comply, he has the Kains evicted from their apartment and moves in with his wife.

The rooms and the site of the Kains' home are modeled after the Canettis' place Himmelstra8e 30 in Vienna's 19th district situated in the midst of hills and vineyards (Wachinger 2005, 72).[8] Eva and Andreas are reflections of Veza and Elias Canetti, and their neighbor Hilde of the attractive and impetuous Frieda Benedikt, the daughter of Ernst Martin Benedikt, formerly the owner of the *Neue Freie Presse.* Veza Canetti thematizes the fabulous wealth of her neighbors, which is quickly depleted, and the arrest of the Hilde's father, who once was a pillar of society. Werner appears to be a conglomerate of several persons--scholars, scientists, and artists, in the Canetti circle.[9] He works with stones and thus calls to mind Elias Canetti's friend, the sculptor Fritz Wotruba. However, his arrest and tragic fate are reminiscent of other friends of the Canettis as well, some of whom had been unable to escape Nazi occupied Austria. The Canettis knew from the developments in Germany what could be expected from the Nazis and that they faced the kind of dangers and hardships that had driven their German associates Wieland Herzfelde, George Grosz, Lion Feuchtwanger, and Bertolt Brecht into exile.

Prior to 1938 the Canettis' world had been turned upside down several times. After the demise of the Habsburg Empire, Social Democrats took the leadership role in Vienna. In 1927 the republic was gradually transformed into a fascist state. Considering that these political changes went hand in hand with fundamental social paradigm shifts that called into question concepts of national and individual identity, it is not surprising that the themes of insanity and criminality play an important role the most diverse literary works of that era. One strategy of addressing the social and political problems at hand included satire and black humor. The Canettis availed themselves of these techniques to establish an emotional distance as they analyzed the changes in cultural values and the social fabric.

Long before Charlie Chaplin's film *The Great Dictator* (1940) the Nazis, and notably Hitler, had often been made a laughing stock by their opponents. Karl Kraus's posthumously published *The Third Witches' Sabbath* (*Die dritte Walpurgisnacht*), written in 1933, represents an attempt at exposing Nazi mentality through satire. However, he also recognized that perspicacity was no remedy against the brute force of the Nazi regime.[10] In Elias and Veza Canetti's fiction Nazis and Nazi-like characters such as the janitor and former policeman Benedikt Pfaff in *Auto-da-Fé* and the SA-man Pilz in *The Tortoises* share the grotesque features of Nazi characters in the works of anti-fascist authors such as Lion Feuchtwanger, Alfred Kerr, and Friedrich Wolf. Yet, especially Veza Canetti's novel emphasizes the lethal potential of these characters; their ability and determination to kill and to destroy an entire way of life.

In *The Tortoises* Veza Canetti portrays the hardships of living under Nazi rule with a special focus on Eva Kain. Until the time when Veza left Vienna, her works, although serious and critical, had included characters or episodes that suggested that progress was possible, and that there was reason for hope as long as reason and common sense prevailed. Elias Canetti's outlook, in contrast, had been thoroughly pessimistic and misanthropic from the start, for example his first drama *The Wedding* (*Die Hochzeit*, 1932) and *Auto-da-Fé*. His skepticism regarding progress and human achievement had engendered his detached, cerebral, and literary approach. To distill from his texts a particular social or political conviction seems an impossible task; his pervasive criticism precludes a specific ideological or educational message. There remains little to say after the self-destruction of Peter Kien and the systematic dismantling of all of the other characters in intellectual and moral terms. The emotional detachment with which *Auto-da-Fé* is presented precludes reader identification with any of the characters. The authoritative intellectual agency is positioned outside the plot and lies with the narrator/author. This constellation empowers the readers to recognize all of the characters' pathologies and the absurdity of the events.

During his exile years Elias Canetti did not publish. He recorded his experiences and impressions in his diaries, notes, and aphorisms.[11] He also resumed his research on crowds, crowd dynamics, and related phenomena, which he had begun in Vienna and resulted in his philosophical-anthropological treatise *Crowds and Power* (*Masse und Macht*).[12] His personal life, the difficulties in exile and his complicated relationships, took up much of his energy. He stayed a few weeks with his Viennese friend Anna Mahler, continued his relationship with Frieda Benedikt, who had come to England in 1938 (Hanuschek 2005, 315), and established a network of new friends and associates that he describes in *Party in the Blitz* (*Party im Blitz*, 2003).[13] Veza Canetti initially lived with her brother, "Bucky" Calderon in Surrey and completed the *The Tortoises* in November 1939 (Hanuschek 2005, 314). She had passed a "'bad time' by the ocean" with Georg and Elias Canetti (Hanuschek 2005, 312). There had been a fight between the brothers, apparently involving money, and Veza left for London together with Georg.[14] The uncertainty of their circumstances affected the Canettis severely. Veza's state of mind is reflected in her protagonist Eva.

Eva's fear and depression escalate into a kind of emotional paralysis and silent desperation. Veza Canetti's literary alter ego in *The Tortoises* differs markedly from the women characters of her earlier works, many of whom coped with difficult situations by skillful maneuvering. Frau Andrea and her daughter Diana in *Yellow Street* exemplify the wit and worldliness that impoverished women of the interwar period needed in order to cope in their misogynistic society.[15] In contrast, Eva Kain is robbed of all of her optimism when she boards the train from Vienna through Germany to

France. She "was in a state of profound turmoil [. . .] and she sat paralyzed" (V.Canetti 2001a, 231). When asked to declare her valuables to a German border official she states with trembling lips: "We have one object of value. Yes. The ashes of our brother!" (231). Eva, characterized as a "tormented woman," appears inconsolable (232).

The horrors of the final days in Vienna left indelible traces also on Veza Canetti's face as well. A series of photographs in Wachinger's *Elias Canetti. Pictures from his Life* (*Elias Canetti. Bilder aus seinem Leben*, 2005) reveal the psychological and physical changes Veza underwent between 1937 and 1939 (Wachinger 2005, 82-84). The three photos dated 1937 show a mature yet playful woman with an irresistible smile. In a photo of 1938 the same face is overshadowed by melancholy and worry. Finally, the portrait "Veza Canetti, 'July 1938, still in Grinzing but after the regime change'" represents a dramatically aged woman with features bearing an expression of mourning, worry, and depression. Compared to the careful makeup and grooming in the 1937 photos the later ones show signs of neglect. Veza looks careworn and tired. All these physical changes can be interpreted as manifestations of depression and inner turmoil. Dejection and confusion are the very emotions Veza Canetti ascribes to her autobiographical narrator in the posthumously published short narrative "Toogoods or the Light" ("Toogoods oder das Licht)."[16] "For I was so intimidated, so bombed out by life, that I actually thought that the house of the Toogoods was an asylum just because there were no bombs falling close to it" (V. Canetti 2001, 203).[17] Photographs taken later than 1938 reveal that Veza Canetti never regained her earlier exuberance—within a few months of extreme stress she had mentally and physically become transformed.

Contrary to Veza's life in Vienna, where she had lived until her escape to London, Elias Canetti's character was shaped by his exposure to different countries—Bulgaria, England, Austria, Switzerland—and the linguistic and cultural readjustments. Also in professional terms he was a free spirit. He had received his doctorate in Chemistry from the University of Vienna but never worked in this discipline. He was never employed by an academic organization, institute, or university and did not identify with an intellectual movement, school, or program. His analytical method eclectically combines insights and approaches from different fields; literature, anthropology, natural sciences, philosophy, and history. This broad intellectual base corresponds to his conviction that coming to grips with the mass phenomena of the twentieth century and the continued threat of war required more than specialized knowledge. Wary of social visions shaped by a specific ideology, he paid special attention to intellectuals on the periphery. In other words, Elias Canetti designed an intellectual reference system all his own as a context for his writing.

A glance at the persons whom he credits for his intellectual development sheds further light on the position he carved out for himself. In his autobiography, notably the second and third part, *The Torch in my Ear* (*Die Fackel im Ohr*) and *The Play of the Eyes* (*Das Augenspiel*), he sketches an intellectual panorama closely linked to the cultural territory of the former Habsburg Empire. Vienna being his intellectual center, Canetti's major reference points appear marginal from a German point of view. Sigmund Freud, the Frankfurt School, and Bertolt Brecht, all of whom Canetti knew but rejected, play only a minor role in his autobiography. Even within the Viennese context he shows a propensity for marginal and idiosyncratic individuals such as the paraplegic Herbert Patek, whom he portrays in great detail as a man he admires (Hanuschek 2005, 191). Towards members of the establishment and the rich and famous, including Alma Mahler Werfel and her husband Franz Werfel, he expresses contempt and dislike (Hanuschek 2005, 256). He refers to one of the most celebrated writers of the period, Stephan Zweig, as one of "the worst" authors he know and "not even worth [. . .] being mentioned by name" (Hanuschek 2005, 161). In other instances Elias Canetti changed allegiances. Intellectuals whom he had initially revered as he had the journalist Karl Kraus and the novelist and critic Hermann Broch, eventually earned his disapproval.

The heroes in *The Torch in my Ear* and *The Play of the Eyes* consist of persons of local fame. Often they are personal acquaintances associated with the interwar bohème. Among them are almost forgotten individuals such as the writer Ibolya (Ibby) Gordon, about whom Hanuschek writes that she was by-passed by the many feminist rediscoveries, and that Canetti provides most of the information known about her today (Hanuschek 2005, 150). It is characteristic of Canetti's representational strategy to place all of the individuals in question on a level playing field. He discusses members of his extended family with the same thoroughness and critical acumen as he does members of the intelligentsia be it the self-styled Buddhist and poet Alfred Waldinger, the sculptors Fritz Wotruba and Anna Mahler, the Berlin-born conductor Hermann Scherchen, and the novelist and mass theorist Hermann Broch (E. Canetti 1980, 89-95 and 1985, 145-165; Wachinger 2005, 73). Canetti's unquestioned admiration belongs to the obscure poet Abraham Sonne, who under the name Avraham Ben Yitzak published Hebrew poetry. Canetti met Sonne in the mid-1930s on a regular basis at the Café Museum and came to idolize him. In Canetti's eyes Sonne is the most astute critic and the most impressive and humane thinker among his contemporaries. The predilection for unusual personalities and little known intellectuals leave Elias Canetti free to design his own intellectual methodology and an independent creative reference system.

In exile Canetti continued along the same path. He chose his friends from widely diverse circles. His London friends included Austrian exile writers, artists, and scholars such as H.G. Adler, author of path-breaking studies of Nazi concentration camps and the bureaucracy of the Final Solution,[18] Canetti's lover Frieda Benedikt, who soon became a successful novelist, and the painter Marie-Louise von Motesiczky, another Viennese exile. Among his acquaintances and friends were also British writers such as Iris Murdoch and Kathleen Raine, and aristocrats such as the film producer Aymer Maxwell and the author Gavin Maxwell. Even in Vienna Veza Canetti seems to have been less gregarious than her husband, but she had close ties with Leftist intellectuals, Socialists like herself, who came under attack after the 1934 February revolts when the Dollfuß government began to take drastic measures against the political Left. In England, Veza, who disliked the English parties Elias avidly attended, moved primarily in Central European exile and Shoah survivor circles, among them H.G. Adler and Erich Fried.

Veza Canetti's publications in Vienna's *Arbeiter-Zeitung* are informed by a Socialist point of view and emphasized issues of class and gender. Her foremost concern was reforming the existing class system, its gender and economic structure. Through the appropriate reforms, her fiction implies, it will be possible to meet the Nazi threat head-on. In contrast to other German-speaking Jewish writers as for example Lion Feuchtwanger, who presented a detailed account of Nazi ideology and Nazi excesses in his documentary novel *The Oppenheims* (*Die Geschwister Oppenheim*, 1933), Veza Canetti's narratives of the early 1930s thematize neither the Nazi ideology nor its concepts of race, nation, blood and soil, and anti-Semitism.[19]

In keeping with the revolutionary optimism of Socialist ideology regarding the perfectibility of human beings, Veza Canetti emphasized education, reason, strategic thinking, political consciousness, and class and gender solidarity as ways to combat patriarchy and capitalism. Eccentric or pathological characters such as Herr Iger (*Yellow Street*) who is obsessed with money and power and abuses his wife and children, or the sadistic and vindictive small-time capitalist, "the Runkel," who resents able-bodied women, represent deviations from the norm of mental and physical health implied in Veza Canetti's writings.[20] The novel *Yellow Street* contains an entire collection of obsessive and oppressive types including Mr. Tiger, who eventually falls victim to his illicit desires, Mrs. Hatvany, a racist at heart, who exploits poor women, and finally the amorphous mob that attacks a little girl because she was not raped and murdered as had been assumed (V. Canetti 1999, 138).

> Chairs were waved at her [Helli Wunderer], she was threatened with umbrellas, she was jostled, shaken and sworn at, because she was alive and not dead; the donors demanded their money back from her, swore they would have the police down on her, and finally they knocked the child down off the stage. (V. Canetti 1999, 139)

The spectacle ends with a remarkable sentence that suggests that Veza Canetti, despite her political convictions, had a low opinion of most of her fellow human beings: "For man walks erect, lofty spiritual qualities etched into his countenance" (139).

Overall, *Yellow Street* expresses the notion that men and women have the potential to become predators and exploiters. In cunning and ruthlessness, the disabled shop owner "Die Runkel" is equal to her male counterparts, Iger and Tiger. Other female oppressors of women include a procuress, Mrs. Hatvany, who runs her sex trade under the guise of an employment agency, and a Baroness, who hires an attractive young woman as a maid, whom she intends to use her for her sexual gratification. Most of the male and female villains prey on inexperienced females from the country, who seek employment in the city.

Until 1938 Veza Canetti had conceptualized the abuse of power in terms of economic oppression and gender based oppression. By highlighting gender inequality, she also pointed at the remedy for the many social ills: the redistribution of wealth, legal and social emancipation for women, and educational reform. Written at a time when the democratic structures of the First Republic of Austria were still in place but in jeopardy, Veza Canetti's early works showed that much remained to be done to establish and secure an egalitarian system. Only when society no longer sanctions, promotes, and rewards aberrant behavior and exploitation, she illustrates in her works, only then can the abuses be stopped.

In *Yellow Street* examples of the social ills include criminality, corruption, and prostitution.[21] The novel establishes a link between gender, social status, and the perception of crime and insanity. While some of her texts of that era contain moments of hope that suggest that positive change may be possible through concerted action and vigilance, many of her stories end on a pessimistic note. In one of her most upbeat narratives, "The New Guy," politics and criminality are linked. Justice prevails in the end because the seller of a Nazi newspaper is convicted of a theft for which he had framed his Socialist colleague. The truth comes out, and even the police support the falsely accused Socialist.[22] Stories such as these demonstrate that integrity and a commitment to the common good bring about positive change. Yet, more frequently, Veza Canetti's stories deal with missed opportunities that destroy innocent persons. The attempted suicide of Emilie Jaksch in *Yellow Street*, one of the abused and socially abandoned maids in the text, exemplifies the failure of society to protect its weakest members (V. Canetti 1999, 90-91). Emilie is only one of the many unmarried women in *Yellow Street* who seek to improve their lot by coming to Vienna. They take menial jobs and many of them end up in the sex trade.[23]

Complementing the narratives about the dangers facing single women, the episode "The Ogre" in *Yellow Stree*t and the drama *The Ogre* (*Der Oger*) thematize the plight of a married immigrant woman. The central character is a young Bosnian named Maya Iger (in the narrative) and Draga Iger (in the drama). Having been married off by her father, Draga/Maya is taken to Vienna by her ruthless and greedy husband. Once in the big city, Iger, who married his wife for her dowry and inheritance, oppresses and tyrannizes her. Far away from family and friends, the woman is without recourse. In the drama Draga prevails against her despotic father and abusive husband with the help of a friend and the family's loyal business manager. Her victory suggests that the dispossessed must work together to better their lot. The respective episode in the novel ends tragically: Maya loses all her money to her tormentor. After a nervous breakdown she is confined to a mental institution. Her insanity serves as a mere pretext to rob her of her money and her freedom.

The story reveals an ingrained meanness that prevents individuals from recognizing that they are members of the same class and facing the same basic conditions. Ill will, gender bias, and jealousy on the part of male and female characters preclude solidarity. The bawd Mrs. Hatvany surmises that Maya "always was mad, and she could have driven him crazy too, with all her evil ways," and Mr. Koppstein, who has always had an eye on Draga, notes: "Ah, she really was a fair-looking lass" (V. Canetti 1999, 60). The grocer's wife, who helped him to gain access to Maya's inheritance, trivializes Iger's crimes towards his family, wife beating and extortion. She expresses the generally agreed-upon notion that Maya should have surrendered her money to Iger because "he's her husband after all" (61). Also the policeman whom Maya called to protect her children from their father's cruelty takes the husband's side: "The inspector looked at him. Herr Iger winked and pointed to his forehead. 'Calm down, my dear!'" (58). In the Iger episode Veza Canetti uncovers a gender-based social conspiracy. Gender identity and perceptions of madness and criminality are shown to be linked in the following manner: a woman's resistance to male abuse is likely to result in her being declared incompetent, but a man is not held accountable for crimes against a woman, especially if she is his wife. Veza Canetti's texts underlies a social critical program, hence her portrayal of criminality, obsession, and mental illness as by-products of an unfair society. Social inequities drive the oppressed individuals in her stories to depression and suicide and instill in the privileged megalomania and sadism, which cause them to become criminals. The view that Elias Canetti sets forth, namely, that insanity is a dignified and even hopeful state, runs counter to Veza's notion that it is part of a syndrome that social reforms could cure.

Having lived since 1925 in the Haidgasse close to Veza's Ferdinandstraβe apartment in the Leopoldstadt (Ferdinandstraße was the model for her Yellow Street), Elias Canetti relocated in 1927 to Hagenberggasse 47, in Vienna's 13th district, two months before the so-called "bloody Friday" uprising (Hanuschek 2005, 130, 138-142). Canetti devoted a separate chapter in his autobiography to this historical event that transformed Austria's political landscape (E. Canetti 1980, 268-273). The window of Canetti's suburban abode faced the grounds of *Am Steinhof*, the psychiatric hospital of the City of Vienna. Canetti lived there until 1933, completed his doctorate in Chemistry, worked on literary works, and tried to publish. For a long time, he had been fascinated with Vienna's "city of the insane" and relished the opportunity of observing it from his window (Canetti 1980, 261).

At the time, Steinhof housed approximately 6,000 persons the majority of whom perished in the Nazi killing programs.[24] In addition to the profound impression Steinhof and its inhabitants made on Elias Canetti, the mass frenzy during the riots of July 15, 1927 provided a new urgency to his studies of altered states of consciousness produced by mass events on the one hand, and isolation and the condition of being singled out from the crowd on the other. The insights Canetti developed during this time inform his eccentric characters' deranged and criminal behavior in *Auto-da-Fé*. Overall, his approach differs markedly from Veza Canetti's social criticism. In his novel the fascination with insanity and the insane is manifest throughout. Extreme characters such as Kien, Therese, the ape-man, and Fischerle may be anti-social, but they are also impressive in their cohesiveness that allows them to forge reference systems all their own in the absence of viable social norms. One of the previously mentioned characters expresses the same awe, the psychiatrist Georges Kien, who fosters a patient's attempts to regress to the developmental stage of an ape.

Kien envies the man's transformation into an apeman, which he perceives as an increase in sexual and emotional powers. Georges even reaches the point where he no longer wants to treat his patient.[25] Compared to Veza, who remained faithful to his Socialist principles, Elias Canetti's fiction is the work of a proponent of radical individualism. Phenomena that are socially stigmatized as insanity or crime appear as expressions of the uncensored individual—as expressions of inner freedom and independence. This kind of freedom is at the heart of the apeman episode in *Auto-da-Fé*. The patient, an educated man, is motivated by his desire to escape from the restrictions modern society imposes upon him.[26] He experiences social norms as the disease of the age in which he lives.

In his discussion of the design of his literary characters with *Am Steinhof* as his major source of inspiration, Canetti articulates the special position he accords insanity:

> Thinking of a cure seemed demeaning to them [his envisioned fictional madmen]. None of them should return to the irrelevance of ordinary everyday life. Adapting to the likes of us would degrade them, and to allow that I had a too high regard for the uniqueness of their experience. (E. Canetti 1980, 356)

With Steinhof before eyes (E. Canetti 1980, 356) and troubled by disquieting impressions he had gathered during a trip to Berlin, Canetti planned to write a *Comédie Humaine an Irren* (355), a cycle of novels about different kinds of obsessions. Not coincidentally, he chose a working title reminiscent of Dante and Balzac. Similar to the classical authors, he intended to capture the very essence of his time. Insanity was the leading theme for the project with which he hoped to combat the premonitions of impending doom he had had in the capital of the Weimar Republic:

> I had not come to terms with anything that filled me with horror and alarming premonitions since my Berlin trip. What else but a terrible inferno could come of it? I felt how merciless life was. That everything ran past everything else and nothing actually interacted with anything else. (355)

The characters around which Canetti planned to build his individual novels of included a "man of truth," a "visionary," a "religious fanatic," a "collector," a "wastrel," an "enemy of death," an "actor," and a "man of books." Only the latter was realized in the protagonist of Peter Kien in *Auto-da-Fé* (E. Canetti 1980, 354). In their one-sidedness these figures function as an expression and a diagnosis of the state of their author's society and historical period.

Designed as linear, Canetti's characters are propelled by a single impetus and move into a single direction like "live one-man-rockets" (E. Canetti 1980, 355). Such figures do appear in the author's dramas and notebooks. They seem to emerge from witticisms and apercus and become the embodiment of a surprising idea. For each one of them Canetti forged a specialized language "comprehensible, to be sure, but in such a way that no one else spoke like that" (355). His method of character construction calls to mind the technique of the acoustic mask in his dramas. Helga Kraft writes:

> Not only the words and sentences a character is in the habit of speaking constitute the acoustic mask, but the sound and modulation of the voice as well as the gestures accompanying the utterances."[27]

Auto-da-Fé was intended to be the first novel of the cycle but ended up being the last. The German and Austrian publication venues closed their doors to Jewish writers. In exile Elias Canetti focused on his philosophical anthropological project on crowds and power and turned to a more personal genre, his notes and notations. During the war he did not publish but helped Frieda Benedikt with her English novels.[28] Benedikt's protagonists bear a distinct resemblance to the literary characters Canetti describes in his autobiography.

The separate pavilions of Steinhof inspired Canetti's imagination. He thought of the mental patients inside and associated them with his literary characters that in their over-individualization and emotional isolation appear deranged. Reflecting upon their insanity, he writes that he developed a profound respect for people who had distanced themselves so radically from others that their society considered them insane (E. Canetti 1980, 356). He confessed that he was becoming so attached to his "insane" characters that he avoided eliminating them from his imagined sanatorium pavilion: "I did not have the heart to kill off a single one of my characters. None of them had developed far enough for me to envision their demise" (356). He even attributed a utopian perspective to insanity:

> If the inhabitants of these individualized languages could find something to say to each other that would make sense to them, then there would be hope for ordinary people like us who are lacking the dignity of insanity. (356)

The concept of the "dignity of insanity" is foreign to Veza Canetti. Even in her exile novel *The Tortoises*, which conveys detailed descriptions of the megalomaniac insanity of the Nazis and their supporters and the despair and depression of their intended victims, mental health is the implied norm. The Jewish characters are ousted by the Austrian majority and made objects of contempt and ridicule. Eva Kain almost breaks down under the pressure and comes to losing her mind. Nowhere is this condition labeled insanity, nor does it appear particularly dignified.

Certain characters and themes in Elias and Veza Canetti may appear similar, suggesting mutual influences or collaboration between the two authors. For example, the chapter “The Kind Father” in *Auto-da-Fé* (367-378) calls to mind Veza Canetti’s *Der Oger*. These texts have as their common theme wife-and-child abuse in the claustrophobic structures of an isolated nuclear family in a lower middle class Vienna milieu. The episode in *Auto-da-Fé* is extremely radical and revolting. It involves incest, torture, and brainwashing with no way out for the two women, a mother and her daughter. The wife of the abuser dies of the mistreatment, and a similar fate awaits the daughter. Maya Iger in *Yellow Street*, as mentioned earlier, is driven into a psychosis by her husband. Veza Canetti exposes the deep-seated misogyny within Austrian society, the reason why Maya is blamed for her own misfortune. Elias Canetti’s episode lacks the transparency of *The Ogre*. There does not seem to be a remedy to the oppression, and the insights into the mindset of the characters leave little hope for change.

As soon as Veza Canetti reached her London exile she processed the traumatic memories of the last days in Grinzing by writing *The Tortoises*. Completed in record time, the novel may have served a therapeutic function for the author, and it reveals profound changes in Veza Canetti’s outlook on society and the human species. In the closing episode Eva and Andreas Kain leave Vienna without hopes of ever returning to Austria. Eva has but one fear, that the train might turn back to Nazi Germany (V. Canetti 2001a, 232). *The Tortoises* explicitly identifies the protagonists as Jews and takes issue with the racial ideology of National Socialism, which none of Elias Canetti’s works do. The physical traits of Veza Canetti’s Eva Kain and her reactions mirror those of the author. Dark-haired and dark-eyed, Eva epitomizes Jewishness. The SA-man Pilz represents the paradigmatic Nazi. His many transgressions are legal under the new regime. His tall tales about hunting wild animals in Africa and his killing “useless” animals in public to set an example for children foreshadow the fate he intends for the Jewish characters: in Vienna he hunts Eva and her family and friends as he earlier did animals. The Nazi actions in *The Tortoises* may seem irrational, but they succeed in their ultimate objective to spread terror and disenfranchise Jews. The gratuitous cruelty on the part of the invaders reveals how much pleasure they take in tormenting their victims. All of their attacks are carried out with extreme cruelty—cruelty becomes an end itself. This is most obvious during the pogrom and concentration camp episodes.

In *The Tortoises,* Veza Canetti's earlier convictions based on Socialist ideology break down. There is a notable correction of her earlier low opinion of wealthy people. The Nazis are indiscriminate in their persecution of the rich girl Hilde, the Kains, members of the middle class, and the indigent Felberbaum. Conversely, Pilz and his wife, products of the lower middle class aspire to the privilege and wealth that are suddenly within their reach. Neither cultural identity, achievement, nor self-identification matter if the person in question is Jewish by Nazi definition.

The effect of the Nazi brutality on the Jewish protagonists is a central concern in *The Tortoises*. The persecuted individuals respond to enormous pressures in irrational ways: Andreas becomes preoccupied with the disfigured tortoises—saving them becomes his priority even though his and Eva's life is in danger; Werner chooses total denial and refuses to believe that he is in danger. Only Eva is fully aware of the situation. Underneath her stoic mask, she suffers the most. Yet she appears "ice-cold" (V. Canetti 2001a, 12). Expecting disaster to strike any moment, she is emotionally cut her off from those around her.

> Fully conscious, and with a deathly chill upon you, you make your way to the door when the bell rings. You open it and stand in their way, because their way is strewn with corpses. (11)

To emphasize her Jewish appearance Eva is often contrasted with blond, exuberant, and athletic women like Hilde (11). Also Hilde is Jewish, but she can "pass" as a non-Jew and does not suffer the kind of panic that is taking hold of Eva. Throughout the novel Hilde interacts with Jews and non-Jews, even with Nazis.

The social and psychological impact of anti-Semitic stereotyping is a recurrent theme. Clearly, the awareness of the impact the racist ideology has on everyone has undermined Veza Canetti's earlier trust in progress. Anti-Semitism in *The Tortoises* has the effect of a murderous mass psychosis. No argument, no rational intervention can stop the fanaticism. The Jewish protagonists are powerless against the mass madness. Their helplessness increasingly causes irrational and pathological responses, while their opponents devise actions that are ever more brutal.

Elias Canetti, while not addressing racism, anti-Semitism, and Nazi ideology directly, studied the mental states associated with crowd phenomena and the mentality of the paranoid leader, all of which are central to National Socialism. Yet, even in his major oeuvre *Crowds and Power (Masse und Macht)* he chose to discuss the case of the paranoid Daniel Paul Schreber rather than Adolf Hitler. In contradistinction to Elias's position, Veza Canetti increasingly identified herself through the Jewish fate and her affinity to the Central European survivor community in London. The long-range effects of having to leave her home and her native city, and the trauma caused by the revelations about the Holocaust changed the way Veza Canetti experienced reality. She lost the optimism that is an integral part of Socialism. Elias Canetti, on the other hand, was confirmed in his position as a cosmopolitan and a detached analyst of humankind that had characterized his stance from the start, as he recorded crimes and madness carefully and without illusion in *Auto-da-Fé*.

Works Cited

Adler, H[ans] G[ünter]. 1955. *Theresienstadt. 1941-1945. Das Antlitz einer Zwangsgemeinschaft.* Tübingen: Mohr.
—. 1974. *Der verwaltete Mensch. Studien zur Deportation der Juden aus Deutschland.* Tübingen: Mohr.
Aly, Götz, et al. 1994. *Cleansing the fatherland. Nazi medicine and racial hygiene*. Baltimore: Johns Hopkins UP, 1994.
Barnow, Dagmar. 2000. "Elias Canetti—Poet and Intellectual." In *Critical essays on Elias Canetti*. New York: Hall: 15-34.
Beckermann, Ruth. 1989. *Unzugehörig. Österreicher und Juden nach 1945.*Vienna: Löcker.
Benedikt, Frieda (ps. Anna Sebastian). 1944. *The monster.* London: Cape.
—. *Let thy moon arise.* London: Cape.
Bettauer, Hugo. 1924. *Die freudlose Gasse*. Vienna: Gloriette.
Bunzl, John and Bernd Marin. 1983. *Antisemitismus in Österreich.* Innsbruck: Inn Verlag.
Canetti, Elias. 1935. *Die Blendung.* Vienna: Reichner. [1948. Munich: Weismann; 1963. Munich: Hanser]
—. 1950. *Komödie der Eitelkeit.* Munich: Weismann.
—. 1960. *Masse und Macht.* Hamburg: Claassen.
—. 1980. *Die Fackel im Ohr.* Munich: Hanser.
—. 1981. *Auto-da-Fé*, transl. by C. V. Wedgwood. New York: Continuum.
—. 1985. *Das Augenspiel.* Munich; Hanser.
—. 2003. *Party im Blitz. Die englischen Jahre.* Munich: Hanser.

—. 2005. *Party in the Blitz. The English years*, translated by Michael Hofmann. New York: New Directions.

Canetti, Veza and Elias.2006. *Briefe an Georges*, edited by Karen Lauer and Kristian Wachinger. Munich: Hanser.

Canetti, Veza. 1989. *Die gelbe Sraße.* Munich: Hanser.

—. 1990. *Der Oger.* Munich: Hanser.

—. 1992. *Geduld bringt Rosen.* Munich: Hanser.

—. 1999. *Die Schildkröten.* Munich: Hanser.

—. 2001. *Der Fund.* Munich: Hanser, 2001.

—. 2001a. *The tortoises*, translated by Ian Mitchell. New York: New Directions.

—. 1999. *Yellow street. A novel in five scenes*, translated by Ian Mitchell. New York: New Directions.

—. Veza Canetti. 1999a. "The New Guy," in *Contemporary Jewish writing in Austria*, edited by Dagmar C. G. Lorenz. Lincoln: U of Nebraska P, 1999: 43-48.

Chaplin, Charlie. Dir. 1940. *The great dictator.* USA 1940.

Conradi, Peter J. 1998. *Iris. A memoir of Iris Murdoch.* London: Duckworth, 1998.

Donahue, William C. 2001.*The end of modernism. Elias Canetti's Auto-da-Fé.* Chapel Hill: U of North Carolina P.

Douma, Eva. 1998. *Deutsche Anwälte zwischen Demokratie und Diktatur.* Frankfurt: Fischer 1998.

Feuchtwanger, Lion. 1933. *Die Geschwister Oppenheim.* Amsterdam: Querido.

Freud, Sigmund. 1930. *Das Unbehagen in der Kultur.* Vienna: Internationaler Psychoanalytischer Verlag.

Hanuschek, Sven. 2005. *Elias Canetti.* Munich: Hanser: 196-197.

Kraft, Helga. 2004. "Staging a critique of modernism: Canetti's plays." In *A companion to the works of Canetti.* Rochester: Camden House: 135-155.

Kraus, Karl. 1952. *Die dritte Walpurgisnacht.* Munich: Kösel.

Meidl, Eva M. *Veza Canettis Sozialkritik in der revolution≅ren Nachkriegszeit.* Frankfurt: Lang, 1998.

Pabst, Georg Wilhelm. 1925. Dir. *Die freudlose Gasse.* Germany.

Pappenheim, Bertha. 1924. *Sisyphus-Arbeit: Reisebriefe aus den Jahren 1911 und 1912.* Leipzig: Lindner.

Schedel, Angelika. 2005. "'Buch ist von mir keines erschienen . . . ' Veza Canetti verliert ihr Werk und hilft einem Dichter_zu ηberleben." In *Dossier Veza Canetti*, edited by Ingrid Sp rk and Alexandra Strohmaier. Graz: Droschl: 191-210.

Scheiber, Nicole. 2005. "Bibliographie von Veza Canetti." In *Dossier Veza Canetti*: 219-232.
Wachinger, Kristian. Ed. 2005. *Elias Canetti. Bilder aus seinem Leben.* Munich: Hanser: 82-84.

Notes

[1] Veza Canetti, *The tortoises,* translated by Ian Mitchell (New York: New Directions, 2001); Elias Canetti, *Auto-da-f9*, transl. by C. V. Wedgwood (New York: Continuum, 1981).
[2] See: Götz Aly et al., *Cleansing the fatherland. Nazi medicine and racial hygiene* (Baltimore: Johns Hopkins U P, 1994); Eva Douma, *Deutsche Anwälte zwischen Demokratie und Diktatur* (Frankfurt: Fischer 1998).
[3] The chapter "A madhouse" (395-414) reveals that Georges Kien is unable to maintain boundaries between him and his patients.
[4] Hanuschek 2005, 196-197, discusses the relationship between the Canettis and Fischer. Scheiber 2005, 221-222, lists the works the author published under the pen names Veza Magd, Martha Murner, and Veronika Knecht in *Arbeiter-Zeitung.*
[5] William C. Donahue, *The end of modernism. Elias Canetti's* Auto-da-fé (Chapel Hill: U of North Carolina P, 2001).
[6] Kristian Wachinger, ed. *Elias Canetti. Bilder aus seinem Leben* (Munich: Hanser, 2005), 82-84, contains a series of photographs of Veza Canetti. Compared to the earlier pictures, the March 1938 image shows a visibly aged, depressed woman.
[7] Ruth Beckermann, *Unzugehörig. Österreicher und Juden nach 1945* (Vienna: Löcker, 1989), 51 writes: "It was an orgiastic pogrom. Orthodox Jews had to clean the streets with toothbrushes; the wigs of orthodox women were burned in public [. . .]. In Vienna, which had a Jewish population of approximately 180,000 Jews, it was a lucrative event—ranging from personal robbery and enrichment campaigns to the improvement of the social situation for the rest of the population" (my own translation).
[8] Wachinger, 72, contains a photography of the house on Himmelstra8e, which Canetti characterizes in a letter to his brother Georges from 1935 as "eine herrliche Wohnung . . . wohl an der schönsten Stelle Wiens."
[9] Peter J. Conradi, *Iris. A memoir of Iris Murdoch* (London: Duckworth, 1998), 349.
[10] Karl Kraus, *Die dritte Walpurgisnacht* (Munich: Kösel, 1952). Charlie Chaplin, dir. *The great dictator*. USA 1940.
[11] The first new work that appeared after the English translation of *Auto-da-Fé,* by C. V. Wedgwood (London: Cape, 1946) was *Comedy of vanity* (*Komödie der Eitelkeit.* Munich: Weismann, 1950).
[12] Elias Canetti, *Masse und Macht* (Hamburg: Claassen, 1960).
[13] Elias Canetti, *Party im Blitz. Die englischen Jahre* (Munich: Hanser, 2003) was translated by Michael Hofmann as *Party in the Blitz* (New York: New Directions, 2005).

[14] The volume of letters, *Veza and Elias Canetti. Briefe an Georges*, ed. Karen Lauer and Kristian Wachinger (Munich: Hanser, 2006) contains no correpondence from the time between May 23,1939 and May 18, 1940.

[15] Veza Canetti, "The Tiger," in *Yellow street* (New York: New Directions, 1999, 93-114.

[16] Veza Canetti, "Toogoods oder das Licht" in *Der Fund* (Munich: Hanser, 2001), 197-204. The translations from this text are my own.

[17] "Denn so eingeschüchtert war ich, so verbombt vom Leben, daß ich wirklich dachte, das Haus der Toogoods sei ein Asyl, bloß weil es ringsum nicht von Bomben regnete."

[18] H.G. Adler, *Theresienstadt. 1941-1945. Das Antlitz einer Zwangsgemeinschaft* (Tübingen: Mohr, 1955) and *Der verwaltete Mensch. Studien zur Deportation der Juden aus Deutschland* (Tübingen: Mohr, 1974).

[19] Lion Feuchtwanger, *Die Geschwister Oppenheim* (Amsterdam: Querido, 1933).

[20] Veza Canetti, *Der Oger* (Munich: Hanser, 1990).

[21] In "Der Neue," in *Geduld bringt Rosen* (Munich: Hanser, 1992), 67-72, Veza Canetti describes the underhanded tactics of a Nazi newspaper vendor against a Socialist colleague. She shows that by helping one another the rightwing extremist can be neutralized. The film *Die freudlose Gasse*, dir. Georg Wilhelm Pabst, Germany, 1925, provides a similarly decadent portrait of interwar Vienna replete with crime and prostitution as *Yellow street* shows.

[22] Veza Canetti, "The New Guy," in *Contemporary Jewish writing in Austria*, ed. Dagmar C. G. Lorenz (Lincoln: U of Nebraska P, 1999), 43-48.

[23] "The Ogre," in *Yellow Street*, 29-62. The problems facing female migrants, notably of Jewish background, from Eastern Europe and parts of the former Habsburg Empire, had been a matter of concern since the turn of the century as activist and social worker Bertha Pappenheim revealed. See for example Pappenheim's letters, *Sisyphus-Arbeit: Reisebriefe aus den Jahren 1911 und 1912* (Leipzig: Lindner, 1924).

[24] See: "Der Krieg gegen die 'Minderwertigen.' Zur Geschichte der Nazi-Medizin in Wien." Eine Ausstellung des Dokumentationsarchivs des Österreichischen Widerstandes im Otto-Wagner Spital der Stadt Wien. <http://www.spiegelgrund.at/>

[25] See "A Madhouse" in *Auto-da-Fé*, 395-414.

[26] Sigmund Freud detailed the limitations and sources of discontent in modernity in *Civilization and its discontents* [*Das Unbehagen in der Kultur* (Vienna: Internationaler Psychoanalytischer Verlag, 1930)] half a decade before the publication of *Auto-da-fé*.

[27] Helga Kraft, "Staging a critique of modernism: Canetti's plays," in *A companion to the works of Canetti* (Rochester: Camden House, 2004), 135-155. Here: 144.

[28] Frieda Benedikt published under the pseudonym Anna Sebastian *The Monster* (London: Cape, 1944) and *Let thy moon arise* (London: Cape, 1944).

CHAPTER EIGHTEEN

CRIME IN THOMAS BERNHARD'S NOVELS: A CRITIQUE OF THE FATHERS

JOSEPH MOSER

Thomas Bernhard, Austria's most prolific and controversial writer of the second half of the twentieth century, is known to many for his criticism of Austria. Belonging to the first generation to experience adulthood in Austria's newly founded Second Republic after 1945, he sought to uncover the failings of past generations in his novels. Crime plays a central role in this endeavor, for most of his critique is directed at the crimes that the father generation had perpetrated. While some have labeled Bernhard a *Nestbeschmutzer* (someone who soils his own nest), much of his criticism was out of love for his country and a deep rooted desire to change Austria for the better. It is common for adolescents and young adults to rebel against their parents; however, in Bernhard's case this is complicated by his difficult relationship with his mother and the fact that he never met his father, as well as that his grandfather's anachronistic world view left an important mark on Bernhard. Emerging from the legacy of the Holocaust and war crimes committed by Austrians during the Third Reich, Bernhard's critique of the fathers seeks to reject this generation's past and have an honest reckoning with their failings rather than trying to forget the past and to stylize Austria as the first victim of Hitler's aggression, which had been the official doctrine of Austria after 1945.

The critique of the father is particularly strong in both Bernhard's first successful novel, *Frost* (1963), and his last novel, *Extinction* (*Auslöschung,* 1986). In both there is a strong romanticization of the country's past in the Austro-Hungarian Empire and an unease with the present state of the country. His critique of the fathers praises and romanticizes his grandfather's generation, particularly in *Frost.* In order to understand Bernhard's rejection of his father's generation, it is important to realize that Bernhard had a special relationship with his grandfather, Johannes Freumbichler, who had pursued the life of a bohemian at the turn of the century and continued to struggle to survive as a writer in the early 1930's.[1] Bernhard never knew his father, Alois Zuckerstätter, who, having fallen victim to alcoholism, committed suicide in 1940. He grew up with his grandparents and his mother, Herta Bernhard. While he adored his grandfather for most of his life, there are significant differences that separated them. Freumbichler did not achieve any public recognition as a writer until the Austro-Fascist *Ständestaat* (Corporate State) awarded him the state prize for literature in 1937 for his novel *Philomena Ellenhub*. Despite the fact that he rejected National Socialism, his literature was mostly set in the rural milieu and compatible with the Nazi's *Blut-und-Boden* (Blood and Soil) ideology. Freumbichler was also very proud of the German language, which Bernhard later came to reject in *Extinction*. While Bernhard set most of his writings in rural areas, just like his grandfather, hiss writing is tremendously critical of country people, almost to the extent of demonizing rural settings, a result of Nazis war crimes and genocide. Bernhard is interested in uncovering the failings of his country and people.

In Bernhard's autobiographical pentalogy *Die Ursache* (*The Cause* 1975), *Der Keller* (*The Cellar*; 1976), *Der Atem* (*The Breath* 1978), *Die Kälte* (*The Cold*; 1981), and *Ein Kind* (*A Child*; 1982), collected in David McLintock's English translation *Gathering Evidence* (1985), Bernhard chronicles his life from the time of his birth in 1931 until 1952, just before he started his career as a writer. In these texts, he clearly expresses his affection for his grandfather, who also exerted an important influence politically on Bernhard. He admired Freumbichler's resistance to pursuing a petit-bourgeois lifestyle. In *A Child* he writes: "My grandfather loved chaos; he was an anarchist, if only in spirit. My mother, on the other hand, spent all her life trying to secure a foot in the middle-class world, or at least in the world of the lower middle-class—an endeavor in which she naturally could not succeed" (McClintock, 19). His mother represented for him the world of the petit-bourgeoisie, which he criticized in several of his works. As an individualist and libertarian, a rather uncommon position in Austria, Bernhard disliked assimilating his interests to those of mass trends, and therefore his view of life stood in radical opposition to that of his mother, who wanted to belong to middle-class Austrian society.

Bernhard blames many of Austria's problems on the failings of the "Vätergeneration" (fathers' generation), and this also includes his mother to an extent. He considers this generation, which was born roughly between 1900 and 1910, to bear the responsibility for World War II and the Holocaust. As much as he despises his father's generation, he praises his grandfather's generation, the last to reach adulthood still under the monarchy. This is in part due to the autobiographical fact that Bernhard had a very close relationship to his grandfather, while he never knew his father, who had abandoned his mother before Bernhard was born. Bernhard's view of history is shaped by a vision of a good Europe before 1914 and a miserable post-World War I continent. This is certainly a romanticized historical perspective that ignores the realities of the history before 1914 and is part of the fictional setting of his texts. It is undoubtedly a reactionary position as well, though his libertarian world view kept him from becoming affiliated with a specific Austrian political party.

Almost following a tradition in Austrian literature from Joseph Roth and Karl Kraus to more contemporary writers such as Alexander Lernet-Holenia and later Peter Handke and Gerhard Roth, Bernhard presents a romanticized view of Austria-Hungary—but note that he never explicitly refers to *Österreich-Ungarn* (Austria-Hungary) in any of his literary texts, but rather alludes to this aspect of his country's past. The past glory of a multi-ethnic empire that was ostensibly clean of having committed genocide and war crimes intrigued many of these writers. With this idealization of the monarchy's past, Bernhard embraces Imperial Austria as a major player in world politics and the antithesis of the tiny, provincial, and mono-ethnic (German-)Austrian republic after 1918. After World War II and the atrocities committed during the Holocaust, Bernhard sees very few redeeming qualities in his country and his compatriots, and he is thus ashamed of his nationality. Yet, while his critics label him a *Nestbeschmutzer*, he loves his country and feels sorry for himself that being an Austrian after 1945 did not permit him to feel proud of it, like a French or an English person might. Thus, Bernhard is not interested in Austria's imperial origins for the sake of knowing more about history, but rather out of his dissatisfaction with the present status of Austria.

This romanticization of Austria-Hungary is also the cause of Bernhard's admiration for the multi-ethnic monarchy, and his literary figures tend to think very fondly of Poles, Yugoslavs, and Italians, all of whom were former peoples of the Habsburg Empire. While Bernhard's figures throughout his literary oeuvre adore these nationalities, these figures also vehemently express their dislike of all things German. This is especially the case in *Extinction*, where the protagonist's name, Franz Josef Murau, is a very unsubtle reference to Emperor Franz Josef I. This monarch, whose reign lasted from 1848 to 1914, not only marked the last period of the Austrian Empire, but also was the head of a multi-ethnic and fervently non-nationalist government, not unlike the European Union's stance towards multiculturalism today. It would be incorrect, however, to deduce from this that Bernhard was a monarchist. His interest in pre-World War I Europe and the monarchy originates solely *ex negativo*, from his dissatisfaction with the present and the crimes committed by his father's generation.

Bernhard clearly stated his objections against the present, when he received the *Rudolf-Alexander-Schröder-Stiftung-Literaturpreis der Freien Hansestadt Bremen* in 1965. In his speech, entitled "Mit der Klarheit nimmt die Kälte zu" (With clarity coldness increases), he writes: "The last half century is a single pain, now our mental pain" (244). The wars and scientific innovations may have made people's perceptions of the world clearer, but they also destroyed the warm, fairy-tale-like Europe before World War I. Bernhard does not necessarily understand this time period because he was born seventeen years after that war began, but he feels very uncomfortable with both the recent past and the present. He disconnects himself from the previous generation of blind fathers and stupid teachers. In the natural sciences, he sees the blame for the coldness in the present: "With clarity, coldness increases. This clarity und this coldness will rule from now on. The science of nature will give us a higher form of clarity and a much more grim coldness than we could imagine" (245). Bernhard expresses a very conservative view, suspicious of both his own generation and that of his father. He is inherently afraid and suspicious of innovation and change. This conservatism facilitated his longing for the monarchy.

In *Frost*, memories of past and present crimes and a deep despair leading to suicide present a very dark and sinister view of post-war Austria. The result of this despair is both physical and mental illness. The criminal nature and pathologies of some of the residents of the small Alpine village of Weng cannot be separated from recent wartime experiences. Strauch, a painter, who spent the war together with his sister in Weng is being observed by his brother's *Famulant* (doctor's assistant) in an attempt to medically record and evaluate Strauch's condition; however, the *Famulant*'s observations lack both the ethics and the structure of a legitimate medical study. The memories of the war bring Strauch back to this small Alpine village. He wants to return, as he puts it, "[to] primitive living. Unassumingness." (26) The deprivations of the war can still be felt in Weng at the end of the 1950s. Strauch explains to the *Famulant*: "'If the walls could talk,' he said, 'every room has seen its own atrocity. The war has soaked into these walls. I mean, the room where you're staying ..." (26). The *Famulant* is thus confronted by the omnipresence of the wartime past, inescapable in Weng. This only increases the *Famulant*'s curiosity about it, but Strauch remains silent on this topic. The *Famulant* becomes aware that something uncanny must have happened during the war and profoundly disturbed the people and their personal interaction in the village. Because of his relatively young age, very much like Bernhard himself, the *Famulant* has only a sketchy knowledge of the past, and the generations that know more about the war are not able or willing to talk about it. The German concept of *Schweigen* (not communicating) hovers over this small community. Even the many conversations that the *Famulant* strikes up with Strauch and the other villagers do not remedy this inability to express ideas and emotions.

Traces of past crimes, however, can be found everywhere, not only in the little village but also in the forest. Strauch claims, "The war had left grisly traces up and down the valley. 'Even today you keep encountering skulls or entire skeletons, covered over by a thin layer of pine needles'" (149). He is referring to the regiments that starved in the forest during the war. Strauch, however, still defends the German soldiers, claiming that they were not murderers, but rather that murder had been the trade of the "dark elements out of the East." He even accuses the inmates from the nearby penal facility. Strauch only knows third-hand what actually happened during the war, and that is why he defends the soldiers and accuses the so-called *Ostarbeiter* (forced laborers from Eastern Europe) and other inmates while using terms reminiscent of the Nazi past. The prejudice against Eastern Europeans, and particularly Poles, who could have been subjects of the Austro-Hungarian Empire, underlines the lingering resentment against people from the East and is a direct result of Nazi rule in Austria, which had further removed the country from its multi-ethnic origins.

When confronted with this hazy perception of the past, one naturally wonders what the people in Weng still know about their village during the war. There are obvious facts that most seem to be informed about, such as that the factory, which worked primarily for the arms industry, was a target for Allied bombing raids. Many of the Allied airplanes, though, crashed in the mountains due to the perpetually bad weather in the region. Other war relics, such as human remains or abandoned equipment left behind in the woods also make up this memory of the war. This testifies to the ignorance of many Austrians at the end of the 1950s, who can locate memories of the war, but yet completely lack an understanding of their recent history.[2] Strauch makes the *Famulant* aware of the fact that the villagers do not want to be enlightened about the past. He analyzes this ignorance by asking in reference to a person's fantasy: "Someone who doesn't know anything, is such a thing possible? A man who never knew anything?" (35). Even though Strauch is asking this question about people's fantasy, this also needs to be seen in reference to a person's general knowledge and thus one's historical knowledge. Strauch says: "Everything, every smell, is chained to a crime of some sort, an abuse, the war, some piece of infamy or other … Even if it's all buried under the snow just now" (54). The snow covers up the ugly wartime memories. The people in Weng are still being influenced by events that happened in the war. Strauch continues, "And all wartime experiences, you know, everything these people have to talk about is to do with the war … [for] the war is an inexpungible inheritance. The war is properly the third sex. Do you understand!" (55-56). Strauch considers the war to be an elementary component of the consciousness of the people.

The war is very important for the historical context of the novel, because it permanently changed the people of Weng.[3] Strauch searches for true descriptions of the war, which prove difficult to find, since everyone whom he interviews tells a different story. The search for the truth plays a fundamental part in all of Bernhard's works. Talking to the knacker (harness-maker or saddler), Strauch puts these war narratives to the test by asking trick questions. If he asks if something happened in Poltawa and the knacker answers that it was in Odessa, then Strauch knows that the knacker is telling the truth, because he had previously also referred to Odessa (102). In contrast to this trivial check of the truth of an historical account, Strauch asserts: "I often tried to come closer to the truth, to this understanding of truth, even if only through silence" (179). It is not easy to find the truth and there is also fear of uncovering the truth. While looking at the snowfall Strauch observes agitatedly:

> Unworthy, you know. I'm unable to explain myself, the truth, the propensity for the truth is so difficult, that human facilities aren't sufficient … it's all a matter of fragments, suggestions, all of thought is just one never experienced clarity … for nothing. So much material. Those vast proportions! This unworthy orientation … all human misery struck me as luminous enough! A blizzard is certainly a deathly process … but what is a blizzard? How does it come about? A mutiny, miraculous … my account is nothing but fear, nothing but a child's fear of an uncommon spectacle …. (194)

The snow evokes memories of death and fear of the unknown and the uncanny, and with this Strauch thinks not only of the snow, but also of the war and of understanding the past. He cannot grasp the proportions of the atrocities and the suffering. His knowledge is limited to a few reference points. The society's and state's dishonest treatment of the past further complicates the process of finding the truth. The ability to grasp the truth is hindered by fear of the uncanny. The people of Weng are also afraid of this truth, because they subconsciously feel guilty. Strauch claims: "Country people are the underclass [*Untermenschen*] of today. The underclass. And the country is degenerate, debased, so much more debased than the city! The last war has been the ruination of country people!" (165).[4] Strauch uses the Nazi term "Untermensch" to criticize the rural people. Bernhard thus brings up a comparison between the city and the countryside. The war and despair drove people in the countryside to commit crimes. However, reading between the lines shows that participation in National Socialism was also considered to be a crime, and therefore Strauch describes the people on the countryside as "Untermenschen." The use of this term, which the Nazis used against Jews and foreigners from the East, is used here to disparage the countryfolk, who had been idealized in the Fascist era. In this context, it is also important to note that the knacker has a long-standing tradition as an untouchable figure in German literature since Heinrich von Kleist's novella *Michael Kohlhaas* (1808). Bernhard very likely chose the knacker in this role in his novel, because just like the one in Kleist's novella, he spoils everything he touches. The knacker confirms Strauch's idea that the locals committed numerous crimes during the war.

> In the war, there was no lack of criminality here. And even after the war, when I was back home, people were brained over a bicycle or a piece of bread. And imagine this: the French let the convicts out of the prisons, and they flooded the entire country; every little place saw killings over a blanket, or an old horse. Not to mention the acts of vengeance! […] During and after the war, he was in Weng with his sister. The farmers did not treat him at all well.' The painter had been forced to sleep in an attic of the inn for a while, 'because the rooms were all full of soldiers.' (105)

The blame for a part of the crimes committed towards the end of the war is still being put on the actual victims, namely the prison inmates. According to this, the French as the occupying power caused chaos in the village when they released these prisoners. They are also being blamed for Strauch and his sister losing their room. This passage shows the greed of the locals in the postwar period and it turns out that through this avarice, people were injured and wounds opened that have not yet healed. The people in this small mountain village used the chaos at the end of the war to their advantage. Compared to a large city, people in this village live close to each other and also know each other well, which after the crimes that these villagers perpetrated on each other during the war estranged all these close relationships. Strauch declares to the *Famulant* that no generation is too young to have memories of the war:

> "The war was finished by the time you were ready to think. You know nothing about the war. You know nothing, period. And these people, all of them on the lowest level, often the lowest level of character, these people are all prize witnesses to the great crimes that were perpetrated." (55)

The locals of Weng, whom Strauch refers to as "these people," know very well what happened during the war. He considers their refusal to remember to be a character flaw. "The great crimes" refer to war crimes and the crimes committed by the Nazis. However, the multitude of petty crimes committed in Weng also belongs to this listing, and the microcosm Weng represents Austria. The small crimes committed in Weng represent the larger crimes that Austrians sought to hide after the war. Thus, this passage also alludes to the founding myth of an innocent Austria that was put to sleep from 1938 to 1945. This uncanny view of the post-war era in Austria that Bernhard presents in *Frost* explains Bernhard's longing for a more glorious past.

The novel abounds in regular, everyday, almost absurd mean acts that Strauch and the *Famulant* experience in the small town, all of which are a product of the father's generation. It would be impossible to name them all, but I will examine a few that document the pathological disturbance of personal relationships in Weng. Strauch suffers from the roughness of the people in Weng. The lady who owns the local inn, whom Strauch describes as a typical example of an inn hostess in Salzburg, serves her guests dog meat which she receives from her lover, the knacker. Her husband is in prison for murder, but his release is foreseeable in the coming years. Strauch is deeply affected by the inn hostess's refusal to send money to her husband and her reluctance to mail packages to him in prison. The case of the imprisoned innkeeper poses the question of rehabilitating convicted criminals. Strauch claims: "But you have to help someone like that, who's been taken out of society, and held up to all as a criminal, don't you?" (239). Strauch says that he supports the rehabilitation of criminals. He wants to help outcasts of society who have served their time for a crime. One may also find references to Bernhard's angst regarding the justice system which resulted from the libel case brought against him by Peter Stanchina in the second half of the 1950s.[5] Strauch announces: "Do you know what I hear now? I can hear charges being brought against the big ideas, a great court has been convoked to hear the case, I can hear them slowly beginning to arraign all the big ideas" (34). Bernhard, who was to endure two more libel cases, criticized already in *Frost* the overwhelming power of judicial courts and the lack of unlimited freedom of speech.

Strauch mourns the collapse of the Habsburg monarchy by saying: "And finally, as we know, frost may also signify the *end of a world empire*" (280). He recognizes that Austria played hardly any role in the world after 1918 and especially after 1945, and he believes that the country became icy because of the historical turmoil and the wartime crimes. He claims about the state, the government, and Austria's neutrality:

> As far as our own state was concerned, then, aside from the fact that it wasn't a state ('no longer a state!'), it was something as ridiculous as a 'squeaking little rhesus monkey in a big zoo,' in which, naturally enough, only the well-fed and beautiful specimens of lions and tigers and leopards attracted any interest: it was their roaring. Only roaring counted, squeaking was ridiculous! (288)

Austria's relative lack of importance on the international stage is made quite clear with this animal analogy. The country, which tried to assert itself in the post-war period internationally as a cultured nation, is being ridiculed for its insignificant size. Strauch longs for a stronger Austria that does not only "squeak" but can "roar" instead. This again proves the longing of many of Bernhard's literary figures for a stronger Austria without a troubled past. However, Strauch sees no hope of that:

> [T]he state itself is cretinous, and the people are pitiful. Our state is ludicrous. On top of everything, the presence of musicality. Petit bourgeois sordidness [....] we are at a stage of absolute degradation. Our state [...] is a hotel of ambivalence, the bordello of Europe, enjoying an excellent reputation, especially overseas. (289)

Strauch is discontent with the self-complacency of Austrians. He criticizes Austria's desire to market itself as a musical *Kulturnation* and thus thematizes the duality of clean culture and war crimes. At the beginning of the 1960s, especially after the state treaty of 1955 and the Kennedy and Khrushchev summit in 1961, Austria was quite respected in the world. The inclination to refer to the country as a bordello probably stems from the idea that Austria had come to regard itself as the host of important international meetings and events. Strauch accuses the politicians of not speaking the truth and makes them responsible for the lies in the Austrian society.

> Our head of state was a 'co-op manager,' our chancellor 'a market-day brothel attendant.' The people had the choice of butchers, apprentice electricians, dully blown-up waistcoat wearers, between grave-robbers and grave-robbers' assistants. Democracy, 'our democracy,' was the biggest swindle. (288)

This quote refers to the Federal President Adolf Schärf, a Social Democrat, and Federal Chancellor Julius Raab, a Conservative. Bernhard's characters, very much like Bernhard himself, refused to align themselves with one of the two large parties. This comment was unusual in the post-war period when Austria was politically divided, and thus confused readers and reviewers who sought to associate Bernhard with one political affiliation. Bernhard and almost all of his main characters are individualists who are opposed to the collectivity. The difference between Social Democrats and Conservatives is nebulous to Bernhard, as he considered all politicians to be mean-spirited. Bernhard's attitude may be misunderstood as being elitist and anti-democratic. However, it is rather a criticism of his compatriots and a desire for his country to rise from mediocrity. He sees no difference between the two main political parties and the monarchy, which both suppress the individuality that is of such importance to an artist. The reference to his compatriots as grave-robbers has to be seen in connection with the Nazi crimes, and Bernhard uses this term even more pronouncedly in his *Politische Morgenandacht* (*Political Morning Prayer*).

Frost is different from Bernhard's great novels of the 1970s, *Granite (Das Kalkwerk*, 1970) and *Correction* (*Korrektur*, 1975), in that its historical context is post-war Austria before the arrival of *Wirtschaftswunder* prosperity. War experiences, even when these are being partially suppressed, are the main source of the people's pain and suffering, which in turn cause illnesses. The social class of the suffering characters in the novels following *Frost* is elevated, as they are mostly Upper Austrian landowners and scientists. The war has moved into greater distance in these novels. In his roman-à-clef *Extinction* (*Auslöschung*, 1986), Bernhard again deals with the past and his critique of the fathers intensifies with the temporal distance from his grandfather.

In the fragment "Der Italiener" (The Italian), which was published in 1964 and was the template for *Extinction*, Bernhard further develops his uneasiness with contemporary Austria. The narrator in this very short text has a conversation with an Italian visitor who has come to attend the funeral of the narrator's parents. As they stroll around the estate, the narrator tells the Italian about plays which he as a child wrote with his siblings and then performed in the family's *Lustgarten*. The Austrian connects with the Italian, who also participated in this kind of summer activity as a child. Suddenly, the narrator senses a level of comfort with his Italian friend that leads him to show this man the location of the mass grave near the woods, where two dozen Polish corpses lie buried. He goes on to confide in the Italian that his father used to refer to the *Lusthaus* as a slaughterhouse. As a child, for years the narrator heard the crying of the Polish victims before he could fall asleep. The Italian describes this mass murder as a "Greuel" [atrocity]. The narrator says: "There are 'no means to flee from oneself.' What he meant with this at this precise moment, I did not know. We were standing in front of the window, exactly in front of the dead man [his father]." (trans. of *Der Italiener*, 40). This text differs from *Frost*, because the Poles are the victims and the Austrians and Germans are the perpetrators. The Italian understands his Austrian friend. Both men have grown up in post-Fascist countries. There is no escape from this past for either Austrians or Italians in their respective countries. The narrator explains further to his friend that he also confided his family's secret to a friend from Hungary and one from Freistadt, Upper Austria. History connects these three confidants through their pre-Fascist past in the Habsburg Empire. Thus, rather than connecting with Germans through their shared language and the recently shared past in Nazi Germany, the Austrian in this text feels culturally connected to the former peoples of Austria-Hungary.

In *Extinction*, Bernhard's final novel, which he published more than twenty years later, in 1986, he picks up the "Italiener" fragment and writes a roman-à-clef that incorporates many of the themes of his earlier works. Bernhard fleshes out the close relationship between the Austrian narrator, Franz-Josef Murau, and his Italian student, Gambetti, whom he gives private lessons in Rome. In her essay "The Established Outsider: Bernhard," Dagmar Lorenz points out that Murau's elitist pose as a private scholar for whom the liberal arts are the only prerogative, and who thus depends on the monarchial hierarchy fits better into the period *ante quem* (34). Murau does not fit into the present, but longs for this glorious past. In many ways this is autobiographical, as Bernhard felt similarly about Austria. The plot of *Extinction* centers on Murau, who has just returned to Rome when he receives the news that his parents have died in a car accident. He dreads having to return to his family's estate, and in his mind he prepares to explain his sudden return to Austria to his student. Murau has left Austria and prefers to live in Italy, where he is in the company of the Austrian poet Maria, a character much resembling Ingeborg Bachmann. Murau and Maria share their love for Italy, a foreign country, but not foreign enough to feel culturally disconnected. Murau is following in the footsteps of his uncle Georg, who turned his back on his family and lived abroad in various Mediterranean countries and thus remained the only relative clear of a Nazi past. The uncle serves as a mentor for Murau, and the mutual rejection of Murau's parents' ideology unites these two figures. The uncle's rejection of his brother alienated him from the rest of his family, a position similar to that of those Austrians who rejected Nazism in that particular generation. Georg is the exception and not the rule for his generation, and so is his rejection of Austria and the German language. Murau says about his uncle: "Das Deutsche ist das Unerträglichste, sagte er [Georg]. Ich war begeistert, wenn er *Die mediterranen Länder* sagte. Es ist ein Schock, sagte er, hierher [nach Österreich] zurückzukommen" (42). The German language and all things German are unbearable for Georg because he feels that they are irrevocably linked to the mass murder committed by the Nazi regime. Murau and his uncle are unable to disassociate the language from these crimes. This sentiment is also connected to the fact that the Nazis bombastically used the German language to express their desire for racial superiority, thereby degrading their victims. This invalidated the use of German for many after 1945. Murau feels that his mother tongue has weighed him down, and he is not yet able to recognize that German is not only the language of the Nazi perpetrators, but also the mother tongue of many murdered Jewish victims. Despite Murau's interest in literature, he has not yet picked up on post-war Jewish writers like Paul Celan and Walter Benjamin, just two of the many whose writings could have helped Murau accept the language as not solely connected with these crimes and their perpetrators. Murau tells Gambetti:

> German words hang like lead weights on the German language, I had said to Gambetti, and constantly drag the mind down to a level that can only be harmful to it. German thought and German speech soon became paralyzed under the intolerable weight of the language, which suppresses any thought before it can find expression. Under the German language, I said, German thought had developed only with difficulty and never came to full efflorescence, as Romance thought had under Romance languages—as witness the centuries of effort that the Germans had invested in their thinking. (4)

Murau claims that German has hindered the thinking and the historical development of the people who speak the language. This is certainly a self-loathing position for Murau, but it stems from an Austrian desire to disassociate from Germany and German nationalism that is both at the root of the collapse of the multi-ethnic Habsburg Empire and fundamental to the development of Nazism. Murau admires Romance languages, and this is certainly contrary to the Nazi idea of the superiority of the German language. This break with the German language is not only a critique of his father, but also of his grandfather who had praised the German language. With the temporal distance from his grandfather's death increased by twenty years, Bernhard started to feel comfortable criticizing both his father and grandfather in a way that he would not have been able to do in *Frost* (see Judex, 234). Italy and the Italian language, which used to be one of the many languages of the old Austria, are both different enough from the contemporary Austrian republic, and yet there is a connection through history.

Since Bernhard never explicitly refers to the Habsburg monarchy, one could argue that there are also other cultural connections between these Central European countries, such as the shared Roman Catholic religion. Despite Bernhard's conservatism, he was very suspicious of the church's role in Austria in almost all of his texts. In fact in *Auslöschung*, Murau considers Austria's Catholic/National Socialist heritage to be at the root of all the evil deeds perpetrated there. In defense of himself Murau writes:

> I am always dragging Austria in the dirt, they [his critics responding to his editorials in newspapers] say, denigrating my own country in the most outrageous fashion and crediting the Austrians with base and despicable Catholic and National Socialist opinions whenever and wherever I can, whereas according to the writers, no such base and despicable opinions exist in Austria. Austria is not base and despicable, they say; it has *never been anything but beautiful*, and the Austrians are decent people. (9-10)

Fascism and Roman-Catholicism, which most former countries of the Habsburg Empire experienced in their histories may also link these countries, especially in the way they failed to confront this aspect of their past. In opposition to this past, Bernhard and his literary protagonists uphold a positivist historical conceptualization of the distant Habsburg Empire that both struggles to boost Austria's self-image over the unspeakable crimes committed in the country's more recent past and also links Austrians to their neighbors in Central Europe. The criticism of Austria in this novel is also strengthened in comparison to *Frost* by the fact that Murau explicitly refers to Austria's National Socialist past. The protagonist is ashamed of his country and despises his parents for their involvement;

> It's natural to love one's parents, and it's equally natural to love one's brothers and sisters, I thought [...] We therefore fail to notice that from a

certain moment onward we hate them, without wanting to, just as normally as we previously loved them, for all kinds of reasons that we become aware of only years later, often decades later. (6)

The open criticism of his parents and the clear accusation of many Austrians' allegiance to National Socialism is spelled out very clearly in *Extinction*. Murau does not shy away from comparing Nazi Fascism and Roman Catholicism and finding similarities in how these ideologies oppress people. In fact, Bernhard first expressed this idea in his autobiographical novel *Die Ursache* (1975), where he chronicles his stay at the boarding school in Salzburg's Schrannengasse just before and after the war. Here, he claims, there was no difference in the cruelties committed by the Nazi principal and his Catholic successor. In *Extinction* Murau picks up on this theme and complains that he has been receiving letters in which people criticize him for saying that Austrians have a *katholisch-nationalsozialistische Gesinnung* (a Catholic/National Socialist mind-set). In the twentieth century, Austria experienced two Fascist regimes: the Clerico-Fascist Corporate State (1934-38) and the *Anschluss* to Hitler Germany (1938-45). However, while many regarded the Corporate State authoritarian, after the 1945 no one initially compared this regime to Nazi Germany. Murau's conception of equating Roman Catholicism with National Socialism was still a new phenomenon in Austrian literature in 1986, and it rejected the idea that Fascism was forcibly imported to Austria from Germany.

While the frankness and clarity of Bernhard's criticism is most distinct in his final novel, it was clearly present in his first novel as well. Over the years he became more comfortable formulating his critique more directly. This change came about through his public reception, which over the twenty-three years between *Frost* and *Extinction* turned him from a rising young author into an old critic of his country, thus making him more comfortable living up to the image of a critic. Perhaps needless to say, the public failed to understand the reasons for his criticism and that in many ways he loved his country more than the people labeling him a *Nestbeschmutzer*.

Works Cited

Bernhard, Thomas. *Extinction*. Chicago: University of Chicago Press [Translation of *Auslöschung* (1986).]

—. *Frost*. 1963. Translated by Michael Hofmann. New York: Knopf, 2006.

—. *Gathering Evidence*. Translated by David McClintock. New York: Knopf, 1985. [Translation including *Die Ursache* (1975), *Der Keller* (1976), *Der Atem* (1978), *Die Kälte* (1981), and *Ein Kind* (1982).]

—. "Mit der Klarheit nimmt die Kälte zu." *Jahresring*. Stuttgart: DVA, 1965 (74-89).

Dowden, Stephen. *Understanding Thomas Bernhard*. Columbia, SC: University of South Carolina Press, 1991.

Judex, Bernhard. *Der Schriftsteller Johannes Freumbichler 1881-1949*. Vienna: Böhlau, 2006.

Ludewig, Alexandra. *Grossvaterland*. Bern: Peter Lang, 1999

Markolin, Caroline. *Thomas Bernhard and His Grandfather*. Riverside: Ariadne, 1993

Pfabigan, Alfred. "*Frost* als zeitgeschichtliche Quelle: Versuch einer Parallellektüre des Bernhardschen Erstlings und der *Unfähigkeit zu trauern* von Alexander und Margarethe Mitscherlich." *Österreich und andere Katastrophen*. Edited by Jeanne Benay and Pierre Béhar. St. Ingbert: Röhrig, 2001 (74-89).

Notes

[1] Several studies have examined the relationship between Bernhard and his grandfather in great detail. Some of the most noteworthy are Caroline Markolin's *Thomas Bernhard and His Grandfather*, Alexandra Ludewig's *Grossvaterland*, and Bernhard Judex's *Der Schriftsteller Johannes Freumbichler 1881-1949*.

[2] Alfred Pfabigan claims that the development of *Frost* falls into the period of the Eichmann and Auschwitz trials, but this novel still seems to respect the collective feeling of seeing Austria as the first victim of Hitler's aggression (see Pfabigan, 80).

[3] Stephen Dowden refers to Strauch's comment that the privations of wartime were the reason for moral decay (see Dowden, 23).

[4] Michael Hofmann translates *Untermenschen* as underclass. This is not necessarily correct in English, as Bernhard was not writing about a social class, but rather a sort of degraded and inferior human being.

[5] From 1956 to 1959 the director of the Salzburg State Theater, Peter Stanchina, pursued a libel case against Bernhard on account of an article that he had published about the theater in the newspaper *Die Furche*. After several appeals the case was dropped in 1959. This was the first of three major libel cases brought against Bernhard during his lifetime.

CHAPTER NINETEEN

THE RETURN OF THE REPRESSED AS DIAGNOSIS AND CURE IN DORON RABINOVICI'S *SEARCH FOR M*

REBECCA S. THOMAS

National Forgetting and the Return of the Repressed

The Austrian presidential election of 1986 and its cultural reverberations precipitated a radical shift in Austrian history and cultural consciousness. As the Waldheim affair[1] destroyed once and for all the myth of Austrian innocence by exposing the distortions of post-war historiography, Austrians were forced to re-examine and revise long standing notions of national and personal identity. The election of Dr. Kurt Waldheim to the Austrian presidency was a watershed event in that it brought to light knowledge of Austrian ties to Nazism that had long been repressed or denied. The reaction generated by the very public revelations about Waldheim's past and, more significantly, the omissions in his account thereof in his memoir, led ultimately to a new direction in Austrian literary and political discourse. For the first time since 1945, Austrian politicians, artists and intellectuals conducted open and heated discussion about Austria's willing embrace of Nazism as ideology and practice.

The net effect of these revelations was the palliative if often difficult experience of bringing events to consciousness that had long been hidden in revisionism or banished entirely from memory. In his essay "Taboos and Self-Deception The Second Republic's Reconstruction of History," Anton Pelinka follows the threads of memory and forgetting back to the Moscow Declaration (1943) and the early days of Austrian post-war identity formation

> The victim hypothesis of the Moscow Declaration, isolated from the hypothesis of joint responsibility, has become the basis for Austria's identity as a victim. What has been forgotten more or less is the second part of the Moscow Declaration which holds Austria responsible for National Socialism and its crimes. This process of forgetting started as early as 27 April 1945, when in the preface of the Declaration of Independence only the victim hypothesis was formulated, while the hypothesis of joint responsibility was almost hidden at the end of the document. Another part of this forgetfulness was that the State Treaty no longer included any reference to the concept of joint responsibility (Pelinka, 95).

Austria's characteristic refrain "*Glücklich ist, wer vergisst*" ["happy the one who forgets"] became untenable in a post- Holocaust world.[2]

The politically engaged authors and intellectuals who played a central role in combating a relapse into repression of national history in the wake of the Waldheim Affair were often reviled as "*Nestbeschmutzer*" (birds that foul their own nest) by those who feared being exposed or resented the "unpatriotic" criticism of Austria. The demands from private citizens and public officials alike that these authors be silenced or even driven from the country was in reality an attempt to keep repressed knowledge and information from becoming public. [3] The desire to defame, silence or remove the agents of historical memory represented an attack on the historical facts themselves as enemies of the false self-image of the Second Republic. The vitriolic backlash against the messengers of historical truth reproduced the dynamics of classic Freudian repression on a national scale. Austrian post-war identity, the national ego, depended on the continued repression of its ties with National Socialism.

The Search for M and Freudian Repression

In his novel, *The Search for M.* [*Suche nach M.*] (1999), Doron Rabinovici reveals the mechanisms and consequences of forgetting for Jews and non-Jews alike in the postwar era. He contrasts forgetting as willful revisionism by non-Jewish Austrians with Holocaust victims' forgetting as repression of trauma. The recovery of memory becomes a potential locus of healing, as well as the vehicle for creating and restoring meaningful personal and national narratives. In this sense, the entire novel can be read as a masterfully ironic working through of the implications of Freud's theory of repression, transferred here from the individual to the national scale.

In Rabinovici's novel, repression becomes a complex extended metaphor for Austrian post-war history. The novel's structure and symbolic schema rest on two prongs of Freud's theory of trauma and hysteria: the persistence of repressed traumatic memory expressed as hysterical symptom, and the healing of hysteria through a cognitive and affective return of the repressed:

> We must presume [...] that the psychical trauma—or more precisely the memory of the trauma—acts like a foreign body which long after its entry must continue to be regarded as an agent that is still at work; and we find the evidence for this in a highly remarkable phenomenon which at he same time lends an important *practical* interest to our findings. For we found, to our great surprise at first, that *each individual hysterical symptom immediately and permanently disappeared when we had succeeded in bringing clearly to light the memory of the event by which it was provoked and in arousing its accompanying affect, when the patient had described that event in the greatest possible detail and had put the affect into words*" (Freud, *Hysteria* 6).

Bringing the truth to consciousness and *language* is the source of healing. Silence is the enemy, and is therefore logically associated with everything dysfunctional in the novel. The moments of healing invariably involve a listener, an "other" who, like an analyst, prompts, recognizes and acknowledges the reality of the depths being disclosed, an other to receive the telling. This structural element underscores the necessity of dialogue, of speaking and listening, for healing, and as such both suggests and mirrors the talking cure popularized by Freud's therapeutic practice. The link between the talking cure and post-holocaust testimonials is explicit. The telling brings transfiguration, is the "liberating, although frightening" encounter with memory and history (Felman, 47).

Rabinovici's novel also mirrors psychoanalytic models in its fulsome use of dreams, slips and jokes that both conceal and reveal the truth of hidden thoughts and desires. Like the interpretation of dreams, the interpretation of the novel reveals the repressed. But whereas Freud's turn-of-the-century work was principally concerned with exploring taboos regarding sexuality, Rabinovici's post-Waldheim novel explores the taboo topic of Austria's Holocaust experience, which does not seem "entirely dissimilar to the many sexual secrets" (18).[4] Like Freud, Rabinovici seeks to reveal what culture hides from its self. Austria after the trauma of World War II is the patient on the couch.[5] [6]

The figures of this novel are joint witnesses to a trauma, and are afflicted with what Shoshan Felman refers to as the "sickness of the one who 'knows'" (Felman, 12). While the physical location of the novel alternates between Vienna and Tel Aviv, the novel's emotional and thematic cite is the domain of unacknowledged knowledge, that is, what is hidden within "one who knows." The traumatic site is bifurcated: on one side, the victims of the Holocaust, and on the other, Austrians who want to forget what they know about what they or their fellow Austrians did to the victims. [7]

In his 1914 essay "Remembering, Repeating and Working Through," Freud explores the effects of repressed memory through an evaluation of psychosomatic symptoms broadly referred to as signs of "traumatic neurosis" (Freud, "Remembering," 145). The traumatic event, which is not remembered or even available to consciousness, is repeated through seemingly unrelated tics or repetitive behaviors. The repeating behaviors are the physical eruption of a repressed memory event through which the victim acts out the trauma over and over again, reliving the sensory experience without volition or conscious memory.

Trauma is imprinted on both body and psyche in Rabinovici's text. The physical marks of the Shoah show up on Mosche Morganthau's x-rays, in which his deformed spinal column tells the story of days and months spent hunched in a hiding place on Warsaw's city limits. The contortion upon which his survival depended has left a memorial of pain and disfiguration, "the stigmata of his lack of motion as a child" (16)[8] about which he doesn't wish to speak, but that is real and immediate. His chronic back pain is a sign that the past is not past but persists in the present in tangible ways. The persistence of this suffering then becomes the metaphor for the continuing effects of the unspoken past in contemporary Austrian culture generally. The physical mark borne by Mosche's spine parallels the psychological disfiguration borne by individuals as well as the collective in Rabinovici's narrative.

In his *Of Memory, Reminiscence, and Writing On the Verge*, David Farrell Krell presents an insightful analysis of the intersection of "memory, malady and therapy" for Freud (Krell, 106). Krell takes special note of Freud's assertion that "hysterical patients are suffering from reminiscences" (Freud, *Hysteria,* 7). The suffering of the patients treated by Freud and Joseph Breuer at this time was often accompanied by somatic symptoms without physiological causes:

> He [Freud] explained that whatever complaints hysterics might have, a facial tic, chronic nausea, numbness in the limbs, the complaints could be regarded—a purely physiological, "medical" cause having been excluded—as vestiges of remembrance. Freud called them *Erinnerungssymbole*, "symbols of remembrance."...Freud compared these

> symptoms to monuments or memorials—like ancient herms, serving as both burial crypts and pathmarkers—that affect the patient in a mysteriously persistent and overpowering way (Krell, 106).

These symbols of remembrance are evident in the first generation Holocaust survivors in Rabinovici's text. Mosche Morgenthau is hampered not only by the physical deformation of his spine, but by an increasingly severe and disabling speech disorder in which his inflection indicates the opposite of his desires. This verbal tic can be "attributed…to the *incompleteness* of amnesia, the *failure* to achieve total forgetfulness, the ultimate futility of resistance," that is to say, the futility of the attempt to hold the past at bay (Krell, 107).[9]

Symptoms as Symbols of Memory

Rabinovici gives us a detective novel and psychological thriller. Generations of Jews and non-Jews alike have been robbed of memory and identity, the parents through an inability or unwillingness to remember and testify to their trauma, and the children through the narrative void created in the parents' silence. Jakob Scheinowitz survived the Holocaust in which his ex-wife and daughter perished. Plagued by the trauma he witnessed as well as his guilt over the accident of his survival, he attempts to escape the history that has been his defining destiny. In the post-war years, he endeavors to re-invent himself outside the memory and identity of the Jewish community to which he remains only briefly and loosely in contact before disappearing into his new identity as Jakob Fandler. He spurns the future of joint suffering he sees represented by his friends who re-marry other survivors. Incapable of forming meaningful relationships with women, he spends the years after the war engaged in a series of meaningless love affairs with much younger women, all the while smoking and drinking to excess. This clear pattern of willful self-destruction expresses through action the death wish (*thanatos*) and nihilism he can not acknowledge or articulate overtly.

In her groundbreaking book *Unclaimed Experience Trauma, Narrative, and History*, Cathy Caruth's interpretation of repression defers the moment of cognitive awareness of the traumatic event itself. It is not that the mind represses the memory of trauma after the event is experienced, but rather that the traumatic event causes a radical disassociation of consciousness at the very time of the event such that the trauma is never really *experienced* at the time of the occurrence at all. It was and remains literally absent from memory, but utterly present as "reminiscence" (unknown knowledge or memory) that expresses itself somatically through physical symptoms beyond the control or comprehension of the sufferer.

By this analysis of Freud's theory, the history of the traumatic event is not present to consciousness until the "return of the repressed" can be achieved, at which time the sufferer actually *experiences* the event *for the first time*. Only after this experiencing of the trauma simultaneously on emotional and cognitive planes can the victim "work through" the event towards a recovery. The silence of the fathers in Rabinovici's text thus represents a past that can not be spoken, both because the horror surpasses language and because the experience is not cognitively available in a form that can be narrated. The trajectory of the text impels its figures towards a return of the repressed that will make limited healing, history and narrative possible again.

In the meantime, however, the repressed can not be integrated, but remains as a fragmentary symptom of failed forgetting. Associations that drag unwanted memory fragments to the surface continually undermine the work of repression. Common articles and experiences of everyday life revive unwanted recollection not as coherent narrative but as shards of the past striped pajamas, confining spaces, an empty larder all evoke past horror. Dani, Mosche's son and the novel's central figure, serves the function of unwanted prod to memory throughout. His refusal to eat as a child results in his emaciated appearance, a frightening, living recollection of starving camp inmates for his parents. In addition, his Grandmother is often silenced for noting that he reminds her strongly of this or that relative deceased in the Holocaust.

The suppression of the survivor's history as transmuted through memory is both a pathology and an act of defiance against the perpetrators, an attempt to withdraw from the continuing sphere of influence radiating from past traumatic experience. Mosche is desperate to construct a new narrative for his child *ex nihilo*, from a fictional Zero Hour in which his story is not deformed and defined by the trauma and humiliation of the parents' generation

> "'Once upon a time there was a little boy and his name was Dani' 'No!' The four year old shrieks as if his throat were on fire. 'I want a real story!'" (14).[10]

But the real story to which Mosche's wounds bear witness can not be told, and the utopian narrative of the second generation unbound from history is an impossibility, so Mosche's stories remain fixed in the aporia of an idealized future that can not materialize without the roots of its forgotten past.

Similarly, Jakob Fandler/Scheinowitz tries to protect his son from his past, saying he won't let "them" (the Nazis) define and destroy the boy. Like Dani, Arieh grows up in the oral tradition of silence, disconnected from both his Jewish history and the contemporary Jewish community from which his father has remained alienated. He can only allude to the horrors of his own experience by telling and retelling the story of persecution and exile contained in the Passover liturgy, a story which is his, but not his. The emotional distance he achieves allows him to relate the events of his suffering as thought speaking of someone else. He transfers the impact of his trauma to a narrative that stands in for his own experience. The defense mechanism of silence and dissociation on the part of the parents ultimately robs the children of personal or group identity and cultural memory, and this leads to crippling psychological consequences. The attempted liberation through denial and resistance to the past backfires in deeply disturbing ways that are visited upon the second generation of survivors.

The fragmentary nature of these unwanted remembrances along with the fierce compulsion to repel and silence those memories as they intrude on consciousness all correspond to the psychological profiles of survivors as victims of trauma. While therapeutic interventions encourage Holocaust survivors, as well as other survivors of abuse and trauma, to recover unwanted fragmentary memories and to integrate them into a personal narrative, the absence of mediation between memory and consciousness leaves the survivor adrift. Without the anchor of emotional and cognitive context, painful memories must be held at bay by whatever distancing devices the sufferer can marshal. The past, like Mosche's silence, is "a coffin" (16) and should be left to rest in peace.

But the past will not rest, let alone peacefully. The survivors' children sense the anxiety and dislocation of their elders, but are alienated from their personal history and identity. Dani and Arieh, the children of Mosche and Jakob, end up as second-generation Holocaust survivors who, as Navah, Arieh's wife, points out, were *also* born with blue numbers on their arms. They, too, suffer the pain and dislocation bequeathed by their parents, but without the emotional context of even repressed experience. They, too, are a lost generation, without history, historical memory, or a solid foundation for identity (Felman, 47). Consequently, they are left with a vague emptiness, and it does not surprise that both Dani and Arieh are afflicted with the unwanted "gift" of taking on the identity of others. Nature abhors a vacuum, and their lack of identity rooted in lost history and memory leaves them as empty vessels. The empty rootlessnes and its psychological and physical symptoms for these young men replicates the failure of post-war Austrian identity.

Arieh, Jakob's son, is the very cipher for the search for self in the novel, and in this search, he takes on the identity of his arch-foes in an attempt to subdue, envelope and control them. Throughout the novel, his father, his father's best friend, and his wife all warn that he can not find himself in others. And yet he is compulsively driven to seek "the other" and to annihilate him, whether it be the racist thug Wernherr in Vienna whom he ultimately stalks and murders, or the Palestinian agents he stalks for the Israeli secret service. His wife, Navah, the historian who researches the history of the Jews of Czernowitz, urges him to look for himself in the history of his people. Leon Fischer, his father's lifelong friend, urges him to return to Cracow after Jakob's death, to see the ghetto and the camps and to begin to re-construct his identity out of the ashes of suffering and survival. Jakob's seemingly cryptic remark that: "If you are you because you are you, and I am I, because I am I, then you are you and I am I. If, however, you are you because I am I and I am I because you are you, then you are not you and I am not I" (37)[11] is the first admonition Arieh receives not to seek himself in others or to let himself be defined in the negative. It is not until the end of the novel that Arieh can embrace this path to identity through recovery of what his ancestors have repressed. In the meantime, he experiences his failed identity as an affliction from which he seeks the "cure" in his flight to Israel.

Meanwhile, Dani, Mosche and Gita's son, recedes behind the mummy-like gauze bandages of Mullemann, literally Bandage (Mulle) Man, the public persona who takes the guilt of the world upon himself, and whose police record ultimately reads "Identity unknown" (171). Dani is the victim of an inexplicable sickness in which his skin flares up in a horrible rash whenever he is in the presence of guilt. When his rash erupts, he takes on the experiences of the perpetrator, and somehow knows not only the details of how the crime was committed, but also the innermost thoughts of the criminal before, during and after the act. All of this he is able to reflect and articulate. The more guilt he encounters, the more he suffers. The more bandages he has to wear, the more Dani disappears into the mass of gauze

> Maybe I'm nothing more than bandages and compresses, totally consumed by them. It seems to me at times that Mullemann is a clump of pains made of numerous deaths and nothing more than a commemorative bundle of various rolls of gauze accidentally woven together. At some points Mullemann thinks: Maybe there is no me (76). [12]

Both Arieh and Dani disappear behind masks that conceal the void of self and meaningful connection to the world. The personal search for self embodied in these characters parallels the post-war search for Austrian identity in the vacuum of historical memory.

Crime as Symptom

Immediately striking in Rabinovici's narrative is the pervasive psychological dysfunction of the characters. Nurtured in an environment of secrecy and hypocrisy, they have either developed symptoms of a psychosomatically induced physical illness or pathologically disturbed criminal behavior. The disabling forces of repressed memory and lost history cripple the texts characters: the Jews suffer myriad physical and emotional maladies, while the majority community is awash in various criminal, anti-social, or pathological behaviors. Both communities suffer a breakdown in interpersonal relations. Crime and psychological disorders from the trivial (kleptomania) to the grave (rape and murder) pervade the novel as metaphors, symptoms of social and political disease. Crime and mental illness are linked in multiple ways throughout, and each has reality based as well as metaphorical meaning. Crime shows up both as a continuation of Nazi culture in an unreconstructed present and also as a pathological symptom of a society out of joint. Mental illness functions as a metaphor for what Gerhard Roth refers to as the "open insanity" of contemporary Austrian culture, as well as a realistic symptom of repression of traumatic memory. While Mosche's speech defect is the eruption of his unresolved status as victim, his son's vicious skin rash takes on a more universal significance. Dani's (Mullemann's) abilities to detect and, more importantly, reflect and articulate guilt make him a mirror not only of the parents' past, but for the society at large. He registers not only the survivor trauma and guilt of the Jewish community, but the crimes past and present of the non-Jewish community. The criminal element that forms the subtext and background for the novel is a metaphor for the interconnectedness of past and present social ills. The skin-heads' violent attack on a foreigner represent the consequences of an unreconstructed mentality in post-war Austria that mirrors and perpetuates the ideology that made the Holocaust possible. For Rabinovici, this mentality is a cancer on the social body, an illness that must be treated. The past erupts in the guise of hatred, violence and corruption into the present, a social parallel to the personal diagnosis of somatic conversion: crime is a symptom of society's underlying malady and dysfunction just as physical symptoms of neurosis point to an underlying psychological condition.

The main action of the story takes place in the Austria of the mid 1990s in the post-Waldheim era. Waldheim himself embodies the historical continuity between un-repented war crimes and contemporary systemic corruption. Rabinovici makes the unambiguous connection that Austria's failure to pursue, prosecute or even acknowledge Austrian perpetrators of war crimes after the war provided the political cover for the openly xenophobic political atmosphere of the late twentieth century, and in effect created an environment corruption in both politics and law:

> [...] [skinheads] got off scot-free in this country, even found sympathy and support in parts of the judicial system and from the police. War criminals were not brought to court and everything recalling the crimes once committed as well as actions provoking persecution and mass murder was deliberately ignored rather than prosecuted. Guilty parties were just not to be found in a country that claimed to be without blemish (29).[13]

The targets have changed but the jackboots and rubber truncheons continue to meet with a tacit acceptance that translates into official protection for the criminal rather than the victim. The political, legal and financial establishments are complicit in concealing the original crime and in sanctioning the perpetuation of resentments and prejudice that lead to injustice. In short, the criminal has become the norm in spite of a facade of respectability and order.

Old resentments and unresolved prejudices persist, and there is plenty of anti-Semitism to be found, yet the most public disruptions of civil society are not rote repetitions of anti-Semitism. Instead, they represent the transference of the underlying attitudes of that made Austria's embrace of Nazism possible onto the ethnic, socio-political realities of the childrens' generation.

Overt anti-Semitism is portrayed as politically incorrect, and, indeed, there are several scenes in which non-Jewish characters are at pains to avoid giving offence to Jews. Part of the humor of the novel results from the eruption of repressed anti-Semitism in jokes, Freudian slips of tactless humor or artificial, self-conscious and stilted discourse that are bound to offend. However, although explicit anti-Semitism is taboo, anti-Turkish sentiments, for example, are openly tolerated and expressed. Crass stereotyping of "foreign" culture is not relegated to isolated bigots, but is institutionalized in politics and law.

After hearing of xenophobic crimes committed but not prosecuted in Vienna of the 1990's, Arieh is driven to stalk the perpetrator. In the process, he begins to dress in the jackboots and leather attire of his skinhead prey, and, filled with racist loathing, begins to wash himself obsessively. Repelled by inchoate revulsion, he recoils from the touch of the Turkish newspaper salesman. Overcome by the aggressive excess of hate he has imbibed, he overzealously pushes the neo-Nazi through a window, killing him with the blow.

Subsequent to the murder, Arieh is forced to flee to Israel, where he hopes to be able to be free to be himself in a realm absent the "other." As a Jew among Jews, he hopes to locate a core of authenticity within himself. His efforts are in vain, however, as the Israeli secret service blackmails him into becoming an Israeli agent stalking the Palestinian enemy. Now, under the assumed name Arthur Bein, he undertakes missions in which he assumes tertiary identities as part of his covert operations. This chain of events repeats his father's paradoxical flight from and search for himself.

In addition, when Arieh takes on the persona of the perpetrator, and then, indeed becomes a perpetrator. As he murders out of revenge, he enters into a cycle of violence that amounts to a criminal compulsion. Rabinovici levels a scathing critique at the economy of violence as either a personal or political tool of vengeance or hatred when he has the now "wanted" Arieh flee to Israel, where he becomes an agent in the perpetuation of the Middle-East conflict and the seemingly endless cycle of violence that imbues that culture.[14] The ultimately self-destructive and self-cancelling nature of the violent solution is vividly portrayed in the chapter "Jael," named for Arieh's daughter. Here, the hunter becomes the hunted, and Arieh's own daughter is used to inform against him in the same way in which he persuades his victims' children to inform against their fathers. The space between victim and perpetrator has been erased, and the moral imperative for action lost. The wheel of events has devolved into senselessness that extends beyond national borders and reaches relentlessly into future generations.

The contrast between the apparent respectability of everyday relations and a hidden, violent reality reflects the rift between appearance and reality in Austrian post-war culture generally. The seemingly unrelated chapter entitled "Keysser" that immediately precedes the "Jael" chapter in *Search for M.* provides a non-Jewish parallel to Arieh's double life. Keysser has no direct relationship to the war, the Holocaust, issues of Jewish identity or Austrian complicity in war crimes. Instead, the chapter is a frightening voyage into the thoughts and habits of a successful businessman, family man, and psychopath. In Keysser, the causes and effects of failed identity formation on a national level crystallize in one very disturbed individual: failed authenticity causes his descent into criminality.

The chapter opens with a scene involving the unfortunate psychoanalyst Caro Sandner who is a failure at therapeutic intervention:

> When she discussed cases with colleagues in a supervisory capacity, cases whose files she had studied, or when she illuminated the inner life of a person who had just left a session, she amazed everyone. In a patient's presence, however, in the isolation of a therapy session, Caro Sandner was often a failure (81).[15]

Her inability to "know" and reach her patients during their sessions is summed up in her pathetically comical inability to spell their names, a cipher for understanding. Upon leaving one such session from which both patient and analyst emerge distraught, Caro is secretly stalked by the murderous rapist Keysser, whose malicious mission is temporarily disrupted by the ring of his cell phone.

Keysser represents the deep alienation of individuals in a contemporary Austrian society whose fundamental brokenness profoundly disrupts or prohibits normal interpersonal relations and psychological development. Keysser is not only alienated from his wife, he also remains fundamentally unknown to and isolated from everyone in his life, including himself. His utter dislocation is reflected in the fact that no one, even long time colleagues, can spell his name, and the constant, symbolic confrontation with this lack of identity in the form of his misspelled name on paychecks, bills and rent notices leaves him frustrated and enraged.

His alienation from the world has both cause and effect in his alienation from himself, which is represented by a radical split in his personality. Keysser appears to be painfully normal and respectable in his roles as devoted father and businessman, but his hidden identity is that of rapist and murderer. On one level, this behavior is the eruption of personal wounds stemming from his utter isolation from meaningful relationships made impossible by the unwillingness to acknowledge the lies at the foundation of his marriage and life as a whole. As such, the psychopathology of Keysser is metaphorical for a dangerous neurosis on the body politic of Austria that is both cause and effect of repressed truth. Beyond this, Keysser's double life is metaphorical for the hypocrisy of bourgeois Austrian society with its façade of respectability, but the underlying truth of xenophobia, racism, and other anti-social, destructive attitudes that emerge in slips and jokes in political platforms endorsed at the voting booth.

An odd thing happens on Keysser's way to a murder, however. When the hapless psychologist Sandner becomes Keysser's target for the second time, she takes note of him, and mistakes him for Mullemann, the man who has been publicly confessing to Keysser's crimes. When he emphatically proclaims his identity as Keysser, she not only accepts it, but correctly spells his name. In this moment of recognition, exposition, and confrontation with the totality of his identity, he suddenly loses the desire to kill, and throws down his knife. This scene depicts a double healing in the moment of crisis that reveals threatening truths, Keysser is brought face to face with himself, is presented with a mirror that clarifies and heals, and he "no longer felt the desire to murder this woman"[16] (92). Simultaneously, Sandner's encounter with revealed truth personified by the immanent threat posed by Keysser cures her of the block that inhibits effective therapy. In this moment, revealed knowledge of themselves and the other brings a cure.

Placed in relationship to the depictions of neo-Nazi, skinhead violence against Jews and minorities depicted in the opening chapters of the novel, this chapter reveals the palliative properties of knowing the *other* as an antidote to violence, racial or otherwise. Jakob Fandler's insight that "if you are you because I am I and I am I because you are you, then you are not you and I am not I"(37)[17] takes on significance in this context. A completely new paradigm of identity formation that does not rely on contrast with an *other* is demanded by the text.

Exposure of the secret of his identity provides the cure for Keysser's pathological outbursts. Similarly, Sina Mohn, the art historian, would seem to have everything going for her, yet she is driven to bouts of kleptomania. When Dani/Mullemann confesses in her place, and she takes him in, the two of them begin to know one another, to share their innermost secrets. In short order, the revelation of concealed wrongdoing and hidden identity acts as a cleansing balm. Sina no longer feels the need to steal, Dani begins to emerge from the Mullemann mummy as the bandages unwind and his rash, the "inexplicable sickness" abates. Healing comes with unwrapping the secrets, the mysteries, exposing the weaknesses and wounds. Only then can the individual connect in healthy ways to the community. This healing begins with the therapeutic encounter with a caring listener, who can bring one face to face with the wound.

The importance of both confessor and unbiased listener in this analogy to the talking cure is key, whether the listening party is an individual or a state. Mosche's speech tic has gotten increasingly worse since he began his futile quest for recognition of his victim status. The search for acknowledgement of state involvement in the Holocaust and corroboration of his personal history is a search for truth that is also the search for healing. Official acknowledgement would bring public and private perceptions of reality, history, and memory into harmony, eliminating the need for the *Erinnerungssymbol* of his linguistic quirk, thus healing his tick. Continued repression of the truth exacerbates his dysfunction.

Return of the Repressed and Healing

For both Freud and Rabinovici, memory is both the cause of the symptoms and the path to a cure. The symptoms actually "constitute the first stage of genuine recollection and recovery" (Krell, 109), and healing proceeds through the recovery of these recollections. The seemingly ancillary figures of Navah, with her study of Jewish History, and Leon Fleischer with his urgent pleas for Arieh to return to Poland to reclaim his past, are the bearers of the message of redemption through memory. However it is Mullemann as a herald for claiming identity and history with his mantra "it was me, I did it!" who brings the sacrifice and cure for the society at large.

The returning Jew provokes unwanted memory of past crimes by his mere presence in Austrian society. For the majority population, his very existence is the reminder of all that this society wants to forget. Dani, like the Jews returning to Austria from imposed exile, becomes a physical *Erinnerungssymbol*, a present manifestation of what is hidden, an eruption of repressed truth into consciousness. Rudi Kreuz, the erstwhile Nazi informant who also profited from the Aryanization of Jewish property, is the novel's prime representative of persistent Anti-semitic tendencies that have actually worsened in the climate of repressed truth:

> It was only after the war that Kreuz's hatred of the Jews erupted into the open. in every one that returned he saw a debt collector, someone who had come to collect what Kreuz withheld from the victimes (112).[18]

Parallel to a patient in analysis, Kreuz and the Austrian public fear and resist revelation, which threatens the defensive fortress of repression:

> It was not merely a matter of a phantom criminal, but of the web of politics, the entanglements of high finance, the embroilment of parliament that had steered and restrained the people for decades. All these had to be drastically trimmed with one ruthless stroke. listening to their sons from their rocking chairs while watching the evening news, however, a few grandfathers warned that if all that should be brought into the open there would be terrible consequences. If these things began to unwind, the very

> bindings holding the community together would dissolve[...] Should all the efforts of their generation have been in vain? Hadn't theycovered over all the tracks during reconstruction, blottedout all the memories wih their determined silence?[...] We really ought to deport this Mullemann, drive him out, if not shoot him[...] (125).[19]

The desire to silence Mulleman here mirrors both the pateint's resistance to traumatic revelations in analysis as well as resistance to revelations of the *Nestbeschmutzer*, those who would unwind the bandages of Austria's concealed past. The intensity of the desire to silence the messenger is proportional to the fear of what might be revealed.

Mullemann is a construct, monstrous and fearful because he reveals all that has been repressed. But this particular Jew in the guise of Mullemann is not content to be a silent reminder, but instead broadcasts wrongdoing, making it impossible for the perpetrators to remain in hiding. It is interesting, however, that his mode is not accusatory, but rather confessional. In his incessant "confessions" of the crimes of others, he not only reveals the truth about hidden wrongs in the society, but he also teaches by example the simple words that establish responsibility for personal actions, and the connection of people to deeds, and experience to identity "It was me. I did it. I'm guilty." This message is meant for Jew and non-Jew alike, to embrace and acknowledge their past and their complicity in perpetuating untenable fictions about personal and collective identity, guilt and history.[20]

Mullemann not only preaches the lesson as he spreads panic of disclosure, but he too bears the imprint of society's wounds on his body. Arieh, who, like a patient in analysis, has been locked in a personal dialectic of resisting and seeking self disclosure fears Mullemann's disclosures when they are in the hospital together and he senses Mullemann "knows" him in some profound and frightening way. In spite of his fear, he is drawn to the truth, which he seeks to read "like a filmstrip" (79) from the discarded bandages Mullemann has left on the floor. The history of everything Mullemann knows is excreted through his wounds and imprinted on the gauze that both hides and heals the oozing sores. The dialectic of hide and seek that Arieh performs parallels the hiding and revealing that characterize the bandages, as well as the potential for aesthetics to simultaneously disguise and reveal truths about that which is otherwise unspeakable and unknowable.

Dani/Mullemann is clearly the key character binding all of the seemingly disparate threads of the story together. He shows up in all of the scenes, accurately reflecting the guilt or innocence of a multi-ethnic culture. In turn, the paintings of the eccentric artist Otto Toot who paints portraits that he then disguises in gauze and bandages until they are unrecognizable by their physical features reflect Mullemann. His self-portrait, entitled *Ahasver* or the eternal Jew, parallels the appearance and function of Mullemann in society and leaves clues about how Mullemann is to be interpreted as well as to the role of literature and art in reclaiming memory. The self-referentiality of the novel itself, along with the metaphor of the filmstrip and the episode surrounding the painter Otto Toot, links artistic language and media to the project of recovery. Literature finds a new relevance and significance in recovering history, identity and memory via its unique representational status. This is the meaning of Jakob's recital of the *Haggadah*, the text of the Passover in which he "told about the exodus from Egypt, about the trek through the Sinai desert as if he had experienced everything himself" (31).[21] The story of persecution, exile and return is *his* story, swaddled in the guise of history. The narrative contains and conceals his trauma, maintaining it just beyond the reach of cognitive recall.

The bandages of Mullemann and in Otto Toot's painting *Ahasver* are the key to the novel. They both conceal and reveal the site of injury. In Shoshana Felman's terms, it is "within the wound, from within the woundedness, that the event, incomprehensible though it may be, becomes accessible" (Felman , 28). Thus, attention to the wound gives access to the event of its infliction, the historical specificity of the Holocaust. Mullemann's bandaging, "pointed to an injury, yet beyond to its healing" (149).[22] However, in order for healing to take place, the bandages must be removed. This will involve revealing those wounds which Austrian society has been as pains to keep hidden. The bandages "disclose all of [a body's] injuries, lay open its breakdowns and defects, but its recovery as well. The blood, the pus, the ointments – they're all memory traces...you can hide…someone by bandages, or recognize him. You can mask and reveal him at the same time" (149-150).[23]

The painting, like Mullemann's uncanny truth and guilt detection, is a mirror. Sina Mohn the art historian went to the gallery "to discover him, but in the meantime it was she who had been discovered...Otto Toot's "Ahasuerus" was a kind of mirror that, instead of the observer's exterior, reflected an inner light and blind spot on one's own conscience" (138).[24] Mullemann's confessions after Sina is caught shoplifting echo Sina's guilt the way Toot's paintings represent and reflect guilt. The painterly trick creating the illusion that the painting's eyes follow the spectator mirrors Mullemann's relentless psychological pursuit of the guilty who, ultimately broken by the confrontation with the truth of their crimes and identities, are left no choice but to confess and claim the hidden secrets of their past, and thus be made whole. Paradoxically, what is concealed in the text of bandage and art makes visible that which the perpetrators wish to conceal. While the psyche flees direct confrontation with trauma and guilt, they can be mediated to consciousness through the symbolic universe of art that provokes self-analysis either therapy or art. *The Search for M.* functions like Toot's paintings and like Mullemann himself. It conceals aspects of Austrian history and culture in a collage of interconnected stories all bound together by Mullemann's gauze, that is part detective thriller and part *roman-a-clef*. When the layers of interpretation are peeled back, like the encounter with Toot's painting, everyone recognizes or finds him or herself. The search for "M" is simultaneously the search for Mullemann and "me" [mir] the gauze thread leads back through the labyrinth of history and experience to the self.

It is telling that Rabinovici's novel ends on the optimistic note of Mullemann breaking away from his duties at the prison, presumably to rejoin Sina and recover Dani, once and for all, to shed the bandages and the guilt, be healed, and seize life. In the final paragraph, Karl Siebert, a mediating figure among the various communities, and not coincidentally a criminal investigator associated with uncovering crimes, stands at a window, "looking through the bars at the open spaces."[25] This final image is a gesture of hope that society, like Mullemann and the others, will one day liberate itself from the prison of self-deception, and emerge into the open spaces in which culture can recover history and identity.

Works Cited

Bernhard, Thomas. *Heldenplatz*. 1988. Frankfurt: Suhrkamp.

Cantor, Jay. *The Space Between Literature and Politics*. 1981. Baltimore: Johns Hopkins UP.

Carruth, Cathy. *Unclaimed Experience Trauma, Narrative and History*. 1996. Baltimore: Johns Hopkins UP.

Codde, Phillippe. 2007. "Burned by the History of the Twentieth Century Trauma and Narrative, Containment in Daniel Stern's Holocaust Novels," *Partial Answers Journal of Literature and the History of Ideas* 5.1 (51-75).

Felman, Shoshana and Dori Laub. 1992. *Testimony. Crises of Witnessing in Literature, Psychoanalysis, and History*. New York: Routledge.

Freud, Sigmund. 1953-1974. "Remembering, Repeating and Working Through: Further Recommendations on the Technique of Psychoanalysis." *The Standard Edition of the Complete Psychological*

Works of Sigmund Freud, Vol.XII. Trans. James Strachey. London: Hogarth (147-156).

—. with Joseph Breuer. 1955. *Studies on Hysteria. The Standard Edition of the Complete Works of Sigmund Freud*, Vol. II. Trans. James Strachey. London: The Hogarth Press.

Krell, David Farrell. 1990. *Of Memory, Reminiscence and Writing*. Bloomington: Indiana UP.

Pelinka, Anton. 1997. "Taboos and Self-Deception The Second Republic's Reconstruction of History." Bischoff, Günter and Anton Pelinka, eds. *Historical Memory and National Identity*. Contemporary Austrian Studies, Vol. 5. New Brunswick: Transaction Publishers (95-102).

Rabinovici, Doron. 1997. *Suche nach M.* Frankfurt am Main: Suhrkamp.

—. 2000. *The Search for M.* Trans. Francis Sharp. Riverside: Ariadne Press.

—. "Der Richtige Riecher" [The Right Nose]. *Papirnik*. 1994. Frankfurt: Suhrkamp.

Roth, Michael S. 1998. *Sigmund Freud: Conflict and Culture*. New York: Alfred Knopf.

Thomas, Rebecca. 2005. "Literatur, Politik, und Liebe: Doron Rabinovici im Gespräch." in *Praesent 2005: Das Österreichische Literaturjahrbuch*. Ed. Michael Ritter. Wien: Edition Praesens (65-72).

Notes

[1] In 1986, Kurt Waldheim ran for and was elected President of Austria. During the electoral campaign, it was revealed that he had lied about his activities during World War II, and that he had had knowledge of war crimes committed in the Balkans during the time of his service. Waldheim vigorously disputed revelations about his membership in Nazi organizations and knowledge of the atrocities committed by the German army unit of which he was an officer in Yugoslavia. The public debate that emerged from the Waldheim affair put Austria's victim status under scrutiny and unleashed a new era of national self-examination among Austrian intellectuals, artists and politicians.

[2] This lighthearted refrain from Johann Strauss's operetta *Die Fledermaus* (1874) characterized Austria's escape into operetta and champagne as the empire hurtled towards collapse before World War I. It is paradigmatic for Austria's historic reticence not to engage openly with its cultural and political realities.

[3] The most widely publicized incident of this phenomenon involved the scandal surrounding Thomas Bernhard's play *Heldenplatz* (1988), which also treated the theme of continuing Anti-Semitism in post-war Austria. Kurt Waldheim referred to the drama as an insult to all Austrians, and the mere rumors of the play's critical

content provoked a public demonstrations and official calls for the play to be withdrawn from the *Burgtheater*.

[4] "nicht unähnlich den vielen sexuellen Geheimnissen" (32).

[5] Rabinovici's allusion to Freud is vital both as text and subtext: as text, it provides a structural matrix linking the disparate parts and characters of the novel in a metaphor of illness and healing; as subtext, it underscores the continuity of Austrian Jewish intellectuals from the turn of the century to the contemporary day as pivotal contributors to and critics of modern Austrian identity.

[6] Trauma was always central to Freud's project of disclosing repressed memory While Janet's and Freud's research focused initially on female hysteria and neurosis, Freud's attention was soon drawn by soldiers returning from World War I whose pathological condition he considered akin to the syndromes of neurotics. Hence, the soldier's post-war psychological problems became known as "war neurosis," also known as "shell shock." With every new major war, the terminology changed, from "shell shock" after World War I, to "combat fatigue" and "survivor syndrome" after World War II, and finally to post-traumatic stress disorder (PTSD) after the Vietnam war, a condition officially recognized by the American Psychiatric Association in 1980. Trauma, in short, has always been closely allied to crises of war (Codde, 51). The word "trauma" comes from the Greek word for "wound." Trauma is a wound to the psyche so profound that the conscious mind can not assimilate or confront it. The mind's defense mechanism is to repress the memory of the traumatic event in order to protect consciousness from the confrontation with the wound, to prevent a reliving of the traumatic event.

[7] The question of repressed and recovered memory is one of the most hotly debated quarrels in psychology today. In contemporary psychology, both the model and efficacy of repressed and recovered memory have come under serious scrutiny. However, within a historically verifiable arena of events such as war or genocide in which the victim's presence at the site of trauma can be confirmed, the therapeutic effects of recovering memory continue to have currency and relevance. Victims of post-traumatic stress disorder (PTSD), of which Holocaust survivors and soldiers make up significant sub-sets, continue to benefit not only from drug therapy for depression, anxiety and sleep disorders, but also from what is a modern adaptation of Freud's psychoanalytic concepts. Therapies in this arena may range from dialog and working through of disturbing images and memories with the therapist, to various forms of art therapy and therapeutic creative writing or story telling. Each of these therapeutic interventions is indebted to Freud's original notion of the "talking cure." Some current trends in psychology seek to link observations regarding memory and the unconscious to the neurosciences and brain mapping, that is to say, to remove analysis from the realm of pseudo-science and to bridge the gap between mind and brain. For a thorough discussion of the debates surrounding contemporary reception of Freud's theories see, *Sigmund Freud: Conflict andCulture*, the volume edited by Michael S. Roth, the currator of the controversial Freud exhibit mounted by the Smithsonian Institute.

[8] "[...]die Stigmata seiner Kindlichen Unbeweglichkeit" (29).

[9] The symptom of facial tic which appears in Freud's case study of Frau Emmy von N., in *Studies on Hysteria* (91-93) may have served as a model for Mosche's disorder.
[10] "'Nein', schreit der Vierjährige auf, ein Brand geht durch seine Kehle. 'Ich will eine richtige Geschichte'" (27).
[11] "Wenn du du bist, weil du du bist, und ich ich bin, weil ich ich bin, dann bist du du, und ich bin ich; wenn aber du du bist, weil ich ich bin, und ich ich bin, weil du du bist, dann bist du nict du, und ich bin nicht ich" (59).
[12] "Zuweilen schein mir, als wäre Mullemann ein Schmerzpaket zahlloser Tode; nichts als ein Erinnerungsbündel aus verschiedenen, zufällig verwobenen Mullrollen. In manchen Momenten denkt Mullemann: Vielleicht gibt es mich nicht" (114-115).
[13] "Ihn wunderte nicht, wenn solche Gruppen in diesem land meist ungeschoren blieben, Verständnis und Fürsprache fanden bei Teilen der Justiz und der Polizei. Kriegsverbrecher wurden nicht vor Geicht gestellt, und alles, was sich auf die Untaten, die hier einst begangen worden waren, berief, zu Hatz und Massenmord aufforderte, wurde nicht verfolgt, sondern geflissentlich übersehen. Schuldige durften nicht zu finden sein in einem Land, das allgemeine Unbeflecktheit beanspruchte" (47).
[14] It should be noted that Rabinovici makes the distinction in other works between the violence of hatred and revenge, and necessary moments of self-defense. In his short story "The Right Nose" [Der Richtige Riecher], the Jewish protagonist, known for his gift for language and persuasion, is forced to deliver a nose-breaking punch to a friend whose latent anti-Semitic attitudes prove impervious to words of reason. As Rabinovici noted in a 2004 Interview "Sometimes a blow can have a clarifying effect" ["Manchmal wirkt ein Schlag klärend"], (Interview, 69).
[15] "Besprach sie im Kreis der Kollegenschaft, in Supervision, die Fälle, deren Akten sie studiert hatte, oder leuchtete sie das Innere einer Person aus, die eine Sitzung eben verlassen hatte, so versetzte sie mit ihren Einsichten alle in erstaunen, doch in Gegenwart eines Patienten, in der Einsamkeit mit einer Person, die Caro Sandner aufgesucht hatte, versagte sie nicht selten" (120).
[16] "war ihm alle Lust, die Frau zu ermorden, vergangen" (136).
[17] "[...]wenn aber du du bist, weil ich ich bin, und ich ich bin, weil du du bist, dann bist du nicht du, und ich bin nicht ich" (59).
[18] "Erst nach dem Krieg entbrannte Kreuz in offenen Haß auf Juden, sah er in jedem, der zurückkehrte, einen Schuldeneintreiber, einen, der gekommen war, zu holen, was Kreuz den Opfern vorentheilt" (164).
[19] [...]hier ging es nicht nur um ein Phantom des Verbrechens, sondern um den Filz der Politik, um die Verstrickungen der Finanz, die Seilschaften des Parlaments, die das Volk seit Jahrzehnten Lenkten und gängelten...Doch einige Groβväter...hörten die Worte ihrer Söhne und warnten im Schaukelstuhl vor den Abendnachrichten, wenn all das nun aufgerollt werden sollte, würde Schrecklichstes geschehen, würde sich bei solch einer Abwicklung der Gesamtverband der Gemeinschaft auflösen...Wer...wäre in diesem Land denn frei von Schuld? Sollten all die Anstrengungen ihrer Generation vergeblich gewesen

sein? Hatten sie nicht alle Spuren im Wiederaufbau verwischt, alle Erinnerungen mit verbissenem Schweigen ausgelöscht? ...vertreiben müβte man diesen Mullemann" (182-183).

[20] The Christ imagery in this text is striking. Mosche's scars from the Ghetto are referred to as stigmata, and Dani literally takes the sins of the world upon himself and ultimately atones and brings redemption to the people. Simultaneously, Dani can also be read as a protective but potentially threatening Golem figure.

[21] "vom Auszug aus Ägypten, vom weg durch die Wüste Sinai, als hätte er alles selbst erlebt" (50).

[22] "[...]wies auf eine Verletzung hin, doch auch auf deren Heilung" (216).

[23] "[...]tragen eine Niederschrift des Körpers an sich. Sie sind die Bekenntnisse aller Verletzungen, die Offenlegung von Versagen und Makel, doch ebenfalls der Genesung. Das Blut, das Eiter, die Salben...all das sind Erinnerungsspuren...Mit einem Verband kannst du jemanden verstecken und bestimmen oder wieder erkennen; du kannst ihn vermummen und enthüllen zugleich" (216).

[24] "Sie war ausgezogen, ihn zu entdecken, doch mittlerweile war sie es, die entdeckt wurde. ...Ihr dämmerte es, dass Ott Toots 'Ahasver' eine Art Spiegel war; in dem er nicht das Äußere des Betrachters reflektierte, sondern sein Augenlicht und blinder Fleck: das Eigene Gewissen" (201).

[25] "[...]durch das Gitter ins Freie" (269).

CHAPTER TWENTY

THE DESTRUCTION OF IDYLLIC AUSTRIA IN WOLF HAAS'S DETECTIVE NOVELS

HELGA SCHRECKENBERGER

In the German-speaking countries, the detective novel has traditionally been relegated to the realm of popular fiction and deemed not worthy of serious literary consideration (see Nusser, 7; Düsing, 7).[1] However, the postmodern challenge to the division between high and low culture has resulted in a change in the dismissive attitude towards detective fiction, especially in Austrian literature,[2] and over the last decade, a significant number of Austrian writers have chosen the detective novel as their preferred literary genre.[3] Moreover, their novels have met with great success, achieving both reader popularity and critical acclaim in Austria as well as in Germany.[4] In contrast to earlier "detective writers" like Peter Handke, Gerhard Roth and Peter Rosei, these authors—Paulus Hochgatterer, Thomas Glavinic, Wolf Haas, Alfred Komarek, Lisa Lercher, Stefan Slupetzky, and Heinrich Steinfest among others—are not interested in deconstructing the generic conventions of the detective narrative, but rather in utilizing its potential to elicit both pleasure and social insight.

This is certainly true for Wolf Haas, whose six novels featuring Simon Brenner, former police detective turned private eye, rank among the most successful and popular of the contemporary Austrian detective novels.[5] Haas entertains and intrigues readers by embroiling his protagonist in the most unusual and complicated murder cases, and with the rather unorthodox manner in which the cases are solved. However, solving the murders does not result in a "happy ending." Unlike the traditional mystery, the old order, which has been upset by the crime, is not reestablished at the end. Rather, Haas's detective novels exemplify Richard Alewyn's definition of the detective story as a "parable of the destruction of an ideal world" (343).[6] The investigation of the murders unearths too much guilt and criminal activity and too many embarrassing details for the idyll ever to be credibly restored again. Haas aims his destruction at the official image and narrative of an idyllic Austria as the sum of its beautiful landscapes, rich culture, traditional values, and cheerful, wholesome inhabitants. Each of his novels satirically exposes these perceptions as clichéd constructions and pretensions that bear little resemblance to reality. In doing so, Haas masterfully appropriates the formal and thematic conventions of the traditional detective story for his satirical criticism of Austrian society.

In his study *Murder from an Academic Angle,* Heta Pyrhönen points out the dynamic nature of all literary genres and applies it to detective fiction

> In fact, each new instance in a genre constitutes an addition to an existing corpus and entails a selection from the repertoire of generic elements available at any one time. Some elements are included, others excluded; some even become mutually incompatible. Each new novel aims to extend or to modify the repertoire, either by adding a new element or by transgressing one of the old ones. (41)

According to Pyrhönen detective fiction constantly redefines the boundaries of the genre. He thus rejects the structuralists' understanding of the detective genre as repetitions of the same text as a too uniform view of "the internal relations *within* the genre" and views it "as a plethora of innovation within certain limits" (30). This aptly describes Haas's detective stories. While adhering to the basic conventions of the detective genre, the Brenner novels do not fit neatly in any of the subgenres of detective fiction, neither the classical analytical novel nor the hard-boiled detective stories which originated in the United States in the 1930s. Rather, Haas incorporates elements of both subgenres. For example, his protagonist shows some similarities to the lonely hero of the hard-boiled novel, but like the detective of the analytical detective story, he also relies on his intuition and powers of deduction to solve cases. Moreover, Haas's complex narrative perspective, which encompasses two distinct types of narration—first-person and omniscient—constitutes a stylistic innovation with regard to the narrative strategies of detective fiction. These innovations and crossings of boundaries not only have aesthetic consequences, but contribute to the novels' critical agenda. Haas's modifications are aimed at integrating his criticism structurally and thematically rather than imposing it as a separate entity on his novels.

While Haas's novels display the generic plot structure of the detective narrative—a crime has occurred, the detective undertakes the investigation, the perpetrator is revealed and brought to justice—each of these generic features is invested with a critical function. The crime—in all of Haas's novels it is a murder—is the central event of the detective narrative, setting all other events in motion. Haas pays tribute to this stock feature of the detective narrative by formulaically starting his novels with the sentence "Again, something has happened."[7] The initial murder is not only the starting point for the detective narrative, it is crucial for its success. It catches the attention of the readers, makes them curious, and challenges them to find the solution to the mystery.

Accordingly, each initial murder of the six Brenner-novels is spectacular and highly constructed, eliciting the reader's admiration for the ingenuity of the author's imagination. In the first novel of the series, *Auferstehung der Toten* (*Resurrection of the Dead*, 1996), the first morning run of the ski lift has the frozen corpse of an American tourist arriving simultaneously at the top and at the bottom of the mountain. In *Der Knochenmann* (*Skeleton Man*, 1997), human bones are found among the mountains of discarded chicken carcasses in a popular restaurant. This gruesome evidence is trumped by the discovery of a local soccer player's head among the soccer balls of the club. In *Komm, süßer Tod* (*Come, Sweet Death*, 1998), a single bullet kills a couple engaged in a kiss. *Silentium!* (1999) begins with the discovery of twenty-three human body parts wrapped in nylon bags in the table for foosball located in a boys school. In *Wie die Tiere* (*Like Animals*, 2001), a dog ironically tears the throat of a young woman who is collecting money in behalf of an animal-aid organization called "Tierfamilie" (animal family). In the last novel, *Das ewige Leben* (*Eternal Life,* 2003), Brenner awakens in a psychiatric clinic in his home town Graz with a bullet in his head supposedly the result of a suicide attempt, which he however cannot remember.

More important than the murders themselves is their setting. It is quite evident that the scenes of the crimes are chosen to challenge conventional images of Austria. In the first novel the murder takes place in Zell am See, one of the most popular ski resorts in the Austrian Alps. The crime scene of *Der Knochenmann* is a restaurant famous for its grilled chicken located in a small town beautifully situated in the eastern part of Styria. In *Komm, süßer Tod* and *Wie die Tiere* the murders occur in Vienna, which because of its historical and cultural tradition is Austria's main tourist attraction. Salzburg, Mozart's hometown and host of the famous Festspiele, is turned into a crime scene in *Silentium!* For the last novel in the series, Haas chose the idyllic provincial town Graz, which in 2003 was named the cultural capital of Europe ("Europäische Kulturhauptstadt") as his crime scene.

As the murders are supposed to pose an enigma for the detective and the reader, they typically occur in unusual places that enhance their mysteriousness or render them especially sacrilegious. However, Colin Watson points out another function of the selection of the murder scene: they are often chosen to disturb and disrupt the reader's sense of security. For example, British detective novels frequently are situated at locations associated with safety and familiarity country estates, colleges, or exclusive London clubs, and a murder taking place in these locations upsets and challenges the feeling of safety (Watson, 169). Haas's selection of crime scenes seems similarly motivated in that they represent the stereotypical tourist-Austria which is marketed all over the world. An example of this is the way the town Klöch, location of *Der Knochenmann*, is introduced by the TV announcer

> "Klöch is a sleepy little town in eastern Styria, close to the border of Hungary and Slovenia. In Austria we associate this gently hilly landscape with an idyll that today hardly exists any longer in a similar unspoiled manner. Not far from the well-known Styrian Tuscany, the wine route of Klöch is becoming more and more popular with every year. An appropriate number of stops for excursions and picnics exist in the area, as well as idyllic wine restaurants. [...]" (29f.)[8]

The report sounds like an advertisement for tourism, stressing the unspoiled beauty of this part of Austria, its suitability for daytrips, and its great culinary offerings. By situating his murders in such well-known locations in Austria, Haas not only destroys the idyllic notion attributed to them, but also irritates the readers by challenging their sense of familiarity with these places.

Moreover, as Dennis Porter asserts, the relationship between the scene of the crime and the event can be either conjunctive or disjunctive "Landscapes appear either as the source and extension of the crimes reported or as their antithesis" (190). The former is the case in Haas's novel *Silentium!* where the first murder is discovered at a Catholic seminary for boys. As the narrator states at the beginning of the novel, a Catholic boarding school is a rather unusual place for such a gruesome crime

> And in the Marianum of all places, where you imagine that the nice ten-year-old farm boy enters on one side and exits on the other side eight years later, semi-ready to be a priest. It is no wonder that nobody suspected anything for such a long time. Because it is incredible that something like this could possibly happen in the cleanest boarding-school in Salzburg of all places. (5) [9]

However, the irony of this statement is unmistakable and signals to the reader that there might be more going on in the boarding-school than meets the eye. While insisting that it is inconceivable that something criminal could happen in a Catholic boarding-school "of all places," the narrator draws attention to the fact that this "clean" school has the purpose of turning young, healthy boys into catholic priests. That means, that the boys are instructed to deny or suppress their sexuality. The narrator depicts this as a natural, almost automatic process—the boys enter on one side and exit "semi-ready" eight years later—glancing over the methods employed to achieve this semi-readiness. Moreover, he emphasizes the "cleanness" of the school, by which as he is quick to point out he does not mean cleanliness or hygiene, but rather moral cleanness, drawing attention to the Catholic Church's condemnation of sexuality. Brenner's investigation, however, reveals this as hypocrisy. While the Catholic Church preaches sexual abstinence, one of its representative institutions, the Marianum, is profiting from the forced prostitution of young Filipina girls brought to Austria under the pretense of offering them work at the seminary. Haas links the forced prostitution directly to the Catholic Church's attitude toward sexuality, as the following dialogue between Simon Brenner and his sidekick in this novel, René, shows

> "These idiots pray day and night to a virgin! Do you know what this leads to?"
> "They believe once the hymen is broken, it does not make any difference any more."
> "Might as well destroy the entire doll." (206)[10]

Indeed, the Catholic seminary does not function like W. H. Auden's "Great Good Place," where the contradiction between murder and place serves to underscore that crime is but the exception that proves the rule (151). Rather, the location of the crime is also its source. By selecting the seminary as the crime site and by linking it to the crime, Haas attacks the moral credibility of the Catholic Church, one of the most powerful institutions in Austria.

A similar conjunctive relationship between crime and crime scene can be established for all of Haas's Brenner novels. In *Komm, Süßer Tod*, the ambulance service, supposedly a non-profit organization established to save lives, murders patients after having talked them into naming the ambulance service as sole beneficiary in their wills. The affluence of the idyllic tourist town which is the murder scene in *Auferstehung der Toten* is the result of a long history of exploitation and opportunism. The huge chicken restaurant with its gigantic meal portions in *Der Knochenmann* symbolizes the attempts of the owner to compensate for his impotence by murdering four people. In addition, the little village on the border to Hungary and Slovenia has become a haven for prostitution and other illegal activities. In *Das ewige Leben* the perpetrator comes from within the police. Haas chooses the crime scenes not only with the intention of destroying idyllic pretense, but also to implicate and therefore attack many of Austria's revered institutions and cherished traditions: the tourist industry in *Auferstehung der Toten,* the Catholic Church as well as the Salzburg Festivals in *Silentium!*, ambulance services in *Komm, süßer Tod*, and the police in *Das ewige Leben.* The proverbial Austrian love for dogs becomes suspect in *Wie die Tiere*, while *Der Knochenmann* deals Austrians' culinary partiality for "Backhendel" (fried chicken) a fatal blow.

In addition, all of Haas's novels allude to contemporary Austrian issues: the impact of tourism, especially ski tourism, on the environment (*Auferstehung der Toten*); the revelation of sex scandals within the Catholic Church (*Silentium!*); Austria's involvement in the Balkan War and sex-trafficking at the border towns to former Eastern Bloc countries (*Der Knochenmann*); the dominance of an aging population in Vienna (*Komm, süßer Tod*[11] and *Wie die Tiere*); remodeling of Nazi war towers (*Wie die Tiere*);[12] and right-wing attacks against the Roma population (*Das ewige Leben*). By linking these current events and issues to crimes, Haas brings them to the forefront of the readers' consciousness and invites their critical evaluation.

Crime not only constitutes the starting-point of the detective narrative, but also engenders the basic narrative configuration by positioning the detective against the perpetrator of the crime. The convention of the genre ensures the triumph of the detective; consequently the myth of the hero is imbedded in the narrative structure (Porter, 155). Two prototypes of detectives have emerged, the cerebral detective of the analytical crime novel who relies solely on his powers of observation and deduction to solve the crime and who is hardly touched by the events himself; and the action-oriented detective of the hard-boiled school whose hands-on approach to crime-solving often involves him in dangerous, violent situations.

Haas's Simon Brenner shares a number of similarities with the detectives of the hard-boiled school, who, as critics have pointed out, embody criticism of a society that is characterized primarily by its strive for power and profit and has little compassion for the victims of such a system (Porter, 174ff.; Nusser, 119ff). The popularity of hard-boiled detective fiction rose in the twenties and thirties, a time of socioeconomic hardship in America which led to a widespread distrust of institutions and the government. The private eye became the lonely hero who fought the criminal forces that infested all structures of society: business, politics, law, and the police. Hired by "respectable" society to rescue it from the threats posed by criminal elements, he soon finds out that respectable society itself is deceitful, corrupt, and guilty. His resistance to power and money, reflected in his own modest circumstances, perseverance, and moral choices in face of deadly danger, contribute to the hero status of the private eye. Dennis Porter states with regard to Dashiell Hammett and Raymond Chandler, the creators of the best-known representatives of the hard-boiled detectives Sam Spade and Philip Marlowe

> The private eyes of both authors are, then, genuinely popular heroes, because while they have remained small men by choice; as a point of honor, they also always manage in the end to have the last word against the class enemies of ordinary people—the rich, the powerful, and the official police. The apparent loser for once is the moral winner. (174)

Wolf Haas created a similar hero with his Simon Brenner, who has left the police department after nineteen years of service, tired of the presumptuous authority and prejudices of his superior. His choice to work as a private detective seems rather a necessity than a true calling. Like the private eyes of the hard-boiled school, Brenner lives on the margin of society. He has no fixed address or regular income, but constantly moves around taking on odd jobs to make ends meet. He also has no respect for authority, wealth, power, social standing, or institutions. His lack of ambition and his awkward decency enable him to expose people, situations, and institutions for what they are without regard for personal consequences. Like the private eye of the hard-boiled novel, Brenner embodies individualism, independence, and stubborn integrity, which come with the price of financial instability and lack of any type of permanent relationship.

Brenner also shares with the detectives of the hard-boiled school that he repeatedly falls victim to violence during his investigations. These incidents serve to emphasize the determination, perseverance, and hyper-masculinity of the detective. In Haas's novels, while potentially fatal, these encounters with violence are not without a comical element suggesting the author's satirical intent. For example, the perpetrator of *Silentium!* attempts to eliminate Brenner by locking him into a shower and dousing him with boiling hot water; in *Wie die Tiere*, Brenner looses half of his calf to a pit bulldog; in *Der Knochenmann*, the perpetrator attempts to slaughter Brenner with a meat cleaver. But even the loss of his little finger does not deter Brenner from his mission to prevent the death of another victim, nor do the beatings and other attempts on his life stop him from pursuing his cases. Instead, they only provoke a stubborn determination. Again, he displays the same perseverance and moral rectitude when faced with danger as his hard-boiled counterparts.

It has been pointed out that the private eye of the hard-boiled novel is a law unto himself, often crossing legal boundaries to follow his own code of justice. Likewise, Brenner is not averse to bending the law when it does not agree with his own sense of justice. In *Auferstehung der Toten* he neglects to report a young girl's involvement in the murder

> Because Elfi now had a dead father who officially never had been her father. And she quit school. And of course she did not have a job any more. And Lorenz was dead. And the only one who had cared for her was in prison. And Brenner was thinking, Elfi is stuck in Zell, and she has been punished enough. (152)[13]

The fact that Brenner agrees to the blackmail of a reporter not to contact a woman in whom both are romantically interested (like earlier private eyes, Brenner proves quite irresistible for women) in order to protect the girl's secret shows the proverbial "soft spot" of the tough private eye. Brenner repeatedly covers for perpetrators whose crimes he considers justified or insignificant in face of the wrongs done to them. More serious, however, is his involvement in the death of the perpetrator in *Silentium!* While this murderer is quite despicable—he not only has murdered four people but is also responsible for the forced prostitution of young Filipinas and has just attempted to boil Brenner to death—his murder does challenge Brenner's integrity. However here, too, Brenner follows the code of protecting the innocent from suffering unduly. He acts out of concern for the wife and five children of the murderer who would be destitute if the man were convicted. Just like the hard-boiled detectives, Brenner represents a position between that of the police and the criminal. Like them, he is a people's champion who stands "on the margin of the law as representative of a higher law" (Porter, 169).

Despite all of his heroic qualities, Brenner appears quite ordinary, sharing the average appearance of the hard-boiled detective

> A stocky type, with shoulders that are almost wider than his legs are long. Not tall, not short, and a real square-head with two vertical lines in his cheeks. And such a red, scarred skin [...]. (*Auferstehung der Toten*, 15)[14]

In addition to his looks, Brenner's speech, education, and interests underscore his averageness, which invites reader identification.[15] Moreover, Brenner is endowed with some typical "Austrian" traits and habits. Although quick-witted, he is habitually cranky and suffers frequently from migraines. He is not averse to using the system to his advantage. For example, in *Auferstehung der Toten* he attempts to keep the subsidized apartment provided for state employees even after leaving the police force. In *Wie die Tiere* he looks to escape the financial straits which force him to take on all kinds of odd jobs by trying to qualify for early retirement. However, the system proves always more corrupt, and Brenner's attempts to con the system which invariably fail seem insignificant in comparison to the larger issues he uncovers during his investigations. He represents a protagonist whom Austrian readers recognize and with whom they might even identify. His lack of ambition, his precarious financial situation, his innate rebellion against presumptuous authority position him on the margin of society. Since this society in large part is fraught with hypocrisy, corruption, greed, local injustice, and false ambition, Brenner provides a positive counter-image. He preserves his individualism, his personal integrity, and especially his humanity in an increasingly self-serving, deceitful, and inauthentic world.

One of Brenner's most distinctive characteristics is his intuition, which differentiates him from both the ruthless hero-detective of the hard-boiled novel and the personified rationality of the analytical detective. Already early on, Brenner intuitively knows the solution—it presents itself in the form of a song that he can't get out of his mind. The narrator states that Brenner is aware "that the subconscious often gave him a little tip. He whistles something, like, a catchy tune, and possibly the solution to the murder is hiding in the catchy tune" (*Wie die Tiere*, 111).[16] However, Brenner lacks the ability to decode this clue correctly, mainly because of his faulty memory. For example, in *Komm, süßer Tod* he only understands at the end that his incorrect recall of a line from Bach's *St. Matthew's Passion* ("come, sweet death" instead of "come, sweet cross") contained the solution to the murders, because the ambulance staff killed their diabetic patients by injecting them with a sugar solution.[17] While this tick with the catchy tune distinguishes Brenner from other detectives, it also serves to build up suspense. The reader is challenged to make the connection before Brenner and solve the enigma.

Following wrong clues and harboring false suspicions is part of the narrative convention of the detective story as it prolongs the plot and builds suspense. Another of Brenner's peculiarities is his digressive method of investigation that often has him head in the wrong direction. He clearly lacks the analytical discipline and linearity of the detective of the classical whodunit, as the narrator repeatedly observes

> And if there was a roundabout way, then Brenner was sure to take it. That's what had always made his superiors at the police so livid. And sometimes I have even suspected he's doing it on purpose. But then I always have to admit, he really just can't concentrate on the essential things. (*Komm, süßer Tod*, 124)[18]

Brenner's investigative detours, which usually are the result of involuntary associations and memories, are deemed inefficient by official detectives (his superiors at the police). However, they do eventually lead to the solving of the crime, thus favoring Brenner's associative and intuitive method over the straightforward, simplifying method of the police.

Brenner's digressions have an additional function. While his observations and discoveries are often unrelated to his case, they reveal other, sometimes equally grave and reprehensible crimes. For example, in *Der Knochenmann* Brenner comes across war-profiteering, manipulation of art prices, exploitation of foreign workers, forced prostitution, and exploitation of the loneliness and fear of senior citizens. In *Silentium!* he looks behind the façade of the Salzburger Festspiele to discover questionable attempts by the organizers to cater to the whims a self-indulgent, overly-satiated clientele. In *Die Auferstehung der Toten* his investigation reveals a long history of local injustices and exploitations. In *Das ewige Leben* he infiltrates a group of citizens intent on defending themselves against the perceived threat of local Roma. Brenner's investigations reveal the pervasive nature of crime and its permutation of society. Critics of the analytical detective story have pointed out that its tendency to emphasize the power of logic and analytical deduction isolates the crime and reduces it to a technical problem which can be solved purely by intellect (Moretti, 144). Brenner's digressive investigation prevents such an isolation and thus a trivialization of the crime.

With that Haas's novels achieve a social-critical function that Peter Nusser sees realized in the thriller

> The thriller suggests that criminality in society is not an exception. Based on this structural feature it has the possibility to take on a social critical function (which many of its best authors have realized) and to show crimes not just as simple stimulus (as in the normal case) but to use it to denunciate a corrupt or altogether "disturbed" society. (46)[19]

Thus, Haas's Austria is not the idyllic place of unspoiled beauty and innocence, but a country with its share of contemporary issues, problems, and shortcomings.

The most defining feature of Haas's detective novels is their narrative perspective, which contributes to both the suspense and the critical insight of the novels. A nameless first-person narrator imparts all of Brenner's cases to the reader. He speaks a distinct Austrian German which contains many characteristics of oral speech. It appears as if he were recounting Brenner's adventures to a fellow customer at his favorite bar. The sentences are elliptical, grammatically incorrect (for example the use of subordinating conjunctions in main clauses); they contain many idiomatic expressions such as "praktisch" (practically), "natürlich" (of course, naturally), and "frage nicht" (don't ask) and fillers like "ding," thus simulating an actual conversation taking place. Another conversational feature employed by the narrator is his direct address of the reader with expressions like "Jetzt pass auf" (pay attention now), "Du musst wissen" (you need to know), and "Du darfst eines nicht vergessen" (You must not forget). These formulaic expressions create an intimate relationship between narrator and reader. They also suggest that the narrator possesses superior knowledge and thus increases his narrative authority.

At first Haas's narrator reminds of Conan Doyle's Dr. Watson, who also records and narrates Sherlock Holmes's cases. However, there is a decisive difference between the two narrators. While Watson is part of the crime story, Haas's narrator is not. His only function seems to be to narrate Brenner's adventures. The reader does not learn his identity or his relationship to Brenner until the end of the sixth novel, when he interferes with the action of the crime story. He has been subletting an apartment from Brenner's grandfather in Graz, and for many years he has taken a certain interest in Brenner and his adventures. His entrance into the crime story coincides with the end of his narration as he is shot and killed. Consequently, the reader learns the final details of Brenner's case not from the narrator but from a newspaper article. The death of the narrator has another consequence as it marks the end of the Brenner series.

However, Haas's narrator does not simply narrate from the first-person perspective, but combines two distinctive types of narration the I-narration and the omniscient narration (see Martens).[20] The omniscience of the narrator is especially evident with regard to Brenner. The narrator is informed about details from his childhood and adolescence; he knows his habits and shortcomings, his thoughts, emotions and motives. He shares this knowledge eagerly and in great detail with the reader. In the following passage he explains why Brenner really asked about one of the suspects after waking up from a coma

> One thing is very interesting. When you have been in a coma for a longer period, you don't wake up in all places at the same time. Rather in one place after the other. And Brenner was already almost awake all over but the morality was still a bit in a coma. Because he did not care if they also got Milovanovic and Jurasic or not. He was only interested if Kaspar Krennek [the investigating police officer] was onto them, hence his ambition was already awake. (*Der Knochenmann*, 146)[21]

The narrator not only divulges Brenner's thoughts and motivations, he also comments on and evaluates them for the reader. Gunther Martens points out the uniqueness of Haas's omniscient narrator in the context of detective fiction. It is usual for this genre to employ either a third-person narrator who has no special insight into the detective or the detective himself to tell the story as a first-person narration. Both types of narration are limited, which enhances the suspense of the novel (Martens, 67). Haas, however, achieves suspense by combining omniscient and first-person narration.[22]

Retardation is one of the most common and effective ways to build suspense in detective fiction. Haas's narrator fulfills this function by his tendency to digress from the main storyline. This he shares with the protagonist, Brenner. Moritz Baβler has pointed to the parallels between the investigative and the narrative digressions in Haas's novels. Like Brenner, the narrator uses every opportunity to take a detour and to break away from the murder plot. In *Auferstehung der Toten* the reader learns about the operation of ski lifts, the privilege of subsidized housing for civil servants, rules of curling on asphalt, and the insufficient preparation of the volunteer fire-fighters. In *Der Knochenmann* the narrator discusses soccer, the times when there wasn't a television set in every living room, the advantages of "Kellerstüberln" (a basement room with a bar).

Baβler reads these digressions of the narrator as examples of archiving local knowledge and contemporary everyday culture, which for him characterizes the contemporary popular novel

> In the Brenner novels, the micro-digressions of the narrator take on the archiving function of the catalogue. They draw the spatial net of the encyclopedia over the very conventional, linear, action-rich, suspenseful crime story. [...] And in this net there is [...] no sub-structure, no hidden meaning. Even the Nazi-period is not, as it was in the post-war literature, the monstrous backdrop but rather just another knot, another aspect among many. (195)[23]

For Baβler the narrative digressions have no meaning beyond the obvious. They have purely "archival" function. However, he misses the critical potential of the narrator's observations and commentaries. They do not merely inform about local peculiarities or contemporary cultural habits and fads, but also about certain attitudes and views with regard to social and political questions. For example, the narrator comments as follows on the dam of Karprun in *Auferstehung der Toten*

> "Symbol of the republic," the newspaper said, that was in 1951 when they had the opening ceremony. Now, of course, you cannot build a high mountain reservoir within six years, or maybe you could do it today, but not then. Of course, the politicians did not mention one word about the fact that it—but I also don't want to go on about the Nazi period again. (32)[24]

The commentary of the narrator not only intimates Nazi involvement in the construction of the "symbol of the republic," but also reflects how this information is habitually suppressed. While Baβler is correct in his observation that the Nazi period is not the central theme of *Auferstehung der Toten*, there is a certain relationship to Brenner's case. The narrator tells about the Ukrainian forced laborers who were invited to the forty-year anniversary of the reservoir, "because hundreds of them of course had died up there at the construction site during the war" (32), revealing the exploitation of the forced laborers during Austria's involvement with the Nazi regime. Exploitation and past guilt are also central themes of the dectective plot in *Auferstehung der Toten*.[25]

But even those digressions which cannot be related to the plot of the crime novel have a critical function, as many of the commentaries reflect commonly held opinions which the narrator tends to turn into universal truths with phrases such as "Da sieht man wieder" (It's obvious again). For example, the narrator comments on a soccer game between a small provincial club and a more prominent opponent in *Der Knochenmann*

> Now naturally these games tend to be a bit on the more brutal side. Because when the underdogs sense a chance, they go all out. That's not only true in soccer. That's also sometimes true for a small country. That it gets into a murderous frenzy if the opportunity presents itself. But I don't mean specifically the Austrians; it's more a general thought. (14-15)[26]

The narrator explains the "natural" violent character of the local soccer game because of the constellation of the underdog fighting to triumph against a mightier opponent. He tries to show the universality of such behavior by pointing to small countries and their "murderous frenzy" if they get a chance to seize power. He immediately emphasizes that he did not mean Austrians but was just making a general observation. However, with this Haas makes sure that the reader is thinking about Austria and its role during the Nazi period. By defending Austria, the narrator actually draws attention to its past transgressions. Moreover, by emphasizing the "naturalness" of an event or action, the narrator makes clear that in reality there is nothing natural about it. Violence at a sport event is not necessarily natural; it is also not naturally understandable that politicians do not acknowledge Austria's past, and it is even less natural that hundreds of forced laborers died during the construction of the Karprun dam.

The narrator also echoes the Brenner novels' general intention to discredit the Austrian idyll

> But riding in the empty mail bus through Styria as Brenner was doing it now, that is still one of the most beautiful things that you can experience in this world: the sun, the fields, the vineyards, the two-story toy farmhouses of which every single one could have won the floral decoration competition. And I don't want anyone to start about the suicide statistics again, because suicide statistics are everywhere but floral decoration competition not everywhere. (*Der Knochenmann*, 97-98)[27]

The narrator's comment evokes the stereotypical image of the Austrian idyll and elevates it to the most beautiful experience on earth. Again, by disparaging the criticism of the shallowness of this idyll given the high rate of suicide in Austria, he draws attention to it.

Some critics have pointed out that the narrator often harbors some rather questionable ideas and opinions which one would find in the *Kronenzeitung*, Austria's right-wing populist newspaper with a readership of a lower educational level (F. Haas, 130). Thus the narrator at times seems to be the embodiment of the "average Austrian mind" and its prejudices and racist and sexist sentiments. For example, the narrator concludes his admiration of the Brazilian soccer player Pelé with these predictions

> There won't be anything like that in the near future because they're doing much too well over there today, and if you grow up in a slum today, then you also have everything, color TV, video, the people in the slums have already everything. So, the boy doesn't work so hard at soccer, the last important effort is missing if you no longer have a real slum. (*Der Knochenmann*, 25)[28]

The irony of this comment is less visible than in the previous examples. However, by imitating the style of the so-called "Stammtischrede" (bar talk), Haas continues the Austrian tradition of *Sprachkritik* (criticism of language). He makes prejudices visible and renders them ridiculous by suggesting that a lower poverty rate or the absence of "real" slums is deplorable because it makes people less desperate.

At other times the narrator's lack of education and thus understanding of the complexity of issues contributes to his inability to explain causalities

> Now a party. For a few years now the daughter of the vice president of the festivals has been president herself, not of the festivals but, like, charity president. Because charity is never for nothing. Rather, the money, that came in, only for the weak, either weak because of social stuff, or let's say, down there in Africa, where they save the condoms for the next papal visit and use them as welcoming balloons. Then, of course, more and more illnesses occur, you have to send tons of medication, that all costs a fortune, now where does it come from, if you don't steal it; thus the people from the festival said during a contemplative moment, you know what, let's have a charity party. (*Silentium!,* 106)[29]

The fragmented sentence "Rather, the money, that came in, only for the weak, either weak because of social stuff, or let's say, down there in Africa, where they save the condoms for the next papal visit and use them as welcoming balloons" differs from the elliptical style the narrator usually employs. Here the reason for the poverty of the "weak" is not explained with a minimum of words, but the narrator stumbles over his words because he is incapable of formulating a precise thought. He has no real insight why people "down there in Africa" are poor and need help. But he quickly blames their adherence to the teaching of the Catholic Church for it, suggesting that it is their own fault. However, the idea that a lavish party could be construed as charitable work—an event where the public consumes lavishly in order to help the starving population in Africa—reveals the absurdity of the concept. Again, Haas uses linguistic means to uncover prejudices and hypocrisy.

The narrator's digressions fulfill two functions in Haas's novel: they build suspense by interrupting the denouement of the detective plot, and they reinforce the general critical intent of the novels. The unique narrative voice, the irony, and the subversive humor of the narrator's reflections make both enjoyable for the reader.

In interviews Wolf Haas tends to downplay the critical aspect of his novels in favor of their entertaining qualities (F. Haas, 129). While his novels are extremely entertaining and their social criticism is hidden behind satire and subversive humor, it is just as potent as that of more serious literature. Thus Wolf Haas's novels demonstrate that the boundaries between low and high culture, between popular and serious literature no longer exist. Haas succeeds in combining innovative narrative strategies with conventional features of a popular genre to present his readers with an entertaining as well a thought-provoking literary dissection of the Austrian myth of an ideal world.

Works Cited

Alewyn, Richard. "Der Ursprung des Detektivromans." *Probleme und Gestalten.* Frankfurt a. M. Insel Verlag, 1974. 341-60.

Auden, Wystan Hugh. "The Guilty Vicarage." *The Dyer's Hand.* London Faber and Faber, 1963. 146-58.

Baβler, Moritz. *Der deutsche Pop-Roman. Die neuen Archivisten.* Munich Verlag C. H. Beck, 2002.

Düsing, Wolfgang, ed. *Experimente mit dem Kriminalroman.* Frankfurt a. M. Peter Lang, 1993.

Haas, Franz. "Aufklärung in Österreich. Die erhellenden Kriminalromane von Wolf Haas." *Mord als kreativer Prozess. Zum Kriminalroman der Gegenwart in Deutschland, Österreich und der Schweiz.* Edited by Sandro Moraldo. Heidelberg Winter, 2005. 127-34.

Haas, Wolf. *Auferstehung der Toten.* Reinbek/Hamburg Rowohlt, 1996.

—. *Der Knochenmann.* Reinbek/Hamburg Rowohlt, 1997

—. *Komm, süßer Tod.* Reinbek/Hamburg Rowohlt, 1998.

—. *Silentium!* Reinbek/Hamburg Rowohlt, 2000.

—. *Wie die Tiere.* Reinbek/Hamburg Rowohlt, 2001.

—. *Das ewige Leben.* Reinbek/Hamburg Rowohlt, 2003.

Martens, Gunther. "'Aber wenn du von einem Berg springst, ist es wieder umgekehrt.' Zur Erzählerprofilierung in den Meta-Krimis von Wolf Haas." *Modern Austrian Literature* 39.1 (2006) 65-80.

Moretti, Franco. "Clues." *Signs Taken For Wonders. Essays in the Sociology of Literary Forms.* Translatedby Susan Fischer, David Forgacs, and David Miller. London NLB—Verso Editions, 1983. 130-50.

Most, Glenn W., and William W. Stowe, eds. *The Poetics of Murder. Detective Fiction and Literary Theory.* San Diego Harcourt Brace Jovanovich, 1983.

Nusser, Peter. *Der Kriminalroman.* 3rd Edition. Stuttgart J. B. Metzler, 2003.

Porter, Dennis. *The Pursuit of Crime. Art and Ideology in Detective Fiction*. New Haven Yale University Press, 1981.

Pyrhönen, Heta. *Murder from an Academic Angle An Introduction to the Study of the Detective Narrative*. Columbia, SC Camden House, 1994.

Watson, Colin. *Snobbery with Violence. Crime Stories and Their Audience.* London Eyre and Spottiswoode, 1971.

Notes

[1] Swiss author Friedrich Dürrenmatt is seen as the exception.

[2] Already in the 1960s and 1970s several young Austrian writers turned to the detective story, but with the intention of deconstructing and subverting its conventional structure and revealing its ideological connotations. Examples include Peter Handke's *Der Hausierer* (1967) and *Die Angst des Tormanns vor dem Elfmeter* (1970); Gerhard Roth's *how to be a detective* (1972), *Der große Horizont* (1973), *Ein neuer Morgen* (1976), *Am Abgrund* (1986), and *Der Untersuchungsrichter* (1988); and Peter Rosei's *Wer war Edgar Allan?* (1979). These novels challenge the inherent realism of the detective narrative by creating a chaotic world devoid of order and causality, and by blurring the positions of victim, perpetrator, and detective

[3] One of the major bookstores in Vienna, Thalia, has created a separate shelf space for Austrian detective novels.

[4] Heinrich Steinfest was awarded third place in the German detective novel competition for his novel *Ein sturer Hund* in 2004.

[5] Haas received the "Deutsche Krimi-Preis" (German Detective Novel Award) in 1997 (*Auferstehung der Toten)*, 1999 (*Der Knochenmann*), and 2000 (*Silentium!*).

[6] "Gleichnis der Zerstörung einer heilen Welt." If not otherwise indicated, all translations from German into English are mine.

[7] "Jetzt ist schon wieder was passiert." All but the first novel of the Brenner series, *Auferstehung der Toten*, start with this sentence.

[8] "Klöch ist ein kleiner verschlafener Ort in der Oststeiermark, knapp an der Grenze zu Ungarn und Slowenien. In Österreich verbindet man mit dieser sanfthügeligen Landschaft eine Idylle, wie sie heutzutage kaum noch wo in ähnlich unverdorbener Weise anzutreffen ist. Unweit der bekannten Steirischen Toskana erfreut sich auch die Klöcher Weinstraβe von Jahr zu Jahr gröβerer Beliebtheit. Dementsprechend viele Ausflugs- und Jausenstationen sowie die idyllischen *Buschenschanken* gibt es in der Gegend. [...]."

[9] "Und ausgerechnet im Marianum, wo man glauben möchte, da kommt der brave Bauernbub als Zehnjähriger auf der einen Seite hinein und acht Jahre später als halbfertiger Pfarrer auf der anderen Seite wieder heraus. Kein Wunder, daβ so lange niemand Verdacht geschöpft hat. Weil eigentlich unfaβbar, daβ ausgerechnet

in der saubersten Internatsschule von ganz Salzburg so etwas möglich war" (*Silentium!*, 5).

[10] "Diese Gestörten beten Tag und Nacht eine Jungfrau an! Und weißt du, wohin das führt?" "Sie glauben, wenn das Jungfernhäutchen einmal verletzt ist, ist es schon egal." "Kann man gleich die ganze Puppe zerfetzen."

[11] There was also a highly publicized case where nurses in a Viennese hospital administered non-voluntary euthanasia to their elderly patients.

[12] The remodeling of the Flakturm in the Augarten Park, one of the six towers constructed by the Nazis as firing towers and bomb shelters, for the use of animals is the motivating force behind the murders in *Wie die Tiere*. There has been an ongoing discussion about the use of these towers. The Augarten Flakturm is currently closed for safety reasons. However, part of the Flakturm in the Esterházy Park was turned into an aquarium in 1956. Haas might have also been inspired by the remodeling of the Gasometers, four large depots for natural gas, which were turned into apartment buildings and shopping malls in 2001, and which are now tourist stops.

[13] "Weil die Elfi, die hat jetzt einen toten Vater gehabt, der offiziell nie ihr Vater gewesen ist. Und die Schule abgebrochen. Und Stelle natürlich auch keine mehr. Und der Lorenz tot. Und die einzige, die sich um sie gekümmert hat, im Gefängnis. Und der Brenner hat sich gedacht, die Elfi sitzt jetzt in Zell, die ist gestraft genug."

[14] "So ein untersetzter Typ, wo die Schultern fast breiter sind als die Beine lang. Nicht groß, nicht klein und einen richtigen Kantschädel mit zwei senkrechten Falten in den Wangen. Und so eine rote, narbige Haut [...].

[15] Dennis Porter points out that Chandler's Philip Marlow and Hammett's Sam Spade, for example, were created to resemble the average American (male) reader in speech, taste, life-style, and values (165). This differentiates the hard-boiled detective from the heroes of the classic analytical detective story, who are intellectual, eccentric, and upper-class and do not invite identification from the average reader.

[16]"Dass ihm das Unbewusste oft einen kleinen Tipp gibt. Er pfeift irgendetwas, quasi Ohrwurm, und da steckt womöglich im Ohrwurm die Mordlösung drinnen."

[17] However, even the correct text contains a clue since the ambulance service's name is "Kreuzritter" (knights of the cross). Critics have pointed out the allusion to the Red Cross (Martens, 78).

[18] "Und wo ein Umweg gewesen ist, dann hat ihn der Brenner garantiert genommen. Das hat ja seine Vorgesetzten bei der Polizei immer so zur Weißglut getrieben. Und manchmal habe ich schon den Verdacht gehabt, er tut es absichtlich. Aber dann muß ich immer wieder zugeben, er kann sich einfach wirklich nicht auf das Wesentliche konzentrieren."

[19] "Der Thriller deutet an, daß das Verbrechen in der Gesellschaft nicht die Ausnahme ist. Er hat damit aufgrund einer formalen Voraussetzung die von seinen besten Autoren ergriffene Möglichkeit, sozialkritische Funktionen zu übernehmen, das Verbrechen also nicht als bloßen Reiz (wie im Normalfall), sondern zur Denunziation einer korrupten oder insgesamt 'gestörten' Gesellschaft einzusetzen."

[20] Baßler distinguishes 3 types of narration omniscient, third-person, and I-narration (190f.). I follow Martens as I consider omniscient what Baßler sees as third-person narration.

[21] "Eines ist hochinteressant. Wenn du längere Zeit im Koma gelegen bist, dann wachst du nicht an allen Stellen gleichzeitig auf. Sondern der Reihe nach. Und beim Brenner ist schon fast alles wach gewesen, aber die Moral noch ein bißchen im Koma. Weil es ist ihm egal gewesen, ob sie den Milovanovic und die Jurasic auch schnappen oder nicht. Es hat ihn nur interessiert, ob der Kaspar Krennek ihnen auf die Schliche gekommen ist, also der Ehrgeiz schon wieder munter [...]."

[22] Martens' close readings of some passages from *Das ewige Leben* show that the narrator's omniscient insights into the thoughts and motivations of other characters in the novels function mainly to interrupt the action or slow it down (69). Haas also uses the conventional way of creating suspense from an omniscient position by means of prediction. Since Haas's omniscient narrator already knows all the details of the case, he is able to tantalize the reader by alluding to events about to happen. For example, he concludes chapter 4 of *Silentium!* by hinting that two people are about to be murdered. With regard to detective fiction, Martens observes that Haas's narrator challenges the inherent realism of the genre.

[23] "Die archivierende Funktion des Katalogs übernehmen in den Brenner-Romanen die Mikrodigressionen des Erzählers. Sie spannen das räumliche Netze der Enzyklopädie über die ganz traditionell lineare, actionreiche, spannungsgeladene Krimihandlung. [...] Und in diesem Netz gibt es [....] keine Substruktur, keinen unter oder hinter irgendwas verborgenen Sinn. Selbst die Nazizeit ist nicht, wie in der Nachkriegsliteratur, das ungeheure Dahinter, sondern nur ein weiterer Knoten, ein Aspekt unter vielen."

[24] "'Symbol der Republik'" ist in der Zeitung gestanden, das war 1951, wie sie ihn eröffnet haben. Jetzt kann man natürlich in sechs Jahren keinen Hochgebirgsstausee bauen, oder vielleicht könnte man es heute, aber damals nicht. Die Politiker haben natürlich kein Wort darüber verloren, daß er—aber ich möchte jetzt auch nicht wieder mit der Nazizeit anfangen."

[25] The murdered American couple were owners of a company that caused the death of many of their workers because of unsafe working conditions. The same company delivered the materials for the dam whose construction caused the death of many laborers. The third murder victim had sexually exploited his sister and had left her when she was pregnant to marry the daughter of the American couple. The ruthless destruction of the Alps by ski tourism continues the exploitation in the present.

[26] "Jetzt sind diese Spiele natürlich gern ein bißchen auf der brutaleren Seite. Weil wenn die Kleinen eine Chance wittern, dann kennen sie nichts. Das gilt nicht nur für den Fußball. Das gilt auch oft einmal für ein kleines Land. Daß es gern einmal den Blutrausch kriegt, wenn die Gelegenheit günstig ist. Aber ich meine jetzt nicht speziell die Österreicher, mehr so eine generelle Überlegung."

[27] "Aber im leeren Postauto durch die Steiermark, wie es der Brenner jetzt gemacht hat, das ist immer noch etwas vom Schönsten, was du auf dieser Welt erleben kannst: die Sonne, die Felder, die Weinhügel und die einstöckigen Spielzeug-

Bauernhäuser, von denen jedes einzelne den Blumenschmuckwettbewerb hätte gewinnen können. Und da soll mir nicht wieder einer mit der Selbstmordstatistik daherkommen, weil Selbstmordstatistik gibt es schließlich überall, aber Blumenschmuckwettbewerb nicht überall." (In some provinces in Austria, the post office also provides transportation service.)

[28] "Und so was wird es nicht mehr so schnell geben, weil denen geht es ja heute auch schon viel zu gut drüben, und wenn du heute in einem Slum aufwächst, da hast du auch schon alles, Farbfernsehen,Video, alles haben die Leute schon im Slum. Und da strengt sich der Bub auch nicht so an beim Kicken, der letzte Einsatz fehlt, wenn es kein richtiger Slum mehr ist."

[29] "Jetzt Party. Seit ein paar Jahren war die Tochter vom Festspielvize selber auch ein bißchen Präsidentin, nicht von den Festpielen, sondern quasi Wohltätigkeitspräsidentin. Weil Wohltätigkeit nie für den Hugo. Sondern das Geld, das hereingekommen ist, nur für den Schwachen, entweder vom sozialen dings her schwach, oder sagen wir Afrika unten, wo sie die Kondome lieber aufsparen als Willkommensluftballone für den nächsten Papstbesuch. Dann natürlich Krankheiten noch und noch, muß man wieder tonnenweise Medikamente hinunterschicken, das kostet ja alles ein Vermögen, jetzt woher nehmen, wenn nicht stehlen, haben die Festspielleute in einer besinnlichen Stunde gesagt, wißt ihr was, machen wir eine Wohltätigkeitsparty."

CHAPTER TWENTY-ONE

UNDER THE IMAGE: CRIMINALITY, GUILT AND NATIONAL ALLEGORY IN ALOIS HOTSCHNIG'S *LEONARDO'S HANDS*

ROBERT VON DASSANOWSKY

The single questionable aspect of the English-language translation of Alois Hotschnig's novel *Leonardos Hände* (*Leonardo's Hands*) can be found in the publisher's blurbs on the back cover of the book. A seemingly petty issue to be sure, but for this particular text, which delves into the concepts of reality and escape, it becomes a significant error that demands an introduction to the author and to the specific literary genealogy of his work. The *Frankfurter Allgemeine Zeitung* is quoted as stating that the original release "places Alois Hotschnig in the first rank of German writers." What must certainly be meant is German-*language* writers, for Hotschnig is *Austrian*, and regardless of whether this was an error in translation or in the original, the corrected nationality is an essential key to the stylistic and allegorical comprehension of this text.

Hotschnig is among the latest voices traceable to an Austrian literary tradition that began at the start of the last century and so influenced international modernist writing. He is clearly a descendent of Arthur Schnitzler, whose Viennese Impressionism fostered a century of attempting a more realistic style or more effective realism in literary form. Far more than just parroting the original concept, Hotschnig re-visions this modernist school of art/philosophy filtered through the particular crisis of reason that is our postmodern sensibility. *Leonardo's Hands* focuses on the psychological transformation of a young Austrian engineer, Kurt Weyrath, who causes a highway accident that kills an elderly couple and places their twenty-four year old daughter, Anna, in a coma. Racked with remorse for having fled the scene of the disaster, Kurt abandons his well-ordered professional and personal life to join an ambulance service so that he might come into close contact with Anna. He subsequently assists in her therapies, learns all he can about her past, and attempts to reconstruct her existence. Over a year after the accident, Anna awakens from her coma, and Kurt becomes her companion as she pieces together the elements of her interrupted life and crisscrosses Austria and Europe as an art scholar, studying the paintings of Leonardo da Vinci. Kurt discovers a very different being than his perceptions had led him to believe. Anna's painful reconnection with her shadowy former lover whose child she carried but lost, and who encouraged her drug addiction, ultimately makes Kurt subservient to her difficult rebirth. Her desire for personal closure, which results in the killing of her ex-lover, and Kurt's desire to take on responsibility for the death in order to be punished for his original crime, dooms them both.

My sociopolitical reading of *Leonardo's Hands* as an examination of guilt and social self-definition would suggest that the novel is as potently critical of Austrian society and culture in both style and content at the start of our century as Arthur Schnitzler's *Lieutenant Gustl* (Lieutenant Gustl) was at the inception of the last. Published in 1900, Schnitzler's was the first German-language novella to be told completely by internal monologue, a stream-of-consciousness experience that made such later works as Joyce's *Ulysses* possible. It also signaled a forthcoming rationalist mass society that would celebrate the existential power of humanity and the overthrow of monolithic value systems. Hotschnig now gives us a literary signal of the postmodern century to come. Perception and existentialism are thrown into question in a manner similar to the way surface "reality" was attacked at the start of the previous century. The irony of Schnitzler's Gustl and, by projection, of a civilization on the verge of a Great War, was that he retreated from a possible reinvention of self, which might have saved him, for the sake of a traditional and ultimately disastrous self-definition. In Hotschnig, the irony of Kurt's self-reinvention is that it matters little in a world where what passes for reality is so virtualized that it is no longer a traceable or even a particularly meaningful destination. The author clearly rejects the modernist notion of "a delirium of many," which is how Austrian author Robert Musil defined reality, in favor of a collage of individual mythologies that climb out of the Lyotardian rubble of the modernist social meta-narratives.[1]

Hotschnig's epistemological novel is also satisfyingly postmodern in its complex and intricate structure, which increases the reader's sense of

Kurt's lack of center. The novel's mix of multiple narrative perspectives and interruptions, as Peter Filkins explains, often sets "a newspaper account next to a journal entry next to a medical definition next to an analysis of a painting next to a dialogue"(ix), yet it still fails to give its questing characters any solid information or direction. What this suggests to us, however, is the limitation of human knowledge and the slippery nature of our scholarships—on history, society, the body, the mind, and existence as a whole. The banal elements of everyday life are elevated to the most enigmatic mysteries as if to say that all the questions we have answered since the Enlightenment, all the reason-based scientific methodologies, all the psychological analysis may have yet missed the point. Hotschnig counts Max Frisch among his influences, and there is an inter-textual relation between his novel and the early postmodern literary exercise of that author's 1979 fictional diary-collage, *Der Mensch erscheint im Holozän* (Man in the Holocene; see Decloedt). There, a man living in a remote village who fears he is cut off from the world by a landslide collects knowledge for "posterity" by papering his environment with pertinent cuttings from encyclopedias, newspapers, and books, which are reproduced as part of Frisch's text. The attempt to understand humanity and re-construct the world through fragments of knowledge fails to provide any intellectual direction for the victim, who then suffers cerebral apoplexy. The fear of the landslide is ultimately exposed as the character's fear of his own uncontrollable loss of memory. In *Leonardo's Hands*, Hotschnig's central characters, Kurt and Anna, are recall-obsessed as well and attempt to correct or negate memory—Kurt through his reinvention of himself and Anna; Anna in seeking revenge against her former lover—to make life bearable. While the opposite of Frisch's literary exercise occurs—memory is stubborn and refuses to be "lost"—there is a similar message: Kurt's technology and Anna's cultural knowledge provide neither character with the tools to successfully deal with their traumas. Their individualities remain unarticulated in a society that frames its values in corporate consumerism, transitory hyperrealism, and virtualization. Yet this transitory aspect also creates the illusion of the ability to morph into new identities and to dispose of an unwanted past.

Hotschnig's references to Frisch and to his other great influence, Kafka, are also part of the subversion of the corporate/consumerist socio-culture and the resulting personal non-identity the novel posits (see Decloedt, 332). There is the echo of Ingeborg Bachmann's questioning of gender roles and a male-dominated society, particularly in Hotschnig's gendering of the symbolic victim-half of Austria as female (Anna). There are the dreaded labyrinths of society that suffocated Kafka's "K" and here capture Kurt as well. Add to those elements traces of the Romantic novel as *Gesamtkunstwerk* (total work of art) and its picaresque artist-adventurer, the fairy tale (Anna as Sleeping Beauty and Kurt as her savior prince), and imagery that reflects Anna's art scholarship, evoking Giorgio de Chirico's barren surrealism and Picasso's intentionally artificial "synthetic cubism." Often the novel generates highly cinematic moments with its mix of film noir-style narration interrupted by multidirectional interior monologues. What results is angst, suspense, and revelation played out in a literary translation of the jump-cut, dissolve, and montage, creating a mood best described as Sartre directed by Hitchcock. Hotschnig's central artistic subtext for the exploration of the illusion of image, however, is not cinema but painting—for its static *Schein und Sein* (appearance and being) quality and because religious art iconizes myth as transcendent knowledge. Taking Kurt to the Uffizi museum in Florence, Anna confesses her ideological connection with painting. Da Vinci's *Verkündigung* (*The Annunciation*) becomes her projected self-portrait, in which the destructive folly of her past but also Kurt's criminality and self-delusion are transcended: "[F]or me the world exists within these hands, orderly and obedient, what in love we call humble and grateful, felt toward a god, a person, who is mistaken about everything."[2]

Born in an Austrian town bordering Italy and Slovenia (then Yugoslavia) in 1959, Alois Hotschnig learned first-hand that the Middle-Europe nostalgia and postwar promotion of the country as the "Alpine Republic," a neutral mirror of multicultural Switzerland, had little basis in actuality. Rather, the imperial inner colonization of other ethnicities by the German(ic)-Austrians was still apparent, and the remnants of Austria's provincialization under Nazism continued to hold sway. "Confronted and entrusted with restrictions since childhood, such as the discrimination against the Slovenian-speaking minority, but also regarding outsiders and the handicapped in close personal circles, I have concentrated on the narrowness of the familiar in my texts; with the Carinthian, the Tyrolian, the Austrian narrowness. ..."[3] This creative attempt to rattle the barriers of the Austrian experience brought Hotschnig to authors dealing with the limits of language and stylistic traditions (Celan and Joyce) and of self-realization (Beckett), and to those critical of an official-national cultural imaginary (Brecht, Bachmann, and Frisch). In these he located the very center of his own desire to write and to approach society and existence filtered through his earlier medical studies as "the assault against unhealthy, i.e. pathogenic structures."[4] But it is Franz Kafka, and in particular his *Tagebücher* (*Diaries*), that particularly informs Hotschnig's style in the diary-like fragmentary verbal and imagistic landscape of *Leonardo's Hands*. The absurdity of social and political structures, but also the concept of self-reflection in Hotschnig, stems from Kafka's existentialist anxieties and the failure of his literary characters to articulate identity and control over personal definition: "All my texts deal with the questions and forms of reinsuring personal identity."[5]

My comparison of *Leonardo's Hands* to Schnitzler's *Gustl* in style-as-revolt and through a shared sociocritical trajectory is based in Hotschnig finding resources in students of Schnitzler (Joyce and Bachmann), and in the very process of literary impressionism that frames the author's creative process of constructing narrative from years of collected fragmentary ideas and themes. Instead of formulating pre-determined characterizations that give rise to dialogue and representation, a "playful observation phase" precedes the solidification of characters that grow from the forest of archived phrases and impressions.[6] In this way, Hotschnig's observations become reactions to the human condition that over time are elevated into a pantheon of personal mythology. It is a Lyotardian collection of random events that come to transmit a "reality." Hotschnig's writings are also reflected in the meaning he gives visual art in *Leonardo's Hands*. Arising from a process of experimentation, paintings are not rigidly pre-determined (even if so attempted) and therefore fascinate Anna and reflect her interrupted, partially planned, partially improvised life.

Reading Hotschnig allegorically, as an examination of the Austrian nation, must begin with *Aus. Eine Erzählung* (Out/Over. A Story). This first important work dating from 1989 recalls the character studies of Thomas Bernhard that so critically moved beyond individual consciousness towards the conscience of a national *Weltanschauung*. Hotschnig's near-expressionistic father/son conflict in *Aus*, where a younger generation must transform itself to survive the real and perceived pressures of the older (Kafka's relationship with his father might well be the intertext here), can also be read as Austria's difficult role in the horrors of Europe in the twentieth century. As the son awaits his father's death, he comes to the realization that this event will not free him from the past. Moreover, he admits to being a victim but has found himself to be an oppressive perpetrator as well. In *Ludwigs Zimmer* (Ludwig's Room), from 2000, Hotschnig returns to the concepts of dying und inheritance. As with the simultaneous status of victim and perpetrator in *Aus* and the idealistic/artistic Anna who is capable of murderous revenge in *Leonardo's Hands*, there is a multivalence of personality and national interpretation. No one quality may overshadow the other.

In *Ludwigs Zimmer*, Kurt Weber inherits more than a family villa in Carinthia; he is sentenced to guardianship over a space where the dead do not simply haunt the landscape, they *are* the landscape. Returning to the home of his childhood, which is slowly revealed to the reader as a link to National Socialist crimes, Weber feels the inevitability of a long-delayed coming-to-terms with the past: "I knew they would collect me, as I was forced to remain at this place, and to wait for them, like a judgment which would be passed on me, and was passed."[7] A member of the postwar generation, Weber represents a memory-less Second Republic, romanticizing the villa and the surrounding territory until he discovers a past of torture and death which opposes his own construction of life, his Austrian imaginary. The connection between these two poles is an old woman who continues to live in the villa and often locks herself into the room of her long-dead lover, a resistance fighter interned at Mauthausen concentration camp who perished in forced labor on the Loibl-Pass to Slovenia—a chapter of history neither country wishes to examine. The author's comment in 2000 regarding the novel, "that one can manage to get by with no [self-]examination is for me a basis for such workaday fascism,"[8] was obviously aimed at the province's governor and then Freedom Party leader Jörg Haider and illuminates his literary character-existentialism as national allegory. As Heinz Hug contextualizes: "The family is the germ-cell of sociopolitical power, silence the basis for the development of human suffering and social injustice."[9] Hotschnig's allegorical Second Republic characters, the son in *Aus*, Kurt Weber in *Ludwigs Zimmer*, and, most compellingly, Kurt Weyrath in *Leonardo's Hands*, are all denuded of their illusions of autonomy from or control of the repercussions of the past. There is no escape clause, and the attempt to create one only serves to drain the present of authenticity and ultimately to destroy the subject.

Leonardo's Hands is the most complex of the author's writing from a sociopolitical viewpoint. Like the paintings encountered in the novel that represent and/or distort reality, Hotschnig's multivalent text can be deciphered as a personification of Austria's fascist past and the Second Republic's problematic national reinvention. Kurt Weyrath is an idealistic technocrat with little sympathy for the human condition beyond what can be dealt with through his expertise. After joining the ambulance service in order to remain close to Anna and remove his guilt by helping to understand and care for her, he expects to comprehend and (re)construct her being on the basis of limited information:

> She's an art historian, now I know. She studies art history. Here in Innsbruck. [...] For weeks I dragged myself to every lecture I could find, knowing that she had seen something of what I was seeing while attending them, hoping also to meet someone there whom she got to know. (70)[10]

And later:

> Now I also know what to talk about with her. Next to her bed I've stacked up art books which I run her hand over. I hold the pictures in front of her eyes and read out loud from the books, or I tell her about the lectures that I visit and about the professors there whom she must know. (70)[11]

Kurt's process, which enacts Lyotard's "speculative philosophy" of the metanarratives inherent in modernism, the expectation of a rational, determinable outcome, mirrors the postwar reconstruction of or reconnection with Austria's national identity from the external, trivialized representation rather than through an internal realization and organic reconstruction.[12] Kurt's use of the art books as signifiers of Anna reduces her to a fictionalized, idealized art student, regardless of what her actual relationship with that aspect of her life may have been. His own criminal act is repressed with a union in her rebirth: "Tell me, what have I done? Your parents lie in the cemetery, but why should we worry about your parents? You are here, you have survived. I am here, I have survived. We simply belong together" (82).[13] Kurt justifies his communication attempts with Anna through confidence in a simplistic cause-and-effect process (again a metanarrative construct) which conveys his arbitrary external "knowledge" as well as the desire for reward: "I know you, for I have taken care of you. I know every part of your body, and you will let me get to know your mind. I will share mine with you. Here's to us, Anna" (82).[14] While Kurt tenderly attempts to be a vital presence to her, Anna can only "speak" in her incomprehensible non-language, which underscores her damage and difference and, above all, forever links her very being to Kurt's discarded past: "Diagnosis: Partial aphasia. Muteness is what they call it. It can continue, but also suddenly disappear. I try to speak, but I only end up speaking to myself" (86).[15] In response to her heavily bandaged and tenuous physical state, but also to Kurt's conscientious albeit reductionist expectations of her rebirth, she remarks (in inner monologue):

> Such bandages manifest themselves on the inside, not just on the outside of the body, and that's why I need you when it appears that I'm cutting

> myself off. I have survived, and yet it still is as if I am lame, mummified, because of what I was before you. You know yourself that when one takes off the bandages, the body falls apart. So be careful, but do it. (93)[16]

In this statement, Anna-Austria can be understood as a "body" of ethnocultures which once before "fell apart" when the bandages were removed (following the sociopolitical "mummification" brought on by reactionary aspects of the monarchy in the nineteenth century and the "injuries" of the First World War). Surviving Nazism and the Second World War, Austria is "as if lame" under a long Allied occupation and through repression of guilt. Anna's recovery suggests that she can never be the same again, at least in any previous concept of her "totality."

Allegorically speaking, reinvention is necessary to break with those pasts and deal with the scarring—as the new Austrian Nation and Alpine Republic. Anna insists they visit the sites of the automobile accident and her parents' graves in a manner that precludes reflection—"without explaining them" (94)[17]—and simply accepts "their past" as a path into the present: "Let's start with you. That will work. We share many of the same places" (94).[18] She hints, however, that her reality is in truth neither created nor resolved by Kurt's actions. Their new life together may begin at this juncture, but Anna harbors a history of abuse that she permitted, and the source continues to linger: "My real murderer is in fact alive" (95).[19] His difficult work in aiding her "healing" has given Kurt a sense of ownership of Anna. As she gains strength, however, she opposes his control and reductionism, but also admits her previous self-destructive patterns:

> You think you should have a right to me, but there's no reason that you should, no, none at all.... I am not a piece of property, Kurt. I was at one time, that's why it's so hard for me, that's why I don't know who I am. I was a piece of property and wanted it that way, for a long time, and then later was forced to remain one.... (100)[20]

Linked as they now are, in a dialogue nearly undifferentiated by spacing so that it appears to be schizoid monologue, Anna's self-examination ultimately underscores Kurt's guilt. The culpability for the destruction of lives cannot be removed by an idealistic re-vision of self or nation; the fanciful creation of a new façade does not change the nature of actual identity. A coming to terms with the past can only be dealt with actively, as Anna suggests: "We've already been sick, Kurt. Now we're slowly getting better" (101).[21] Nevertheless, there is here no simple process of determinable cause and effect, no hope of liberation in self-confrontation, only the promise of knowledge through an irrational journey. "Where are you taking me? I'd walk through hell with you, you know that, " Kurt reassures Anna, who responds: "That's where we will end up. But the path through it leads through heaven" (102).[22] The "heaven" is Florence, where Anna can escape into the art she so loves and in which she finds meaning.

Fatima Naqvi compares Kurt's conflicts to Max Frisch's 1957 *Homo Faber*, in which that novel's postwar engineer Walter Faber comes to represent a persistent fascistic modernity. Kurt's technocratic idealism is already unsatisfying and problematic for him at the start of Hotschnig's novel, as his discarded partner Gerda relates: "Engineering has gotten to you again" (30).[23] With his work on barrage projects, Kurt embodies the technological/progressive Austria that has been promoted by governments and in popular culture as a break from previous political incarnations since the immediate post-imperial era. Like the worker's housing constructions of Red Vienna in the First Republic and the highway constructions of the Austro-fascist period that appeared on tourist placards and in feature films,[24] the early Second Republic's Austrian Nation was characterized by the state-of-the-art power plant at Kaprun, which is presented in the traditional/provincial Austrian *Heimatfilm* in the 1955 *Das Lied der Hohen Tauern*/The Song of Kaprun. This film's romance with a new "national technology" creates a pseudo-progressive identity that at once attempts to rescue the kitsch-tradition of the provincial idyll and break with the immediate National Socialist past (see Büttner and Dewald, 315-18, and Dassanowsky, 165). Gerda's prediction of the danger of Kurt's self-definition in soulless technology, like the technocratic-Nazi correlation in *Homo Faber*, is fulfilled by a life-altering disaster that in its commonplace technological quality and intellectual/emotional response (a careless hit-and-run automobile accident) wryly suggests the most banal allegorization of Hannah Arendt's banality of evil.

Klaus Zeyringer finds a more contemporary criticism in the work's relationship with the concept of the Second Republic as a response to the avoidance of the Nazi past and the collapse of that "reality" in the Waldheim Era of the late 1980s. The final line of Hotschnig's novel, "But it was not so" (146),[25] which ultimately deflates any hope for the central characters, is for Zeyringer a signal of resistance to Austria's recent political culture, especially the xenophobia that came with the ascent of Jörg Haider and the Freedom Party in the late 1990s. It is part of a literary-based sociopolitical discourse which has a long tradition in Austria but which has been particularly vocal since the 1980s in works by Handke, Bernhard, and Jelinek: "[It is] an intellectual tradition in which aesthetics provide a substitute for morality and the language of poetry is understood as being the language of the 'morally better' members of society." Zeyringer also posits that Hotschnig attacks the consumerist culture as an accessory to official hyperreality:

> … at a significant point, namely when Kurt Weyrath is, or so he believes, beginning "a new life" with Anna. At that point the first thing they do together is: "We are going shopping." In the light of the first sentence ["When someone dies, then here that means that he doesn't go shopping again"] what this means is: we are alive.

Anna's wish to escape first the limitations of her injuries and then her previous life, coupled with Kurt's attempt to reinvent self, motivates their desire to flee into a newer and "purer" identity beyond the illusions of their tainted world. The strengthening of Anna's voice throughout the novel, from the abstract/inner monologue to direct dialogue ("a leitmotif called: 'Get me out of here'" [Zeyringer]) is a movement towards a painful but perhaps more authentic life coming in a novel that begins, like the Second Republic, with death and incomplete endings.

The other intriguing facet of *Leonardo's Hands* as a postmodern existentialistic exercise is its meditation on the nature of the visual as an aspect of human control. Certainly one thinks immediately of Riefenstahl's *Triumph of the Will* or of any agitprop performance or artwork ever created. However, the author is broader in his focus and questions the nature of painting humanity, of utilizing beauty *as* national escapism. Austria's postwar desire to blot out historical realities and be *seen* as an Alpine tourist paradise with dashes of high-art and a trivialized imperial legacy is undeniably Hotschnig's target. Naqvi comments that Thomas Bernhard symbolized the Catholic-fascist connection in Austria in the politicization of religious aesthetics as *Staatskunst* (state art) in his novel *Alte Meister* (Old Masters; 1985): "Not only is the art industry and Austria's self-comprehension promoted by such exhibitions, but in the same manner also the continuing influence of Catholic structures" (49).[26] For Hotschnig, however, there is a liberating truth in personal relationship with and in interpretation of such art. Anna, who studies da Vinci to comprehend his veiled ideology (ironically, this artist has since become an international pop-icon of suggested cryptic information through Dan

Brown's trivial mystic/adventure novel *The Da Vinci Code*), instinctually understands the creation of identity manipulation and perception in such a visually codified manner. She tells Kurt: "What are you doing all this for, Kurt, only to make me into an image of what you want?" (100)[27] She also admits this in regard to her fascination with da Vinci, which represents her own reflection of "rebirth" and, on an allegorical level, the concept of a placid Alpine Republic "painting" over difficult postwar realities: "Here it's the same as in Florence, those lovely hands.... What is actually going on in the painting is hidden by this beauty and painted over, such that it cannot really be seen" (107).[28] Later, regarding the same painting, Anna infuses the escapism with Catholicism:

> And her hand rests upon the head of her son like unatoned guilt, his blood, as they say. Spilling down to us and our children, again and again, to lead us not into temptation, but to deliver us from evil. All of that has much more to do with us than you can imagine, Kurt, you'll see. (108)[29]

Naqvi analyses Hotschnig's novel as a statement of contemporary alienation in an Austria where near-official Catholicism and modernity collide, where form and function of a religiously underpinned *Weltanschauung* no longer relate (39). She posits that Kurt's post-accident involvement with "rescuing" (the ambulance service and Anna) is an attempt to escape technocracy and reconnect with an emotionally-based humanism. In a reading where Kurt and Anna play out the problem of Austrian dystopic reinventions in the mid- and late twentieth century, Kurt fights disenchantment with a lost and damaged past by creating a new rebirth myth around his self-definition and that of his victim.

Mirroring Kurt's benevolent construction of Anna is her own re-construction of self and the relationship with Kurt. Both rationalize these creations to represent "Rettung," a word the author plays with in its ambiguous meanings: as *rescue* regarding Kurt's efforts with the ambulance service, and as *salvation*, for which both characters search and for which they justify their actions as pathway. As in the author's examination of the father/son relationship in *Aus*, the crime, done in an effort to assert self, to forgive self, to comprehend self, to justify self—whether as individual or as nation—is a generational and co-dependent synthesis. Without seeing the irony in her own actions, Anna, who is in the process of manipulating Kurt to serve her goals, writes him about the manipulations of her returned ex-lover:

> I treat myself to you, he always said, in order to make up for all those who dream of having me. He victimized me, you understand, and I played the victim. No longer a free will. And that is what I am afraid of Kurt, its starting again.... If you let me stay here, you'll be my murderer, we have to get away. (126)[30]

A Catholic-critical reading of the novel also applies to the concept of the (re-)constructed national imaginary of Kurt and Anna as Second Republic Austria: "But form remains without substance; faith is not church ceremony.... The Catholic rhetoric that influences private and public spheres of existence allows Kurt to dare a return to the Catholic community, but this fails" (Naqvi, 40).[31] Faith becomes formula and is subverted by science and technology just as Austrian national identity is undercut by a selective memory and constructions that attempt to reframe and explain away guilt. One of the many non-specific narrators early in the text is specific with advice: "Life, Herr Weyrath, plays out the past" (34).[32] More than an "unredeemed past" (42), Austria has too long had a selectively unapproachable one.

Peter Filkins writes that "Hotschnig's realism holds little truck with the pseudorealism that pretends to explain the causes of catastrophe, or that reflects with false sobriety upon its consequences" (x). Here is the paradox of life and living in the post-Holocaust world and the examination of it through the multivalent postmodernist understanding of identity construction and even artistic subversion of that construction. Indeed, the work is so deliberately ambiguous in style and voice that it demonstrates what Umberto Eco calls "the provocation of Chance, the Indeterminate, the Probable, the Ambiguous" in postmodernity. A modern literature that is "still the exercise of a reason which tries to reduce things to a discursive clarity" is utterly ruptured by Hotschnig in *Leonardo's Hands* (qtd. in Cannon, 31). The final line, "But it was not so," provides the polysemic closure of the text in regard to the illusions of (sociopolitical) reality and more specifically in response to Anna's defense of her life and Kurt's, and against the possible murder charges for the death of her ex-lover. Her hope for escape/salvation ("Rettung") and for a life together with Kurt will, of course, be dashed. Her own "life painting," in which she hopes to escape into a da Vinci-like obscuration of the terrible knowledge she recognizes beneath Leonardo's placid hands with one of beauty and peace, is untenable. The novel arrives at the realization of the collapse of the grand narrative in the Lyotardian sense as it denies the totalizing of modernist form as text, as character narrative, and as representation of Austrian national escapism.

While the work does not go so far as to be aware of itself as fiction, it does dramatize the inevitable fiction of experience, personal and national. In its depiction of Kurt and Anna's existential angst, as well as in their alienation from self-definition through consumerism, they choose to become "nothing" rather than the "something" assigned them (by the national culture or by Kurt's fantasy of Anna) as "productive" members of a society that would wipe away their own individual meaning. Kurt and Anna's transference of their value system to the metaphysical and out of the constructions of perception-reality and hyper-reality speaks for a difficult but still possible self-determination. Hotschnig's allegory of the re-visioned postwar Austrian nation attempting to paint over history and guilt is also the failure of a modernism, which would tell us that we control our lives to an extent that would have been unimaginable in Schnitzler's time. In our crisis of reason, however, we may discover that realities are only agenda-laden simulacrums, and what passes for rationalism might well need to be transcended.

Works Cited

Büttner, Elisabeth, and Christian Dewald. *Anschluss an Morgen. Eine Geschichte des österreichischen Films von 1945 bis zur Gegenwart.* Salzburg: Residenz, 1997.

Cannon, JoAnn. *Postmodern Italian Fiction: The Crisis of Reason in Calvino, Eco, Sciascia, Malerba.* Rutherford: Fairleigh Dickenson University Press, 1989.

Dassanowsky, Robert von. *Austrian Cinema: A History.* Jefferson, NC: McFarland, 2005.

Decloedt, Leopold. "Ein Gespräch mit Alois Hotschnig." In *Hinter den Bergen eine andere Welt. Österreichische Literatur des 20. Jahrhunderts.* Edited by Anke Bosse and Leopold Decloedt. Amsterdam: Rodopi, 2004.

Filkins, Peter. Foreword. *Leonardo's Hands.* By Alois Hotschnig. Lincoln: University of Nebraska Press, 1999. vii-xi.

Frisch, Max. *Der Mensch erscheint im Holozän.* Frankfurt a. M.: Suhrkamp, 2001.

Hotschnig, Alois. *Aus. Eine Erzählung.* Frankfurt a. M.: Luchterhand, 1989.

—. *Leonardo's Hands.* Translated by Peter Filkins. Lincoln: University of Nebraska Press, 1999.

—. *Leonardos Hände.* Hamburg: Luchterhand, 1992.

—. *Ludwigs Zimmer*. Cologne: Kiepenheuer & Witsch, 2000.

Hug, Heinz. "Eine Erbschaft in Kärnten." Review of *Ludwigs Zimmer*, by Alois Hotschnig. *Der Landbote* (Winterthur), 10 October 2000. <http://www.landbote.ch/news/landbote?ressort=786artikel=66534>. (accessed January 27, 2007)

Kafka, Franz. *Tagebücher 1910-1923*. Edited by Max Brod. Frankfurt a. M.: Fischer, 1967.

Mohr, Peter. "Mit einem Fingerzeig auf Haider." Review of *Ludwigs Zimmer*, by Alois Hotschnig. *Saarbrücker Zeitung*, 9 September 2000. <http://sz.sol.de>. (accessed January 27, 2007)

Naqvi, Fatima. "Die Verzauberung der Welt: Tradierte Religion in Alois Hotschnigs *Leonardos Hände*. *Modern Austrian Literature* 33.2 (2000): 37-54.

Schnitzler, Arthur. *Leutnant Gustl*. 1900. Frankfurt a. M.: Fischer, 2001.

Zeyringer, Klaus. "Österreichische Literatur seit 1986." *The Liffey Project*. http//www.liffeyproject.net. (accessed October 6, 2006)

Notes

[1] Jean-Francois Lyotard rejects the system of thought built around modernist grand generalizations about how things should function. He defines postmodernism as incredulity towards such meta-narratives and posits that reality cannot be accurately represented by rational theory.

[2] Filkins, 106. "Für mich findet in diesen Händen die Welt statt, verstehst du, Anordnung und Gehorsam, in Liebe, wie wir es nennen, in Demut und Dankbarkeit, einem Gott gegenüber, einem Menschen, der sich in allem geirrt hat" (170). All English translations of *Leonardos Hände* are taken from the Peter Filkins translation and hereafter referenced with parenthetical page references in the text and the corresponding original German in an endnote.

[3] "Von Kind an mit Einschränkungen und Ausgrenzungen konfrontiert und vertraut, wie etwa der Diskriminierung der sprachlichen Minderheit der Slowenen, aber auch von Außenseitern und Behinderten im nahen persönlichen Umfeld, habe ich mich in meinen Texten mit der familiären Enge befasst, mit der kärntnerischen, der tirolischen, der österreichischen Enge..." (Decloedt, "Ein Gespräch mit Alois Hotschnig," 329; all translations from this source mine).

[4] "Das Anrennen gegen ungesunde bzw. Krankmachende Strukturen" (Decloedt, 331). Hotschnig was a medical student at the University of Innsbruck before turning to writing (see Filkins, viii).

[5] "In allen meinen Texten geht es um diese Fragen und um Formen der Rückversicherung der eigenen Identität" (Decloedt, 333).
[6] "spielerische Beobachtungsphase" (Decloedt, 333-34).
[7] "Doch ich wußte, sie holen mich ein, indem ich gezwungen war, an diesem Ort stehenzubleiben und auf sie zu warten wie auf ein Urteil, das über mich kommen sollte und kam" (42-43; my translation).
[8] "Dass man mit sich auskommt, nichts hinterfragt, ist für mich ein Grund für den Alltagsfaschismus" (see Peter Mohr; my translation).
[9] "Die Familie als Keimzelle sozio-politischer Gewalt, das Schweigen als Grundlage für die Entwicklung menschlichen Leids und sozialer Ungerechtigkeit" (my translation).
[10] "Sie ist Kunsthistorikerin, weiß ich jetzt. Sie studiert Kunstgeschichte. Hier in Innsbruck. [...] Seit Wochen quäle ich mich durch alle möglichen Vorlesungen, etwas davon wird sie gesehen haben, und vielleicht lerne ich dort jemanden kennen, den sie gekannt hat" (115) .
[11] "Jetzt weiß ich auch was mit ihr reden. An ihrem Bett stapeln sich Kunstbände, die ich mit ihrer Hand abtaste. Ich halte ihr die Bilder vor das Gesicht und lese aus den Büchern laut vor, oder erzähle ihr von den Vorlesungen, die ich besuche, und rede über den Professoren dort, die sie ja kennen muß" (117).
[12] The external constructions I refer to regarding Austria's postwar revision include the 1943 Moscow Declaration indicating Austria as victim of Nazism, Western Allied interests in rebuilding an independent Austria to serve their interests in the Cold War, and the concept of Austria as a neutral, Swiss-like "Alpine Republic" in order to attract investment and tourism and to escape past sociocultural and political linkages.
[13] "Was habe ich getan, sag, deine Eltern liegen auf dem Friedhof, was kümmern uns deine Eltern, du bist da, du hast überlebt, die Zeit bis zum Unfall und seither, wir gehören ganz einfach zusammen" (135).
[14] "Ich kenne dich ja, denn ich habe dich gepflegt, jeder Teil deines Körpers ist mir bekannt, und in deinen Kopf wirst du mich führen. Ich zeig dir den meinen. Stoßen wir an auf uns, Anna" (135).
[15] "Diagnose: Partielle Aphasie. Wortstummheit, sagt man den Kranken. Es kann bleiben, ebenso auch vergehen. Ich versuche zu sprechen, spreche ausschließlich mit mir selbst" (141).
[16] "Diese Binden bekommt man von innen heraus nicht vom Körper ab, dazu brauche ich Dich, wenn es auch ausseiht, als wehrte ich mich. Ich habe überlebt, bin aber doch immer wie gelähmt, durch das, was bisher mit mir war, vor Dir, mumifiziert. Du weißt, wenn man die Binden abnimmt, zerfallen die Körper, so gib also acht, aber tu es" (151-52).
[17] "ohne sie zu erklären" (152).
[18] "Geh von dir aus, Es wird stimmen. Wir haben gemeinsame Orte" (152).

[19] "Mein wirklicher Mörder lebt auch" (154).
[20] "Du Kurt, und ein Recht haben wollen auf mich, woran denn an mir, nein.... Ich bin kein Besitz, ich war es, deshalb tue ich mich so schwer, deshalb habe ich mich nicht, ich war ein Besitz und wollte es sein, lange und dann unter Zwang" (160).
[21] "Eine Krankheit täte jetzt gut. Die hatten wir, Kurt. Jetzt werden wir langsam gesund" (162).
[22] "Wohin führst du mich? Ich gehe mit dir in die Hölle, das weißt du. Dort landen wir. Aber der Weg dorthin führt in den Himmel" (164).
[23] "Deine Technik zerstört Dich wieder einmal" (67).
[24] Especially the Großglockner Hochalpenstraße, which is promoted in the film *Singende Jugend* (Singing Youth), aka *An Orphan Boy of Vienna* (1936). See Dassanowsky, 71.
[25] "Aber das stimmte nicht" (232).
[26] "Nicht nur die Kulturindustrie und das österreichische Selbstverständnis als Kulturnation werden durch diese ausgestellten Kunstwerke gefördert, sondern in gleicher Weise das Weiterwirken katholischer Formen" (my translation).
[27] "Wofür benützt du Dich, Kurt, indem Du mich einem Sinn für Dich zuführen willst?" (161).
[28] "Auch hier, es ist wie in Florenz, ideale Hände....Was eigentlich abspielt im Bild, ist gerade durch diese Schönheit verdeckt und übermalt und so gar nicht sichtbar.... (171-72).
[29] "Und ihre Hand fährt wie eine ungesühnte Schuld auf den Kopf ihres Sohnes herab, sein Blut, heißt es, kommt über uns und unsere Kinder, und führe uns nicht in Versuchung, sondern erlöse uns von allem Übel. Mit uns hat das alles mehr zu tun, als Dir lieb sein kann, Kurt, Du wirst sehen" (173).
[30] "Ich leiste dich mir, hat er immer gesagt, als Entschuldigung vor den anderen, die auch von mir träumten. Er hat mich geopfert, verstehst du, und ich habe ihm das Opfer gemacht. Nicht mehr freiwillig dann. Und davor habe ich jetzt Angst Kurt, es fängt wieder an .... Wenn du mich hierläßt, bist du mein Mörder, wir müssen hier weg" (201).
[31] "Aber Form bleibt ohne Substanz, aus dem kirchlichen Zeremoniell kein Glaube.... Die katholische Rhetorik, die private und öffentliche Sphären durchdringt, läßt ihn [Kurt] eine Rückkehr in die katholische Gemeinschaft wagen; aber diese schlagt fehl" (my translation).
[32] "Das Leben, Herr Weyrath, spielt sich als Vergangenheit ab" (60).

Chapter Twenty-Two

The New Order: The Method of Madness in the Cinema of Michael Haneke

Oliver Speck

In a relatively short period of time, Michael Haneke's oeuvre developed from critically acclaimed films with a small distribution, co-produced by Austrian and German television, to works of French cinema, without doubt the most sophisticated cinema in Europe in terms of public image, distribution, and star-power. Now accosted by French stars (Juliette Binoche, Daniel Auteuil, Isabelle Huppert) to make movies showcasing them, Haneke's name is synonymous with European art house cinema. It should be added that Haneke himself is quite media-savvy, insisting in interviews and in the short documentary features that accompany the DVD-editions of his films that he, as the filmmaker, can only give one of many possible interpretations of the films he wrote and directed, adding to the image of himself as the heir to the European tradition of the socially critical *auteur*.[1] Like other European directors who previously took this spot in the imagination of the *feuilletons* (e.g., Peter Greenaway and Theo Angelopoulos), Haneke is addressing topics considered difficult measured by the standards of commercial cinema: the traumatic effects of violence, racism, sexism, and alienation. Considering his well-documented contempt for television and Hollywood cinema with its generic system (see Cieutat and Rouyer, Grabner, Sharett), which by critics and scholars alike are seen as postmodern excesses lacking in substance, it is not surprising that Michael Haneke has been labeled a modernist.

This reputation in turn clearly dictates the reception of Haneke's films, which are judged by their ability to take a readily identifiable stance against phenomena perceived as "typically postmodern," i.e., the reifying effects of consumer capitalism and the role of mass-media in it. One critic, representative of such a judgment, attests to "Haneke's perverse modernist desire to punish us for our collusion with the commodified—and thus, for Haneke at least, mendacious—narrative certainties of dominant cinema."[2] While there are certainly signature shots typical of Haneke (a close-up on the exchange of goods and money), typical scenarios (an oedipal triangle, often sharing the same names—Anna/Anne, Georg/Georges, and Ben), and recurring motifs (the droning of television and/or reference to current events such as the war in Bosnia) that warrant such a reading, I would argue that these surface phenomena are merely symptoms, and that it would be more fruitful to concentrate on madness, the one *topos* that appears in one form or another in all of Haneke's films. Therefore, instead of expecting a critique of our culture that we can apply when needed, we should accept, with regard to Haneke, Nietzsche's famous insight that philosophers and artists are "physicians of culture," an insight with which Haneke, who studied psychology and philosophy at the University of Vienna, is certainly familiar. In other words, instead of the normative demand for a cure, we should first accept the *auteur*'s ability to diagnose a disease in our culture by reading the symptoms.

With this shift in perspective in mind, we can readily see that there are two forms of madness in Haneke's films that need to be held apart: the everyday craziness of life in our fragmented, postmodern world and the madness of a criminal act, often linked to a violent, traumatic event that cuts all social bonds. Haneke seems to play here on the two German words for being mad: *wahnsinnig* (meaning "insane"), whose more commonly encountered noun form, *Wahnsinn*, could be translated literally as "delusional sense"—with the same double meaning of "sense" as in English—and the more colloquially used adjective *verrückt*, crazy, literally "out of joint." It is in this latter sense that madness in film is generally depicted: as a character's state of un-reason (*Ver-rücktheit*). It is important to point out that this craziness which befalls the evil stock character of virtually all action films is never motivated psychologically—the prototypical "bad guy" of Hollywood action films is evil incarnate in himself—but instead provides the hero's motivation for violence in the form of a morally justified revenge. In Haneke's cinema, however, madness becomes a new order that provides a new *sense*: we can locate this new sense, for example, in the form of a new code in the everyday craziness of racism in, for example, *Code inconnu: Récit incomplet de divers voyages* (*Code unknown*, 2000). When the civil order breaks down in *Le Temps du loup* (*Time of the Wolf*, 2003) only mad actions still make sense. And, cynically, the new order of madness provides perverse rules of the game in the *Familienroman*, the Freudian family romance of the tortured family in *Funny Games* (1997). This article will look at the instances of this "new-order" madness in the cinema of cruelty that Michael Haneke unfolds and explore its subversive uses, especially as concerns not only Haneke's cultural analyses, but—on another and less understood level—his very stance concerning cinema spectatorship and the pedagogical role cinema plays for the viewer.

What is remarkable here is the affinity that Haneke's conceptual framework shows to philosophers like Michel Foucault, Jean Baudrillard, Jacques Derrida, Gilles Deleuze, Shoshana Felman, or Alain Badiou, who have been dismissed with the label "postmodern." Badiou, for example, calls for an "ethics of truths," while Felman reflects on the pedagogical use of trauma.[3] This does not mean that Haneke's films can be explained by reading these philosophers and "applying" their thought to his films; instead, it should be stressed that these films make a similar attempt with aesthetic means as does the philosophy of the above-mentioned thinkers. This attempt can be described as the thinking of a possible alternative to the global culture of so-called postmodernity.[4]

The basis for Haneke's unique take on madness can be found already in his first three films, the trilogy about alienation which he baptized "glaciation of feelings" ("*Vergletscherung der Gefühle*"): *Der Siebente Kontinent* (*The Seventh Continent*, 1989), *Benny's Video* (1992) and *71 Fragmente einer Chronologie des Zufalls* (*71 Fragments of a Chronology of Chance*, 1994), as well as in *Funny Games* (1997), the last German language film Haneke wrote and directed.[5] Noticeably, the family's murder/suicide in *The Seventh Continent*—apparently inspired by a real event—as well as the shooting spree and suicide in *71 Fragments of a Chronology of Chance* indeed *do not make sense. The Seventh Continent*'s nuclear family is socially on the rise, with a long-awaited and hard-earned promotion for the father adding to their economic security, a well-established daily routine and, apparently, a comfortable life in their house. When the couple destroys all their goods and flushes the money down the toilet before killing their young daughter and committing suicide, their motives cannot be explained. Likewise, Max's humiliation at the bank at the hands of an aggressive customer in *71 Fragments* certainly does not justify his taking out his aggression on innocent bystanders. However, if we take Michael Haneke as a "physician of culture," what Gilles Deleuze calls a "clinician of civilization" (*Logic*, 237), we can establish a point of view from which this clinical picture does make sense. In short, we need to identify this new disease by carefully analyzing its symptoms.

The clinician of civilization, as Daniel W. Smith explains in his excellent introduction to Deleuze's *Essays Critical and Clinical*, "distinguishes cases that had hitherto been confused by dissociating symptoms that were previously grouped together, and by juxtaposing them with others that were previously dissociated. In this way, the doctor constructs an original clinical concept for the disease [...]" (xvi). In the following, I bring out the most important of Michael Haneke's clinical concepts, still prevalent in his French-language films, by concentrating on the different forms of madness in his first four cinematic feature films. I focus on two concepts: trauma, which always results from a failed integration into the symbolic framework, and symbolic exchange, an objectifying (market) force that expresses itself in the infinite substitutability of object for object and object for money. As I argue, these concepts do not provide a cure, or a single identifiable cause for the disease, but rather introduce a pedagogy of the image, where the viewer is led away from seeking a transcendent, true image, or Truth, and instead is initiated into the (painful) taking of perspectives that yields unexpected, plural truths. The clinical concepts of exchange and trauma are only the first steps in the process of finding a possible cure, providing not a punctual event constituting a radical shift, but rather the bringing on of a different mode of thinking and praxis.

In his films, Haneke attempts what Deleuze calls a pedagogy, educating the viewer to more complex ways of reading, thus enabling the diagnostic work performed by the image: "There is a pedagogy of the image, especially with Godard, when the function is made explicit, when the frame serves as an opaque surface of information, sometimes blurred by saturation, sometimes reduced to the empty set, to the white or black screen" (*Cinema 1*, 13).[6] This pedagogy of the image appears in Haneke's films in the insertion of black film, but also in the painfully long sequences of the table-tennis player and the old man's phone conversation in *71 Fragments*. In *Benny's Video*, it appears as the repeated slaughter of the pig (which we must assume is real, not "all Ketchup," as Benny calls cinematic bloodshed) and as the fictive slaughter of the girl, which we simultaneously see and do not see, being out of the field of vision of Benny's video camera, in turn the object of the film camera. This space that is not shown but that nevertheless exists in the fiction is known as *hors champ* ("out of field") in cinematic terms. In all these cases of video-in-film, the image is revealed *as* image with its manipulative power, thus drawing attention to the materiality of the *hors cadre*, the outside of the cinematic frame itself, the space of enunciation: What is it the director does not allow us to see? Do we really want to see it?

In the framework of clinical diagnoses, it is not surprising that in *The Seventh Continent* we do not partake in the couple's planning of the suicide and no psychological motive is ever given, while only the wife's letters to her in-laws are heard as voice-over. Benny, in *Benny's Video*, pressured to give an explanation for the slaughter of a young girl he encountered by chance, can only say that he "wanted to know how it is." Instead, Haneke's camera—which has often been compared to a diagnostic instrument (Seeßlen, 52)—dissociates and isolates the protagonist's daily routines in order to facilitate the diagnoses. These routines—with some significant exceptions—are symbolic exchanges: buying and consuming food, leaving a note with some lunch money, renting videos, exchanging money for drugs, etc. In each instance, the camera focuses on the object of exchange, sometimes in extreme close-up. As an example, repeated scenes of shopping come to mind, or the long chain of hands in *Benny's Video*, passing on the goods and the money from one choirboy to the next.

The isolating focus on the object of exchange has the curious effect that the object as the actual agent seems to stand still, while the world revolves around it. Here, Haneke shows another kinship with Jean-Luc Godard insofar as a careful differentiation needs to be upheld between what Godard famously calls "*juste une image*" ("just/only an image") and "*une image juste*" ("a just/true image"). While the "just image" attempts to find a perfect expression for a concept, the images Godard and Haneke construct are "only images" that do not point to a transcendent point of view, but rather question it.[7] This differentiation in turn allows two different but not mutually exclusive readings or, rather, perspectives. One perspective that establishes itself in the foreground—and here the images certainly provide a "just" illustration—concerns the lack of meaning in this routine, stressing, as Adam Bingham aptly puts it, the "emotional vacuity of modern life":

> "By showing only shots of hands turning off alarm clocks, hands preparing food, etc., the film very effectively states just how mechanically such tasks, the everyday tasks that make up these characters' lives, are performed. And thus just how empty their lives really are."

This perspective, however, provides the foil for a second perspective, which, since it is an abstract concept, cannot be shown, but is constructed by the constant repetition and insertion of a black screen that syncopates *The Seventh Continent* and *71 Fragments*: the exchange of commodities. More akin to Eisenstein's famous plan to adapt Marx's *Capital* for the screen, Haneke crosses over in these moments to the genre of essay-film, effectively filming the paradoxical impossibility of showing the concept of exchange.

Michael Haneke's educated viewer, enabled to "see" the concept of exchange at work, must now be equally capable of seeing the exceptional.

That this network of symbolic exchange is firmly grounded in consumer capitalism and that words are used sparingly and entirely for the purpose of basic communication is not remarkable in itself. But the notable exception to this circulation of goods, seemingly a rupture of exchange, is the family's murder/suicide in *The Seventh Continent*, which takes the form of a suicidal potlatch with a carefully planned exchange of all moveable goods for money, withdrawal of cash and a final feast, followed by a methodical destruction of all furniture and the flushing of the cash down the toilet. This absolute annulment of the family's economic existence, however, is already foreshadowed by some breaks in the otherwise smooth symbolic exchange. When the brother-in-law's inability to get over their mother's death manifests itself at the dinner table, the couple responds to his emotional breakdown with an embarrassed silence. More telling, when the young daughter, Eva, feigns blindness at school, her mother promises Eva that she will go unpunished if she admits her guilt. Ignoring her promise as well as the daughter's obvious attempt to get attention—we see a newspaper with the headline "Blind Girl Earns Sympathy"—the mother slaps her in the face.

This violation of a symbolic debt finds its most disturbing manifestation in the rationalization that we witness in the suicide note that is left for the parents. Here, the couple explains that they pondered whether they should "take Eva with them" or not. After asking their daughter whether she is afraid of death, and obtaining her response in the negative, they decide that killing her would be in her best interest. A visual illustration of this decision is provided by the fish, whose agonizing death is shown in extreme close-up. At this point, Eva begins to understand her imminent death and resists when she is forced to drink the poisonous cocktail of sleeping pills. Eva as the child, however, is exactly that which escapes the symbolic exchange in the paradoxical form of the gift. As Jacques Derrida points out in *Given Time*, there can be no gift since every gift introduces its receiver into a vicious circle of gift and counter-gift, in short, an economic exchange which denies the very definition of gift as something that is given freely, without ulterior motive. Following Marcel Mauss's play on the etymology of gift, leading to the different meanings that the word gained in English, where it refers to something that is given, and German, where *Gift* means poison, Derrida states:

> In order to be gift, not only must the donor or donee not perceive or receive the gift as such, have no consciousness of it, no memory, no recognition; he or she must also forget it right away [*à l'instant*] and moreover this forgetting must be so radical that it exceeds even the psychoanalytic categoriality of forgetting. (18)

The only gift—and Haneke clearly points to it in the final sequence of *The Seventh Continent*—is therefore the impossible gift of existence that Eva as the child cannot perceive or recognize, but which in turn puts her parents into debt. Contrary to this debt—what we might call an ethical debt—the parents, by giving poison to their child, act on Eva as if she were a commodity in their possession, like the furniture or the fish, not something that is indeed given in the other, radical sense. Thus, the viewer realizes that, in fact, the family murder/suicide is not a rupture in the chain of exchange, but rather a radical form of it, radical because it takes the logic of exchange to a new, undeniably "logical" end, and radical because, as image, it calls attention to that very logic of exchange that the couple fails to overcome.

With this perversion of the gift in mind, we can now better determine Michael Haneke's clinical concept of the exchange. The repeated focus on the exchange of goods shows that the objects of exchange not only provide meaning, but that the protagonists in this circle also fully identify with this logic of exchange, thereby defining themselves as goods—a true perversion in the sense of Lacan's pun of the *père-version*, the father's version, where the subject denies its own excessive sexual enjoyment, its *jouissance*, and instead makes itself into an instrument of the Other's *jouissance*. The perverse logic of the parents' actions becomes apparent here: since the Other as the site of absolute alterity does not exist and cannot be appropriated by identification, serving as an instrument of the Other's *jouissance* means serving a pure projection of an inhuman logic. Characteristically, the (self-)destruction is carried out without any apparent emotional involvement. Indeed, instead of seeing the potlatch as an alternative to the capitalist exchange of goods, one that replaces the utilitarian economy of lack with one of excess, as Georges Bataille famously suggests in *The Accursed Share*, the parents in *The Seventh Continent* fully identify with the exchange. Any forms of excess, be they emotional or other, have no place in this logic. The reaction to the brother's breakdown and the slap in the face that the spouse receives after declaring her love to her husband in *71 Fragments* also bear witness to this. And the cool reaction of the father in *Benny's Video* is telling. He sarcastically remarks: "*Nicht gerade die ideale Imagepflege!* (Not especially ideal for our public image!)" The problem is one of dealing with the excess, the non-exchangeable—or, as Bataille calls it, expenditure—which threatens the family's symbolic capital. Hence, the body of the victim in *Benny's Video* is entirely perceived as a problem of waste-disposal: "The pieces have to be small enough so that they don't clog the drain."

The audience, by virtue of Haneke's clinical camera, is pushed into the role of Polonius, who has to admit: "Though this be madness, yet there is method in it." Or, as the father at the beginning of the suicidal potlatch perceives: "We can only do this if we approach it methodically!" Only from this limited perspective—from the point of view of the exchange—does it make sense, *Wahnsinn*, to define the family entirely as a closed and dispensable economic circle that can be taken off the circuit without hurting the overall exchange. The sense of delusion stems from the logic of exchange, not a rupture with it, thus making "delusional sense."

This inability to deal with excess and the subsequent identification with the logic of exchange leading to a perversion points to a traumatic, i.e., failed, integration into the psyche's conceptual framework, a failure that Freud famously linked to the death drive. Here, we encounter a second recurring clinical concept, that of trauma, which in Haneke's oeuvre is already discernible in *71 Fragments* but is developed later in his French films, especially *Caché* (*Hidden*, 2005). According to Laplanche and Pontalis, trauma is "[a]n event in the subject's life, defined by its intensity, by the subject's incapacity to respond adequately to it and by the upheaval and long-lasting effects that it brings about in the psychical organization" (465). These traumas which appear in all of Haneke's films and are always linked to a violent crime, however, should not be confused with the trauma of the typical traumatized character that we encounter in many Hollywood films and whose trauma is usually eliminated or "solved" by the violent annihilation of the trauma's cause.[8] *Caché*, for example, goes to great lengths to establish George's, the main character's, innocence, who, as a 6 year old, out of jealousy contributed to the removal of an Algerian boy, Majid, to an orphanage, but who was of course too young at that point to understand the effects of his actions. In their concise introduction to the notion of trauma, Baranger et al. point out that in Freud's definition the traumatic should not be confused with the pathogenic. The trauma is instead an event that needs to be "historicized," that is, explained in the form of a history. However, as Baranger et al. stress, the resulting history is only valid from a very limited point of view: "This does not mean that historization is an arbitrary process. As analysts, we cannot propose to anyone any history that is not his own" (124). The historization that happens in Haneke's cinema is also not arbitrary but belongs to the mad point of view, the only point of view that provides a meaning. Much like an analyst, the audience of a Haneke film has to accept and identify with the mad point of view in order to avoid an arbitrary, i.e., relativistic, reading.

In *Caché* the actual traumata, always resulting from a failed integration into the symbolic framework, appear on three levels. The trigger for the events depicted in the film is the real trauma brought about by the brutal murder of up to 200 Algerians and the subsequent cover-up by French police in Paris on 17 October 1961. On a second, extradiegetic level, the audience can only imagine the abuse Majid must have received as a young Algerian boy, recently orphaned because of a massacre that was committed and covered up by the authorities. Majid's incapacity to deal with the traumatic loss of his parents and the abuse at the orphanage results in an apparently arrested development and his blaming Georges for his misery. The third type of trauma, finally, is the one to which Majid subjects Georges—and by extension the viewer—by his shocking and bloody suicide.

To take another example of Haneke's depiction of trauma, *Le Temps du loup* puts this depiction of the violent event that traumatizes the viewer right at the beginning of the film when the father, a figure of calm and sincere authority, is suddenly shot down by a squatter, an event which we witness only through the sound of the gunshot, the blood on the mother's face, and her vomiting in reaction to the slaughter of her husband. The camera carefully avoids a shot of the body. The unknown event that caused the civil order to break down is never explained and, as in the case of Majid's imagined past, stays outside the frame of events unfolding on the screen, always present (we see burning livestock) but unexplained.

Another example of this extradiegetic trauma is certainly the incredible hardship and abuse the young fugitive in *71 Fragments* must have suffered and to which he alludes in an interview he is giving on television. Again, it is an imagined trauma, requiring an act of imagination on the part of the audience. Apparently unfazed by his ordeals or the interview situation, the fugitive talks about his past. However, if a girl his age already works regularly as a prostitute, how desolate must his own life be? Likewise, the trauma of real historical event is, of course, omnipresent in Haneke's oeuvre in the form of news about violent conflicts that play unobserved in the background in, for example, Benny's room in *Benny's Video*, or the Laurents' living room in *Caché*. As in Godard's films—*Notre musique/Our Music* (2004) and *For Ever Mozart* (1996) come to mind—the war in Bosnia and the Gulf War are omnipresent here. And like Godard and other leading intellectuals, Haneke seems to suggest that the West has not dealt adequately with these traumatic events, that is, has failed to integrate them in its symbolic framework by appropriately historicizing them.[9]

One could object, of course, that establishing trauma as the limit of representation is not exactly a new idea, especially in light of the paradoxes involved in representing the unimaginable of the Holocaust. What Haneke avoids with his complex strategy is the creation of a third, overarching position, one that embraces relativism in order to pursue a meta-truth. This relativism would indeed provide the closure that Haneke's films regularly deny. Again, Deleuze provides a theoretical rationale for this shift which he calls "perspectivism" and which he finds in the Baroque. As Deleuze puts it:

> [P]erspectivism amounts to a relativism, but not the relativism we take for granted. It is not a variation of truth according to the subject, but the condition in which the truth of a variation appears to the subject. This is the very idea of Baroque perspective. (*The Fold*, 20)

Instead of the omniscient perspective of traditional narrative cinema, Haneke's films create conditions in which a truth appears to the viewer, as uncomfortable as this truth might be. The truth espoused by this position is not "capital t" Truth, but a plural truth that appears, sometimes briefly, in a given perspective and that is not subjective: just images, and definitely not a just image. Avoiding an image that somehow "captures" a transcendent truth is key here. The clichéd "life is crazy," for example, is inverted and appears as a life that suddenly makes sense when the viewer is forced to take the perspective of the senseless event.

As is the case especially in *71 Fragments* and *Code inconnu*, the events unfolding on the screen make sense only from the paradoxical point of view of the traumatic event, the *Wahnsinn*, that provides the only link for the different storylines. While in *71 Fragments* the characters are finally connected by the rampage and the contingency of being in the wrong place at the wrong time, *Code inconnu* adds another dimension by linking different kinds of racism: the thoughtless cruelty of Jean's action and the policeman who automatically takes Jean's side, but also the sexism and projected racism of the young Arab who attacks Anne. This perspective that is forced on the viewer is puzzling for many critics who seem to resist what Haneke's pedagogy of the image effectively demands, a thinking from the mad perspective of the traumatic event.[10] Here again we need to acknowledge that Georges and Anne in their different incarnations are objectively innocent. From the point of view of the event, however, their inability to work through or "historicize" the traumas makes them guilty. In this sense *Crash*, by Paul Haggis (2004), could be considered the exact opposite of Haneke's *71 Fragments* and *Code Inconnu*, with which it shares some structural similarities. *Crash* attempts to find "just images" in order to purvey a strong message, while Haneke's films question the entire concept of the "just," overarching image.

That the appearance of trauma in different forms in Haneke's films can easily be mapped onto Lacan's well-known topology of the Borromean knot, which illustrates the formation of the subject using the entwined circles of Real/Imaginary/Symbolic, underlines the importance of this concept, enabling us to see even better the significance of the perspectival shifts in Haneke's films.[11] If we take the filmic text as a form of the Symbolic and the unseen traumas as the Imaginary, the Real appears mostly in the form of a historic event that is mediated by television. There is, however, another image that Haneke carefully constructs in his films, with the notable exception of the *Le Temps du loup* and *La Pianiste/The Piano Teacher* (2001). This pedagogical image appears *just* briefly with the shock of realizing that we are not gazing *at* something but *with* something, thereby traumatizing the viewer with an abrupt shift in perspective.

At the beginning of *Caché*, for example, a perfectly innocent shot of a tranquil urban neighborhood is suddenly revealed to be a surveillance video by a fast-forwarding of the tape and voices that comment on what can be seen on it. Here the gazes of spectator, surveillance- and film camera, characters, and unknown agent find themselves suddenly aligned—except that, of course, each of them sees something different. A similar moment appears twice in *Benny's Video*, first when the video of the killing is shown to the parents, and then when Benny shows a video of his parents to the police. And in *Code inconnu* we must realize that a puzzling scene showing Anne frolicking in a pool with another man and a dramatic last-minute rescue of a little boy is only a film in which she stars. The function of this shift is pedagogical in that it educates the viewer about trauma, giving him or her a wake-up call, a taste of trauma first-hand. It short-circuits viewer identification by suddenly putting the viewer in the subjective position of first-person narrative. This is doubly traumatizing because he or she never expected to occupy this position, and because it is also occupied by the unknown agent. The viewer is thus made to bear and confront a troubled ethical position with which he or she must identify at that moment.

However, the most pronounced instance of this traumatizing shift in perspective appears in *Funny Games*, certainly Haneke's most controversial film so far, shocking audiences and critics since its release.[12] While it might be possible for an audience to take a distanced stance towards the violent events depicted in *Le Temps du loup* and *La Pianiste*, *Funny Games* refuses any relieving perspective. Again, this refusal of closure works on several levels, the most surprising being, of course, the mastery on the intradiegetic level over the diegesis that one of the sadistic killers suddenly deploys. When the mother can grab the shotgun and at least partially avenge the slaughter of her son, the other killer frantically looks for the remote control. He then proceeds to rewind the scene until the crucial moment and thus prevents the mother from reaching the gun in the rerun. This, along with the other self-referential moments, not only destroys the phantasm of an imagined, possible happy-ending, but also the spectator's mastery over the text.

In his perceptive reading of *Funny Games*, Brian Price recognizes that the theme of mastery is established already in the first game of *Funny Games*, the family's classical music guessing-game: "The satisfaction the couple takes in correctly matching name to sound, sign to signifier, is both an expression of cultural mastery and an expression of confidence in an essential bond between the word and sound, speech and authentic self" (26). This bond relates also to the mastery of the spectator, who expects a bond between the text and self, authentication of self by the filmic text. This expectation is mocked by the killers' discussion about the reality of fiction, which "is as real as the reality that you see likewise," right after they throw the mother overboard.

Read on a superficial level, the smug superiority of Peter and Paul, the killers, combined with the film's self-referentiality, would point to a "fallacious allegory," as an enraged reviewer has remarked. Tellingly, it is especially Haneke's refusal to show the acts of violence, focusing only on the effects, that angers this critic: "It is an immoral procedure and a lie to show the victim's bodies as the sole place of violence" (Masson, 39; my translation). Price is correct here in insisting that *Funny Games* is not about violence but about the unrepresentability of pain. As he explains, pain that is linked to a cathartic effect in the end serves an ideology: "Instead, pain here mobilizes thought, but ironically does so by its refusal to find a word or image identical to it" (29). A traditional moralist perspective would seek to provide a meaning, a transcendent point of view, while *Funny Games* insists that the body of the victim is indeed the only space where the image of violence can be found. The conscience of the perpetrator certainly stays clean. Hence the repeated instances of paradoxically innocent guilty persons, like Georges in *Caché*. The young black man in *Code inconnu* who berates Jean for his insulting gesture unwittingly condemns the woman whose dignity he wanted to protect to being deported. And even Benny's deed, as horrible as it is, would not count as premeditated murder, while the parents' careful planning of their criminal act is perfectly rationalized by the reference to a higher order.

It seems, then, that the two clinical concepts that Haneke diagnoses—and that are here called "exchange" and "trauma"—are related in *Funny Games* insofar as there is a class conflict carrying the events. Interestingly enough, this class conflict relates to the audience, not the killers. Not only are the two killers familiar with their victims' way of life, easily able to turn the gated community into a prison camp, but, as their knowledge of golf and sailing shows, they are not impostors but clearly part of the upper-middle-class that they are murdering. Ultimately, the audience's envy of the life of the rich is punished by the traumatizing events we are forced to see, or, what is worse, the spectacle of which we are denied. Again, the killers' actions do not make sense unless we accept the point of view of the exchange fully. Indeed, the only difference between killer and victim seems to be that Peter and Paul do not buy into the values of high culture and morality but fully identify with completely free-floating, fully exchangeable rules of the game that they change at will, even breaking the basic rule of fiction when they break "the fourth wall" by addressing the spectator and changing the diegetic reality. To come back to the viewer of Haneke's films in general, he or she is thus forced to follow the logic of exchange to its end and to confront it in all its traumatic "fullness," thus gaining insight into his or her own implication in this exchange. Or, to follow through the metaphor of the physician of culture, the viewer gains a bill of (ill) health regarding his or her stance on—and in—exchange.

What Haneke shows might be summarized thus: it is not so much that late capitalist culture is characterized by the disease of madness as regards the logic of exchange, but rather that the logic of exchange proceeds prosaically, sanely to its end. Furthermore, to invoke the task of the physician of culture introduced at the beginning, through the concept of trauma newly associated to that of exchange, the viewer is given a unique perspective or view, a brief but true image of that madness and his or her position, both ethical and structural, in it such that the "perspectivality" of the perspective—its constructedness, the manner of its production—is itself briefly visible. The view is thus also a view into the production of this (produced) perspective.

Inevitably, what follows Haneke's clinical diagnosis is the demand for a cure. However, here we need to resist again the temptation to find a cure in the form of a transcendent perspective. As was shown above, by reading the symptoms, Haneke's cinema proceeds in two related steps necessary to diagnose the disease in our culture, whereby the filmic text appears as a form of the Symbolic and the unseen traumas to which the characters are subjected as the Imaginary, while the Real appears mostly in the form of a historic violent event mediated by television. First, Haneke's cinema forces the spectator to accept the only perspective that makes sense, the mad perspective of the *Wahnsinn*. Second, it employs a pedagogy of the image that teaches its audience new ways of seeing in order to avoid the construction of a finalizing—that is, true and just—perspective instead showing "just images."

However, the formulation "just images" should not be understood as irrelevant images or images that convey a relativistic truth that, in the end, is as good as any other truth. As already stated, perspectival truth, while not the same as metaphysical Truth, does have a truth-value appearing in the perspective. To put it in other words, the value of the "cure" lies in the viewer's renewed critical stance that arises from the pedagogical initiation of Haneke's films. These mad—*wahnsinnige*—images demand that the spectator situate him- or herself vis-à-vis the new order that they create. The pedagogical initiation through these images is thus such that the viewer is made to look critically not only at the filmic images, but at his or her own extradiegetic reality implicated by the diegetic madness.

Works Cited

Badiou, Alain. "What is a Philosophical Institution? Or: Address, Transmission, Inscription." *Cosmos and History: The Journal of Natural and Social Philosophy* 2.1/2 (2006): 9-14.

Baranger, Madeleine, Willy Baranger, and Jorge M. Mom. "The Infantile Psychic Trauma from Us to Freud: Pure Trauma, Retroactivity, and Reconstruction." *The International Journal of Psychoanalysis* 69 (1988): 113-28.

Bartlett, A. J. "Conditional Notes on a New Republic." *Cosmos and History: The Journal of Natural and Social Philosophy* 2.1/2 (2006): 39-67.

Bataille, Georges. *The Accursed Share: An Essay on General Economy. Volume 1: Consumption*. New York: Zone Books, 1988.

Baudrillard, Jean. *The Gulf War Did Not Take Place*. Bloomington, IN: Indiana University Press, 1995.

Bingham, Adam. "Life, or Something Like It: Michael Haneke's *Der siebente Kontinent* (*The Seventh Continent*, 1989)." *KINOEYE* 4.1 (8 March 2004): <http://www.kinoeye.org/04/01/bingham01_no2.php>. Accessed January 2007.

Birchall, Bridget. "From Nude to Metteuse-en-scène: Isabelle Huppert, Image, and Desire in *La Dentellière* (Goretta, 1977) and *La Pianiste* (Haneke, 2001)." *Studies in French Cinema* 5.1 (2005): 5-15.

Cieutat, Michel. "Funny Games." In *50 Films qui ont fait scandale*. Edited and introduced by Gérard Camy. Condé-sur-Noireau, France: Corlet, 2002. 203-06.

Cieutat, Michel, and Philippe Rouyer. "Entretien avec Michael Haneke: On ne montre pas la réalité, juste son image manipulée." *Positif: Revue Mensuelle de Cinéma* 536 (Oct. 2005): 21-25.

Deleuze, Gilles. *Cinema 1: The Movement Image*. Minneapolis: University of Minnesota Press, 1986.

—. *Cinema 2: The Time Image*. Minneapolis: University of Minnesota Press, 1989.

—. *The Fold: Leibniz and the Baroque*. Minneapolis: University of Minnesota Press, 1993.

—. *Logic of Sense*. London: Athlone Press, 2001.

—. "Three Questions on Six Times Two." In *Negotiations 1972-1990*. New York: Columbia University Press, 1995. 37-45.

Derrida, Jacques. Given *Time: 1. Counterfeit Money*. Chicago, IL: University of Chicago Press, 1992.

Falcon, Richard. Review of *Code Unknown*. *Sight & Sound* May 2001: 46.

Felman, Shoshana. "Education and Crisis, or the Vicissitudes of Teaching." In *Trauma: Explorations in Memory*. Edited by Cathy Caruth. Baltimore, MD: Johns Hopkins University Press, 1995. 13-60.

Frey, Mattias. "Supermodernity, Capital, and Narcissus: The French Connection to Michael Haneke's Benny's Video." *cinetext* (Sept. 2002): <http://cinetext.philo.at/magazine/frey/bennysvideo.html>. Accessed January 2007.

Grabner, Franz. "'Der Name der Erbsünde ist Verdrängung': Ein Gespräch mit Michael Haneke." In *Michael Haneke und seine Filme*. Edited by Christian Wessely, Gerhard Larcher, and Franz Grabner. Magdeburg: Schüren Verlag, 2005. 33-46.

Haneke, Michael. "*71 Fragments of a Chronology of Chance*: Notes to the Film." In *After Postmodernism: Austrian Literature and Film in Transition*. Edited by Willy Riemer. Riverside, CA: Ariadne Press, 2000. 171-75.

Jakovljevic, Branislav. "Theatre of War in the Former Yugoslavia: Event, Script, Actors." *The Drama Review* 43.3 (1999): 5-13.

Knauß, Stefanie. "Vom Fremdsein, der Befremdlichkeit und der Einsamkeit: DAS SCHLOSS von Michael Haneke." In *Michael Haneke und seine Filme*. Edited by Christian Wessely, Gerhard Larcher, and Franz Grabner. Magdeburg: Schüren Verlag, 2005. 261-82.

Landy, Marcia. "Just an Image: Godard, Cinema, and Philosophy." *Critical Quarterly* 43.3 (Oct. 2001): 9-31.

Laplanche, J., and J. B. Pontalis. *The Language of Psycho-Analysis*. New York: W. W. Norton, 1967.

"Special Cannes." *Positif: Revue Mensuelle de Cinéma* 437/438 (juillet/août 1997): 94/95.

Le Cain, Maximilian. "Do the Right Thing: The Films of Michael Haneke." *Senses of Cinema* 26 (May-June 2003): <http://esvc001106.wic016u.serverweb.com/contents/03/26/haneke.html>. Accessed December 2007.

Masson, Alain. "*Funny Games*: Une allégorie fallacieuse." *Positif: Revue Mensuelle de Cinéma* 443 (janvier 1998): 39-40.

Peucker, Brigitte. "Fragmentation and the Real: Michael Haneke's Family Trilogy." In *After Postmodernism: Austrian Literature and Film in Transition*. Edited by Willy Riemer. Riverside, CA: Ariadne Press, 2000. 176-88.

Price, Brian. "Pain and the Limits of Representation." *Framework: The Journal of Cinema and Media* 47.2 (2006): 22-29.

Rayns, Tony. Review of *The Piano Teacher. Sight & Sound* Nov. 2001: 54.

Seeßlen, Georg. "Strukturen der Vereisung." In *Michael Haneke und seine Filme*. Edited by Christian Wessely, Gerhard Larcher, and Franz Grabner. Magdeburg: Schüren Verlag, 2005. 47-65.

Sharrett, Christopher. "The World That Is Known: An Interview with Michael Haneke." *Cineaste* (Summer 2003): 28-31.

Smith, David. "Introduction: 'A Life of Pure Immanence': Deleuze's 'Critique et Clinique' Project." In *Gilles Deleuze, Essays Critical and Clinical*. Edited by David Smith. Minneapolis: University of Minnesota Press, 1997. xi-liii.

Walsh, David. "Michael Haneke's *Caché*: The Artist Has Not Done the Most Difficult Work." *World Socialist Web Site*, 21 April 21 2006: <http://www.wsws.org/articles/2006/apr2006/cach-a21.shtml>. Accessed December 2006.

Wheately, Catherine, "The Masochistic Fantasy Made Flesh: Michael Haneke's *La Pianiste* as Melodrama." *Studies in French Cinema Journal* 6.2 (2006): 117-27.

Wood, Robin. "In Search of the Code inconnu." *Cineaction* 62 (Oct. 2003): 41-49.

Wyatt, Jean. "Jouissance and Desire in Michael Haneke's *The Piano Teacher*." *American Imago* 62.4 (2006): 453-82.

Films Cited

71 Fragmente einer Chronologie des Zufalls (*71 Fragments of a Chronology of Chance*) by Michael Haneke, 1994
Benny's Video by Michael Haneke, 1992
Caché (*Hidden*) by Michael Haneke, 2005
Code inconnu: Récit incomplet de divers voyages (*Code unknown*) by Michael Haneke, 2000
C*rash* by Paul Haggis, 2004
For Ever Mozart by Jean-Luc Godard, 1996
Funny Games by Michael Haneke, 1997
Le Temps du loup (*Time of the Wolf*) by Michael Haneke, 2003
Notre musique (*Our Music*) by Jean-Luc Godard, 2004
Pianiste, La (*The Piano Teacher*) by Michael Haneke, 2001
Siebente Kontinent, Der (The Seventh Continent) by Michael Haneke, 1989

Notes

[1] Haneke, "*71 Fragments*," 171: "I provide a construct and nothing more—its interpretation and its integration into a value and belief system is always the work of the recipient."
[2] Falcon, "*Code Unknown*," 46. For a convincing reading of Haneke as modernist see also Peucker. As further proof of my thesis I would like to point to the interesting fact that critics on a regular basis vehemently attack one film in Haneke's oeuvre that they perceive as bad, because it does not deliver the modernist critique they expect: "Without considerable reflection and inner struggle, serious social analysis, and compassion for human difficulty, one ends up with a mirror that merely reflects back at the spectator a vision of the world that is far too familiar, far too unmediated" (Walsh); "*Funny Games* (1997) stands as the one truly bad film on Haneke's otherwise consistently excellent filmography. […] *Funny Games* puts a naive faith in the confrontational power of the spectacle of sadistic violence, which Tarantino had already definitively tamed and thus undermined in his first two films" (Le Cain); "The conspicuously humourless Haneke started working with stars only in *Code Unknown*, one film ago, and hasn't yet found a credible way to reconcile his determinedly dark-side view of humanity with his new-found need to attract the mass arthouse audience" (Rayns). What I suggest is a reading that takes seeming "exceptions" seriously and sees how they make sense in the entire oeuvre.
[3] For an in-depth analysis of Badiou's concept of pedagogy in relation to art and philosophy see Bartlett.

[4] To put it bluntly, Haneke formulates his concepts in images. I would therefore strongly disagree with Frey, who, referring amongst others to Baudrillard, Foucault, and Deleuze, claims in his "Supermodernity, Capital, and Narcissus": "Haneke and these thinkers share an important common perspective in their respective endeavors, seeking to revive moribund fields with a respective cinematic/theoretical shock therapy."

[5] I exclude here the films Michael Haneke made for television. However, my arguments can certainly be extended for his adaptation of Kafka's *The Castle, Das Schloß* (1997), where Haneke also points to the madness and lack of meaning the protagonist encounters in the castle with his use of fragmentation and black screen. For an analysis of this film, see Knauß. I will not address the music in Haneke's films, which could also be seen as taking another perspective (see Wood, Wheatley).

[6] See also Deleuze, *Cinema 2*, 248. For a detailed reading of Deleuze and Godard's pedagogy, see Landy.

[7] Deleuze points out that the just images, or "just ideas," as he calls them, have to be understood in the form of questions (see "Three Questions," esp. 38-40).

[8] As a tongue-in-cheek reference in *Caché*, Haneke puts posters in the son's bedroom, amongst others, of *The Matrix Reloaded* (2003), *The Chronicles of Riddick* (2004), *In Hell* (2003), and *Van Helsing* (2004), all action-films whose plot revolves around the violent destruction of an evil, sometimes literally inhuman adversary.

[9] See here esp. Baudrillard. An interesting and very personal perspective on the event of war and its mise-en-scène can be found in Jakovljevic.

[10] In an otherwise insightful exploration of Isabelle Huppert's image, Bridget Birchall concludes "that her status as subject, as manifest in *La Pianiste*, remains frustratingly problematic" (6). I would argue that *La Pianiste* only makes sense from the perspective of the traumatized character of the piano teacher. Jean Wyatt seems to be the only critic who remarked on the necessary shift in perspective (466).

[11] This should be understood as a pedagogy: Badiou uses Lacan's Borromean knot to explain the vocation of the philosophical institution.

[12] The film apparently divided the jury in Cannes ("Special Cannes"; see also Cieutat). At the time of this writing, Haneke is finishing an American remake of *Funny Games*.

CONTRIBUTORS

Katherine Arens is professor of Germanic Studies, Comparative Literature, Women's and Gender Studies, and Science and Technology Studies at the University of Texas at Austin. Her principal areas are split between intellectual history and literature of the eighteenth through twentieth centuries (Austria and Germany), and curriculum development. Recent book publications include *Remapping the Foreign Language Curriculum: A Multi-Literacies Approach* (with Janet Swaffar; MLA, 2005) and *Empire in Decline: Fritz Mauthner's Critique of Wilhelminian Germany* (Lang, 2001); recent articles include "*Stadtwollen*: Benjamin's *Arcades Project* and the Problem of Method." (*PMLA*, 122, #1 [January 2007]: 43-60), "The Four-Fold Way to Internationalism: Grillparzer's Non-National Historical Literacy" (in: *Aneignungen, Entfremdungen: The Austrian Playwright Franz Grillparzer*, eds. Raleigh Whitinger and Clemens Ruthner. [Lang, 2007]. 21-48), and "'Glücklich ist, wer [nicht] vergißt': From Museum Culture to *Broadway-an-der-Wien*" (in: *Mediating Germany: Popular Culture between Tradition and Innovation.*, ed. Gerd Bayer [Cambridge Scholars Press, 2006]: 73-91).

Lyle Barkhymer is a Professor of Music at Otterbein College, Westerville, Ohio, USA. He earned his doctorate from Indiana University, Bloomington, and did further work at the Universität für Musik und Darstellende Kunst in Vienna. He has also studied in NEH sponsored seminars with William P. Malm at the University of Michigan, Reinhold Brinkmann at Harvard University, and Regina Kecht and Dorothy James in Vienna. From his special interest in Austrian culture, he developed a senior year capstone course for his college that culminates in a two-week interterm December seminar in Vienna.

Lesley Bart received her Bachelor's degree in Sociology from Pacific University in Oregon. She is currently pursuing a Master's degree in Women's Studies at The Ohio State University. Her current research interests include constructions of transgender identity in mental health and medical discourses and feminist politics and activism in the queer pornography industry.

Robert von Dassanowsky is Professor of German and Film Studies, and Director of the Film Studies Program at the University of Colorado, Colorado Springs. He has published widely on European literature, culture and cinema, and is co-founder of the International Alexander Lernet-Holenia Society. He is also active as an independent producer. His most recent book is the first English language examination of Austria's film art and industry, *Austrian Cinema: A History* (2005). He is currently co-editing a collection on *New Austrian Film* with Oliver C. Speck for publication in 2009, and developing a study on the cinema of Austrofascism.

Theodore Fiedler is Professor of German and Chair of the Department of Modern and Classical Languages, Literatures and Cultures, University of Kentucky. From 1993 through 2002 he served as editor of the international journal *Colloquia Germanica*, a role he has recently resumed. He has written on film and various aspects of 20th century literature and culture of the German-speaking countries. In addition to papers on Trakl, Hofmannsthal, Brecht, Alexander Kluge, and Volker Braun, his publications include an edition of Rilke's correspondence with Ellen Key, Swedish feminist and educational reformer, major articles on Rilke's reception of Nietzsche and psychoanalysis, and two essays on Harry Graf Kessler, Weimar, and the politics of modernism in Wilhelminian Germany. He is presently at work on a book-length study of Peter Handke and Yugoslavia.

Lorely French is Distinguished University Professor of German at Pacific University. Her publications include a book entitled "German Women Letter Writers 1750 to 1850" and numerous articles on topics such as Roma writing in Austria, Afro-German women writers, and German women writers in Romanticism, including Bettine von Arnim, Sophie Mereau, Dorothea Schlegel, and Rahel Varnhagen. She is presently co-author of "Pacific Coast Philology," the journal of the Pacific Ancient and Modern Languages Association (PAMLA).

Hans Gabriel holds the College German Faculty position at the North Carolina School of the Arts, the performing arts and filmmaking campus of the University of North Carolina. His research interests include narrative theory and German-language literary realism. He has published articles on the nineteenth-century German-language *Novelle* and the Preface as a literary device, and is currently working on a book that examines the efforts of nineteenth-century German-language realism to locate an aesthetic space for its own literary representations.

Winfried R. Garscha was born in 1952 in Linz, Upper Austria. He studied history and linguistics at the University of Vienna, where he received his PhD in 1983 with a thesis about the "Anschluss" movement in the 1920's and 1930's in Germany and Austria. Currently, he is an archivist and supervisor for scholarly projects at the Documentation Center of Austrian Resistance/DÖW (1987-) and the co-director of the Austrian Research Center for Postwar Trials (1998-). He has served as deputy secretary (1978-), vice president (1990-) and treasurer (1994-) of the International Conference of Labour and Social History (ITH). He is author of numerous lectures, books and essays about Austrian history, the labor movement and about dealing with the Nazi past in Austrian arts, politics and the judiciary. His recent publications include "Linker Widerstand—'Rote Hilfe'—Arbeiterwiderstand" in Stefan Karner/Karl Duffek (Eds.), *Widerstand in Österreich 1938-1945. Die Beiträge der Parlaments-Enquete 2005* (2007). He was the co-author of *Justiz in Oberdonau (vol. 7*) (2007), and the co-editor of *Holocaust und NS-Kriegsverbrechen vor Gericht: Der Fall Österreich* (2006). His article entitled "The Trials of Nazi War Criminals in Austria" will be appearing in the forthcoming volume *Nazi Crimes and the Law* to be published by Cambridge University Press.

Georg Grote is College Lecturer in the School of Languages & Literatures in University College Dublin. His research areas include Western European History with special focus on historical and contemporary collective organisation of peoples through nationalisms and regionalisms. He is the author of *Torn Between Politics and Culture: The Gaelic League 1893-1993* (1994), "Die grosse Hungersnot in Irland 1845-1849," in Jörg Rademacher (ed.), *Irlands grosser Hunger,* (1996), *Anglo-Irish Theatre and the Formation of a Nationalist Political Culture between 1890-1930* (2003) and has co-edited *German Memory Contests. The Quest for Identity in Literature, Film, and Discourse since 1990* (with Anne Fuchs, Mary Cosgrove 2006). Publications on the South Tyrol issue in the 20th century include "Gehen oder Bleiben? – Die Identitätskrise der deutschsprachigen Südtiroler in Optanten- und Dableibergedichten der Optionszeit, 1939-1943," in Modern Austrian Literature, Vol.37, No. 1/2, 2004, "Vielsprachigkeit in Südtirol – Modell für Europa oder Kapitulation vor der Geschichte?" Acta Germanica, Band 33, 2005. He is currently completing a monograph on South Tyrolean identity in the 20th century.

Günter Haika teaches German and Photography at the Vienna Program of Wake Forest University, and courses on Austrian literature, film, and Austrian women writers at IES Vienna. He is a regular contributor to "praesent. das österreichische literaturjahrbuch", and has mainly published on recent Austrian literature, with occasional essays about older literature (e.g., Goethe, Lenau, and Meyern). He is currently editing *brutal real – Neuer Realismus in der Österreichischen Literatur der Gegenwart* (forthcoming later in 2008) as well as a critical edition of a 1787 novel by W. F. Meyern. His first book as a photographer will feature black-and-white images of Prague and will be published later in 2008.

Luke Heighton is currently completing a PhD on 'Art and the Asylum, Vienna 1890-1914' at Birkbeck College University of London. He has previously studied at the Courtauld Institute of Art, London, University College, Oxford and the University of Liverpool. Other areas of interest include Foucault's treatment of madness in relation to subjectivity, madness as a trope within cultural and philosophical discourse, and contemporary art.

Susanne Hochreiter is Assistant Professor at the University of Vienna (Department of German Studies). Her research interests: modern Austrian literature, literature by women, Theatre, Gender Studies, Queer Studies. Her publications include: *Frank Kafka: Raum und Geschlecht*. Würzburg: Königshausen & Neumann, 2007; *Literatur, Lehren, Lernen. Hochschuldidaktik und germanistische Literaturwissenschaft.* (Co-Editor.). Wien: Böhlau, 2006.

Geoffrey C. Howes (Ph.D. University of Michigan, 1985) is Professor of German at Bowling Green State University in Ohio. From 2000 to 2005 he was co-editor with Jacqueline Vansant of *Modern Austrian Literature*. He has published on a variety of topics in Austrian studies including Robert Musil, Joseph Roth, Ingeborg Bachmann, Peter Rosei, Lilian Faschinger, Thomas Bernhard, Michael Scharang, and recent Austrian essays, and is working on a book about the representation of madness in Austrian fiction. His translations into English include texts by Rosei, Faschinger, Margret Kreidl, Gerhard Kofler, and Doron Rabinovici.

Julie M. Johnson is Assistant Professor of Art History at the University of Texas at San Antonio. Her essays have appeared in the Oxford Art Journal, The Woman's Art Journal, Nineteenth-Century Art Worldwide,

The Austrian History Yearbook, and edited volumes and museum catalogues. She was a Research Fellow at the IFK in Vienna in Fall 2007.

Stefan Kutzenberger is Lecturer at the Institute for Comparative Literature (University of Vienna) and co-editor of Robert Musil's Diaries for the digital edition of his Collected Works (Klagenfurter Ausgabe). His main areas of research and publication are the contemporary reception of Robert Musil, intermedial relations of Fin de siècle Vienna, literary interrelations between Latin America and the German-Speaking world and Latin American Boom- and Postboomliterature.

Dagmar C. G. Lorenz, Professor of Germanic Studies and Director of Jewish Studies at the University of Illinois at Chicago, publishes on Austrian, German and German-Jewish literature and culture, and Holocaust Studies. She served as editor of *The German Quarterly* (1997-2003) and held offices with MLA, GSA, MALCA, and AATG. Recent publications include *Keepers of the Motherland: German Texts by Jewish Women Writers* (1997), and *Verfolgung bis zum Massenmord. Diskurse zum Holocaust in deutscher Sprache* (1992) and edited volumes, *Elsa Porges-Bernstein alias Ernst Rosmer: Woman,Writer, Holocaust Survivor:a Critical Anthology* (coedited with Helga W. Kraft, 2006), *A Companion to the Works of Elias Canetti* (2004), *A Companion to the Works of Arthur Schnitzler* (2003), *Contemporary Jewish Writing in Austria* (1999). *Transforming the Center, Eroding the Margins: Essays on Ethnic and Cultural Boundaries in German Speaking Countries* (coedited with Renate S. Posthofen (1998), *Insiders and Outsiders. Jewish and Gentile Culture in Germany and Austria* (1994).

Moser, Joseph W.: Ph.D. (2004) in German from the University of Pennsylvania with dissertation on Thomas Bernhard's dialogue with the public sphere. Assistant Professor of German, Coordinator of German Program, Washington & Jefferson College, Washington, PA. Book Review Editor for Modern Austrian Literature. He recently published the following article on Thomas Bernhard: "Literaturskandal als Dialog mit der Öffentlichkeit: Der Fall Thomas Bernhard," In: *Literatur als Skandal.* Ed. Stefan Neuhaus. Göttingen: Vandenhoeck & Ruprecht, 2007: 503-512.

Sarah Painitz is Visiting Assistant Professor of German and Comparative Literature at Butler University. She received her Ph.D. in German from the University of Virginia in 2007. Her scholarship focuses on 20th-century German literature, modernism, gender studies, and narrative theory and she is currently working on a book project on Austrian women writers of the interwar years. She will begin employment as Assistant Professor of German at Wabash College in fall 2008.

Pamela S. Saur has taught German and various literature and linguistics courses since 1988 at Lamar University in Beaumont, Texas. Lamar named her University Professor in 2007. She holds a Ph.D. in German from the University of Iowa and an M.Ed. in English teaching from the University of Massachusetts. She has published numerous scholarly articles and book chapters on Gerhard Roth and other Austrian authors, translated three Austrian works with Ariadne Press, and co-edited *Visions and Visionaries in Contemporary Austrian Literature and Film* with Margarete Lamb-Faffelberger (Lang, 2004). She served for several years as Editor of Schatzkammer der deutschen Sprache, Dichtung und Geschichte and the Texas Foreign Language Association Bulletin.

Helga Schreckenberger, Professor of German at the University of Vermont. Research interests focus on contemporary Austrian literature and Exile Studies. Publications on Lilian Faschinger, Elisabeth Reichart, Marlene Streeruwitz, Gerhard Roth, Felix Mitterer, Arnold Zweig, Adrienne Thomas, Erich Maria Remarque, Erika Mann. Most recent publications include the edited volume *Alchemie des Exils. Exil als schoepferischer Impuls*(2006) and the article "Frauen an der Front. Der Erste Weltkrieg und seine Folgen fuer weibliches Selbstverstaendnis."

Oliver C. Speck is a professor at Virginia Commonwealth University in Richmond, Va., where he teaches European Cinema and German at the School of World Studies. Oliver Speck's scholarly writing focuses on narrative strategies and the representation of memory and history in French, German and other European cinema. Currently, he is working on a book on Michael Haneke and is also co-editing a volume on New Austrian Cinema.

Rebecca S. Thomas (Ph.D. The Ohio State University, 1992) is Associate Professor of German at Wake Forest University and member at large to the Executive Committee of the Modern Austrian Literature and Culture Association. Her research and publications focus on contemporary Austrian studies. She has published on Franz Kafka as well as numerous contemporary Austrian authors, including Gerhard Roth, Elfriede Jelinek, Doron Rabinovici and Kathrin Röggla, and is currently translating Röggla's novel *we never sleep* [*wir schlafen nicht*] for Ariadne Press.

INDEX

Note: *Madness* is also used as a synonym for *mental illness,* and *crime* for *criminality.* Figures and tables are indicated by an italicized *f* and *t,* respectively.

L